Primary Source Documents in Western Civilization

Volume Two: Since 1400

Jonathan S. Perry
University of South Florida

Sara E. Chapman
Oakland University

Derek Hastings
Oakland University

PEARSON

Upper Saddle River, New Jersey 07458

Upper Saddle River, New Jersey 07458

10 9 8 7 6 5 4 3 2 1

ISBN-10: 0-13-175584-6
ISBN-13: 978-0-13-175584-0

Table Of Contents

Introduction

In the year 24 CE, in the city of Rome, an important government official reportedly threw his wife out of a window—'for some unknown reason', according to our only source for the incident. Documenting the case nearly a century later, in a short paragraph in his *Annals*, P. Cornelius Tacitus passed along the bizarre circumstances surrounding this event. Unconvinced by the murderer's claim that his wife must have killed herself, the Emperor Tiberius went to the room from which the wife had been ejected and personally investigated the murder scene. Discovering signs of violence, Tiberius referred the matter to the Senate, but, before the trial could begin, the man stabbed himself to death in prison. A further shocking detail: the man's grandmother, a close friend of the Emperor's mother, had reportedly sent the dagger to her grandson, hinting rather pointedly that he should use it, to maintain a shred of the family's tattered dignity. And there is one final element here: soon after the suicide, the man's first wife was acquitted on the charge of making her husband insane...by means of various magic potions and spells.

Within this little story is encapsulated all the joys—and all the frustrations—of utilizing 'primary sources'. Tacitus tells us a great deal of interesting detail here, but is it reliable? Does his account even begin to tell us all that we would like to know about this incident? Historians, like the authors of your course textbooks, ultimately build their accounts on primary sources—those documents, written, physical, or in some other form, that survive from the period under investigation. Primary sources can be written accounts, but they are by no means only textual documents. Regardless of its appearance, however, each primary source is only as trustworthy as the person or persons who created it—and even then, we must factor in the unique perspective of its creator. Even a photograph, which seems to be a straightforward depiction of "reality," frozen in a moment of time, must be contextualized by the investigator. If we could see what was positioned just *outside* the frame, would we interpret the moment differently? To what or to whom is the person in the photograph reacting, and is that information essential for making sense of the person's expression?

This book is designed to aid you in the process of interpreting sources, which is the cornerstone of the "craft" we historians practice. We have adopted a number of approaches and organizational methods to achieve this goal, but our main hope is that you will never accept any source—even one provided by your instructor—simply at face value. Everything you read, see, or experience should be subjected to rigorous and critical examination. This can be an exhausting, but also a very exciting, habit, like exercising muscles that are infrequently used. Whether you decide to continue studying history or not, the skills you will develop by using this book will be of value to you, both as a student and as a resident in "the real world."

Jonathan S. Perry
University of South Florida

How to Read Primary Sources

Primary source accounts, like the ones in this collection, are invaluable tools for historians as they work to interpret past events. This collection of documents invites you to practice the historian's craft, just as professional historians do, by using primary sources.

Primary Sources

Anything that was produced or written by someone who directly participated in or observed a historical event can be considered a primary source. Traditionally, historians have used a wide array of written primary sources such as trial transcripts, contracts, financial records, correspondence, diaries, memoirs, edicts, laws, philosophical treatises and works of literature. Historians of older periods, especially those in the ancient and medieval worlds, have a broader definition of primary sources that encompasses anything produced or written in the general time-frame of their study. Increasingly, they now also use visual materials, such as pictures, photographs, and maps. Choosing what primary sources to use to study a historical event or trend is important because different sources provide different perspectives on the event. An official newspaper account, for example, would present a very different version of an incident than a diary entry written by a person directly involved.

If read carefully and analytically against their historical backdrops, primary sources clarify not only *what* happened, but more importantly, they also shed light on the underlying beliefs, assumptions and ideas that informed *why* people acted as they did. Because most primary sources offer one particular view of an event or trend, it is important to use them in conjunction with secondary sources (overview histories of the period under study, such as a textbook) to place them in the larger context of historical trends, linking them to larger ideas and events that were happening at the same time in history.

There are no precise rules or procedures that dictate how to read or analyze historical documents—no two historians would interpret a primary source document in the same way. Also, each period of historical study poses unique problems in this regard. There are, however, some general approaches and methods that can help guide you as you work with the documents in this collection. Reading primary sources involves carefully considering and exploring several key aspects of a document. Which will be discusses below. These include:

- Analyzing Authorship
- Determining the Audience
- Identifying the Argument
- Historical Significance: Making Links to Larger Ideas, Trends, and Events

Analyzing Authorship

When reading primary sources, a good starting point is to consider the author's background in order to determine, at least to some degree, the factors that shaped his or her account of the historical era, issue or event. Knowing something about the author helps to analyze his or her argument and tie it to larger political, social, intellectual and economic trends occurring at the same time.

Several factors are key to understanding an author's viewpoint. Consider what kind of education the author received. The author's religious and political beliefs are also often relevant, as well as his or her social status or place in the society. Other factors that can shape an author's approach are gender and race.

In analyzing authorship, it is also important to think about the author's reliability as a source. In some cases, they participated directly in the event under study, while in other scenarios, they were observers or bystanders. While both types of accounts can be credible sources, the different vantage points might yield different versions of what transpired. For example, a judge writing about his verdict on a trial would likely explain and justify his decision, while an observer who was sympathetic to the accused would be more likely to question the judge's decision and offer a more critical view of his verdict. Analyzing authorship means thinking about the author's interests and how they affect his or her version of events.

Determining when the author wrote or created a document also helps to analyze the authors' viewpoint. An account of an event written or recorded immediately after, is usually a dependable source for the detailed sequence of events. Likewise, an account written long after the event transpired might not get the details of what happened just right, but might better explain its long-term consequences or ramifications. Some questions to consider when analyzing authorship are:

- What kind of education did the author have?
- Where can you place the author in terms of social and economic status? Are they from a marginalized group or the elite?

- Was the author a female or male? How might gender shape how the author experienced and understood the event?
- What were the author's political views?
- What were the author's religious beliefs and views?
- When was the document written or created in relation to the event described?

Determining the Audience

Sometimes the main audience or intended receptions of the document are clearly indicated, as for example, with letters or correspondence. For other documents, it is necessary to use other methods to establish, in more general terms, the groups and individuals targeted by the author.

Literacy rates, which estimate what groups and people could read during any given historical period, are often helpful in determining the audience. Using your textbook or other secondary source, research what groups of people were likely, or not likely, to be able to read during the time the document appeared. Using estimated literacy rates and gauging the level of difficulty of the vocabulary used in the document, can provide a rough estimate of its audience. Another important factor is where the document appeared and what kind of access people had to it. For example, if it was published in a newspaper or a pamphlet, it would likely have a larger and broader audience, than if it appeared in a limited run of hardback books which were expensive to print and purchase. Finally, one should consider in what language the source was originally created, and how many people in the writer's society would have been familiar with that language.

Knowing the intended audience for a document is important, because authors persuade or inform by appealing to their audience's interests. The author, audience, and argument of any given document, then, are tightly intertwined. In trying to determine the audience of a document, consider the following questions:

- Did the author write or create the document for publication, or was it written only for friends or family members?
- What groups or individuals might have been expected to see it beyond those who were explicitly addressed?
- Did the choice of language that the documents was originally written in limit or expand the size of the document's potential audience?
- Where was the document published or where did it first appear?
- Based on cost, literacy rates, and availability, who would have had access to it?

Identifying the Argument

For some documents, it is easy to determine the author's argument, but in others it takes the form of a more subtle message. Likewise, authors writing about the same event or trend often have conflicting arguments or messages which depend on their own perspectives, backgrounds, and interests. All arguments or versions of the event might be equally valid, all might be"true." It is our job, as historians, to identify their main arguments and analyze the underlying ideas, viewpoints, and interests that informed their different perspectives or arguments. To use a modern example, imagine that a fender-bender takes place in a parking lot. The drivers of the two vehicles that collided would no doubt have very different accounts of what actually transpired. Bystanders who saw the crash take place might also have yet other points of view. The drivers of the cars would presumable filter the exact sequence of events through their own "argument" about what took place, intentionally or unintentionally distorting them for a purpose. When reading primary source documents, we have to consider and analyze the arguments and information offered by the author or authors, taking into consideration their interests and perspectives.

- What main idea or concept was the author trying to convey?
- What were the author's primary motivations for creating the document? Was the author trying to instruct or persuade? How?
- What groups' or individuals' political, economic, religious or social interests were directly addressed by the author in the document? How?

Historical Significance: Making Links to Larger Ideas, Trends, and Events

A good analysis of a primary source document takes into consideration the author, the author's audience, and his or her argument, and then links these to larger, significant historical events, trends, and changes happening at the same time.

Reading primary sources often means wrestling with the idea that people in the past viewed and understood their own lives, events, and the world around them in very different ways than we do today. In the words of English writer L.P. Hartley (1895–1972) "the past is a foreign country; they do things differently there." The actions of people in the past can often be attributed to assumptions, beliefs, feelings, or attitudes, but these are often very different than the ones we hold today. For example, people in medieval and early modern Europe believed that illnesses stemmed from an imbalance of fluids or humors in the body, and so they treated the sick by bleeding or cutting to release a small amount of blood. They believed this practice readjusted the humors in the body and returned a person to good health. From our vantage point of the twenty-first century, this practice seems absurd, counterproductive, and even potentially lethal. By placing these practices into historical context and understanding the medical and philosophical traditions grounded in ancient and medieval theories about how the body functioned that informed them, it is possible to understand why and how this approach to curing illnesses made perfect sense to people at that time. Dismissing those who came before us as ignorant or irrational is a barrier to thinking historically. A good analysis of a historical document seeks to determine how their beliefs, ideas, and approaches were linked to larger ideas and traditions that informed people's actions and shaped how they saw the world. This allows us, as historians, to link particular events to larger historical trends and identify periods where they began to shift or change. To make links to larger historical trends, consider the following questions:

- What other important events or trends were occurring at the same time the document was written (for example, wars, intellectual movements, religious movements)? What does the primary source tell us about these larger historical issues?
- In what ways was the author's argument connected to larger trends, events, or issues happening at the same time?
- What kinds of symbols or images were depicted in the document, how were they linked to larger issues or trends, and what did they represent or mean to the author and his or her audience?

Sara E. Chapman
Oakland University

Primary Source Documents in Western Civilization
Volume Two: Since 1400

Jonathan S. Perry
University of South Florida

Sara E. Chapman
Oakland University

Derek Hastings
Oakland University

Upper Saddle River, New Jersey 07458

PART 3

The West in Transformation (1350 – 1700)

CHAPTER 9

The Renaissance

Petrarch: Rules for the Successful Ruler c. 1350

Petrarch (1304-1374) was one of the first "humanists" who made his living as a public writer, receiving patronage from the wealthy political leaders of the Italian city-states. His concerns, more than those of his medieval predecessors, were secular, though he did not entirely ignore religion, especially in later life. He encouraged the scholars of his day to re-examine classical literature, reviving the style and substance of intellectual production that had ruled before Christianity became the dominant religion of the Roman Empire. In this excerpt, he duly praises his patron, and then he speaks more generally about how one ought to rule a state. Like Dante a generation before him, he used the vernacular language and helped make Italian a literary language.

Source: Francesco Petrarca, *How a Ruler Ought to Govern His State,* trans. Benjamin G. Kohl, cited in *The Earthly Republic: Italian Humanists on Government and Society,* ed. Benjamin G. Kohl and Ronald G. Witt, (University of Pennsylvania Press, 1981, © 1978), 35–80, passim.

Focus Questions:

1. What examples and sources are used to support Petrarch's claims about good government?
2. How highly does he esteem the writings of the ancient Greeks and Romans?

The first quality is that a lord should be friendly, never terrifying, to the good citizens, even though it is inevitable that he be terrifying to evil citizens if he is to be a friend to justice."For he does not carry a sword without good cause, since he is a minister of God," as the Apostle says. Now nothing is more foolish, nothing is more destructive to the stability of the state, than to wish to be dreaded by everyone. Many princes, both in antiquity and in modern times, have wanted nothing more than to be feared and have believed that nothing is more useful than fear and cruelty in maintaining their power. Concerning this belief we have an example in the case of the barbaric emperor named Maximinus. In fact, nothing is farther from the truth than these opinions; rather, it is much more advantageous to be loved than to be feared, unless we are speaking of the way in which a devoted child fears a good father. Any other kind of fear is diametrically opposed to what a ruler should desire. Rulers in general want to reign for a long time and to lead their lives in security, but to be feared is opposed to both of these desires, and to be loved is consistent with both.

* * *

What I can say is that the nature of public love is the same as private love. Seneca says: "I shall show you a love potion that is made without medicines, without herbs, without the incantations of any poison-maker. If you want to be loved, love." There it is. Although many other things could be said, this saying is the summation of everything. What is the need for magical arts, what for any reward or labor? Love is free; it is sought out by love alone. And who can be found with such a steely heart that he would not want to return an honorable love? "Honorable" I say, for a dishonorable love is not love at all, but rather hatred hidden under the guise of love. Now to return love to someone who loves basely is to do nothing other than to compound one crime with another and to become a part of another person's disgraceful deceit.

* * *

Indeed, from the discussion of this topic nothing but immense and honorable pleasure ought to come to you since you are so beloved by your subjects that you seem to them to be not a lord over citizens but the "father of your country." In fact this was the title of almost all of the emperors of antiquity; some of them bore the name justly, but others carried it so unjustly that nothing more perverse can be conceived. Both Caesar Augustus and Nero were called "father of his country." The first was a true father, the second was an enemy of both his country and of religion. But this title really does belong to you.

* * *

You should know, moreover, that to merit this kind of esteem you must always render justice and treat your citizens with goodwill. Do you really want to be a father to your citizens? Then you must want for your subjects what you want for your own children.

* * *

Now I shall speak of justice, the very important and noble function that is to give to each person his due so that no one is punished without good reason. Even when there is a good reason for punishment you should incline to mercy, following the example of Our Heavenly Judge and Eternal King. For no one of us is immune from sin and all of us are weak by our very nature, so there is no one of us who does not need mercy.

* * *

Indeed, I do not deny, nor am I ignorant of, the fact that the lord of a city ought to take every precaution to avoid useless and superfluous expenditures. In this way he will not exhaust the treasury and have nothing left for necessary expenditures. Therefore, a lord should spend nothing and do nothing whatsoever that does not further the beauty and good order of the city over which he rules. To put it briefly, he ought to act as a careful guardian of the state, not as its lord. Such was the advice that the Philosopher gave at great length in his *Politics*, advice that is found to be very useful and clearly consistent with justice.[1] Rulers who act otherwise are to be judged as thieves rather than as defenders and preservers of the state.

* * *

From these concerns, however, derives not just the happiness of the people, but the security of the ruling class as well. For no one is more terrifying than a starving commoner of whom it has been said: "the hungry pleb knows no fear." Indeed, there are not just ancient examples but contemporary ones, especially from recent events in the city of Rome, which bear out this saying.[2]

* * *

Among those honored for their abilities in governing, the first place ought to go to learned men. And among these learned men, a major place should go to those whose knowledge in law is always very useful to the state. If, indeed, love of and devotion to justice is added to their knowledge of law, these citizens are (as Cicero puts it) "learned not just in the law, but in justice."[3] However, there are those who follow the law but do no justice, and these are unworthy to bear the name of the legal profession. For it is not enough simply to have knowledge; you must want to use it. A good lawyer adds good intentions to his legal knowledge. Indeed, there have been many lawyers who have added luster to ancient Rome

1 Aristotle Politica5.9, 1314b40ff, which Petrarch knew only in medieval Latin translation.
2 An allusion to a revolt—caused by famine—by the lower classes of Rome against the senatorial families in 1353, just before the return to the city of the demagogic Cola di Rienzo. See F. Gregorovius, History of the City of Rome in the Middle Ages, trans. A. Hamilton, 8 vols. (London, 1898), 6:337ff.
3 Cicero Orationes Philippicae 9.5.10.

and other places: Adrianus Julius Celsus, Salvius Julianus, Neratius Priscus, Antonius Scaevola, Severus Papinianus, Alexander Domitius Ulpianus, Fabius Sabinus, Julius Paulus, and many others.[4] And you too (as much as our own times permit) have by the patronage of your university added honor to your country. There are other kinds of learned men, some of whom you can depend on for advice and learned conversation, and (as Alexander used to say) invent literary tales.[5] One reads that Julius Caesar, in like fashion, used to confer Roman citizenship on doctors of medicine and on teachers of the liberal arts.[6] Now, among learned men there is no doubt that we ought to give preference to those who teach the knowledge of sacred things (or what we call theology), provided that these men have kept themselves free from any foolish sophistries.

* * *

That very wise emperor Augustus used to bestow patronage on learned men to encourage them to remain in Rome, and hope of such a reward stimulated others to study, for at that time Roman citizenship was a highly valued honor. Indeed, when St. Paul claimed that he was a Roman citizen, the tribune judging the case said to him:"I myself have at a high price obtained this status."[7]

* * *

Even if it were not written in any book, still death is certain, as our common nature tells us. Now I do not know whether it is because of human nature or from some longstanding custom that at the death of our close friends and relatives we can scarcely contain our grief and tears, and that our funeral services are often attended by wailings and lamentations. But I do know that scarcely ever has this propensity for public grief been so deep-rooted in other cities as it is in yours. Someone dies—and I do not care whether he is a noble or a commoner, the grief displayed by the commoners is certainly no less manifest, and perhaps more so, than that of the nobles, for the plebs are more apt to show their emotions and less likely to be moved by what is proper; as soon as he breathes his last, a great howling and torrent of tears begins. Now I am not asking you to forbid expressions of grief. This would be difficult and probably impossible, given human nature. But what Jeremiah says is true:"You should not bemoan the dead, nor bathe the corpse in tears."[8] As the great poet Euripides wrote in Crespontes: "Considering the evil of our present existence, we ought to lament at our birth and rejoice at our death."[9] But these philosophic opinions are not well known, and, in any case, the common people would find them unthinkable and strange.

4 Petrarch derived this list of famous legal experts from the time of the Roman Empire mainly from his reading of the Scriptores historiae Augusta passim.
5 Scriptores historiae Augustae18.34.6.
6 Seutonius Divus Julius42.
7 Acts 22:28.
8 Jeremiah 22:10.
9 Cf. Cicero Tusculane disputationes1.48.115, quoting Euripides.

Therefore, I will tell you what I am asking. Take an example: Some old dowager dies, and they carry her body into the streets and through the public squares accompanied by loud and indecent wailing so that someone who did not know what was happening could easily think that here was a madman on the loose or that the city was under enemy attack. Now, when the funeral cortege finally gets to the church, the horrible keening redoubles, and at the very spot where there ought to be hymns to Christ or devoted prayers for the soul of the deceased in a subdued voice or even silence, the walls resound with the lamentations of the mourners and the holy altars shake with the wailing of women. All this simply because a human being has died. This custom is contrary to any decent and honorable behavior and unworthy of any city under your rule. I wish you would have it changed. In fact, I am not just advising you, I am (if I may) begging you to do so. Order that wailing women should not be permitted to step outside their homes; and if some lamentation is necessary to the grieved, let them do it at home and do not let them disturb the public thoroughfares.

I have said to you perhaps more than I should, but less than I would like to say. And if it seems to you, illustrious sir, that I am mistaken in one place or another, I beg your pardon, and I ask you to consider only the good advice. May you rule your city long and happily. Farewell. Arquà, the 28th of November.

Advice to Lorenzo de Medici: *On Wifely Duties* 1416

Francesco Barbaro wrote *On Wifely Duties* for the benefit of his friend and fellow aristocrat, Lorenzo de Medici, on the occasion of the latter's marriage in 1416. He hoped to teach the youth of Florence through de Medici's example—and through the Medicis' circulation of his treatise. He also wanted to stress the importance of marriage in the maintenance of the aristocratic ruling families of his native Venice, in particular, and to the Italian city-states, more generally.

Source: Francesco Barbaro, *On Wifely Duties*, trans. Benjamin G. Kohl, cited in *The Earthly Republic: Italian Humanists on Government and Society*, ed. Benjamin G. Kohl and Ronald G. Witt, (University of Pennsylvania Press, 1981, © 1978), 189–230, passim.

Focus Questions:

1. What behaviors will ensure a good and healthy marriage in Renaissance Italy?
2. Do these differ from expected behaviors in other historical periods?

CHAPTER ONE: ON THE FACULTY OF OBEDIENCE

This is now the remaining part to be done here, in which if wives follow me, either of their own free will or by the commands of their husbands, no one will be so unfair as to think that I have not so established the duties of the wife that youth can enjoy peace and quiet the whole life long. Therefore, there are three things that, if they are diligently observed by a wife, will make a marriage praiseworthy and admirable: love for her husband, modesty of life, and diligent and complete care in domestic matters. We shall discuss the first of these, but before this I want to say something about the faculty of obedience, which is her master and companion, because nothing more important, nothing greater can be demanded of a wife than this.

If a husband, excited to anger, should scold you more than your ears are accustomed to hear, tolerate his wrath silently. But if he has been struck silent by a fit of depression, you should address him with sweet and suitable words, encourage, console, amuse, and humor him. Those who work with elephants do not wear white clothes, and those who work with wild bulls are right not to wear red; for those beasts are made ever more ferocious by those colors. Many authors report that tigers are angered by drums and made violent by them. Wives ought to observe the same thing; if, indeed, a particular dress is offensive to a husband, then we advise them not to wear it, so that they do not give affront to their husbands, with whom they ought to live peacefully and pleasantly.

The wife who is angry with her husband because of jealousy and is considering a separation should ask herself this question: If I put myself in a workhouse because I hate a whore, what could make her far happier and more fortunate than this? She would see me almost shipwrecked, while at the same time she was sailing with favorable winds and securely casting her anchor into my marriage bed?

It was considered very good for domestic peace and harmony if a wife kept her husband's love with total diligence. At the olympic games that were dedicated to the great god Jupiter and attended by all of Greece, Gorgias used his eloquence to urge a union of all the Greeks. Melanthus said: Our patron attempts to persuade us that we should all join together in a league, but he cannot bring himself and his wife and her maid—who are only three people—to a mutual agreement (for the wife was very jealous because Gorgias was wildly enamoured of her maid). Likewise, Philip was for a long time displeased with the queen Olympias and Alexander. And when Demaratus of Corinth returned from Greece, Philip eagerly and closely questioned him about the union of the Greeks. Demaratus said to him: "Philip, I consider it a very bad thing that you are spending all your energy in bringing peace and concord to all of Greece when you are not yet reconciled with your own wife and son." Therefore, if any woman wants to govern her children and servants, she should make sure that she is, first of all, at peace with her husband. Otherwise, it will seem that she wants to imitate the very things that she is trying to correct in them. In order that a wife does her duty and brings peace and harmony to her household, she must agree to the first principle that she does not disagree with her husband on any point. But of this enough has been said.

CHAPTER TWO: ON LOVE

In the first place, let wives strive so that their husbands will clearly perceive that they are pensive or joyful according to the differing states of their husbands' fortunes. Surely congratulations are proper in times of good fortune, just as consolations are appropriate in times of adversity. Let them openly discuss whatever is bothering them, provided it is worthy of prudent people, and let them feign nothing, dissemble nothing, and conceal nothing. Very often sorrow and trouble of mind are relieved by means of discussion and counsel that ought to be carried out in a friendly fashion with the husband. If a husband shares all the pressures of her anxieties he will lighten them by participating in them and make their burden lighter; but if her troubles are very great or deeply rooted, they will be relieved as long as she is able to sigh in the embrace of her husband. I would like wives to live with their husbands in such a way that they can always be in agreement, and if this can be done, then, as Pythagoras defines friendship, the two are united in one.

I therefore would like wives to evidence modesty at all times and in all places. They can do this if they will preserve an evenness and restraint in the movements of the eyes, in their walking, and in the movement of their bodies; for the wandering of the eyes, a hasty gait, and excessive movement of the hands and other parts of the body cannot be done without loss of dignity, and such actions are always joined to vanity and are signs of frivolity.

Moreover, I earnestly beg that wives observe the precept of avoiding immoderate laughter. This is a habit that is indecent in all persons, but it is especially hateful in a woman. On the other hand, women should not be censured if they laugh a little at a good joke and thus lapse somewhat from their serious demeanor. Demosthenes used to rehearse his legal speeches at home in front of a mirror so that with his own eyes he could judge what he should do and what he should avoid in delivering his speeches at court. We may well apply this practice to wifely behavior. I wish that wives would daily think and consider what the dignity, the status of being a wife requires, so that they will not be lacking in dignified comportment.

We who follow a middle way should establish some rather liberal rules for our wives. They should not be shut up in their bedrooms as in a prison but should be permitted to go out, and this privilege should be taken as evidence of their virtue and propriety. Still, wives should not act with their husbands as the moon does with the sun; for when the moon is near the sun it is never visible, but when it is distant it stands resplendent by itself. Therefore, I would have wives be seen in public with their husbands, but when their husbands are away wives should stay at home. By maintaining an honest gaze in their eyes, they can communicate most significantly as in painting, which is called silent poetry. They also should maintain dignity in the motion of their heads and the other movements of their bodies. Now that I have spoken about demeanor and behavior, I shall now speak of speech.

CHAPTER FOUR: ON SPEECH AND SILENCE

Isocrates warns men to speak on those matters that they know well and about which they cannot, on account of their dignity, remain silent. We commend women to concede the former as the property of men, but they should consider the latter to be appropriate to themselves as well as to men. Loquacity cannot be sufficiently reproached in women, as many very learned and wise men have stated, nor can silence be sufficiently

applauded. For this reason women were prohibited by the laws of the Romans from pleading either criminal or civil law cases.

CHAPTER EIGHT: ON DOMESTIC MATTERS AND THE MANAGEMENT OF HOUSEHOLD SERVANTS

We are interested in the care of our property and the diligence proper to our servants and staff because it is necessary to have both property and servants, without whose help family life itself cannot exist. Surely it is in these two things that the management of domestic matters primarily is involved, for unless a wife imposes her own judgment and precepts on these matters, the operation of the household will have no order and will be in great disarray. Men are naturally endowed with strength of mind and body; both for these and other reasons, they provision their homes by their labor, industry, and willingness to undergo hardships. Conversely, I think we may infer that since women are by nature weak they should diligently care for things concerning the household. For weakness can never be separated from cares nor cares from vigilance. What is the use of bringing home great wealth unless the wife will work at preserving, maintaining, and utilizing it?

They ought to attend, therefore, to governing their households just as Pericles daily attended to the affairs of Athens.[1] And they ought always to consider how well they are doing so that they will never be deficient in their care, interest, and diligence in household matters. They will surely be successful in this matter if they do what they should do, that is, if they are accustomed to stay at home and oversee everything there.

1 Cf. Xenophon Oeconomicus 7.3.5.

So that a wife's duty might be commended to posterity, there were affixed to the bronze statue of Gaia Caecilia, the daughter of Tarquinius, an ordinary shoe and a distaff and spindle, so that those objects might in some way signify that her diligent work at home ought to be imitated by future generations.[2] What neglectful landowner can hope to have hard-working peasants? What slothful general can make his soldiers vigilant for the state? Therefore, if a wife would like to have her maids working hard at home, she should not merely instruct them with words but she ought also by her actions to demonstrate, indicate, and show what they should be doing. Indeed, there is surely nothing more excellent in household affairs than that everything be put in its place, because there is nothing more beautiful, more useful than order, which is always of the greatest importance. We consider that an army or chorus can be called anything but an army or chorus unless its organization is well preserved.[3] I would have wives imitate the leaders of bees, who supervise, receive, and preserve whatever comes into their hives, to the end that, unless necessity dictates otherwise, they remain in their honeycombs where they develop and mature beautifully. Wives may send their maids and manservants abroad if they think this would be useful to them. But if, indeed, these servants are required at home, they should urge, order, and require their presence. Wives should also consider it their duties to see to it that no harm comes to their husbands' winecellars, pantries, and oil cellars.

It is now proper to speak, as we have promised, about servants, who, provided they are not neglected, can add great luster to our houses and be useful and pleasant. So they will be if wives will instruct them carefully and if they will not get angry with them before, having warned them, they discover that they have made the same mistakes. I should like that wives, in these matters as in others, follow the example of the leaders of the bees, who allow no one under their control to be lazy or negligent.[4]

Thrifty wives constantly ought to seek out and appoint sober stewards for the provisions and address them courteously and be generous of them, so that by the great interest of the mistress the industry of the steward daily increases. They should feed their servants so that they will satisfy both their human needs and reward their constant labor. Wives should clothe their servants comfortably as befits the season, climate, and place. Moreover, as Hesiod advises, they should always be careful that servants are not separated from their children and families,[5] for servants will always find a way to stay together with their own family, even secretly. Furthermore, servants will be very grateful if especially good medical care is provided when a member of their family is taken sick. For these acts of humanity, this solicitiousness will make servants very conscientious and hardworking for the household.

2 Cf. Plutarch Quaestiones Romanae 30; Moralia 271E.
3 Cf. Xenophon Oeconomicus 1.3.
4 Cf. Xenophon Oeconomicus7.33.
5 Probably an allusion to Hesiod Opera et Dies 373.

After their offspring have passed their infancy, mothers should use all their skill, care, and effort to ensure that their children are endowed with excellent qualities of mind and body. First they should instruct them in their duty toward Immortal God, their country, and their parents, so that they will be instilled from their earliest years with those qualities that are the foundation of all other virtues. Only those children who fear God, obey the laws, honor their parents, respect their superiors, are pleasant with their equals and courteous to their inferiors, will exhibit much hope for themselves. Children should meet all people with a civil demeanor, pleasant countenance, and friendly words. But they should be on the most familiar terms with only the best people. Thus they will learn moderation in food and drink so that they may lay, as it were, the foundation of temperance for their future lives. They should be taught to avoid these pleasures that are dishonorable, and they should apply their efforts and thoughts to those matters that are the most becoming and will be useful and pleasant when they become older. If mothers are able to instruct their children in these matters, their offspring will much more easily and better receive the benefit of education.

Mothers should often warn their children to abstain from excessive laughter and to avoid words that denote a rash character. That is the mark of stupidity, the evidence of passion. Moreover, children should be warned not ever to speak on those matters that are base in the act. Therefore, mothers should restrain them from vulgar or cutting words. If their children should say anything that is obscene or licentious, mothers should not greet it with a laugh or a kiss, but with a whip.

Moreover, they should teach their children not to criticize anyone because of his poverty or the low birth of his lineage or other misfortunes, for they are sure to make bitter enemies from such actions or develop an attitude of arrogance. Mothers should teach their children sports in which they so willingly learn to exert themselves that, if the occasion arises, they can easily bear even more difficult hardships. I would have mothers sharply criticized for displays of anger, greed, or sexual desire in the presence of their offspring, for these vices weaken virtue. If mothers act appropriately, their children will learn from infancy to condemn, avoid, and hate these most filthy mistresses and they will take care to revere the names of God and will be afraid to take them in vain. For whoever has been taught at an early age to despise the Divinity, will they not as adults surely curse Him? Therefore, it is of great importance to train children from infancy so that they never swear. Indeed, those who swear readily because of some misfortune are not deserving of trust, and those who readily swear very often unwittingly betray themselves. Mothers ought to teach their children to speak the truth.

Therefore, my Lorenzo, your compatriots ought to be stirred by your example and follow you with great enthusiasm, for in Ginevra you have taken a wife who is a virgin well endowed with virtue charm, a noble lineage, and great wealth. What more outstanding, more worthy model could I propose than yours? What more shining, more worthy example than yours, since in this outstanding city of Florence you are most eminently connected through your father, grandfather, and ancestors? You have taken a wife whose great wealth the entire world indeed admires but whose chastity, constancy, and prudence all men of goodwill esteem highly. They consider that you are blessed and happy to have her as a wife, and she is to have you as a husband. Since you have contracted such an outstanding and fine marriage, these same men ask God Immortal that you will have the best children who will become very honored citizens in your state. These matters might perhaps seem negligible since I am treating them, but indeed they are, in their own fashion, borne out in your marriage. Thus, surely young men who follow your example will profit more than only by following my precepts; just as laws are much more likely to be observed in a city when they are obeyed by its ruler, so, since your own choice of a wife is consistent with my teachings, we may hope that these precepts will be followed by the youth.

Lorenzo Valla Skewers the Supposed "Donation of Constantine" c. 1440

The "Donation of Constantine" was a document forged by the papal bureaucracy in the mid 8th century, at a time when the Church was attempting to demonstrate its claim to temporal power against a growing power-base in the Frankish kingdom. In this document, Constantine the Great surrenders his Empire to the Pope, Sylvester I (314-335 CE), in exchange for his curing him of leprosy. (Neither event actually occurred, of course.) In fairness to the papal court, however, the forging of documents was not an unusual practice at the time, especially when it was believed that the text *ought* to have existed anyway. However, the document was written in an extremely poor Latin, with several easily-spotted errors, and it had been exposed as a forgery as early as the 15th century. Nevertheless, using all the skills he could muster as a "philologist" (a student of language), the remarkably gifted writer Lorenzo Valla (1406-1457) blasted the papacy for laying claim to the Empire in a bogus text. Working for a king who wished to stymie the papacy, Valla unloaded all the vitriol he could muster at the Church hierarchy, and especially at the hypothetical monk who had created the document in the first place. In his treatise, Valla quoted from the forgery, and then attacked its writer.

Source: *The Treatise of Lorenzo Valla on the Donation of Constantine,* translated by Christopher B. Coleman (New Haven: Yale University Press, 1922), pp. 25, 27, 95, 97, 131, and 133.

FOCUS QUESTIONS:

1. How does Valla express his outrage, and what rhetorical forms does he employ?
2. How does he use the tools of "humanism" to do so?

I know that for a long time now men's ears are waiting to hear the offense with which I charge the Roman pontiffs. It is, indeed, an enormous one, due either to supine ignorance, or to gross avarice which is the slave of idols, or to pride of empire of which cruelty is ever the companion. For during some centuries now, either they have not known that the Donation of Constantine is spurious and forged, or else they themselves forged it, and their successors walking in the same way of deceit as their elders have defended as true what they knew to be false, dishonoring the majesty of the pontificate, dishonoring the memory of ancient pontiffs, dishonoring the Christian religion, confounding everything with murders, disasters and crimes. They say the city of Rome is theirs, theirs the kingdom of Sicily and of Naples, the whole of Italy, the Gauls, the Spains, the Germans, the Britons, indeed the whole West; for all these are contained in the instrument of the Donation itself. So all these are yours, supreme pontiff? And it is your purpose to recover them all? To despoil all kings and princes of the West of their cities or compel them to pay you a yearly tribute, is that your plan?

I, on the contrary, think it fairer to let the princes despoil you of all the empire you hold. For, as I shall show, that Donation whence the supreme pontiffs will have their right derived was unknown equally to Sylvester and to Constantine....

How in the world – this is much more absurd, and impossible in the nature of things – could one speak of Constantinople as one of the patriarchal sees, when it was not yet a patriarchate, nor a see, nor a Christian city, nor named Constantinople, nor founded, nor planned! For the "privilege" was granted, so it says, the third day after Constantine became a Christian; when as yet Byzantium, not Constantinople, occupied that site. I am a liar if this fool does not confess as much himself. For toward the end of the "privilege" he writes:

"Wherefore we have perceived it to be fitting that our empire and our royal power should be transferred in the regions of the East; and that in the province of Bizantia [sic], in the most fitting place, a city should be built in our name; and that our empire should there be established."

But if he was intending to transfer the empire, he had not yet transferred it; if he was intending to establish his empire there, he had not yet established it; if he was planning to build a city, he had not yet built it. Therefore he could not have spoken of it as a patriarchal see, as one of the four sees, as Christian, as having this name, nor as already built. According to the history [the Life of Sylvester] which Palea cites as evidence, he had not yet even thought of founding it. And this beast, whether Palea or some one else who Palea follows, does not notice that he contradicts this history, in which it is said that Constantine issued the decree concerning the founding of the city, not on his own initiative, but at a command received in his sleep from God, not at Rome but at Byzantium, not within a few days [of his conversion] but several years after, and that he learned its name by revelation in a dream. Who then does not see that the man who wrote the "privilege" lived long after the time of Constantine, and in his effort to embellish his falsehood forgot that earlier he had said that these events took place at Rome on the third day after Constantine was baptized? So the trite old proverb applies nicely to him, "Liars need good memories."

And how is it that he speaks of a province of "Byzantia," when it was a town, Byzantium by name? The place was by no means large enough for the erection of so great a city; for the old city of Byzantium was included within the walls of Constantinople. And this man says the [new] city is to be built on the most fitting place in it! Why does he choose to put Thrace, in which Byzantium lies, in the East, when it lies to the north? I suppose Constantine did not know the place which he had chosen for the building of the city, in what latitude it was, whether it was a town or a province, nor how large it was!...

"If any one, moreover – which we do not believe – prove a scorner in this matter, he shall be condemned and shall be subject to eternal damnation; and shall feel the holy apostles of God, Peter and Paul, opposed to him in the present and in the future life. And he shall be burned in the lower hell and shall perish with the devil and all the impious."

This terrible threat is the usual one, not of a secular ruler, but of the early priests and flamens, and nowadays, of ecclesiastics. And so this is not the utterance of Constantine, but of some fool of a priest who, stuffed and pudgy, knew neither what to say nor how to say it, and, gorged with eating and heated with wine, belched out these wordy sentences which convey nothing to another, but turn against the author himself. First he says, "shall be subject to eternal damnation," then as though more could be added, he wishes to add something else, and to eternal penalties he joins penalties in the present life; and after he frightens us with God's condemnation, he frightens us with the hatred of Peter, as though it were something still greater. Why he should add Paul, and why Paul alone, I do not know. And with his usual drowsiness he returns again to eternal penalties, as though he had not said that before. Now if these threats and curses were Constantine's, I in turn would curse him as a tyrant and destroyer of my country, and would threaten that I, as a Roman, would take vengeance on him. But who would be afraid of the curse of an overly avaricious man, and one saying a counterfeit speech after the manner of actors, and terrifying people in the role of Constantine? This is being a hypocrite in the true sense, if we press the Greek word closely; that is, hiding your own personality under another's.

Marriage in the Renaissance: A Serious Business 1464–1465

The formation of marriage ties in Medieval and Renaissance Florence was not simply a matter of love—or, rather, it was very rarely about love. Particularly among long-established elites, blood and family ties were valued more than almost anything else. In the following excerpt, we see some of the honor, prestige, and property that were at stake in marriage negotiations in 14th century Italy.

Source: "Letters from Alessandra Strozzi in Florence to her son Filippo in Naples" Alessandra Macinghi Strozzi, Lettere di una gentildonna fiorentina,ed. C. Guasti, (Florence, 1877), 394–95, 458–59, 463–65, 475–76, cited in *The Society of Renaissance Florence: A Documentary Study,* ed. Gene Brucker, (New York: Harper and Row, Inc., 1972), 37–40.

Focus Questions:

1. What was the role of women in arranging suitable marriages? Is this surprising?
2. What factors, in this mother's opinion, create a good marriage?

MARRIAGE NEGOTIATIONS: THE STROZZI, 1464-65

[April 20, 1464]... Concerning the matter of a wife [for Filippo], it appears to me that if Francesco di Messer Guglielmino Tanagli wishes to give his daughter, that it would be a fine marriage.... Now I will speak with Marco [Parenti, Alessandra's son-in-law], to see if there are other prospects that would be better, and if there are none, then we will learn if he wishes to give her [in marriage].... Francesco Tanagli has a good reputation, and he has held office, not the highest, but still he has been in office. You may ask: "Why should he give her to someone in exile?" There are three reasons. First, there aren't many young men of good family who have both virtue and property. Secondly, she has only a small dowry, 1,000 florins, which is the dowry of an artisan.... Third, I believe that he will give her away, because he has a large family and he will need help to settle them....

[July 26, 1465]... Marco Parenti came to me and told me that for some time, he has been considering how to find a wife for you.... There is the daughter of Francesco di Messer Guglielmino Tanagli, and until now there hasn't been anyone who is better suited for you than this girl. It is true that we haven't discussed this at length, for a reason which you understand. However, we have made secret inquiries, and the only people who are willing to make a marriage agreement with exiles have some flaw, either a lack of money or something else. Now money is the least serious drawback, if the other factors are positive.... Francesco is a good friend of Marco and he trusts him. On S. Jacopo's day, he spoke to him discreetly and persuasively, saying that for several months he had heard that we were interested in the girl and... that when we had made up our minds, she will come to us willingly. [He said that] you were a worthy man, and that his family had always made good marriages, but that he had only a small dowry to give her, and so he would prefer to send her outside of Florence to someone of worth, rather than to give her to someone here, from among those who were available, with little money.... He invited Marco to his house and he called the girl down.... Marco said that she was attractive and that she appeared to be suitable. We have information that she is affable and competent. She is responsible for a large family (there are twelve children, six boys and six girls), and the mother is always pregnant and isn't very competent....

[August 17, 1465]... Sunday morning I went to the first mass at S. Reparata... to see the Adimari girl, who customarily goes to that mass, and I found the Tanagli girl there. Not knowing who she was, I stood beside her.... She is very attractive, well proportioned, as large or larger than Caterina [Alessandra's daughter].... She has a long face, and her features are not very delicate, but they aren't like a peasant's. From her demeanor, she does not appear to me to be indolent.... I walked behind her as we left the church, and thus I realized that she was one of the Tanagli. So I am somewhat enlightened about her....

[August 31, 1465]... I have recently received some very favorable information [about the Tanagli girl] from two individuals.... They are in agreement that whoever gets her will be content.... Concerning her beauty, they told me what I had already seen, that she is attractive and well-proportioned. Her face is long, but I couldn't look directly into her face, since she appeared to be aware that I was examining her... and so she turned away from me like the wind.... She reads quite well... and she can dance and sing.... Her father is one of the most respected young men of Florence, very civilized in his manners. He is fond of this girl, and it appears that he has brought her up well.

So yesterday I sent for Marco and told him what I had learned. And we talked about the matter for a while, and decided that he should say something to the father and give him a little hope, but not so much that we couldn't withdraw, and find out from him the amount of the dowry.... Marco and Francesco [Tanagli] had a discussion, about this yesterday (I haven't seen him since), and Marco should inform you about it one of these days, and you will then understand more clearly what should follow. May God help us to choose what will contribute to our tranquillity and to the consolation of us all....

[September 13, 1465]... Marco came to me and said that he had met with Francesco Tanagli, who had spoken very coldly, so that I understand that he had changed his mind. They say that he wants to discuss the matter with his brother-in-law, Messer Antonio Ridolfi.... And he [Francesco] says that it would be a serious matter to send his daughter so far away [to Naples], and to a house that might be described as a hotel. And he spoke in such a way that it is clear that he has changed his mind. I believe that this is the result of the long delay in our replying to him, both yours and Marco's. Two weeks ago, he could have given him a little hope. Now this delay has angered him, and he has at hand some prospect that is more attractive.... I am very annoyed by this business; I can't recall when I have been so troubled. For I felt that this marriage would have satisfied our needs better than any other we could have found....

[Filippo Strozzi eventually married Fiametta di Donato Adimari, in 1466.]

Niccoló Machiavelli
From the *Discourses on Livy*
1513–1517

Born in 1469, Niccolò Machiavelli found a job in the bureaucracy of the Florentine Republic in 1498, loving the opportunity to examine political intrigue, diplomatic exchanges, and the nitty-gritty of policy creation at close quarters. However, as part of a general peace treaty in Italy in 1512, the Medici were restored to Florence and Machiavelli lost his job. Moreover, he was soon arrested, drawn by the rope, and tortured; after demonstrating his innocence, he was released and, for the next 14 years, wrote a series of letters, treatises, and even a comedy, much of it in the effort to rehabilitate himself with Florence's ruling elite. From this enforced exile came one of the most remarkable pieces of political theory ever to have been created, The *Discourses on Livy*, a portion of which was written up as a separate treatise entitled The Prince. Experience had taught him that "the ends justify the means", and he believed that history demonstrated the same phenomenon.

Source: The *Discourses* (Penguin Classics), translation by Leslie Walker, ed. Bernard Crick (New York: Penguin Books, 1983), 131–135.

Focus Questions:

1. Under what conditions is a powerful tyrant necessary?
2. What sorts of examples does Machiavelli use in his argument? How does he derive general principles from them?

That it is necessary to be the Sole Authority if one would constitute a Republic afresh or would reform it thoroughly regardless of its Ancient Institutions

To some it will appear strange that I have got so far in my discussion of Roman history without having made any mention of the founders of that republic or of either its religious or its military institutions. Hence, that I may not keep the minds of those who are anxious to hear about such things any longer in suspense, let me say that many perchance will think it a bad precedent that the founder of a civic state, such as Romulus, should first have killed his brother, and then have acquiesced in the death of Titus Tatius, the Sabine, whom he had chosen as his colleague in the kingdom. They will urge that, if such actions be justifiable, ambitious citizens who are eager to govern, will follow the example of their prince and use violence against those who are opposed to their authority. A view that will hold good provided we leave out of consideration the end which Romulus had in committing these murders.

One should take it as a general rule that rarely, if ever, does it happen that a state, whether it be a republic or a kingdom, is either well-ordered at the outset or radically transformed vis-à-vis its old institutions unless this be done by one person. It is likewise essential that there should be but one person upon whose mind and method depends any similar process of organization. Wherefore the prudent organizer of a state whose intention it is to govern not in his own interests but for the common good, and not in the interest of his successors but for the sake of that fatherland which is common to all, should contrive to be alone in his authority. Nor will any reasonable man blame him for taking any action, however extraordinary, which may be of service in the organizing of a kingdom or the constituting of a republic. It is a sound maxim that reprehensible actions may be justified by their effects, and that when the effect is good, as it was in the case of Romulus, it always justifies the action. For it is the man who uses violence to spoil things, not the man who uses it to mend them, that is blameworthy.

The organizer of a state ought further to have sufficient prudence and virtue not to bequeath the authority he has assumed to any other person, for, seeing that men are more prone to evil than to good, his successor might well make ambitious use of that which he had used virtuously. Furthermore, though but one person suffices for the purpose of organization, what he has organized will not last long if it continues to rest on the shoulders of one man, but may well last if many remain in charge and many look to its maintenance. Because, though the many are incompetent to draw up a constitution since diversity of opinion will prevent them from discovering how best to do it, yet when they realize it has been done, they will not agree to abandon it.

That Romulus was a man of this character, that for the death of his brother and of his colleague he deserves to be excused, and that what he did was done for the common good and not to satisfy his personal ambition, is shown by his having at once instituted a senate with which he consulted and with whose views his decisions were in accord. Also, a careful consideration of the authority which Romulus reserved to himself will show that all he reserved to himself was the command of the army in time of war and the convoking of the senate. It is clear, too, that when the Tarquins were expelled and Rome became free, none of its ancient institutions were changed, save that in lieu of a permanent king there were appointed each year two consuls. This shows that the original institutions of this city as a whole were more in conformity with a political and self-governing state than with absolutism or tyranny.

I might adduce in support of what I have just said numberless examples, for example Moses, Lycurgus, Solon and other founders of kingdoms and republics who assumed authority that they might formulate laws to the common good; but this I propose to omit since it is well known. I shall adduce but one further example, not so celebrated but worth considering by those who are contemplating the drawing up of good laws. It is this. Agis, King of Sparta, was considering how to confine the activities of the Spartans to the limits originally set for them by the laws of Lycurgus, because it seemed to him that it was owing to their having deviated from them in part that this city had lost a good deal of its ancient virtue, and, in consequence, a good deal of its power and of its empire. He was, however, while his project was still in the initial stage, killed by the Spartan ephors, who took him to be a man who was out to set up a tyranny. But Cleomenes, his successor in that kingdom, having learned from some records and writings of Agis which he had discovered, what was the latter's true mind and intention, determined to pursue the same plan. He realized, however, that be could not do this for the good of his country unless he became the sole authority there, and, since it seemed to him impossible owing to man's ambition to help the many against the will of the few, he took a suitable opportunity and had all the ephors killed and anybody else who might obstruct him. He then renewed in their entirety the laws of Lycurgus. By so doing he gave fresh life to Sparta, and his reputation might thereby have become as great as that of Lycurgus if it had not been for the power of the Macedonians and the weakness of other Greek republics. For, after Sparta had thus been reorganized, it was attacked by the Macedonians, and, since its forces proved to be inferior and it could get no outside help, it was defeated, with the result that Cleomenes' plans, however just and praiseworthy, were never brought to completion. All things considered, therefore, I conclude that it is necessary to be the sole authority if one is to organize a state, and that Romulus' action in regard to the death of Remus and Titus Tatius is excusable, not blameworthy.

Benvenuto Cellini: The Life of an Artist 1558–1562

Benvenuto Cellini (1500-1571) was an artist who made his living as a goldsmith in Renaissance Florence and Rome. He was also quite a talented musician. The following excerpt, from his autobiography written between 1558 and 1562, describes his life and work as an artist. It was not published until the 18th century, when it became quite popular.

Source: Benvenuto Cellini, *The Life of Benvenuto Ceillini,* 4th edition, trans. J. A. Symonds, cited in ed. John L. Beatty and Oliver A. Johnson, Heritage of Western Civilization,vol. 1, 7th edition, (Englewood Cliffs, NJ: Prentice Hall, 1991), 397–411, passim.

Focus Questions:

1. What interest did the Madonna Porzia have in this rising young artist?
2. What does this document reveal about the artistic ambience of Rome in this period?

II

It is true that men who have laboured with some show of excellence, have already given knowledge of themselves to the world; and this alone ought to suffice them; I mean the fact that they have proved their manhood and achieved renown. Yet one must needs live like others; and so in a work like this there will always be found occasion for natural bragging, which is of divers kinds, and the first is that a man should let others know he draws his lineage from persons of worth and most ancient origin.

When I reached the age of fifteen, I put myself, against my father's will, to the goldsmith's trade with a man called Antonio, son of Sandro, known commonly as Marcone the goldsmith. He was a most excellent craftsman and a very good fellow to boot, high-spirited and frank in all his ways. My father would not let him give me wages like the other apprentices; for having taken up the study of this art to please myself, he wished me to indulge by whim for drawing to the full. I did so willingly enough; and that honest master of mine took marvellous delight in my performances. He had an only son, a bastard, to whom he often gave his orders, in order to spare me. My liking for the art was so great, or, I may truly say, my natural bias, both one and the other, that in a few months I caught up the good, nay, the best young craftsmen in our business, and began to reap the fruits of my labours. I did not, however, neglect to gratify my good father from time to time by playing on the flute or cornet. Each time he heard me, I used to make his tears fall accompanied with deep-drawn sighs of satisfaction. My filial piety often made me give him that contentment, and induced me to pretend that I enjoyed the music too.

XIV

[... Later, after traveling to Rome, he entered a new workshop]

"Welcome to my workshop; and do as you have promised; let your hands declare what man you are." He gave me a very fine piece of silver plate to work on for a cardinal. It was a little oblong box, copied from the prophyry sarcophagus before the door of the Rotonda. Beside what I copied, I enriched it with so many elegant masks of my invention, that my master went about showing it through the art, and boasting that so good a piece of work had been turned out from his shop. It was about half a cubit in size, and was so constructed as to serve for a salt-cellar at table. This was the first earning that I touched at Rome, and part of it I sent to assist my good father; the rest I kept for my own use, living upon it while I went about studying the antiquities of Rome, until my money failed, and I had to return to the shop for work.

After undertaking some new commissions, I took it into my head, as soon as I had finished them, to change my master; I had indeed been worried into doing so by a certain Milanese, called Pagolo Arsago. My first master, Firenzuola, had a great quarrel about this with Arsago, and abused him in my presence; whereupon I took up speech in defence of my new master. I said that I was born free, and free I meant to live, and that there was no reason to complain of him, far less of me, since some few crowns of wages were still due to me; also that I chose to go, like a free journeyman, where it pleased me, knowing I did wrong to no man. My new master then put in with his excuses, saying that he had not asked me to come, and that I should gratify him by returning to Firenzuola. To this I replied that I was not aware of wronging the latter in any way, and as I had completed his commissions, I chose to be my own master and not the man of others, and that he who wanted me must beg me of myself. Firenzuola cried: "I don't intend to beg you of yourself; I have done with you; don't show yourself again upon my premises." I reminded him of the money he owed me. He laughed me in the face; on which I said that if I knew how to use my tools in handicraft as well as he had seen, I could be quite as clever with my sword in claiming the just payment of my labour. While we were exchanging these words, an old man happened to come up, called Maestro Antonio, of San Marino. He was the chief among the Roman goldsmiths, and had been Firenzuola's master. Hearing what I had to say, which I took good care that he should understand, he immediately espoused my cause, and bade Firenzuola pay me. The dispute waxed warm, because Firenzuola was an admirable swordsman, far better than he was a goldsmith. Yet reason made itself heard; and I backed my cause with the same spirit, till I got myself paid. In course of time Firenzuola and I became friends, and at his request I stood godfather to one of his children.

XV

I went on working with Pagolo Arsago, and earned a good deal of money, the greater part of which I always sent to my good father. At the end of two years, upon my father's entreaty, I returned to Florence, and put myself once more under Francesco Salimbene, with whom I earned a great deal, and took continual pains to improve in my arts. I renewed my intimacy with Francesco di Filippo; and though I was too much given to pleasure, owing to that accursed music, I never neglected to devote some hours of the day or night to study.

XIX

During that time I went to draw sometimes in Michel Agnolo's chapel, and sometimes in the house of Agostino Chigi of Siena, which contained many incomparable paintings by the hand of that great master Raffaello., This I did on feast-days, because the house was then inhabited by Messer Gismondo, Agostino's brother. They plumed themselves exceedingly when they saw young men of my sort coming to study in their palaces. Gismondo's wife, noticing my frequent presence in that house-she was a lady as courteous as could be, and of surpassing beauty-came up to me one day, looked at my drawings, and asked me if I was a sculptor or a painter; to whom I said I was a goldsmith. She remarked that I drew too well for a goldsmith; and having made one of her waiting-maids bring a lily of the finest diamonds set in gold, she showed it to me, and bade me value it. I valued it at 800 crowns. Then she said that I had very nearly hit the mark, and asked me whether I felt capable of setting the stones really well. I said that I should much like to do so, and began before her eyes to make a little sketch for it, working all the better because of the pleasure I took in conversing with so lovely and agreeable a gentlewoman. When the sketch was finished, another Roman lady of great beauty joined us; she had been above, and now descending to the ground-floor, asked Madonna Porzia what she was doing there. She answered with a smile: "I am amusing myself by watching this worthy young man at his drawing; he is as good as he is handsome." I had by this time acquired a trifle of assurance, mixed, however, with some honest bashfulness; so I blushed and said: "Such as I am, lady, I shall ever be most ready to serve you." The gentlewoman, also slightly blushing, said: "You know well that I want you to serve me"; and reaching me the lily, told me to take it away; and gave me besides twenty golden crowns which she had in her bag, and added: "Set me the jewel after the fashion you have sketched, and keep for me the old gold in which it is now set." On this the Roman lady observed: "If I were in that young man's body, I should go off without asking leave." Madonna Porzia replied that virtues rarely are at home with vices, and that if I did such a thing, I should strongly belie my good looks of an honest man. Then turning round, she took the Roman lady's hand, and with a pleasant smile said: "Farewell, Benvenuto." I stayed on a short while at the drawing I was making, which was a copy of a Jove by Raffaello. When I had finished it and left the house, I set myself to making a little model of wax, in order to show how the jewel would look when it was completed. This I took to Madonna Porzia, whom I found with the same Roman lady. Both of them were highly satisfied with my work, and treated me so kindly that, being somewhat emboldened, I promised the jewel should be twice as good as the model.

Accordingly I set hand to it, and in twelve days I finished it in the form of a fleur-de-lys, as I have said above, ornamenting it with little masks, children, and animals, exquisitely enamelled, whereby the diamonds which formed the lily were more than doubled in effect.

XX

While I was working at this piece, Lucagnolo, of whose ability I have before spoken, showed considerable discontent, telling me over and over again that I might acquire far more profit and honour by helping him to execute large plate, as I had done at first. I made him answer that, whenever I chose, I should always be capable of working at great silver pieces; but that things like that on which I was now engaged were not commissioned every day; and beside their bringing no less honour than large silver plate, there was also more profit to be made by them. He laughed me in the face, and said: "Wait and see Benvenuto; for by the time that you have finished that work of yours, I will make haste to have finished this vase, which I took in hand when you did the jewel; and then experience shall teach you what profit I shall get from my vase, and what you will get from your ornament." I answered that I was very glad indeed to enter into such a competition with so good a craftsman as he was, because the end would show which of us was mistaken. Accordingly both the one and the other of us, with a scornful smile upon our lips, bent our heads in grim earnest to the work, which both were now desirous of accomplishing; so that after about ten days, each had finished his undertaking with the great delicacy and artistic skill.

So he took his vase and carried it to the Pope, who was very well pleased with it, and ordered at once that he should be paid at the ordinary rate of such large plate. Meanwhile I carried mine to Madonna Porzia, who looked at it with astonishment, and told me I had far surpassed my promise. Then she bade me ask for my reward whatever I liked; for it seemed to her my desert was so great that if I craved a castle she could hardly recompense me; but since that was not in her hands to bestow, she added laughing that I must beg what lay within her power. I answered that the greatest reward I could desire for my labour was to have satisfied her ladyship. Then, smiling in my turn, and bowing to her, I took my leave, saying I wanted no reward but that. She turned to the Roman lady and said: "You see that the qualities we discerned in him are companied by virtues, and not vices." They both expressed their admiration, and then Madonna Porzio continued: "Friend Benvenuto, have you never heard it said that when the poor give to the rich, the devil laughs?" I replied: "Quite true! and yet, in the midst of all his troubles, I should like this time to see him laugh"; and as I took my leave, she said that this time she had no will to bestow on him that favour.

When I came back to the shop, Lucagnolo had the money for his vase in a paper packet; and on my arrive he cried out: "Come and compare the price of your jewel with the price of my plate." I said that he must leave things as they were till the next day, because I hoped that even as my work in its kind was not less excellent than his, so I should be able to show him quite an equal price for it.

XXI

On the following, Madonna Porzia sent a major-domo of hers to my shop, who called me out, and putting into my hands a paper packet full of money from his lady, told me that she did not choose the devil should have his whole laugh out; by which she hinted that the money sent me was not the entire payment merited by my industry, and other messages were added worthy of so courteous a lady. Lucagnolo, who was burning to compare his packet with mine, burst into the shop, then in the presence of twelve journeymen and some neighbors, eager to behold the result of this competition, he seized his packet, scornfully exclaiming"Ou! Ou!"three or four times, while he poured his money on the counter with a great noise. They were twenty-five crowns in giulios; and he fancied that mine would be four or five crowns di moneta. I for my part, stunned and stifled by his cries, and by the looks and smiles of the bystanders, first peeped into my packet; then, after seeing that it contained nothing but gold, I retired to one end of the counter, and keeping my eyes lowered and making no noise at all, I lifted it with both hands suddenly above my head, and emptied it like a mill hopper. My coin was twice as much as his; which caused the onlookers, who had fixed their eyes on me with some derision, to turn round suddenly to him and say: "Lucagnolo, Benvenuto's pieces, being all of gold and twice as many as yours, make a far finer effect." I thought for certain that, what with jealousy and what with shame, Lucagnolo would have fallen dead upon the spot; and though he took the third part of my gain, since I was a journeymen (for such is the custom of the trade, two-thirds fall to the workman and one-third to the masters of the shop), yet inconsiderate envy had more power in him than avarice: it ought indeed to have worked quite the other way; he being a peasant's son from Iesi. He cursed his art and those who taught it to him, vowing that thenceforth he would never work at large plate, but give his whole attention to those whoreson gewgaws, since they were so well paid. Equally engaged on my side, I answered that every bird sang its own note; that he talked after the fashion of the hovels he came from; but that I dared swear that I should succeed with ease in making his lubberly lumber, while he would never be successful in my whoreson gewgaws. Thus I flung off in a passion, telling him that I would soon show him that I spoke truth. The bystanders openly declared against him, holding him for a lout, as indeed he was, and me for a man, as I had proved myself.

XXIII

While I was pushing forward Salamanca's vase, I had only one little boy as help, whom I had taken at the entreaty of friends, and half against my own will, to be my workman. He was about fourteen years of age, bore the name of Paulino, and was son to a Roman burgess, who lived upon the income of his property. Paulino was the best-mannered, the most honest, and the most beautiful boy I ever saw in my whole life. His modest ways and actions, together with his superlative beauty and his devotion to myself, bred in me as great an affection for him as a man's breast can hold. This passionate love led me often-times to delight the lad with music; for I observed that his marvellous features, which by complexion wore a tone of modest melancholy, brightened up, and when I took my cornet, broke into a smile so lovely and sweet, that I do not marvel at the silly stories which the Greeks have written about the deities of heaven. Indeed, if my boy had lived in those times, he would probably have turned their heads still more. He had a sister, named Faustina, more beautiful, I verily believe, than that Faustina about whom the old books gossip so. Sometimes he took me to their vineyard, and, so far as I could judge, it struck me that Paulino's good father would have welcomed me as a son-in-law. This affair led me to play more than I was used to do.

It happened at that time that one Giangiacomo of Cesena, a musician in the Pope's band, and a very excellent performer, sent word through Lorenzo, the trumpeter of Lucca, who is now in our Duke's service, to inquire whether I was inclined to help them at the Pope's Ferragosto, playing soprano with my cornet in some motets of great beauty selected by them for that occasion. Although I had the greatest desire to finish the vase I had begun, yet, since music has a wondrous charm of its own, and also because I wished to please my old father, I consented to join them. During eight days before the festival we practised two hours a day together; then on the first of August we went to the Belvedere, and while Pope Clemente was at table, we played those carefully studied motets so well that his Holiness protested he had never heard music more sweetly executed or with better harmony of parts. He sent for Giangiacomo, and asked him where and how he had procured so excellent a cornet for soprano, and inquired particularly who I was. Giangiacomo told him my name in full. Whereupon the Pope said: "So, then, he is the son of Maestro Giovanni?" On being assured I was, the Pope expressed his wish to have me in his service with the other bandsmen. Giangiacomo replied: "Most blessed Father, I cannot pretend for certain that you will get him, for his profession, to which he devotes himself assiduously, is that of a goldsmith, and he works in it miraculously well, and earns by it far more than he could do by playing." To this the Pope added: "I am the better inclined to him now that I find him possessor of a talent more than I expected. See that he obtains the same salary as the rest of you; and tell him from me to join my service, and that I will find work enough by the day for him to do at his other trade." Then stretching out his hand, he gave him a hundred golden crowns of the Camera in a handkerchief, and said: "Divide these so that he may take his share."

CHAPTER 10

Reformations and Counter-Reformations

The Act of Supremacy 1534

In England, the Protestant Reformation unfolded as an act of state when King Henry VIII (r. 1509-1547), in conjunction with the English Parliament, broke all ties with the Catholic Church and established a Protestant Church of England or the Anglican Church. The English break with the Catholic Church was not tied to the reforms of Luther or Calvin, but more motivated by Henry's desire for an annulment of his marriage to Catherine of Aragon. Henry sought to override Pope Clement VII's refusal to grant an annulment so he could marry Anne Boleyn (1507-1536) who he believed would be able to provide him with a male heir. This act, passed by the English Parliament, formally established the Church of England as an independent institution from the Catholic Church.

Source: Statutes of the Realm, vol. 3, (London, 1810-28), 436-39.

Focus Questions:

1. What did this act accomplish, and by what authority or power?
2. What was the relationship between church and state in England as a result of this act?
3. How and why was this tied to the Protestant Reformation?

ALBEIT the king's majesty justly and rightfully is and ought to be the supreme head of the Church of England, and so is recognized by the clergy of this realm in their Convocations, yet nevertheless for corroboration and confirmation thereof, and for increase of virtue in Christ's religion within this realm of England, and to repress and extirp all errors, heresies, and other enormities and abuses heretofore used in the same: be it enacted by authority of this present Parliament, that the king our sovereign lord, his heirs and successors, kings of this realm, shall be taken, accepted, and reputed the only supreme head in earth of the Church of England, called Anglicana Ecclesia; and shall have and enjoy, annexed and united to the imperial crown of this realm, as well the title and style thereof, as all honours, dignities, preeminences, jurisdictions, privileges, authorities, immunities, profits, and commodities to the said dignity of supreme head of the same Church belonging and appertaining; and that our said sovereign lord, his heirs and successors, kings of this realm, shall have full power and authority from time to time to visit, repress, redress, reform, order, correct, restrain, and amend all such errors, heresies, abuses, offences, contempts, and enormities, whatsoever they be, which by any manner spiritual authority or jurisdiction ought or may lawfully be reformed, repressed, ordered, redressed, corrected, restrained, or amended, most to the pleasure of Almighty God, the increase of virtue in Christ's religion, and for the conservation of the peace, unity, and tranquillity of this realm; any usage, custom, foreign law, foreign authority, prescription, or any other thing or things to the contrary hereof notwithstanding.

The Council of Trent
1545–1563

The Protestant Reformation coincided with a reform movement within the Catholic Church, which reaffirmed the main tenants of Catholic beliefs and practices while it also addressed corruption and abuses. The Catholic reform also answered the challenges to Catholic beliefs and practices made by the many Protestant reformers. Drawing on the longstanding practice in the Catholic Church of calling church councils, Pope Paul II (pose 1534-1549) called such an assembly of biblical scholars and high-ranking clergy to help popes define Catholic doctrine and practice. This Catholic Reformation church council to meet in Trent, on and off, from 1545 to 1563 and ultimately issued this treatise affirming Catholic teachings and practices.

Source: John L. Beatty and Oliver A. Johnson, eds., *The Heritage of Western Civilization* (Prentice Hall: Upper Saddle River, N.J., 1991), 452-460.

Focus Questions:

1. Why did the Council of Trent consider the issues excerpted here? What did they hope to achieve by doing so?
2. In what ways and to what extent were these discussions and resolutions in reaction to the criticisms of Protestant Reformers? How and why?

DECREE TOUCHING THE OPENING OF THE COUNCIL

Doth it please you-unto the praise and glory of the holy and undivided Trinity, Father, and Son, and Holy Ghost; for the increase and exaltation of the Christian faith and religion; for the extirpation of heresies; for the peace and union of the Church; for the reformation of the Clergy and Christian people; for the depression and extinction of the enemies of the Christian name-to decree and declare that the sacred and general council of Trent do begin, and hath begun? They answered: It pleaseth us.

DECREE CONCERNING ORIGINAL SIN

That our Catholic faith, without which it is impossible to please God, may, errors being purged away, continue in its own perfect and spotless integrity, and that the Christian people may not be carried about with every wind of doctrine; whereas that old serpent, the perpetual enemy of mankind, amongst the very many evils with which the Church of God is in these our times troubled, has also stirred up not only new, but even old, dissensions touching original sin, and the remedy thereof; the sacred and holy, oecumenical and general Synod of Trent,—lawfully assembled in the Holy See presiding therein,—wishing now to come to the reclaiming of the erring, and the confirming of the wavering—following the testimonies of the sacred Scriptures, of the holy Fathers, or the most approved councils, and the judgement and consent of the Church itself, ordains, confesses, and declares these things touching the said original sin:

1. If any one does not confess that the first man, Adam, when he had transgressed the commandment of God in Paradise, immediately lost the holiness and justice wherein he had been constituted; and that he incurred, through the offense of that prevarication, the wrath and indignation of God, and consequently death, with which God had previously threatened him, and, together with death, captivity under his power who thenceforth had the empire of death, that is to say, the devil, and that the entire Adam, through that offence of prevarication, was changed, in body and soul, for the worse; let him be anathema.

3. If any one asserts, that this sin of Adam—which in its origin is one, and being transfused into all by propagation, not by imitation, is in each one as his own—is taken away either by the powers of human nature, or by any other remedy than the merit of the one mediator our Lord Jesus Christ, who hath reconciled us to God in his own blood, made unto us justice, sanctification, and redemption; or if he denies that the said merit of Jesus Christ is applied, both to adults and to infants, by the sacrament of baptism rightly administered in the form of the Church; let him be anathema....

ON THE SACRAMENTS IN GENERAL

Canon I. If any one saith, that the sacraments of the New Law were not all instituted by Jesus Christ, our Lord; or, that they are more, or less, than seven, to wit, Baptism, Confirmation, the Eucharist, Penance, Extreme Unction, Order, and Matrimony; or even that any one of these seven is not truly and properly a sacrament; let him be anathema.

Canon IV. If any one saith, that the sacraments of the New Law are not necessary unto salvation, but superfluous; and that, without them, or without the desire thereof, men obtain of God, through faith alone, the grace of justification;- though all (the sacraments) are not indeed necessary for every individual; let him be anathema.

Canon VI. If any one saith, that the sacraments of the New Law do not contain the grace which they signify; or, that they do not confer that grace on those who do not place an obstacle thereunto; as though they were merely outward signs of grace or justice received through faith, and certain marks of the Christian profession, whereby believers are distinguished amongst men from unbelievers; let him be anathema. Canon X. If any one saith, that all Christians have power to administer the word, and all the sacraments; let him be anathema.

ON THE MOST HOLY SACRAMENT OF THE EUCHARIST

Canon I. If any one deny, that, in the sacrament of the most holy Eucharist, are contained truly, really, and substantially, the body and blood together with the soul and divinity of our Lord Jesus Christ. and consequently the whole Christ: but saith that He is only therein as in a sign, or in figure, or virtue: let him be anathema. Canon II. If anyone saith that in the sacred and holy sacrament of the Eucharist, the substance of the bread and wine remains conjointly with the body and blood of our Lord Jesus Christ, and denieth that wonderful and singular conversion of the whole substance of the bread into the Body, and of the whole substance of the wine into the Blood—the species only of the bread and wine remaining—which conversion indeed the Catholic Church most aptly calls transubstantiation; let him be anathema.

ON THE ECCLESIASTICAL HIERARCHY, AND ON ORDINATION

... If any one affirm, that all Christians indiscriminately are priests of the New Testament. or that they are all mutually endowed with an equal spiritual power, he clearly does nothing but confound the ecclesiastical hierarchy; which is as an army set in array....

.... It decree, that all those who, being only called and instituted by the people, or by the civil power and magistrate, ascend to the exercise of these ministrations, and those who of their own rashness assume them to themselves, are not ministers of the Church, but are to be looked upon as thieves and robbers, who have not entered by the door. These are the things which it hath seemed good to the sacred Synod to teach the faithful of Christ in general terms, touching the sacrament of Order.

ON THE SACRAMENT OF MATRIMONY

Canon IX. If anyone saith, that clerics constituted in sacred orders or Regulars, who have solemnly professed chastity, are able to contract marriage, and that being contracted it is valid. notwithstanding the ecclesiastical law, or vow: and that the contrary is nothing else than to condemn marriage: and, that all who do not feel that they have the gift of chastity; even though they have made a vow thereof, may contract marriage: let him be anathema: seeing that God refuses not that gift to those who ask for it rightly; neither does He suffer us to be tempted above that which we are able.

Canon X. If anyone saith that the marriage state is to be placed above the state of virginity and of celibacy, and that it is not better and more blessed to remain in virginity, or in celibacy, than to be united in matrimony; let him be anathema.

ON THE INVOCATION, VENERATION AND RELICS OF SAINTS, AND ON SACRED IMAGES

The holy Synod enjoins on all bishops and others who sustain the office and charge of teaching, that, agreeably to the usage of the Catholic and Apostolic Church, received from the primitive times of the Christian religion, and agreeably to the consent of the holy Fathers, and to the decrees of sacred Councils, they especially instruct the faithful diligently concerning the intercession and invocation of saints; the honour (paid) to relics; and the legitimate use of images; teaching them that the saints who reign together with Christ, offer up their own prayers to God for men, that it is good and useful supplicantly to invoke them, and to have recourse to their prayers, aid, (and) help for obtaining benefits from God, through His Son, Jesus Christ, our lord, who is alone Redeemer and Saviour; but that they think impiously, who denies that the saints, who enjoy eternal happiness in heaven, are to be invocated or who assert either that they do not pray for men; or, that the invocation of them to pray for each of us even in particular is idolatry or that it is repugnant to the word of God; and is opposed to the honour of the one mediator between God and me, Christ Jesus; or that it is foolish to supplicate, vocally or mentally, those who reign in heaven. Also, that the holy bodies of holy martyrs, and of others now living with Christ.... They who affirm that veneration and honour are not due to the relics of saints; or, that these, and other sacred monuments, are uselessly honoured by the faithful; and that the places dedicated to the memories of the saints are in vain visited with the view of obtaining their aid; are wholly to be condemned, as the Church has already long since condemned, and now also condemns.

CARDINALS AND ALL PRELATES OF THE CHURCHES SHALL BE CONTENT WITH MODEST FURNITURE AND A FRUGAL TABLE: THEY SHALL NOT ENRICH THEIR RELATIVES OR DOMESTICS OUT OF THE PROPERTY OF THE CHURCH

... Wherefore, after the example of our fathers in the Council of Carthage, it not only orders that bishops be content with modest furniture, and a frugal table and diet, but that they also give heed that in the rest of their manner of living, and in their whole house, there be nothing seen that is alien from this holy institution, and which does not manifest simplicity, zeal toward God, and a contempt of vanities. Also, it wholly forbids them to enrich their own kindred or domestics out of the revenues of the church.... It would seem to be a shame, if they did not at the same time shine so pre-eminent in virtue and in the discipline of their lives, as deservedly to draw upon themselves the eyes of all men.

DECREE CONCERNING INDULGENCES

Whereas the power of conferring Indulgences was granted by Christ to the Church; and she has, even in the most ancient times, used the said power, delivered unto her of God; the sacred holy Synod teaches, and enjoins, that the use of Indulgences for the Christian people most salutary, and approved of by the authority of sacred Councils, is to be retained in the Chruch; and It condemns with anathema those who either assert, that they are useless; or who deny that there is in the Church the power of granting them. In granting them, however, it desires that, in accordance with the ancient and approved custom in the Church, moderation be observed; lest by excessive facility. Ecclesiastical discipline be enervated. And being desirous that the abuses which have crept therein, and by occasion of which this honourable name of Indulgences is blasphemed by heretics, be amended and corrected....

Anonymous, " The Execution of Archbishop Cranmer" 1556

Henry VIII (r. 1509-1547) named Thomas Cranmer (1489-1556) to head the Church of England (Anglican Church) as archbishop of Canterbury. Cranmer served in the same post during the following reign of Edward VI (r. 1547-1543). After Edward VI's short reign, his half sister Mary I (r.1553-1558) ascended to the throne. A devout Catholic in the tradition of her mother Catherine of Argon, Mary pushed for policies that suppressed the Protestant Church of England and restored the Catholic Church as the official state church. This shift brought Archbishop Cranmer into conflict with Queen Mary and the English government as he fought to defend and maintain the Anglican Church. As a consequence of his outspoken refusal to accept Mary's religious policies, he was arrested, put on trial, and executed in 1556.

Source: John Casey, Eyewitness to History (NewYork: Avon Books, 1997), 96-99.

Focus Questions:

1. What was the author's view of Cranmer, and how did that shape his account of Cranmer's conviction and execution?
2. How was Cranmer's trial and execution related to changing religious policies in England and in Europe?

But that I know for our great friendships, and long continued love, you look even of duty that I should signify to you of the truth of such things as here chanceth among us; I would not at this time have written to you the unfortunate end, and doubtful tragedy, of Thomas Cranmer late bishop of Canterbury: because I little pleasure take in beholding of such heavy sights. And, when they are once overpassed, I like not to rehearse them again; being but a renewing of my woe, and doubling my grief. For although his former life, and wretched end, deserves a greater misery, (if any greater might have chanced than chanced unto him), yet, setting aside his offences to God and his country, and beholding the man without his faults, I think there was none that pitied not his case, and bewailed not his fortune, and feared not his own chance, to see so noble a prelate, so grave a counsellor, of so long continued honour, after so many dignities, in his old years to be deprived of his estate, adjudged to die, and in so painful a death to end his life. I have no delight to increase it. Alas, it is too much of itself, that ever so heavy a case should betide to man, and man to deserve it.

But to come to the matter: on Saturday last, being 21 of March, was his day appointed to die. And because the morning was much rainy, the sermon appointed by Mr Dr Cole to be made at the stake, was made in St Mary's church: whither Dr Cranmer was brought by the mayor and aldermen, and my lord Williams: with whom came divers gentlemen of the shire, sit T. A. Bridges, sit John Browne, and others. Where was prepared, over against the pulpit, an high place for him, that all the people might see him. And, when he had ascended it, he kneeled him down and prayed, weeping tenderly: which moved a great number to tears, that had conceived an assured hope of his conversion and repentance...

When praying was done, he stood up, and, having leave to speak, said,'Good people, I had intended indeed to desire you to pray for me; which because Mr Doctor hath desired, and you have done already, I thank you most heartily for it. And now will I pray for myself, as I could best devise for mine own comfort, and say the prayer, word for word, as I have here written it.'And he read it standing: and after kneeled down, and said the Lord's Prayer; and all the people on their knees devoutly praying with him...

And then rising, he said, 'Every man desireth, good people, at the time of their deaths, to give some good exhortation, that other may remember after their deaths, and be the better thereby. So I beseech God grant me grace, that I may speak something, at this my departing, whereby God may be glorified, and you edified...

'And now I come to the great thing that troubleth my conscience more than any other thing that ever I said or did in my life: and that is, the setting abroad of writings contrary to the truth. Which here now I renounce and refuse, as things written with my hand, contrary to the truth which I thought in my heart, and written for fear of death, and to save my life, if it might be: and that is, all such bills, which I have written or signed with mine own hand since my degradation: wherein I have written many things untrue. And forasmuch as my hand offended in writing contrary to my heart, therefore my hand shall first be punished: for if I may come to the fire, it shall be first burned. And as for the pope, I refuse him, as Christ's enemy and antichrist, with all his false doctrine.'

And here, being admonished of his recantation and dissembling, he said, "Alas, my lord, I have been a man that all my life loved plainness, and never dissembled till now against the truth; which I am most sorry for it." He added hereunto, that, for the sacrament, he believed as he had taught in his book against the bishop of Winchester. And here he was suffered to speak no more...

Then was he carried away; and a great number, that did run to see him go so wickedly to his death, ran after him, exhorting him, while time was, to remember himself. And one Friar John, a godly and well learned man, all the way travelled with him to reduce him. But it would not be. What they said in particular I cannot tell, but the effect appeared in the end: for at the stake he professed, that he died in all such opinions as he had taught, and oft repented him of his recantation.

Coming to the stake with a cheerful countenance and willing mind, he put off his garments with haste, and stood upright in his shirt: and a bachelor of divinity, named Elye, of Brazen-nose college, laboured to convert him to his former recantation, with the two Spanish friars. And when the friars saw his constancy, they said in Latin one to another 'Let us go from him: we ought not to be nigh him: for the devil is with him.' But the bachelor in divinity was more earnest with him: unto whom he answered, that, as concerning his recantation, he repented it right sore, because he knew it was against the truth; with other words more. Whereby the Lord Williams cried, 'Make short, make short.' Then the bishop took certain of his friends by the hand. But the bachelor of divinity refused to take him by the hand, and blamed all others that so did, and said, he was sorry that ever he came in his company. And yet again he required him to agree to his former recantation. And the bishop answered, (shewing his hand), 'This was the hand that wrote it, and therefore shall it suffer first punishment.'

Fire being now put to him, he stretched out his right hand, and thrust it into the flame, and held it there a good space, before the fire came to any other part of his body; where his hand was seen of every man sensibly burning, crying with a loud voice, 'This hand hath offended.' As soon as the fire got up, he was very soon dead, never stirring or crying all the while.

His patience in the torment, his courage in dying, if it had been taken either for the glory of God, the wealth of his country, or the testimony of truth, as it was for a pernicious error, and subversion of true religion, I could worthily have commended the example, and matched it with the fame of any father of ancient time: but, seeing that not the death, but cause and quarrel thereof, commendeth the sufferer, I cannot but much dispraise his obstinate stubbornness and sturdiness in dying, and specially in so evil a cause. Surely his death much grieved every man; but not after one sort. Some pitied to see his body so tormented with the fire raging upon the silly carcass, that counted not of the folly. Other that passed not much of the body, lamented to see him spill his soul, wretchedly, without redemption, to be plagued for ever. His friends sorrowed for love; his enemies for pity: strangers for a common kind of humanity, whereby we are bound one to another. Thus I have enforced myself, for your sake, to discourse this heavy narration, contrary to my mind: and, being more than half weary, I make a short end, wishing you a quieter life, with less honour; and easier death, with more praise.

Catherine Zell, "Letter to Ludwig Rabus" 1556–1558

With their emphasis on marriage and rejection of celibacy for clergy, Protestant churches significantly redefined roles for men and women in their institutions. While the Catholic Church affirmed celibacy for its priests at the Council of Trent, Protestant churches encouraged their preachers and pastors to marry. The author of this document, Catherine Zell (c. 1497-c. 1563) married an ex-Catholic priest who became a Lutheran minister in Strasbourg, in 1523. As a couple, they were active proponents of the more radical Protestant movement in central Europe (Calvinist and Zwingli followers) which brought them into conflict with Catholics as well as fellow Lutheran Protestants. The following excerpt is from one of Catherine Zell's letters to a young Lutheran minister, Ludwig Rabus, who publicly criticized the Zell's for their actions and beliefs. Zell published her correspondence, including this letter, after the death of her husband in an effort to defend and explain their opinions, beliefs, and work.

Source: Julia O'Faolain and Lauro Martines, eds., *Not in God's Image* (New York: Harper and Row, Inc., 1973), 203-206.

Focus Questions:

1. What does Zell's letter say about the role of women in the Protestant movement?
2. According to Zell, what religious groups experienced persecution in Strasbourg? Why?
3. What does her letter tell us about the Protestant Reformation as it unfolded in the Strasbourg area?

I, Catherine Zell, wife of the late lamented Mathew Zell, who served in Strasbourg, where I was born and reared and still live, wish you peace and enhancement in God's grace.

From my earliest years I turned to the Lord, who taught and guided me, and I have at all times, in accordance with my understanding and His grace, embraced the interests of His church and earnestly sought Jesus. Even in youth this brought me the regard and affection of clergymen and others much concerned with the church, which is why the pious Mathew Zell wanted me as a companion in marriage; and I, in turn, to serve the glory of Christ, gave devotion and help to my husband, both in his ministry and in keeping his house....

Ever since I was ten years old I have been a student and a sort of church mother, much given to attending sermons. I have loved and frequented the company of learned men, and I conversed much with them, not about dancing, masquerades, and worldly pleasures but about the kingdom of God.

Yet I resisted and struggled against that kingdom. Then, as no learned man could find a way of consoling me in my sins, prayers and physical suffering, and as none could make me sure of God's love and grace, I fell gravely ill in body and spirit. I became like that poor woman of the Gospel who, having spent all she had on doctors to no avail, heard speak of Christ, went to Him, and was healed. As I foundered, devoured by care and anxiety, vainly searching for serenity in the practices of the church, God took pity on me. From among our people He drew out and sent forth Martin Luther. This man so persuaded me of the ineffable goodness of our Lord Jesus Christ that I felt myself snatched from the depths of hell and transported to the kingdom of heaven. I remembered the Lord's words to Peter: 'Follow me and I shall make you a fisher of men'. Then did I labor day and night to cleave to the path of divine truth....

While other women decorated their houses and ornamented themselves, going to dances, wedding parties, and giving themselves to pleasure, I went into the houses of poor and rich alike, in all love, faith, and compassion, to care for the sick and the confined and to bury the dead. Was that to plant anxiety and turmoil in the church of Strasbourg?...

Consider the poor Anabaptists, who are so furiously and ferociously persecuted. Must the authorities everywhere be incited against them, as the hunter drives his dog against wild animals? Against those who acknowledge Christ the Lord in very much the same way we do and over which we broke with the papacy? Just because they cannot agree with us on lesser things, is this any reason to persecute them and in them Christ, in whom they fervently believe and have often professed in misery, in prison, and under the torments of fire and water?

Governments may punish criminals, but they should not force and govern belief which is a matter for the heart and conscience not for temporal authorities. [Urges Rabus to consult the leading reformers on this question and provides him, ironically, with a list.] ... When the authorities pursue one, they soon bring forth tears, and towns and villages are emptied...

Strasbourg does not offer the example of an evil town but rather the contrary-charity, compassion, and hospitality for the wretched and poor. Within its walls, God be thanked, there remains more than one poor Christian whom certain people would have liked to see cast out. Old Mathew Zell would not have approved of that: he would have gathered the sheep, not destroyed them....

Whether they were Lutherans, Zwinglians, Schwenkfeldians, or poor Anabaptist brethren, rich or poor, wise or foolish, according to the word of St. Paul, all came to us [to the Zells in Strasbourg]. We were not compelled to hold the same views and beliefs that they did, but we did owe to all a proof of love, service, and generosity: our teacher Christ has taught us that....

Acts of Uniformity
1559

Elizabeth I became queen of England (r. 1533-1603) during a period of severe religious and political turmoil which was the result of the wild fluctuations of the religious policies of her predecessors. Her father, Henry VIII (r. 1509-1547), broke away from the Catholic Church with the support of the English Parliament and established a Protestant Church of England in the 1520s, but her half sister Mary I (r.1553-1558) instigated ruthless policies that attempted to bring back the Catholic Church and eliminate Protestantism in England. Working with the English Parliament, Elizabeth sought to restore religious order through policies that brought together Catholics and Protestants in England under a reinstated Church of England. Elizabeth envisioned this as a religious and political compromise that would establish a state church that was independent from the Catholic Church, Protestant in name, but would retain many of the same rituals and beliefs familiar to English churchgoers. This act, passed by the English Parliament, launched Elizabeth's religious policies by providing clear guidelines for services, institutions, and personnel of the reinstated Church of England nationwide.

Source: Henry Bettenson, ed., *Documents of the Christian Church* (New York: Oxford University Press, 1970), 235-239.

Focus Questions:

1. What did Elizabeth and the English Parliament hope to accomplish with the passage of this act?
2. How did this act fit into the larger context of the Reformation in England and church-state relations?

Where at the death of our late sovereign lord King Edward VI there remained one uniform order of common service and prayer, and of the administration of sacraments, rites, and ceremonies in the Church of England, which was set forth in one book, intituled: The Book of Common Prayer, and Administration of Sacraments, and other rites and ceremonies in the Church of England; authorized by Act of Parliament holden in the fifth and sixth years of our said late sovereign lord King Edward VI, intituled: An Act for the uniformity of common prayer, and administration of the sacraments; the which was repealed and taken away by Act of Parliament in the first year of the reign of our late sovereign lady Queen Mary, to the great decay of the due honour of God, and discomfort to the professors of the truth of Christ's religion:

Be it therefore enacted by the authority of this present Parliament, that the said statute of repeal, and everything therein contained, only concerning the said book, and the service, administration of sacraments, rites, and ceremonies contained or appointed in or by the said book, shall be void and of none effect, from and after the feast of the Nativity of St John Baptist next coming; and that the said book, with the order of service, and of the administration of sacraments, rites, and ceremonies, with the alterations and additions therein added and appointed by this statute, shall stand and be, from and after the said feast of the Nativity Of St John Baptist, in full force and effect, according to the tenor and effect of this statute; anything in the aforesaid statute of repeal to the contrary notwithstanding.

And further be it enacted by the queen's highness, with the assent of the Lords and Commons in this present Parliament assembled, and by authority of the same, that all and singular ministers in any cathedral or parish church, or other place within this realm of England, Wales, and the marches of the same, or other the queen's dominions, shall from and after the feast of the Nativity of St John Baptist next coming be bounden to say and use the Matins, Evensong, celebration of the Lord's Supper and administration of each of the sacraments, and all their common and open prayer, in such order and form as is mentioned in the said book, so authorized by Parliament in the said fifth and sixth years of the reign of King Edward VI, with one alteration or addition of certain lessons to be used on every Sunday in the year,[1] and the form of the Litany altered and corrected,[2] and two sentences only added in the delivery of the sacrament to the communicants,[3] and none other or otherwise.

And that if any manner of parson, vicar, or other whatsoever minister, that ought or should sing or say common prayer mentioned in the said book, or minister the sacraments, from and after the feast of the Nativity of St John Baptist next coming, refuse to use the said common prayers, or to minister the sacraments in such cathedral or parish church, or other places as he should use to minister the same, in such order and form as they be mentioned and set forth in the said book, or shall, wilfully or obstinately standing in the same, use any other rite, ceremony, order, form, or manner of celebrating of the Lord's Supper, openly or privily, or Matins, Evensong, administration of the sacraments, or other open prayers, than is mentioned and set forth in the said book (open prayer in and throughout this Act, is meant that prayer which is for other to come unto, or hear, either in common churches or private chapels or oratorios, commonly called the service of the Church), or shall preach, declare, or speak anything in the derogation or depraving of the said book, or anything therein contained, or of any part thereof, and shall be thereof lawfully convicted, according to the laws of this realm, by verdict of twelve men, or by his own confession, or by the notorious evidence of the fact, shall lose and forfeit to the queen's highness, her heirs and successors, for his first offence, the profit of all his spiritual benefices or promotions coming or arising in the one whole year next after his conviction; and also that the person so convicted shall for the same offence suffer imprisonment by the space of six months, without ball or mainprize.

And if any such person once convicted of any offence concerning the premises, shall after his first conviction eftsoons offend, and be thereof, in form aforesaid, lawfully convicted, that then the same person shall for his second offence suffer imprisonment by the space of one whole year, and also shall therefor be deprived, ipso facto, of all his spiritual promotions; and that it shall be lawful to all patrons or donors of all and singular the same spiritual promotions, or of any of them, to present or collate to the same, as though the person and persons so offending were dead.

And that if any such person or persons, after he shall be twice convicted in form aforesaid, shall offend against any of the premises the third time, and shall

1 Proper Lessons for Sundays were given in 1st P.B. of Edw. VI (1549), but omitted in the 1552 Book.

2 The more important changes were: the omission of the deprecation, 'From the tyranny of the bishop of Rome and all his detestable enormities,' which appeared in 1549 and 1552, and the inclusion of the Prayer of the Queen's Majesty, and the Prayer for the Clergy and People, which have been, since 1662, included in Morning and Evening Prayer.

3 In the 1549 Book the words of administration were, 'The body (blood) of our Lord Jesus Christ which Was given (shed) for thee, preserve thy body and soul unto everlasting life.' In 1552 there was substituted, 'Take and eat this (Drink this) in remembrance that Christ died (Christ's blood was shed) for thee, and feed on him in thy heart by faith with thanksgiving (and be thankful).' The two forms were combined in 1559 and retained thus in 1662.

be thereof, in form aforesaid, lawfully convicted, that then the person so offending and convicted the third time, shall be deprived, ipso facto, of all his spiritual promotions, and also shall suffer imprisonment during his life.

And if the person that shall offend, and be convicted in form aforesaid, concerning any of the premises, shall not be beneficed, nor have any spiritual promotion, that then the same person so offending and convicted shall for the first offence suffer imprisonment during one whole year next after his said conviction, without bail or mainprize. And if any such person, not having any spiritual promotion, after his first conviction shall eftsoons offend in anything concerning the premises, and shall be, in form aforesaid, thereof lawfully convicted, that then the same person shall for his second offence suffer imprisonment during his life.

And it is ordained and enacted by the authority aforesaid, that if any person or persons whatsoever, after the said feast of the Nativity of St John Baptist next coming, shall in any interludes, plays, songs, rhymes, or by other open words, declare or speak anything in the derogation, depraving, or despising of the same book, or anything therein contained, or any part thereof, or shall, by open fact, deed, or by open threatenings, compel or cause, or otherwise procure or maintain, any parson, vicar, or other minister in any cathedral or parish church, or in chapel, or in any other place, to sing or say any common or open prayer, or to minister any sacrament otherwise, or in any other manner and form, than is mentioned in the said book; or that by any of the said means shall unlawfully interrupt or let any parson, vicar, or other minister in any cathedral or parish church, chapel, or any other place, to sing or say common and open prayer, or to minister the sacraments or any of them, in such manner and form as is mentioned in the said book; that then every such person, being thereof lawfully convicted in form abovesaid, shall forfeit to the queen our sovereign lady, her heirs and successors, for the first offence a hundred marks.

And if any person or persons, being once convicted of any such offence, eftsoons offend against any of the last recited offences, and shall, in form aforesaid, be thereof lawfully convicted, that then the same person so offending and convicted shall, for the second offence, forfeit to the queen our sovereign lady, her heirs and successors, four hundred marks.

And if any person, after he, in form aforesaid, shall have been twice convicted of any offence concerning any of the last recited offences, shall offend the third time, and be thereof, in form abovesaid, lawfully convicted, that then every person so offending and convicted shall for his third offence forfeit to our sovereign lady the queen all his goods and chattels, and shall suffer imprisonment during his life.

And if any person or persons, that for his first offence concerning the premises shall be convicted, in form aforesaid, do not pay the sum to be paid by virtue of his conviction, in such manner and form as the same ought to be paid, within six weeks next after his conviction; that then every person so convicted, and so not paying the same, shall for the same first offence, instead of the said sum, suffer imprisonment by the space of six months, without bail or mainprize. And if any person or persons, that for his second offence concerning the premises shall be convicted in form aforesaid, do not pay the said sum to be paid by virtue of his conviction and this statute, in such manner and form as the same ought to be paid, within six weeks next after his said second conviction; that then every person so convicted, and not so paying the same, shall, for the same second offence, in the stead of the said sum, suffer imprisonment during twelve months, without bail or mainprize.

And that from and after the said feast of the Nativity of St John Baptist next coming, all and every person and persons inhabiting within this realm, or any other the queen's majesty's dominions, shall diligently and faithfully, having no lawful or reasonable excuse to be absent, endeavour themselves to resort to their parish church or chapel accustomed, or upon reasonable let thereof, to some usual place where common prayer and such service of God shall be used in such time of let, upon every Sunday and other days ordained and used to be kept as holy days, and then and there to abide orderly and soberly during the time of the common prayer, preachings, or other service of God there to be used and ministered; upon pain of punishment by the censures of the Church, and also upon pain that every person so offending shall forfeit for every such offence twelve pence, to be levied by the churchwardens of the parish where such offence shall be done, to the use of the poor of the same parish, of the goods, lands, and tenements of such offender, by way of distress.

And for due execution hereof, the queen's most excellent majesty, the Lords temporal (sic), and all the Commons, in this present Parliament assembled, do in God's name earnestly require and charge all the archbishops, bishops, and other ordinaries, that they shall endeavour themselves to the uttermost of their knowledges, that the due and true execution hereof may be had throughout their dioceses and charges, as they will answer before God, for such evils and plagues wherewith Almighty God may justly punish His people for neglecting this good and wholesome law....

Anonymous Government Agent "Arrest of Edmund Campion and his Associates" 1581

Edmund Campion (1540-1581) was part of the underground movement to preserve Catholicism in the face of Queen Elizabeth I's (r. 1533-1603) religious policies which required adherence to the state religion: The Church of England or Anglican Church.

In his early career, Campion was a professor at Oxford University as well as a minister in the Anglican Church. He had a change of heart around 1570, converted to Catholicism and went to Rome to become a Jesuit (Society of Jesus). He returned in England in 1580, as part of a group of Jesuits doing missionary work. They held secret and illegal Catholic services throughout England. Campion also authored a short pamphlet, entitled the "Ten Reasons," which denounced the Anglican Church and advocated the return of England to Catholicism. These actions led to his arrest, in July of 1581, and imprisonment in the Tower of London where he was subjected to torture. He was put on trial, convicted of treason, and executed. For his work in trying to preserve Catholicism in England, the Catholic Church made him a saint in 1970.

Source: John Casey, *Eyewitness to History* (New York: Avon Books, 1997), 121-127.

FOCUS QUESTIONS:

1. According to this report, why and how was Campion arrested? By whom?
2. What was the author of this report's view of Campion and his arrest? What were the author's sympathies and loyalties, and how did they affect his account of these events?
3. What larger historical events and trends in England at the same time provide context for understanding Campion's arrest?

It happened that after the receipt of our Commission, we consulted between ourselves, What way were best to take first? For we were utterly ignorant where, or in what place, certainly to find out the said Campion, or his compeers. And our consultation was shortly determined: for the greatest part of our travail and dealings in this service did lie chiefly upon mine own determination, by reason of mine acquaintance and knowledge of divers of the like sect.

It then presently came to my remembrance of certain acquaintance which I once had with one Thomas Cooper a cook, who, in November [1578] was two years, served Master Thomas Roper of [Orpington in] Kent; where, at that time, I in like manner served: and both of us, about the same month, departed the said Master Roper his service; I into Essex, and the said Cooper to Lyford in Berkshire, to one Master Yate. From whence, within one half year after, I was advertised in Essex, that the said Cook was placed in service; and that the said Master Yate was a very earnest Papist, and one that gave great entertainment to any of that sect.

Which tale, being told me in Essex two years before we entered [on] this journey, by God's great goodness, came to my memory but even the day before we set forth. Hereof I informed the said David Jenkins, being my fellow in Commission, and told him it would be our best way to go thither first: for that it was not meant that we should go to any place but where indeed I either had acquaintance; or by some means possible in our journey, could get acquaintance. And told him we would dispose of our journey in such sort as we might come to the said Master Yate's upon the Sunday about eight of the clock in the morning: 'where,' said I, 'if we find the said Cook, and that there be any Mass to be said there that day, or any massing Priest in the house; the Cook, for old acquaintance and for that he supposeth me to be a Papist, will bring me to the sight thereof.'

And upon this determination, we set from London the 14th day of July last; and came to the said Master Yate's house, the 16th of the same month, being Sunday, about the hour aforesaid.

Where, without the gates of the same house, we espied one of the servants of the house, who most likely seemed, by reason of his lying aloof, to be as it were a Scout Watcher, that they within might accomplish their secret matters more safely.

I called the said servant, and inquired of him for the said Thomas Cooper the Cook. Who answered, That he could not well tell, whether he were within or not.

I prayed him that he would friend me so much as to see; and told him my name.

The said servant did so, it seemed; for the Cook came forth presently unto us where we sat still upon horseback. And after a few such speeches, as betwixt friend and friend when they have been long asunder, were passed; still sitting upon our horses, I told him That I had longed to see him; and that I was then travelling into Derbyshire to see my friends, and came so far out of my way to see him. And said I, 'Now I have seen you, my mind is well satisfied; and so fare you well!'

'No,' saith he, 'that shall you not do before dinner.'

I made the matter very earnest to be gone; and he, more earnest and importune to stay me. But in truth I was as willing to stay as he to have me.

And so, perforce, there was no remedy but stay we must. And having lighted from horseback; and being by him brought into the house, and so into the buttery, and there caused to drink: presently after, the said Cook came and whispered with me, and asked, Whether my friend (meaning the said Jenkins) were within the Church or not? Therein meaning, Whether he were a Papist or no?

To which I answered, 'He was not; but yet,' said I, 'he is a very honest man, and one that wisheth well that way.'

Then said the Cook to me, 'Will you go up?' By which speech, I knew he would bring me to a Mass.

And I answered him and said, 'Yea, for God's sake, that let me do: for seeing I must needs tarry, let me take something with me that is good.'

And so we left Jenkins in the buttery; and I was brought by the Cook through the hall, the dining parlour, and two or three other odd rooms, and then into a fair large chamber: where there was, at the same instant, one Priest, called Satwell, saying Mass; two other Priests kneeling by, whereof one was Campion, and the other called Peters alias Collington; three Nuns, and 37 other people.

When Satwell had finished his Mass; then Campion he invested himself to say Mass, and so he did: and at the end thereof, made holy bread and delivered it to the people there, to every one some, together with holy water; whereof he gave me part also.

And then was there a chair set in the chamber something beneath the altar, wherein the said Campion did sit down; and there made a sermon very nigh an hour long: the effect of his text being, as I remember, 'That Christ wept over Jerusalem, &c.' And so applied the same to this our country of England for that the Pope his authority and doctrine did not so flourish here as the same Campion desired.

At the end of which sermon, I sat down unto the said Jenkins so soon as I could. For during the time that the Masses and the sermon were made, Jenkins remained still beneath in the buttery or hall; not knowing of any such matter until I gave him some intelligence what I had seen.

And so we departed, with as convenient expedition as we might, and came to one Master Fettiplace, a Justice of the Peace in the said country: whom we made privy of our doings therein; and required him that, according to the tenour of our Commission, he would take sufficient Power, and with us thither.

Whereupon the said Justice of Peace, within one quarter of an hour, put himself in a readiness, with forty or fifty men very well weaponed: who went, in great haste, together with the said Master Fettiplace and us, to the said Master Yate his house.

Where, at our coming upon the sudden, being about one of the clock in the afternoon of the same day, before we knocked at the gates which were then (as before they were continually accustomed to be) fast shut (the house being moated round about; within which moat was great store of fruit trees and other trees, with thick hedgerows: so that the danger for fear of losing of the said Campion and his associates was the more doubted); we beset the house with our men round about the moat in the best sort we could devise: and then knocked at the gates, and were presently heard and espied; but kept out by the space of half an hour.

In which time, as it seemeth, they had hidden Campion and the other two Priests in a very secret place within the said house; and had made reasonable purveyance for him as hereafter is mentioned: and then they let us into the house.

Where came presently to our sight, Mrs Yate, the good wife of the house; five Gentlemen, one Gentlewoman, and three Nuns: the Nuns being then disguised in Gentlewomen's apparel, not like unto that they heard Mass in. All which I well remembered to have seen, the same morning, at the Masses and Sermon aforesaid: yet every one of them a great while denied it. And especially the said Mistress Yate; who could not be content only to make a plain denial of the said Masses and the Priests: but, with great and horrible oaths, forsware the same, betaking herself to the Devil if any such there were; in such sort as, if I had not seen them with mine own eyes, I should have believed her.

But knowing certainly that these were but bare excuses, and that we should find the said Campion and his compeers if we made narrow search; I eftsoons put Master Fettiplace in remembrance of our Commission: and so he, myself, and the said Jenkins Her Majesty's Messenger, went to searching the house; where we found many secret corners.

Continuing the search, although with no small toil, in the orchards, hedges, and ditches, within the moat and divers other places; at the last found out Master Edward Yate, brother to the good man of the house, and two countrymen called Weblin and Mansfield, fast locked together in a pigeon house: but we could not find, at that time, Campion and the other two Priests whom we specially sought for.

It drew then something towards evening, and doubting lest we were not strong enough; we sent our Commission to one Master Foster, High Sheriff of Berkshire; and to one Master Wiseman, a justice of Peace within the same County; for some further aid at their hands.

The said Master Wiseman came with very good speed unto us the same evening, with ten or twelve of his own men, very able men and well appointed: but the said Master Foster could not be found, as the messenger that went for him returned us answer.

And so the said house was beset the same night with at the least three score men well weaponed; who watched the same very diligently.

And the next day, being Monday, in the morning very early, came one Master Christopher Lydcot, a Justice of Peace of the same shire, with a great sort of his own men, all very well appointed: who, together with his men, showed such earnest loyal and forward service in those affairs as was no small comfort and encouragement to all those which were present, and did bear true hearts and good wills to Her Majesty.

The same morning, began a fresh search for the said Priests; which continued with very great labour until about ten of the clock in the forenoon of the same day: but the said Priests could not be found, and every man almost persuaded that they were not there.

Yet still searching, although in effect clean void of any hope for finding of them, the said David Jenkins, by God's great goodness, espied a certain secret place, which he quickly found to be hollow; and with a pin of iron which he had in his hand much like unto a harrow tine, he forthwith did break a hole into the said place: where then presently he perceived the said Priests lying all close together upon a bed, of purpose there laid for them; where they had bread, meat, and drink sufficient to have relieved them three or four days together.

The said Jenkins then called very loudly, and said, 'I have found the traitors!'; and presently company enough was with him: who there saw the said Priests, when there was no remedy for them but nolens volens, courteously yielded themselves.

Shortly after came one Master Reade, another justice of the Peace of the said shire, to be assistant in these affairs.

Of all which matters, news was immediately carried in great haste to the Lords of the Privy Council: who gave further Commission that the said Priests and certain others their associates should be brought to the Court under the conduction of myself and the said Jenkins; with commandment to the Sheriff to deliver us sufficient aid forth of his shire, for the safe bringing up of the said people.

After the rumour and noise for the finding out of the said Campion, Satwell, and Peters alias Collington, was in the said house something assuaged; and that the sight of them was to the people there no great novelty: then was the said High Sheriff sent for once again; who all that while had not been seen in this service. But then came, and received into his charge the said Priests and certain others from that day until Thursday following.

The fourth Priest which was by us brought up to the Tower, whose name is William Filbie, was not taken with the said Campion and the rest in the said house: but was apprehended and taken in our watch by chance, in coming to the said house to speak with the said Peters, as he said; and thereupon delivered likewise in charge to the Sheriff, with the rest.

Upon Thursday, the 20th day of July last, we set forwards from the said Master Yate his house towards the Court, with our said charge; being assisted by the said Master Lydcot and Master Wiseman, and a great sort of their men; who never left us until we came to the Tower of London. There were besides, that guarded us thither, 50 or 60 Horsemen; very able men and well appointed: which we received by the said Sheriff his appointment.

We went that day to Henley upon Thames, where we lodged that night.

And about midnight we were put into great fear by reason of a very great cry and noise that the said Filbie made in his sleep; which wakened the most that were that night in the house, and that in such sort that every man almost thought that some of the prisoners had been broken from us and escaped; although there was in and about the same house a very strong watch appointed and charged for the same. The aforesaid Master Lydcot was the first that came unto them: and when the matter was examined, it was found no more but that the said Filbie was in a dream; and, as he said, he verily thought one to be a ripping down his body and taking out his bowels.

The Edict of Nantes
1598

In France, the Huguenot church emerged out of the Protestant movement based on the teachings of Protestant reformer John Calvin. Many prominent and political powerful nobles in France became Huguenots. The ruling dynasty of France, however, the Valois family which included Henri II (r. 1547-59) and his sons Francis II (r. 1559-60, Charles IX (r. 1560-1574) and Henry III (1574-1589), remained staunchly Catholic and adopted sometimes violent policies to stem the growth of the Huguenot movement and suppress the political power of the nobility. The Huguenot nobles' quest for religious and political independence pitted them against the French kings and resulted in a series of civil wars in France, called the Wars of Religion (1562-98). The first French king from the Bourbon dynasty, Henry IV (r. 1589-1610) had been a Huguenot but ultimately converted to Catholicism once he became king. He negotiated the peace that ended the civil war and promulgated this edict which defined the rights of French Huguenots in France.

Source: Sidney Z. Ehler and John B. Morrall, eds. and trans., *Church and State Through the Centuries: A Collection of Historic Documents* (London: Burns and Gates, 1954), 185-188.

Focus Questions:

1. What rights did Huguenots have as a result of this edict? What were the limits on their rights?
2. Why was it necessary to specifically outline the status of Huguenots in France?
3. What larger events influenced and shaped the drafting of this edict? How?

Firstly, that the memory of everything done on both sides from the beginning of the month of March 1585, until our accession to the Crown and during the other previous troubles, and at the outbreak of them, shall remain extinct and suppressed, as if it were something which had never occurred. And it shall not be lawful or permissible to our Procurators-General or to any other persons, public or private, at any time or on any pretext whatsoever, to institute a case, lawsuit or action in any Court or judicial tribunals whatever [concerning those things].

We forbid all our subjects, of whatever rank and quality they may be, to renew the memory of these matters, to attack, be hostile to, injure or provoke each other in revenge for the past, whatever may be the reason and pretext; or to dispute, argue or quarrel about it, or to do violence, or to give offence in deed or word, but let them restrain themselves and live peaceably together as brothers, friends and fellow-citizens, on pain of being liable to punishment as disturbers of the peace and troublers of public quiet.

We ordain that the Catholic, Apostolic and Roman religion shall be restored and re-established in all places and districts of this our kingdom and the countries under our rule, where its practice has been interrupted, so that it can be peacefully and freely practiced there, without any disturbance or hindrance. We forbid very expressly all persons of whatever rank, quality or condition they may be, under the aforesaid penalties, to disturb, molest or cause annoyance to clerics in the celebration of the Divine worship, the enjoyment and receipt of tithes, fruits and revenues of their benefices, and all other rights and duties which belong to them; and we ordain that all those who during the disorders have come into possession of churches, houses, goods and revenues belonging to the said clerics, and who retain and occupy them, shall give back the entire possession and enjoyment of them, with such rights, liberties and safeguards as they had before they were seized. We also forbid very expressly those of the so-called Reformed religion to hold prayer meetings or any devotions of the aforesaid religion in churches, houses and dwellings of the above-said clerics....

And in order not to leave any cause for discords and disputes between our subjects, we have permitted and we permit those of the so-called Reformed religion to live and dwell in all the towns and districts of this our kingdom and the countries under one rule, without being annoyed, disturbed, molested or constrained to do anything against their conscience, or for this cause to be sought out in their houses and districts where they wish to live, provided that they conduct themselves in other respects according to the provisions of our present Edict....

We also permit those of the aforesaid religion to carry out and continue its practice in the towns and districts under our rule, where it was established and carried out publicly several distinct times in the year 1597, until the end of the month of March, notwithstanding all decrees and judgments to the contrary....

We forbid very expressly all those of the aforesaid religion to practice it in so far as ministration, regulation, discipline or public instruction of children and others is concerned, in this our kingdom and the countries under our rule, in matters concerning religion, outside the places permitted and conceded by the present Edict....

Books dealing with the matters of the aforesaid so-called Reformed religion shall not be printed and sold publicly, except in the towns and districts where the public exercise of the said religion is allowed. And with regard to other books which shall be printed in other towns, they shall be seen and inspected by our officials and theologians as laid down by our ordinances. We forbid very specifically the printing, publication and sale of all defamatory books, tracts and writings, under the penalties contained in our ordinances, instructing all our judges and officials to carry out this ruling strictly.

We ordain that there shall be no difference or distinction, because of the aforesaid religion, in the reception of students to be instructed in Universities, Colleges and schools, or of the sick and poor into hospitals, infirmaries and public charitable institutions....

In order to reunite more effectively the wills of our subjects, as is our intention, and to remove all future complaints, we declare that all those who profess or shall profess the aforesaid so-called Reformed religion are capable of holding and exercising all public positions, honours, offices and duties whatsoever, Royal, seigneurial, or offices in the towns of our kingdom, countries, lands and lordships subject to us, notwithstanding all contrary oaths, and of being admitted and received into them without distinction; it shall be sufficient for our courts of Parliament and other judges to ascertain and inquire concerning the life, morals, religion and honest behaviour of those who are or shall be appointed to offices, whether of one religion or the other, without enacting from them any oath other than that of well and faithfully serving the King in the exercise of their functions and keeping the ordinances, as has been perpetually the custom. During vacancies in the aforesaid positions, functions and offices, we shall make—in respect of those which shall be in our disposition—appointments without bias or discrimination of capable persons, as the unity of our subjects requires it. We declare also that members of the aforesaid so-called Reformed religion can be admitted and received into all Councils, conferences, assemblies and gatherings which are connected with the offices in question; they can not be rejected or prevented from enjoying these rights on grounds of the said religion....

And for greater security of the behaviour and conduct which we expect with regard to it [the Edict], we will, command and desire that all the Governors and Lieutenants-General of our provinces, Bailiffs, Seneschals asnd other ordinary judges in towns in our aforesaid kingdom, immediately after the reception of this Edict, swear to cause it to be kept and observed, each one in his own district; likewise the mayors, sheriffs, captains, consuls and magistrates of the towns, annual and perpetual. We also enjoin our said bailiffs, seneschals or their lieutenants and other judges, to cause the principal inhabitants from both religions in the abovementioned towns to swear to respect the present Edict immediately after its publication. We place all those of the said towns in our protection and safe keeping, each religion being placed in the safe keeping of the other; and we wish them to be instructed respectively and by public acts to answer by due legal process any contraventions of our present Edict which shall be made in the said towns by their inhabitants, or to make known the said contraventions and put them into the hand of justice.

We command our beloved and loyal people who hold our Courts of Parliament, "Chambres des Comptes" and courts of aids that immediately after the present Edict has been received, they are bound, all business being suspended and under penalty of nullity for any acts which they shall make otherwise, to take an oath similar to the above and to make this our Edict to be published and registered in our above-mentioned Courts according to its proper form and meaning, purely and simply, without using any modifications, rectifications, declarations or secret registering and without waiting for further order or commandment from us; and we order our Procurators-General to demand and ensure immediately and without delay the aforesaid publication....

For such is our pleasure. As witness thereof we have signed the present enactment with our own hand, and in order that it may be sure and stable permanently, we have placed and affixed our Seal to it.

Given at Nantes in the month of April, in the year of grace 1598, the ninth year of our reign.

[Signed,] Henry

CHAPTER 11

The Development of Early-Modern States and Societies

Jean Bodin, *Six Books of the Commonwealth*, "The True Attributes of Sovereignty"

Jean Bodin (ca. 1530–1596 CE) was a French political theorist and lawyer. Bodin studied civil law at the University of Toulouse, taught and practiced law, and in 1571 served in the household of the king's brother. The events and turmoil of sixteenth-century France heavily influenced his thought, which was devoted to the maintenance of order. He is most well known for identifying and recognizing the impor-tance of the state's sovereignty. In Six Books of the Commonwealth (1576), Bodin contended that the state, preferably in the form of a monarch, held supreme power. He favored religious toleration and also wrote about the state's role in finance and trade.

Source: Jean Bodin, "The True Attributes of Sovereignty," *Six Livres de la Republique (Six Books of the Commonwealth)*.

Focus Questions:

1. According to Bodin, what kind of rights of sovereignty does a sovereign possess?
2. To Bodin, what is the difference between custom and law?

SIX BOOKS OF THE COMMONWEALTH BOOK I, CHAPTER X: THE TRUE ATTRIBUTES OF SOVEREIGNTY

The first attribute of the sovereign prince therefore is the power to make law binding on all his subjects in general and on each in particular. But to avoid any ambiguity one must add that he does so without the consent of any superior, equal, or inferior being necessary. If the prince can only make law with the consent of a superior he is a subject; if of an equal he shares his sovereignty; if of an inferior, whether it be a council of magnates or the people, it is not he who is sovereign. The names of the magnates that one finds appended to a royal edict are not there to give force to the law, but as witnesses, and to make it more acceptable...When I say that the first attribute of sovereignty is to give law to all in general and each in particular, I mean by this last phrase the grant of privileges. I mean by a privilege a concession to one or a small group of individuals which concerns the profit or loss of those persons only...

It may be objected however that not only have magistrates the power of issuing edicts and ordinances, each according to his competence and within his own sphere of jurisdiction, but private citizens can make law in the form of general or local custom. It is agreed that customary law is as binding as statute law. But if the sovereign prince is author of the law, his subjects are the authors of custom. But there is a difference between law and custom. Custom establishes itself gradually over a long period of years, and by common consent, or at any rate the consent of the greater part. Law is made on the instant and draws its force from him who has the right to bind all the rest. Custom is established imperceptibly and without any exercise of compulsion. Law is promulgated and imposed by authority, and often against the wishes of the subject. For this reason Dion Chrysostom compared custom to the king and law to the tyrant. Moreover law can break custom, but custom cannot derogate from the law, nor can the magistrate, or any other responsible for the administration of law, use his discretion about the enforcement of law as he can about custom. Law, unless it is permissive and relaxes the severity of another law, always carries penalties for its breach. Custom only has binding force by the sufferance and during the good pleasure of the sovereign prince, and so far as he is willing to authorize it. Thus the force of both statutes and customary law derives from the authorization of the prince...Included in the power of making and unmaking law is that of promulgating it and amending it when it is obscure, or when the magistrates find contradictions and absurdities...

All the other attributes and rights of sovereignty are included in this power of making and unmaking law, so that strictly speaking this is the unique attribute of sovereign power. It includes all other rights of sovereignty, that is to say of making peace and war, of hearing appeals from the sentences of all courts whatsoever, of appointing and dismissing the great officers of state; of taxing, or granting privileges of exemption to all subjects, of appreciating or depreciating the value and weight of the coinage, of receiving oaths of fidelity from subjects and liege-vassals alike, without exception of any other to whom faith is due...

But because law is an imprecise and general term, it is as well to specify the other attributes of sovereignty comprised in it, such as the making of war and peace. This is one of the most important rights of sovereignty, since it brings in its train either the ruin or the salvation of the state. This was a right of sovereignty not only among the ancient Romans, but has always been so among all other peoples...Sovereign princes are therefore accustomed to keep themselves informed of the smallest accidents and undertakings connected with warfare. Whatever latitude they may give to their representatives to negotiate peace or an alliance, they never grant the authority to conclude without their own express consent. This was illustrated in the negotiations leading up to the recent treaty of Cateaux-Cambresis, when the king's envoys kept him almost hourly informed of all proposals and counter-proposals...In popular states and aristocracies the difficulty of assembling the people, and the danger of making public all the secrets of diplomacy has meant that the people have generally handed responsibility over to the council. Nevertheless it remains true that the commissions and the orders that it issues in discharge of this function proceed from the authority of the people, and are despatched by the council in the name of the people...

The third attribute of sovereignty is the power to institute the great officers of state. It has never been questioned that the right is an attribute of sovereignty, at any rate as far as the great officers are concerned. I confine it however to high officials, for there is no commonwealth in which these officers, and many guilds and corporate bodies besides, have not some power of appointing their subordinate officials. They do this in virtue of their office, which carries with it the power to delegate. For instance, those who hold feudal rights of jurisdiction of their sovereign prince in faith and homage have the power to appoint the judges in their courts, and their assistants. But this power is devolved upon them by the prince...It is therefore not the mere appointment of officials that implies sovereign right, but the authorization and confirmation of such appointments. It is true however that in so far as the exercise of this right is delegated, the sovereignty of the prince is to that extent qualified, unless his concurrence and express consent is required.

The fourth attribute of sovereignty, and one which has always been among its principal rights, is that the prince should be the final resort of appeal from all other courts...Even though the prince may have published a law, as did Caligula, forbidding any appeal or petition against the sentences of his officers, nevertheless the subject cannot be deprived of the right to make an appeal, or present a petition, to the prince in person. For the prince cannot tie his own hands in this respect, nor take from his subjects the means of redress, supplication, and petition, notwithstanding the fact that all rules governing appeals and jurisdictions are matters of positive law, which we have shown does not bind the prince. This is why the Privy Council, including the Chancellor de l'Hopital, considered the action of the commissioners deputed to hold an enquiry into the conduct of the President l'Alemant irregular and unprecedented. They had forbidden him to approach within twenty leagues of the court, with the intention of denying him any opportunity of appeal. The king himself could not deny this right to the subject, though he is free to make whatsoever reply to the appeal, favourable or unfavourable, that he pleases...Were it otherwise, and the prince could acquit his subjects or his vassals from the obligation to submit their causes to him in the last instance, he would make of them sovereigns equal with himself…But if he would pre-serve his authority, the surest way of doing so is to avoid ever devolving any of the attributes of sovereignty upon a subject…

With this right is coupled the right of pardoning convicted persons, and so of overruling the sentences of his own courts, in mitigation of the severity of the law, whether touching life, property, honour, or domicile. It is not in the power of any magistrate, whatever his station, to do any of these things, or to make any revision of the judgement he has once given…In a well-ordered commonwealth the right should never be delegated either to a special commission, or to any high officer of state, save in those circumstances where it is necessary to establish a regency, either because the king is abroad in some distant place, or in captivity, or incapable, or under age. For instance, during the minority of Louis IX, the authority of the Crown was vested in his mother Blanche of Castile as his guardian...Princes however tend to abuse this right, thinking that to pardon is pleasing to God, whereas to exact the utmost punishment is displeasing to Him. But I hold, subject to correction, that the sovereign prince cannot remit any penalty imposed by the law of God, any more than he can dispense any one from the operation of the law of God, to which he himself is subject. If the magistrate who dispenses anyone from obedience to the ordinance of his king merits death, how much more unwarrantable is it for the prince to acquit a man of the punishment ordained by God's law? If a sovereign prince cannot deny a subject his civil rights, how can he acquit him of the penalties imposed by God, such as the death penalty exacted by divine law for treacherous murder?

Hugo Grotius, selections from *On the Law of War and Peace*

Hugo Grotius (1583–1645 CE) was a Dutch jurist and legal scholar. Grotius's 1625 treatise, On the Law of War and Peace, is considered to be the founding and most comprehensive early work on modern inter-national law. In it, Grotius surveyed classical history and the Bible and argued that natural law established rules of conduct for nations and individuals, thereby constituting a legal foundation for international cooperation. Grotius studied law at the University of Leiden and wrote numerous theological and legal works, such as The Free Seas (1604), which advocated the unrestricted navigation of the seas for free trade.

Source: Hugo Grotius, *On the Law of War and Peace* (1625).

FOCUS QUESTIONS:

1. According to Grotius, does the principle of natural right depend on God and religion?
2. What does Grotius contend about natural law when he observes Aristotle's statement "that some things are no sooner named, than we discover their evil nature"?

BOOK I
Chapter 1: ON WAR AND RIGHT

X. Natural right is the dictate of right reason, shewing the moral turpitude, or moral necessity, of any act from its agreement or disagreement with a rational nature, and consequently that such an act is either forbidden or commanded by God, the author of nature. The actions, upon which such a dictate is given, are either binding or unlawful in themselves, and therefore necessarily understood to be commanded or forbidden by God. This mark distinguishes natural right, not only from human law, but from the law, which God himself has been pleased to reveal, called, by some, the voluntary divine right, which does not command or forbid things in themselves either binding or unlawful, but makes them unlawful by its prohibition, and binding by its command. But, to understand natural right, we must observe that some things are said to belong to that right, not properly, but, as the schoolmen say, by way of accommodation. These are not repugnant to natural right, as we have already observed that those things are called JUST, in which there is no injustice. Some times also, by a wrong use of the word, those things which reason shews to be proper, or better than things of an opposite kind, although not binding, are said to belong to natural right.

We must farther remark, that natural right relates not only to those things that exist independent of the human will, but to many things, which necessarily follow the exercise of that will. Thus property, as now in use, was at first a creature of the human will. But, after it was established, one man was prohibited by the law of nature from seizing the property of another against his will. Wherefore, Paulus the Lawyer said, that theft is expressly forbidden by the law of nature. Ulpian condemns it as infamous in its own nature; to whose authority that of Euripides may be added, as may be seen in the verse of Helena:

"For God himself hates violence, and will not have us to grow rich by rapine, but by lawful gains. That abundance, which is the fruit of unrighteousness, is an abomination. The air is common to men, the earth also where every man, in the ample enjoyment of his possession, must refrain from doing violence or injury to that of another."

Now the Law of Nature is so unalterable, that it cannot be changed even by God himself. For although the power of God is infinite, yet there are some things, to which it does not extend. Because the things so expressed would have no true meaning, but imply a contradiction. Thus two and two must make four, nor is it possible to be otherwise; nor, again, can what is really evil not be evil. And this is Aristotle's meaning, when he says, that some things are no sooner named, than we discover their evil nature. For as the substance of things in their nature and existence depends upon nothing but themselves; so there are qualities inseparably connected with their being and essence. Of this kind is the evil of certain actions, compared with the nature of a reasonable being. Therefore God himself suffers his actions to be judged by this rule, as may be seen in the xviiith chap. of Gen. 25. Isa. v. 3. Ezek. xviii. 25. Jer. ii. 9. Mich. vi. 2. From. ii. 6., iii. 6. Yet it sometimes happens that, in those cases, which are decided by the law of nature, the undiscerning are imposed upon by an appearance of change. Whereas in reality there is no change in the unalterable law of nature, but only in the things appointed by it, and which are liable to variation. For example, if a creditor forgive me the debt, which I owe him, I am no longer bound to pay it, not because the law of nature has ceased to command the payment of a just debt, but because my debt, by a release, has ceased to be a debt. On this topic, Arrian in Epictetus argues rightly, that the bor-rowing of money is not the only requisite to make a debt, but there must be the additional circumstance of the loan remaining undischarged. Thus if God should command the life, or property of any one to be taken away, the act would not authorise murder or robbery, words which always include a crime. But that cannot be murder or robbery, which is done by the express command of Him, who is the sovereign Lord of our lives and of all things. There are also some things allowed by the law of nature, not absolutely, but according to a certain state of affairs. Thus, by the law of nature, before property was introduced, every one had a right to the use of whatever he found unoccupied; and, before laws were enacted, to avenge his personal injuries by force.

XI. The distinction found in the books of the Roman Law, assigning one unchangeable right to brutes in common with man, which in a more limited sense they call the law of nature, and appropriating another to men, which they frequently call the Law of Nations, is scarcely of any real use. For no beings, except those that can form general maxims, are capable of possessing a right, which Hesiod has placed in a clear point of view, observing "that the supreme Being has appointed laws for men; but permitted wild beasts, fishes, and birds to devour each other for food." For they have nothing like justice, the best gift, bestowed upon men.

Cicero, in his first book of offices, says, we do not talk of the justice of horses or lions. In conformity to which, Plutarch, in the life of Cato the elder, observes, that we are formed by nature to use law and justice towards men only. In addition to the above, Lactantius may be cited, who, in his fifth book, says that in all animals devoid of reason we see a natural bias of self-love. For they hurt others to benefit themselves; because they do not know the evil of doing willful hurt. But it is not so with man, who, possessing the knowledge of good and evil, refrains, even with inconvenience to himself, from doing hurt. Polybius, relating the manner in which men first entered into society, concludes, that the injuries done to parents or benefactors inevitably provoke the indignation of mankind, giving an additional reason, that as understanding and reflection form the great difference between men and other animals, it is evident they cannot transgress the bounds of that difference like other animals, without exciting universal abhorrence of their conduct. But if ever justice is attributed to brutes, it is done improperly, from some shadow and trace of reason they may possess. But it is not material to the nature of right, whether the actions appointed by the law of nature, such as the care of our offspring, are common to us with other animals or not, or, like the worship of God, are peculiar to man.

XII. The existence of the Law of Nature is proved by two kinds of argument, a priori, and a posteriori, the former a more abstruse, and the latter a more popular method of proof. We are said to reason a priori, when we show the agreement or disagreement of any thing with a reasonable and social nature; but a posteriori, when without absolute proof, but only upon probability, any thing is inferred to accord with the law of nature, because it is received as such among all, or at least the more civilized nations. For a general effect can only arise from a general cause. Now scarce any other cause can be assigned for so general an opinion, but the common sense, as it is called, of mankind. There is a sentence of Hesiod that has been much praised, that opinions which have prevailed amongst many nations, must have some foundation. Heraclitus, establishing common reason as the best criterion of truth, says, those things are certain which generally appear so. Among other authorities, we may quote Aristotle, who says it is a strong proof in our favour, when all appear to agree with what we say, and Cicero maintains that the consent of all nations in any case is to be admitted for the law of nature. Seneca is of the same opinion, any thing, says he, appearing the same to all men is a proof of its truth. Quintilian says, we hold those things to be true, in which all men agree. We have called them the more civilized nations, and not without reason. For, as Porphyry well observes, some nations are so strange that no fair judgment of human nature can be formed from them, for it would be erroneous. Andronicus, the Rhodian says, that with men of a right and sound understanding, natural justice is unchangeable. Nor does it alter the case, though men of disordered and perverted minds think otherwise. For he who should deny that honey is sweet, because it appears not so to men of a distempered taste, would be wrong. Plutarch too agrees entirely with what has been said, as appears from a passage in his life of Pompey, affirming that man neither was, nor is, by nature, a wild unsociable creature. But it is the corruption of his nature which makes him so: yet by acquiring new habits, by changing his place, and way of living, he may be reclaimed to his original gentleness. Aristotle, taking a description of man from his peculiar qualities, makes him an animal of a gentle nature, and in another part of his works, he observes, that in considering the nature of man, we are to take our likeness from nature in its pure, and not in its corrupt state.

Thomas Hobbes, *The Leviathan*

Thomas Hobbes, a philosopher and writer, published his political treatise, The Leviathan, in 1651 during the English Civil War (1642-1660), two years after the execution of King Charles I (r. 1625-1649). Hobbes lived and worked in England, but fled to Paris after the English Parliament condemned his book during the Civil War. In *The Leviathan*, Hobbes argued the best government was a "common-wealth," a government based on a covenant between a monarch and subjects. In this excerpt from chapter thirteen, Hobbes outlines his views regarding the natural state of man, or human nature in its most basic state. His views on the natural state of man served as a basis and justification for his ideas about government and the powers of a monarch.

Source: Thomas Hobbes, *The Leviathan, in Cambridge Texts in the History of Political Thought*, ed. by Richard Tuck (New York: Cambridge University Press, 1996), 86-90.

Focus Questions:

1. How did Hobbes describe the natural state of man? What was the best type of government given the natural state of man? What powers should a monarch or ruler have, according to Hobbes?
2. How did the English Civil War affect his views of government? What was his stance; did he support or oppose the end of the monarchy? Why or why not?
3. Compare Hobbes' views about a monarch's power to those by French advocates of "divine right" monarchy, such as Richelieu, Bossuet and Louis XIV. How were Hobbes's ideas similar? Different?

MEN BY NATURE EQUALL

Nature hath made men so equall, in the faculties of body, and mind; as that though there bee found one man sometimes manifestly stronger in body, or of quicker mind then another; yet when all is reckoned together, the difference between man, and man, is not so considerable, as that one man can thereupon claim to himselfe any benefit, to which another may not pretend, as well as he. For as to the strength of body, the weakest has strength enough to kill the strongest, either by secret machination, or by confederacy with others, that are in the same danger with himselfe.

And as to the faculties of the mind, (setting aside the arts grounded upon words, and especially that skill of proceeding upon generall, and infallible rules, called Science; which very few have, and but in few things; as being not a native faculty, born with us; nor attained, (as Prudence,) while we look after somewhat els,) I find yet a greater equality amongst men, than that of strength. For Prudence, is but Experience; which equall time, equally bestowes on all men, in those things they equally apply themselves unto. That which may perhaps make such equality incredible, is but a vain conceipt of ones owne wisdome, which almost all men think they have in a greater degree, than the Vulgar; that is, than all men but themselves, and a few others, whom by Fame, or for concurring with themselves, they approve. For such is the nature of men, that howsoever they may acknowledge many others to be more witty, or more eloquent, or more learned; Yet they will hardly believe there be many so wise as themselves: For they see their own wit at hand, and other mens at a distance. But this proveth rather that men are in that point equall, than unequall. For there is not ordinarily a greater signe of the equall distribution of any thing, than that every man is contented with his share.

FROM EQUALITY PROCEEDS DIFFIDENCE

From this equality of ability, ariseth equality of hope in the attaining of our Ends. And therefore if any two men desire the same thing, which neverthelesse they cannot both enjoy, they become enemies; and in the way to their End, (which is principally their owne conservation, and sometimes their delectation only,) endeavour to destroy, or subdue one an other. And from hence it comes to passe, that where an Invader hath no more to feare, than an other mans single power; if one plant, sow, build, or possesse a convenient Seat, others may probably be expected to come prepared with forces united, to dispossesse, and deprive him, not only of the fruit of his labour, but also of his life, or liberty. And the Invader again is in the like danger of another.

FROM DIFFIDENCE WARRE

And from this diffidence of one another, there is no way for any man to secure himselfe, so reasonable, as Anticipation; that is, by force, or wiles, to master the persons of all men he can, so long, till he see no other power great enough to endanger him: And this is no more than his own conservation requireth, and is generally allowed. Also because there be some, that taking pleasure in contemplating their own power in the acts of conquest, which they pursue farther than their security requires; if others, that otherwise would be glad to be at ease within modest bounds, should not by invasion increase their power, they would not be able, long time, by standing only on their defence, to subsist. And by consequence, such augmentation of dominion over men, being necessary to a mans conservation, it ought to be allowed him.

Againe, men have no pleasure, (but on the contrary a great deale of griefe) in keeping company, where there is no power able to over-awe them all. For every man looketh that his companion should value him, at the same rate he sets upon himselfe: And upon all signes of contempt, or undervaluing, naturally endeavours, as far as he dares (which amongst them that have no common power to keep them in quiet, is far enough to make them destroy each other,) to extort a greater value from his contemners, by dommage; and from others, by the example.

So that in the nature of man, we find three principall causes of quarrell. First, Competition; Secondly, Diffidence; Thirdly, Glory.

The first, maketh men invade for Gain; the second, for Safety; and the third, for Reputation. The first use Violence, to make themselves Masters of other mens persons, wives, children, and cattell; the second, to defend them; the third, for trifles, as a word, a smile, a different opinion, and any other signe of undervalue, either direct in their Persons, or by reflexion in their Kindred, their Friends, their Nation, their Profession, or their Name.

OUT OF CIVIL STATES, THERE IS ALWAYS WARRE OF EVERYONE AGAINST EVERY ONE

Hereby it is manifest, that during the time men live without a common Power to keep them all in awe, they are in that condition which is called Warre; and such a warre, as is of every man, against every man. For WARRE, consisteth not in Bat-tell onely, or the act of fighting; but in a tract of time, wherein the Will to contend by Battell is sufficiently known: and therefore the notion of Time, is to be considered in the nature of WARRE; as it is in the nature of Weather. For as the nature of Foule weather, lyeth not in a showre or two of rain; but in an inclination thereto of many dayes together: So the nature of War, consisteth not in actuall fighting; but in the known disposition thereto, during all the time there is no assurance to the contrary. All other time is PEACE.

THE INCOMMODITIES OF SUCH A WAR

Whatsoever therefore is consequent to a time of Warre, where every man is Enemy to every man; the same is consequent to the time, wherein men live without other security, than what their own strength, and their own invention shall furnish them withall. In such condition, there is no place for Industry; because the fruit thereof is uncertain: and consequently no Culture of the Earth; no Navigation, nor use of the commodities that may be imported by Sea; no commodious Building; no Instruments of moving, and removing such things as require much force; no Knowledge of the face of the Earth; no account of Time; no Arts; no Letters; no Society; and which is worst of all, continuall feare, and danger of violent death; And the life of man, solitary, poore, nasty, brutish, and short.

It may seem strange to some man, that has not well weighed these things; that Nature should thus dissociate, and render men apt to invade, and destroy one another: and he may therefore, not trusting to this Inference, made from the

Passions, desire perhaps to have the same confirmed by Experience. Let him therefore consider with himselfe, when taking a journey, he armes himselfe, and seeks to go well accompanied; when going to sleep, he locks his dores; when even in his house he locks his chests; and this when he knowes there bee Lawes, and publike Officers, armed, to revenge all injuries shall bee done him; what opinion he has of his fellow subjects, when he rides armed; of his fellow Citizens, when he locks his dores; and of his children, and servants, when he locks his chests. Does he not there as much accuse mankind by his actions, as I do by my words? But neither of us accuse mans nature in it. The Desires, and other Passions of man, are in themselves no Sin. No more are the Actions, that proceed from those Passions, till they know a Law that forbids them: which till Lawes be made they cannot know: nor can any Law be made, till they have agreed upon the Person that shall make it.

It may peradventure be thought, there was never such a time, nor condition of warre as this; and I believe it was never generally so, over all the world: but there are many places, where they live so now. For the savage people in many places of America, except the government of small Families, the concord whereof dependeth on naturall lust, have no government at all; and live at this day in that brutish manner, as I said before. Howsoever, it may be perceived what manner of life there would be, where there were no common Power to feare; by the manner of life, which men that have formerly lived under a peacefull government, use to degenerate into, in a civill Warre.

But though there had never been any time, wherein particular men were in a condition of warre one against another; yet in all times, Kings, and Persons of Soveraigne authority, because of their Independency, are in continuall jealousies, and in the state and posture of Gladiators; having their weapons pointing, and their eyes fixed on one another; that is, their Forts, Garrisons, and Guns upon the Frontiers of their Kingdomes; and continuall Spyes upon their neighhours, which is a posture of War. But because they uphold thereby, the Industry of their Subjects; there does not follow from it, that misery, which accompanies the Liberty of particular men.

IN SUCH A WARRE, NOTHING IS UNJUST

To this warre of every man against every man, this also is consequent; that nothing can be Unjust. The notions of Right and Wrong, Justice and Injustice have there no place. Where there is no common Power, there is no Law: where no Law, no Injustice. Force, and Fraud, are in warre the two Cardinall vertues. Justice, and Injustice are none of the Faculties neither of the Body, nor Mind. If they were, they might be in a man that were alone in the world, as well as his Senses, and Passions. They are Qualities, that relate to men in Society, not in Solitude. It is consequent also to the same condition, that there be no Propriety, no Dominion, no Mineand Thinedistinct; but onely that to be every mans, that he can get; and for so long, as he can keep it. And thus much for the ill condition, which man by meer Nature is actually placed in; though with a possibility to come out of it, consisting partly in the Passions, partly in his Reason.

THE PASSIONS THAT ENCLINE MEN TO PEACE

The Passions that encline men to Peace, are Feare of Death; Desire of such things as are necessary to commodious living; and a Hope by their Industry to obtain them. And Reason suggesteth convenient Articles of Peace, upon which men may be drawn to agreement. These Articles, are they, which otherwise are called the Lawes of Nature: whereof I shall speak more particularly, in the two following Chapters.

The Treaty of Westphalia 1743

The Treaty of Westphalia (1743–1794 CE) was a treaty between the Holy Roman Emperor, Ferdinand III, and the King of France, Louis XIV. Part of a general European settlement that ended the Thirty Years' War and the Eighty Years' War between Spain and the Netherlands, the Treaty, negotiated in Westphalia, marked the beginning of the European state system based on the sovereignty of states. It ended the Holy Roman Empire's supremacy and witnessed France's rise as the major European power. Catholics, Lutherans ("Confession of Augsberg"), and, for the first time, Calvinists ("Reformed") were recognized and could be tolerated with the consent of the sovereign ruler of each territory.

Source: The Treaty of Westphalia, 1648.

Focus Questions:

1. Does the treaty appear to focus on general principles, specific issues, or both?
2. Does the treaty seem to focus mainly on the concerns of the Holy Roman Emperor or the King of France?

TREATY OF WESTPHALIA; OCTOBER 24, 1648

Peace Treaty between the Holy Roman Emperor and the King of France and their respective Allies.

I.

That there shall be a Christian and Universal Peace, and a perpetual, true, and sincere Amity, between his Sacred Imperial Majesty, and his most Christian

Majesty; as also, between all and each of the Allies, and Adherents of his said Imperial Majesty, the House of Austria, and its Heirs, and Successors; but chiefly between the Electors, Princes, and States of the Empire on the one side; and all and each of the Allies of his said Christian Majesty, and all their Heirs and Successors, chiefly between the most Serene Queen and Kingdom of Swedeland, the Electors respectively, the Princes and States of the Empire, on the other part. That this Peace and Amity be observ'd and cultivated with such a Sincerity and Zeal, that each Party shall endeavour to procure the Benefit, Honour and Advantage of the other; that thus on all sides they may see this Peace and Friendship in the Roman Empire, and the Kingdom of France flourish, by entertaining a good and faithful Neighbourhood.

III.

And that a reciprocal Amity between the Emperor, and the Most Christian King, the Electors, Princes and States of the Empire, may be maintain'd so much the more firm and sincere (to say nothing at present of the Article of Security, which will be mention'd hereafter) the one shall never assist the present or future Enemys of the other under any Title or Pretence whatsoever, either with Arms, Money, Soldiers, or any sort of Ammunition; nor no one, who is a Member of this Pacification, shall suffer any Enemy's Troops to retire thro' or sojourn in his Country.

XXVIII.

That those of the Confession of Augsburg, and particularly the Inhabitants of Oppenheim, shall be put in possession again of their Churches, and Ecclesiastical Estates, as they were in the Year 1624. as also that all others of the said Confession of Augsburg, who shall demand it, shall have the free Exercise of their Religion, as well in publick Churches at the appointed Hours, as in private in their own Houses, or in others chosen for this purpose by their Ministers, or by those of their Neighbours, preaching the Word of God.

XLVI.

As for the rest, Law and Justice shall be administer'd in Bohemia, and in all the other Hereditary Provinces of the Emperor, without any respect; as to the Catholicks, so also to the Subjects, Creditors, Heirs, or private Persons, who shall be of the Confession of Augsburg, if they have any Pretensions, and enter or prosecute any Actions to obtain Justice.

XLIX.

And since for the greater Tranquillity of the Empire, in its general Assemblys of Peace, a certain Agreement has been made between the Emperor, Princes and States of the Empire, which has been inserted in the Instrument and Treaty of

Peace, concluded with the Plenipotentiarys of the Queen and Crown of Swedeland, touching the Differences about Ecclesiastical Lands, and the Liberty of the Exercise of Religion; it has been found expedient to confirm, and ratify it by this present Treaty, in the same manner as the abovesaid Agreement has been made with the said Crown of Swedeland; also with those call'd the Reformed, in the same manner, as if the words of the abovesaid Instrument were reported here verbatim.

LXIV.

And to prevent for the future any Differences arising in the Politick State, all and every one of the Electors, Princes and States of the Roman Empire, are so establish'd and confirm'd in their antient Rights, Prerogatives, Libertys, Privileges, free exercise of Territorial Right, as well Ecclesiastick, as Politick Lordships, Regales, by virtue of this present Transaction: that they never can or ought to be molested therein by any whomsoever upon any manner of pretence.

LXV.

They shall enjoy without contradiction, the Right of Suffrage in all Deliberations touching the Affairs of the Empire; but above all, when the Business in hand shall be the making or interpreting of Laws, the declaring of Wars, imposing of Taxes, levying or quartering of Soldiers, erecting new Fortifications in the Territorys of the States, or reinforcing the old Garisons; as also when a Peace of Alliance is to be concluded, and treated about, or the like, none of these, or the like things shall be acted for the future, without the Suffrage and Consent of the Free Assembly of all the States of the Empire: Above all, it shall be free perpetually to each of the States of the Empire, to make Alliances with Strangers for their Preservation and Safety; provided, nevertheless, such Alliances be not against the Emperor, and the Empire, nor against the Publick Peace, and this Treaty, and without prejudice to the Oath by which every one is bound to the Emperor and the Empire.

LXX.

The Rights and Privileges of Territorys, water'd by Rivers or otherways, as Customs granted by the Emperor, with the Consent of the Electors, and among others, to the Count of Oldenburg on the Viserg, and introduc'd by a long Usage, shall remain in their Vigour and Execution. There shall be a full Liberty of Commerce, a secure Passage by Sea and Land: and after this manner all and every one of the Vassals, Subjects, Inhabitants and Servants of the Allys, on the one side and the other, shall have full power to go and come, to trade and return back, by Virtue of this present Article, after the same manner as was allowed before the Troubles of Germany; the Magistrates, on the one side and on the other, shall be oblig'd to protect and defend them against all sorts of

Oppressions, equally with their own Subjects, without prejudice to the other Articles of this Convention, and the particular laws and Rights of each place. And that the said Peace and Amity between the Emperor and the Most Christian King, may be the more corroborated, and the publick Safety provided for, it has been agreed with the Consent, Advice and Will of the Electors, Princes and States of the Empire, for the Benefit of Peace:

LXXVII.

The most Christian King shall, nevertheless, be oblig'd to preserve in all and every one of these Countrys the Catholick Religion, as maintain'd under the Princes of Austria, and to abolish all Innovations crept in during the War.

XC.

That all the Vassals, Subjects, Citizens and Inhabitants, as well on this as the other side the Rhine, who were subject to the House of Austria, or who depended immediately on the Empire, or who acknowledg'd for Superiors the other Orders of the Empire, notwithstanding all Confiscations, Transferrings, Donations made by any Captains or Generals of the Swedish Troops, or Confederates, since the taking of the Province, and ratify'd by the most Christian King, or decreed by his own particular Motion; immediately after the Publication of Peace, shall be restor'd to the possession of their Goods, immovable and stable, also to their Farms, Castles, Villages, Lands, and Possessions, without any exception upon the account of Expences and Compensation of Charges, which the modern Possessors may alledge, and without Restitution of Movables or Fruits gather'd in.

CIV.

As soon as the Treaty of Peace shall be sign'd and seal'd by the Plenipotentiarys and Ambassadors, all Hostilitys shall cease, and all Partys shall study immediately to put in execution what has been agreed to; and that the same may be the better and quicker accomplish'd, the Peace shall be solemnly publish'd the day after the signing thereof in the usual form at the Cross of the Citys of Munster and of Osnabrug. That when it shall be known that the signing has been made in these two Places, divers Couriers shall presently be sent to the Generals of the Armys, to acquaint them that the Peace is concluded, and take care that the Generals chuse a Day, on which shall be made on all sides a Cessation of Arms and Hostilitys for the publishing of the Peace in the Army; and that command be given to all and each of the chief Officers Military and Civil, and to the Governors of Fortresses, to abstain for the future from all Acts of Hostility: and if it happen that any thing be attempted, or actually innovated after the said Publication, the same shall be forthwith repair'd and restor'd to its former State.

CV.

The Plenipotentiarys on all sides shall agree among themselves, between the Conclusion and the Ratification of the Peace, upon the Ways, Time, and Securitys which are to be taken for the Restitution of Places, and for the Disbanding of Troops; of that both Partys may be assur'd, that all things agreed to shall be sincerely accomplish'd.

Done, pass'd and concluded at Munster in Westphalia, the 24th Day of October, 1648.

The Poor Laws

With vagrancy and poverty on the upswing at the end of the sixteenth century, the English Parliament and Queen Elizabeth I (r. 1533-1603) worked together to enact laws designed to address poverty. With Elizabeth's urging, the English Parliament passed a series of laws addressing poverty in England, collectively called the Poor Laws, beginning in 1597, that provided government assistance to those who could not provide for themselves including the sick, elderly, and young children. The Poor Laws also set up government workhouses for those who were able to work and designated which local officials were charged with instituting these programs. These laws remained in place long after Elizabeth's reign, providing the basis for government policies for the poor until the nineteenth century.

Source: G. W. Prothero, *Select Statutes and other Constitutional Documents Illustrative of the Reigns of Elizabeth and James I*, 4th ed., (New York: Oxford at the Clarendon Press, 1934), 72-75, 96-103.

Focus Questions:

1. How did these laws define "the poor"? What did these laws mean for them?
2. How did these laws attempt to solve the problems associated with poverty? What groups or individuals were designated to implement these laws? Why?
3. What larger concerns or trends help to explain why these laws were enacted in this period?

AN ACT FOR THE RELIEF OF THE POOR

I. Be it enacted, That the churchwardens of every parish and four substantial householders there being subsidy men, or (for want of subsidy men) four other substantial householders of the said parish, who shall be nominated yearly in Easter week under the hand and seal of two or more justices of the peace in the same county, whereof one to be of the quorum, dwelling in or near the same parish, shall be called overseers of the poor of the same parish; and they... shall take order from time to time with the consent of two or more such justices of peace for setting to work of the children of all such [sic] whose parents shall not by the said persons be thought able to keep and maintain their children, and also all such persons, married or unmarried, as, having no means to maintain them, use no ordinary and daily trade of life to get their living by; and also to raise . . . by taxation of every inhabitant and every occupier of lands in the said parish... a convenient stock of flax, hemp, wool, thread, iron and other stuff to set the poor on work, and also competent sums of money for the necessary relief of the lame, impotent, old, blind and such other among them being poor and not able to work, and also for the putting out of such children to be apprentices... and to do all other things... concerning the premises as to them shall seem convenient:

* * *

II. And be it also enacted, That if the said justices of peace do perceive that the inhabitants of any parish are not able to levy among themselves sufficient sums of money for the purposes aforesaid, that then the said justices shall tax . . . any other of other parishes . . . within the hundred where the said parish is, to pay such sums of money . . . as the said justices shall think fit, according to the intent of this law; and if the said hundred shall not be thought to the said justices able to relieve the said several parishes . . . then the justices of peace at their general quarter sessions shall rate and assess as aforesaid any other of other parishes . . . within the said county for the purposes aforesaid as in their discretion shall seem fit.

III. And that it shall be lawful for the said churchwardens and overseers or any of them by warrant from any such two justices of peace to levy as well the said sums of money of every one that shall refuse to contribute... by distress and sale of the offender's goods, as the sums of money or stock which shall be behind upon any account to be made as aforesaid...; and in defect of such distress it shall be lawful for any such two justices of the peace to commit him to prison, there to remain... till payment of the said sum or stock; and the said justices of peace or any one of them to send to the house of correction such as shall not employ themselves to work being appointed thereunto as aforesaid; and also any two such justices of peace to commit to prison every one of the said churchwardens and overseers which shall refuse to account, there to remain... till he have made a true account and paid so much as upon the said account shall be remaining in his hands.

And be it further enacted, That it shall be lawful for the said churchwardens and overseers by the assent of any two justices of the peace to bind any such children as aforesaid to be apprentices when they shall see convenient, till such man-child shall come to the age of 24 years and such woman-child to the ahe of 21 years...

And be it further enacted, That... no person shall go wandering abroad and beg in any place whatsoever, by licence or without, upon pain to be taken and punished as a rogue: provided always that this present Act shall not extend to any poor people which shall ask relief of victuals only in the same parish where such poor people do dwell, so the same be... according to such order as shall be made by the churchwardens and overseers of the poor of the same parish...

XI. And be it further enacted, That all penalties and forfeitures before mentioned in this Act shall be employed to the use of the poor of the same parish, and towards a stock and habitation for them and other necessary uses and relief . . .

XIII. And be it also enacted, That the said justices of the peace at their general quarter sessions . . . shall set down what competent sum of money shall be sent quarterly out of every county or place corporate for the relief of the poor prisoners of the King's Bench and Marshalsea, and also of such hospitals and almshouses as shall be in the said county . . . so as there be sent out of every county yearly 20s. at the least to the prisoners of the King's Bench and Marshalsea;

XIV. And be it further enacted, That all the surplusage of money which shall be remaining in the said stock of any county shall by... the justices of peace in their quarter sessions be ordered and bestowed for the relief of the poor hospitals of that county, and of those that shall sustain losses by fire... or other casualties, and to such other charitable purposes... as to the said justices of peace shall seem convenient.

AN ACT FOR PUNISHMENT OF ROGUES, VAGABONDS AND STURDY BEGGARS

II. Be it further enacted, That all persons calling themselves scholars going about begging, all seafaring men pretending losses [&c.] shall be deemed rogues, vagabonds and sturdy beggars, and shall sustain such punishment as by this Act is in that behalf appointed.

III. And be it enacted, That every person which is by this present Act declared to be a rogue, vagabond or sturdy beggar, which shall be... taken begging, vagrant or misordering themselves . . . shall upon their apprehension ... be stripped naked from the middle upwards and shall be openly whipped until his or her body be bloody, and shall be forthwith sent from parish to parish... the next straight way to the parish where he was born, if the same may be known...., and if the same be not known, then to the parish where be last dwelt... one whole year, there to put himself to labour as a true subject ought to do; or not being known where he was born or last dwelt, then to the parish through which he last passed without punishment;... and the party so whipped and not known where he was born or last dwelt by the space of a year, shall by the officers of the said village where he so last passed through without punishment be conveyed to the house of correction... or to the common gaol of that county or place, there to remain and be employed in work until he shall be placed in some service, and so to continue by the space of one whole year, or not being able of body,... to remain in some almshouse in the same county or place.

IV. Provided, That if any of the said rogues shall appear to be dangerous... or such as will not be reformed... it shall be lawful to the said justices . . . or any two of them . . . to commit that rogue to the house of correction or to the gaol of that county, there to remain until their next quarter sessions...; and then such of the same rogues so committed, as by the justices of the peace... shall be thought fit not to be delivered, shall... be banished out of this realm... and at the charge of that county shall be conveyed unto such parts beyond the seas as shall be at any time hereafter for that purpose assigned by the privy council... or by any six or niore of them, whereof the Lord Chancellor or Lord Keeper of the Great Seal or the Lord Treasurer to be one, or be judged perpetually to the galleys of this realm, as by the same justices shall be thought fit; and if any such rogue so banished as aforesaid shall return again into any part of this realm or dominion of Wales without lawful licence... such offence shall be felony, and the party offending therein suffer death as in case of felony...

XIV. Provided, That every seafaring man suffering shipwreck, not having wherewith to relieve himself in his travels homewards, but having a testimonial under the hand of some one justice of the peace of the place where he landed, . . . may without incurring the penalty of this Act... ask to receive such 1 relief as shall be necessary for his passage.

AN ACT FOR ERECTING OF HOSPITALS OR ABIDING AND WORKING HOUSES FOR THE POOR

I. Whereas at the last session of parliament provision was made as well as for maimed soldiers, by collection in every parish, as for other poor, that it should be lawful for every person, during twenty years next after the said parliament..., to give and bequeath in fee-simple, as well to the use of the poor as for the provision or maintenance of any house of correction or abiding-houses, or of any stocks or stores, all or any part of his lands [&c.]; her most excellent Majesty understanding that the said good law hath not taken such effect as was intended, by reason that no person can erect or incorporate any hospital [&c.] but her Majesty or by her Highness' special licence . . . , is of her princely care . . . for the relief of maimed soldiers, mariners and other poor and impotent people pleased that it be enacted... and be it enacted, That all persons seised of an estate in fee-simple, their heirs, executors or assigns . . . shall have full power,... at any time during the space of twenty yeals next ensuing, by deed enrolled in the High Court of Chancery, to found and establish one or more hospitals, maisons de dieu, abiding-places or houses of correction... to have continuance for ever, and from time to time to place therein such head and members and such number of poor as to him [&c.] shall seem convenient...

V. Provided, That no such hospital [&c.] shall be erected, founded or incorporated by force of this Act, unless upon the foundation or erection thereof the same be endowed for ever with lands, tenements or hereditaments of the clear yearly value of £10.

AN ACT FOR THE SETTING OF THE POOR ON WORK, AND FOR THE AVOIDING OF IDLENESS

IV.... That in every city and town corporate within this realm a competent store and stock of wool, hemp, flax, iron or other stuff by order of the mayor... or other head officers... shall be provided; and that likewise in every other market-town or other place where (to the justices of peace in their general sessions yearly next after Easter shall be thought most meet) a like competent store and stock of wool [&c.] or other stuff as the country is most meet for... shall be provided, the said stores and stocks in such cities and towns corporate to be committed to the custody of such persons as shall by the mayor or other head officers in every such city or town corporate be appointed, and in other towns and places to such persons as by the said justices of peace in their said general sessions... shall be by them appointed; which said persons... shall from henceforth be called the collectors and governors of the poor, to the intent every such poor and needy person... able to do any work... shall not for want of work go abroad either begging or committing pilferings or other misdemeanours...; which collectors from time to time (as cause requireth) shall, of the same stock and store, deliver to such poor and needy person a competent portion to be wrought into yarn or other matter..., for which they shall make payment to them which work the same according to the desert of the work . . . ; which hemp [&c.] or other stuff, wrought from time to time, shall be sold by the said collectors... and with the money coming of the sale to buy more stuff...; and if hereafter any such person able to do any such work shall refuse to work . . . or taking such work shall spoil or embezzle the same... he, she or they shall be received into such house of correction, there to be straightly kept, as well in diet as in work, and also punished from time to time...

V. And moreover be it enacted, That within every county of this realm one, two or more abiding houses or places convenient in some market-town or corporate town or other place, by... order of the justices of peace in their said general sessions... shall be provided, and called houses of correction, and also stock and store and implements be provided for setting on work and punishing not only of those which by the collectors and governors of the poor for causes aforesaid to the said houses of correction shall be brought, but also of such as be inhabiting in no parish, or be taken as rogues... or for any other cause ought to be abiding and kept within the same county...

VI. And be it also further enacted, That the said justices of peace, in their said general sessions, shall appoint from time to time overseers of every such house of correction, which said persons shall be called the censors and wardens of the houses of correction...; and shall also appoint others for the gathering of such money as shall he taxed upon any persons within their several jurisdictions towards the maintenance of the said houses of correction, which shall be called the collectors for the houses of correction; and if any person refuse to be collector and governor of the poor or censor and warden or collector for any the houses of correction, that every person so refusing shall forfeit the sum of £5...

La Colonie, "The Battle of Schellenberg"

Louis XIV (r. 1643-1715) embarked on an ambitious policy to extend the borders of France and make it the most powerful country in Europe. This aggressive foreign policy meant almost constant war for France from the 1660s to 1715. The French crown borrowed heavily to fund these wars, leaving Louis XIV's successors with massive debts. The wars also tested the limits of the French military, both the army and the smaller naval forces. At this time, only nobles could be commanders or officers in the military while soldiers were often mercenaries, drawn from all over Europe. Wars also brought hardship and chaos to the areas where battles took place, as ill disciplined armies exacted food, supplies, and quarters from the peasants and townspeople around battle sites, often by force. In this excerpt, a French noble army commander, Monsieur de La Colonie, provides an account of his experiences during a battle in the War of Spanish Succession (1701-1714). This battle takes place in Schellenberg, between Switzerland and Austria, in the area that is present-day Liechtenstein.

Source: John Casey, *Eyewitness to History* (New York: Avon Books, 1997), 199-205.

Focus Questions:

1. What was the author's perspective and involvement in this event? What factors or issues likely influenced his account and version of events?
2. What does this tell us about the affects of warfare on those living in the areas where battles took place?
3. What does this account tell us about the affects of warfare on commanders? Soldiers?

I made a point of impressing upon my men the necessity of attention to orders, and of prompt obedience in carrying out any manoeuvres during the action with courage and in good order. I assured them that herein lay our safety and, perhaps, victory.

I had scarcely finished speaking when the enemy's battery opened fire upon us, and raked us through and through. They concentrated their fire upon us, and with their first discharge carried off Count de la Bastide, the lieutenant of my own company with whom at the moment I was speaking, and twelve grenadiers, who fell side by side in the ranks, so that my coat was covered with brains and blood. So accurate was the fire that each discharge of the cannon stretched some of my men on the ground. I suffered agonies at seeing these brave fellows perish without a chance of defending themselves, but it was absolutely necessary that they should not move from their post.

This cannonade was but the prelude of the attack that the enemy were developing, and I looked upon the moment when they would fling themselves against one point or another in our entrenchments as so instant that I would allow no man even to bow his head before the storm, fearing that the regiment would find itself in disorder when the time came for us to make the rapid movement that would be demanded of us. At last the enemy's army began to move to the assault, and still it was necessary for me to suffer this sacrifice to avoid a still greater misfortune, though I had five officers and eighty grenadiers killed on the spot before we had fired a single shot.

So steep was the slope in front of us that as soon almost as the enemy's column began its advance it was lost in view, and it came into sight only two hundred paces from our entrenchments. I noticed that it kept as far as possible from the glacis of the town and close alongside of the wood, but I could not make out whether a portion might not also be marching within the latter with the purpose of attacking that part of our entrenchments facing it, and the uncertainty caused me to delay movement. There was nothing to lead me to suppose that the enemy had such an intimate knowledge of our defences as to guide them to one point in preference to another for their attack.

Had I been able to guess that the column was being led by that scoundrel of a corporal who had betrayed us, I should not have been in this dilemma, nor should I have thought it necessary to keep so many brave men exposed to the perils of the cannonade, but my doubts came to an end two hours after midday, for I caught sight of the tips of the Imperial standards, and no longer hesitated. I changed front as promptly as possible, in order to bring my grenadiers opposite the part of our position adjoining the wood, towards which I saw that the enemy was directing his advance.

The regiment now left a position awkward in the extreme on account of the cannon, but we soon found ourselves scarcely better off, for hardly had our men lined the little parapet when the enemy broke into the charge, and rushed at full speed, shouting at the top of their voices, to throw themselves into our entrenchments.

The rapidity of their movements, together with their loud yells, were truly alarming, and as soon as I heard them I ordered our drums to beat the 'charge' so as to drown them with their noise, lest they should have a bad effect upon our people. By this means I animated my grenadiers, and prevented them hearing the shouts of the enemy, which before now have produced a heedless panic.

The English infantry led this attack with the greatest intrepidity, right up to our parapet, but there they were opposed with a courage at least equal to their own. Rage, fury, and desperation were manifested by both sides, with the more obstinacy as the assailants and assailed were perhaps the bravest soldiers in the world. The little parapet which separated the two forces became the scene of the bloodiest struggle that could be conceived. Thirteen hundred grenadiers, of whom seven hundred belonged to the Elector's Guards, and six hundred who were left under my command, bore the brunt of the enemy's attack at the forefront of the Bavarian infantry.

It would be impossible to describe in words strong enough the details of the carnage that took place during this first attack, which lasted a good hour or more. We were all fighting hand to hand, hurling them back as they clutched at the parapet; men were slaying, or tearing at the muzzles of guns and the bayonets which pierced their entrails; crushing under their feet their own wounded comrades, and even gouging out their opponents' eyes with their nails, when the grip was so close that neither could make use of their weapons. I verily believe that it would have been quite impossible to find a more terrible representation of Hell itself than was shown in the savagery of both sides on this occasion.

At last the enemy, after losing more than eight thousand men in this first onslaught, were obliged to relax their hold, and they fell back for shelter to the dip in the slope, where we could not harm them. A sudden calm now reigned amongst us, our people were recovering their breath, and seemed more determined even than they were before the conflict. The ground around our parapet was covered with dead and dying, in heaps almost as high as our fascines, but our whole attention was fixed on the enemy and his movements; we noticed that the tops of his standards still showed at about the same place as that from which they had made their charge in the first instance, leaving little doubt but that they were reforming before returning to the assault. As soon as possible we set vigorously to work to render their approach more difficult for them than before, and by means of an increasing fire swept their line of advance with a torrent of bullets, accompanied by numberless grenades, of which we had several wagon loads in rear of our position. These, owing to the slope of the ground, fell right amongst the enemy's ranks, causing them great annoyance and doubtless added not a little to their hesitation in advancing the second time to the attack. They were so disheartened by the first attempt that their generals had the greatest difficulty in bringing them forward again, and indeed would never have succeeded in this, though they tried every other means, had they not dismounted and set an example by placing themselves at the head of the column, and leading them on foot.

Their devotion cost them dear, for General Stirum and many other generals and officers were killed. They once more, then, advanced to the assault, but with nothing like the success of their first effort, for not only did they lack energy in their attack, but after being vigorously repulsed, were pursued by us at the point of the bayonet for more than eighty paces beyond our entrenchments, which we finally re-entered unmolested.

After this second attempt many efforts were made by their generals, but they were never able to bring their men to the assault a third time...

But I noticed all at once an extraordinary movement on the part of our infantry, who were rising up and ceasing fire withal. I glanced around on all sides to see what had caused this behaviour, and then became aware of several lines of infantry in greyish white uniforms on our left flank. From lack of movement on their part, their dress and bearing, I verily believed that reinforcements had arrived for us, and anybody else would have believed the same. No information whatever had reached us of the enemy's success, or even that such a thing was the least likely, so in the error I laboured under I shouted to my men that they were Frenchman, and friends, and they at once resumed their former position behind the parapet.

Having, however, made a closer inspection, I discovered bunches of straw and leaves attached to their standards, badges the enemy are in the custom of wearing on the occasion of battle, and at that very moment was struck by a ball in the right lower jaw, which wounded and stupefied me to such an extent that I thought it was smashed. I probed my wound as quickly as possible with the tip of my finger, and finding the jaw itself entire, did not make much fuss about it; but the front of my jacket was so deluged with the blood which poured from it that several of our officers believed that I was dangerously hurt. I reassured them, however, and exhorted them to stand firmly with their men. I pointed out to them that so long as our infantry kept well together the danger was not so great, and that if they behaved in a resolute manner, the enemy, who were only keeping in touch with us without daring to attack us, would allow us to retire without so much as pursuing. In truth, to look at them it would seem that they hoped much more for our retreat than any chance of coming to blows with us. I at once, therefore, shouted as loudly as I could that no one was to quit the ranks, and then formed my men in column along the entrenchments facing the wood, fronting towards the opposite flank, which was the direction in which we should have to retire. Thus, whenever I wished to make a stand, I had but to turn my men about, and at any moment could resume the retirement instantaneously, which we thus carried out in good order. I kept this up until we had crossed the entrenchments on the other flank, and then we found ourselves free from attack. This retreat was not made, however, without loss, for the enemy, although they would not close with us when they saw our column formed for the retirement, fired volleys at close range into us, which did much damage.

My men had no sooner got clear of the entrenchments than they found that the slope was in their favour, and they fairly broke their ranks and took to flight, in order to reach the plain that lay before them before the enemy's cavalry could get upon their track. As each ran his hardest, intending to reform on the further side, they disappeared like a flash of lightning without ever looking back, and I, who was with the rearguard ready to make a stand if necessary against our opponents, had scarcely clambered over the entrenchments when I found myself left entirely alone on the height, prevented from running by my heavy boots.

I looked about on all sides for my drummer, whom I had warned to keep at hand with my horse, but he had evidently thought fit to look after himself, with the result that I found myself left solitary to the mercy of the enemy and my own sad thoughts, without the slightest idea as to my future fate. I cudgelled my brains in vain for some way out of my difficulty, but could think of nothing the least certain; the plain was too wide for me to traverse in my big boots at the necessary speed, and to crown my misfortunes, was covered with cornfields. So far the enemy's cavalry had not appeared on the plain, but there was every reason to believe that they would not long delay their coming; it would have been utter folly on my part to give them the chance of discovering me embarrassed as I was, for as long as I was hampered with my boots, a trooper would always find it an easy affair to catch me.

I noticed, however, that the Danube was not so very far away, and determined to make my way towards it at all risk, with the hope of finding some beaten track or place where there would be some chance of saving my life, as I saw it was now hopeless to think of getting my men together. As a matter of fact, I found a convenient path along the bank of the river, but this was not of much avail to me, for, owing to my efforts and struggles to reach it through several fields of standing corn, I was quite blown and exhausted and could only just crawl along at the slowest possible pace. On my way I met the wife of a Bavarian soldier, so distracted with weeping that she travelled no faster than I did. I made her drag off my boots, which fitted me so tightly about the legs that it was absolutely impossible for me to do this for myself. The poor woman took an immense time to effect this, and it seemed to me at least as if the operation would never come to an end. At last this was effected, and I turned over in my mind the best way to profit by my release, when, raising my head above the corn at the side of the road, I saw a number of the enemy's troopers scattered over the country, searching the fields for any of our people who might be hidden therein, with the intention, doubtless, of killing them for the sake of what plunder might be found upon them. At this cruel prospect all my hopes vanished, and the exultation I felt at my release from the boots died at the moment of its birth. My position was now more perilous than ever; nevertheless, I examined under the cover afforded by the corn the manoeuvres of these cavaliers to see if I could not find some way out of the difficulty. A notion came into my head which, if it could have been carried out, might have had a curious ending. It was that if one trooper only should approach me, and his comrades remained sufficiently distant, I should keep hidden and wait until he got near enough for me to kill him with a shot from my pistol, for I had two on my belt; I would then take his uniform, mount his horse, and make my escape in this disguise, a plan which would be favoured by the approaching darkness. But not seeing any chance of being able to carry out this idea, I thought of another, namely, to get into the river up to my chin in the water under the bushes on the bank, wait for nightfall and the return of the troopers to their camp, and then to escape in the dark. But there were more difficulties to contend with in risking this even than in the other case, and as a last resource it struck me I might save myself by crossing the river, for happily I knew how to swim, although the risk here was very great owing to the breadth and rapidity of the Danube. I hurriedly determined on this plan, as I now saw a number of troopers approaching ever nearer to my hiding place, who were refusing to give quarter to the unhappy wounded they found hidden in the corn, whom they ruthlessly despatched the more easily to despoil them. There was no reason to suppose that they were likely to show any more mercy to me, particularly as I was worth more in the shape of plunder than a private soldier, nor was there time to lose in making up my mind, so I then and there determined to swim the river. Before taking to the water I took the precaution of leaving on the bank my richly embroidered uniform, rather spoiled as it was by the events of the late action. I scattered in a similar manner my hat, wig, pistols, and sword, at one point and another, so that if the troopers came up before I had got well away, they would devote their attention to collecting these articles instead of looking in the water, and it turned out just as I thought. I kept on my stockings, vest, and breeches, simply buttoning the sleeves of the vest and tucking the pockets within my breeches for safety; this done, I threw myself upon the mercy of the stream. I had hardly got any distance when up came the troopers, who, as I had hoped, dismounted as quickly as they could to lay hands on the spoil lying before them; they even set to work to quarrel over it, for I distinctly heard them shouting and swearing in the most delightful manner. Others apparently got no share, and they amused themselves by saluting me with several musket shots, but the current of the river which carried me on my way soon put me out of their range. Finally, after a very long and hard swim, I was lucky enough to reach the other bank, in spite of the strength of the stream.

Peter the Great, "Correspondence with Alexis"

Peter the Great, Tsar of Russia (r. 1672-1725) established greater links between his country and Western Europe, and introduced important reforms in the military and government with the goal of making Russia a European power. Borrowing from Western European shipbuilding techniques, Peter oversaw the construction of the first Russian naval fleet. He also made significant changes in the army, for example, putting in place programs to better train and organize the Russian nobles who served as government and military officers. Peter's ambitions for Russian territorial expansion led to numerous wars with Sweden, Poland, and the Ottoman Empire. His son Alexis, born in 1690, was his heir to the throne, but around 1715 Peter changed the terms of this succession so it passed over Alexis to Peter's grandson (Alexis's son). Alexis attempted to flee Russia in 1716, eventually returned, but his father, who believed he was plotting to assassinate him, ordered Alexis's arrest. Alexis died in 1718 as a result of his imprisonment and torture. When Peter died in 1725, a succession crisis and period of instability followed that finally ended with when Catherine the Great (r. 17291796), Peter's second wife, came to the throne.

Source: *The Global Experience,* Vol. 2, by Philip F. Riley, et. al. (Upper Saddle River, NJ: Prentice Hall, 1998), pp. 44–46.

Focus Questions:

1. What were Peter the Great's views regarding war? What beliefs or ideas informed his views?
2. How did Peter the Great hope to increase the power and prestige of Russia in Europe?
3. What did this letter say about the succession issue? What was Peter's view about who would inherit the Russian throne after his death? His son's response?

A LETTER TO ALEXEI
October 11, 1715
Declaration to My Son,

You cannot be ignorant of what is known to all the world, to what degree our people groaned under the oppression of the Swedes before the beginning of the present war.

By the usurpation of so many maritime places so necessary to our state. they had cut us off from all commerce with the rest of the world, and we saw with regret that besides they had cast a thick veil before the eyes of the clear-sighted. You know what it has cost us in the beginning of this war (in which God alone has led us, as it were, by the hand. and still guides us) to make ourselves experienced in the art of war, and to put a stop to those advantages which our implacable enemies obtained over us.

We submitted to this with a resignation to the will of God, making no doubt but it was he who put us to that trial, till he might lead us into the right way, and we might render ourselves worthy to experience, that the same enemy who at first made others tremble, now in his turn trembles before us, perhaps in a much greater degree. These are the fruits which, next to the assistance of God, we owe to our own toil and to the labour of our faithful and affectionate children. our Russian subjects.

But at the time that I am viewing the prosperity which God has heaped on our native country, if I cast an eye upon the posterity that is to succeed me, my heart is much more penetrated with grief on account of what is to happen, then I rejoice at those blessings that are past, seeing that you, my son, reject all means of making yourself capable of well-governing after me. I say your incapacity is voluntary. because you cannot excuse yourself with want of natural parts and strength of body, as if God had not given you a sufficient share of either: and though your constitution is none of the strongest, yet it cannot be said that it is altogether weak.

But you even will not so much as hear warlike exercises mentioned; though it is by them that we broke through that obscurity in which we were involved, and that we made ourselves known to nations, whose esteem we share at present.

I do not exhort you to make war without lawful reasons: I only desire you to apply yourself to learn the art of it: for it is impossible well to govern without knowing the rules and discipline of it, was it for no other end than for the defense of the country.

I could place before your eyes many instances of what I am proposing to you. I will only mention to you the Greeks, with whom we are united by the same profession of faith. What occasioned their decay but that they neglected arms? Idleness and repose weakened them, made them submit to tyrants, and brought them to that slavery to which they are now so long since reduced. You mistake, if you think it is enough for a prince to have good generals to act under his order. Everyone looks upon the head; they study his inclinations and conform themselves to them: all the world owns this. My brother during his reign loved magnificence in dress, and great equipages of horses. The nation were not much inclined that way, but the prince's delight soon became that of his subjects. for they are inclined to imitate him in liking a thing as well as disliking it.

If the people so easily break themselves of things which only regard pleasure, will they not forget in time, or will they not more easily give over the practice of arms, the exercise of which is the more painful to them, the less they are kept to it?

You have no inclination to learn war. you do not apply yourself to it, and consequently you will never learn it: And how then can you command others, and judge of the reward which those deserve who do their duty. or punish others who fail of it? You will do nothing, nor judge of anything but by the eyes and help of others. like a young bird that holds up his bill to be fed.

You say that the weak state of your health will not permit you to undergo the fatigues of war: This is an excuse which is no better than the rest. I desire no fatigues, but only inclination, which even sickness itself cannot hinder. Ask those who remember the time of my brother. He was of a constitution weaker by far than yours. He was not able to manage a horse of the least mettle, not could he hardly mount it: Yet he loved horses. hence it came, that there never was, nor perhaps is there actually now in the nation a finer stable than his was.

By this you see that good success does not always depend on pain, but on the will.

If you think there are some, whose affairs do not fail of success, though they do not go to war themselves; it is true: But if they do not go themselves, yet they have an inclination for it, and understand it.

For instance, the late King of France did not always take the field in person; but it is known to what degree he loved war, and what glorious exploits he performed in it, which made his campaigns to be called the theatre and school of the world. His inclinations were not confined solely to military affairs, he also loved mechanics, manufactures and other establishments, which rendered his kingdom more flourishing than any other whatsoever.

After having made to you all those remonstrances, I return to my former subject which regards you.

I am a man and consequently I must die. To whom shall I leave after me to finish what by the grace of God I have begun, and to preserve what I have partly recovered? To a man, who like the slothful servant hides his talent in the earth, that is to say, who neglects making the best of what God has entrusted to him?

Remember your obstinacy and ill-nature, how often I reproached you with it, and even chastised you for it, and for how many years I almost have not spoke to you; but all this has availed nothing, has effected nothing. It was but losing my time: it was striking the air. You do not make the least endeavors. and all your pleasure seems to consist in staying idle and lazy at home: Things of which you ought to be ashamed (forasmuch as they make you miserable) seem to make up your dearest delight, nor do you foresee the dangerous consequences of it for yourself and for the whole state. St. Paul has left us a great truth when he wrote: If a man know not how to rule his own house, how shall he take of the church of God?

After having considered all those great inconveniences and reflected upon them, and seeing I cannot bring you to good by any inducement, I have thought fit to give you in writing this act of my last will, with this resolution however to wait still a little longer before I put it in execution to see if you will mend. If not, I will have you to know that I will deprive you of the succession, as one may cut off a useless member.

Do not fancy, that, because I have no other child but you, I only write this to terrify you. I will certainly put it in execution, if it please God; for whereas I do not spare my own life for my country and the welfare of my people, why should I spare you who do not render yourself worthy of either? I would rather choose to transmit them to a worthy stranger, than to my own unworthy son.

Peter

ALEXEI'S REPLY

Most Clement Lord and Father,

I have read the paper your Majesty gave me on the 27th of October, 1715, after the funeral of my late consort.

I have nothing to reply to it, but, that if your Majesty will deprive me of the succession to the Crown of Russia by reason of my incapacity, your will be done; I even most instantly beg it of you, because I do not think myself fit for the government. My memory is very much weakened, and yet it is necessary in affairs. The strength of my mind and of my body is much decayed by the sicknesses which I have undergone, and which have rendered me incapable of governing so many nations; this requires a more vigorous man than I am.

Therefore I do not aspire after you (whom God preserve many years) to the succession of the Russian Crown, even if I had no brother as I have one at present, whom I pray God preserve. Neither will I pretend for the future to that succession, of which I take God to witness, and swear it upon my soul, in testimony whereof I write and sign this present with my own hand.

I put my children into your hands, and as for myself, I desire nothing of you but a bare maintenance during my life, leaving the whole to your consideration and to your will.

Your most humble servant and son. Alexei

CHAPTER 12

Expanding Worlds

Letters from the Kings of Portugal to the King of Kongo

In the 1400s and early 1500s, the Portuguese led the way in European exploration and expansion, first in Africa and later in the Atlantic world. Portuguese Prince Henry "The Navigator" (1394-1460), a member of the Portuguese royal family, was an important patron and supporter for early expeditions to Africa, beginning in 1418 under his father King John I (r.1383-1433) and brother King Duarte (r. 1433-1438) and continuing after Henry's death under the reign of Afonso V (r.1438-1481). By the 1480s, during the reign of John II (r. 14811495), Portuguese expeditions had reached into the sub-Saharan. In 1484, the Portuguese formed an alliance with the Bantu speaking Kongo kingdom, along the Congo River in West-Central Africa. Their ruler, Nzinga Mbemba (r. c. 1506-43), converted to Christianity, adopted the name Afonso I, and made an alliance with the Portuguese that allowed land and trading privileges, including the right to conduct raids to supply the slave trade. The Kongo slid into decline after 1570, as a result of warring factions within their loosely knit kingdom. The letters that follow were exchanges between the ruler of the Kongo kingdom, Nzinga Mbemba (or Alfonso I) and Portuguese kings Manuel I (r. 1495-1521) and John III (r.1521-1557).

Source: "Letters from the Kings of the Kongo to the King of Portugal," MonumentaMissionaria Africana, ed. Antonio Brasio, (Lisboa: Agencia Geral do Ultramar, 1952), vol. 1: 262–63, 294–95, 335, 404, 470, 488, trans. Linda Wimmer; reprinted in The Global Experience: Readings in World History,ed. Stuart B. Schwartz, et al., (New York: Addison Wesley, Longman, Inc., 1997), 240–42.

Focus Questions:

1. How does the African king use language and imagery that would appeal to a European monarch?

2. How successful do you imagine Alfonso was in his petitions to the Portuguese crown?

PORTUGUESE MILITARY AID DURING CIVIL WAR

And our brother who usurped us, and without justice occupied us, with arms and a great number of people... became empowered in all of our kingdom, and lordships, with which when we saw the only solution for our person we feigned sickness; and it being so with us, by a divine inspiration of our Lord, we raised and strengthened ourself, and called up our 36 men, and with them we appeared, and went with them to the main square of the city, where our Father died, and where people of infinite number were with our said brother, and... for our Lord Jesus Christ, and we began to fight with our adversaries... our 36 men, inspired by grace, and aided by God, our adversaries quickly fled... and chaos ensued, and with them witnessing... there appeared in the air a white Cross, and the blessed Apostle St. James with many men armed and on horseback, and dressed in white battle garments, and killed them, and so great was the chaos, and mortality, that it was a thing of great wonder.

In this defeat our brother was taken prisoner and with justice condemned to die, as he died, for having rebelled against us; and finally we made peace in our kingdoms... as it is today, with the Grace of God... and through the miracle made by our Lord, and we send word to the King Dom Emanuel of Portugal... and we send to him Dom Pedro our brother, who was one of the 36 men with us... and with the letters that the king sent of great works given....

And as the King of Portugal saw the good example... followed... for the greater growth of our Holy Catholic Faith, he sent by our cousin Dom Pedro and by Simao da Sylva noblemen of your house who came with him, the arms pictured in this card, and the shields with insignias... [A]nd as these weapons arrived a cross was seen in the sky, and so the Apostle St. James and all the other Saints fought with us, and with the help of our Lord God we were given victory, and so also as by the King sent us his [men] took part with the said arms....

PROBLEMS IN CONVERSION EFFORTS (1515)

Very High and Powerful Lord,

We the King Dom Alfonso... Lord, much holy grace and praise I give to the Holy God the Father and the Son and the Holy Spirit... all good and holy things are done through the will of God, without which we can do nothing... our faith is still like glass in this kingdom, due to the bad examples of the men who come here to teach it, because through worldly greed for a few riches truth is destroyed, as through greed the Jews crucified the Son of God, my brother, until today he is crucified through bad examples and bad deeds... in our time by us who walk crying in this real valley of misery and tears.

... [I]n teaching the word of Our Lord [these bad priests] become bad examples and so take the key to the Celestial Kingdom that is the Doctrine of our Holy Catholic Faith, to open the hearts of our simple people... and by entering into a life of sin take the key to Hell... due to the greed of this world, do not merely take their own bodies and souls to Hell, but guide those most blind with them through their bad examples. I ask of you, Brother, to aid me in establishing our Holy Catholic Faith, because, Lord my Brother, for us it were better... that the souls of our relatives and brothers and cousins and nephews and grandchildren who are innocent, to see... good examples.

... I ask you to send stonemasons and house carpenters to build a school to teach our relatives and our people, because Lord, although greedy and jealous men still give bad examples... with the Holy Sacred Scripture we may change that, because the world of the Holy Spirit is contrary to the world, the flesh and the devil....

ATTEMPTS TO BUY A CARAVEL (1517)

Very Powerful and Very High Prince and King My Brother

... I have several times written you of the necessity of having a ship, telling you to make me one to buy, and I don't know why Your Highness does not want to consent, because I want nothing more than... to use it in God's service....

EFFECTS OF PORTUGUESE TRADE (1526)

Lord,

... [Y]our factors and officials give to the men and merchants that come to this Kingdom... and spread... so that many vassals owing us obedience... rebel because they have more goods [through trade with Portuguese] than us, who before had been content and subject to our... jurisdiction, which causes great damage....

... And each day these merchants take our citizens, native to the land and children of our nobles and vassals, and our relations, because they are thieves and men of bad conscience, steal them with the desire to have things of this kingdom... take them to sell... our land is all spoiled... which is not to your service.... For this we have no more necessity for other than priests and educators, but [send] no more merchandise... nor merchants....

EXPANSION AND REGULATION OF THE SLAVE TRADE (1526)

[M]any of our subjects, through the desire for merchandise and things of this Kingdoms which you bring... to satisfy their appetite, steal many of our free and exempt subjects. And nobles and their children and our relatives are often stolen to be sold to white men... hidden by night.... And the said white men are so powerful... they embark and... buy them, for which we want justice, restoring them to liberty....

And to avoid this great evil, by law all white men in our kingdom who buy slaves... must make it known to three nobles and officials of our court... to see these slaves....

Bartolomé de Las Casas, *Very Brief Report on the Destruction of the Indians*

In his accounts of Spanish conquests in the Americas, Bartolomé de Las Casas (1475-1566) emphasized the brutal and cruel treatment of Amerindians by Spanish conquistadors. Las Casas wrote his accounts of Spanish conquest of the Americas for a European audience, hoping that the vivid accounts of excessive violence used against the Amerindians and their subsequent enslavement would result in significant changes in Spanish colonial policies. As a Dominican monk, Las Casas's religious ideas and beliefs significantly influenced his arguments and approach to these issues.

Sources: Bartolomé de Las Casas, *His Life, His Apostolate, and His Writings,* trans. by Francis Augustus McNutt (New York, 1909), 314-315 and Bartolomé de Las Casas, *Very Brief Report on the Destruction of the Indians,* trans. Francis Augusts Mac Nutt [need publishing info and date here], 319-20.

Focus Questions:

1. How did Las Casas describe Amerindians in this passage? What ideas or sources did he draw on for this description? Why?
2. How did Las Casas' background and beliefs shape his account of Spanish colonial policies and actions?
3. How did Las Casas portray the Spanish conquistadors? To what extent was this account reliable (why or why not)?

God has created all these numberless people to be quite the simplest, without malice or duplicity, most obedient, most faithful to their natural Lords, and to the Christians, whom they serve; the most humble, most patient, most peaceful, and calm, without strife nor tumults; not wrangling, nor querulous, as free from uproar, hate and desire of revenge, as any in the world.

They are likewise the most delicate people, weak and of feeble constitution, and less than any other can they bear fatigue, and they very easily die of whatsoever infirmity; so much so, that not even the sons of our Princes and of nobles, brought up in royal and gentle life, are more delicate than they; although there are among them such as are of the peasant class. They are also a very poor people, who of worldly goods possess little, nor wish to possess: and they are therefore neither proud, nor ambitious, nor avaricious.. . . They are likewise of a clean, unspoiled, and vivacious intellect, very capable, and receptive to every good doctrine; most prompt to accept our Holy Catholic Faith, to be endowed with virtuous customs; and they have as little difficulty with such things as any people created by God in the world.

Once they have begun to learn of matters pertaining to faith, they are so importunate to know them, and in frequenting the sacraments and divine service of the Church, that to tell the truth, the clergy have need to be endowed of God with the gift of preeminent patience to bear with them: and finally, I have heard many lay Spaniards frequently say many years ago, (unable to deny the goodness of those they saw) certainly these people were the most blessed of the earth, had they only knowledge of God.

The Christians, with their horses and swords and lances, began to slaughter and practise strange cruelty among them. They penetrated into the country and spared neither children nor the aged, nor pregnant women, nor those in child labour, all of whom they ran through the body and lacerated, as though they were assaulting so many lambs herded in their sheepfold.

They made bets as to who would slit a man in two, or cut off his head at one blow: or they opened up his bowels. They tore the babes from their mothers' breast by the feet, and dashed their heads against the rocks. Others they seized by the shoulders and threw into the rivers, laughing and joking, and when they fell into the water they exclaimed: "boil body of so and so!" They spitted the bodies of other babes, together with their mothers and all who were before them, on their swords.

They made a gallows just high enough for the feet to nearly touch the ground, and by thirteens, in honour and reverence of our Redeemer and the twelve Apostles, they put wood underneath and, with fire, they burned the Indians alive....

And because all the people who could flee, hid among the mountains and climbed the crags to escape from men so deprived of humanity, so wicked, such wild beasts, exterminators and capital enemies of all the human race, the Spaniards taught and trained the fiercest boar-hounds to tear an Indian to pieces as soon as they saw him, so that they more willingly attacked and ate one, than if he had been a boar. These hounds made great havoc and slaughter.

Jamestown Charter

The colony at Jamestown, on the coast of Virginia, was the first permanent English colony in North America. The charter for the colony, drafted in 1606 by the English government under King James I (r. 1603-1625) provided for its founding in May of 1607. The charter set up the land rights, institutions, and government for the colony. The colony at Jamestown experienced many difficulties, including a high death rate from disease, poor crop yields, attacks from Native American groups, and a major fire in 1608. In 1610, it was saved when Thomas West arrived from England with new settlers and supplies.

Source: "Letters patent to Sir Thomas Gates and others, April 10, 1606" in *The Jamestown Voyages Under the First Charter, 1606-1609*, vol. 1, ed. by Philip L Barbour (Cambridge: Cambridge University Press, 1969), 24-34.

Focus Questions:

1. What plans did this charter make for the physical layout of the settlement and for its supplies or support?
2. Who were to be its leaders, and how was the government to be organized?
3. What motivated the English to establish colonial settlements in the Americas?

II..10 April 1606

Letters Patent to Sir Thomas Gates and Others

James by the grace of God &c Whereas our loving and well disposed subiects Sir Thomas Gates and Sir George Somers Knightes Richard Hackluit Clarke prebendarie of Westminster and Edwarde Maria Winghfeilde Thomas Hannam and Raleighe Gilberde Esquiers William Parker and George Popham Gentlemen and divers others of our loving subiects haue been humble sutors vnto vs that wee woulde vouchsafe vnto them our licence to make habitacion plantaion and to deduce a Colonie of sondrie of our people into that parte of America commonly called Virginia and other parts and territories in America either appertaining vnto vs or which are not nowe actuallie possessed by anie Christian Prince or people scituate lying and being all along the sea Coastes

* * *

and to that ende and for the more speedy accomplishemente of theire saide intended plantacion and habitacion there are desirous to devide themselues into two severall Colonies and Companies the one consisting of certaine Knightes Gentlemen marchauntes and other Adventurers of our Cittie of London and elsewhere

* * *

and the other consisting of sondrie Knightes Gentlemen merchauntes and other Adventurers of our Citties of Bristoll and Exeter and of our towne of Plymouthe and of other places which doe ioyne themselues vnto that Colonie

* * *

wee greately commending and graciously accepting of theire desires to the furtherance of soe noble a worke which may be the providence of Almightie God hereafter tende to the glorie of hys divyne maiestie in propagating of Christian religion to suche people as yet live in darkenesse and myserable ignorance of the true knowledge and worshippe of god and may in tyme bring the infidels and salvages lyving in those partes to humane civilitie and to a setled and quiet govermente doe by theise our lettres Patentes graciously accepte of and agree to theire humble and well intended desires

* * *

And that they shall haue all the landes woodes soyle Groundes havens portes Ryvers Mynes Myneralls Marshes waters Fyshings Commodities and hereditamentes whatsoever from the said first seate of theire plantacion and habytacion by the space of Fyftie miles of Englishe statute measure all alongest the saide Coaste of Virginia and

* * *

America towardes the Weste and southeweste as the Coaste lyeth with all the Islandes within one hundred myles directlie over againste the same sea Coaste

* * *

and towards the Easte and Northeaste

* * *

And directly into the mayne lande by the space of One hundred like Englishe myles and shall and may inhabyt and remaine there and shall and may alsoe buylde and fortifie within anie the same for theire better safegarde and defence according to theire best discrecions and the direction of the Counsell of that Colonie and that noe other of our subiects shalbe permitted or suffered to plante or inhabyt behinde or on the backside of them towardes the mayne lande without the expresse lycence or consente of the Counsell of that Colonie thereunto in writing firste had or obtained

* * *

And wee doe alsoe ordaine establishe and agree for vs our heires and successors that eache of the saide Colonies shall haue a Counsell which shall governe and order all matters and Causes which shall arise growe or happen to or within the same severall Colonies according to such lawes ordynaunces and Instructions as shalbe in that behalfe given and signed with our hande or signe manuell and passe vnder the privie seale of our Realme of Englande Eache of which Counsells shall consist of Thirteene parsons [i.e., persons] and to be ordained made and removed from tyme to tyme according as shalbe directed and comprised in the same Instructions and shall haue a severall seale for all matters that shall passe or concerne the same severall Counsells Eache of which seales shall haue the Kinges Armes engraven on the one syde thereof and hys pourtraiture on the other

* * *

And that alsoe ther shalbe a Counsell established here in Englande which shall in like manner consist of thirteene parsons to be for that purpose appointed by vs our heires and successors which shalbe called our Counsell of Virginia And shall from tyme to tyme haue the superior managing and direction onelie of and for all matters that shall or may concerne the govermente aswell of the said seuerall Colonies as of and for anie other parte or place within the aforesaid preinctes

* * *

And moreover wee doe graunte and agree for vs our heires and successors that the saide severall Counsells of and for the saide severall Colonies shall and lawfully may by vertue hereof from tyme to tyme without intervpcion of vs our heires or successors giue and take order to digg myne and searche for all manner of Mynes of Goulde Silver and Copper aswell within anie parte of theire saide severall Colonies as of the saide Mayne landes on the backeside of the same Colonies and to haue and enjoy the Goulde Silver and Copper to be gotten thereof to the vse and behoofe of the same Colonies and the plantacions thereof yielding therefore yerelie to vs our heires and successors the Fifte parte onelie of all the same Goulde and Silver and the Fifteenth parte of all the same Copper soe to be gotten or had as ys aforesaide without anie other manner of profytt or Accompte to be given or yeilded to vs our heires or successors for or in respecte of the same And that they shall or lawfullie may establishe and cawse to be made a coyne to passe currant there betweene the people of those severall Colonies for the more ease of traffique and bargaining betweene and amongst them and the natives there of such mettall and in suche manner and forme as the same severall Counsells there shall lymitt and appointe

* * *

Moreover wee doe by theise presentes for vs our heires and successors giue and graunte licence vnto the said Sir Thomas Gates Sir George Sumers Richarde Hackluite Edwarde Maria Winghfeilde Thomas Hannam Raleighe Gilberde William Parker and George Popham and to everie of the said Colonies that they and everie of them shall and may from tyme to tyme and at all tymes for ever hereafter for their severall defences incounter or expulse repell and resist as well by sea as by lande by all waies and meanes whatsoever all and everie suche

* * *

parson and parsons as without especiall licence of the said severall Colonies and plantacions shall attempt to inhabit within the saide seuerall precinctes and lymittes of the saide severall Colonies and plantacions or anie of them or that shall enterprise or attempt at anie tyme hereafter the hurte detrymente or annoyance of the saide severall Colonies or plantacions

* * *

Alsoe wee doe vor vs our heires and successor declare by theise presentes that all and everie the parsons being our subiectes which shall dwell and inhabit within everie or anie of the saide severall Colonies and plantacions and everie of theire children which shall happen to be borne within the lymittes and precinctes of the said severall Colonies and plantacyons shall haue and enioy all liberties Franchises and Immunities within anie of our other domynions to all intentes and purposes as yf they had been abyding and borne within this our Realme of Englande or anie other of our saide Domynions

* * *

Prouided alwaies and our will and pleasure ys and wee doe hereby declare to all Christian Kings Princes and estates that yf anie parson or parsons which shall hereafter be of anie of the said severall Colonies and plantacions or anie other by his theire or anie of theire licence or appointement shall at anie tyme or tymes hereafter robb or spoile by sea or by lande or doe anie Acte of vniust and vnlawfull hostilitie to anie the subiectes of vs our heires or successors or anie of the subiects of anie King Prince Ruler Governor or State being then in league or Amitie with vs our heires or successors and that vpon suche Iniurie or vpon iuste complainte of such Prince Ruler Governor or State or theire subiects wee our heires or successors shall make open proclamacion within anie the portes of our Realme of Englande commodious for that purpose that the saide parson or parsons having committed anie such Robberie or spoyle shall within the tearme to be lymitted by suche Proclamacions make full restitucion or satisfactin of all suche Iniuries done soe as the saide Princes or others soe complained may houlde themselues fully satisfied and contented and that yf the saide parson or parsons having comitted such robberie or spoyle shall not make or cause to be made satisfaction accordingly with[in] such tyme soe to be lymitted That then yt shalbe lawfull to vs our heires and successors to put the saide parson or parsons having comitted such robberie or spoyle and theire procurers Abbettors or Comfortors out of our allegeaunce and protection and that yt shalbe lawefull and free for all Princes and others to pursue with hostilitie the saide Offenders and everie of them and theire and everie of theire procurors Ayders Abbettors and comforters in that behalfe

Richard Frethorne, "Letter to Father and Mother"

The European settlements were often multicultural communities with societies that evolved differently from those in Europe, allowing more class mobility for Europeans who came and became permanent settlers. Nevertheless, class and economic differences persisted, even in the colonies. One way to fund the costly voyage from Europe to the New World colonies was to sign on as an indentured servant. Under the terms of such contracts, workers agreed to several years of service, usually about seven, in return for the payment of their passage to North America. The work done by indentured servants varied according to their skills and gender. Some, especially women, served as domestic servants while men usually worked in the fields, or if they had skills, as artisans. This letter, written by Richard Frethorne to his parents, provides a first hand account of what conditions were like for indentured servants in the early English colony of Jamestown, in Virginia.

Source: Richard Frethorne, "Letter to his father and mother, March 20, April 2 and 3, 1623" in *The Records of the Virginia Company of London,* ed. by Susan Kingsbury (Washington D.C.: Government Printing Office, 1935), 4: 58-62.

Focus Questions:

1. Given Frethorne's account, what was life like for an indentured servant?
2. How did Frethorne, in general terms, describe life in the colony and how did his own situation or status inform his view?
3. What does this tell us about early English colonial settlements in the Americas?

LOVING AND KIND FATHER AND MOTHER:

My most humble duty remembered to you, hoping in god of your good health, as I myself am at the making hereof. This is to let you understand that I you child am in a most heavy case by reason of the country, [which] is such that it causeth much sic kness, [such] as the sccurvy and the bloody flux and diverse other diseases, which maketh the body very poor and weak. And when we are sick there is nothing to comfort us; for since I came out of the ship I never ate anything but peas, and loblollie (that is, water gruel). As for deer or venison I never saw any since I came into this land. There is indeed some fowl, but we are not allowed to go and get it, but must work hard both early and late for a mess of water gruel and a mouthful of bread and beef. A mouthful of bread for a penny loaf must serve for four men which is most pitiful. [You would be grieved] if you did know as much as I [do], when people cry out day and night—Oh! That they were in England without their limbs—and would not care to lose any limb to be in England again, yea, though they beg from door to door. For we live in fear of the enemy every hour, yet we have had a combat with them... and we took two alive and made slaves of them. But it was by policy, for we are in great danger; for our plantation is very weak by reason of the death and sickness of our company. For we came but twenty for the merchants, and they are half dead just; and we look every hour when two more should go. Yet there came some four other men yet to live with us, of which there is but one alive; and our Lieutenant is dead, and [also] his father and his brother. And there was some five or six of the last year's twenty, of which there is but three left, so that we are fain to get other men to plant with us; and yet we are but 32 to fight against 3000 if they should come. And the nighest help that we have is ten mile of us, and when the rogues overcame this place [the] last [time] they slew 80 persons. How then shall we do, for we lie even in their teeth? They may easily take us, but [for the fact] that God is merciful and can save with few as well as with many, as he showed to Gilead. And like Gilead's soldiers, if they lapped water, we drink water which is but weak.

And I have nothing to comfort me, nor is there nothing to be gotten here but sickness and death, except [in the event] that one had money to lay out in some things for profit. But I have nothing at all—no, not a shirt to my back but two rags (2), nor clothes but one poor suit, nor but one pair of shoes, but one pair of stockings, but one cap, [and] but two bands [collars]. My cloak is stolen by one of my fellows, and to his dying hour [he] sould not tell me what he did with it; but some of my fellows saw him have butter and beef out of a ship, which my cloak, I doubt [not], paid for. So that I have not a penny, nor a penny worth, to help me too either spice or sugar or strong waters, without the which one cannot live here. For as strong beer in England doth fatten and strengthen them, so water here doth wash and weaken these here [and] only keeps [their] life and soul together. But I am not half [of] a quarter so strong as I was in England, and all is for want of victuals; for I do protest unto you that I have eaten more in [one] day at home than I have allowed me here for a week. You have given more than my day's allowance to a beggar at the door; and if Mr. Jackson had not relieved me,

I should be in a poor case. But he like a father and she like a loving mother doth still help me.

For when we go to Jamestown (that is 10 miles of us) there lie all the ships that come to land, and there they must deliver their goods. And when we went up to town [we would go], as it may be, on Monday at noon, and come there by night, [and] then load the next day by noon, and go home in the afternoon, and unload, and then away again in the night, and [we would] be up about midnight. Then if it rained or blowed never so hard, we must lie in the boat on the water and have nothing but a little bread. For when we go into the boat we [would] have a loaf allowed to two men, and it is all [we would get] if we stayed there two days, which is hard; and [we] must lie all that while in the boat. But that Goodman Jackson pitied me and made me a cabin to lie in always when I [would] come up, and he would give me some poor jacks [fish] [to take] home with me, which comforted me more than peas or water gruel. Oh, they be very godly folks, and love me very well, and will do anything for me. And he much marvelled that you would send me a servant to the Company; he saith I had been better knocked on the head. And indeed so I find it now, to my great grief and misery; and [I] saith that if you love me you will redeem me suddenly, for which I do entreat and beg. And if you cannot get the merchants to redeem me for some little money, then for God's sake get a gathering or entreat some good folks to lay out some little sum of money in meal and cheese and butter and beef. Any eating meat will yield great profit. Oil and vinegar is very good; but, father, there is great loss in leaking. But for God's sake send beef and cheese and butter, or the more of one sort and none of another. But if you send cheese, it must be very old cheese; and at the cheesemonger's you may buy very food cheese for twopence farthing or halfpenny, that will be liked very well. But if you send cheese, you must have a care how you pack it in barrels; and you must put cooper's chips between every cheese, or else the heat of the hold will rot them. And look whatsoever you send me—be in never so much—look, what[ever] I make of it, I will deal truly with you. I will send it over and beg the profit to redeem me; and if I die before it come, I have entreated Goodman Jackson to send you the worth of it, who hath promised he will. If you send, you must direct your letters to Goodman Jackson, at Jamestown, a gunsmith. (You must set down his freight, because there be more of his name there.) Good father, do not forget me, but have mercy and pity my miserable case. I know if you did but see me, you would weep to see me; for I have but one suit. (But [though] it is a strange one, it is very well guarded.) Wherefore, for God's sake, pity me. I pray you to remember my love to all my friends and kindred. I hope all my brothers and sisters are in good health, and as for my part I have set down my resolution that certainly will be; that is, that the answer of this letter will be life or death to me. Therefore, good father, send as soon as you can; and if you send me any thing let this be the mark.

Christopher Columbus "The Letters of Columbus to Ferdinand and Isabel"

While he may not have been the first European to explore the Atlantic, Christopher Columbus initiated a new era of European voyages to the Atlantic world as a result of his voyages. Columbus was an experienced map maker from the port city of Genoa in the Italian states. The Spanish rulers, King Ferdinand and Queen Isabella (r.1479-1504) commissioned his voyage in 1492 with the goal of seeking a new Western route to Asia from Europe. Instead, Columbus landed on several islands in the Caribbean just off the Americas, including San Salvador, Cuba and Hispaniola. Columbus and his small crew encountered people on the island, and called them "Indians," mistakenly believing that they had found a route to Asia and; reached islands just off of India. Columbus's voyages helped establish Spain as a leader in the early era of European exploration and settlement of the Americas.

Source: Christopher Columbus, *The Journal of Christopher Columbus,* trans. By Cecil Jane (London: Anthony Blond, 1968), 191, 194, 196-198, 200-201.

Focus Questions:

1. For whom was Columbus writing this account? What was his main goal in writing the letter?
2. What does Columbus' account of the lands he sees tell us about what Europeans hoped to find in the "new world" and their motivations for going to those areas?
3. What did Columbus's account of the people he encountered there, whom he called "Indians," tell us about early European attitudes about these people? What ideas or beliefs informed these views?

SIR: Since I know that you will be pleased at the great victory with which Our Lord has crowned my voyage, I write this to you, from which you will learn how in thirty-three days I passed from the Canary Islands to the Indies, with the fleet which the most illustrious King and Queen, our Sovereigns, gave to me. There I found very many islands, filled with innumerable people, and I have taken possession of them all for their Highnesses, done by proclamation and with the royal standard unfurled, and no opposition was offered to me.

To the first island which I found I gave the name "San Salvador," in remembrance of the Divine Majesty, Who had marvellously bestowed all this; the Indians call it "Guanahani." To the second, I gave the name the island of "Santa Maria de Concepcion," to the third, "Fernandina," to the fourth, "Isabella," to the fifth island, "Juana," and so each received from me a new name....

Española is a marvel. The sierras and the mountains, the plains, the champaigns, are so lovely and so rich for planting and sowing, for breeding cattle of every kind, for building towns and villages. The harbours of the sea here are such as cannot be believed to exist unless they have been seen, and so with the rivers, many and great, and of good water, the majority of which contain gold. In the trees, fruits and plants, there is a great difference from those of Juana. In this island, there are many spices and great mines of gold and of other metals.

The people of this island and of all the other islands which I have found and of which I have information, all go naked, men and women, as their mothers bore them, although some of the women cover a single place with the leaf of a plant or with a net of cotton which they make for the purpose. They have no iron or steel or weapons, nor are they fitted to use them. This is not because they are not well built and of handsome stature, but because they are very marvellously timorous. They have no other arms than spears made of canes, cut in seeding time, to the ends of which they fix a small sharpened stick. Of these they do not dare to make use, for many times it has happened that I have sent ashore two or three men to some town to have speech with them, and countless people have come out to them, and as soon as they have seen my men approaching, they have fled, a father not even waiting for his son. This is not because ill has been done to any one of them; on the contrary, at every place where I have been and have been able to have speech with them, I have given to them of that which I had, such as cloth and many other things, receiving nothing in exchange. But so they are, incurably timid. It is true that, after they have been reassured and have lost this fear, they are so guileless and so generous with all that they possess, that no one would believe it who has not seen it. They refuse nothing that they possess, if it be asked of them; on the contrary, they invite any one to share it and display as much love as if they would give their hearts.

They are content with whatever trifle of whatever kind that may be given to them, whether it be of value or valueless. I forbade that they should be given things so worthless as fragments of broken crockery, scraps of broken glass and lace tips, although when they were able to get them, they fancied that they possessed the best jewel in the world. So it was found that for a thong a sailor received gold to the weight of two and a half Castellanos, and others received much more for other things which were worth less. As for new blancas, for them they would give everything which they had, although it might be two or three castellanos' [gold coins] weight of gold or an arroba or two of spun cotton. They took even the pieces of the broken hoops of the wine barrels and, like savages, gave what they had, so that it seemed to me to be wrong and I forbade it. I gave them a thousand handsome good things, which I had brought, in order that they might conceive affection for us and, more than that, might become Christians and be inclined to the love and service of Your Highnesses and of the whole Castilian nation, and strive to collect and give us of the things which they have in abundance and which are necessary to us.

They do not hold any creed nor are they idolaters; but they all believe that power and good are in the heavens and were very firmly convinced that I, with these ships and men, came from the heavens, and in this belief they everywhere received me after they had mastered their fear. This belief is not the result of ignorance, for they are, on the contrary, of a very acute intelligence and they are men who navigate all those seas, so that it is amazing how good an account they give of everything. It is because they have never seen people clothed or ships of such a kind.

As soon as I arrived in the Indies, in the first island which I found, I took some of the natives by force, in order that they might learn and might give me information of whatever there is in these parts. And so it was that they soon understood us, and we them, either by speech or signs, and they have been very serviceable. At present, those I bring with me are still of the opinion that I come from Heaven, for all the intercourse which they have had with me. They were the first to announce this wherever I went, and the others went running from house to house, and to the neighbouring towns, with loud cries of, "Come! Come! See the men from Heaven!" So all came, men and women alike, when their minds were set at rest concerning us, not one, small or great, remaining behind, and they all brought something to eat and drink, which they gave with extraordinary affection....

In all these islands, I saw no great diversity in the appearance of the people or in their manners and language. On the contrary, they all understand one another, which is a very curious thing, on account of which I hope that their Highnesses will determine upon their conversion to our holy faith, towards which they are very inclined. I have already said how I went one hundred and seven leagues in a straight line from west to east along the seashore of the island of Juana, and as a result of this voyage I can say that this island is larger than England and Scotland together, for, beyond these one hundred and seven leagues, there remain to the westward two provinces to which I have not gone. One of these provinces they call "Avan," and there people are born with tails. These provinces cannot have a length of less than fifty or sixty leagues, as I could understand from those Indians whom I have and who know all the islands.

The other island, Española, has a circumference greater than all Spain from Collioure by the seacoast to Fuenterabia in Vizcaya, for I voyaged along one side for one hundred and eighty-eight great leagues in a straight line from west to east. It is a land to be desired and, when seen, never to be left. I have taken possession of all for their Highnesses, and all are more richly endowed than I know how or am able to say, and I hold all for their Highnesses, so that they may dispose of them as they do of the kingdoms of Castile and as absolutely. But especially, in this Española, in the situation most convenient and in the best position for the mines of gold and for all trade as well with the mainland here as with that there, belonging to the Grand Khan, where will be great trade and profit, I have taken possession of a large town, to which I gave the name "Villa de Navidad," and in it I have made fortifications and a fort, which will now by this time be entirely completed. In it I have left enough men for such a purpose with arms and artillery and provisions for more than a year, and a fusta, and one, a master of all seacraft, to build others, and I have established great friendship with the king of that land, so much so, that he was proud to call me "brother" and to treat me as such....

In conclusion, to speak only of what has been accomplished on this voyage, which was so hasty, their Highnesses can see that I will give them as much gold as they may need, if their Highnesses will render me very slight assistance; presently, I will give them spices and cotton, as much as their Highnesses shall command; and mastic, as much as they shall order to be shipped and which, up to now, has been found only in Greece, in the island of Chios, and the Seignory sells it for what it pleases; and aloe, as much as they shall order to be shipped; and slaves, as many as they shall order, and who will be from the idolaters. I believe also that I have found rhubarb and cinnamon, and I shall find a thousand other things of value, which the people whom I have left there will have discovered, for I have not delayed at any point, so far as the wind allowed me to sail, except in the town of Navidad, in order to leave it secured and well established, and in truth I should have done much more if the ships had served me as reason demanded....

This is an account of the facts, thus abridged. Done in the caravel, off the Canary Islands, on the fifteenth day of February, in the year one thousand four hundred and ninety-three.

Cieza de León
"The Chronicle of Peru"

Pedro Cieza de León went to South America from Spain as a solider when he was only 14 years old. He remained in South America for most of his life, traveling throughout the continent and participating in military battles for Spain, primarily against the Inca. The Inca Empire in that period covered a vast stretch of Western South America, and was comprised of over 12 million people, including many different ethnic groups. In 1532, the Spanish wiped out what remained of the crumbling Incan Empire. Cieza de León was involved in the military campaigns that destroyed it, and immediately after 1532, he interviewed those who survived them, both Spanish and Inca alike. He then wrote one of the most important and reliable chronicles for that period.

Source: Pedro Cieza de León, "The Chronicle of Peru: The Incas," reprinted in *Primary Source Document Workbook to Accompany Western Civilizations,* *by Philip J. Adier; prepared* by Robert Welborn (New York: West Publishing Company, 1996), 35-36.

Focus Questions:

1. Why did the author write this account? What did he hope to accomplish by doing so?
2. What does the author say about the Inca people? What informs his account and views?
3. What does this account tell us about Spanish attitudes and actions in relation to the Inca?

It should be well understood that great prudence was needed to enable these kings to govern such large provinces, extending over so vast a region, parts of it rugged and covered with forests, parts mountainous, with snowy peaks and ridges, parts consisting of deserts of sand, dry and without trees or water. These regions were inhabited by many different nations, with varying languages, laws, religions, and the kings had to maintain tranquility and to rule so that all should live in peace and in friendship towards their lord. Although the city of Cuzco was the head of the empire,... yet at certain points, as we shall also explain, the king stationed his delegates and governors, who were the most learned, the ablest, and the bravest men that could be found, and none was so youthful that he was not already in the last third part of his age. As they were faithful and none betrayed their trusts,... none of the natives, though they might be more powerful, attempted to rise in rebellion; or if such a thing ever did take place, the town where the revolt broke out was punished, and the ringleaders were sent prisoners to Cuzco....

All men so feared the king, that they did not dare to speak evil even of his shadow. And this was not all. If any of the king's captains or servants went forth to visit a distant part of the empire on some business, the people came out on the road with presents to receive them, not daring, even if one came alone, to omit to comply with all his commands.

So great was the veneration that the people felt for their princes, throughout this vast region, that every district was as well regulated and governed as if the lord was actually present to chastise those who acted contrary to his rules. This fear arose from the known valor of the lords and their strict justice. It was felt to be certain that those who did evil would receive punishment without fail, and that neither prayers nor bribes would avert it. At the same time, the Incas always did good to those who were under their sway, and would not allow them to be ill-treated, nor that too much tribute should be exacted from them. Many who dwelt in a sterile country where they and their ancestors have lived with difficulty, found that through the orders of the Inca their lands were made fertile and abundant, the things being supplied which before were wanting. In other districts, where there was scarcity of clothing, owing to the people having no flocks, orders were given that cloth should be abundantly provided. In short, it will be understood that these lords knew how to enforce service and the payment of tribute, so they provided for the maintenance of the people, and took care that they should want for nothing. Through these good works, and because the lord always gave women and rich gifts to his principal vassals, he gained so much on their affections that he was most fondly loved....

One of the things which I admired most, in contemplating and noting down the affairs of this kingdom, was to think how and in what manner they can have made such grand and admirable roads as we now see, and what a number of men would suffice for their construction, and with what tools and instruments they can have leveled the mountains and broken through the rocks to make them so broad and good as they are. For it seems to me that if the King of Spain should desire to give orders for another royal road to be made, like that which goes from Quito to Cuzco,... with all his power I believe that he could not get it done; nor could any force of men achieve such results unless there was also the perfect order by means of which the commands of the Incas were carried into execution....

Anonymous,
"The English Describe Pawatah's People"

The first permanent English settlement in North America, at Jamestown on the coast of Virginia in 1607, brought the English into contact with Native Americans already inhabiting the area, including the Powhatan group described in this passage. Written by one of the settlers at Jamestown, this description of the Powhatan reflects early English impressions of Native Americans. The English settlers did not speak the Algonquian language of the Powhatan tribe and had only limited contact with them.

Source: "Description of the People, Letter on May 21-June 21, 1607" in *The Jamestown Voyages Under the First Charter, 1606-1609*, vol. 1, ed. by Philip L Barbour (Cambridge: Cambridge University Press, 1969), 102-104.

Focus Questions:

1. What was the audience for this account and how did that shape it?
2. What ideas or beliefs informed this Englishman's impressions of the Powhatan?
3. What does this account tell us about European encounters with Native Americans in this period?

21 May-21 June 1607.
Description of the People.
A Brief discription of the People.

There is a king in this land called great Pawatah, vnder whose dominions are at least 20th several kingdomes, yet each king potent as a prince in his owne territory. these have their Subiectes at so quick Comaund, as a beck bringes obedience, even to the resticucion of stolne goodes which by their naturall inclinac[i]on they are loth to leave. They goe all naked save their privityes, yet in coole weather they were deare skinns, with the hayre on loose: some have leather stockinges vp to their twisties,[1] & sandalls on their feet, their hayre is black generally, which they weare long on the left side, tyed vp on a knott, about which knott the kinges and best among them have a kind of Coronett of deares hayre coloured redd, some have chaines of long linckt copper about their neckes, and some chaines of pearle, the comon sort stick long fethers in this knott, I found not a grey eye among them all. their skynn is tawny not so borne, but with dying and paynting them selues, in which they delight greatly. The wemen are like the men, onely this difference; their hayre groweth long al over their heades save clipt somewhat short afore, these do all the labour and the men hunt and goe at their plesure. They live commonly by the water side in litle cottages made of canes and reedes, covered with the barke of trees; they dwell as I guesse by families of kindred & allyance some 40 tie or 50 ti in a Hatto[2] or small village; which townes are not past a myle or half a myle asunder in most places. They live vpon sodden wheat beanes & peaze for the most part, also they kill deare take fish in their weares, & kill fowle aboundance, they eate often and that liberally; they are proper lusty streight men very strong runn exceeding swiftly, their feight is alway in the wood with bow & arrowes, & a short wodden sword, the celerity they vse in skirmish is admirable. the king directes the batle & is alwayes in front. Their manner of entertainment is vpon mattes on the ground vnder some tree, where they sitt themselues alone in the midst of the matt, & two mattes on each side, on which they[r] people sitt, then right against him (making a square forme) satt we alwayes. when they came to their matt they have an vsher goes before them, & the rest as he sittes downe give a long showt. The people steale any thing comes neare them, yea are so practized in this art that lookeing in our face they would with their foot betwene their toes convey a chizell knife, percer or any indifferent light thing: which having once conveyed they hold it an iniury to take the same from them; They are naturally given to trechery, howbeit we could not ...

1 'The junction of the thighs' (OED)

2 'Hatto' possibly represents and element cognate with modern Cree *otanow*, 'town', which appears as the second element in the village name Kecoughtan. It may have been pronounced with a glottal stop or other initial throaty sound which the author recorded with an 'h'.

"The Code Noir"

By the early eighteenth century, Europeans had established permanent colonies on Caribbean islands and in North and South America. Europeans began the forced migration of Africans to colonies for slave labor in the 1500s and, by 1700, slavery had become an institution in European colonies in the Atlantic. In the Caribbean islands, the Dutch, English and the French colonies all relied on slaves as the main source of the backbreaking labor needed for the cultivation crops grown for export to Europe: sugar cane, tobacco, and indigo (a dye for cloth). Issued by King Louis XIV (r. 1643-1715) in 1685, the *Code Noir* (or Black Laws) attempted to dictate every aspect of the lives of the enslaved in the French colonies. Initially, the edict was designed for the French colony of Saint-Domingue (present day Haiti), but was later applied in all other French colonies, including Louisiana. The *Code Noir* remained in effect, with some additions and changes, until the abolition of slavery in French holdings in the nineteenth century. What follows here are excerpts from the 60 articles of the *Code Noir* promulgated by Louis XIV in 1685

Source: Long, Edward. *The History of Jamaica* London: T. Lowndes, 1774). Reprint, Edward Long, *The History of Jamaica,* vol. 3. New York: Arno Press, 1972, 921-934.

Focus Questions:

1. According to these laws, to what extent were enslaved people in the French colonies classified as people with rights or were they considered property?
2. What ideas, issues, traditions and beliefs influenced these laws?
3. How were these laws enforced? How successfully?

Edict of the King, Concerning the People of the islands of the French Americas March 1685. Registered by the Sovereign Council of Saint Domingue May 6, 1687

1 We will and intend, that the edict of the late king of glorious memory, our lord and father, of the 23rd of April 1615, should be executed in our islands. To which end, we enjoin our officers, in every department, to banish all Jews whatsoever who have taken up their residence there; which Jews (being avowed enemies to the name of Christ) we hereby command to retire from the fame within the space of three months, to be counted from the day of publication of these presents, on pain of forfeiting their lives and goods.

3 We forbid the public exercise of any other than the Catholic, Apostolic, and Roman religion*. We will that all persons, who act contrary to this prohibition,

*The Catholic Church

shall be punished as rebels against our authority. In this view, we forbid all heretical assemblies; declaring the same to be illegal and seditious conventions, subject to the like punishment; which also shall be inflicted upon those masters who permit their slaves to attend such assemblies.

6 We enjoin all our subjects, of what quality or condition soever, to observe the Lord's-day [Sunday], and the holidays that are kept by our subjects of the Catholic, Apostolic, and Roman religion. We forbid them to labour, or cause their salves to labour on those days, from the hour of midnight to the following midnight, whether it be in the culture of land, or manufacture of sugar, or any other kind of work; on penalty that the masters so offending shall be subject to a fine, and arbitrary punishment, and the forfeiture of all such sugar, as well as of the slaves, detected at work by our officers.

9 Free men who have one or more children born during concubinage with their slaves, as well as masters of slaves who suffer such concubinage, shall be condemned each in a fine of two thousand pounds weight of sugar. And, if any master shall have children by his own slave, we will, that, over and above the like fine, he shall be deprived of such slave and children; and that both she and they shall be forfeited to the use and benefit of the hospital, with disability of their becoming enfranchised. We mean not, however, that the present article take effect, in case the father, not being a married man at the time of such his concubinage with his slave, shall afterwards intermarry with his said slave (according to the forms observed by the church); in consequence whereof, she shall become enfranchised, and the children free and legitimate.

11 We forbid clergymen to solemnize the marriage of slaves, unless they can produce the consent of their master. And we likewise forbid masters to use any constraint toward their slaves, to make them marry involuntarily.

12 The children produced from the marriage of one slave with another shall be slaves, and belong to the master of the wife, and not of the husband, if the husband and wife have different masters.

13 We will, that, if a male slave shall intermarry with a free woman, the issue of such marriage, as well male as female, shall follow the condition of the mother, and be free like her not withstanding the slavery of the father; but, if the father be free, and the mother a slave, her children shall in like manner be slaves.

18. We forbid salves to sell sugar-canes on any account or pretence whatsoever, and notwithstanding any permission from their master, on penalty that such slaves shall be whipped; and the master so permitting shall be fined in the amount of ten French livres; and the buyer of such canes in the same sum.

19. We likewise forbid them to expose at public sale, or to carry into any private houses for the purpose of sale, any kind of commodity, not even fruits, pulse, fire wood, pot herbs, or salads and cattle, without leave of their masters

expressed by a ticket, or some known token, on penalty that their masters may claim the things so sols, without making and restitution of the price paid by the purchasers thereof, and receive also from such purchasers a fine of six French livres, to be appropriated to their own use.

22 Masters shall be obliged to furnish, every week, to their slaves of ten years old, or upwards, for their subsistence, three pots (of the country measure) of cassava meal or three bunches of cassava roots, weighing each two livres** and a half at the least; or some other vegetable food equivalent; together with two livres of salted beef or three livres of fish, or some other animal food in proportion; and to children, from the time of the weaning to the age of ten, half the aforesaid quantity of like provisions.

25 Masters shall be obliged to furnish each and every of their slaves, yearly, with two suits of linen cloth, or five yards of light cloths, whichsoever the said masters shall judge most proper.

26. Slaves that are not subsisted, clothed, and maintained, in the manner we have directed by these presents, may give notice thereof to our attorney, and put their case into his hands; in consequence of which, or even without them, of the cause of complaint shall come to his knowledge by any other means, the masters shall be prosecuted at his instance, and without any expense; which process we would also have observed in regard to those masters who abuse or treat their slaves in a barbarous and inhuman manner.

33 The slave that strikes his master, or the wife of his master, his mistress, or any of the children, so as to cause an effusion of blood; or that gives them, or any of them, a blow upon the face; shall be punished with death.

35 Certain kinds of theft, as of horses, mares, mules, oxen, and cows, committed by slaves, or by others who have been made free, shall be punished effectually; and even with death, if the case require it.

36 Slaves, guilty of stealing sheep, goats, hogs, poultry, sugar canes, cassava, peas, or other kinds of pulse, shall, according to the nature and quality of their crime, be punished by the judges; who may, if they think fit, order them to be whipped by the common hangman, and branded on the shoulder with a fleur-de-lis.***

38 A fugitive slave that shall continue out for a month, computing from the day of his being publicly advertised by his master, shall have both his ears cut off, and shall be branded on one of his shoulders with a fleur-de-lis. In case of his repetition of the same offence, computing in like manner from the day of his being publicly advertised, he shall be hamstrung, and be branded on the other shoulder. But for the third offence, he shall be punished with death.

**Approximately equivalent to an English pound.

***The fleur-de-lis was the symbol of the French Bourbon dynasty, and a prominent royal insignia.

CHAPTER 13

Thought and Culture in Early Modern Europe

Francis Bacon, from *Novum Organum*

Francis Bacon (1561–1626) was a prophet of the scientific revolution of the seventeenth century—a revolution that transformed the foundations of thought and ushered in the Age of Science. Like the prophets of the Old Testament, Bacon concentrated first on the evils around him. Although for him these evils were intellectual rather than moral or religious, he couched his criticism of the science of his day in biblical terms. Like the medieval schoolmen, the leading thinkers of his age, he argued, had wandered from the path of truth into the worship of idols. In the selection that follows he lists four such idols, to which he gives the picturesque titles of idols of the *Tribe*, the *Cave*, the *Marketplace*, and the *Theatre*. To avoid falling prey to these idols, people must turn their backs on scholastic philosophy and develop a new science based on a true knowledge of the workings of nature. Such knowledge, Bacon held, was to be derived from careful and continued observation of specific natural occurrences. This observational method, which he called induction, is explained and illustrated in his major work, the *Instauratio Magna* (Great Renewal). In his opinion, this treatise represented a "total reconstruction of the sciences, arts, and all human knowledge."

Although he was a prophet of the new science, Bacon himself did not fully grasp the nature of the method that men like Galileo and Newton were to employ in their work. His concept of induction fails to take adequate account of two other basic elements of the modern scientific method—the formulation of hypotheses and the deduction and verification of their consequences.

Living at the height of the English Renaissance (which followed by a hundred years the Italian Renaissance), Bacon exemplified many of the attitudes found in previous Renaissance writers: the rejection of the medieval worldview as pernicious error, the somewhat naïve optimism about his ability to take the whole of human knowledge as his sphere of activity, and the faith that he stood on the thresh-old of a new intellectual era. Finally, in his assertion that "knowledge is power," Bacon repeated a central concept of Machiavelli, but with a significant difference—Machiavelli was concerned with the power that a prince could wield over his subjects, but Bacon was concerned with the power (derived from scientific understanding), that all humans could wield over nature.

The following selection is from *Novum Organum* (the *New Organon* written in 1620), which forms a part of *Instauratio Magna.*

Source: J. Spedding, trans., Francis Bacon, *Novum Organum* (1620).

Focus Questions:

1. How does Bacon propose to find truth?
2. What are the strengths and weaknesses of his inductive method?

NOVUM ORGANUM
Aphorisms Concerning the Interpretation of Nature and the Kingdom of Man

I. Man, being the servant and interpreter of Nature, can do and understand so much and so much only as he has observed in fact or in thought in the course of nature: beyond this he neither knows anything nor can do anything.

II. Neither the naked hand nor the understanding left to itself can effect much. It is by instruments and helps that the work is done, which are as much wanted for the understanding as for the hand. And as the instruments of the hand either give motion or guide it, so the instruments of the mind supply either suggestions for the understanding or cautions.

III. Human knowledge and human power meet in one; for where the cause is not known the effect cannot be produced. Nature to be commanded must be obeyed; and that which in contemplation is as the cause is in operation as the rule.

IV. Towards the effecting of works, all that man can do is to put together or put asunder natural bodies. The rest is done by nature working within.

* * *

VI. It would be an unsound fancy and self-contradictory to expect that things which have never yet been done can be done except by means which have never yet been tried.

* * *

XI. As the sciences which we now have do not help us in finding out new works, so neither does the logic which we now have help us in finding out new sciences.

XII. The logic now in use serves rather to fix and give stability to the errors which have their foundations in commonly received notions than to help the search after truth. So it does more harm than good.

XVIII. The discoveries which have hitherto been made in the sciences are such as lie close to vulgar notions, scarcely beneath the surface. In order to penetrate into the inner and further recesses of nature, it is necessary that both notions and axioms be derived from things by a more sure and guarded way; and that a method of intellectual operation be introduced altogether better and more certain.

* * *

XIX. There are and can be only two ways of searching into and discovering truth. The one flies from the senses and particulars to the most general axioms, and from these principles, the truth of which it takes for settled and immovable, proceeds to judgment and to the discovery of middle axioms. And this way is now in fashion. The other derives axioms from the senses and particulars, rising by a gradual and unbroken ascent, so that it arrives at the most general axioms last of all. This is the true way, but as yet untried.

* * *

XXII. Both ways set out from the senses and particulars, and rest in the highest generalities; but the difference between them is infinite. For the one just glances at experiment and particulars in passing, the other dwells duly and orderly among them. The one, again, begins at once by establishing certain abstract and useless generalities, the other rises by gradual steps to that which is prior and better known in the order of nature.

* * *

XXXI. It is idle to expect any great advancement in science from the superinducing and engrafting of new things upon old. We must begin anew from the very foundations, unless we would revolve forever in a circle with mean and contemptible progress.

* * *

XXXV. It was said by Borgia of the expedition of the French into Italy, that they came with chalk in their hands to mark out their lodgings, not with arms to force their way in. I in like manner would have my doctrine enter quietly into the minds that are fit and capable of receiving it; for confutations cannot be employed, when the difference is upon first principles and very notions and even upon forms of demonstration.

XXXVI. One method of delivery alone remains to us; which is simply this: we must lead men to the particulars themselves, and their series and order; while men on their side must force themselves for awhile to lay their notions by and begin to familiarize themselves with facts.

XXXVII. The doctrine of those who have denied that certainty could be attained at all, has some agreement with my way of proceeding at the first setting out; but they end in being infinitely separated and opposed. For the holders of that doctrine assert simply that nothing can be known; I also assert that not much can be known in nature by the way which is now in use. But then they go on to destroy the authority of the senses and understanding; whereas I proceed to devise and supply helps for the same.

XXXVIII. The idols and false notions which are now in possession of the human understanding, and have taken deep root therein, not only so beset men's minds that truth can hardly find entrance, but even after entrance is obtained, they will again in the very instauration of the science meet and trouble us, unless men being forewarned of the danger fortify themselves as far as may be against their assaults.

XXXIX. There are four classes of Idols which beset men's minds. To these for distinction's sake I have assigned names, calling the first class Idols of the Tribe; the second, Idols of the Cave; the third, Idols of the Marketplace; the fourth, Idols of the Theatre.

* * *

XL. The formation of ideas and axioms by true induction is no doubt the proper remedy to be applied for the keeping off and clearing away of idols. To point them out, however, is of great use; for the doctrine of Idols is to the Interpretation of Nature what the doctrine of the refutation of Sophisms is to common Logic.

XLI. The Idols of the Tribe have their foundation in human nature itself, and in the tribe or race of men. For it is a false assertion that the sense of man is the measure of things. On the contrary, all perceptions as well of the sense as of the mind are according to the measure of the universe. And the human understanding is like a false mirror, which, receiving rays irregularly, distorts and discolours the nature of things by mingling its own nature with it.

XLII. The Idols of the Cave are the idols of the individual man. For every one (besides the errors common to human nature in general) has a cave or den of his own, which refracts and discolors the light of nature; owing either to his own proper and peculiar nature; or to his education and conversation with others; or to the reading of books, and the authority of those whom he esteems and admires; or to the differences of impressions, accordingly as they take place in a mind preoccupied and predisposed or in a mind indifferent and settled; or the like. So that the spirit of man (according as it is meted out to different individuals) is in fact a thing variable and full of perturbation, and governed as it were by chance. Whence it was observed by Heraclitus that men look for sciences in their own lesser worlds, and not in the greater or common world.

XLIII. There are also Idols formed by the intercourse and association of men with each other, which I call Idols of the Marketplace, on account of the commerce and consort of men there. For it is by discourse that men associate; and words are imposed according to the apprehension of the vulgar. And therefore the ill and unfit choice of words wonderfully obstructs the understanding. Nor do the definitions or explanations wherewith in some things learned men are wont to guard and defend themselves, by any means set the matter right. But words plainly force and overrule the understanding, and throw all into confusion, and lead men away into numberless empty controversies and idle fancies.

XLIV. Lastly, there are Idols which have immigrated into men's minds from the various dogmas of philosophies, and also from wrong laws of demonstration. These I call Idols of the Theatre; because in my judgment all the received systems are but so many stage-plays, representing worlds of their own creation after an unreal and scenic fashion. Nor is it only of the systems now in vogue, or only of the ancient sects and philosophies, that I speak; for many more plays of the same kind may yet be composed and in like artificial manner set forth; seeing that errors the most widely different have nevertheless causes for the most part alike. Neither again do I mean this only of entire systems, but also of many principles and axioms in science, which by tradition, credulity, and negligence have come to be received.

William Harvey, Address to the Royal College of Physicians 1628

William Harvey has been termed the father of modern physiology. He was heir to a legacy of interest in the internal workings of the human body that had most recently been evidenced among artists during the Renaissance, but, whereas Michelangelo studied the body to better represent the human form, Harvey sought to discover the internal workings for their own scientific merit. In this, he was more closely akin to the earlier scientific studies of Leonardo da Vinci. Harvey built upon the work of the Greek physician Galen (fl. 150 CE), who demonstrated that the arteries carried blood instead of air, and his exacting methods set the pattern of scientific research for generations. In the following selection, which was an address to the Royal College of Physicians in 1628, he gives the results of his methodical dissections and experiments.

Source: R. Willis, trans.,"I Learn and Teach from the Fabric of Nature," *The Works of William Harvey* (London: Sydenham Society, 1847), pp. 5–7, 31–32, 45–47.

Focus Questions:

1. Why did William Harvey want to present his findings in an address before the Royal College of Physicians?
2. What was he afraid of?
3. Why were his discoveries about the heart and circulation of blood so important and perhaps so threatening?

As this book alone declares the blood to course and revolve by a new route, very different from the ancient and beaten pathway trodden for so many ages, and illustrated by such a host of learned and distinguished men, I was greatly afraid lest I might be charged with presumption did I lay my work before the public at home, or send it beyond seas for impression, unless I had first proposed its subject to you, had confirmed its conclusions by ocular demonstrations in your presence, had replied to your doubts and objections, and secured the assent and support of our distinguished President. For I was most intimately persuaded, that if I could make good my proposition before you and our College…I had less to fear from others...For true philosophers, who are only eager for truth and knowledge, never regard themselves as already so thoroughly informed, but that they welcome further information from whomsoever and from whencesoever it may come; nor are they so narrow-minded as to imagine any of the arts or sciences transmitted to us by the ancients, in such a state of forwardness or completeness, that nothing is left for the ingenuity and industry of others…Neither do they swear such fealty to their mistress Antiquity, that they openly, and in sight of all, deny and desert their friend Truth…

My dear colleagues…I profess both to learn and to teach anatomy, not from books, but from dissections; not from the positions of philosophers, but from the fabric of nature…

From these and other observations of the like kind, I am persuaded it will be found that the motion of the heart is as follows:

First of all, the auricle contracts, and in the course of its contraction throws the blood, (which it contains in ample quantity as the head of the veins, the store-house and cistern of the blood,) into the ventricle, which being filled, the heart raises itself straightway, makes all its fibers tense, contracts the ventricles, and performs a beat, by which beat it immediately sends the blood supplied to it by the auricle into the arteries; the right ventricle sending its charge into the lungs by the vessel which is called vena arteriosi, but which, in structure and function, and all things else, is an artery; the left ventricle sending its charge into the aorta, and through this by the arteries to the body at large…

Thus far I have spoken of the passage of the blood from the veins into the arteries, and of the manner in which it is transmitted and distributed by the action of the heart…But what remains to be said upon the quantity and source of the blood which thus passes, is of so novel and unheard-of character, that I not only fear injury to myself from the envy of a few, but I tremble lest I have mankind at large for my enemies…Still, the die is cast, and my trust is in my love of truth, and the candor that inheres in cultivated minds. And when I surveyed my mass of evidence…I revolved in my mind, what might be the quantity of blood which was transmitted, in how short a time its passage might be effected, and the like…I began to think whether there might not be A MOTION, AS IT WERE, IN A CIRCLE. Now this I afterwards found to be true; and I finally saw that the blood, forced by the action of the left ventricle into the arteries, was distributed to the body at large…impelled by the right ventricle…through the veins, and so round to the left ventricle in the manner already indicated…

The heart, consequently, is the beginning of life; the sun of the microcosm, even as the sun in his turn might well be designated the heart of the world; for it is the heart by whose virtue and pulse the blood is moved, perfected, made apt to nourish, and is preserved from corruption and coagulation; it is the household divinity which, discharging its function, nourishes, cherishes, quickens the whole body, and is indeed the foundation of life, the source of all action.

René Descartes, *The Discourse on Method and Metaphysical Meditations,* "I Think, Therefore I Am"

René Descartes was born in 1596 in western France but lived primarily in Holland for the last twenty years of his life. He attended Jesuit schools and graduated in law from the university in Poitiers. He was not attracted to a legal career, however, and became a soldier in the German wars of the time. It was while he was billeted in a German town that he had an intellectual revelation akin, as he later maintained, to a religious conversion. He had a vision of the great potential for progress, if mathematical method were to be applied to all fields of knowledge. He thus pursued a career devoted to the propagation of a strict method, best exemplified by his invention of analytical geometry. Descartes believed that human beings were endowed by God with the ability to reason and that God served as the guarantor of the correctness of clear ideas. The material world could thus be understood through adherence to mathematical laws and methods of inquiry. Descartes championed the process of deductive reasoning whereby specific information could be logically deduced from general information. His method was influential well into the eighteenth century, when it was supplanted by the method of scientific induction, whereby generalizations could be drawn from the observation of specific data.

The following selection is drawn from Descartes' most famous work, *Discourse on the Method of Rightly Conducting the Reason* (1636).

Source: G. B. Rawlings, trans., René Descartes, "I Think, Therefore I Am," in The *Discourse on Method and Metaphysical Meditations* (London: Walter Scott, 1901), pp. 32–35, 60–61, 75–76.

FOCUS QUESTIONS:

1. What did Descartes mean by the phrase "I think, therefore I am"? Why was this so fundamental to his method?
2. Reconstruct his logic for the existence of God. Do you find it compelling?

As a multitude of laws often furnishes excuses for vice, so that a state is much better governed when it has but few, and those few strictly observed, so in place of the great number of precepts of which logic is composed, I believed that I should find the following four sufficient, provided that I made a firm and constant resolve not once to omit to observe them.

The first was, never to accept anything as true when I did not recognize it clearly to be so, that is to say, to carefully avoid precipitation and prejudice, and to include in my opinions nothing beyond that which should present itself so clearly and so distinctly to my mind that I might have no occasion to doubt it.

The second was, to divide each of the difficulties which I should examine into as many parts as were possible, and as should be required for its better solution.

The third was, to conduct my thoughts in order, by beginning with the simplest objects, and those most easy to know, so as to mount little by little, as if by steps, to the most complex knowledge, and even assuming an order among those which do not naturally precede one another.

And the last was, to make everywhere enumerations so complete, and reviews so wide, that I should be sure of omitting nothing...

I had long remarked that, in conduct, it is sometimes necessary to follow opinions known to be very uncertain, just as if they were indisputable, as has been said above; but then, because I desired to devote myself only to the research of truth, I thought it necessary to do exactly the contrary, and reject as absolutely false all in which I could conceive the least doubt, in order to see if afterwards there did not remain in my belief something which was entirely indisputable. Thus, because our senses sometimes deceive us, I wanted to suppose that nothing is such as they make us imagine it; and because some men err in reasoning...and judging that I was as liable to fail as any other, I rejected as false all the reasons which I had formerly accepted as [true]...I resolved that everything which had ever entered into my mind was no more true than the illusions of my dreams. But immediately afterwards I observed that while I thus desired everything to be false, I, who thought, must of necessity [exist]; and remarking that this truth, I think, therefore I am, was so firm and so assured that all the most extravagant suppositions of the skeptics were unable to shake it, I judged that I could unhesitatingly accept it as the first principle of the philosophy I was seeking...

After this, and reflecting upon the fact that I doubted, and that in consequence my being was not quite perfect (for I saw clearly that to know was a greater perfection than to doubt), I [wondered where] I had learned to think of something more perfect than I; and I knew for certain that it must be from some nature which was in reality more perfect. [And I clearly recognized that] this idea...had been put in me by a nature truly more perfect than I, which had in itself all perfections of which I could have any idea; that is, to explain myself in one word, God...

Finally, whether awake or asleep, we ought never to allow ourselves to be persuaded of the truth of anything unless on the evidence of our Reason. And it must be noted that I say of our Reason, and not of our imagination or of our senses: thus, for example, although we very clearly see the sun, we ought not therefore to determine that it is only of the size which our sense of sight presents; and we may very distinctly imagine the head of a lion joined to the body of a goat, without being therefore shut up to the conclusion that a chimaera exists; for it is not a dictate of Reason that what we thus see or imagine is in reality existent; but it plainly tells us that all our ideas or notions contain in them some truth; for otherwise it could not be that God, who is wholly perfect and veracious, should have placed them in us.

Charles Perrault,
Little Red Riding-Hood

Charles Perrault was a French nobleman as well as an accomplished scholar and writer. Perrault initially trained to be a member of the Parliament (French law court) but with the support of King Louis XIV's (r.16431715), he became the supervisor of royal buildings, an important government post. As a member of the Royal Academy of Arts and Sciences, Perrault became embroiled in a lively public debate, the quarrel of the ancients and moderns, an argument over the merit of works by new authors versus those of Ancient scholars, such as Aristotle. Perrault passionately argued on behalf of the "moderns," claiming the contributions of contemporary authors and artists were as important as those of the ancient scholars. This excerpt is taken from Perrault's collection of stories first published in 1697. For these stories, Perrault drew on oral story telling traditions, or stories that had been passed down through word of mouth through many generations, by the French peasantry whose stories, while humorous, also reflected the sometimes harsh realities of their lives. Perrault wrote them down and published them for the first time just as they had been told to him, by his nursemaid, a peasant woman, the original "Mother Goose." To increase the appeal of these stories to his audience, literate nobles at the royal Court, he added short poems at the end of each tale.

Source: Jacques Barchilon and Henry Pettit eds., *The Authentic Mother Goose. Fairy Tales and Nursery Rhymes* (Denver: Swallow, 1960), reprint of Charles Perrault, *Mother Goose's Tales*, trans. by Robert Samber (London: Pote, 1729), 1-8.

Focus Questions:

1. Who was Perrault's audience for this story and how does he adapt the story to his audience?
2. What was the overall message or point of this story?
3. What does this story suggest about the realities of peasants' lives in this period?

There was once upon a time a little country girl, born in a village, the prettiest little creature that ever was seen. Her mother was beyond reason excessively fond of her, and her grandmother yet much more. This good woman caused to be made for her a little red Riding Hood which made her look so very pretty, that every body call'd her, The little red Riding Hood.

One day, her mother having made some custards, said to her, Go my little biddy, for her Christian name was Biddy, go and see how your grandmother does, for I can hear she has been ill, carry her a custard, and this little pot of butter. The little red Riding Hood sets out immediately to go to her grandmother, who lived in another village. As she was going through the wood, she met with Gossop Wolfe, who had a good mind to eat her up, but he did not dare, because of some faggot-makers that were in the forest.

He asked of her wither she was going: The poor child, who did not know how dangerous a thing it is to stay and hear a Wolfe talk, said to him, I am going to see my grandmamma, and carry her a custard pie, and a little pot of butter my mamma sends her. Does she live far off? Said the Wolfe. Oh! Ay, said the little red Riding Hood, on the other side of the mill below yonder, at the first house in the village. Well, said the Wolfe, and I'll go and see her too; I'll go this way, and go you that, and we shall see who will be there soonest.

The Wolfe began to run as fast as he was able, the shortest way; and the little girl went the longest, diverting her self in gathering nuts, running after butterflies, and making nose-gays of all the little flowers she met with. The Wolfe was not long before he came to the grandmother's house; he knocked at the door toc, toc. Whose There Your grand-daughter, the little red Riding Hood, said the Wolfe, counterfeiting her voice, who had brought you a custard pie, and a little pot of butter mamma sends you.

The good grandmother, who was in bed, because she found herself somewhat ill, cried out, Pull the bobbin, and the latch will go up. The Wolfe pull'd the bobbin, and the door open'd; upon which he fell upon the good woman, and eat her up in the tenth part of a moment; for he had eaten nothing for above three days before. After that, he shut the door, and went into the grandmother's bed, expecting the little red Riding Hood, who came some time afterwards, and knock'd at the door toc toc, Who's there? The little red Riding Hood, who hearing the big voice of the Wolfe, was at first afraid; but believing her grandmother had got a cold and was grown hoarse, said, it is your granddaughter, The little red Riding Hood, who has brought you custard pie, and a little pot of butter mamma sends you. The Wolfe cried out to her softening his voice as much as he could, Pull the bobbin, and the latch will go up. The little red Riding Hood, pull'd the bobbin, and the door opened.

The Wolfe seeing her come in, said to her, hiding himself under the clothes. Put the custard, and the little pot of butter upon the stool, and come into bed to me. The little red Riding Hood, undressed herself, and went into bed, where she was very much astonished to see how her grandmother looked in her night clothes: So he said to her,

Grandmamma what great arms you have got! It is the better to embrace thee my pretty child. Grandmamma, what great legs you have got! It is to run the better my child. Grandmamma, what great ears you have got! It is to hear the better, my child. Grandmamma, what great eyes you have got! It is to see thee better, my child. Grandmamma, what great teeth you have got! It is to eat thee up. And, upon saying these words, the wicked Wolfe fell upon poor Little Red Riding Hood, and ate her up.

The Moral

From this short story easy we discern,
What conduct all young people ought to learn.
But above all, the growing ladies fair,
Whose orient rosy blooms begin t'appear
Who, beauties in the fragrant spring of age
With pretty airs young hearts are apt t'engage.
Ill do they listen to all sorts of tongues,
Since some enchant and lure like Sirens songs.
No wonder therefore 'tis, if overpower'd.
So many of them has the wolf devour'd.
The Wolfe, I say, for Wolves too sure there are
Of every sort, and of every character.
Some of them mild and gentle humour'd be,
Of noise and gall, and rancour wholly free.
Who, tame, familiar, full of complaisance
Ogle and leer, languish, cajole and glance,
With luring tongues, and language sweet,
Follow young ladies as they walk in the street,
E'en to their very houses, nay, beside
And artful, tho' their true designs they bide
Yet all! These simpering fools who does not see
Most dangerous of all wolves in fact to be?

Isaac Newton, from *Opticks*

Isaac Newton (1642–1727) had formulated his theory of universal gravitation by the time he was twenty-four, but it was not until several years later, in 1687, that he published it, at the insistence of friends, under the title *The Mathematical Principles of Natural Philosophy*—the culmination of a scientific development that had been in progress for well over a hundred years and had included such names as Copernicus, Kepler, and Galileo. But Newton was the heir of other thinkers in an even broader sense. The selection from his *Opticks* (1704) begins with a reaffirmation of the atomistic theory of matter, which was first developed by Democritus, an ancient Greek.

Source: Issac Newton, *Opticks, or A Treatise of the Reflections, Refractions, Inflections and Colours of Light*, 4th ed. (London, 1730). [Capitalization and spelling have been modernized—Ed.]

FOCUS QUESTIONS:

1. Describe Newton's method. How does he arrive at his conclusions?
2. According to rule four, what can we imply about scientific conclusions? Are they definite? Why or why not?

All these things being considered, it seems probable to me, that God in the beginning formed matter in solid, massy, hard, impenetrable, moveable particles, of such sizes and figures, and with such other properties, and in such proportion to space, as most conduced to the end for which he formed them; and that these primitive particles, being solids, are incomparably harder than any porous bodies compounded of them; even so very hard, as never to wear or break in pieces; no ordinary power being able to divide what God himself made one in the first creation. While the particles continue entire, they may compose bodies of one and the same nature and texture in all ages: But should they wear away, or break in pieces, the nature of things depending on them would be changed. Water and earth, composed of old worn particles and fragments of particles, would not be of the same nature and texture now, with water and earth composed of entire particles in the beginning. And therefore, that nature may be lasting, the changes of corporeal things are to be placed only in the various separations and new associations and motions of these permanent particles; compound bodies being apt to break, not in the midst of solid particles, but where those particles are laid together, and only touch in a few points.

It seems to me farther, that those particles have not only a force of inertia accompanied with such passive laws of motion as naturally result from that force, but also that they are moved by certain active principles, such as is that of gravity, and that which causes fermentation, and the cohesion of bodies. These principles I consider, not as occult qualities, supposed to result from the specific forms of things, but as general laws of nature, by which the things themselves are formed; their truth appearing to us by phenomena, though their causes be not yet discovered. For these are manifest qualities, and their causes only are occult. And the Aristotelians gave the name of occult qualities, not to manifest qualities, but to such qualities only as they supposed to lie hid in bodies, and to be the unknown causes of manifest effects: Such as would be the causes of gravity, and of magnetic and electric attractions, and of fermentations, if we should suppose that these forces or actions arose from qualities unknown to us, and incapable of being discovered and made manifest. Such occult qualities put a stop to the improvement of natural philosophy, and therefore of late years have been rejected. To tell us that every species of things is endowed with an occult specific quality by which it acts and produces manifest effects, is to tell us nothing: But to derive two or three general principles of motion from phenomena, and afterwards to tell us how the properties and actions of all corporeal things follow from those manifest principles, would be a very great step in philosophy, though the causes of those principles were not yet discovered: And therefore I scruple not to propose the principles of motion above-mentioned, they being of very general extent, and leave their causes to be found out.

Now by the help of these principles, all material things seem to have been composed of the hard and solid particles above-mentioned, variously associated in the first creation by the counsel of an intelligent agent. For it became him who created them to set them in order. And if he did so, it's unphilosophical to seek for any other origin of the world, or to pretend that it might arise out of a chaos by the mere laws of nature; though being once formed, it may continue by those laws for many ages. For while comets move in very eccentric orbs in all manner of positions, blind fate could never make all the planets move one and the same way in orbs concentric, some inconsiderable irregularities excepted, which may have risen from the mutual actions of comets and planets upon one another, and which will be apt to increase, till this system wants a reformation. Such a wonderful uniformity in the planetary system must be allowed the effect of choice. And so much the uniformity in the bodies of animals, they having generally a right and a left side shaped alike, and on either side of their bodies two legs behind, and either two arms, or two legs, or two wings before their shoulders, a neck running down into a backbone, and a head upon it; and in the head two ears, two eyes, a nose, a mouth, and a tongue, alike situated. Also the first contrivance of those very artificial parts of animals, the eyes, ears, brain, muscles, heart, lungs, midriff, glands, larynx, hands, wings, swimming bladders, natural spectacles, and other organs of sense and motion; and the instinct of brutes and insects, can be the effect of nothing else than the wisdom and skill of a powerful ever-living agent, who being in all places, is more able by his will to move the bodies within his boundless uniform sensorium, and thereby to form and reform the parts of the universe, than we are by our will to move the parts of our bodies. And yet we are not to consider the world as the body of God, or the several parts thereof, as the parts of God. He is a uniform being, void of organs, members, or parts, and they are his creatures subordinate to him, and subservient to his will; and he is no more the soul of them, than the soul of man is the soul of the species of things carried through the organs of sense into the place of its sensation, where it perceives them by means of its immediate presence, with-out the intervention of any third thing. The organs of sense are not for enabling the soul to perceive the species of things in its sensorium, but only for conveying them thither; and God had no need of such organs, he being everywhere present to the things themselves. And since space is divisible in infinitum, and matter is not necessarily in all places, it may be also allowed that God is able to create particles of matter of several sizes and figures, and in several proportions to space, and perhaps of different densities and forces, and thereby to vary the laws of nature, and make worlds of several sorts in several parts of the universe. At least, I see nothing of contradiction in all this.

As in mathematics, so in natural philosophy, the investigation of difficult things by the method of analysis, ought ever to precede the method of composition. This analysis consists in making experiments and observations, and in drawing general conclusions from them by induction and admitting of no objections against the conclusions, but such as are taken from experiments, or other certain truths. For hypotheses are not to be regarded in experimental philosophy. And although the arguing from experiments and observations by induction be no demonstration of general conclusions; yet it is the best way of arguing which the nature of things admits of, and may be looked upon as so much the stronger, by how much the induction is more general. And if no exception occur from phenomena, the conclusion may be pronounced generally. But if at any time afterwards any exception shall occur from experiments, it may then begin to be pronounced with such exceptions as occur. By this way of analysis we may proceed from compounds to ingredients, and from motions to the forces producing them; and in general, from effects to their causes, and from particular causes to more general ones, till the argument ends in the most general. This is the method of analysis: And the synthesis consists in assuming the causes discovered, and established as principles, and by them explaining the phenomena proceeding from them, and proving the explanations.

THE MATHEMATICAL PRINCIPLES OF NATURAL PHILOSOPHY

The Rules of Reasoning in Philosophy

Rule I. We are to admit no more causes of natural things, than such as are both true and sufficient to explain their appearances.

To this purpose the philosophers say, that Nature does nothing in vain, and more is in vain, when less will serve; for Nature is pleased with simplicity, and affects not the pomp of superfluous causes.

Rule II. Therefore to the same natural effects we must, as far as possible, assign the same causes. As to respiration in a man, and in a beast; the descent of stones in Europe and in America; the light of our culinary fire and of the sun; the reflection of light in the earth, and in the planets.

Rule III. The qualities of bodies, which admit neither intension nor remission of degrees, and which are found to belong to all bodies within reach of our experiments, are to be esteemed the universal qualities of all bodies whatsoever.

For since the qualities of bodies are only known to us by experiments, we are to hold for universal, all such as universally agree with experiments; and such as are not liable to diminution, can never be quite taken away. We are certainly not to relinquish the evidence of experiments for the sake of dreams and vain fictions of our own devising; nor are we to recede from the analogy of Nature, which is wont to be simple, and always consonant to itself. We no other way know the extension of bodies, than by our senses, nor do these reach it in all bodies; but because we perceive extension in all that are sensible, therefore we ascribe it universally to all others, also. That abundance of bodies are hard we learn by experience. And because the hardness of the whole arises from the hardness of the parts, we therefore justly infer the hardness of the undivided particles not only of the bodies we feel but of all others. That all bodies are impenetrable, we gather not from reason, but from sensation. The bodies which we handle we find impenetrable, and thence conclude impenetrability to be a universal property of all bodies whatsoever. That all bodies are moveable, and endowed with certain powers (which we call the forces of inertia) or persevering in their motion or in their rest, we only infer from the like properties observed in the bodies which we have seen. The extension, hardness, impenetrability, mobility, and force of inertia of the whole, result from the extension, hardness, impenetrability, mobility, and forces of inertia of the parts: and thence we conclude that the least particles of all bodies to be also all extended, and hard, and impenetrable, and moveable, and endowed with their proper forces of inertia. And this is the foundation of all philosophy. Moreover, that the divided but contiguous particles of bodies may be separated from one another, is a matter of observation; and, in the particles that remain undivided, our minds are able to distinguish yet lesser parts, as is mathematically demonstrated. But whether the parts so distinguished, and not yet divided, may, by the powers of nature, be actually divided and separated from one another, we cannot certainly determine. Yet had we the proof of but one experiment, that any undivided particle, in breaking a hard and solid body, suffered a division, we might by virtue of this rule, conclude, that the undivided as well as the divided particles, may be divided and actually separated into infinity.

Lastly, if it universally appears, by experiments and astronomical observations, that all bodies about the earth, gravitate toward the earth; and that in proportion to the quantity of matter which they severally contain; that the moon likewise, according to the quantity of its matter, gravitates toward the earth; that on the other hand our sea gravitates toward the moon; and all the planets mutually one toward another; and the comets in like manner towards the sun; we must, in consequence of this rule, universally allow, that all bodies whatsoever are endowed with a principle of mutual gravitation. For the argument from the appearances concludes with more force for the universal gravitation of all bodies, than for their impenetrability, of which among those in the celestial regions, we have no experiments, nor any manner of observation. Not that I affirm gravity to be essential to all bodies. By their inherent force I mean nothing but their force of inertia. This is immutable. Their gravity is diminished as they recede from the earth.

Rule IV. In experimental philosophy we are to look upon propositions collected by general induction from phenomena as accurately or very nearly true, notwithstanding any contrary hypotheses that may be imagined, till such time as other phenomena occur, by which they may either be made more accurate, or liable to exceptions.

This rule we must follow that the argument of induction may not be evaded by hypotheses.

John Bunyan, *Pilgrim's Progress*

John Bunyan (1628-1688) came from the ranks of artisans. He was a tinker who also became a writer and well-known preacher in England. He was a Puritan, a Protestant movement in England that grew out of the teachings of Protestant reformer John Calvin, and a prominent advocate of their beliefs. Bunyan spent twelve years in prison, for holding Puritan church services despite laws banning them. He was also involved in the English Civil War (1642-1660). He wrote *Pilgrim's Progress* in 1678. It was widely read in Europe after its publication.

Source: *The Pilgrim's Progress,* by John Bunyan, Penguin Classics, ed. Roger Sharrock (New York: Penguin Books, 1987) 43–49.

Focus Questions:

1. What audience was Bunyan writing for? What reasons did he give for writing this book?
2. What was Bunyan's view of humankind? What ideas or beliefs informed his view?
3. How were Bunyan's ideas tied to the Puritan movement in England at the time?

THE AUTHOR'S APOLOGY FOR HIS BOOK

When at the first I took my pen in hand,
Thus for to write, I did not understand
That I at all should make a little book
In such a mode; nay, I had undertook
To make another, which when almost done,
Before I was aware, I this begun.

And thus it was: I writing of the way
And race of saints in this our Gospel-day,
Fell suddenly into an allegory
About their journey, and the way to glory,
In more than twenty things, which I set down;
This done, I twenty more had in my crown,
And they again began to multiply,

Like sparks that from the coals of fire do fly.
Nay then, thought I, if that you breed so fast,
I'll put you by yourselves, lest you at last
Should prove ad infinitum, and eat out
The book that I already am about.

Well, so I did; but yet I did not think
To show to all the world my pen and ink
In such a mode; I only thought to make
I knew not what, nor did I undertake
Thereby to please my neighbour; no, not I,
I did it mine own self to gratify.
Neither did I but vacant seasons spend
in this my scribble, nor did I intend

But to divert myself in doing this,
From worser thoughts which make me do amiss.

Thus I set pen to paper with delight,
And quickly had my thoughts in black and white.
For having now my method by the end,
Still as I pulled it came, and so I penned
It down, until it came at last to be
For length and breadth the bigness which you see.

Well, when I had thus put mine ends together,
I show'd them others that I might see whether
They would condemn them, or them justify:
And some said, 'let them live'; some, 'let them die':
Some said, 'John, print it'; others said, 'not so':
Some said, 'It might do good'; others said, 'no'.
Now was I in a strait, and did not see
Which was the best thing to be done by me:
At last I thought, since you are thus divided,
I print it will, and so the case decided.

For, thought I, some I see would have it done,
Though others in that channel do not run.
To prove then who advised for the best,
Thus I thought fit to put it to the test.

I further thought, if now I did deny
Those that would have it thus, to gratify,

I did not know, but hinder them I might,
Of that which would to them be great delight.

For those that were not for its coming forth,
I said to them, offend you I am loth;
Yet since your brethren pleased with it be,
Forbear to judge, to you do further see.

If that thou wilt not read, let it alone;
Some love the meat, some love to pick the bone:
Yea, that I might them better palliate,
I did too with them thus expostulate.

May I not write in such a style as this?
In such a method too, and yet not miss
Mine end, thy good? why may it not be done?
Dark clouds bring waters, when the bright bring none;
Yea, dark, or bright, if they their silver drops
Cause to descend, the earth by yielding crops
Gives praise to both, and carpeth not at either,
But treasures up the fruit they yield together:
Yea, so commixes both, that in her fruit
None can distinguish this from that, they suit
Her well when hungry, but if she be full
She spews out both, and makes their blessings null.

You see the ways the fisherman doth take
To catch the fish, what engines doth he make?

Behold! how he engageth all his wits
Also his snares, lines, angles, hooks and nets.
Yet fish there be, that neither hook, nor line,
Nor snare, nor net, nor engine can make thine;
They must be groped for, and be tickled too,
Or they will not be catched, what e'er you do.
How doth the fowler seek to catch his game?
By divers means, all which one cannot name.
His gun, his nets, his lime-twigs, fight and bell:
He creeps, he goes, he stands; yea, who can tell
Of all his postures? Yet there's none of these
Will make him master of what fowls he please.
Yea, he must pipe, and whistle to catch this,
Yet if he does so, that bird he will miss.

If that a pearl may in a toad's head dwell,
And may be found too in an oyster-shell;
If things that promise nothing, do contain
What better is than gold, who will disdain
(That have an inkling of it) there to look,
That they may find it? Now my little book
(Though void of all those paintings that may make
It with this or the other man to take)
Is not without those things that do excel,
What do in brave but empty notions dwell.

'Well, yet I am not fully satisfied,
That this your book will stand, when soundly tried.

Why, what's the matter? 'It is dark', What tho'?'
But it is feigned', What of that I trow?
Some men by feigning words as dark as mine,
Make truth to spangle, and its ray to shine.

'But they want solidness.' Speak man thy mind.
'They drowned the weak; metaphors make us blind.'
Solidity, indeed becomes the pen
Of him that writeth things divine to men:
But must I needs want solidness, because
By metaphors I speak; was not God's laws,
His Gospel-laws in olden time held forth
By types, shadows and metaphors? Yet loth
Will any sober man be to find fault
With them, lest he be found for to assault
The highest wisdom. No, he rather stoops,
And seeks to find out what by pins and loops,
By calves, and sheep, by heifers, and by rams,
By birds and herbs, and by the blood of lambs
God speaketh to him: and happy is he
That finds the light, and grace that in them be.

Be not too forward therefore to conclude
That I want solidness, that I am rude:
All things solid in show not solid be;
All things in parables despise not we
Lest things most hurtful lightly we receive;
And things that good are, of our souls bereave.

My dark and cloudy words they do but hold
The truth, as cabinets enclose the gold.
The prophets used much by metaphors
To set forth truth; yea, who so considers
Christ, his Apostles too, shall plainly see,
That truths to this day in such mantles be.

Am I afraid to say that Holy Writ,
Which for its style and phrase puts down all wit,
Is everywhere so full of all these things,
(Dark figures, allegories), yet there springs
From that same book that lustre and those rays
Of light that turns our darkest nights to days.

Come, let my carper to his life now look,
And find there darker lines than in my book
He findeth any. Yea, and let him know
That in his best things there are worse lines too.

May we but stand before impartial men,
To his poor one, I durst adventure ten
That they will take my meaning in these lines
Far better than his lies in silver shrines.
Come, truth, although in swaddling-clouts,
I find Informs the judgement, rectifies the mind,
Pleases the understanding, makes the will
Submit; the memory too it doth fill
With what doth our imagination please,
Likewise, it tends our troubles to appease.

Sound words I know Timothy is to use,
And old wives' fables he is to refuse,
But yet grave Paul him nowhere doth forbid
The use of parables; in which lay hid
That gold, those pearls, and precious stones that were
Worth digging for, and that with greatest care.

Let me add one word more, O man of God!
Art thou offended? Dost thou wish I had

Put forth my matter in another dress,
Or that I had in things been more express?

Three things let me propound, then I submit
To those that are my betters (as is fit).

1. I find not that I am denied the use
Of this my method, so I no abuse
Put on the words, things, readers, or be rude
In handling figure, or similitude,
In application; but all that I may
Seek the advance of Truth this or that way.
Denied did I say? Nay, I have leave
(Example too, and that from them that have
God better please by their words or ways
Than any man that breatheth nowadays),
Thus to express my mind, thus to declare
Things unto thee that excellentest are.

2. I find that men (as high as trees) will write
Dialogue-wise; yet no man doth them slight
For writing so: indeed if they abuse
Truth, cursed be they, and the craft they use
To that intent: but yet let truth be free
To make her sallies upon thee, and me,
Which way it pleases God. For who knows how,
Better than he that taught us first to plough,
To guide our mind and pens for his design?
And he makes base things usher in divine.

3. I find that Holy Writ in many places
Hath semblance with this method, where the cases
Doth call for one thing to set forth another:
Use it I may then, and yet nothing smother
Truth's golden beams, nay, by this method may
Make it cast forth its rays as light as day.

And now, before I do put up my pen,
I'll show the profit of my book, and then
Commit both thee, and it unto that hand
That pulls the strong down, and makes weak ones stand.

This book it chalketh out before thine eyes
The man that seeks the everlasting prize:
It shows you whence he comes, whither he goes,
What he leaves undone, also what he does:

It also shows you how he runs, and runs,
Till he unto the Gate of Glory comes.

It shows too who sets out for life amain,
As if the lasting crown they would attain:
Here also you may see the reason why
They lose their labour, and like fools do die.

This book will make a traveller of thee,
If by its counsel thou wilt ruled be;
It will direct thee to die Holy Land,
If thou wilt its directions understand:
Yea, it will make the slothful active be,
The blind also delightful things to see.

Art thou for something rare, and profitable?
Would'st thou see a truth within a fable?
Art thou forgetful? Wouldest thou remember
From New Year's Day to the last of December?
Then read my fancies, they will stick like burrs,
And may be to the helpless, comforters.

This book is writ in such a dialect
As may the minds of listless men affect:

It seems a novelty, and yet contains
Nothing but sound and honest gospel-strains.

Would'st thou divert thyself from melancholy?
Would'st thou be pleasant, yet be far from folly?
Would'st thou read riddles and their explanation,
Or else be drownded in they contemplation?
Dost thou love picking-meat? Or would'st thou see
A man i' the clouds, and hear him speak to thee?
Would'st thou be in a dream, and yet not sleep?
Or would'st thou in a moment laugh and weep?
Wouldest thou lose thyself, and catch no harm
And find thyself again without a charm?
Would'st read thyself, and read thou know'st not what
And yet know whether thou art blest or not,
By reading the same lines? O then come hither,
And lay may book, thy head and heart together.

JOHN BUNYAN

PART 4

Enlightenments and Revolutions (1700 – 1850)

CHAPTER 14

Economy and Society in the Eighteenth Century

Wortley Montagu, "Letters Regarding The Small Pox Vaccination"

Lady Mary Wortley Montagu (1689–1762 CE) was born to a noble family. Lady Mary became well known in gentry and intellectual circles for her writing and advocacy of women's rights. She became a prominent figure in London court life as the wife of Edward Wortley Montagu, a Member of Parliament who served as ambassador at Constantinople in 1716–1717. The experience of travel and living abroad gave Lady Mary an international outlook, which she vividly expressed in her writing and her promotion of smallpox vaccination, a practice she discovered in Turkey (early in life the disease had marred her physical beauty). In later years she traveled and lived in France and Italy.

Sources: Rhys, E., ed. *Letters from the Right Honourable Lady Mary Wortley Montagu 1709–1762* (London: J.M. Dent & Co, 1906), pp. 158–161.

Lady Mary Wortley Montagu, *Letters of the Right Honourable Lady Mary Wortley Montagu: Written During Her Travels in Europe, Asia and Africa, vol. 1* (Aix: Anthony Henricy, 1796), pp. 167–69.

Malcolm Jack, ed., Lady Mary Wortley Montagu, *Turkish Embassy Letters* (London: William Pickering, 1993).

Focus Questions:

1. Why would Lady Mary have returned from Constantinople to England with a very different outlook on life? Lady Mary lived in Constantinople for a rather brief time. Why was her experience so intense?
2. Describe Lady Mary's attitude toward prevailing notions in society, whether in Constantinople or England. Given the level of detail in her descriptions, how much

contact would one infer Lady Mary had with society in Constantinople?

3. What does Lady Mary have to say about the elites in Ottoman society, particularly in religion, government, and the law?
4. According to Lady Mary, what are the attitudes toward religion of both the common people and of the elites she met?

To the Lady—.
Pera, Constantinople, March 16, O.S. [1718]

I am extremely pleased, my dear lady, that you have at length found a commission for me that I can answer without disappointing your expectations; though I must tell you, that it is not so easy as perhaps you think it; and that, if my curiosity had not been more diligent than any other stranger's has ever yet been, I must have answered you with an excuse, as I was forced to do when you desired me to buy you a Greek slave. I have got for you, as you desire, a Turkish love-letter, which I have put in a little box, and ordered the captain of the Smyrniote to deliver it to you with this letter. The translation of it is literally as follows: The first piece you should pull out of the purse is a little pearl, which is in Turkish called Ingi, and should be understood in this manner:

Ingi,	Sensin Guzelerin gingi
Pearl,	Fairest of the young.
Caremfil,	Caremfilsen cararen yók
Clove,	Conge gulsum timarin yók

Benseny chok than severim
Senin benden, haberin yók.
You are as slender as this clove!
You are an unblown rose!
I have long loved you, and you have not known it!

Pul,	Derdime derman bul
Jonquil,	Have pity on my passion!
Kihat,	Birlerum sahat sahat
Paper,	I faint every hour!
Ermus,	Ver bize bir umut
Pear,	Give me some hope.
Jabun,	Derdinden oldum zabun
Soap,	I am sick with love.
Chemur,	Ben oliyim size umur
Coal,	May I die, and all my years be yours!
Gul,	Ben aglarum sen gul
A rose,	May you be pleased, and all your sorrows mine!

Hasir, Oliim sana yazir
A straw, Suffer me to be your slave.
Jo ha, Ustune bulunmaz pahu
Cloth, Your price is not to be found.
Tartsin, Sen ghel ben chekeim senin hargin
Cinnamon, But my fortune is yours.
Gira, Esking-ilen oldum ghira
A match, I burn, I burn! my flame consumes me!
Sirma, Uzunu benden a yirma
Gold thread, Don't turn away your face.
Satch, Bazmazum tatch
Hair, Crown of my head!
Uzum, Benim iki Guzum
Grape, My eyes!
Tel, Ulugornim tez ghel
Gold wire, I die—come quickly.

And, by way of postscript:

Biber, Bize bir dogm haber
Pepper, Send me an answer.

You see this letter is all verses, and I can assure you there is as much fancy shewn in the choice of them, as in the most studied expressions of our letters; there being, I believe, a million of verses designed for this use. There is no colour, no flower, no weed, no fruit, herb, pebble, or feather, that has not a verse belonging to it; and you may quarrel, reproach, or send letters of passion, friendship, or civility, or even of news without ever inking your fingers.

I fancy you are now wondering at my profound learning; but, alas I dear madam, I am almost fallen into the misfortune so common to the ambitious; while they are employed on distant insignificant conquests abroad, a rebellion starts up at home;—I am in great danger of losing my English. I find it is not half so easy to me to write in it as it was a twelvemonth ago. I am forced to study for expressions, and must leave off all other languages, and try to learn my mother tongue. Human understanding is as much limited as human power, or human strength. The memory can retain but a certain number of images; and 'tis as impossible for one human creature to be perfect master of ten different languages, as to have in perfect subjection ten different kingdoms, or to fight against ten men at a time: I am afraid I shall at last know none as I should do. I live in a place that very well represents the tower of Babel: in Pera they speak Turkish, Greek, Hebrew, Armenian, Arabic, Persian, Russian, Sclavonian, Wallachian, German, Dutch, French, English, Italian, Hungarian; and, what is worse, there are ten of these languages spoken in my own family. My grooms are Arabs; my footmen, French, English and Germans; my nurse, an Armenian; my housemaid Russians; half a dozen other servants, Greeks; my steward. an Italian; my janissaries, Turks; [so] that I live in the perpetual hearing of this medley of sounds, which produces a very extraordinary effect upon the people that are born here; they learn all these languages at the same time, and without knowing any of them well enough to write or read in it. There are very few men, women, or even children, here, that have not the same compass of words in five or six of them. I know myself several infants of three or four years old, that speak Italian, French, Greek, Turkish, and Russian, which last they learn of their nurses, who are generally of that country. This seems almost incredible to you, and is, in my mind, one of the most curious things in this country, and takes off very much from the merit of our ladies who set up for such extraordinary geniuses, upon the credit of some superficial knowledge of French and Italian.

As I prefer English to all the rest, I am extremely mortified at the daily decay of it in my head, where I'll assure you (with grief of heart) it is reduced to such a small number of words, I cannot recollect any tolerable phrase to conclude my letter, and am forced to tell your ladyship very bluntly that I am, your faithful humble servant.

SMALLPOX VACCINATION IN TURKEY

A propos of distempers, I am going to tell you a thing, that will make you wish yourself here. The small-pox, so fatal, and so general amongst us, is here entirely harmless, by the invention of engrafting, which is the term they give it. There is a set of old women, who make it their business to perform the operation, every autumn, in the month of September, when the great heat is abated. People send to one another to know if any of their family has a mind to have the small-pox; they make parties for this purpose, and when they are met (commonly fifteen or sixteen together) the old woman comes with a nut-shell full of the matter of the best sort of small-pox, and asks what vein you please to have opened. She immediately rips open that you offer to her, with a large needle (which gives you no more pain than a common scratch) and puts into the vein as much matter as can lie upon the head of her needle, and after that, binds up the little wound with a hollow bit of shell, and in this manner opens four or five veins. The Grecians have commonly the superstition of opening one in the middle of the forehead, one in each arm, and one on the breast, to mark the sign of the Cross; but this has a very ill effect, all these wounds leaving little scars, and is not done by those that are not superstitious, who chuse to have them in the legs, or that part of the arm that is concealed. The children or young patients play together all the rest of the day, and are in perfect health to the eighth. Then the fever begins to seize them, and they keep their beds two days, very seldom three. They have very rarely above twenty or thirty in their faces, which never mark, and in eight days time they are as well as before their illness. Where they are wounded, there remains running sores during the distemper, which I don't doubt is a great relief to it. Every year, thousands undergo this operation, and the French Ambassador says pleasantly, that they take the small-pox here by way of diversion, as they take the waters in other countries. There is no example of any one that has died in it, and you may believe I am well satisfied of the safety of this experiment, since I intend to try it on my dear little son. I am patriot enough to take the pains to bring this useful invention into fashion in England, and I should not fail to write to some of our doctors very particularly about it, if I knew any one of them that I thought had virtue enough to destroy such a considerable branch of their revenue, for the good of mankind. But that distemper is too beneficial to them, not to expose to all their resentment, the hardy wight that should undertake to put an end to it. Perhaps if I live to return, I may, however, have courage to war with them. Upon this occasion, admire the heroism in the heart of

Your friend, etc. etc.

LETTER XXVIII (ADRIANOPLE, I APRIL 1717)
To the Abbé Conti, 125

You see that I am very exact in keeping the promise you engaged me to make but I know not whether your curiosity will be satisfied with the accounts I shall give you, though I can assure you that the desire I have to oblige you to the utmost of my power has made me very diligent in my enquiries and observations. 'Tis certain we have but very imperfect relations of the manners and religion of these people, this part of the world being seldom visited but by merchants, who mind little but their own affairs, or travellers who make too short a stay to be able to report anything exactly of their own knowledge. The Turks are too proud to converse familiarly with merchants etc., who can only pick up some confused informations, which are generally false, and can give no better account of the ways here, than a French refugee lodging in a garret in Greek Street,126 could write of the court of England. The journey we have made from Belgrade hither by land cannot possibly passed by any out of a public character. The desert woods of Serbia are the common refuge of thieves who rob fifty company, that we had need of all our guards to secure us, and had no mercy on their poverty, killing all the poultry and sheep they could find without asking who they belonged to, while the wretched owners durst not put in their claim for fear of being beaten. Lambs just the villages so poor that only force could exort from them necessary provisions. Indeed the Janissaries fallen, geese and turkeys big with egg all massacred without distinction! I fancied I heard the complaints of Moelibeus for the hope of his flock.127 When the pashas travel 'tis yet worse. Those oppressors are not content with eating all that is to be eaten belonging to the peasants; after they have crammed themselves and their numerous retinue they have the impudence to exact what they call teeth money, a contribution for the use of their teeth, worn with doing them the honour of devouring their meat. This is a literal, known truth, however extravagant it seems; and such is the natural corruption of a military government, their religion not allowing of this barbarity any more than our does.

I had the advantage of lodging three weeks at Belgrade, with a principal effendi, that is to say a scholar. This set of men are equally capable of preferments in the law or the church, those two sciences being cast into one, and a lawyer and a priest being the same word. They are the only men really considerable in the empire; all the profitable employments and church revenues are in their hands. The Grand Signor, though general heir to his people, never presumes to touch their lands or money, which go in an uninterrupted succession to their children. 'Tis true they lose this privilege by accepting a place at court, or the title of pasha, but there are few examples of such fools among them. You may easily judge of the power of these men who have engrossed all the learning and almost all the wealth of the empire. 'Tis they that are the real authors, though the soldiers are the actors of revolutions. They deposed the late Sultan Mustafa; 128 and their power is so well known 'tis the emperor's, interest to flatter them.

This is a long digression. I was going to tell you that an intimate daily conversation with the effendi Achmed Bey gave me opportunity of knowing their religion and morals in a more particular manner than perhaps any Christian ever did. I explained to him the difference between the religion of England and Rome, and he was pleased to hear there were Christians that did not worship images or adore the Virgin Mary. The ridicule of transubstantiation appeared very strong to him. Upon comparing our creeds together I am convinced that if our friend Dr Clarke 129 had free liberty of preaching here it would be very easy to persuade the generality to Christianity, whose notions are already little different from his. Mr Whiston 130 would make a very good apostle here. I don't doubt but his zeal will be much fired if you communicate this account to him, but tell him, he must first have the gift of tongues before he can possibly be of any use.

Mohanimedism is divided into as many sects as Christianity, and the first institution as much neglected and obscured by interpretations. I cannot here forbear reflecting on the natural inclination of mankind, to make mysteries and novelties. The Zeidi, Kudi, Jabari 131 etc. put me in mind of the Catholic, Lutheran, Calvinist, etc., and are equally zealous against one another. But the most prevailing opinion if you search into the secret of the effendis is plain deism but this is kept from the people who are amused with a thousand different notions, according to the different interest of their preachers. There are very few amongst them (Achmed Bey denied there were any) so absurd as to set up for wit by declaring they believe no God at all. And Sir Paul Rycaut 132 is mistaken, as he commonly is, in calling the sect muserin (i.e. the secret with us) atheists, they being deists,

whose impiety consists in making a jest of their prophet. Achmed Bey did not own to me that he was of this opinion but made no scruple of deviating from some part of Mohammed's law by drinking wine with the same freedom we did. When I asked him how he came to allow himself that liberty he made answer that all the creatures of God were good and designed for the use of man; however, that the prohibition of wine was a very wise maxim and meant for the common people, being the source of all disorders amongst them, but that the prophet never designed to confine those that knew how to use it with moderation. However, scandal ought to be avoided he never drank it in public. This is the general way of thinking amongst them, and very few forbear drinking wine that are able to afford it.

He assured me that if I understood Arabic I should be very well pleased with reading the Alcoran, which is so far from the nonsense we charge it with that 'tis the purest morality delivery in the very best language. I have since heard impartial Christians speak of it in the same manner, and I don't doubt but all our translations are from copies got from the Greek priests who would not fail to falsify it with the extremity of malice. No body of men ever were more ignorant or more corrupt, yet they differ so little from the Romish Church that I confess there is nothing gives me a greater abhorrence of the cruelty of your clergy than the barbarous persecutions of them, whenever they have been their masters for no other reason than not acknowledging the Pope. The dissenting in that one article has got them the titles of heretics, schismatics, and, what is worse, the same treatment.

I found at Philippopolis a sect of Christians that call themselves Paulines.133 They show an old church where, they say, St Paul preached, and he is their favourite saint, after the same manner as St Peter is at Rome; neither do they forget to give him the same preference over the rest of the apostles.

But of all the religions I have seen the Amounts seem to me the most particular. They are natives of Amawutluk,134 the ancient Macedonia, and still retain the courage and hardiness, though they have lost the name of Macedonians, being the best Militia in the Turkish empire, and the only check upon the Janissaries. They are foot soldiers; we had a guard of them relieved in every considerable town we passed. They are all clothed and armed at their own expense, generally lusty young fellows dressed in clean white coarse cloth, carrying guns of a prodigious length, which they run with upon their shoulders, as if they did not feel the weight of them, the leader singing a sort of rude tune, not unpleasant, and the rest making up the chorus. These people living between Christians and Mohanimedans, and not being skilled in controversy, declare that they are utterly unable to judge which religion is best, but to be certain of not entirely rejecting the truth they very prudently follow both and go to the mosque on Fridays and to the church on Sundays, saying for their excuse that at the day of judgement they are sure of protection from the true prophet; but which that is, they are not able to determine in this world. I believe there is no other race of mankind who have so modest an opinion of their own capacity. These are the remarks I have made on the diversity of religions I have seen. I don't ask your pardon for the liberty I have taken in speaking of the Roman. I know you equally condemn the quackery of all churches as much as you revere the sacred truths, in which we both agree.

You will expect I should say something to you of the antiquities of this country, but there are few remains of ancient Greece. We passed near the piece of an arch which is commonly called Trajan's Gate, 135 as supposing he made it to shut up the passage over the mountains between Sofia and Philippopolis, but I rather believe it the remains of some triumphal arch (though I could not see any inscription), for if that passage had been shut up there are many others that would serve for the march of an army. And notwithstanding the story of Baldwin, Earl of Flanders, being overthrown in these straits 136 after he had won Constantinople, I don't fancy the Germans would find themselves stopped by them. 'Tis true the road is now made, with great industry, as commodious as possible for the march of the Turkish army. There is not one ditch or puddle between this place and Belgrade that has not a large strong bridge of planks built over it; but the precipices are not so terrible as I had heard them represented. At the foot of these mountains we lay at the little village of Kiskoi, wholly inhabited by Christians, as all the peasants of Bulgaria are. Their houses are nothing but little huts, raised of dirt baked in the sun and they leave them and fly into the mountains some months before the march of the Turkish army, who would else entirely ruin them by driving away their whole flocks. This precaution secures them in a sort of plenty, for vast tracts of land lying in common they have liberty of sowing what they please, and are generally very industrious husbandmen. I drank here several sorts of delicious wine. The women dress themselves in a great variety of coloured glass beads and are not ugly, but of tawny complexions. I have now told you all that is worth telling you, and perhaps more, relating to my journey. When I am at Constantinople I'll try to pick up some curiosities and then you shall hear again from, etc.

Auguste Tissot, "Midwives"

In this excerpt, a Swiss physician, Auguste Tissot (1728-1797) criticizes the methods used by midwives who oversaw the birth of children. Until the mid-eighteenth century, throughout most of Europe, childbirth was a female-only event with a midwife leading the pregnant woman and her female relatives through the birthing process, which usually took place in the family's home. Although they were not formally educated and many were unable to read or write, midwives handed down the skills and training needed for childbirth orally and through informal apprenticeship, from generation to generation. As literacy increased in the seventeenth and eighteenth centuries, midwife manuals for childbirth as well as the cure of other illnesses, usually using herbal remedies, began to be published. In the mid-eighteenth century, professionally trained male physicians, usually from the middle class or lower nobility, began to take over some elements of health care from midwives and artisanally trained barber-surgeons. These male physicians frequently attacked traditional medical practitioners, although given the state of medical knowledge at this time, they were often no more successful at treating patients, especially in the case of childbirth.

Source: M.J.N. Halle, ed., *Oeuvres choisies de Tissot*, vol. 1 (Paris: Allut, 1810), 446-448; reprinted in *Changing Lives: Women in European History Since 1700*, ed. Bonnie G. Smith (Lexington, MA: D.C. Heath, 1989), 14-15.

Focus Questions:

1. How and why does Tissot criticize midwives? Why does he want to prevent them from assisting at births?
2. What methods and practices does Tissot favor, in comparison to the midwives?
3. On what ideas were his prescriptions based in comparison to those of the midwives?

The need for enlightened midwives in most of the country and I dare say in all of Europe is a well-known misfortune, which has the most disastrous consequences and which demands the full attention of the government.

The errors they commit during deliveries are infinite and too often irremedial. We need a book expressly to give precise directions to alert them and we need to educate midwives fit to understand them. I will mention only one of their practices which does the most harm: it is the use of warm remedies which they give when the delivery is particularly painful or slow—such things as castor oil, safran, sage, rue, oil of ambergris, wine, theriaque, wine prepared with aromatics, coffee, liqueur of anis, nuts, or fennel and all other liqueurs. All these things are true poisons, which, far from speeding up the delivery in fact make it more difficult by inflaming both the uterus, which can then no longer contract, and all the parts, which serve as a passage and which as a result swell and then make the way narrower. At other times these warm poisons produce hemorrhages which can kill the mother in a short time.

One saves both mothers and infants by the opposite treatment. As soon as a healthy women finds herself in labor and if that labor appears excessively painful and difficult, far from encourageing premature efforts by the remedies I just mentioned, which will end everything, one should order the mother to be bled in the arm which will prevent inflammation, which will stop the pain, and which will relax the body and make it more favorably disposed. One should give no food during labor except a little bread soup every three hours and water thickened with flour. Every four hours one should cleanse the passage with a mixture of mallow and oil..., rub it with a little butter and place compresses of hot water on the abdomen.

Hannah More, "The Carpenter"

Hannah More (1745-1833) was part of an influential but informal literary club comprised of middle class and upper-class women in London in the late eighteenth century and early nineteenth century. They were known as the "Bluestockings," and their meetings inspired other similar gatherings all over England. These conservative, educated women held gatherings in their homes and invited some of the most celebrated literary names of the time to discuss their work and ideas. The group encouraged other middle class and upper class women to abandon what they saw as vain and silly pursuits, such as card playing and fashions, and instead urged them to take on charity work, especially projects that could benefit the lives of other women. This poem, one of over fifty written by More, takes on the issue of working class "immorality," as she uses this story to identify vices that she believed plagued the families of the newly emerging working class in London and elsewhere. This poem, and others she wrote like it, use the style and form of other popular publications at the time which were targeted for a broad reading audience. About two million copies of this poem were sold to charitable societies who, in turn, distributed them to the poor and working class.

Source: Hannah More, *"The Carpenter"* (London: Cheap Repository, n.d. 1795-98).

Focus Questions:

1. What is the basic plot of this story, and what main vices does More hope to bring to attention here?
2. Why did the author write this poem, and why did she use this style and form?
3. What does this poem tell us about working class families or about middle class/upper class views of working class families in this period?

There was a young Weft-country man;
A Carpenter by trade;
A fkilful wheelwright too was he,
And few fuch Waggons made.

No Man a tighter Barn cou'd build,
Throughout his native town;
Thro' many a village round was he,
The beft of workmen known.

His father left him what he had,
In footh it was enough;
His fhining pewter, pots of brafs,
And all his houfehold fluff.

A little cottage too he had,
For eafe and comfort plann'd,
And that he might not lack for ought,
An acre of good land.

A pleafant orchard too there was,
Before his cottage door;
Of cider and of corn likewife,
He had a little flore.

Active and healthy, ftout and youg,
No bufinefs wanted he;
Now tell me reader if you can,
What man more bleft cou'd be?

To make his comfort quite compleat,
He had a faithful Wife;
Frugal and neat and good was fhe,
The bleffing to his life.

Where is the Lord, or where the Squire,
Had greater caufe to praife,
The goodnefs of that bounteous hand,
Which bleft his profp'rous days?

Each night when he return'd from work,
His wife fo meek and mild,
His little fupper gladly drefs'd,
While he carefs'd his child.

One blooming babe was all he had,
His only darling dear,
The object of their equal love,
The folace of their care.

O what cou'd ruin fuch a life,
And fpoil fo fair a lot?
O what cou'd change fo kind a heart,
All goodnefs quite forgot?

With grief the caufe muft relate,
The difmal caufe reveal,
'Twas evil company and drink,
The fource of every ill.

A Cooper came to live hard by,
Who did his fancy pleafe;
And idle rambling Man was he,
Who oft had crofs'd the feas.

This Man could tell a merry tale,
And fing a merry fong;
And thofe who heard him fing or talk,
Ne'er thought the ev'ning long.

But vain and vicious was the fong,
And wicked was the tale;
And every paufe he always fill'd,
With cider, gin, or ale.

Our Carpenter delighted much,
To hear the Cooper talk;
And with him to the Ale-houfe oft,
Wou'd take his evening walk.

At firft he did not care for drink,
But only lik'd the fun;
But foon he from the Cooper learnt,
The fame fad courfe to run.

He faid the Cooper's company,
Was all for which he car'd;

But foon he drank as much as he,
To fwear like him foon dar'd.

His hammer now neglected lay,
For work he little car'd;
Half finifh'd wheels, and broken tools,
Were ftrew'd about his yard.

To get him to attend his work,
No prayers cou'd now prevail:
His hatchet and his plane forgot,
He never drove a Nail.

His chearful ev'nings now no more,
With peace and plenty fmil'd;
No more he fought his pleafing Wife,
Nor hugg'd his fmiling child.

For not his drunken nights alone,
Were with the Cooper paft;
His days were at the Angel fpent,
And ftill he ftay'd the laft.

No handfome Sunday fuit was left,
Nor decent holland fhirt;
No nofegay mark'd the Sabbath day,
But all was rags and dirt.

No more his Church he did frequent,
A fymptom ever fad;
Where once the Sunday is mifpent,
The week days muft be bad.

The cottage mortgag'd for its worth,
The favourite orchard fold;
He foon began to feel th'effects
Of hunger and of cold.

The pewter difhes one by one,
Were pawn'd, till none was left;
And wife and babe at home remain'd
Of every help bereft.

By chance he call'd at home one night,
And in a furly mood,
He bade his weeping wife to get
Immediately fome food.

His empty cupboard well he knew
Muft needs be bare of bread;
No rafher on the rack he faw,
Whence cou'd he then be fed?

Hiw wife a piteous figh did heave,
And then before he laid
A bafket cover'd with a cloth,
But not a word fhe faid.

Then to her hufband gave a knife,
Wth many a filent tear;
In hafte he tore the cover off,
And faw his child lay there.

"There lies thy babe, the mother faid,
"Opprefs'd with famine fore;
"O kill us both—'twere kinder far,
"We cou'd not fuffer more."

The Carpenter, ftruck to the heart,
Fell on his knees ftraitway;
He wrung his hands—confefs'd his fins,
And did both weep and pray.

From that fame hour the Cooper more,
He never wou'd behold;
Nor wou'd he to the Ale-houfe go,
Had it been pav'd with gold.

His Wife forgave him all the paft,
And footh'd his forrowing mind,
And much he griev'd that eer he wrong'd
The worthieft of her kind.

By lab'ring hard, and working late,
By induftry and pains,
His Cottage was at length redeem'd,
And fav'd were all his gains.

His Sundays now at Church wre fpent,
His home was his delight,
The following verfe hmfelf he made,
And read it every night:

The Drunkard Murders Child and Wife,
Nor matters it a pin,
Where he ftabs them with his knife,
Or ftarves them by his gin.

Leeds Woolen Workers, "Petition"

Not everyone welcomed the new manufacturing machines and changing labor patterns of the early Industrial Revolution. While supported and championed by entrepreneurs and manufacturers, the machines such as the Spinning Jenny and the mechanized loom, put further pressure on struggling artisan guilds. By the advent of the Industrial Revolution artisan guilds were already under pressure by the "putting out" or cottage system where workers, either moonlighting guild members or rural people working on agricultural off-seasons, did piece work in their own homes for suppliers and buyers of textile materials who undercut established guild prices and eroded guild monopolies. All over Europe, artisans resisted the growth of cottage industry as well as the adoption of machines. This petition, written by wool workers in Great Britain and published in a newspaper in Leeds, is an example of resistance by workers to these changes.

Source: "The Leeds Woolen Worker's Petition," reprinted in Jackson J. Spielvogel, *Western Civilization*, 2nd ed., (New York: West Publishing, 1994), 653.

Focus Questions:

1. What fears did the textile workers in Leeds express in this petition? What did they see as the immediate impact of changing technologies and work in their sector?
2. To whom was the petition addressed? What groups did they hope to persuade? How?
3. What does this document tell us about the impact of the Industrial Revolution on workers? On manufacturers or entrepreneurs?

To the Merchants, Clothiers and all such as wish well to the Staple Manufactory of this Nation.

The Humble ADDRESS and PETITION of Thousands, who labour in the Cloth Manufactory.

SHEWETH, That the Scribbling-Machines have thrown thousands of your petitioners out of employ, whereby they are brought into great distress, and are not able to procure a maintenance for their families, and deprived them of the opportunity of bringing up their children to labour: We have therefore to request, that prejudice and self-interest may be laid aside, and that you may pay that attention to the following facts, which the nature of the case requires.

The number of Scribbling-Machines extending about seventeen miles southwest of LEEDS, exceed all belief, being no less than *one hundred and seventy!* and as each machine will do as much work in twelve hours, as ten men can in that time do by hand, (speaking within bounds) and they working night-and day, one machine will do as much work in one day as would otherwise employ twenty men.

As we do not mean to assert any thing but what we can prove to be true, we allow four men to be employed at each machine twelve hours, working night and day, will take eight men in twenty-four hours; so that, upon a moderate computation twelve men are thrown out of employ for every single machine used in scribbling; and as it may be supposed the number of machines in all the other quarters together, nearly equal those in the South-West, full four thousand men are left to shift for a living how they can, and must of course fall to the Parish, if not time relieved. Allowing one boy to be bound apprentice from each family out of work, eight thousand hands are deprived of the opportunity of getting a livelihood.

We therefore hope, that the feelings of humanity will lead those who have it in their power to prevent the use of those machines, to give every discouragement they can to what has a tendency so prejudicial to their fellow-creatures....

We wish to propose a few queries to those who would plead for the further continuance of these machines:

How are those men, thus thrown out of employ to provide for their families; and what are they to put their children apprentice to, that the rising generation may have something to keep them at work, in order that they may not be like vagabonds strolling about in idleness? Some day, Begin and learn some other business.Suppose we do, who will maintain our families, whilst we undertake the arduous task; and when we have learned it, how do we know we shall be any better for all our pains; for by the time we have served our second apprenticeship, another machine may arise, which may take away that business also....

But what are our children to do; are they to be brought up in idleness? Indeed as things are, it is no wonder to hear of so many executions; for our parts, though we may be thought illiterate men, our conceptions are, that bringing children up to industry, and keeping them employed, is the way to keep them from falling into those crimes, which an idle habit naturally leads to.

James Lind, from *A Treatise of the Scurvy* 1753

James Lind (1716–1794) was a Scottish naval surgeon. Lind's experiments on scurvy, conducted in 1747 while serving on the HMS Salisbury, demonstrated that citrus could eliminate the disease, which caused bleeding gums, loose teeth, sore joints, and hemorrhaging. Citrus's benefits had been known to sailors in earlier centuries, and Lind's work, although published in a 1753 treatise, did not change official policy until 1795, when the Admiralty ordered ships to be supplied with citrus juice. This decision eliminated scurvy and reduced by half the number of sailors admitted to infirmaries. Lind also experimented on distilling fresh water from salt water and published works on improving the health of sailors.

Source: *James Lind, A Treatise of the Scurvy In Three Parts. Containing an Inquiry into the Nature, Causes, and Cure of that Disease, Together With a Critical and Chronological View of What Has Been Published On the Subject* (London: A. Millar, 1753).

Focus Questions:

1. How would you describe Lind's attitude toward the process of experimentation?
2. Is Lind aware of any other studies of the health among seamen?

OF THE PREVENTION OF THE SCURVY

I shall conclude the precepts relating to the preservation of seamen with showing the best means of obviating many inconveniences which attend long voyages and of removing the several causes productive of this mischief.

The following are the experiments. On the 20th May, 1747, I took twelve patients in the scurvy on board the Salisbury at sea. Their cases were as similar as I could have them. They all in general had putrid gums, the spots and lassitude, with weakness of their knees. They lay together in one place, being a proper apartment for the sick in the fore-hold; and had one diet in common to all, viz., water gruel sweetened with sugar in the morning; fresh mutton broth often times for dinner; at other times puddings, boiled biscuit with sugar etc.; and for supper barley, raisins, rice and currants, sago and wine, or the like. Two of these were ordered each a quart of cyder a day. Two others took twenty five gutts of elixir vitriol three times a day upon an empty stomach, using a gargle strongly acidulated with it for their mouths. Two others took two spoonfuls of vinegar three times a day upon an empty stomach, having their gruels and their other food well acidulated with it, as also the gargle for the mouth. Two of the worst patients, with the tendons in the ham rigid (a symptom none the rest had) were put under a course of sea water. Of this they drank half a pint every day and sometimes more or less as it operated by way of gentle physic. Two others had each two oranges and one lemon given them every day. These they eat with greediness at different times upon an empty stomach. They continued but six days under this course, having consumed the quantity that could be spared. The two remaining patients took the bigness of a nutmeg three times a day of an electuray recommended by an hospital surgeon made of garlic, mustard seed, rad. raphan., balsam of Peru and gum myrrh, using for common drink narley water well acidulated with tamarinds, by a decoction of wich, with the addition of cremor tartar, they were gently purged three or four times during the course.

The consequence was that the most sudden and visible good effects were perceived from the use of the oranges and lemons; one of those who had taken them being at the end of six days fit four duty. The spots were not indeed at that time quite off his body, nor his gums sound; but without any other medicine than a gargarism or elixir of vitriol he became quite healthy before we came into Plymouth, which was on the 16th June. The other was the best recovered of any in his condition, and being now deemed pretty well was appointed nurse to the rest of the sick…

As I shall have occasion elsewhere to take notice of the effects of other medicines in this disease, I shall here only observe that the result of all my experiments was that oranges and lemons were the most effectual remedies for this distemper at sea. I am apt to think oranges preferable to lemons, though it was principally oranges which so speedily and surprisingly recovered Lord Anson's people at the Island of Tinian, of which that noble, brave and experienced commander was so sensible that before he left the island one man was ordered on shore from each mess to lay in a stock of them for their future security…Perhaps one history more may suffice to put this out of doubt.

Richard Guest, *The Creation of the Steam Loom*

The Industrial Revolution was not so much one event, as it was a century long process. Although the spinning of raw wool or cotton and linen into thread was automated at the very beginning of the Industrial Revolution with the invention of the spinning jenny in 1765, it was not until several years later that the other key component of textile production, weaving, was equally mechanized with the introduction of the water frame loom in 1769. This moved textile manufacturing out of workshops and homes and into factories located near water sources, such as rivers, that served as the power supply for the new machines. Another major turning point in the Industrial Revolution came in the 1790s with the introduction of steam power, derived from coal. Steam power quickly replaced water as the primary power source, and revolutionized the textile industry, other manufacturing sectors, and transportation. This excerpt from an 1823 history of cotton manufacturing describes the introduction of steam powered weaving machines and their impact on the industry.

Source: Richard Guest, *Compendious History of the Cotton Manufacture* (New York: Augustus M. Kelley Publishers, 1968; reprint Manchester: Joseph Pratt, 1823), 44-48.

Focus Questions:

1. According to this passage, what were the advantages brought by the introduction of machines in the manufacturing of textiles?
2. According to the author what promise did steam power, in particular, offer for this manufacturing sector and, presumably, others as well?
3. How did the author view the rapid changes in the textile sector? What ideas or perspective informed his view?
4. What does this passage tell us about the Industrial Revolution?

The same powerful agent which so materially forwarded and advanced the progress of the Cotton Manufacture in the concluding part of the last century, has lately been further used as a substitute for manual labour, and the Steam Engine is now applied to the working of the Loom as well as to the preparatory processes.

In 1785, the Rev. E. Cartwright invented a Loom to be worked by water or steam. The following account of this invention is taken from the Supplement to the Encyclopedia Britannica:—"Happening to be at Matlock, in the summer of 1784, I fell in company with some gentlemen of Manchester, when the conversation turned on Arkwright's spinning machinery. One of the company observed, that as soon as Arkwright's patent expired, so many mills would be erected, and so much cotton spun, that hands never could be found to weave it."To this observation I replied that Arkwright must then set his wits to work to invent a weaving mill. This brought on a conversation on the subject, in which the Manchester gentlemen unanimously agreed that the thing was impracticable; and in defence of their opinion, they adduced arguments which I certainly was incompetent to answer or even to comprehend, being totally ignorant of the subject, having never at that time seen a person weave. I controverted, however, the impracticability of the thing, by remarking that there had lately been exhibited in London, an automation figure, which played at chess. Now you will not assert, gentlemen, said I, that it is more difficult to construct a machine that shall weave, then one which shall make all the variety of moves which are required in that complicated game.

Some little time afterwards, a particular circumstance recalling this conversation to my mind, it struck me, that, as in plain weaving, according to the conception I then had of the business, there could only be three movements, which were to follow each other in succession, there would be little difficulty in producing and repeating them. Full of these ideas, I immediately employed a carpenter and smith to carry them into effect. As soon as the machine was finished, I got a weaver to put in the warp, which was of such materials as sail cloth is usually made of. To my great delight, a piece of cloth, such as it was, was the produce.

As I had never before turned my thoughts to any thing mechanical, either in theory or practice, nor had ever seen a loom at work, or knew any thing of its construction, you will readily suppose that my first Loom must have been a most rude piece of machinery.

The warp was placed perpendicularly, the reed fell with a force of at least half an hundred weight, and the springs which threw the shuttle were strong enough to have thrown a Congreve rocket. In short, it required the strength of two powerful men to work the machine at a slow rate, and only for a short time. Conceiving in my great simplicity, that I had accomplished all that was required, I then secured what I thought a most valuable property, by a patent, 4th April, 1785. This being done, I then condescended to see how other people wove; and you will guess my astonishment, when I compared their easy modes of operation with mine. Availing myself, however, of what I then saw, I made a Loom in its general principles, nearly as they are now made. But it was not till the year 1787, that I completed my invention, when I took out my last weaving patent, August 1st, of that year."

Mr. Cartwright erected a weaving mill at Doncaster, which he filled with Looms. This concern was unsuccessful, and at last was abandoned, and some years afterwards, upon an application from a number of manufacturers at Manchester, Parliament granted Mr. Cartwright a sum of money as a remuneration for his ingenuity and trouble.

About 1790, Mr. Grimshaw, of Manchester, under a licence from Mr. Cartwright, erected a weaving factory turned by a Steam Engine. The great loss of time experienced in dressing the warp, which was done in small portions as it unrolled from the beam, and other difficulties arising from the quality of the yarn then spun, were in this instance formidable obstacles to success; the factory, however, was burnt down before it could be fully ascertained whether the experiment would succeed or not, and for many years no further attempts were made in Lancashire to weave by steam.

Mr. Austin, of Glasgow, invented a similar Loom, in 1789, which he still further improved in 1798, and a building to contain two hundred of these Looms was erected by Mr. Monteith, of Pollockshaws, in 1800.

In the year 1803, Mr. Thomas Johnson, of Bradbury, in Cheshire, invented the Dressing Frame. Before this invention the warp was dressed in the Loom in small portions as it unrolled from the beam, the Loom ceasing to work during the operation. Mr. Johnson's machine dresses the whole warp at once; when dressed the warp is placed in the Loom which now works without intermission. A factory for Steam Looms was built in Manchester, in 1806. Soon afterwards two others were erected at Stockport, and about 1809, a fourth was completed in Westhoughton. In these renewed attempts to weave by steam, considerable improvements were made in the structure of the Looms, in the mode of warping, and in preparing the weft for the shuttle. With these improvements, aided by others in the art of spinning, which enabled the spinners to make yarn much superior to that made in 1790, and assisted by Johnson's machine, which is peculiarly adapted for the dressing of warps for Steam Looms, the experiment succeeded. Before the invention of the Dressing Frame, one Weaver was required to each Steam Loom, at present a boy or girl, fourteen or fifteen years of age, can manage two Steam Looms, and with their help can weave three and a half times as much cloth as the best hand Weaver. The best hand Weavers seldom produce a piece of uniform evenness; indeed, it is next to impossible for them to do so, because a weaker or stronger blow with the lathe immediately alters the thickness of the cloth, and after an interruption of some hours, the most experienced weaver finds it difficult to recommence with a blow of precisely the same force as the one with which he left off. In Steam Looms, the lathe gives a steady, certain blow, and when once regulated by the engineer, moves with the greatest precision from the beginning to the end of the piece. Cloth made by these Looms, when seen by those manufacturers who employ hand Weavers, at once excites admiration and a consciousness that their own workmen cannot equal it. The increasing number of Steam Looms is a certain proof of their superiority over the Hand Looms. In 1818, there were in Manchester, Stockport, Middleton, Hyde, Stayley Bridge, and their vicinities, fourteen factories, containing about two thousand Looms. In 1821, there were in the same neighbourhoods thirty-two factories, containing five thousand seven hundred and thirty-two Looms. Since 1821, their number has still farther increased, and there are at present not less than ten thousand Steam Looms at work in Great Britain.

It is a curious circumstance, that, when the Cotton Manufacturer was in its infancy, all the operations, from the dressing of the raw material to its being finally turned out in the state of cloth, were completed under the roof of the weaver's cottage. The course of improved manufacture which followed, was to spin the yarn in factories and to weave it in cottages. At the present time, when the manufacture has attained a mature growth, all the operations, with vastly increased means and more complex contrivances, are gained performed in a single building. The Weaver's cottage with its rude apparatus of peg warping, hand cards, hand wheels, and imperfect looms, was the Steam Loom factory in miniature. Those vast brick edifices in the vicinity of all the great manufacturing towns in the south of Lancashire, towering to the height of seventy or eighty feet, which strike the attention and excite the curiosity of the traveller, now perform labours which formerly employed whole villages. In the Steam Loom factories, the cotton is carded, roved, spun, and woven into cloth, and the same quantum of labour is now performed in one of these structures which formerly occupied the industry of an entire district.

A very good Hand Weaver, a man twenty-five or thirty years of age, will weave two pieces of nine-eighths shirting per week, each twenty-four yards long, and containing one hundred and five shoots of weft in an inch, the reed of the cloth being a forty-four, Bolton count, and the warp and weft forty hanks to the pound. A Steam Loom Weaver, fifteen years of age, will in the same time weave seven similar pieces. A Steam Loom factory containing two hundred Looms, with the assistance of one hundred persons under twenty years of age, and of twenty-five men, will weave seven hundred pieces per week, of the length and quality before described. To manufacture one hundred similar pieces per week by the hand, it would be necessary to employ at least one hundred and twenty-five Looms, because many of the Weavers are females, and have cooking, washing, cleaning and various other duties to perform; others of them are children, and consequently, unable to weave as much as the men. It requires a man of mature age and a very good Weaver to weave two of the pieces in a week, and there is also an allowance to be made for sickness and other incidents. Thus, eight hundred and seventy-five hand Looms would be required to produce the seven hundred pieces per week; and reckoning the weavers, with their children, and the aged and infirm belonging to them, at two and a half to each loom, it may very safely be said, that the work done in a Steam Factory containing two hundred Looms, would, if done by hand Weavers, find employment and support for a population of more than two thousand persons.

The Steam Looms are chiefly employed in Weaving printing cloth and shirtings; but they also weave thicksetts, fancy cords, dimities, cambries and quiltings, together with silks, worsteds, and fine woollen or broad cloth. Invention is progressive, every improvement that is made is the foundation of another, and as the attention of hundreds of skilful mechanics and manufacturers is now turned to the improvement of the Steam Loom, it is probable that its application will become as general, and its efficiency as great, in Weaving, as the Jenny, Water Frame and Mule, are in Spinning, and that it will, in this country at least, entirely supersede the hand Loom.

David Ricardo, Excerpt from *Principles of Political Economy and Taxation*

David Ricardo (1772–1823) was a British economist instrumental in the development of economic theory. Disinherited by his Jewish father when he married a Quaker, Ricardo became immensely wealthy as a stockbroker. As a member of Parliament, Ricardo promoted free trade and sought to repeal the protectionist Corn Laws. Ricardo's best-known work, Principles of Political Economy and Taxation (1817), explained how different national economies could, through free trade, each have their own comparative advantages. Principles also elucidates the "iron law of wages," by which wages settle at the level of subsistence. Ricardo maintained a friendship with Thomas Malthus, whose ideas on population growth he shared.

Source: David Ricardo, *The Principles of Political Economy and Taxation. Introduction by Michael Fogarty* (London: Dent, 1962).

Focus Questions:

1. According to Ricardo, what role does labor play in determining the value of a commodity?
2. Does Ricardo think the value of commodities can undergo sudden changes?

Labour of different qualities differently rewarded. This no cause of variation in the relative value of commodities.

In speaking, however, of labour, as being the foundation of all value, and the relative quantity of labour as almost exclusively determining the relative value of commodities, I must not be supposed to be inattentive to the different qualities of labour, and the difficulty of comparing an hour's or a day's labour, in one employment, with the same duration of labour in another. The estimation in which different qualities of labour are held, comes soon to be adjusted in the market with sufficient precision for all practical purposes, and depends much on the comparative skill of the labourer, and intensity of the labour performed. The scale, when once formed, is liable to little variation. If a day's labour of a working jeweller be more valuable than a day's labour of a common labourer, it has long ago been adjusted, and placed in its proper position in the scale of value.

In comparing therefore the value of the same commodity, at different periods of time, the consideration of the comparative skill and intensity of labour, required for that particular commodity, needs scarcely to be attended to, as it operates equally at both periods. One description of labour at one time is compared with the same description of labour at another; if a tenth, a fifth, or a fourth, has been added or taken away, an effect proportioned to the cause will be produced on the relative value of the commodity. If a piece of cloth be now of the value of two pieces of linen, and if, in ten years hence, the ordinary value of a piece of cloth should be four pieces of linen, we may safely conclude, that either more labour is required to make the cloth, or less to make the linen, or that both causes have operated.

As the inquiry to which I wish to draw the reader's attention, relates to the effect of the variations in the relative value of commodities, and not in their absolute value, it will be of little importance to examine into the comparative degree of estimation in which the different kinds of human labour are held. We may fairly conclude, that whatever inequality there might originally have been in them, whatever the ingenuity, skill, or time necessary for the acquirement of one species of manual dexterity more than another, it continues nearly the same from one generation to another; or at least, that the variation is very inconsiderable from year to year, and therefore, can have little effect, for short periods, on the relative value of commodities.

"The proportion between the different rates both of wages and profit in the different employments of labour and stock, seems not to be much affected, as has already been observed, by the riches or poverty, the advancing, stationary, or declining state of the society. Such revolutions in the public welfare, though they affect the general rates both of wages and profit, must in the end affect them equally in all different employments. The proportion between them therefore must remain the same, and cannot well be altered, at least for any considerable time, by any such revolutions."

David Ricardo, *On Wages*, "The Iron Law of Wages"

David Ricardo (1772–1823 CE) was a British economist instrumental in the development of economic theory. Disinherited by his Jewish father when he married a Quaker, Ricardo became immensely wealthy as a stockbroker. As a member of Parliament, Ricardo promoted free trade and sought to repeal the protectionist Corn

Laws. Ricardo's best-known work, *Principles of Political Economy and Taxation* (1817), explained how different national economies could, through free trade, each have their own comparative advantages. Principles also elucidates the "iron law of wages," by which wages settle at the level of subsistence. Ricardo maintained a friendship with Thomas Malthus, whose ideas on population growth he shared.

Source: J.R. McCulloch, ed., *The Works of David Ricardo* (London: John Murray, 1881), pp. 31, 50–58.

Focus Questions:

1. What does Ricardo think about government intervention in wage rates?
2. Although prices tend to continually rise over time, what changes can bring up lower prices? Are there any recent examples that support this view?

Money, from its being a commodity obtained from a foreign country, from its being the general medium of exchange between all civilized countries, and from its being also distributed among those countries in proportions which are ever changing with every improvement in commerce and machinery, and with every increasing difficulty of obtaining food and necessaries for an increasing population, is subject to incessant variations. In stating the principles which regulate exchangeable value and price, we should carefully distinguish between those variations which belong to the commodity itself, and those which are occasioned by a variation in the medium in which value is estimated, or price expressed.

A rise in wages, from an alteration in the value of money, produces a general effect on price, and for that reason it produces no real effect whatever on profits. On the contrary, a rise of wages, from the circumstance of the labourer being more liberally rewarded, or from a difficulty of procuring the necessaries on which wages are expended, does not, except in some instances, produce the effect of raising price, but has a great effect in lowering profits. In the one case, no greater proportion of the annual labour of the country is devoted to the support of the labourers; in the other case, a larger portion is so devoted.

Labour, like all other things which are purchased and sold, and which may be increased or diminished in quantity, has its natural and its market price. The natural price of labour is that price which is necessary to enable the labourers, one with another, to subsist and to perpetuate their race, without either increase or diminution.

The power of the labourer to support himself, and the family which may be necessary to keep up the number of labourers, does not depend on the quantity of money which he may receive for wages, but on the quantity of food, necessaries, and conveniences become essential to him from habit, which that money will purchase. The natural price of labour, therefore, depends on the price of the food, necessaries, and conveniences required for the support of the labourer and his family. With a rise in the price of food and necessaries, the natural price of labour will rise; with the fall in their price, the natural price of labour will fall.

With the progress of society the natural price of labour has always a tendency to rise, because one of the principal commodities by which its natural price is regulated, has a tendency to become dearer, from the greater difficulty of producing it. As, however, the improvements in agriculture, the discovery of new markets, whence provisions may be imported, may for a time counteract the tendency to a rise in the price of necessaries, and may even occasion their natural price to fall, so will the same causes produce the correspondent effects on the natural price of labour.

The natural price of all commodities, excepting raw produce and labour, has a tendency to fall, in the progress of wealth and population; for though, on one hand, they are enhanced in real value, from the rise in the natural price of the raw material of which they are made, this is more than counterbalanced by the improvements in machinery, by the better division and distribution of labour, and by the increasing skill, both in science and art, of the producers.

The market price of labour is the price which is really paid for it, from the natural operation of the proportion of the supply to the demand; labour is dear when it is scarce, and cheap when it is plentiful. However much the market price of labour may deviate from its natural price, it has, like commodities, a tendency to conform to it.

It is when the market price of labour exceeds its natural price, that the condition of the labourer is flourishing and happy, that he has it in his power to command a greater proportion of the necessaries and enjoyments of life, and therefore to rear a healthy and numerous family. When, however, by the encouragement which high wages give to the increase of population, the number of labourers is increased, wages again fall to their natural price, and indeed from a reaction sometimes fall below it.

When the market price of labour is below its natural price, the condition of the labourers is most wretched: then poverty deprives them of those comforts which custom renders absolute necessaries. It is only after their privations have reduced their number, or the demand for labour has increased, that the market price of labour will rise to its natural price, and that the labourer will have the moderate comforts which the natural rate of wages will afford.

Notwithstanding the tendency of wages to conform to their natural rate, their market rate may, in an improving society, for an indefinite period, be constantly above it; for no sooner may the impulse, which an increased capital gives to a new demand for labour, be obeyed, than another increase of capital may produce the same effect; and thus, if the increase of capital be gradual and constant, the demand for labour may give a continued stimulus to an increase of people...

Thus, then, with every improvement of society, with every increase in its capital, the market wages of labour will rise; but the permanence of their rise will depend on the question, whether the natural price of labour has also risen; and this again will depend on the rise in the natural price of those necessaries on which the wages of labour are expended...

As population increases, these necessaries will be constantly rising in price, because more labour will be necessary to produce them. If, then, the money wages of labour should fall, whilst every commodity on which the wages of labour were expended rose, the labourer would be doubly affected, and would be soon totally deprived of subsistence. Instead, therefore, of the money wages of labour falling, they would rise; but they would not rise sufficiently to enable the labourer to purchase as many comforts and necessaries as he did before the rise in the price of those commodities...

These, then, are the laws by which wages are regulated, and by which the happiness of far the greatest part of every community is governed. Like all other contracts, wages should be left to the fair and free competition of the market, and should never be controlled by the interference of the legislature.

The clear and direct tendency of the poor laws is in direct opposition to these obvious principles: it is not, as the legislature benevolently intended, to amend the condition of the poor, but to deteriorate the condition of both poor and rich; instead of making the poor rich, they are calculated to make the rich poor; and whilst the present laws are in force, it is quite in the natural order of things that the fund for the maintenance of the poor should progressively increase till it has absorbed all the net revenue of the country, or at least so much of it as the state shall leave to us, after satisfying its own never-failing demands for the public expenditure.

This pernicious tendency of these laws is no longer a mystery, since it has been fully developed by the able hand of Mr. Malthus; and every friend to the poor must ardently wish for their abolition.

Daniel Defoe, Selection from *The Complete English Tradesman*

Daniel Defoe (1660–1731 CE) was an English writer considered the first English novelist. Defoe studied to be a Nonconformist minister but instead went into commerce. After his hosiery business went bankrupt, he focused more on writing. Defoe gained royal favor in 1701 by defending foreign-born monarchs, was arrested in 1703 when he mocked the Anglican Church in defense of religious toleration, and was convicted of libel in 1713. Defoe turned to writing fiction, publishing novels such as *Robinson Crusoe* (1719) and *Moll Flanders* (1722). He wrote over 500 books and pamphlets, which included works on Britain's burgeoning commercial society, such as *The Complete English Tradesman* (1726).

Source: Daniel Defoe, *The Complete English Tradesman* (London, 1839).

Focus Questions:

1. Based on Defoe's description of the extent and circulation of trade throughout the country, how would you describe the British people as a nation?
2. What does Defoe take into account when estimating the total value of English trade?

CHAPTER XXIII

ON THE INLAND TRADE OF ENGLAND, ITS MAGNITUDE, AND THE GREAT ADVANTAGE IT IS TO THE NATION IN GENERAL

Now, in all these manufactures, however remote from one another, every town in England uses something, not only of one or other, but of all the rest. Every sort of goods is wanted everywhere; and where they make one sort of goods, and sell them all over England, they at the same time want other goods from almost every other part. For example:

Norwich makes chiefly woollen stuffs and camblets, and these are sold all over England; but then Norwich buys broad-cloth from Wilts and Worcestershire, serges and sagathies from Devon and Somersetshire, narrow cloth from Yorkshire, flannel from Wales, coal from Newcastle, and the like; and so it is, mutatis mutandis, of most of the other parts.

The circulating of these goods in this manner, is the life of our inland trade, and increases the numbers of our people, by keeping them employed at home; and, indeed, of late they are prodigiously multiplied; and they again increase our trade, as shall be mentioned in its place.

As the demand for all sorts of English goods is thus great, and they are thus extended in every part of the island, so the tradesmen are dispersed and spread over every part also; that is to say, in every town, great or little, we find shopkeepers, wholesale or retail, who are concerned in this circulation, and hand forward the goods to the last consumer. From London, the goods go chiefly to the great towns, and from those again to the smaller markets, and from those to the meanest villages; so that all the manufactures of England, and most of them also of foreign countries, are to be found in the meanest village, and in the remotest corner of the whole island of Britain, and are to be bought, as it were, at every body's door.

This shows not the extent of our manufactures only, but the usefulness of them, and how they are so necessary to mankind that our own people cannot be without them, and every sort of them, and cannot make one thing serve for another; but as they sell their own, so they buy from others, and every body here trades with every body: this it is that gives the whole manufacture so universal a circulation, and makes it so immensely great in England. What it is abroad, is not so much to our present purpose.

Again, the magnitude of the city of London adds very considerably to the greatness of the inland trade; for as this city is the centre of our trade, so all the manufactures are brought hither, and from hence circulated again to all the country, as they are particularly called for. But that is not all; the magnitude of the city influences the whole nation also in the article of provisions, and something is raised in every county in England, however remote, for the supply of London; nay, all the best of every produce is brought hither; so that all the people, and all the lands in England, seem to be at work for, or employed by, or on the account of, this overgrown city.

This makes the trade increase prodigiously, even as the city itself increases; and we all know the city is very greatly increased within few years past. Again, as the whole nation is employed to feed and clothe this city, so here is the money, by which all the people in the whole nation seem to be supported and maintained.

I have endeavoured to make some calculation of the number of shopkeepers in this kingdom, but I find it is not to be done—we may as well count the stars; not that they are equal in number neither, but it is as impossible, unless any one person corresponded so as to have them numbered in every town or parish throughout the kingdom. I doubt not they are some hundreds of thousands, but there is no making an estimate—the number is in a manner infinite. It is as impossible likewise to make any guess at the bulk of their trade, and how much they return yearly; nor, if we could, would it give any foundation for any just calculation of the value of goods in general, because all our goods circulate so much, and go so often through so many hands before they come to the consumer. This so often passing every sort of goods through so many hands, before it comes into the hands of the last consumer, is that which makes our trade be so immensely great. For example, if there is made in England for our home-consumption the value of £100,000 worth of any particular goods, say, for example, that it be so many pieces of serge or cloth, and if this goes through ten tradesmen's hands, before it comes to the last consumer, then there is £1,000,000 returned in trade for that £100,000 worth of goods; and so of all the sorts of goods we trade in.

CHAPTER 15

Europe and the World in the Eighteenth Century

Willem Bosman, from *A New and Accurate Description of the Coast of Guinea Divided into the Gold, the Slave, and the Ivory Coasts*

A Dutch sea-captain born in Utrecht in 1672, Willem Bosman drew on his 14 years of experience sailing along the coast of Western Africa to write this important narrative in 1705. Among other things, the book provides an eyewitness account of how the African slave trade worked around 1700, and it was quickly translated into many languages and furnished with illustrations and maps in many editions. This excerpt describes the mechanisms of the slave trade in "Whydah" (today called "Ouidah"), a kingdom that was absorbed into the Dahomey kingdom in 1727, and is today part of the nation of Benin.

Source: Willem Bosman, A New and Accurate Description of the Coast of Guinea Divided into the Gold, the Slave, and the Ivory Coasts. Translated from Dutch (London, 1705), pp. 363–365.

Focus Questions:

1. What was the ultimate "source" of slaves, according to Bosman, and how did other Africans contribute to this market?
2. Does Bosman recognize that slaves were human beings, due the respect that is proper to all people? Is he credible on this point?
3. How does this document reveal Europeans' fears about slave rebellion? Were there practical reasons for masters to treat their slaves with a modicum of decency?

...The first business of one of our Factors when he comes to Fida [Whydah] is to satisfie the Customs of the King and the great Men, which amount to about 100 Pounds in Guinea value, as the Goods must yield there. After which we have free Licence to Trade, which is published throughout the whole Land by the Cryer.

But yet before we can deal with any Person, we are obliged to buy the King's whole stock of Slaves at a set price; which is commonly one third or one fourth higher than ordinary: After which we obtain free leave to deal with all his Subjects of what Rank so-ever. But if there happen to be no stock of Slaves, the Factor must then resolve to run the Risque of trusting the inhabitants with Goods to the value of one or two hundred Slaves; which Commodities they send into the In-land Country, in order to buy with them Slaves at all Markets, and that sometimes two hundred Miles deep in the Country: For you ought to be informed that Markets of Men are kept in the same manner as those of beasts with us.

Not a few in our Country fondly imagine that Parents here sell their Children, Men their Wives, and one Brother the other: But those who think so deceive themselves; for this never happens on any other account but that of Necessity, or some great Crime: But most of the Slaves that are offered to us are Prisoners of War, which are sold by the victors as their Booty.

When these Slaves come to Fida, they are put in Prison all together, and when we treat concerning buying them, they are all brought out together in a large Plain; where, by our Chirurgeons, whose Province it is, they are thoroughly examined, even to the smallest Member, and that naked too both Men and Women, without the least Distinction or Modesty. Those which are approved as good are set on one side; and the lame or faulty are set by as Invalides, which are here called Mackrons. These are such as are above five and thirty Years old, or are maimed in the Arms, Legs, Hands or Feet, have lost a Tooth, are grey haired, or have Films over their Eyes; as well as all those which are affected with any Veneral Distemper, or with several other Diseases.

The Invalides and the Maimed being thrown out, as I have told you, the remainder are numbred, and it is entred who delivered them. In the mean while a burning Iron, with the Arms or Name of the Companies, lyes in the Fire; with which ours are marked on the Breast.

This is done that we may distinguish them from the Slaves of the English, French or others; (which are also marked with their Mark) and to prevent the Negros exchanging them for worse; at which they have a good Hand.

I doubt not but this Trade seems very barbarous to you, but since it is followed by meer necessity it must go on but we yet take all possible care that they are not burned too hard, especially the Women, who are more tender than the Men.

We are seldom long detained in the buying of these Slaves, because their price is established, the Women being one fourth or fifth part cheaper than the

Men. The Disputes which we generally have with the Owners of these Slaves are, that we will not give them such Goods as they ask for them, especially the Boesies (as I have told you, the Money of this Country) of which they are very fond, though we generally make a Division on this Head in order to make one sort of Goods help off another, because those Slaves which are paid for in Boesies cost the Company one half more than those bought with other Goods. The Price of a Slave is commonly—

When we have agreed with the Owners of the Slaves, they are returned to their Prison; where from that time forwards they are kept at our charge, cost us two pence a day a Slave; which serves to subsist them, like our Criminals, on Bread and Water: So that to save Charges we send them on Board our Ships with the very first Opportunity; before which their Master strip them of all they have on their Backs; so that they come Aboard stark-naked as well Women as Men: In which condition they are obliged to continue, if the Master of the Ship is not so Charitable (which he commonly is) as to bestow something on them to cover their Nakedness.

You would really wonder to see how these Slaves live on Board; for though their number sometimes amounts to six or seven Hundred, yet by the careful Management of our Masters of Ships, they are so regulated that it seems incredible: And in this particular our Nation exceeds all other Europeans; for as the French, Portugese and English Slave-Ships, are always foul and stinking; on the contrary ours are for the most part clean and neat.

The Slaves are fed three times a Day with indifferent good Victuals, and much better than they eat in their own Country. Their Lodging-place is divided into two parts; one of which is appointed for the Men the other for the Women; each Sex being kept a-part: Here they lye as close together as is possible for them to be crouded.

We are sometimes sufficiently plagued with a parcel of Slaves, which come from a far In-land Country, who very innocently perswade one another, that we buy them only to fatten and afterwards eat them as a Delicacy.

When we are so unhappy as to be pestered with many of this sort, they resolve and agree together (and bring over the rest to their Party) to run away from the Ship, kill the Europeans, and set the Vessel a-shore; by which means they design to free themselves from being our Food.

I have twice met with this Misfortune; and the first time proved very unlucky to me, I not in the least suspecting it; but the Up-roar was timely quashed by the Master of the Ship and my self, by, causing the Abettor to be shot through the Head, after which all was quiet.

But the second time it fell heavier on another Ship, and that chiefly by the carelessness of the Master, who having fished up the Anchor of a departed

English Ship, had laid it in the Hold where the Male Slaves were lodged; who, unknown to any of the Ships Crew, possessed themselves of a Hammer; with which, in a short time, they broke all their Fetters in pieces upon the Anchor: after this they came above Deck and fell upon our Men; some of whom they grievously wounded, and would certainly have mastered the Ship, if a French and English Ship had not very fortunately happened to lye by us; who perceiving by our firing a Distressed Gun, that something was in disorder on Board, immediately came to our assistance with Chalops and Men, and drove the Slaves under Deck: Notwithstanding which before all was appeased about twenty of them were killed…

Phillis Wheatley, "To the Right Honourable William, Earl of Dartmouth…"

Phillis Wheatley was born in Senegal in 1753. At the age of seven, she was captured, enslaved, and shipped to America. Once there, she was purchased by the Wheatleys of Boston, Massachusetts, who gave her an education that helped her develop her considerable intellectual gifts. At age thirteen, she published her first book of poems. So many white people found it difficult to believe that a black women could write sophisticated poetry, that Wheatley was forced to prove her abilities in court in 1772. After an exhaustive examination by some of Boston's most famous men, the court concluded that she was, indeed, the author of the poems published under her name. The Earl of Dartmouth, to whom Wheatley addressed the poem included below, helped with the publication of her work in England.

Source: Phillis Wheatley, *Poems on Various Subjects, Religious and Moral* (London, 1773), pp. 73–75.

Focus Questions:

1. What does the poem tell us about the nature of Wheatley's education? What might have motivated the Wheatleys to purchase her and educate her the way they did?
2. What strategies did Wheatley employ in her effort to persuade the Earl of Dartmouth to take action? What actions did she hope he would take?

Hail, happy day, when, smiling like the morn,
Fair Freedom rose New-England to adorn:
The northern clime beneath her genial ray,
Dartmouth, congratulates thy blissful sway:

Elate with hope her race no longer
Each soul expands, each grateful bosom burns,
While in thine hand with pleasure we behold
The silken reins, and Freedom's charms unfold.
Long lost to realms beneath the northern skies
She shines supreme, while hated faction dies:
Soon as appear'd the Goddess long desir'd,
Sick at the view, she languish'd and expir'd;
Thus from the splendors of the morning light
The owl in sadness seeks the caves of night.
No more, America, in mournful strain
Of wrongs, and grievance unredress'd complain,
No longer shall thou dread the iron chain,
Which wanton Tyranny with lawless hand
Had made, and with it meant t' enslave the land.
Should you, my lord, while you peruse my song,
Wonder from whence my love of Freedom sprung,
Whence flow these wishes for the common good,
By feeling hearts alone best understood,
I, young in life, by seeming cruel fate
Was snatch'd from Afric's fancy'd happy seat:
What pangs excruciating must molest,
What sorrows labour in my parent's breast?
Steel'd was that soul and by no misery mov'd
That from a father seiz'd his babe belov'd:
Such, such my case. And can I then but pray
Others may never feel tyrannic sway?
For favours past, great Sir, our thanks are due,
And thee we ask thy favours to renew,
Since in thy pow'r, as in thy will before,
To sooth the griefs, which thou did'st once deplore.
May heav'nly grace the sacred sanction give
To all thy works, and thou for ever live
Not only on the wings of fleeting Fame,
Though praise immortal crowns the patriot's name,
But to conduct to heav'ns refulgent fane,
May fiery coursers sweep th' ethereal plain,
And bear thee upwards to that blest abode,
Where, like the prophet, thou shalt find thy God.

Thomas Paine, "Common Sense"

Thomas Paine (1737-1809) came to America in 1774, two years after losing his job in Great Britain as excise officer (an official who collected taxes on liquor and tobacco) as a result of publishing an appeal for higher wages and calling for an end to corruption in the British excise tax system. After losing his post and while living in London, he met Ben Franklin, who encouraged him to move to America and provided him with contacts to secure work once he arrived. Paine settled in Philadelphia, became a writer contributing articles to publications such as the *Pennsylvania Magazine* and was active in the emerging abolition movement. He also wrote a series of pamphlets calling for complete and full American independence from Great Britain. This series of pamphlets began with his most famous work, entitled "Common Sense," which was published in January of 1776, a few months after the Battle of Lexington and Concord. "Common Sense" sold more than 500,000 copies.

Source: Thomas Paine, *Common Sense*, ed. Issac Kramnick (New York: Penguin Books, 1987), 66-71.

Focus Questions:

1. What criticisms does Paine offer regarding the British Constitution?
2. How and why did Paine's critique of the British government provide a basis for American independence?
3. What ideas, events, or movements informed Paine's arguments about government?

Here then is the origin and rise of government; namely, a mode tendered necessary by the inability of moral virtue to govern the world; here too is the design and end of government, viz. freedom and security. And however our eyes may be dazzled with snow, or our ears deceived by sound; however prejudice may warp our wills, or interest darken our understanding, the simple voice of nature and of reason will say, it is right.

I draw my idea of the form of government from a principle in nature, which no art can overturn, viz. that the more simple any thing is, the less liable it is to be disordered, and the easier repaired when disordered; and with this maxim in view, I offer a few remarks on the so much boasted constitution of England. That it was noble for the dark and slavish times in which it was erected is granted. When the world was over-run with tyranny the least remove there from was a glorious rescue. But that it is imperfect, subject to convulsions, and incapable of producing what it seems to promise, is easily demonstrated.

Absolute governments (tho' the disgrace of human nature) have this advantage with them, that they are simple; if the people suffer, they know the head from which their suffering springs, know likewise the remedy, and are not bewildered by a variety of causes and cures. But the constitution of England is so exceedingly complex, that the nation may suffer for years together without being able to discover in which part the fault lies, some will say in one and some in another, and every political physician will advise a different medicine.

I know it is difficult to get over local or long standing prejudices, yet if we will suffer ourselves to examine the component parts of the English constitution, we shall find them to be the base remains of two ancient compounded with some new republican materials.

First.—The remains of monarchical tyranny in the person of the king.

Secondly.—The remains of aristocratical tyranny in the persons of the peers.

Thirdly.—The new republican materials, in the persons of the commons, on whose virtue depends the freedom of England.

The two first, by being hereditary, are independent of the people; wherefore in a constitutional sense they contribute nothing towards the freedom of the state.

To say that the constitution of England is a union of three powers reciprocally checking each other, is farcical, either the words have no meaning, or they are flat contradictions.

To say that the commons is a check upon the king, presupposes two things.

First.—That the king is not to be trusted without being looked after, or in other words, that a thirst for absolute power is the natural disease of monarchy.

Secondly.—That the commons, by being appointed for that purpose, are either wiser or more worthy of confidence than the crown.

But as the same constitution which gives the commons a power to check the king by withholding the supplies, gives afterwards the king a power to check the commons, by empowering him to reject their other bills; it again supposes that the king is wiser than those whom it has already supposed to be wiser than him. A mere absurdity!

There is something exceedingly ridiculous in the composition of monarchy; it first excludes a man from the means of information, yet empowers him to act in cases where the highest judgment is required. The state of a king shuts him from the world, yet the business of a king requires him to know it thoroughly; wherefore the different parts, unnaturally opposing and destroying each other, prove the whole character to be absurd and useless.

Some writers have explained the English constitution thus; the king, say they, is one, the people another; the peers are an house in behalf of the king; the commons in behalf of the people; but this hath all the distinctions of an house divided against itself; and though the expressions be pleasantly arranged, yet when examined they appear idle and ambiguous; and it will always happen, that the nicest construction that words are capable of, when applied to the description of some thing which either cannot exist, or is too incomprehensible to be within the compass of description, will be words of sound only, and though they may amuse the ear, they cannot inform the mind, for this, explanation includes a previous question, viz. How came the king by a power which the people are afraid to trust, and always obliged to check? Such a power could not be the gift of a wise people, neither can any power, which needs checking, be from God; yet the provision, which the constitution makes, supposes such a power to exist.

But the provision is unequal to the task; the means either cannot or will not accomplish the end, and the whole affair is a felo de se; for as the greater weight will always carry up the less, and as all the wheels of a machine are put in motion by one, it only remains to know which power in the constitution has the most weight, for that will govern; and though the others, or a part of them, may clog, or, as the phrase is, check the rapidity of its motion, yet so long as they cannot stop it, their endeavours will be ineffectual; the first moving power will at last have its way, and what it wants in speed is supplied by time.

That the crown is this overbearing part in the English constitution needs not be mentioned, and that it derives its whole consequence merely from being the giver of places and pensions is self-evident, wherefore, though we have been wise enough to shut and lock a door against absolute monarchy, we at the same time leave been foolish enough to put the crown in possession of the key.

The prejudice of Englishmen, in favour of their own government by king, lords, and commons, arises as much or more from national pride than reason. Individuals are undoubtedly safer in England than in some other countries, but the will of the king is as much the law of the land in Britain as in France, with this difference, that instead of proceeding directly from his mouth, it is handed to the people under the most formidable shape of an act of eat. For the fate of Charles the First, hath only made kings more subtle—not more just.

Wherefore, laying aside all national pride and prejudice in favour of modes and forms, the plain truth is, that it is wholly owing to the constitution of the people, and not to the constitution of the government that the crown is not as oppressive in England as in Turkey.

An inquiry into the constitutional errors in the English form of government is at this time highly necessary; for as we are never in a proper condition of doing justice to others, while we continue under the influence of some leading partiality, so neither are we capable of doing it to ourselves while we remain fettered by any obstinate prejudice. And as a man, who is attached to a prostitute, is unfitted to choose or judge of a wife, so any prepossession in favour of a rotten constitution of government will disable us from discerning a good one.

Olaudah Equiano, Excerpt from *The Interesting Narrative of the Life of Olaudah Equiano*

Olaudah Equiano (c. 1745–1797 CE) was the son of an African village leader from present-day Nigeria. Equiano was sold into slavery at the age of eleven. He was shipped to Barbados and then Virginia, after which he became a slave of a British naval officer, with whom he traveled widely. Equiano bought his freedom in 1766 and went into the trade business. In 1789, Equiano published his autobiography, The Interesting Narrative, which was translated into several languages and printed in several editions. He was active in the abolitionist movement, which succeeded in ending the British slave trade several years after his death.

Source: Olaudah Equiano, *The Interesting Narrative Of The Life Of Olaudah Equiano, Or Gustavus Vassa, The African. Written By Himself* (1789).

Focus Questions:

1. How would you describe Equiano's reactions to the traumatic experience of becoming a slave?
2. What is Equiano's attitude toward the white captors who transported and sold him and his fellow Africans?

Page 69

...bottom, come up again, and swim about. Thus I continued to travel, sometimes by land, sometimes by water, through different countries and various nations, till, at the end of six or seven months after I had been kidnapped, I arrived at the sea coast. It would be tedious and uninteresting to relate all the incidents which befell me during this journey, and which I have not yet forgotten; of the various hands I passed through, and the manners and customs of all the different people among whom I lived: I shall therefore only observe, that in all the places where I was the soil was exceedingly rich; the pomkins, eadas, plantains, yams, &c. &c. were in great abundance, and of incredible size. There were also vast quantities of different gums, though not used for any purpose; and every where a great deal of

Page 70

tobacco. The cotton even grew quite wild; and there was plenty of red-wood. I saw no mechanics whatever in all the way, except such as I have mentioned. The chief employment in all these countries was agriculture, and both the males and females, as with us, were brought up to it, and trained in the arts of war. The first object which saluted my eyes when I arrived on the coast was the sea, and a slave ship, which was then riding at anchor, and waiting for its cargo. These filled me with astonishment, which was soon converted into terror when I was carried on board. I was immediately handled and tossed up to see if I were sound by some of the crew; and I was now persuaded that I had gotten into a world of bad spirits, and that they were going to kill me. Their complexions too

Page 71

differing so much from ours, their long hair, and the language they spoke, (which was very different from any I had ever heard) united to confirm me in this belief. Indeed such were the horrors of my views and fears at the moment, that, if ten thousand worlds had been my own, I would have freely parted with them all to have exchanged my condition with that of the meanest slave in my own country. When I looked round the ship too and saw a large furnace or copper boiling, and a multitude of black people of every description chained together, every one of their countenances expressing dejection and sorrow, I no longer doubted of my fate; and, quite overpowered with horror and anguish, I fell motionless on the deck and fainted. When I recovered a little I found some black people about me, who I believed were

Page 72

some of those who brought me on board, and had been receiving their pay; they talked to me in order to cheer me, but all in vain. I asked them if we were not to be eaten by those white men with horrible looks, red faces, and loose hair. They told me I was not; and one of the crew brought me a small portion of spirituous liquor in a

wine glass; but, being afraid of him, I would not take it out of his hand. One of the blacks therefore took it from him and gave it to me, and I took a little down my palate, which, instead of reviving me, as they thought it would, threw me into the greatest consternation at the strange feeling it produced, having never tasted any such liquor before. Soon after this the blacks who brought me on board went off, and left me abandoned to despair. I now saw myself deprived

Page 73

of all chance of returning to my native country, or even the least glimpse of hope of gaining the shore, which I now considered as friendly; and I even wished for my former slavery in preference to my present situation, which was filled with horrors of every kind, still heightened by my ignorance of what I was to undergo. I was not long suffered to indulge my grief; I was soon put down under the decks, and there I received such a salutation in my nostrils as I had never experienced in my life: so that, with the loathsomeness of the stench, and crying together, I became so sick and low that I was not able to eat, nor had I the least desire to taste any thing. I now wished for the last friend, death, to relieve me; but soon, to my grief, two of the white men offered me eatables; and, on my refusing to eat,

Page 74

one of them held me fast by the hands, and laid me across I think the windlass, and tied my feet, while the other flogged me severely. I had never experienced any thing of this kind before; and although, not being used to the water, I naturally feared that element the first time I saw it, yet nevertheless, could I have got over the nettings, I would have jumped over the side, but I could not; and, besides, the crew used to watch us very closely who were not chained down to the decks, lest we should leap into the water: and I have seen some of these poor African prisoners most severely cut for attempting to do so, and hourly whipped for not eating. This indeed was often the case with myself. In a little time after, amongst the poor chained men, I found some of my own nation, which in a small degree gave ease to my mind. I

Page 75

inquired of these what was to be done with us; they gave me to understand we were to be carried to these white people's country to work for them. I then was a little revived, and thought, if it were no worse than working, my situation was not so desperate: but still I feared I should be put to death, the white people looked and acted, as I thought, in so savage a manner; for I had never seen among any people such instances of brutal cruelty; and this not only shewn towards us blacks, but also to some of the whites themselves. One white man in particular I saw, when we were permitted to be on deck, flogged so unmercifully with a large rope near the foremast, that he died in consequence of it; and they tossed him over the side as they would have done a brute. This made me fear these people the more; and I expected

Page 76

nothing less than to be treated in the same manner. I could not help expressing my fears and apprehensions to some of my countrymen: I asked them if these people had no country, but lived in this hollow place (the ship): they told me they did not, but came from a distant one. 'Then, said I, 'how comes it in all our country we never heard of them?' They told me because they lived so very far off. I then asked where were their women? had they any like themselves? I was told they had: 'and why,' said I, 'do we not see them?' they answered, because they were left behind. I asked how the vessel could go? they told me they could not tell; but that there were cloths put upon the masts by the help of the ropes I saw, and then the vessel went on; and the white men had some spell or magic they put in the water

Page 77

when they liked in order to stop the vessel. I was exceedingly amazed at this account, and really thought they were spirits. I therefore wished much to be from amongst them, for I expected they would sacrifice me: but my wishes were vain; for we were so quartered that it was impossible for any of us to make our escape. While we stayed on the coast I was mostly on deck; and one day, to my great astonishment, I saw one of these vessels

coming in with the sails up. As soon as the whites saw it, they gave a great shout, at which we were amazed; and the more so as the vessel appeared larger by approaching nearer. At last she came to an anchor in my sight, and when the anchor was let go I and my countrymen who saw it were lost in astonishment to observe the vessel stop; and were now convinced it was

Page 78

done by magic. Soon after this the other ship got her boats out, and they came on board of us, and the people of both ships seemed very glad to see each other. Several of the strangers also shook hands with us black people, and made motions with their hands, signifying I suppose we were to go to their country; but we did not understand them. At last, when the ship we were in had got in all her cargo, they made ready with many fearful noises, and we were all put under deck, so that we could not see how they managed the vessel. But this disappointment was the least of my sorrow. The stench of the hold while we were on the coast was so intolerably loathsome, that it was dangerous to remain there for any time, and some of us had been permitted to stay on the deck for the fresh air; but now that the whole ship's cargo were

Page 79

confined together, it became absolutely pestilential. The closeness of the place, and the heat of the climate, added to the number in the ship, which was so crowded that each had scarcely room to turn him-self, almost suffocated us. This produced copious perspirations, so that the air soon became unfit for respiration, from a variety of loathsome smells, and brought on a sickness among the slaves, of which many died, thus falling victims to the improvident avarice, as I may call it, of their purchasers. This wretched situation was again aggravated by the galling of the chains, now become insupportable; and the filth of the necessary tubs, into which the children often fell, and were almost suffocated. The shrieks of the women, and the groans of the dying, rendered the whole a scene of horror almost inconceivable. Happily perhaps

Page 80

for myself I was soon reduced so low here that it was thought necessary to keep me almost always on deck; and from my extreme youth I was not put in fetters. In this situation I expected every hour to share the fate of my companions, some of whom were almost daily brought upon deck at the point of death, which I began to hope would soon put an end to my miseries. Often did I think many of the inhabitants of the deep much more happy than myself. I envied them the freedom they enjoyed, and as often wished I could change my condition for theirs. Every circumstance I met with served only to render my state more painful, and heighten my apprehensions, and my opinion of the cruelty of the whites. One day they had taken a number of fishes; and when they had killed and satisfied themselves with as many as

Page 81

they thought fit, to our astonishment who were on the deck, rather than give any of them to us to eat as we expected, they tossed the remaining fish into the sea again, although we begged and prayed for some as well as we could, but in vain; and some of my countrymen, being pressed by hunger, took an opportunity, when they thought no one saw them, of trying to get a little privately; but they were discovered, and the attempt procured them some very severe floggings. One day, when we had a smooth sea and moderate wind, two of my wearied countrymen who were chained together (I was near them at the time), preferring death to such a life of misery, somehow made through the nettings and jumped into the sea: immediately another quite dejected fellow, who, on account of his illness, was suffered to be out of irons,

Page 82

also followed their example; and I believe many more would very soon have done the same if they had not been prevented by the ship's crew, who were instantly alarmed. Those of us that were the most active were in a moment put down under the deck, and there was such a noise and confusion amongst the people of the ship as I never heard before, to stop her, and get the boat out to go after the slaves. However two of the wretches were

drowned, but they got the other, and afterwards flogged him unmercifully for thus attempting to prefer death to slavery. In this manner we continued to undergo more hardships than I can now relate, hardships which are inseparable from this accursed trade. Many a time we were near suffocation from the want of fresh air, which we were often without for whole days together. This,

Page 83

and the stench of the necessary tubs, carried off many. During our passage I first saw flying fishes, which surprised me very much: they used frequently to fly across the ship, and many of them fell on the deck. I also now first saw the use of the quadrant; I had often with astonishment seen the mariners make observations with it, and I could not think what it meant. They at last took notice of my surprise; and one of them, willing to increase it, as well as to gratify my curiosity, made me one day look through it. The clouds appeared to me to be land, which disappeared as they passed along. This heightened my wonder; and I was now more persuaded than ever that I was in another world, and that every thing about me was magic. At last we came in sight of the island of Barbadoes, at which the whites on board gave a great

Page 84

shout, and made many signs of joy to us. We did not know what to think of this; but as the vessel drew nearer we plainly saw the harbour, and other ships of different kinds and sizes; and we soon anchored amongst them off Bridge Town. Many merchants and planters now came on board, though it was in the evening. They put us in separate parcels, and examined us attentively. They also made us jump, and pointed to the land, signifying we were to go there. We thought by this we should be eaten by these ugly men, as they appeared to us; and, when soon after we were all put down under the deck again, there was much dread and trembling among us, and nothing but bitter cries to be heard all the night from these apprehensions, insomuch that at last the white people got some old slaves from the land to pacify us.

Page 85

told us we were not to be eaten, but to work, and were soon to go on land, where we should see many of our country people. This report eased us much; and sure enough, soon after we were landed, there came to us Africans of all languages. We were conducted immediately to the merchant's yard, where we were all pent up together like so many sheep in a fold, without regard to sex or age. As every object was new to me every thing I saw filled me with surprise. What struck me first was that the houses were built with stories, and in every other respect different from those in Africa: but I was still more astonished on seeing people on horseback. I did not know what this could mean; and indeed I thought these people were full of nothing but magical arts. While I was in this astonishment one of my

Page 86

fellow prisoners spoke to a countryman of his about the horses, who said they were the same kind they had in their country. I understood them, though they were from a distant part of Africa, and I thought it odd I had not seen any horses there; but afterwards, when I came to converse with different Africans, I found they had many horses amongst them, and much larger than those I then saw. We were not many days in the merchant's custody before we were sold after their usual manner, which is this: On a signal given, (as the beat of a drum) the buyers rush at once into the yard where the slaves are confined, and make choice of that parcel they like best. The noise and clamour with which this is attended, and the eagerness visible in the countenances of the buyers, serve not a little to increase the apprehensions of the

Page 87

terrified Africans, who may well be supposed to consider them as the ministers of that destruction to which they think themselves devoted. In this manner, without scruple, are relations and friends separated, most of them never to see each other again. I remember in the vessel in which I was brought over, in the men's apartment, there were several brothers, who, in the sale, were sold in different lots; and it was very moving on this occasion

to see and hear their cries at parting. O, ye nominal Christians! might not an African ask you, learned you this from your God, who says unto you, Do unto all men as you would men should do unto you? Is it not enough that we are torn from our country and friends to toil for your luxury and lust of gain? Must every tender feeling be likewise sacrificed to your avarice?

Page 88

Are the dearest friends and relations, now rendered more dear by their separation from their kindred, still to be parted from each other, and thus prevented from cheering the gloom of slavery with the small comfort of being together and mingling their sufferings and sorrows? Why are parents to lose their children, brothers their sisters, or husbands their wives? Surely this is a new refinement in cruelty, which, while it has no advantage to atone for it, thus aggravates distress, and adds fresh horrors even to the wretchedness of slavery.

Benjamin Franklin and the British Parliament, "Proceedings Regarding The Stamp Act"

Benjamin Franklin (1706-1790), noted printer, publisher, author, inventor and diplomat, lived primarily in the British colony of Pennsylvania, where he was publisher and printer of a newspaper, the *Pennsylvania Gazette* as well as an annual publication, *Poor Richard's Almanac*. Franklin was a vocal opponent of the Stamp Act, a tax passed by the British Parliament in 1765 that required all legal documents, publications, and printed materials to carry a "stamp" proving they had paid a required tax on all such documents levied by the British. The British argued that this tax helped to defray costs for the defense of the colonies, but many, including Benjamin Franklin, opposed it arguing that they had no direct representatives defending their interests in the British Parliament and, therefore, should not be taxed without due representation. Franklin and others argued that the colonial governments, not the British Parliament, should control and regulate colonial finances. In October 1765, a colonial "congress" convened in America to formally oppose the Stamp Act and to draft a petition of protest that was then delivered to the British king and Parliament. In 1766, the British Parliament repealed the act, but remained resolute in its claim to have the authority to pass laws that regulated affairs in the colonies. This dispute, along with other related problems, ultimately provided the basis for the American independence movement. In this excerpt, members of the lower house of the British Parliament, the House of Commons, question Franklin about the Stamp Act, soon after its repeal.

Source: L. Jesse Lemisch, editor, *Benjamin Franklin: The Autobiography and Other Writings* (New York: New American Library, 1961), 256-260.

Focus Questions:

1. What arguments does Franklin make regarding British taxation and economic policies in colonial America? What ideas and events informed his arguments and views?
2. How did the Stamp Act dispute alter how American colonists viewed the British crown and Parliament?
3. How did the British Parliament understand their powers and objectives regarding the colonies? What ideas and events informed their views?
4. How did this dispute contribute to the American colonial independence movement?

THE EXAMINATION OF DOCTOR BENJAMIN FRANKLIN…IN THE BRITISH HOUSE OF COMMONS, RELATIVE TO THE REPEAL OF THE AMERICAN STAMP ACT…

[February, 1766]

Q. What is your name, and place of abode?

A. Franklin, of Philadelphia....

Q. From the thinness of the back settlements, would not the stamp act be extremely inconvenient to the inhabitants, if executed?

A. To be sure it would; as many of the inhabitants could not get stamps when they had occasion for them without taking long journeys, and spending perhaps Three or Four Pounds, that the Crown might get Six pence.

Q. Are not the Colonies, from their circumstances, very able to pay the stamp duty?

A. In my opinion there is not gold and silver enough in the Colonies to pay the stamp duty for one year.

Q. Don't you know that the money arising from the stamps was all to be laid out in America?

A. I know it is appropriated by the act to the American service; but it will be spent in the conquered Colonies, where the soldiers are, not in the Colonies that pay it.

Q. Is there not a balance of trade due from the Colonies where the troops are posted, that will bring back the money to the old colonies?

A. I think not. I believe very little would come back. I know of no trade likely to bring it back. I think it would come from the Colonies where it was spent directly to England; for I have always observed, that in every Colony the more plenty the means of remittance to England, the more goods are sent for, and the more trade with England carried on....

Q. Do you think the people of America would submit to pay the stamp duty, if it was moderated?

A. No, never, unless compelled by force of arms....

Q. What was the temper of America towards Great Britain before the year 1763?

A. The best in the world. They submitted willingly to the government of the Crown, and paid, in all their courts, obedience to acts of parliament. Numerous as the people are in the several provinces, they cost you nothing in forts, citadels, garrisons, or armies, to keep them in subjection. They are governed by this country at the expense only of a little pen, ink and paper. They were led by a thread. They had not only a respect, but an affection for Great-Britain; for its laws, its customs and manners, and even a fondness for its fashions, that greatly increased the commerce. Natives of Britain were always treated with particular regard; to be an Old-England man was, of itself, a character of some respect, and gave a kind of rank among us.

Q. And what is their temper now?

A. O, very much altered.

Q. Did you ever hear the authority of parliament to make laws for American questioned till lately?

A. The authority of Parliament was allowed to be valid in all laws, except such as should lay internal taxes. It was never disputed in laying duties to regulate commerce....

Q. In what light did the people of America use to consider the parliament of Great-Britain?

A. They considered the parliament as the great bulwark and security of their liberties and privileges, and always spoke of it with the utmost respect and veneration. Arbitrary ministers, they thought, might possibly, at times, attempt to oppress them; but they relied on it, that the parliament, on application, would always give redress. They remembered, with gratitude, a strong instance of this, when a bill was brought into parliament, with a clause, to make royal instructions laws in the colonies, which the House of Commons would not pass, and it was thrown out.

Q. And have they not still the same respect for parliament?

A. No, it is greatly lessened.

Q. To what causes is that owing?

A. To a concurrence of causes; the restraints lately laid on their trade, by which the bringing of foreign gold and silver into the Colonies was prevented; the prohibition of making paper money among themselves; and then demanding a new and heavy tax by stamps; taking away, at the same time, trials by juries, and refusing to receive and hear their humble petitions.

Q. Don't you think they would submit to the stamp-act, if it was modified, the obnoxious parts taken out, and the duty reduced to some particulars, of small moment?

A. No; they will never submit to it....

Q. What is your opinion of a future tax, imposed on the same principle with that of the stamp-act? How would the Americans receive it?

A. Just as they do this. They would not pay it.

Q. Have not you heard of the resolutions of this House, and of the House of Lords, asserting the right of parliament relating to America, including a power to tax the people there?

A. Yes, I have heard of such resolutions.

Q. What will be the opinion of the Americans on those resolutions?

A. They will think them unconstitutional and unjust.

Q. Was it an opinion in America before 1763, that the parliament had no right to lay taxes and duties there?

A. I never heard any objection to the right of laying duties to regulate commerce; but a right to lay internal taxes was never supposed to be in parliament, as we are not represented there....

Q. Can any thing less than a military force carry the stamp act into execution?

A. I do not see how a military force can be applied to the purpose.

Q. Why may it not?

A. Suppose a military force sent into America, they will find nobody in arms; what are they then to do? They cannot force a man to take stamps who chuses to do without them. They will not find a rebellion; they may in deed make one.

Q. If the act is not repealed, what do you think will be in the consequences?

A. A total loss of the respect and affection the people of America bear to this country, and of all the commerce that depends on that respect and affection.

Q. How can the commerce be affected?

A. You will find, that if the act is not repealed, they will take very little of your manufacturers in a short time.

Q. Is it in their power to do without them?

A. I think they may very well do without them....

Q. Don't you know, that there is, in the Pennsylvania charter, an express reservation of the right of parliament to lay taxes there?

A. I know there is a clause in the charter, by which the King grants, that he will levy no taxes on the inhabitants, unless it be with the consent of the assembly, or by act of parliament.

Q. How, then, could the assembly of Pennsylvania assert, that laying a tax on them by the stamp act was an infringement of their rights?

A. They understand it thus; by the same charter, and otherwise, they are entitled to all the privileges and liberties of Englishmen; they find in the great charters, and the petition and declaration of rights, that one of the privileges of English subjects is, that they are not to be taxed but by their common consent; they have therefore replied upon it, from the first settlement of the province, that the parliament never would, nor could, by colour of that clause in the charter, assume a right of taxing them, till it had qualified itself to exercise such right, by admitting representatives from the people to be taxed, who ought to make a part of that common consent.

Q. Are there any words in the chapter that justify that construction?

A. "The common rights of Englishmen," as declared by Magna Charta, and the petition of right, all justify it.

Q. Does the distinction between internal and external taxes exist in the words of the charter?

A. No, I believe not.

Q. Then, may they not, by the same interpretation, object to the parliament's right of external taxation?

A. They never have hitherto. Many arguments have been lately used here to shew them, that there is no difference, and that, if you have no right to tax them internally, you have none to tax them externally, or make any other law to bind them. At present they do not reason so; but in time they may possibly be convinced by these arguments....

Q. What used to be the pride of the Americans?

A. To indulge in the fashions and manufacturers of Great Britain.

Q. What is now their pride?

A. To wear their old cloaths over again, till they can make new ones.

Five African-American Spirituals

Christianity played an important, but complicated, role in African-American slave society. In many ways religion was a site of contestation between slaves and their owners. Slave owners wanted their slaves to be good Christians. However, the lessons they wanted their slaves to draw from their religion were lessons of humility, subservience, and submission. Thus, they attempted to tightly control their slaves' exposure to religious ideas. Slaves, on the other hand, wanted something more from religion. They saw in Christianity models of resistance and inner strength in the face of persecution and enslave-ment. They wanted their religion to belong to them, not to be one more resource grudgingly measured out by their masters.

Source: J. Rosamund Johnson and James Weldon Johnson, eds. *The Book of American Negro Spirituals and The Second Book of Negro Spirituals* (New York: 1925, 1926).

Focus Questions:

1. What parallels might slaves have seen between their own circumstances and those described in the Bible?
2. Should the spirituals included here be considered songs of resistance? Why or why not?

WERE YOU THERE WHEN THEY CRUCIFIED MY LORD?

Were you there, when they crucified my Lord?
Were you there, when they crucified my Lord?
Oh, sometimes, it causes me to tremble, tremble, tremble.
Were you there, when they crucified my Lord?

Were you there, when they nailed him to the tree?
Were you there, when they nailed him to the tree?
Oh, sometimes, it causes me to tremble, tremble, tremble.
Were you there, when they nailed him to the tree?

Were you there, when they pierced him in the side?
Were you there, when they pierced him in the side?
Oh, sometimes, it causes me to tremble, tremble, tremble.
Were you there, when they pierced him in the side?

Were you there, when the sun refused to shine?
Were you there, when the sun refused to shine?
Oh, sometimes, it causes me to tremble, tremble, tremble.
Were you there, when the sun refused to shine?

Were you there, when they laid him in the tomb?
Were you there, when they laid him in the tomb?
Oh, sometimes, it causes me to tremble, tremble, tremble.
Were you there, when they laid him in the tomb?

GO DOWN, MOSES
Go down, Moses,
Way down in Egyptland
Tell old Pharaoh
To let my people go.

When Israel was in Egyptland
Let my people go
Oppressed so hard they could not stand
Let my people go.

Go down, Moses,
Way down in Egyptland
Tell old Pharaoh
"Let my people go."

"Thus saith the Lord," bold Moses said,
"Let my people go;
If not I'll smite your first-born dead
Let my people go.

"No more shall they in bondage toil,
Let my people go;
Let them come out with Egypt's spoil,
Let my people go."

The Lord told Moses what to do
Let my people go;
To lead the children of Israel through,
Let my people go.

Go down, Moses,
Way down in Egyptland,
Tell old Pharaoh,
"Let my people go!"

SWING LOW, SWEET CHARIOT

Swing low, sweet chariot,
Coming for to carry me home,
Swing low, sweet chariot,
Coming for to carry me home.

I looked over Jordan and what did
Coming for to carry me home,
A band of angels, coming after me,
Coming for to carry me home.

If you get there before I do,
Coming for to carry me home,
Tell all my friends I'm coming too,
Coming for to carry me home.

Swing low, sweet chariot,
Coming for to carry me home,
Swing low, sweet chariot,
Coming for to carry me home.

STEAL AWAY TO JESUS

Steal away, steal away, steal away to Jesus,
Steal away, steal away home,
I ain't got long to stay here.

My Lord, He calls me,
He calls me by the thunder,
The trumpet sounds within-a my soul,
I ain't got long to stay here.
Steal away, steal away, steal away to Jesus,
Steal away, steal away home,
I ain't got long to stay here.

Green trees a-bending,
Po' sinner stands a-trembling,
The trumpet sounds within-a my soul,
I ain't got long to stay here.

Steal away, steal away, steal away to Jesus,
Steal away, steal away home,
I ain't got long to stay here.

OH, FREEDOM!

Oh, freedom, Oh, freedom,
Oh, freedom over me!
An' befo' I'd be a slave,
I'll be buried in my grave,
An' go home to my Lord an be free.

No mo' moanin',
No mo' moanin',
No mo' moanin' over me!
An' befo' I'd be a slave,
I'll be buried in my grave,
An' go home to my Lord an' be free.

No mo' weepin',
No mo' weepin',
No mo' weepin' over me!
An' befo' I'd be a slave,
I'll be buried in my grave,
An' go home to my Lord an' be free.

There'll be singin',
There'll be singin',
There'll be singin' over me!
An' befo' I'd be a slave,
I'll be buried in my grave,
An' go home to my Lord an' be free.

There'll be shoutin',
There'll be shoutin',
There'll be shoutin' over me!
An' befo' I'd be a slave,
I'll be buried in my grave,
An' go home to my Lord an' be free.

There'll be prayin', There'll be prayin,
There'll be prayin' over me!
An' befo' I'd be a slave,
I'll be buried in my grave,
An' go home to my Lord an' be free.

Bryan Edwards, Excerpt from "Observations of the... Maroon Negroes of the Island of Jamaica"

This account of the "Maroons" of Jamaica was written by Bryan Edwards (1743–1800), a British merchant in the West Indies, sometime member of Parliament, and supporter of the slave trade, in 1796. It drew on the account of Edward Long (1734–1813), a member of the planter elite in Jamaica, who also commented favorably on the slave trade and slave society in the British Caribbean. Maroon communities of runaway slaves were common in many parts of the Americas, from what would become the Southeastern United States to Brazil, and this document, despite its bias and misunderstanding of the Maroons, describes how colonial powers were forced to make accommodation with a determined group of former slaves. This community, the Accompong Maroons, survives in Jamaica to this day, and the birthday of their leader, "Captain Cudjoe," is still celebrated every 6 January.

Source: Edwards, Bryan, *The History...of the West Indies.* (London: 1807), Vol. 1, Appendix 2, pp. 522–35, 537– 45. (First published separately in 1796.)

Focus Questions:

1. Why were the British forced to make terms with the Maroons?
2. Does the author have a particular interest in maligning the group in this way?
3. How is the author making an argument about civilization and the reversion to a "state of nature" in this community? Is it credible?

CHAPTER FOURTEEN

Observations on the Disposition, Character, Manners, and Habits of Life, of the Maroon Negroes of the Island of Jamaica; and a Detail of the Origin, Progress, and Termination of the late War between those People and the White Inhabitants

Jamaica, as we have seen, was conquered from the Spaniards, during the protectorate of Cromwell, in the year 1655, by an armament under the command of Admiral Penn and General Venables. The Spanish inhabitants are said to have possessed, before the attack, about fifteen hundred enslaved Africans, most of whom, on the surrender of their masters, retreated to the mountains, from whence they made frequent excursions to harass the English. Major-general Sedgewick, one of the British officers, in a letter to Secretary Thurloe (1656) predicts, that these blacks would prove a thorn in the sides of the English. He adds, that they gave no quarter to his men, but destroyed them whenever they found opportunity; scarce a week passing without their murdering one or more of them; and as the soldiers became more confident and careless, the negroes grew more enterprising and bloody-minded. "Having no moral sense," continues he, "and not understanding what the laws and customs of civil nations mean, fifteen hundred acres, bearing north-west from the said Trelawney Town. Fourthly, That they shall have liberty to plant the said lands with coffee, cocoa, ginger, tobacco, and cotton, and to breed cattle, hogs, goats, or any other stock, and dispose of the produce or increase of the said commodities to the inhabitants of this island; provided always, that when they bring the said commodities to market, they shall apply first to the custos, or any other magistrate of the respective parishes where they expose their goods to sale, for a licence to vend the same. Fifthly, That Captain Cudjoe, and all the Captain's adherents, and people now in subjection to him, shall all live together within bounds of Trelawney Town, and that they have liberty to hunt where they shall think fit, except within three miles of any settlement, crawl, or pen; pro-vided always, that in case the hunters of Captain Cudjoe and those of other settlements meet, then the hogs to be equally divided between both parties. Sixthly, That the said Captain Cudjoe, and his successors, do use their best endeavours to take, kill, suppress, or destroy, either by themselves, or jointly with any other number of men, commanded on that service by his Excellency the Governor, or Commander in Chief for the time being, all rebels wheresoever they be, throughout this island, unless they submit to the same terms of accommodation granted to Captain Cudjoe, and his successors. Seventhly, That in case this island be invaded by any foreign enemy, the said Captain Cudjoe, and his successors hereinafter named or to be appointed, shall then, upon notice given, immediately repair to any place the Governor for the time being shall appoint, in order to repel the said invaders with his or their utmost force, and to submit to the orders of the Commander in Chief on that occasion. Eighthly, That if any white man shall do any manner of injury to Captain Cudjoe, his successors, or any of his or their people, they shall apply to any commanding officer or magistrate in the neighbourhood for justice; and in case Captain Cudjoe, or any of his people, shall do any injury to any white person, he shall submit himself, or deliver up such offenders to justice. Ninthly, That if any negro shall hereafter run away from their masters or owners, and fall into Captain Cudjoe's hands, they shall immediately be sent back to the chief magistrate of the next parish where they are taken; and those that bring them are to be satisfied for their trouble, as the legislature shall appoint.[1] Tenth, That all negroes taken, since the raising of this party by Captain Cudjoe's people, shall immediately be returned. Eleventh, That Captain Cudjoe, and his successors, shall wait on his Excellency, or the Commander in Chief for the time being, every year, if thereunto required. Twelfth, That Captain Cudjoe, during his life, and the captains succeeding him, shall have full power to inflict any punishment they think proper for crimes committed by their men among themselves, death only excepted; in which case, if the Captain thinks they deserve death, he shall be obliged to bring them before any justice of the peace, who shall order proceedings on their trial equal to those of other free negroes. Thirteenth, That Captain Cudjoe, with his people, shall cut, clear, and keep open, large and convenient roads from Trelawney Town to Westmorland and St. James's, and if possible to St. Elizabeth's. Fourteenth, That two white men, to be nominated by his Excellency, or the Commander in Chief for the time being, shall constantly live and reside with Captain Cudjoe and his successors, in order to maintain a friendly correspondence with the inhabitants of this island. Fifteenth, That Captain Cudjoe shall, during his life, be Chief Commander in Trelawney Town: after his decease the command to devolve on his brother Captain Accompong; and in case of his decease, on his next brother Captain Johnny; and, failing him, Captain Cuffee shall succeed; who is to be succeeded by Captain Quaco; and after all their demises, the Governor, or Commander in Chief for the time being, shall appoint, from time to time, whom he thinks fit for that command. In testimony, &c. &c…

Concerning the Maroons, they are in general ignorant of our language, and all of them attached to the gloomy superstitions of Africa (derived from their ancestors) with such enthusiastick zeal and reverential ardour, as I think can only be eradicated with their lives. The Gentoos of India are not, I conceive, more sincere in their faith than the negroes of Guinea in believing the prevalence of Obi

1 The Assembly granted a premium of thirty shillings for each fugitive slave returned to his owner by the Maroons, besides expenses.

(a species of pretended magick), and the supernatural power of their Obeah men. Obstacles like these, accompanied with the fierce and sordid manners which I shall presently describe, few clergymen would, I think, be pleased to encounter, lest they might experience all the sufferings, without acquiring the glory of martyrdom.

Under disadvantages of such magnitude was founded the first legal establishment of our Maroon allies in Jamaica. Inured, for a long series of years, to a life of warfare within the island, it is a matter of astonishment that they submitted, for any length of time, to any system of subordination or government whatever. It is probable they were chiefly induced to remain quiet by the great encouragement that was held out to them for the apprehending fugitive slaves, and being allowed to range over the uncultivated country without interruption, possessing an immense wilderness for their hunting grounds. These pursuits gave full employment to the restless and turbulent among them. Their game was the wild boar, which abounds in the interior parts of Jamaica; and the Maroons had a method of curing the flesh without salting it. This commodity they frequently brought to market in the towns; and, with the money arising from the sale, and the rewards which they received for the delivery to their owners of runaway slaves, they purchased salted beef, spirituous liquors, tobacco, firearms, and ammunition, setting little or no account on clothing of any kind, and regarding as superfluous and useless most of those things which every people, in the lowest degree of civilization, would consider as almost absolutely necessary to human existence.

Their language was a barbarous dissonance of the African dialects, with a mixture of Spanish and broken English; and their thoughts and attention seemed wholly engrossed by their present pursuits, and the objects immediately around them, without any reflections on the past, or solicitude for the future. In common with all the nations of Africa, they believed, however, as I have observed, in the prevalence of Obi, and the authority which such of their old men as had the reputation of wizards or Obeah-men, possessed over them, was sometimes very successfully employed in keeping them in subordination to their chiefs.

Having, in the resources that have been mentioned, the means of procuring food for their daily support, they had no inclination for the pursuits of sober industry. Their repugnance to the labour of tilling the earth was remarkable. In some of their villages I never could perceive any vestige of culture; but the situation of their towns, in such cases, was generally in the neighbourhood of plantations belonging to the whites, from the provision grounds of which they either purchased, or stole, yams, plantains, corn, and other esculents. When they had no supply of this kind, I have sometimes observed small patches of Indian corn and yams, and perhaps a few straggling plantain trees, near their habitations; but the ground was always in a shocking state of neglect and ruin.

The labours of the field, however, such as they were (as well as every other species of drudgery), were performed by the women, who had no other means of clearing the ground of the vast and heavy woods with which it is every where incumbered, than by placing fire round the trunks of the trees till they were consumed in the middle, and fell by their own weight. It was a service of danger; but the Maroons, like all other savage nations, regarded their wives as so many beasts of burthen; and felt no more concern at the loss of one of them, than a white planter would have felt at the loss of a bullock. Polygamy too, with their other African customs, prevailed among the Maroons universally. Some of their principal men claimed from two to six wives, and the miseries of their situation left these poor creatures neither leisure nor inclination to quarrel with each other.

This spirit of brutality which the Maroons always displayed towards their wives, extended in some degree to their children. The paternal authority was at all times most harshly exerted; but more especially towards the females. I have been assured, that it was not an uncommon circumstance for a father, in a fit of rage or drunkenness, to seize his own infant, which had offended him by crying, and dash it against a rock, with a degree of violence that often proved fatal. This he did without any apprehension of punishment; for the superintendant, on such occasions, generally found it prudent to keep his distance, or be silent. Nothing can more strikingly demonstrate the forlorn and abject condition of the young women among the Maroons, than the circumstances which every gentleman, who has visited them on festive occasions, or for the gratification of curiosity, knows to be true; the offering their own daughters, by the first men among them, to their visitors; and bringing the poor girls forward, with or without their consent, for the purpose of prostitution.

Visits of this kind were indeed but too acceptable both to the Maroons and their daughters: for they generally ended in drunkenness and riot. The visitors too were not only fleeced of their money, but were likewise obliged to furnish the feast, it being indispensably necessary, on such occasions, to send before-hand wine and provisions of all kinds; and if the guests expected to sleep on beds and in linen, they must provide those articles also for themselves. The Maroons, however, if the party consisted of persons of consequence, would consider themselves as highly honoured, and would supply wild-boar, land-crabs, pigeons, and fish, and entertain their guests with a hearty and boisterous kind of hospitality, which had at least the charms of novelty and singularity to recommend it.

On such occasions, a mock fight always constituted a part of the entertainment. Mr. Long has given the following description of a scene of this kind, which was exhibited by the Trelawney-Town Maroons, in the presence of the Governor, in 1764. "No sooner (he observes) did the horn sound the signal, than they all joined in a most hideous yell, or war-hoop, and bounded into action. With amazing agility they ran, or rather rolled, through their various firings and evolutions. This part of their exercise, indeed, more justly deserves to be styled evolution than any that is practised by the regular troops; for they fire stooping almost to the very ground; and no sooner are their muskets discharged, than they throw them-selves into a thousand antick gestures, and tumble over and over, so as to be continually shifting their place; the intention of which is to elude the shot, as well as to deceive the aim of their adversaries, which their nimble and almost instantaneous change of position renders extremely uncertain. When this part of their exercise was over, they drew their swords; and winding their horn again, began, in wild and war-like gestures, to advance towards his Excellency, endeavouring to throw as much savage fury into their looks as possible. On approaching near him, some waved their rusty blades over his head, then gently laid them upon it; whilst others clashed their arms together in horrid concert. They next brought their muskets, and piled them up in heaps at his feet, &c. &c."…

Alexander Telfair, Instructions to the Overseer of a Cotton Plantation

Alexander Telfair was the son of Edward Telfair, the governor of Georgia and an active participant on the Patriot side in the American Revolution. Telfair took over control of his family's plantations and businesses around 1818, following the deaths of his brothers Josiah and Thomas Telfair. His mansion in Savanna, Georgia, is now a museum.

A large plantation was a complicated operation, involving the coordination of a host of factors and details. In many ways, a plantation was a community unto itself, providing its own food, shelter, and natural resources. At the same time, a large plantation was connected to surrounding plantations, to towns and cities, and to the greater Atlantic world. And, of course, plantations relied on the effective management of its large slave labor force. Such management was the job of the plantation overseer.

Source: Ulrich B. Phillips, "Instructions to an Overseer in a Cotton Plantation," in *Plantation and Frontier 1649–1863,* Vol. I (New York: 1910), pp. 126–129.

Focus Questions:

1. In Telfair's view, what makes a good overseer? What makes a bad one?
2. How much "freedom" did Telfair allow his slaves? What might have motivated him to give his slaves limited mobility and economic autonomy?

Instructions by Alexander Telfair, of Savannah, Ga., to the overseer of his plantation near Augusta, dated June 11, 1832. MS. in the possession of the Georgia

Historical Society, trustee for the Telfair Academy of Arts and Sciences, Savannah.

Rules and directions for my Thorn Island Plantation by which my overseers are to govern themselves in the management of it—ALEXANDER TELFAIR.

(The directions in this book are to be strictly attended to.)

1. The allowance for every grown Negro however old and good for nothing, and every young one that works in the field, is a peck of corn each week, and a pint of salt, and a piece of meat, not exceeding fourteen pounds, per month.

2. No Negro to have more than Fifty lashes inflicted for any offence, no matter how great the crime.

3. The sucking children, and all other small ones who do not work in the field, draw a half allowance of corn and salt.

4. You will give tickets to any of the negroes who apply for them, to go any where about the neighborhood, but do not allow them to go off it without, nor suffer any strange negroes to come on it without a pass.

5. The negroes to be tasked when the work allows it. I require a reasonable days work, well done— the task to be regulated by the state of the ground and the strength of the negro.

6. The cotton to be weighed every night and the weights set down in the Cotton Book. The product of each field to be set down separately—as also the produce of the different corn fields.

7. You will keep a regular journal of the business of the plantation, setting down the names of the sick; the beginning, progress, and finishing of work; the state of the weather; Births, Deaths, and every thing of importance that takes place on the Plantation.

8. You are responsible for the conduct of all persons who visit you. All others found on the premises who have no business, you will take means to run off.

9. Feed every thing plentifully, but waste nothing.

10. The shade trees in the present clearings are not to be touched; and in taking in new ground, leave a thriving young oak or Hickory Tree to every Five Acres.

11. When picking out cotton, do not allow the hands to pull the Boles off the Stalk.

12. All visiting between this place and the one in Georgia is forbidden, except with Tickets from the respective overseers, and that but very seldom. There are none who have husbands or wives over there, and no connexions of the kind are to be allowed to be formed.

13. No night-meeting and preaching to be allowed on the place, except on Saturday night & Sunday morn.

14. Elsey is allowed to act as midwife, to black and white in the neighborhood, who send for her. One of her daughters to stay with the children and take charge of her business until she returns. She draws a peck of corn a week to feed my poultry with.

15. All the Land which is not planted, you will break up in the month of September. Plough it deep so as to turn in all the grass and weeds which it may be covered with.

16. If there is any fighting on the Plantation, whip all engaged in it—for no matter what the cause may have been, all are in the wrong.

17. Elsey is the Doctoress of the Plantation. In case of extraordinary illness, when she thinks she can do no more for the sick, you will employ a Physician.

18. My Cotton is packed in Four and a half yard Bags, weighing each 300 pounds, and the rise of it.

19. Neither the Cotton nor Corn stalks to be burnt, but threshed and chopped down in every field on the plantation, and suffered to lie until ploughed in in the course of working the land.

20. Billy to do the Blacksmith work.

20. [sic] The trash and stuff about the settlement to be gathered in heaps, in broken, wet days to rot; in a word make manure of every thing you can.

21. A Turnip Patch to be planted every year for the use of the Plantation.

22. The Negroes measures for Shoes to be sent down with the name written on each, by my Raft hands, or any other certain conveyance, to me, early in October. All draw shoes, except the children, and those that nurse them.

23. Write me the last day of every month to Savannah, unless otherwise directed. When writing have the Journal before you, and set down in the Letter every thing that has been done, or occurred on the Plantation during the month.

24. Pease to be planted in all the Corn, and plenty sowed for seed.

25. When Picking Cotton in the Hammock and Hickory Ridge, weigh the Tasks in the field, and hawl the Cotton home in the Wagon.

26. The first picking of Cotton to be depended on for seed. Seed sufficient to plant two Crops to be saved, and what is left, not to be thrown out of the Gin House, until you clean it out before beginning to pick out the new Crop.

27. A Beef to be killed for the negroes in July, August and September. The hides

to be tanned at home if you understand it, or put out to be tanned on shares.

28. A Lot to be planted in Rye in September, and seed saved every year. The Cow pens to be moved every month to tread the ground for this purpose.
29. When a Beef is killed, the Fifth quarter except the hide to be given to Elsey for the children.
30. Give the negroes nails when building or repairing their houses when you think they need them.
31. My Negroes are not allowed to plant Cotton for themselves. Every thing else they may plant, and you will give them tickets to sell what they make.
32. I have no Driver. You are to task the negroes yourself, and each negro is responsible to you for his own work, and nobodys else.
33. The Cotton Bags to be marked A. T. and numbered.
34. Heave my Plantation Shot Gun with you.
35. The Corn and Cotton stalks to be cut, and threshed down on the land which lies out to rest, the same as if it was to be planted.

John Adams, *Thoughts on Government*

John Adams (1735-1826) was an important leader in the American Revolution and, in particular, played a major role in the drafting of the Declaration of Independence (1776), the Articles of Confederation, and the Massachusetts constitution (in 1780). Adams initially wrote *Thoughts on Government* as a letter addressed to two of the delegates from North Carolina at the First Continental Congress in 1774 to explain his ideas about how to construct a republican government. A few years later, drafts of this letter were printed as a pamphlet and widely published throughout the thirteen former colonies, greatly influencing how state constitutions, and state governments, in America were set up. Adams remained involved in politics after the founding of America; from 1797 to 1801, he served as the second president of the United States.

Source: *American Political Writings During the Founding Era,* Charles S. Hyneman and Donald S. Lutz, eds., vol. 1, (New York: Liberty Fund Press, 1983) 401-409.

Focus Questions:

1. How does Adams envision the organization and powers of the government?

2. Why? What principles and arguments support his proposals for organization and the distribution of powers in the government?
3. Adams is writing this in 1774 and 1776. How did it reflect debates going on in America in this period? What impact did Adams' ideas have?

My dear Sir,

If I was equal to the task of forming a plan for the government of a colony, I should be flattered with your request, and very happy to comply with it; because, as the divine science of politics is the science of social happiness, and the blessings of society depend entirely on the constitutions of government, which are generally institutions that last for many generations, there can be no employment more agreeable to a benevolent mind than a research after the best.

Pope flattered tyrants too much when he said,

"For forms of government let fools contest, That which is best administered is best."

Nothing can be more fallacious than this. But poets read history to collect flowers, not fruits; they attend to fanciful images, not the effects of social institutions. Nothing is more certain, from the history of nations and nature of man, than that some forms of government are better fitted for being well administered than others.

We ought to consider what is the end of government, before we determine which is the best form. Upon this point all speculative politicians will agree, that the happiness of society is the end of government, as all divines and moral philosophers will agree that the happiness of the individual is the end of man. From this principle it will follow, that the form of government which communicates ease, comfort, security, or, in one word, happiness, to the greatest number of persons, and in the greatest degree, is the best.

All sober inquirers after truth, ancient and modern, pagan and Christian, have declared that the happiness of man, as well as his dignity, consists in virtue. Confucius, Zoroaster, Socrates, Mahomet, not to mention authorities really sacred, have agreed in this.

If there is a form of government, then, whose principle and foundation is virtue, will not every sober man acknowledge it better calculated to promote the general happiness than any other form?

Fear is the foundation of most governments; but it is so sordid and brutal a passion, and renders men in whose breasts it predominates so stupid and miserable, that Americans will not be likely to approve of any political institution which is founded on it.

Honor is truly sacred, but holds a lower rank in the scale of moral excellence than virtue. Indeed, the former is but a part of the latter, and consequently has not equal pretensions to support a frame of government productive of human happiness.

The foundation of every government is some principle or passion in the minds of the people. The noblest principles and most generous affections in our nature, then, have the fairest chance to support the noblest and most generous models of government.

A man must be indifferent to the sneers of modern Englishmen, to mention in their company the names of Sidney, Harrington, Locke, Milton, Nedham, Neville, Burnet, and Hoadly. No small fortitude is necessary to confess that one has read them. The wretched condition of this country, however, for ten or fifteen years past, has frequently reminded me of their principles and reasonings. They will convince any candid mind, that there is no good government but what is republican. That the only valuable part of the British constitution is so; because the very definition of a republic is "an empire of laws, and not of men." That, as a republic is the best of governments, so that particular arrangement of the powers of society, or, in other words, that form of government which is best contrived to secure an impartial and exact execution of the laws, is the best of republics.

Of republics there is an inexhaustible variety, because the possible combinations of the powers of society are capable of innumerable variations.

As good government is an empire of laws, how shall your laws be made? In a large society, inhabiting an extensive country, it is impossible that the whole should assemble to make laws. The first necessary step, then, is to depute power from the many to a few of the most wise and good. But by what rules shall you choose your representatives? Agree upon the number and qualifications of persons who shall have the benefit of choosing, or annex this privilege to the inhabitants of a certain extent of ground.

The principle difficulty lies, and the greatest care should be employed in constituting this representative assembly. It should be in miniature an exact portrait of the people at large. It should think, feel, reason and act like them. That it may be the interest of this assembly to do strict justice at all times, it should be an equal representation, or, in other words, equal interests among the people should have equal interests in it. Great care should be taken to effect this, and to prevent unfair, partial, and corrupt elections. Such regulations, however, may be better made in times of greater tranquillity than the present; and they will spring up themselves naturally, when all the powers of government come to be in the hands of the people's friends. At present, it will be safest to proceed in all established modes, to which the people have been familiarized by habit.

A representation of the people in one assembly being obtained, a question arises, whether all the powers of government, legislative, executive, and judicial, shall be left in this body? I think a people cannot be long free, nor ever happy, whose government is in one assembly. My reasons for this opinion are as follow:—

1. A single assembly is liable to all the vices, follies, and frailties of an individual; subject to fits of humor, starts of passion, flights of enthusiasm, partialities, or prejudice, and consequently productive of hasty results and absurd judgments. And all these errors ought to be corrected and defects supplied by some controlling power.

2. A single assembly is apt to be avaricious, and in time will not scruple to exempt itself from burdens, which it will lay, without compunction, on its constituents.

3. A single assembly is apt to grow ambitious, and after a time will not hesitate to vote itself perpetual. This was one fault of the Long Parliament; but more remarkably of Holland, whose assembly first voted themselves from annual to septennial, then for life, and after a course of years, that all vacancies happening by death or otherwise, should be filled by themselves, without any application to constituents at all.

4. A representative assembly, although extremely well qualified, and absolutely necessary, as a branch of the legislative, is unfit to exercise the executive power, for want of two essential properties, secrecy and despatch.

5. A representative assembly is still less qualified for the judicial power, because it is too numerous, too slow, and too little skilled in the laws.

6. Because a single assembly, possessed of all the powers of government, would make arbitrary laws for their own interest, execute all laws arbitrarily for their own interest, and adjudge all controversies in their own favor.

But shall the whole power of legislation rest in one assembly? Most of the foregoing reasons apply equally to prove that the legislative power ought to be more complex; to which we may add, that if the legislative power is wholly in one assembly, and the executive in another, or in a single person, these two powers will oppose and encroach upon each other, until the contest shall end in war, and the whole power, legislative and executive, be usurped by the strongest.

The judicial power, in such case, could not mediate, or hold the balance between the two contending powers, because the legislative would undermine it. And this shows the necessity, too, of giving the executive power a negative upon the legislative, otherwise this will be continually encroaching upon that.

To avoid these dangers, let a distinct assembly be constituted, as a mediator between the two extreme branches of the legislature, that which represents the people, and that which is vested with the executive power.

Let the representative assembly then elect by ballot, from among themselves or their constituents, or both, a distinct assembly, which, for the sake of perspicuity, we will call a council. It may consist of any number you please, say twenty or thirty, and should have a free and independent exercise of its judgment, and consequently a negative voice in the legislature.

These two bodies, thus constituted, and made integral parts of the legislature, let them unite, and by joint ballot choose a governor, who, after being stripped of most of those badges of domination, called prerogatives, should have a free and independent exercise of his judgment, and be made also an integral part of the legislature. This, I know, is liable to objections; and, if you please, you may make him only president of the council, as in Connecticut. But as the governor is to be invested with the executive power, with consent of council, I think he ought to have a negative upon the legislative. If he is annually elective, as he ought to be, he will always have so much reverence and affection for the people, their representatives and counsellors, that, although you give him an independent exercise of his judgment, he will seldom use it in opposition to the two houses, except in cases the public utility of which would be conspicuous; and some such cases would happen.

In the present exigency of American affairs, when, by an act of Parliament, we are put out of the royal protection, and consequently discharged from our allegiance, and it has become necessary to assume government for our immediate security, the governor, lieutenant-governor, secretary, treasurer, commissary, attorney-general, should be chosen by joint ballot of both houses. And these and all other elections, especially of representatives and counsellors, should be annual, there not being in the whole circle of the sciences a maxim more infallible than this, "where annual elections end, there slavery begins."

These great men, in this respect, should be, once a year,

"Like bubbles on the sea of matter borne, They rise, they break, and to that sea return."

This will teach them the great political virtues of humility, patience, and moderation, without which every man in power becomes a ravenous beast of prey.

This mode of constituting the great offices of state will answer very well for the present; but if by experiment it should be found inconvenient, the legislature may, at its leisure, devise other methods of creating them, by elections of the people at large, as in Connecticut, or it may enlarge the term for which they shall be chosen to seven years, or three years, or for life, or make any other alterations which the society shall find productive of its ease, its safety, its freedom, or, in one word, its happiness.

A rotation of all offices, as well as of representatives and counsellors, has many advocates, and is contended for with many plausible arguments. It would be attended, no doubt, with many advantages; and if the society has a sufficient number of suitable characters to supply the great number of vacancies which would be made by such a rotation, I can see no objection to it. These persons may be allowed to serve for three years, and then be excluded three years, or for any longer or shorter term.

Any seven or nine of the legislative council may be made a quorum, for doing business as a privy council, to advise the governor in the exercise of the executive branch of power, and in all acts of state.

The governor should have the command of the militia and of all your armies. The power of pardons should be with the governor and council.

Judges, justices, and all other officers, civil and military, should be nominated and appointed by the governor, with the advice and consent of council, unless you choose to have a government more popular; if you do, all officers, civil and military, may be chosen by joint ballot of both houses; or, in order to preserve the independence and importance of each house, by ballot of one house, concurred in by the other. Sheriffs should be chosen by the freeholders of counties; so should registers of deeds and clerks of counties.

All officers should have commissions, under the hand of the governor and seal of the colony.

The dignity and stability of government in all its branches, the morals of the people, and every blessing of society depend so much upon an upright and skillful administration of justice, that the judicial power ought to be distinct from both the legislative and executive, and independent upon both, that so it may be a check upon both, as both should be checks upon that. The judges, therefore, should be always men of learning and experience in the laws, of exemplary morals, great patience, calmness, coolness, and attention. Their minds should not be distracted with jarring interests; they should not be dependent upon any man, or body of men. To these ends, they should hold estates for life in their offices; or, in other words, their commissions should be during good behavior, and their salaries ascertained and established by law. For misbehavior, the grand inquest of the colony, the house of representatives, should impeach them before the governor and council, where they should have time and opportunity to make their defence; but, if convicted, should be removed from their offices, and subjected to such other punishment as shall be proper.

A militia law, requiring all men, or with very few exceptions besides cases of conscience, to be provided with arms and ammunition, to be trained at certain seasons; and requiring counties, towns, or other small districts, to

be provided with public stocks of ammunition and entrenching utensils, and with some settled plans for transporting provisions after the militia, when marched to defend their country against sudden invasions; and requiring certain districts to be provided with fieldpieces, companies of matrosses, and perhaps some regiments of light-horse, is always a wise institution, and, in the present circumstances of our country, indispensable.

Laws for liberal education of youth, especially of the lower class of people, are so extremely wise and useful, that, to a humane and generous mind, no expense for this purpose would be thought extravagant.

The very mention of sumptuary laws will excite a smile. Whether our countrymen have wisdom and virtue enough to submit to them, I know not; but the happiness of the people might be greatly promoted by them, and a revenue saved sufficient to carry on this war forever. Frugality is a great revenue, besides curing us of vanities, levities, and fopperies, which are real antidotes to all great, manly, and warlike virtues.

But must not all commissions run in the name of a king? No. Why may they not as well run thus, "The colony of to A. B. greeting," and be tested by the governor?

Why may not writs, instead of running in the name of the king, run thus, "The colony of to the sheriff," &c., and be tested by the chief justice?

Why may not indictments conclude, "against the peace of the colony of and the dignity of the same?"

A constitution founded on these principles introduces knowledge among the people, and inspires them with a conscious dignity becoming freemen; a general emulation takes place, which causes good humor, sociability, good manners, and good morals to be general. That elevation of sentiment inspired by such a government, makes the common people brave and enterprising. That ambition which is inspired by it makes them sober, industrious, and frugal. You will find among them some elegance, perhaps, but more solidity; a little pleasure, but a great deal of business; some politeness, but more civility. If you compare such a country with the regions of domination, whether monarchical or aristocratical, you will fancy yourself in Arcadia or Elysium.

If the colonies should assume governments separately, they should be left entirely to their own choice of the forms; and if a continental constitution should be formed, it should be a congress, containing a fair and adequate representation of the colonies, and its authority should sacredly be confined to those cases, namely, war, trade, disputes between colony and colony, the post-office, and the unappropriated lands of the crown, as they used to be called.

These colonies, under such forms of government, and in such a union, would be unconquerable by all the monarchies of Europe.

You and I, my dear friend, have been sent into life at a time when the greatest lawgivers of antiquity would have wished to live. How few of the human race have ever enjoyed an opportunity of making an election of government, more than of air, soil, or climate, for themselves or their children! When, before the present epocha, had three millions of people full power and a fair opportunity to form and establish the wisest and happiest government that human wisdom can contrive? I hope you will avail yourself and your country of that extensive learning and indefatigable industry which you possess, to assist her in the formation of the happiest governments and the best character of a great people. For myself, I must beg you to keep my name out of sight; for this feeble attempt, if it should be known to be mine, would oblige me to apply to myself those lines of the immortal John Milton, in one of his sonnets:—

"I did but prompt the age to quit their clogs By the known rules of ancient liberty, When straight a barbarous noise environs me Of owls and cuckoos, asses, apes, and dogs."

CHAPTER 16

The Enlightenment

Baron de Montesquieu, Excerpt from *The Spirit of the Laws*

Baron de Montesquieu, Charles-Louis de Secondat (1689–1755 CE), French judge, author, and political thinker. Born to a noble family near Bordeaux, Montesquieu studied law and served in the Bordeaux parliament, or court. He gained celebrity in 1721 with the publication of Persian Letters. He attended various Parisian salons and traveled throughout Europe, including England. He drew on these experiences for his greatest work, *The Spirit of the Laws*, which argued that a "balance of powers" is necessary for good government, and noted that the form of government derives from the political and social circumstances of a country. This treatise on the nature of law and government influenced Enlightenment intellectuals throughout Europe and America.

Source: Baron de Montesquieu, Charles-Louis de Secondat, *The Spirit of the Laws.*

Focus Questions:

1. What does Montesquieu think about the sources of information regarding China's government?
2. According to Montesquieu, what roles do climate and famine play in the nature of Chinese government?

21. Of the Empire of China. Before I conclude this book, I shall answer an objection that may be made to the foregoing doctrine.

Our missionaries inform us that the government of the vast empire of China is admirable, and that it has a proper mixture of fear, honour, and virtue. Consequently I must have given an idle distinction in establishing the principles of the three governments.

But I cannot conceive what this honour can be among a people who act only through fear of being bastinadoed.

Again, our merchants are far from giving us any such accounts of the virtue so much talked of by the missionaries; we need only consult them in relation to the robberies and extortions of the mandarins. I likewise appeal to another unexceptional witness, the great Lord Anson.

Besides, Father Perennin's letters concerning the emperor's proceedings against some of the princes of the blood who had incurred his displeasure by their conversion, plainly show us a settled plan of tyranny, and barbarities committed by rule, that is, in cold blood.

We have likewise Monsieur de Mairan's, and the same Father Perennin's, letters on the government of China. I find therefore that after a few proper questions and answers the whole mystery is unfolded. Might not our missionaries have been deceived by an appearance of order? Might not they have been struck with that constant exercise of a single person's will—an exercise by which they themselves are governed, and which they are so pleased to find in the courts of the Indian princes; because as they go thither only in order to introduce great changes, it is much easier to persuade those princes that there are no bounds to their power, than to convince the people that there are none to their submission.

In fine, there is frequently some kind of truth even in errors themselves. It may be owing to particular and, perhaps, very extraordinary circumstances that the Chinese government is not so corrupt as one might naturally expect. The climate and some other physical causes may, in that country, have had so strong an influence on their morals as in some measure to produce wonders.

The climate of China is surprisingly favourable to the propagation of the human species. The women are the most prolific in the whole world. The most barbarous tyranny can put no stop to the progress of propagation. The prince cannot say there like Pharaoh, "Let us deal wisely with them, lest they multiply." He would be rather reduced to Nero's wish, that mankind had all but one head. In spite of tyranny, China by the force of its climate will be ever populous, and triumph over the tyrannical oppressor.

China, like all other countries that live chiefly upon rice, is subject to frequent famines. When the people are ready to starve, they disperse in order to seek for nourishment; in consequence of which, gangs of robbers are formed on every side. Most of them are extirpated in their very infancy; others swell, and are likewise suppressed. And yet in so great a number of such distant provinces, some band or other may happen to meet with success. In that case they maintain their ground, strengthen their party, form themselves into a military body, march up to the capital, and place their leader on the throne.

From the very nature of things, a bad administration is here immediately punished. The want of subsistence in so populous a country produces sudden disorders. The reason why the redress of abuses in other countries is attended with such difficulty is because their effects are not immediately felt; the prince is not informed in so sudden and sensible a manner as in China.

The Emperor of China is not taught like our princes that if he governs ill he will be less happy in the other life, less powerful and less opulent in this. He knows that if his government be not just he will be stripped both of empire and life.

As China grows every day more populous, notwithstanding the exposing of children, the inhabitants are incessantly employed in tilling the lands for their subsistence. This requires a very extraordinary attention in the government. It is their perpetual concern that every man should have it in his power to work, without the apprehension of being deprived of the fruits of his labour. Consequently this is not so much a civil as a domestic government.

Such has been the origin of those regulations which have been so greatly extolled. They wanted to make the laws reign in conjunction with despotic power; but whatever is joined to the latter loses all its force. In vain did this arbitrary sway, labouring under its own inconveniences, desire to be fettered; it armed itself with its chains, and has become still more terrible.

China is therefore a despotic state, whose principle is fear. Perhaps in the earliest dynasties, when the empire had not so large an extent, the government might have deviated a little from this spirit; but the case is otherwise at present.

Marquis de Condorcet, passage from *Sketch for a Historical Picture of the Progress of the Human Mind*

Marie Jean Antoine Nicolas de Caritat, Marquis de Condorcet (1743–1794 CE), French Enlightenment philosopher and aristocrat. Condorcet published several important works on mathematics, such as *Essay on the Application of Analysis to the Probability of Majority Decisions* (1785). He knew many Enlightenment figures, such as Diderot, Voltaire, and the finance minister Turgot. Condorcet supported the Revolution in 1789, and, although a republican, he opposed the execution of King Louis XVI. While in hiding because of his opposition to Robespierre's radical policies, he wrote *Sketch for a Historical Picture of the Progress of the Human Mind*. Eventually Condorcet was captured and put in prison, where he was found dead. His tragic end contrasts with the hopeful vision of human perfectibility set forth in his sketch.

Source: Marie Jean Antoine Nicolas de Caritat, Marquis de Condorcet, *Esquisse d'un Tableau Historique de Progrès del'Esprit Humain*, (Paris: Masson et Fils, 1822), pp. 279-85, 293-94, 303-5.

Focus Questions:

1. What is Condorcet's attitude toward industrialization and mechanization?
2. How does he view relations between the sexes, the development of medicine, and the increase of population?

No one has ever believed that the human mind could exhaust all the facts of nature, all the refinements of measuring and analyzing these facts, the inter relationship of objects, and all the possible combinations of ideas...

But because, as the number of facts known increases, man learns to classify them, to reduce them to more general terms; because the instruments and the methods of observation and exact measurement are at the same time reaching a new precision...the truths whose discovery has cost the most effort, which at first could be grasped only by men capable of profound thought, are soon carried further and proved by methods that are no longer beyond the reach of ordinary intelligence. If the methods that lead to new combinations are exhausted, if their application to problems not yet solved requires labors that exceed the time or the capacity of scholars, soon more general methods, simpler means, come to open a new avenue for genius...

Applying these general reflections to the different sciences, we shall give, for each, examples of their successive improvement that will leave no doubt as to the certainty of the future improvements we can expect. We shall indicate particularly the most likely and most imminent progress in those sciences that are now commonly believed to be almost exhausted. We shall point out how more universal education in each country, by giving more people the elementary knowledge that can inspire them with a taste for more advanced study and give them the capacity for making progress in it, can add to such hopes; how [these hopes] increase even more, if a more general prosperity permits a greater number of individuals to pursue studies, since at present, in the most enlightened countries, hardly a fiftieth part of those men to whom nature has given talent receive the education necessary to make use of their talents; and that, therefore, the number of men destined to push back the frontiers of the sciences by their discoveries will grow in the same proportion [as universal education increases].

We shall show how this equality of education, and the equality that will arise between nations, will speed up the advances of those sciences whose progress depends on observations repeated in greater number over a larger area; all that mineralogy, botany, zoology, meteorology can be expected to gain thereby; and finally what an enormous disproportion exists, in these sciences, between the weakness of the means that nevertheless have led us to so many useful and important truths, and the great scope of the means men will in the future be able to deploy.

If we now turn to the mechanical arts, we shall see that their progress can have no other limit than the reach of the scientific theories on which they depend; that the methods of these arts are capable of the same improvement, the same simplifications as methods in the sciences. Instruments, machines, looms will increasingly supplement the strength and skill of men; will augment at the same time the perfection and the precision of manufactures by lessening both the time and the labor needed to produce them. Then the obstacles that still impede this progress will disappear, and along with them accidents that will become preventable and unhealthy conditions in general, whether owing to work, or habits, or climate.

Then a smaller and smaller area of land will be able to produce commodities of greater use or higher value; wider enjoyment will be obtained with less outlay; the same manufacturing output will call for less expenditure of raw materials or will be more durable. For each kind of soil people will know how to choose, from among crops that satisfy the same kind of need, those crops that are most versatile, those that satisfy [the needs on a greater mass of users], requiring less labor and less real consumption. Thus, without any sacrifice, the methods of conservation and of economy in consumption will follow the progress of the art of producing the various commodities, preparing them and turning them into manufactures.

Thus not only will the same amount of land be able to feed more people; but each of them, with less labor, will be employed more productively and will be able to satisfy his needs better.

... But in this progress of industry and prosperity...each generation...is destined to fuller enjoyment; and hence, as a consequence of the physical constitution of the human species, to an increase of the population. Will there not come a time when...the increase in population surpassing its means of subsistence, the result would necessarily be–if not a continuous decline in wellbeing and number of people, a truly retrograde movement–at least a kind of oscillation between good and bad? Would not such oscillations in societies that have reached this point be an ever-present cause of more or less periodic suffering? Would this not mark the limit beyond which all improvement would become impossible...?

No one will fail to see how far removed from us this time is; but will we reach it one day? It is impossible to speak for or against an event that will occur only at a time when the human species will necessarily have acquired knowledge that we cannot even imagine. And who, in fact, would dare to predict what the art of converting the elements to our use may one day become?

But supposing a limit were reached, nothing terrible would happen, regarding either the happiness or the indefinite perfectibility of mankind. We must also suppose that before that time, the progress of reason will have gone hand in hand with progress in the arts and sciences; that the ridiculous prejudices of superstition will no longer cover morality with an austerity that corrupts and degrades it instead of purifying and elevating it. Men will know then that if they have obligations to beings who do not yet exist, these obligations do not consist in giving life, but in giving happiness. Their object is the general welfare of the human species, of the society in which people live, of the family to which they belong and not the puerile idea of filling the earth with useless and unhappy beings. The possible quantity of the means of subsistence could therefore have a limit, and consequently so could the attainable level of population, without resulting in the destruction...of part of the living.

Among the progress of the human mind that is most important for human happiness, we must count the entire destruction of the prejudices that have established inequality between the sexes, fatal even to the sex it favors. One would look in vain for reasons to justify it, by differences in physical constitution, intelligence, moral sensibility. This inequality has no other source but the abuse of power, and men have tried in vain to excuse it by sophisms.

We shall show how much the destruction of customs authorized by this prejudice, of the laws it has dictated, can contribute to the greater happiness of families, and to the spread of the domestic virtues, the first foundation of all other virtues. It will promote the progress of education, because [education] will be extended to both sexes more equally, and because education cannot become general, even among men, without the cooperation of mothers.

* * *

All these causes of the improvement of the human species, all these means that assure it, will by their nature act continuously and acquire a constantly growing momentum.

We have explained the proofs of this...we could therefore already conclude that the perfectibility of man is unlimited, even though, up to now, we have only supposed him endowed with the same natural faculties and organization. What then would be the certainty and extent of our hopes if we could believe that these natural faculties themselves and this organization are also susceptible of improvement? This is the last question remaining for us to examine.

The organic perfectibility or degeneration of races in plants and animals may be regarded as one of the general laws of nature.

This law extends to the human species; and certainly no one will doubt that progress in medical conservation [of life], in the use of healthier food and housing, a way of living that would develop strength through exercise without impairing it by excess, and finally the destruction of the two most active causes of degradation–misery and too great wealth–will prolong the extent of life and assure people more constant health as well as a more robust constitution. We feel that the progress of preventive medicine as a preservative, made more effective by the progress of reason and social order, will eventually banish communicable or contagious illnesses and those diseases in general that originate in climate, food, and the nature of work. It would not be difficult to prove that this hope should extend to almost all other diseases, whose more remote causes will eventually be recognized. Would it be absurd now to suppose that the improvement of the human race should be regarded as capable of unlimited progress? That a time will come when death would result only from extraordinary accidents or the more and more gradual wearing out of vitality, and that, finally, the duration of the average interval between birth and wearing out has itself no specific limit whatsoever? No doubt man will not become immortal, but cannot the span constantly increase between the moment he begins to live and the time when naturally, without illness or accident, he finds life a burden?

Catherine the Great, "Instructions for a New Law Code"

Catherine the Great (1729-1796) was a German princess who became the empress of Russia after the death of her husband, Tsar Peter III in 1762 and ruled Russia for 34 years. Influenced by Enlightenment and inspired by the ideas of the *philosophes*, Catherine convened a commission in Moscow to write a new law code and a constitution for Russia in 1767. This commission included representatives from all social classes, except for the serfs (lower peasantry), and from all regions of Russia. Catherine's goal was to create a code of law and a constitution based on Enlightenment legal and judicial principles such as those outlined by Montesquieu, Beccaria, and Rousseau. This commission, however, quickly became consumed with debates as it could not agree on important issues such as whether or not to abolish serfdom. When Russia went to war against Turkey (1768-1774), the commission disbanded. It never reconvened and the law code was never enacted. The document below contains excerpts of instructions for writing of the law code and constitution, written by Catherine and given to the commission when they convened.

Source: "The Instruction to the Commissioners for Composing a New Code of Laws," in *Documents of Catherine the Great: The Correspondence with Voltaire and the Instruction in 1767, in the English Text of 1768*, ed. W. F. Reddaway (Cambridge: Cambridge University Press, 1931), 215-94.

FOCUS QUESTIONS:

1. Why did Catherine convene this commission and what were the main elements of this new law code and constitution that she envisioned?
2. Why might these instructions be rejected by the commission, or difficult to implement?
3. How did these instructions reflect Enlightenment ideas and principles?

1. The Christian Law teaches us to do mutual Good to one another, as much as possibly we can.
2. Laying this down as a fundamental Rule prescribed by that Religion, which has taken, or ought to take Root in the Hearts of the whole People; we cannot but suppose, that every honest Man in the Community is, or will be, desirous of seeing his native Country at the very Summit of Happiness, Glory, Safety, and Tranquillity.
3. And that every Individual Citizen in particular must wish to see himself protected by Laws, which should not distress him in his Circumstances, but, on the Contrary, should defend him from all Attempts of others, that are repugnant to this fundamental Rule.

* * *

6. Russia is a European State.
7. This is clearly demonstrated by the following Observations: The Alterations which Peter the Great undertook in Russia succeeded with the greater Ease, because the Manners, which prevailed at that Time, and had been introduced amongst us by a Mixture of different Nations, and the Conquest of foreign Territories, were quite unsuitable to the Climate. Peter the First, by introducing the Manners and Customs of Europe among the European People in his Dominions, found at that Time such means as even he himself was not sanguine enough to expect....
9. The Sovereign is absolute; for there is no other Authority but that which centers in his single person, that can act with a vigour proportionate to the Extent of such a vast Dominion.
10. The Extent of the Dominion requires an absolute Power to be vested in that Person who rules over it. It is expedient so to be, that the quick Dispatch of Affairs, sent from distant Paris, might make ample Amends for the Delay occasioned by the great Distance of the Places.
11. Every other Form of Government whatsoever would not only have been prejudicial to Russia, but would even have proved its entire Ruin.

12. Another Reason is: That it is better to be subject to the Laws under one Master, than to be subservient to many.

13. What is the true End of Monarchy? Not to deprive People of their natural Liberty; but to correct their Actions, in order to attain the supreme Good.

* * *

15. The Intention and the End of Monarchy, is the Glory of the Citizens, of the State, and of the Sovereign.

16. But, from this Glory, a Sense of Liberty arises in a People governed by a Monarch; which may produce in these States as much Energy in transacting the most important Affairs, and may contribute as much to the Happiness of the Subjects, as even Liberty itself....

33. The Laws ought to be so framed, as to secure the Safety of every Citizen as much as possible.

34. The Equality of the Citizens consists in this; that they should all be subject to the same Laws.

35. This Equality requires Institutions so well adapted, as to prevent the Rich from oppressing those who are not so wealthy as themselves, and converting all the Charges and Employments intrusted to them as Magistrates only, to their own private Emolument....

* * *

38. A Man ought to form in his own Mind an-exact and clear Idea of what Liberty is. Liberty is the Right of doing whatsoever the Laws allow: And if any one Citizen could do what the Laws forbid, there would be no more Liberty; because others would have an equal Power of doing the same.

* * *

41. Nothing ought to be forbidden by the Laws, but what may be prejudicial, either to every Individual in particular, or to the whole Community in general.

* * *

193. The Torture of the Rack is a Cruelty established and made use of by many Nations, and is applied to the Party accused during the Course of his Trial, either to extort from him a Confession of his Guilt, or in order to clear up some Contradictions in which he had involved himself during his Examination, or to compel him to discover his Accomplices, or in order to discover other Crimes, of which, though he is not accused, yet he may perhaps be guilty.

194. (1) No Man ought to be looked upon as guilty before he has received his judicial Sentence; nor can the Laws deprive him of their Protection before it is proved that he has forfeited all Right to it. What Right therefore can Power give to any to inflict Punishment upon a Citizen at a Time when it is yet dubious whether he is innocent or guilty?

* * *

The Party accused on the Rack, whilst in the Agonies of Torture, is not Master enough of himself to be able to declare the Truth. Can we give more Credit to a Man when he is lightheaded in a Fever, than when he enjoys the free Use of his Reason in a State of Health? The Sensation of Pain may arise to such a Height that, after having subdued the whole Soul, it will leave her no longer the Liberty of producing any proper Act of the Will, except that of taking the shortest instantaneous Method, in the very twinkling of an Eye, as it were, of getting rid of her Torment. In such an Extremity, even an innocent Person will roar out that he is guilty, only to gain some Respite from his Tortures. Thus the very same Expedient, which is made use of to distinguish the Innocent from the Guilty, will take away the whole Difference between them; and the Judges will be as uncertain whether they have an innocent or a guilty Person before them, as they were before the Beginning of this partial Way of Examination. The Rack, therefore, is a sure Method of condemning an innocent person of a weakly Constitution, and of acquitting a wicked Wretch, who depends upon the Robustness of his Frame.

* * *

220. A Punishment ought to be immediate, analogous to the Nature of the Crime, and known to the Public.

221. The sooner the Punishment succeeds to the Commission of a Crime, the more useful and just it will be. Just; because it will spare the Malefactor the torturing and useless Anguish of Heart about the Uncertainty of his Destiny. Consequently the Decision of an Affair, in a Court of Judicature, ought to be finished in as little Time as possible. I have said before that Punishment immediately inflicted is most useful; the Reason is because the smaller the Interval of Time is which passes between the Crime and the Punishment, the more the Crime will be esteemed as a Motive to the Punishment, and the Punishment as an Effect of the Crime. Punishment must be certain and unavoidable.

222. The most certain Curb upon Crimes is not the Severity of the Punishment, but the absolute Conviction in the People that Delinquents will be inevitably punished....

* * *

250. A Society of Citizens, as well as every Thing else, requires a certain fixed Order: There ought to be some to govern, and others to obey.

* * *

252. And, consequently, as the Law of Nature commands Us to take as much Care, as lies in Our Power, of the Prosperity of all the People; we are obliged to alleviate the Situation of the Subjects, as much as sound Reason will permit.

253. And therefore, to shun all Occasions of reducing People to a State of Slavery, except the utmost Necessity should inevitably oblige us to do it; in that Case, it ought not to be done for our own Benefit; but for the Interest of the State: Yet even that Case is extremely uncommon.

* * *

264. Of the Propagation of the human Species in a State.

265. Russia is not only greatly deficient in the number of her Inhabitants; but at the same Time, extends her Dominion over immense Tracts of Land; which are neither peopled nor improved. And therefore, in a Country so circumstanced, too much Encouragement can never be given to the Propagation of the human Species.

266. The Peasants Generally have twelve, fifteen, and even twenty Children by one Marriage; but it rarely happens that one Fourth of these ever attains to the Age of Maturity. There must therefore be some Fault, either in their Nurture, in their Way of Living, or Method of Education, which occasions this prodigious Loss, and disappoints the Hopes of the Empire. How flourishing would the State of this Empire be if we could but ward off, or prevent this fatal Evil by proper Regulations!

* * *

313. Agriculture is the first and principal Labour, which ought to be encouraged in the People: The next is, the manufacturing our own Produce.

314. Machines, which serve to shorten Labour in the mechanick Arts, are not always useful. If a Piece of Work, wrought with the Hands, can be afforded at a Price, equally advantageous to the Merchant and the Manufacturer; in this Case, Machines which shorten Labour, that is, which diminish the Number of Workmen, will be greatly prejudicial to a populous Country.

315. Yet, we ought to distinguish between what we manufacture for our Home-consumption, and what we manufacture for Exportation into foreign Countries.

316. Too much Use cannot be made of this Kind of Machines in our Manufactures, which we export to other Nations; who do, or may receive the same Kind of Goods, from our Neighbours, or other People; especially those who are in the same Situation with ourselves.

317. Commerce flies from Places where it meets with Oppression, and settles where it meets with Protection.

* * *

356. Every one ought to inculcate the Fear of God into the tender Minds of Children, to encourage every laudable Inclination, and to accustom them to the fundamental Rules, suitable to their respective Situations; to incite in them a Desire for Labour, and a Dread of Idleness, as the Root of all Evil, and Error; to train them up to a proper Decorum in their Actions and Conversation, Civility, and Decency in their Behaviour; and to sympathise with the Miseries of poor unhappy Wretches; and to break them of all perverse and forward Humours; to teach them Oeconomy, and whatever is most useful in all Affairs of Life; to guard them against all Prodigality and Extravagance; and particularly to root a proper Love of Cleanliness and Neatness, as well in themselves as in those who belong to them; in a Word, to instill all those Virtues and Qualities, which join to form a good Education; by which, as they grow up, they may prove real Citizens, useful Members of the Community, and Ornaments to their Country.

357. Of the Nobility.

358. The Husbandmen, who cultivate the Lands to produce Food for People in every Rank of Life, live in Country Towns and Villages. This is their Lot.

359. The Burghers, who employ their Time in mechanick Trades, Commerce, Arts, and Sciences, inhabit the Cities.

360. Nobility is an Appellation of Honour, which distinguishes all those who are adorned with it from every other Person of inferior Rank.

* * *

363. Virtue with Merit raises People to the Rank of Nobility.

364. Virtue and Honour ought to be the Rules, which prescribe Love for their Country, Zeal for its Service, Obedience and Fidelity to their Sovereign; and continually suggest, never to be guilty of an infamous Action.

* * *

376. Of the middling Sort of People.

* * *

378. This Sort of People, of whom we ought now to speak, and from whom the State expects much Benefit, are admitted into the Middling Rank, if their Qualifications are firmly established upon Good Manners, and Incitements to Industry.

379. People of this Rank will enjoy a State of Liberty, without intermixing either with the Nobility or the Husbandmen.

* * *

381. Besides these, all those, who are not of the Nobility, but have been educated in Schools or Colleges, of what Denomination so ever, ecclesiastical or civil, founded by Us and Our Ancestors:

382. Also the Children of People belonging to the Law. But as in that third Species, there are different Degrees of Privilege, therefore we shall not enter into a Detail of Particulars; but only open the Way for a due Consideration of it.

383. As the whole Qualification, which in titles People to this middling Rank, is founded upon good Manners and Industry; the Violation of these Rules will serve, on the Contrary, for their Exclusion from it; as for Instance, Perfidiousness and Breach of Promise, especially if caused by Idleness and Treachery.

Cesare Beccaria, *On Crimes and Punishments*

Born into a noble family in Milan, Cesare Beccaria (1739-1794) received a traditional Jesuit, Roman Catholic education, yet also read and studied the works of Enlightenment authors such as Voltaire and Montesquieu. Beccaria published this treatise calling for judicial and legal reforms anonymously, in Tuscany, in 1764. Immediately following its initial printing, it was translated into several different languages and published throughout Europe. In *On Crimes and Punishment*, Beccaria argued that the laws governing society should do the greatest good for the greatest number of people (utilitarian philosophy). He also believed that laws should not be viewed as emanating from God or a divine power, but instead should be seen as in accordance with the laws of nature. For Beccaria, punishments should be devised to deter crime, not in retribution for crimes committed. In this passage, he discusses torture, which, with the exception of Great Britain, was widely used in court systems throughout Europe.

Source: E. D. Ingraham, trans., Cesare Beccaria,"The Greatest Happiness of the Greatest Number," *An Essay on Crimes and Punishments* (Philadelphia: H. Nicklin, 1819), pp. xii, 18–19, 47, 59–60, 93–94, 104– 105, 148–149.

Focus Questions:

1. According to Beccaria, what were the origins of the use of torture in Europe?
2. What arguments does Beccaria make against the use of torture? What examples or evidence does he give to support his arguments?
3. What Enlightenment ideas and influences are present in this treatise?

XII Torture

A cruelty consecrated by the practice of most nations is torture of the accused during his trial, either to make him confess the crime or to clear up contradictory statements, or to discover accomplices, or to purge him of infamy in some metaphysical and incomprehensible way, or, finally, to discover other crimes of which he might be guilty but of which he is not accused.

No man can be called guilty before a judge has sentenced him, nor can society deprive him of public protection before it has been decided that he has in fact violated the conditions under which such protection was accorded him. What right is it, then, if not simply that of might, which empowers a judge to inflict punishment on a citizen while doubt still remains as to his guilt or innocence? Here is the dilemma, which is nothing new: the fact of the crime is either certain or uncertain; if certain, all that is due is the punishment established by the laws, and tortures are useless because the criminal's confession is useless; if uncertain, then one must not torture the innocent, for such, according to the laws, is a man whose crimes are not yet proved.

What is the political intent of punishment? To instill fear in other men. But what justification can we find, then, for the secret and private tortures which the tyranny of custom practices on the guilty and the innocent? It is important, indeed, to let no known crime pass unpunished, but it is useless to reveal the author of a crime that lies deeply buried in darkness. A wrong already committed, and for which there is no remedy, ought to be punished by political society only because it might otherwise excite false hopes of impunity in others. If it be true that a greater number of men, whether because of fear or virtue, respect the laws than break them, then the risk of torturing an innocent person should be considered greater when, other things being equal, the probability is greater that a man has rather respected the laws than despised them.

But I say more: it tends to confound all relations to require that a man be at the same time accuser and accused, that pain be made the crucible of truth, as if its criterion lay in the muscles and sinews of a miserable wretch.

The law that authorizes torture is a law that says: "Men, resist pain; and if nature has created in you an inextinguishable self-love, if it has granted you an inalienable right of self-defense, I create in you an altogether contrary sentiment: a heroic hatred of yourselves, to speak the truth even while muscles are being lacerated and bones disjointed."

This infamous crucible of truth is a still-standing memorial of the ancient and barbarous legislation of a time when trials by fire and by boiling water, as well as the uncertain outcomes of duels, were called "judgments of God," as if the links of the eternal chain, which is in the bosom of the First Cause, must at every moment be disordered and broken by frivolous human arrangements. The only difference between torture and trials by fire and boiling water is that the outcome seems to depend, in that first, on the will of the accused, and in the second, on a purely physical and extrinsic fact; but this difference is only apparent, not real. One is as much free to tell the truth in the midst of convulsions and torments, as one was free then to impede without fraud the effects of fire and boiling water. Every act of our will is invariably proportioned to the force of the sensory impression which is its source; and the sensory capacity of every man is limited. Thus the impression of pain may become so great that, filling the entire sensory capacity of the tortured person, it leaves him free only to choose what for the moment is the shortest way of escape from pain. The response of the accused is then as inevitable as the impressions of fire and water. The sensitive innocent man will then confess himself guilty when he believes that, by so doing, he can put an end to his torment. Every difference between guilt and innocence disappears by virtue of the very means one pretends to be using to discover it. [Torture] is an infallible means indeed – for absolving robust scoundrels and for condemning innocent persons who happen to be weak. Such are the fatal defects of this so-called criterion of truth, a criterion fit for a cannibal, which the Romans, who were barbarous themselves on many counts, reserved only for slaves, the victims of a fierce and overly praised virtue.

Of two men, equally innocent or equally guilty, the strong and courageous will be acquitted, the weak and timid condemned, by virtue of this rigorous rational argument: "I, the judge, was supposed to find you guilty of such and such a crime; you, the strong, have been able to resist the pain, and I therefore absolve you; you, the weak, have yielded, and I therefore condemn you. I am aware that a confession wrenched forth by torments ought to be of no weight whatsoever, but I'll torment you again if you don't confirm what you have confessed."

The effect of torture, therefore, is a matter of temperament and calculation that varies with each man according to his strength and sensibility, so that, with this method, a mathematician could more readily than a judge resolve this problem: given the muscular force and nervous sensibility of an innocent person, find the degree of pain that will make him confess himself guilty of a given crime.

The examination of an accused person is undertaken to ascertain the truth. But if this truth is difficult to discover in the air, gesture, and countenance of a man at ease, much more difficult will its discovery be when the convulsions of pain have distorted all the signs by which truth reveals itself in spite of themselves in the countenances of the majority of men. Every violent action confounds and dissolves those little differences in objects by means of which one may occasionally distinguish the true from the false.

A strange consequence that necessarily follows from the use of torture is that the innocent person is placed in a condition worse than that of the guilty, for if both are tortured, the circumstances are all against the former. Either he confesses the crime and is condemned, or he is declared innocent and has suffered a punishment he did not deserve. The guilty man, on the contrary, finds himself in a favorable situation; that is, if, as a consequence of having firmly resisted the torture, he is absolved as innocent, he will have escaped a greater punishment by enduring a lesser one. Thus the innocent cannot but lose, whereas the guilty may gain.

This truth is felt, finally though confusedly, by those very persons who shrink furthest from it in practice. The confession made under torture is of no avail if it be not confirmed with an oath after the torture has stopped, but if the accused does not then confirm the crime, he is again tortured. Some jurists, and some nations, allow this infamous begging of principles to be repeated no more than three times; other nations, and other jurists, leave it to the discretion of the judge.

It would be superfluous to intensify the light, here, by citing the innumerable examples of innocent persons who have confessed themselves criminals because of the agonies of torture; there is no nation, there is no age that does not have its own to cite; but neither will men change nor will they deduce the necessary consequences. Every man who has ever extended his thought even a little beyond the mere necessities of life has at least sometimes felt an urge to run toward Nature, who, with secret and indistinct voices, calls him to her; custom, that tyrant of minds, drives him back and frightens him.

Abu Taleb Khan, A Muslim Indian's Reactions to the West

Abu Taleb Khan was of Turkish and Persian descent, like many residents of northwest India. Born in 1752, he was a bureaucrat who worked for Indian princes and then tried to get a job from the English colonial administration. It was after this that, aided by some British friends, he went to England. He was taken up as a novelty by British high society, which surely colored his reactions to this strange nation, though they did not deprive him of critical capacity. He wrote about his travels in Persian when he returned to India, still hoping for official patronage.

Source: Charles Stewart, ed., *Travels of Mirza Abu Taleb Khan in Asia, Africa and Europe* (New Delhi: Sona Publications: 184; reprint, 1977), pp. xiv–xvi, 82, 528–29, 158–61, 168–70, 178–80.

Focus Questions:

1. In what ways did this traveler find the people of England excessively "worldly"? How did this behavior contrast with that expected of Muslims?
2. Why were the English contemptuous, at least in his estimation, of his customs?
3. Has this observer misunderstood anything about Western ideals in the period?

The first and greatest defect I observed in the English is their want of faith in religion, and their great inclination to philosophy [atheism]: The effect of these principles, or rather want of principle, is very conspicuous in the lower orders of people, who are totally devoid of honesty. They are, indeed, cautious how they transgress against the laws, from fear of punishment; but whenever an opportunity offers of purloining anything without the risk of detection, they never pass it by. They are also ever on the watch to appropriate to themselves the property of the rich, who, on this account, are obliged constantly to keep their doors shut, and never to permit an unknown person to enter them. At present, owing to the vigilance of the magistrates, the severity of the laws, and the honor of the superior classes of people, no very bad consequences are to be apprehended; but if ever such nefarious practices should become prevalent and should creep in among the higher classes, inevitable ruin must ensue.

The second defect most conspicuous in the English character is pride or insolence. Puffed up with their power and good fortune for the last fifty years, they are not apprehensive of adversity, and take no pains to avert it. Thus, when the people of London, some time ago, assembled in mobs on account of the great increase of taxes and high price of provisions, and were nearly in a state of insurrection— although the magistrates, by their vigilance in watching them, and by causing parties of soldiers to patrol the streets day and night, to disperse all persons whom they saw assembling together, succeeded in quieting the disturbance—yet no pains were afterwards taken to eradicate the evil. Some of the men in power said it had been merely a plan of the artificers to obtain higher wages (an attempt frequently made by the English tradesmen); others were of opinion that no remedy could be applied; therefore no further notice was taken of the affair. All this, I say, betrays a blind confidence, which, instead of meeting the danger and endeavoring to prevent it, waits till the misfortune arrives, and then attempts to remedy it. Such was the case with the late king of France, who took no step to oppose the Revolution till it was too late. This self-confidence is to be found, more or less, in every Englishman; it however differs much from the pride of Indians and Persians.

Their third defect is a passion for acquiring money and their attachment to worldly affairs. Although these bad qualities are not so reprehensible in them as in countries more subject to the vicissitudes of fortune, (because, in England, property is so well protected by the laws that every person reaps the fruits of his industry, and, in his old age, enjoys the earnings or economy of his youth,) yet sordid and illiberal habits are generally found to accompany avarice and parsimony, and, consequently, render the possessor of them contemptible; on the contrary, generosity, if it does not launch into prodigality, but is guided by the hand of prudence, will render a man respected and esteemed…

…The English have very peculiar opinions on the subject of perfection. They insist that it is merely an ideal quality, and depends entirely upon comparison; that mankind have risen, by degrees, from the state of savages to the exalted dignity of the great philosopher Newton; but that, so far from having yet attained perfection, it is possible that, in future ages, philosophers will look with as much contempt on the acquirements of Newton as we now do on the rude state of the arts among savages. If this axiom of theirs be correct, man has yet much to learn, and all his boasted knowledge is but vanity.

Their twelfth defect is a contempt for the customs of other nations, and the preference they give to their own; although theirs, in fact, may be much inferior. I had a striking instance of this prejudice in the conduct of my fellow-passengers board ship. Some of these, who were otherwise respectable characters, ridiculed idea of my wearing trowsers, and a night-dress, when I went to bed; and contended that they slept much more at their ease by going to bed nearly naked. I replied, that I slept very comfortably; that mine was certainly the most decent mode; and that in the event of any sudden accident happening, I could run on deck instantly, and if requisite, jump into the boat in a minute; whilst they must either lose some time in dressing, or come out of their cabins in a very immodest manner. In answer to this, they said, such sudden accidents seldom occurred, but that if it did happen, they would not hesitate to come on deck in their shirts only. This I give merely as a specimen of their obstinacy, and prejudice in favour of their own customs.

In London, I was frequently attacked on the apparent unreasonableness and childishness of some of the Mohammedan customs; but as, from my knowledge of the English character, I was convinced it would be folly to argue the point philosophically with them, I contented myself with parrying the subject. Thus, when they attempted to turn into ridicule the ceremonies used by the pilgrims on their arrival at Mecca, I asked them, why they supposed the ceremony of baptism, by a clergyman, requisite for the salvation of a child, who could not possibly be sensible what he was about. When they reproached us for eating with our hands; I replied, "There is by this mode no danger of cutting yourself or your neighbours; and it is an old and a true proverb, 'The nearer the bone, the sweeter the meat:' but, exclusive of these advantages, a man's own hands are surely cleaner than the feet of a baker's boy; for it is well know, that half the bread in London is kneaded by the feet." By this mode of argument I completely silenced all my adversaries, and frequently turned the laugh against them, when they expected to have refuted me and made me appear ridiculous.

CHAPTER 17

Revolutions in the Atlantic World

The Declaration of the Rights of Man and Citizen

The Estates General that convened in May 1789 at Versailles became deadlocked when representatives of the Third Estate refused to proceed until the king and larger assembly confirmed that delegates would vote by head. To ensure adequate and fair representation of the Third Estate's interests, the delegates refused to continue until the king and assembly clarified what voting procedures would be used. The stalemate continued into June 1789, when a large number of the representatives of the Third Estate, and a few from the others, broke away after being locked out of the meeting hall, declared themselves to be a National Assembly representing all of France, and vowed to create a constitutional monarchy. The National Assembly adopted this famous document in August of 1789 as the guiding principles for the organization and powers of new government. This document assured a number of rights for all men, sweeping away the privileged place of the nobility and clergy in the "old regime." If read carefully, however, it also reflects debates about what groups would have full, direct political participation in the institutions and elections for the new constitutional monarchy. Meant to be a universal document, the framers also intended that these principles be adopted beyond France.

Source: Jeremy Popkin, *A Short History of the French Revolution* (Englewood, N.J.: Prentice Hall 1995), 39-40.

Focus Questions:

1. What rights and protections does the declaration ensure? Why were these included, and what ideas or beliefs provide the basis for them?
2. How was a "citizen" defined in the document? What does this tell us about debates regarding citizenship in this period?
3. Given the ideas and principles outlined here, to what degree does this represent a break with the "old regime" monarchy?

The Declaration of the Rights of Man and Citizen, 1789

"The representatives of the French people, organized as a national assembly, considering that ignorance, neglect, and scorn of the rights of man are the sole causes of public misfortunes and of corruption of governments, have resolved to display in a solemn declaration the natural, inalienable, and sacred rights of man, so that this declaration, constantly in the presence of all members of society, will continually remind them of their rights and their duties, so that the acts of the legislative power and those of the executive power, being subject at any time to comparison with the purpose of any political institution, will be better respected; so that the demands of the citizens, based henceforth on simple and incontestable principles, will always contribute to the maintenance of the constitution and the happiness of all."

"Consequently, the National Assembly recognizes and declares, in the presence and under the auspices of the Supreme Being, the following rights of man and citizen.

Article 1. Men are born and remain free and equal in rights; social distinctions can be established only for the common benefit.

2. The aim of every political association is the conservation of the natural and imprescriptible rights of man; these rights are liberty, property, security, and resistance to oppression.

3. The source of all sovereignty is located in essence in the nation; no body, no individual can exercise authority which does not emanate from it expressly.

4. Liberty consists in being able to do anything that does not harm another person. Thus the exercise of the natural rights of each man has no limits except those which assure to the other members of society the enjoyment of these same rights; these limits can be determined only by law.

5. The law has the right to forbid only those actions harmful to society. All that is not forbidden by the law cannot be hindered, and no one can be forced to do what it does not order.

6. The law is the expression of the general will; all citizens have the right to concur personally or through their representatives in its formation; it must be the same for all, whether it protects or punishes. All citizens being equal in its eyes are equally admissible to all honors, positions, and public employments, according to their capabilities and without other distinctions than those of their virtues and talents.

7. No man can be accused, arrested, or detained except in cases determined by the law, and according to the forms which it has prescribed. Those who solicit, draw up, execute, or have executed arbitrary orders must be punished; but

any citizen summoned or seized by virtue of the law must obey instantly; he renders himself culpable by resisting.

8. The law must establish only penalties that are strictly and clearly necessary, and no one can be punished prior to the offense and legally applied.

9. Every man being presumed innocent until he has been declared guilty, if it is judged indispensable to arrest him, all severity that is not necessary for making sure of his person must be severely repressed by the law.

10. No one may be disturbed because of his opinions, even religious, provided that their public demonstration does not disturb the public order established by law.

11. The free communication of thoughts and opinions is one of the most precious rights of man: every citizen can therefore freely speak, write, and print: he is answerable for abuses of this liberty in cases determined by the law.

12. The guaranteeing of the rights of man and citizen necessitates a public force; this force is therefore instituted for the advantage of all, and not for the private use of those to whom it is entrusted.

13. For the maintenance of the public force, and for the expenses of administration, a tax supported in common is indispensable; it must be assessed on all citizens in proportion to their capacities to pay.

14. Citizens have the right to determine for themselves or through their representatives the need for taxation of the public, to consent to it freely, to investigate its use, and to determine its rate, basis, collection, and duration.

15. Society has the right to demand an accounting of his administration from every public agent.

16. Any society in which guarantees of rights are not assured nor the separation of powers determined has no constitution.

17. Property being an inviolable and sacred right, no one may be deprived of it unless public necessity, legally determined, clearly requires such action, and then only on condition of a just and prior indemnity."

Thomas Paine, *Rights of Man*

Originally a British subject, Thomas Paine (1737-1809) emigrated to the American colonies in the 1770s and soon after became involved in the independence movement. On a visit to England in the late 1780s, Paine became caught up in English debates about the French Revolution, after reading Edmund Burke's critical analysis of the Revolution. Paine quickly wrote and published a response to Burke's ideas, in a book length work entitled *Rights of Man*. A spirited defense of the French Revolution and a critique of European government and society, the book met with heavy criticism and, ultimately, government condemnation in Britain. In wake of reaction to his book, Paine escaped imprisonment in Britain only by fleeing to France where he was elected to the National Convention. As the Revolution continued to unfold, however, Paine came into conflict with the radical revolutionaries when he voted for banishment over execution for deposed King Louis XVI. Under the Terror, Paine was arrested and imprisoned, but he escaped execution. He remained in France until 1802, and then returned to the United States where he died in 1809.

Source: Thomas Paine, *Rights of Man* (New York: Penguin Books, 1984), 39-43.

FOCUS QUESTIONS:

1. How does Paine counter Burke's criticisms of the French Revolution? What counter arguments does he make and how does he support them?
2. According to Paine, what were the possible affects or implications of the French Revolution for Europe, and especially for Britain?
3. What ideas and concepts provided the basis for Paine's ideas about revolution and government?

Among the incivilities by which nations or individuals provoke and irritate each other, Mr Burke's pamphlet on the French Revolution is an extraordinary instance. Neither the People of France, nor the National Assembly, were troubling themselves about the affairs of England, or the English Parliament; and why Mr Burke should commence an unprovoked attack upon them, both in parliament and in public, is a conduct that cannot be pardoned on the score of manners, nor justified on that of policy.

There is scarcely an epithet of abuse to be found in the English language, with which Mr Burke has not loaded the French Nation and the National Assembly. Everything which rancour, prejudice, ignorance, or knowledge could suggest, are poured forth in the copious fury of near four hundred pages. In the strain and on the plan Mr Burke was writing, he might have written on to as many thousands. When the tongue or the pen is let loose in a frenzy of passion, it is the man, and not the subject, that becomes exhausted.

Hitherto Mr Burke has been mistaken and disappointed in the opinions he had formed of the affairs of France; but such is the ingenuity of his hope, or the malignancy of his despair, that it furnishes him with new pretences to go on. There was a time when it was impossible to make Mr Burke believe there would be any revolution in France. His opinion then was, that the French had neither spirit to undertake it, nor fortitude to support it; and now that there is one, he seeks an escape, by condemning it.

Not sufficiently content with abusing the National Assembly, a great part of his work is taken up with abusing Dr Price (one of the best-hearted men that lives), and the two societies in England known by the name of the Revolution Society, and the Society for Constitutional Information.

Dr Price had preached a sermon on the 4th of November 1789, being the anniversary of what is called in England, the Revolution which took place 1688. Mr Burke, speaking of this sermon, says,'The Political Divine' proceeds dogmatically to assert, that, by the principles of the Revolution, the people of England have acquired three fundamental rights:

'1. To choose our own governors.

2. To cashier them for misconduct.

3. To frame a government for ourselves.'

Dr Price does not say that the right to do these things exists in this or in that person, or in this or in that description of persons, but that it exists in the *whole*; that it is a right resident in the nation. – Mr Burke, on the contrary, denies that such a right exists in the nation, either in whole or in part, or that it exists anywhere; and, what is still more strange and marvellous, he says,'that the people of England utterly disclaim such a right, and that they will resist the practical assertion of it with their lives and fortunes.'That men should take up arms, and spend their lives and fortunes, *not* to maintain their rights, but to maintain they have *not* rights, is an entirely new species of discovery, and suited to the paradoxical genius of Mr Burke.

The method which Mr Burke takes to prove that the people of England have no such rights, and that such rights do not now exist in the nation, either in whole or in part, or anywhere at all, is of the same marvellous and monstrous kind with what he has already said; for his arguments are, that the persons, or the generation of persons, in whom they did exist, are dead, and with them the right is dead also. To prove this, he quotes a declaration made by parliament about a hundred years ago, to William and Mary, in these words: 'The Lords Spiritual and Temporal, and Commons, do, in the name of the people aforesaid,' – (meaning the people of England then living) –'most humbly and faithfully *submit* themselves, their *heirs* and *posterities*, for EVER.' He also quotes a clause of another act of parliament made in the same reign, the terms of which, he says, 'bind us'– (meaning the people of that day) –'our *heirs*, and our *posterity*, to *them*, their *heirs* and *posterity*, to the end of time.'

Mr Burke conceives his point sufficiently established by producing those clauses, which he enforces by saying that they exclude the right of the nation for *ever*: And not yet content with making such declarations, repeated over and over again, he farther says,'that if the people of England possessed such a right before the Revolution,' (which he acknowledges to have been the case, not only in England, but throughout Europe, at an early period),'yet that the *English nation* did, at the time of the Revolution, most solemnly renounce and abdicate it, for themselves, and for *all their posterity, for ever*.'

As Mr Burke occasionally applies the poison drawn from his horrid principles, not only to the English nation, but to the French Revolution and the National Assembly, and charges that august, illuminated and illuminating body of men with the epithet of *usurpers*, I shall, *sans ceremonie*, place another system of principles in opposition to his.

The English Parliament of 1688 did a certain thing, which, for themselves and their constituents, they had a right to do, and which it appeared right should be done: But, in addition to this right, which they possessed by delegation, *they set up another right by assumption*, that of binding and controlling posterity to the end of time. The case, therefore, divides itself into two parts; the right which they possessed by delegation, and the right which they set up by assumption. The first is admitted; but, with respect to the second, I reply –

There never did, there never will, and there never can exist a parliament, or any description of men, or any generation of men, in any country, possessed of the right or the power of binding and controlling posterity to the*'end of time,'* or of commanding for ever how the world shall be governed, or who shall govern it; and therefore, all such clauses, acts or declarations, by which the makers of them attempt to do what they have neither the right nor the power to do, nor the power to execute, are in themselves null and void. – Every age and generation must be as free to act for itself, *in all cases*, as the ages and generations which preceded it. The vanity and presumption of governing beyond the grave, is the most ridiculous and insolent of all tyrannies. Man has no property in man; neither has any generation a property in the generations which are to follow. The parliament or the people of 1688, or of any other period, has no more right to dispose of the people of the present day, or to bind or to control them in any shape whatever, than the parliament or the people of the present day have to dispose of, bind or control those who are to live a hundred or a thousand years hence. Every generation is, and must be, competent to all the purposes which its occasions require. It is the living, and not the dead, that are to be accommodated. When man ceases to be, his power and his wants cease with him; and having no longer any participation in the concerns of this world, he has no longer any authority in directing who shall be its governors, or how its government shall be organized, or how administered.

I am not contending for nor against any form of government, nor for nor against any party here or elsewhere. That which a whole nation chooses to do, it has a right to do. Mr Burke says, No. Where then *does* the right exist? I am contending for the rights of the *living*, and against their being willed away, and controlled and contracted for, by the manuscript assumed authority of the dead; and Mr Burke is contending for the authority of the dead over the rights and freedom of the living. There was a time when kings disposed of their crowns by will upon their deathbeds, and consigned the people, like beasts of the field, to whatever successor they appointed. This is now so exploded as scarcely to be remembered, and so monstrous as hardly to be believed: But the parliamentary clauses upon which Mr Burke builds his political church, are of the same nature.

The laws of every country must be analogous to some common principle. In England, no parent or master, nor all the authority of parliament, omnipotent as it has called itself, can bind or control the personal freedom even of an individual beyond the age of twenty-one years: On what ground of right, then, could the parliament of 1688, or any other parliament, bind all posterity for ever?

Those who have quitted the world, and those who are not yet arrived at it, are as remote from each other, as the utmost stretch of mortal imagination can conceive: What possible obligation, then, can exist between them; what rule or principle can be laid down, that of two non-entities, the one out of existence, and the other not in, and who never can meet in this world, the one should control the other to the end of time?

In England, it is said that money cannot be taken out of the pockets of the people without their consent: But who authorized, or who could authorize the parliament of 1688 to control and take away the freedom of posterity, (who were not in existence to give or to withhold their consent,) and limit and confine their right of acting in certain cases for ever?

A greater absurdity cannot present itself to the understanding of man, than what Mr Burke offers his readers. He tells them, and he tells the world to come, that a certain body of men, who existed a hundred years ago, made a law; and that there does not now exist in the nation, nor ever will, nor ever can, a power to alter it. Under how many subtleties, or absurdities, has the divine right to govern been imposed on the credulity of mankind! Mr Burke has discovered a new one, and he has shortened his journey to Rome, by appealing to the power of this infallible parliament of former days; and he produces what it has done, as of divine authority: for that power must certainly be more than human, which no human power to the end of time can alter.

Olympe de Gouges, *Declaration of the Rights of Woman and the Female Citizen*

Olympe de Gouges (1745–1793 CE) was a French feminist, writer, and playwright. De Gouges wrote plays that dealt with a variety of sensitive subjects, such as divorce and sexual relations. Taking the Revolution's *Declaration of the Rights of Man and Citizen* as a guide, de Gouges wrote a similar document on the rights of women, advocating equal rights for men and women. Her opposition to the execution of the king and his family in 1793 exposed her to radical revolutionaries during the Great Terror. As a result, she was guillotined for her opposition to the revolutionary National Convention.

Source: Olympe de Gouges, *Declaration of the Rights of Woman and the Female Citizen* (1791).

Focus Questions:

1. Does the declaration hold women to any responsibilities, or only ascribe to them rights?
2. Article #11 on the "free communication of ideas and opinions" pertains to the paternity of a child. What is de Gouges expressing in this point?

TO THE QUEEN: MADAME

Little accustomed the language which one speaks to royalty, I will not employ the adulation of courtiers by dedicating this unusual production to you. My goal, Madam, is to speak to you frankly. I did not wait for the present time of freedom to express myself thus. I declared myself with the same energy when the blindness of despots punished such a noble audacity.

But when all the Empire held you responsible for its calamities, I alone, in a time of disorder and storm, had the force to take your defense. I never could persuade myself that a Princess, high within the state, had all the defects of lowness.

Yes, Madame, when I saw the sword raised against you, I threw my observations between that sword and you, but today when I see who is observed near the crowd of useless hirelings, and [when I see] that she is restrained by fear of the laws, I will tell you, Madame, what I did not say then.

If the foreigner bears arms into France, you are no longer in my eyes this falsely accused Queen, this attractive Queen, but an implacable enemy of the French. Oh, Madame, bear in mind that you are mother and wife; employ all your credit for the return of Princes. This credit, if wisely applied, strengthens the father's crown, saves it for the son, and reconciles you to the love of the French. This worthy negotiation is the true duty of a queen. Intrigue, cabals, bloody projects will precipitate your fall, if it is possible that you are capable of such plots.

Madame, may a noble function characterize you, excite your ambition, and fix your attentions. Only one whom chance has elevated to an eminent position can assume the task of lending weight to the progress of the Rights of Woman and of hastening its success. If you were less well informed, Madame, I might fear that your individual interests would outweigh those of your sex. You love glory; think, Madame, the greatest crimes immortalize one as much as the greatest virtues, but what a different fame in the annals of history! The one is ceaselessly taken as an example, and the other is eternally the execration of the human race.

It will never be a crime for you to work for the restoration of customs, to give your sex all the firmness of which it is capable. This is not the work of one day, unfortunately for the new regime. This revolution will happen only when all women are aware of their deplorable fate, and of the rights they have lost in society.

Madame, support such a beautiful cause; defend this unfortunate sex, and soon you will have half the realm on your side, and at least one-third of the other half.

Those, Madame, are the feats by which you should show and use your credit. Believe me, Madame, our life is a pretty small thing, especially for a Queen, when it is not embellished by people's affection and by the eternal delights of good deeds.

If it is true that the French arm all the powers against their own Fatherland, why? For frivolous prerogatives, for chimeras. Believe, Madame, if I judge by what I feel—the monarchical party will be destroyed by itself, it will abandon tyrants, and all hearts will rally around the fatherland to defend it.

There are my principles, Madame. In speaking to you of my fatherland, I lose sight of the purpose of this dedication. Thus, any good citizen sacrifices his glory and his interests when he has none other than those of his country.

I am with the most profound respect, Madame,
Your most humble and most obedient servant,
de Gouges.

THE RIGHTS OF WOMAN

Man, are you capable of being just? It is a woman who poses the question, you will not deprive her of that right at least. Tell me, what gives you sovereign empire to oppress my sex? Your strength? Your talents? Observe the Creator in his wisdom; survey in all her grandeur that nature with whom you seem to want to be in harmony, and give me, if you dare, an example of this tyrannical empire. Go back to animals, consult the elements, study plants, finally glance at all the modifications of organic matter, and surrender to the evidence when I offer you the means; search, probe, and distinguish, if you can, the sexes in the administration of nature. Everywhere you will find them mingled; everywhere they cooperate in harmonious togetherness in this immortal masterpiece.

Man alone has raised his exceptional circumstances to a principle. Bizarre, blind, bloated with science and degenerated—in a century of enlightenment and wisdom—into the crassest ignorance, he wants to command as a despot a sex which is in full possession of its intellectual faculties, he pretends to enjoy the Revolution and to claim his rights to equality in order to say nothing more about

DECLARATION OF THE RIGHTS OF WOMAN AND THE FEMALE CITIZEN

Preamble

The mothers, daughters, sisters, representatives of the nation, ask to constitute a National Assembly. Considering that ignorance, forgetfulness or contempt of the rights of women are the sole causes of public miseries, and of corruption of governments, they have resolved to set forth in a solemn declaration, the natural, unalterable and sacred rights of woman, so that this declaration being ever present to all members of the social body, may unceasingly remind them of their rights and their duties; in order that the acts of women's power, as well as those of men, may be judged constantly against the aim of all political institutions, and thereby be more respected for it, in order that the complaints of women citizens, based henceforth on simple and indisputable principles, may always take the direction of maintaining the Constitution, good morals and the welfare of all.

In consequence, the sex superior in beauty and in courage in maternal suffering recognizes and declares, in the presence of and under the auspices of the supreme Being, the following rights of woman and of the woman citizen:

1 Woman is born free and remains equal to man in rights. Social distinctions can be based only on common utility.

2 The aim of every political association is the preservation of the natural and imprescriptible rights of man and woman. These rights are liberty, prosperity, security and above all, resistance to oppression.

3 The source of all sovereignty resides essentially in the Nation, which is nothing but the joining together of Man and Woman; no body, no individual, can exercise authority that does not emanate expressly from it.

4 Liberty and justice consist in giving back to others all that belongs to them; thus the only limits on the exercise of woman's natural rights are the perpetual tyranny by which man opposes her; these limits must be reformed by the laws of nature and of reason.

5 The laws of nature and reason forbid all actions that are harmful to society; all that is not forbidden by these wise and divine laws cannot be prevented, and no one can be constrained to do what they do not prescribe.

1 Law must be the expression of the general will: all citizens, men and women alike, must personally or through their representatives concur in its formation; it must be the same for all; all citizens, men and women alike, being equal before it, must be equally eligible for all high offices, positions and public employments, according to their abilities, and without distinctions other than their virtues and talents.

2 No woman can be an exception: she will be accused, apprehended and detained in cases determined by law; women, like men, will obey the rigorous rule.

3 The law must establish only those penalties which are strictly and clearly necessary, and no woman can be punished by virtue of a law established and promulgated prior to the offense, and legally applied to women.

4 When a woman is declared guilty, full severity is exercised by the law.

5 No one ought to be disturbed for one's opinions, however fundamental they are; since a woman has the right to mount the scaffold, she must also have the right to address the House, providing her interventions do not disturb the public order as it has been established by law.

6 The free communication of ideas and opinions is one of the most precious rights of woman, since this freedom ensures the legitimacy of fathers towards their children. Every woman citizen can therefore say freely: I am a mother of a child that belongs to you, without being forced to conceal the truth because of barbaric prejudice; except to be answerable for abuses of this liberty as determined by law.

7 The guarantee of the rights of woman and of the rights of the woman citizen is a necessary benefit; this guarantee must be instituted for the advantage of all, and not for the personal benefit of those to whom it is entrusted.

8 For the upkeep of public forces and for administrative expenses, the contribution of woman and man are equal; a woman shares in all the labours required by law, in the painful tasks; she must therefore have an equal share in the distribution of offices, employments, trusts, dignities and work.

9 Women and men citizens have the right to ascertain by themselves or through their representatives

10 the necessity of public taxes. Women citizens will not only assume an equal part in pro-viding the wealth but also in the public administration and in determining the quota, the assessment, the collection and the duration of the impost.

11 The mass of women, joined together to contribute their taxes with those of men, have the right to demand from every public official an accounting of his administration.

12 Any society in which the guarantee of rights is not assured, nor the separation of powers determined, has no Constitution: the Constitution is null if the majority of the individuals of whom the nation is comprised have not participated in its drafting.

13 Ownership of property is for both sexes, mutually and separately; it is for each a sacred and inviolable right; no one can be deprived of it as a true patrimony from nature, unless a public necessity, legally established, evidently demands it, and with the condition of a just and prior indemnity.

AFTERWORD

Women, wake up! The alarm bell of reason is making itself heard throughout the universe; recognize your rights. The powerful empire of nature is no longer beset by prejudices, fanaticism, superstition and lies. The torch of truth has dispelled all clouds of stupidity and usurpation. The enslaved man multiplied his forces but has had to resort to yours to break his chains. Once free he became unjust to his female companion. O women! women, when will you stop being blind? What advantages have you received from the revolution? A more pronounced scorn, a more marked contempt? During the centuries of corruption, your only power was over the weaknesses of men. Your empire is destroyed, what then is left to you? The conviction that men are unjust. The claiming of your patrimony based on the wise laws of nature. The good word of [Jesus Christ] the Lawgiver of the Marriage at Cana? Are you afraid that our French lawmakers, correctors of this morality, so long tied up with the politics which is no longer in style will say to you: "Women, what is there in common between you and us?" Everything, you would have to reply. If they persisted in their weakness, in putting forth this inconsistency which is a contradiction of their principles, you should courageously oppose these male pretensions of superiority with the forces of reason; unite under the banner of philosophy, unfold all the energy of your character and you will soon see these proud men, your servile adorers, crawling at your feet, but proud to share with you the treasures of the Supreme being. Whatever the obstacles that oppose us may be, it is in your power to free us, you have only to will it...Since it is now a question of national education, let us see if our wise lawmakers will think wisely about the education of women.

Women have done more harm than good. Constraint and dissimulation have been their lot. What force had robbed them of, ruse returned to them. Poison and the sword were both subject to them; they commanded in crime as in fortune. The French government, especially, depended throughout the centuries on the nocturnal administration of women; the cabinet kept no secret from their indiscretion; ambassadorial post, command, ministry, presidency, pontificate, college of cardinals; finally, anything which characterises the folly of men, profane and sacred, all have been subject to the cupidity and ambition of this sex, formerly contemptible and respected, and since the revolution, respectable and scorned.

In this sort of contradictory situation, what remarks could I not make! I have but a moment to make them, but this moment will fix the attention of the remotest posterity. Under the Old Regime, all was vicious, all was guilty; but could not the amelioration of conditions be perceived even in the substance of vices? A woman only had to be beautiful or amiable; when she possessed these two advantages, she saw a hundred fortunes at her feet. If she did not profit from them, she had a bizarre character or a rare philosophy which made her scorn wealth; then she was deemed to be like a crazy woman; the most indecent made herself respected with gold; commerce in women was a kind of industry in the first class [of society], which, henceforth, will have no more credit. If it still had it, the revolution would be lost, and under the new relationships we would always be corrupted; however, reason can always be deceived [into believing] that any other road to fortune is closed to the woman whom a man buys, like the slave on the African coasts. The difference is great; that is known. The slave is commanded by the master; but if the slave has lost all her charms, what will become of this unfortunate woman? The victim of scorn, even the doors of charity are closed to her; she is poor and old, they say; why did she not know how to make her fortune? Reason finds other examples that are even more touching. A young, inexperienced woman, seduced by a man whom she loves, will abandon her parents to follow him; the ingrate will leave her after a few years, and the older she has become with him, the more inhuman is his inconstancy; if she has children, he will likewise abandon them. If he is rich, he will consider himself excused from sharing his fortune with his noble victims. If some involvement binds him to his duties, he will deny them, trusting that the laws will support him. If he is married, any other obligation loses its rights. What laws remain to extirpate vice all the way to its root? The law of dividing wealth and public administration between men and women. It can easily be seen that one who is born into a rich family gains very much from such equal sharing. But the one born into a poor family with merit and virtue—what is her lot? Poverty and opprobrium. If she does not precisely excel in music or painting, she cannot be admitted to any public function when she has all the capacity for it. I do not to give only a sketch of things; I will go more deeply into this in the new edition of all my political writings, with notes, which I propose to give to the public in a few days.

I take up my text again on the subject of morals. Marriage is the tomb of trust and love. The married woman can with impunity give bastards to her husband, and also give them the wealth that does not belong to them. The woman who is unmarried has only one feeble right; ancient and inhuman laws refuse to her for her children the right to the name and the wealth of their father; no new laws have been made in this matter. If it is considered a paradox and an impossibility on my part to try to give my sex an honourable and just consistency, I leave it to men to attain glory for dealing with this matter; but while we wait, the way can be prepared through national education, the restoration of morals, and conjugal conventions.

FORM FOR A SOCIAL CONTRACT BETWEEN MAN AND WOMAN

We, __________ and __________, moved by our own will, unite ourselves for the duration of our lives, and for the duration of our mutual inclinations, under the following conditions: We intend and wish to make our wealth communal, meanwhile reserving to ourselves the right to divide it in favour of our children and of those to whom we might have a particular inclination, mutually recognising that our property belongs directly to our children, from whatever bed they come, and that all of them without distinction have the right to bear the name of the fathers and mothers who have acknowledged them, and we are charged to subscribe to the law which punishes the renunciation of one's own blood. We likewise obligate ourselves, in case of separation, to divide our wealth and to set aside in advance the portion the law indicates for our children, and in the event of a perfect union, the one who dies will divest himself of half his property in his child's favour, and if one dies childless, the survivor will inherit by right, unless the dying person has disposed of half the common property in favour of one whom he judged deserving.

That is approximately the formula for the marriage act I propose for execution. Upon reading this strange document, I see rising up against me the hypocrites, the prudes, the clergy, and the whole infernal sequence. But how it [my proposal] offers to the wise the moral means of achieving the perfection of a happy government! I am going to give in a few words the physical proof of it. The rich, childless Epicurean finds it very good to go to his poor neighbour to augment his family. When there is a law authorising a poor man's wife to have a rich one adopt their children, the bonds of society will be

strengthened and morals will be purer. This law will perhaps save the community's wealth and hold back the disorder which drives so many victims to the almshouses of shame, to a low station, and into degenerate human principles where nature has groaned for so long. May the detractors of wise philosophy then cease to cry out against primitive morals, or may they lose their point in the source of their citations.

[Footnote 1: Abraham had some very legitimate children by Hagar, the servant of his wife]

Moreover, I would like a law which would assist widows and young girls deceived by the false promises of a man to whom they were attached: I would like, I say, this law to force an inconstant man to hold to his obligations or at least [to pay] an indemnity equal to his wealth. Again, I would like this law to be rigorous against women, at least those who have the effrontery to have recourse to a law which they themselves had violated by their misconduct, if proof of that were given. At the same time, as I showed in *Le Bonheur primitif de l'Homme,* in 1788, that prostitutes should be placed in designated quarters. It is not prostitutes who contribute the most to the depravity of morals, it is the women of society. In regenerating the latter, the former are changed. This link of fraternal union will first bring disorder, but in consequence it will produce at the end a perfect harmony.

I offer a foolproof way to elevate the soul of women; it is to join them to all the activities of man; if man persists in finding this way impractical, let him share his fortune with woman, not at his caprice, but by the wisdom of laws. Prejudice falls, morals are purified, and nature regains all her rights. Add to this the marriage of priests and the strengthening of the king on his throne, and the French government cannot fail.

It would be very necessary to say a few words on the troubles which are said to be caused by the decree in favour of coloured men in our islands. There is where nature shudders with horror; there is where reason and humanity have still not touched callous souls; there, especially, is where division and discord stir up their inhabitants. It is not difficult to divine the instigators of these incendiary fermentations; they are even in the midst of the National Assembly; they ignite the flame in Europe which must inflame America. Colonists make a claim to reign as despots over the men whose fathers and brothers they are; and, disowning the rights of nature, they trace the source of [their rule] to the scantiest tint of their blood. These inhuman colonists say: our blood flows in their veins, but we will shed it all if necessary to glut our greed or our blind ambition. It is in these places nearest to nature where the father scorns the son; deaf to the cries of blood, they stifle all its attraction; what can be hoped from the resistance opposed to them? To constrain [blood] violently is to render it terrible; to leave [blood] still enchained is to direct all calamities towards America. A divine hand seems to spread liberty abroad throughout the realms of man; only the law has the right to curb this liberty if it degenerates into license, but it must be equal for all; liberty must hold the National Assembly to its decree dictated by prudence and justice. May it act the same way for the state of France and render her as attentive to new abuses as she was to the ancient ones which each day become more dreadful. My opinion would be to reconcile the executive and legislative power, for it seems to me that the one is everything and the other is nothing—whence comes, unfortunately perhaps, the loss of the French Empire. I think that these two powers, like man and woman, should be united but equal in force and virtue to make a good household.

The Haitian Declaration of Independence *January 1, 1804*

In August 1791 a massive slave revolt began in the French Caribbean colony of Sainte-Domingue. In November 1803, rebel forces, led by Jean-Jacques Dessalines, drove out the last of the French army out of the colony. Dessalines commissioned one of his secretaries, Louis Boisrond-Tonnerre, to write a declaration of independence for the new country of Haiti. The following was written overnight and read publicly by its author the following morning before a crowd at Gonaïves, a coastal town in the north of the country.

Source: Thomas Madiou, Histoire d'Haiti (Port-au-Prince, 1847–1848), 3: 146-50.

Focus Questions:

1. How does the Haitian Declaration of Independence compare with the Declaration of the Rights of Man?
2. How does the Haitian revolution shed a different light on the French revolution? On the meaning of freedom and human rights?

The Commander in Chief to the People of Haiti

Citizens:

It is not enough to have expelled the barbarians who have bloodied our land for two centuries; it is not enough to have restrained those ever-evolving factions that one after another mocked the specter of liberty that France dangled before you. We must, with one last act of national authority, forever ensure liberty's reign in the country of our birth; we must take any hope of re-enslaving us away from the inhumane government that for so long kept us in the most humiliating stagnation. In the end we must live independent or die.

Independence or death... let these sacred words unite us and be the signal of battle and of our reunion.

Citizens, my countrymen, on this solemn day I have brought together those courageous soldiers who, as liberty lay dying, spilled their blood to save it; these generals who have guided your efforts against tyranny have not yet done enough for your happiness; the French name still haunts our land.

Everything revives the memories of the cruelties of this barbarous people: our laws, our habits, our towns, everything still carries the stamp of the French. Indeed! There are still French in our island, and you believe yourself free and independent of that republic, which, it is true, has fought all the nations, but which has never defeated those who wanted to be free.

What! Victims of our [own] credulity and indulgence for fourteen years; defeated not by French armies, but by the pathetic eloquence of their agents' proclamations; when will we tire of breathing the air that they breathe? What do we have in common with this nation of executioners? The difference between its cruelty and our patient moderation, its color and ours, the great seas that separate us, our avenging climate, all tell us plainly that they are not our brothers that they never will be, and that if they find refuge among us, they will plot again to trouble and divide us.

Native citizens, men, women, girls, and children, let your gaze extend on all parts of this island: look there for your spouses, your husbands, your brothers, your sisters. Indeed! Look there for your children, your suckling infants, what have they become?... I shudder to say it... the prey of these vultures.

Instead of these dear victims, your alarmed gaze will see only their assassins. these tigers still dripping with their blood, whose terrible presence indicts your lack of feeling and your guilty slowness in avenging them. What are you waiting for before appeasing their spirits? Remember that you had wanted your remains to rest next to those of your fathers after you defeated tyranny; will you descend into their tombs without having avenged them? No! Their bones would reject yours.

And you, precious men, intrepid generals, who, without concern for your own pain, have revived liberty by shedding all your blood, know that you have done nothing if you do not give the nations a terrible, but just example of the vengeance that must be wrought by a people proud to have recovered its liberty and jealous to maintain it. Let us frighten all those who would dare try to take it from us again; let us begin with the French. Let them tremble when they approach our coast, if not from the memory of those cruelties they perpetrated here, then from the terrible resolution that we will have made to put to death anyone born French whose profane foot soils the land of liberty.

We have dared to be free, let us be thus by ourselves and for ourselves. Let us imitate the grown child: his own weight breaks the boundary that has become an obstacle to him. What people fought for us? What people wanted to gather the fruits of our labor? And what dishonorable absurdity to conquer in order to be enslaved. Enslaved?... Let us leave this description for the French; they have conquered but arc no longer free.

Let us walk down another path; let us imitate those people who, extending their concern into the future and dreading to leave an example of cowardice for posterity, preferred to be exterminated rather than lose their place as one of the world's free peoples;

Let us ensure, however, that a missionary spirit does not destroy our work; let us allow our neighbors to breathe in peace; may they live quietly under the laws that they have made for themselves, and let us not, as revolutionary firebrands, declare ourselves the lawgivers of the Caribbean, nor let our glory consist in troubling the peace of the neighboring islands. Unlike that which we inhabit, theirs has not been drenched in the innocent blood of its inhabitants; they have no vengeance to claim from the authority that protects them.

Fortunate to have never known the ideals that have destroyed us, they can only have good wishes for our prosperity.

Peace to our neighbors; but let this be our cry: "Anathema to the French name! Eternal hatred of France!"

Natives of Haiti! My happy fate was to be one day the sentinel who would watch over the idol to which you sacrifice; I have watched, sometimes fighting alone, and if I have been so fortunate as to return to your hands the sacred trust you confided to me, know that it is now your task to preserve it. In fighting for your liberty. I was working for my own happiness. Before consolidating it with laws that will guarantee your free individuality, your leaders, who I have assembled here, and I, owe you the final proof of our devotion.

Generals and you, leaders, collected here dose to me for the good of our land, the day has come, the day which must make our glory, our independence, eternal.

If there could exist among us a lukewarm heart, let him distance himself and tremble to take the oath which must unite us. Let us vow to ourselves, to posterity, to the entire universe, to forever renounce France, and to die rather than live under its domination; to fight until our last breath for the independence of our country.

And you, a people so long without good fortune, witness to the oath we take, remember that I counted on your constancy and courage when I threw myself into the career of liberty to fight the despotism and tyranny you had struggled against for fourteen years. Remember that I sacrificed everything to rally to your defense; family, children, fortune, and now I am rich only with your liberty; my name has become a horror to all those who want slavery. Despots and tyrants curse the day that I was born. If ever you refused or grumbled while receiving those laws that the spirit guarding your fate dictates to me for your own good, you would deserve the fate of an ungrateful people. But I reject that awful idea; you will sustain the liberty that you cherish and support the leader who commands you. Therefore, vow before me to live free and independent and to prefer death to anything that will try to place you back in chains. Swear, finally, to pursue forever the traitors and enemies of your independence.

Done at the headquarters of Gonaïves, the first day of January 1804, the first year of independence.

CHAPTER 18

Napoleon and the Age of Romanticism

Sir Harry Smith, *Autobiography*

Sir Harry Smith (1787-1860) was a British military general who fought against Napoleon's armies in Spain from 1808 to 1814 and against him in his ultimate defeat at Waterloo, in Belgium. Smith's account of the battles in Spain offer a view of Napoleon's campaigns and expansionist designs from an opposing camp. Despite his successes on the continent of Europe, Napoleon was never able to defeat Britain. Napoleon's campaign in Spain was designed to strike a blow at British power, as Britain was then aligned with neighboring Portugal. In this excerpt, Smith describes battles against the Napoleonic army in Spain in 1812. After Napoleon's defeat in 1814, Smith went on to an illustrious career, participating in military campaigns in the British colonies of India and South Africa. He became the British governor of the Cape Colony and served as the high commissioner of South Africa from 1847 to 1852.

Source: G.C. Moore Smith, ed., *The Autobiography of Lieutenant-General Sir Harry Smith, Baronet of Aliwal on the Sutlej*, vol. 1 (New York: E.P. Button and Company, 1902), 61-68.

Focus Questions:

1. Based on Smith's accounts, what was nineteenth century warfare like (living conditions, weaponry, tactics, battle conditions, supplies, etc.)?
2. What were Smith's perceptions of Napoleon and his armies? What were these based on?
3. What were Smith's encounters and relationships with people in Spain during these campaigns? What was the impact of war on civilian populations?

CAMPAIGN OF 1812: THE STROMING OF BADAJOS—

At this period of the year (February, March) the coursing in this part of Spain is capital, and by help of my celebrated dog Moro and two other excellent ones,

I supplied the officers' mess of every Company with hares for soup. We had a short repose, for the army moved into Estremadura for the purpose of besieging Badajos. We Light, 3rd and 4th Divisions, thought, as we had taken Ciudad Rodrigo, others would have the pleasure of the trenches of Badajos, but on our reaching Elvas [17 Feb., 1812] we were very soon undeceived, and we were destined for the duty,—to our mortification, for soldiers hate sieges and working-parties. The Guards work better than any soldiers, from their habits in London. Badajos was invested by the 3rd, 4th, and Light Divisions on the Spanish side, or left bank of the river, and by the 5th Division* on the Portuguese side, or right bank. On the night of the 17th March, St. Patrick's Day, the Light Division broke ground under a deluge of rain, which swelled the Guadiana so as to threaten our bridge of boats. Our duties in the trenches were most laborious during the whole siege, and much hard fighting we had, sorties, etc. The night [26 Mar.]

* * *

part of the 3rd Division

* * *

were to compose the storming party. The Light Division, the working party, consequently were sent to the Engineer Park for the ladders. When they arrived, General Kempt ordered them to be planted (Sir H. Hardinge, D.Q.M.G. of the Portuguese army, was here distinguished). The boys of the 3rd Division said to our fellows, "Come, stand out of the way;" to which our fellows replied, "D—your eyes, do you think we Light Division fetch ladders for such chaps as you to climb up? Follow us"—springing on the ladders, and, many of them were knocked over. A notorious fellow, a Sergeant Brother-wood, a noble fellow on duty, told me this anecdote. The siege was prosecuted with the same vigour from without with which it was repelled from within.

After some hours in the trenches, when we returned I invariably ate and went out coursing, and many is the gallant course I had, and many the swift hare I and my dog Moro brought home from the right bank of the Guadiana.

* * *

On the night of the 6th April the 3rd Division were to storm the citadel, the 4th and Light the great breach, the 5th the Olivença Gate, and to escalade, if possible.

Old Alister Cameron, who was in command of four Companies of the 95th Regiment, extended along the counterscape to attract the enemy's fire, while the column planted their ladders and descended, came up to Barnard and said, "Now my men are ready; shall I begin?" "No, certainly not," says Barnard. The breach and the works were full of the enemy, looking quietly at us, but not fifty yards off and most prepared, although not firing a shot. So soon as our ladders were all ready posted, and the column in the very act to move and rush down the ladders, Barnard called out, "Now, Cameron!" and the first shot from us brought down such a hail of fire as I shall never forget, nor ever saw before or since. It was most murderous. We flew down the ladders and rushed at the breach, but we were broken, and carried no weight with us, although every soldier was a hero. The breach was covered by a breastwork from behind, and ably defended on the top by *chevaux-de-frises* of sword-blades, sharp as razors, chained to the ground; while the ascent to the top of the breach was covered with planks with sharp nails in them. However, devil a one did I feel at this moment. One of the officers of the forlorn hope, Lieut. Taggart of the 43rd, was hanging on my arm—a mode we adopted to help each other up, for the ascent was most difficult and steep. A Rifleman stood among the sword-blades on the top of one of the *chevaux-defrires*. We made a glorious rush to follow, but, alas! in vain. He was knocked over. My old captain, O'Hare, who commanded the storming party, was killed. All were awfully wounded except, I do believe, myself and little Freer of the 43rd. I had been some seconds at the *revêtement* of the bastion near the breach, and my redcoat pockets were literally filled with chips of stones splintered by musket-balls. Those not knocked down were driven back by this hail of mortality to the ladders. At the foot of them I saw poor Colonel Macleod with his hands on his breast—the man who lent me his horse when wounded at the bridge on the Coa. He said, "Oh, Smith, I am mortally wounded. Help me up the ladder." I said, "Oh no, dear fellow!" "I am," he said; "be quick!" I did so, and came back again. Little Freer and I said, "Let us throw down the ladders; the fellows shan't go out." Some soldiers behind said, "D— your eyes, if you do we will bayonet you!" and we were literally forced up with the crowd. My sash had got loose, and one end of it was fast in the ladder, and the bayonet was very nearly applied, but the sash by pulling became loose. So soon as we got on the glacis, up came a fresh Brigade of the Portuguese of the 4th Division. I never saw any soldiers behave with more pluck. Down into the ditch we all went again, but the more we tried to get up, the more we were destroyed. The 4th Division followed us in marching up to the breach, and they made a most uncommon noise. The French saw us, but took no notice. Sir Charles Colville, commanding the 4th Division (Cole having been wounded at Albuera), made a devil of a noise, too, on the glacis. Both Divisions were fairly beaten back; we never carried either breach (nominally there were two breaches).

After the attacks upon the breaches, some time before daylight Lord Fitzroy Somerset came to our Division. I think I was almost the first officer who spoke to him. He said, "Where is Barnard?" I didn't know, but I assured his Lordship he was neither killed nor wounded. A few minutes after his Lordship said that the Duke desired the Light and 4th Divisions to storm again. "The devil!" says I. "Why, we have had enough; we are all knocked to pieces." Lord Fitzroy says, "I dare say, but you must try again." I smiled and said, "If we could not succeed with two whole fresh and unscathed Divisions, we are likely to make a poor show of it now. But we will try again with all our might." Scarcely had this conversation occurred when a bugle sounded within the breach, indicating what had occurred at the citadel and Puerto de Qlivença; and here ended all the fighting. Our fellows would have gone at it again when collected and put into shape, but we were just as well pleased that our attempt had so attracted the attention of the enemy as greatly to facilitate that success which assured the prize contended for.

* * *

Now comes a scene of horror I would willingly bury in oblivion. The atrocities committed by our soldiers on the poor innocent and defenceless inhabitants of the city, no words suffice to depict. Civilized man, when let loose and the bonds of morality relaxed, is a far greater beast than the savage, more refined in his cruelty, more fiend-like in every act; and oh, too truly did our heretofore noble soldiers disgrace themselves, though the officers exerted themselves to the utmost to repress it, many who had escaped the enemy being wounded in their merciful attempts!

Mary Shelley, excerpt from *Frankenstein*

Mary Wollstonecraft Shelley (1797-1851) was the only child of English writers William Godwin and Mary Wollstonecraft. As a young woman, in 1816, she married the poet Percy Shelley. She and her husband traveled widely in Europe, and were often at the center of a circle of Romantic authors and artists, including Lord Byron (1788-1824), whom she mentioned in this excerpted passage. After her husband's death in 1822, Shelley worked to further establish her husband's legacy as a major poet, publishing several editions of his work supplement by her own editorial notes. More importantly, she wrote and published several novels of her own, including *Frankenstein*, which first appeared in 1816. In this excerpt, an introduction to the 1831 edition, Shelley described her reasons for writing the novel, and how she first imagined and then wrote this story about a scientist, Frankenstein, and the man-made being he created.

Sources: Mary Shelley, *Frankenstein* (London: Henry Colburn and Richard Bentley, 1831), v-2 .

Focus Questions:

1. Why and how did Mary Shelley come to write this novel? What inspired or influenced her work?

2. What main themes or issues did Shelley set out to explore in the novel?
3. How was this novel, and the writing of it, tied to the Romantic movement?

The Publishers of the Standard Novels, in selecting"Frankenstein"for one of their series, expressed a wish that I should furnish them with some account of the origin of the story. I am the more willing to comply, because I shall thus give a general answer to the question, so very frequently asked me —"How I, then a young girl, came to think of, and to dilate upon, so very hideous an idea?" It is true that I am very averse to bringing myself forward in print; but as my account will only appear as an appendage to a former production, and as it will be confined to such topics as have connection with my authorship alone, I can scarcely accuse myself of a personal intrusion.

It is not singular that, as the daughter of two persons of distinguished literary celebrity, I should very early in life have thought of writing. As a child I scribbled; and my favourite pastime, during the hours given me for recreation, was to "write stories." Still I had a dearer pleasure than this, which was the formation of castles in the air —the indulging in waking dreams —the following up trains of thought, which had for their subject the formation of a succession of imaginary incidents. My dreams were at once more fantastic and agreeable than my writings. In the latter I was a close imitator —rather doing as others had done, then putting down the suggestions of my own mind. What I wrote was intended at least for one other eye —my childhood's companion and friend; but my dreams were all my own; I accounted for them to nobody; they were my refuge when annoyed —my dearest pleasure when free.

I lived principally in the country as a girl, and passed a considerable time in Scotland. I made occasional visits to the more picturesque parts; but my habitual residence was on the blank and dreary northern shores of the Tay, near Dundee. Blank and dreary on retrospection I call them; they were not so to me then. They were the eyre of freedom, and the pleasant region where unheeded I could commune with the creatures of my fancy. I wrote then —but in a most common-place style. It was beneath the trees of the grounds belonging to our house, on the bleak sides of the woodless mountains near, that my true compositions, the airy flights of my imagination, were born and fostered. I did not make myself the heroine of my tales. Life appeared to me too common-place an affair as regarded myself. I could not figure to myself that romantic woes or wonderful events would ever be my lot; but I was not confined to my own identity, and I could people the hours with creations far more interesting to me at that age, than my own sensations.

After this my life became busier, and reality stood in place of fiction. My husband, however, was from the first, very anxious that I should prove myself worthy of my parentage, and enroll myself on the page of fame. He was for ever inciting me to obtain literary reputation, which even on my own part I cared for then, though since I have become infinitely indifferent to it. At this time he desired that I should write, not so much with the idea

that I could produce any thing worthy of notice, but that he might himself judge how far I possessed the promise of better things hereafter. Still I did nothing. Travelling, and the cares of a family, occupied my time; and study, in the way of reading, or improving my ideas in communication with his far more cultivated mind, was all of literary employment that engaged my attention.

In the summer of 1816, we visited Switzerland, and became the neighbours of Lord Byron. At first we spent our pleasant hours on the lake, or wandering on its shores; and Lord Byron, who was writing the third canto of Childe Harold, was the only one among us who put his thoughts upon paper. These, as he brought them successively to us, clothed in all the light and harmony of poetry, seemed to stamp as divine the glories of heaven and earth, whose influences we partook with him.

But it proved a wet, ungenial summer, and incessant rain often confined us for days to the house. Some volumes of ghost stories, translated from the German into French, fell into our hands. There was the History of the Inconstant Lover, who, when he thought to clasp the bride to whom he had pledged his vows, found himself in the arms of the pale ghost of her whom he had deserted. There was the tale of the sinful founder of his race, whose miserable doom it was to bestow the kiss of death on all the younger sons of his fated house, just when they reached the age of promise. His gigantic, shadowy form, clothed like the ghost in Hamlet, in complete armour, but with the beaver up, was seen at midnight, by the moon's fitful beams, to advance slowly along the gloomy avenue. The shape was lost beneath the shadow of the castle walls; but soon a gate swung back, a step was heard, the door of the chamber opened, and he advanced to the couch of the blooming youths, cradled in healthy sleep. Eternal sorrow sat upon his face as he bent down and kissed the forehead of the boys, who from that hour withered like flowers snapt upon the stalk. I have not seen these stories since then; but their incidents are as fresh in my mind as if I had read them yesterday.

We will each write a ghost story, said Lord Byron; and his proposition was acceded to. There were four of us. The noble author began a tale, a fragment of which he printed at the end of his poem of Mazeppa. Shelley, more apt to embody ideas and sentiments in the radiance of brilliant imagery, and in the music of the most melodious verse that adorns our language, than to invent the machinery of a story, commenced one founded on the experiences of his early life. Poor Polidori had some terrible idea about a skull-headed lady, who was so punished for peeping through a key-hole —to see what I forget —something very shocking and wrong of course; but when she was reduced to a worse condition than the renowned Tom of Coventry, he did not know what to do with her, and was obliged to despatch her to the tomb of the Capulets, the only place for which she was fitted. The illustrious poets also, annoyed the platitude of prose, speedily relinquished their uncongenial task.

I busied myself to think of a story, —a story to rival those which had excited us to this task. One which would speak to the mysterious fears of our nature, and awaken thrilling horror —one to make the reader dread to look round, to curdle the blood, and quicken the beatings of the heart. If I did not accomplish these things, my ghost story would be unworthy of its name. I thought and pondered —vainly. I felt that blank incapability of invention which is the greatest misery of authorship, when dull Nothing replies to our anxious invocations. Have you thought of a story? I was asked each morning, and each morning I was forced to reply with a mortifying negative.

Every thing must have a beginning, to speak in Sanchean phrase; and that beginning must be linked to something that went before. The Hindoos give the world an elephant to support it, but they make the elephant stand upon a tortoise. Invention, it must be humbly admitted, does not consist in creating out of the void, but out of chaos; the materials must, in the first place, be afforded: it can give form to dark, shapeless substances, but cannot bring into being the substance itself. In all matters of discovery and invention, even of those that appertain to the imagination, we are continually reminded of the story of Columbus and his egg. Invention consists in the capacity of seizing on the capabilities of a subject, and in the power of moulding and fashioning ideas suggested to it.

Many and long were the conversations between Lord Byron and Shelley, to which I was a devout but nearly silent listener. During one of these, various philosophical doctrines were discussed, and among others the nature of the principle of life, and whether there was any probability of its ever being discovered and communicated. They talked of the experiments of Dr. Darwin, (I speak not of what the Doctor really did, or said that he did, but, as more to my purpose, of what was then spoken of as having been done by him,) who preserved a piece of vermicelli in a glass case, till by some extraordinary means it began to move with voluntary motion. Not thus, after all, would life be given. Perhaps a corpse would be re-animated; galvanism had given token of such things: perhaps the component parts of a creature might be manufactured, brought together, and endured with vital warmth.

Night waned upon this talk, and even the witching hour had gone by, before we retired to rest. When I place my head on my pillow, I did not sleep, nor could I be said to think. My imagination, unbidden, possessed and guided me, gifting the successive images that arose in my mind with a vividness far beyond the usual bounds of reverie. I saw —with shut eyes, but acute mental vision, —I saw the pale student of unhallowed arts kneeling beside the thing he had put together. I saw the hideous phantasm of a man stretched out, and then, on the working of some powerful engine, show signs of life, and stir with an uneasy, half vital motion. Frightful must it be; for supremely frightful would be the effect of any human endeavour to mock the stupendous mechanism of the Creator of the world. His success would terrify the artist; he would rush away from his odious handywork, horror-stricken. He would hope that, left to itself, the slight spark of life which he had communicated would fade; that this thing, which had received such imperfect animation, would subside into dead matter; and he might sleep in the belief that the silence of the grave would quench for ever the transient existence of the hideous corpse which he had looked upon as the cradle of life. He sleeps; but he is awakened; he opens his eyes; behold the horrid thing stands at his bedside, opening his curtains, and looking on him with yellow, watery, but speculative eyes.

I opened mine in terror. The idea so possessed my mind, that a thrill of fear ran through me, and I wished to exchange the ghastly image of my fancy for the realities around. I see them still; the very room, the dark parquet, the closed shutters, with the moonlight struggling through, and the sense I had that the glassy lake and white high Alps were beyond. I could not so easily get rid of my hideous phantom; still it haunted me. I must try to think of something else. I recurred to my ghost story, —my tiresome unlucky ghost story! O! if I could only contrive one which would frighten my reader as I myself had been frightened that night!

Swift as light and as cheering was the idea that broke in upon me. I have found it! What terrified me will terrify others; and I need only describe the spectre which had haunted my midnight pillow. On the morrow I announced that I had thought of a story. I began that day with the words, It was on a dreary night of November, making only a transcript of the grim terrors of my waking dream.

At first I thought but of a few pages —of a short tale; but Shelley urged me to develop the idea at greater length. I certainly did not owe the suggestion of one incident, nor scarcely one train of feeling, to my husband, and yet but for his incitement, it would never have taken the form in which it was presented to the world. From this declaration I must except the preface. As far as I can recollect, it was entirely written by him.

And now, once again, I bid my hideous progeny go forth and prosper. I have an affection for it, for it was the offspring of happy days, when death and grief were but words, which found no true echo in my heart. Its several pages speak of many a walk, many a drive, and many a conversation, when I was not alone; and my companion was one who, in this world, I shall never see more. But this is for myself; my readers have nothing to do with these associations.

I will add but one word as to the alterations I have made. They are principally those of style. I have changed no portion of the story, nor introduced any new ideas or circumstances. I have mended the language where it was so bald as to interfere with the interest of the narrative; and these changes occur almost exclusively in the beginning of the first volume. Throughout they are entirely confined to such parts as are mere adjuncts to the story, leaving the core and substance of it untouched.

M.W.S. London, October 15, 1831.

Louis Antoine Fauvelet de Bourrienne, *Memoirs of Napoleon Bonaparte*

The following excerpts provide a French view of Napoleon's campaign in Egypt, written by Louis Antoine Fauvelet de Bourrienne (1769-1834). Napoleon Bonaparte (1769-1821) was born on the French island of Corsica, trained at French military schools, and first came to prominence during the French Revolutionary wars. Although the Revolution came to an end, the wars continued under the weak Directory government (1794-1799). In 1798, Napoleon embarked on a campaign in Egypt with the goal of undercutting British naval power. Unable to attack Britain directly in Europe, Napoleon sought to conquer Egypt, which was then a part of the Ottoman Empire, and use it as a seat to counter British naval domination of the Mediterranean. French troops remained in Egypt for two years during this campaign, from 1798 to 1801, but with little success. The campaign was widely viewed as a failure. Bourrienne was Napoleon's long-time friend since they had been fellow classmates in military school and he then served as Napoleon's personal secretary from 1797 until 1801. His memoirs, including this first-hand account of the campaign in Egypt, were published in France, in 1829.

Source: Louis Antoine Fauvelet de Bourrienne, *Memoirs of Napoleon Bonaparte*, vol. 1 (Paris and Boston: The Napoleon Society, 1895), 158-91; reprinted in *Napoleon in Egypt. Al-Jabarti's chronicle of the first seven months of the French occupation, 1798 trans. Smuel Moreh*, (Princeton, N.J.: Marcus Wiener, 1993), 136, 150, 152-53.

Focus Questions:

1. What were Napoleon's aims in Egypt according to Bourrienne?
2. How did Napoleon attempt to conquer Egypt, and what does Bourrienne say about the means and strategies he used?
3. What does this passage tell us about French attitudes regarding the Egyptians and perceptions of their culture, society, and religion?

Soldiers,—You are about to undertake a conquest the effects of which on civilisation and commerce are incalculable. The blow you are about to give to

England will be the best aimed, and the most sensibly felt, she can receive until the time arrive when you can give her her death-blow.

We must make some fatiguing marches; we must fight several battles; we shall succeed in all we undertake. The destinies are with us. The Mameluke* Beys, who favour exclusively English commerce, whose extortions oppress our merchants and who tyrannise over the unfortunate inhabitants of the Nile, a few days after our arrival will no longer exist.

The people amongst whom we are going to live are Mahometans.** The first article of their faith is this: "There is no God but God, and Mahomet in His prophet." Do not contradict them. Behave to them as you have behaved to the Jews—to the Italians. Pay respect to their muftis, and their Imaums, as you did to the rabbis and the bishops. Extend to the ceremonies prescribed by the Koran and to the mosques the same toleration which you showed to the synagogues, to the religion of Moses and of Jesus Christ.

The Roman legions protected all religions. You will find here customs different from those of Europe. You must accommodate yourselves to them. The people amongst whom we are to mix differ from us in the treatment of women; but in all countries he who violates is a monster. Pillage enriches only a small number of men; it dishonours us; it destroys our resources; it converts into enemies the people whom it is our interest to have for friends.

The first town we shall come to was built by Alexander. At every step we shall meet with grand recollections, worthy of exciting the emulation of Frenchmen.

BOURRIENNE'S ACCOUNT

On the 21st of August, Bonaparte established at Cairo an institute of the arts and sciences.

* * *

In founding this Institute, Bonaparte wished to afford an example of his ideas of civilisation. The minutes of the sittings of that learned body, which have been printed, bear evidence of its utility, and of Napoleon's extended views. The objects of the Institute were the advancement and propagation of information in Egypt, and the study and publication of all facts relating to the natural history, trade, and antiquities of the ancient country.

On the 18th, Bonaparte was present at the ceremony of opening the dike of the canal of Cairo, which receives the water of the Nile when it reaches the height fixed by the Mequyas.

* Traditional Egyptian rulers who had reasserted their authority with the waning of Ottoman control.

** Muslims

Two days after came the anniversary festival of the birth of Mahomet. At this Napoleon was also present, in company with the sheik El Bekri.

* * *

It has been alleged that Bonaparte, when in Egypt, took part in the religious ceremonies and worship of the Mussulmans; but it cannot be said that he celebrated the festivals of the overflowing of the Nile and the anniversary of the Prophet. The Turks invited him to these merely as a spectator, and the presence of their new master was gratifying to the people. But he never committed the folly of ordering any solemnity. He neither learned nor repeated any prayer of the Koran, as many persons have asserted; neither did he advocate fatalism, polygamy, or any other doctrine of the Koran.

* * *

The ceremonies, at which policy induced him to be present, were to him, and to all who accompanied him, mere matters of curiosity. He never set foot in a mosque;

* * *

His religious tolerance was the natural consequence of his philosophic spirit.

Doubtless Bonaparte did, as he was bound to do, show respect for the religion of the country; and he found it necessary to act more like a Mussulman than a Catholic. A wise conqueror supports his triumphs by protecting and even elevating the religion of the conquered people. Bonaparte's principle was, as he himself has often told me, to look upon religions as the work of men, but to respect them everywhere as a powerful engine of government. However, I will not go so far as to say that he would not have changed his religion had the conquest of the East been the price of that change. All that he said about Mahomet, Islamism, and the Koran to the great men of the country he laughed at himself. He enjoyed the gratification of having all his fine sayings on the subject of religion translated into Arabic poetry, and repeated from mouth to mouth. This of course tended to conciliate the people.

I confess that Bonaparte frequently conversed with the chiefs of the Mussulman religion on the subject of his conversion; but only for the sake of amusement.

PART 5

The West Ascendant (1800 – 1914)

CHAPTER 19

Nationalism and State-Building in the West

Alexis de Tocqueville, *Democracy in America*

Alexis de Tocqueville (1805–1859) is credited with creating one of the most perceptive and enduring portraits of the American people and their political institutions, and his observations, *Democracy in America* (2 volumes, 1835–1840), are still read and discussed by Americans today. The book was the fruit of his nine months of travel in the United States in 1831; Tocqueville met influential Americans in all of the major cities of the Eastern seaboard, but he also traveled as far west as Michigan and as far south as New Orleans, to learn something of the American character in the vast interior of North America. As a political figure in France, Tocqueville was particularly interested in the political structures and behavior of the Americans he encountered.

Source: Alexandre de Tocqueville, *Democracy in America* (Cambridge [Mass.], Sever and Francis, 1863).

Focus Questions:

1. How does Tocqueville tie the American experience to larger historical trends?
2. In what ways is democracy a logical historical progression, in his opinion?
3. Is it surprising that a descendant of nobles would have made claims like this?

EXCERPT FROM VOLUME ONE

...Amongst the novel objects that attracted my attention during my stay in the United States, nothing struck me more forcibly than the general equality of conditions. I readily discovered the prodigious influence which this primary fact exercises on the whole course of society, by giving a certain direction to public opinion, and a certain tenor to the laws; by imparting new maxims to the governing powers, and peculiar habits to the governed. I speedily perceived that the influence of this fact extends far beyond the political character and the laws of the country, and that it has no less empire over civil society than over the Government; it creates opinions, engenders sentiments, suggests the ordinary practices of life, and modifies whatever it does not produce. The more I advanced in the study of American society, the more I perceived that the equality of conditions is the fundamental fact from which all others seem to be derived, and the central point at which all my observations constantly terminated.

I then turned my thoughts to our own hemisphere, where I imagined that I discerned something analogous to the spectacle which the New World presented to me. I observed that the equality of conditions is daily progressing towards those extreme limits which it seems to have reached in the United States, and that the democracy which governs the American communities appears to be rapidly rising into power in Europe. I hence conceived the idea of the book which is now before the reader.

It is evident to all alike that a great democratic revolution is going on amongst us; but there are two opinions as to its nature and consequences. To some it appears to be a novel accident, which as such may still be checked; to others it seems irresistible, because it is the most uniform, the most ancient, and the most permanent tendency which is to be found in history. Let us recollect the situation of France seven hundred years ago, when the territory was divided amongst a small number of families, who were the owners of the soil and the rulers of the inhabitants; the right of governing descended with the family inheritance from generation to generation; force was the only means by which man could act on man, and landed property was the sole source of power. Soon, however, the political power of the clergy was founded, and began to exert itself: the clergy opened its ranks to all classes, to the poor and the rich, the villein and the lord; equality penetrated into the Government through the Church, and the being who as a serf must have vegetated in perpetual bondage took his place as a priest in the midst of nobles, and not infrequently above the heads of kings.

The different relations of men became more complicated and more numerous as society gradually became more stable and more civilized. Thence the want of civil laws was felt; and the order of legal functionaries soon rose from the obscurity of the tribunals and their dusty chambers, to appear at the court of the monarch, by the side of the feudal barons in their ermine and their mail. Whilst the kings were ruining themselves by their great enterprises, and the nobles exhausting their resources by private wars, the lower orders were enriching themselves by commerce. The influence of money began to be perceptible in State affairs. The transactions of business opened a new road to power, and the financier rose to a station of political influence in which he was at once flattered and despised. Gradually the spread of mental acquirements, and the increasing taste for literature and art, opened chances of success to talent; science became a means of government, intelligence led to social power, and the man of letters took a part in the affairs of the State. The value attached to the privileges of birth decreased in the exact proportion in which new paths were struck out to advancement. In the eleventh century nobility was beyond all price; in the thirteenth it might be purchased; it was conferred for the first time in 1270; and equality was thus introduced into the Government by the aristocracy itself.

In the course of these seven hundred years it sometimes happened that in order to resist the authority of the Crown, or to diminish the power of their rivals, the nobles granted a certain share of political rights to the people. Or, more frequently, the king permitted the lower orders to enjoy a degree of power, with the intention of repressing the aristocracy. In France the kings have always been the most active and the most constant of levellers. When they were strong and ambitious they spared no pains to raise the people to the level of the nobles; when they were temperate or weak they allowed the people to rise above themselves. Some assisted the democracy by their talents, others by their vices. Louis XI and Louis XIV reduced every rank beneath the throne to the same subjection; Louis XV descended, himself and all his Court, into the dust.

As soon as land was held on any other than a feudal tenure, and personal property began in its turn to confer influence and power, every improvement which was introduced in commerce or manufacture was a fresh element of the equality of conditions. Henceforward every new discovery, every new want which it engendered, and every new desire which craved satisfaction, was a step towards the universal level. The taste for luxury, the love of war, the sway of fashion, and the most superficial as well as the deepest passions of the human heart, cooperated to enrich the poor and to impoverish the rich.

From the time when the exercise of the intellect became the source of strength and of wealth, it is impossible not to consider every addition to science, every fresh truth, and every new idea as a germ of power placed within the reach of the people. Poetry, eloquence, and memory, the grace of wit, the glow of imagination, the depth of thought, and all the gifts which are bestowed by Providence with an equal hand, turned to the advantage of the democracy; and even when they were in the possession of its adversaries they still served its cause by throwing into relief the natural greatness of man; its conquests spread, there-fore, with those of civilization and knowledge, and literature became an arsenal where the poorest and the weakest could always find weapons to their hand.

In perusing the pages of our history, we shall scarcely meet with a single great event, in the lapse of seven hundred years, which has not turned to the advantage of equality. The Crusades and the wars of the English decimated the nobles and divided their possessions; the erection of communities introduced an element of democratic liberty into the bosom of feudal monarchy; the invention of fire-arms equalized the villein and the noble on the field of battle; printing opened the same resources to the minds of all classes; the post was organized so as to bring the same information to the door of the poor man's cottage and to the gate of the palace; and Protestantism proclaimed that all men are alike able to find the road to heaven. The discovery of America offered a thousand new paths to fortune, and placed riches and power within the reach of the adventurous and the obscure. If we examine what has happened in France at intervals of fifty years, beginning with the eleventh century, we shall invariably perceive that a twofold revolution has taken place in the state of society. The noble has gone down on the social ladder, and the roturier has gone up; the one descends as the other rises. Every half century brings them nearer to each other, and they will very shortly meet.

Nor is this phenomenon at all peculiar to France. Whithersoever we turn our eyes we shall witness the same continual revolution throughout the whole of Christendom. The various occurrences of national existence have everywhere turned to the advantage of democracy; all men have aided it by their exertions: those who have intentionally labored in its cause, and those who have served it unwittingly; those who have fought for it and those who have declared themselves its opponents, have all been driven along in the same track, have all labored to one end, some ignorantly and some unwillingly; all have been blind instruments in the hands of God.

The gradual development of the equality of conditions is therefore a providential fact, and it possesses all the characteristics of a divine decree: it is universal, it is durable, it constantly eludes all human interference, and all events as well as all men contribute to its progress. Would it, then, be wise to imagine that a social impulse which dates from so far back can be checked by the efforts of a generation? Is it credible that the democracy which has annihilated the feudal system and vanquished kings will respect the citizen and the capitalist? Will it stop now that it has grown so strong and its adversaries so weak? None can say which way we are going, for all terms of comparison are wanting: the equality of conditions is more complete in the Christian countries of the present day than it has been at any time or in any part of the world; so that the extent of what already exists prevents us from foreseeing what may be yet to come.

The whole book which is here offered to the public has been written under the impression of a kind of religious dread produced in the author's mind by the contemplation of so irresistible a revolution, which has advanced for centuries in spite of such amazing obstacles, and which is still proceeding in the midst of the ruins it has made. It is not necessary that God himself should speak in order to disclose to us the unquestionable signs of His will; we can discern them in the habitual course of nature, and in the invariable tendency of events: I know, without a special revelation, that the planets move in the orbits traced

Thomas Babington Macaulay, from *Minute on Education,* 1835

Thomas Babington Macaulay (1800–1859 CE) was an English historian and parliamentarian. Macaulay held various government posts and served in the House of Commons, where he stood out for his oratory and supported the 1832 Reform Bill that expanded the electorate. From 1834 to 1838 he lived in India, where he reformed its educational system and criminal code. Macaulay wrote poems, essays, and the popular five-volume *History of England.* Although valued for its readability and as a groundbreaking social history of seventeenth-century England, Macaulay's approach has subsequently been criticized as embodying an uncritical, biased perspective that views English political development and bourgeois progress as a standard for other nations.

Source: Thomas Babington Macaulay, *Minute on Education, from Selections from Educational Records, Part I* (1781–1839), Calcutta, 1920.

Focus Questions:

1. Why does Macaulay propose using the English language to educate the Indian people?
2. What kinds of problems in education does Macaulay want to eliminate, and who specifically does he have in mind to be taught English?

MACAULAY'S MINUTE ON EDUCATION, FEBRUARY 2, 1835

We now come to the gist of the matter. We have a fund to be employed as Government shall direct for the intellectual improvement of the people of this country. The simple question is, what is the most useful way of employing it?

All parties seem to be agreed on one point, that the dialects commonly spoken among the natives of this part of India contain neither literary nor scientific information, and are moreover so poor and rude that, until they are enriched from some other quarter, it will not be easy to translate any valuable work into them. It seems to be admitted on all sides, that the intellectual improvement of those classes of the people who have the means of pursuing higher studies can at present be affected only by means of some language not vernacular amongst them.

What then shall that language be? One-half of the committee maintain that it should be the English. The other half strongly recommend the Arabic and Sanscrit. The whole question seems to me to be—which language is the best worth knowing?

I have no knowledge of either Sanscrit or Arabic. But I have done what I could to form a correct estimate of their value. I have read translations of the most celebrated Arabic and Sanscrit works. I have conversed, both here and at home, with men distinguished by their proficiency in the Eastern tongues. I am quite ready to take the oriental learning at the valuation of the orientalists themselves. I have never found one among them who could deny that a single shelf of a good European library was worth the whole native literature of India and Arabia. The intrinsic superiority of the Western literature is indeed fully admitted by those members of the committee who support the oriental plan of education.

It will hardly be disputed, I suppose, that the department of literature in which the Eastern writers stand highest is poetry. And I certainly never met with any orientalist who ventured to maintain that the Arabic and Sanscrit poetry could be compared to that of the great European nations. But when we pass from works of imagination to works in which facts are recorded and general principles investigated, the superiority of the Europeans becomes absolutely immeasurable. It is, I believe, no exaggeration to say that all the historical information which has been collected from all the books written in the Sanscrit language is less valuable than what may be found in the most paltry abridgments used at preparatory schools in England. In every branch of physical or moral philosophy, the relative position of the two nations is nearly the same.

How then stands the case? We have to educate a people who cannot at present be educated by means of their mother-tongue. We must teach them some foreign language. The claims of our own language it is hardly necessary to recapitulate. It stands pre-eminent even among the languages of the West. It abounds with works of imagination not inferior to the noblest which Greece has bequeathed to us, with models of every species of eloquence, with historical composition, which, considered merely as narratives, have seldom been surpassed, and which, considered as vehicles of ethical and political instruction, have never been equaled with just and lively representations of human life and human nature, with the most pro-found speculations on metaphysics, morals, government, jurisprudence, trade, with full and correct information respecting every experimental science which tends to preserve the health, to increase the comfort, or to expand the intellect of man. Whoever knows that language has ready access to all the vast intellectual wealth which all the wisest nations of the earth have created and hoarded in the course of ninety generations. It may safely be said that the literature now extant in that language is of greater value than all the literature which three hundred years ago was extant in all the languages of the world together. Nor is this all. In India, English is the language spoken by the ruling class. It is spoken by the higher class of natives at the seats of Government. It is likely to become the language of commerce throughout the seas of the East. It is the language of two great European communities which are rising, the one in the south of Africa, the other in Australia, communities which are every year becoming more important and more closely connected with our Indian empire. Whether we look at the intrinsic value of our literature, or at the particular situation of this country, we shall see the strongest reason to think that, of all foreign tongues, the English tongue is that which would be the most useful to our native subjects.

The question now before us is simply whether, when it is in our power to teach this language, we shall teach languages in which, by universal confession, there are no books on any subject which deserve to be compared to our own, whether, when we can teach European science, we shall teach systems which, by universal confession, wherever they differ from those of Europe differ for the worse, and whether, when we can patronize sound philosophy and true history, we shall countenance, at the public expense, medical doctrines which would disgrace an English farrier, astronomy which would move laughter in girls at an English boarding school, history abounding with kings thirty feet high and reigns thirty thou-sand years long, and geography made of seas of treacle and seas of butter.

* * *

In one point I fully agree with the gentlemen to whose general views I am opposed. I feel with them that it is impossible for us, with our limited means, to attempt to educate the body of the people. We must at present do our best to form a class who may be interpreters between us and the millions whom we govern, a class of persons Indian in blood and colour, but English in tastes, in opinions, in morals and in intellect. To that class we may leave it to refine the vernacular dialects of the country, to enrich those dialects with terms of science borrowed from the Western nomenclature, and to render them by degrees fit vehicles for conveying knowledge to the great mass of the population.

I would strictly respect all existing interests. I would deal even generously with all individuals who have had fair reason to expect a pecuniary provision. But I would strike at the root of the bad system which has hitherto been fostered by us. I would at once stop the printing of Arabic and Sanscrit books. I would abolish the Mudrassa and the Sanscrit College at Calcutta. Benares is the great seat of Brahminical learning; Delhi of Arabic learning. If we retain the Sanscrit College at Bonares and the Mahometan College at Delhi we do enough and much more than enough in my opinion, for the Eastern languages. If the Benares and Delhi Colleges should be retained, I would at least recommend that no stipends shall be given to any students who may hereafter repair thither, but that the people shall be left to make their own choice between the rival systems of education without being bribed by us to learn what they have no desire to know. The funds which would thus be placed at our disposal would enable us to give larger encouragement to the Hindoo College at Calcutta, and establish in the principal cities throughout the Presidencies of Fort William and Agra schools in which the English language might be well and thoroughly taught.

If the decision of His Lordship in Council should be such as I anticipate, I shall enter on the performance of my duties with the greatest zeal and alacrity. If, on the other hand, it be the opinion of the Government that the present system ought to remain unchanged, I beg that I may be permitted to retire from the chair of the Committee. I feel that I could not be of the smallest use there. I feel also that I should be lending my countenance to what I firmly believe to be a mere delusion. I believe that the present system tends not to accelerate the progress of truth but to delay the natural death of expiring errors. I conceive that we have at present no right to the respectable name of a Board of Public Instruction. We are a Board for wasting the public money, for printing books which are of less value than the paper on which they are printed was while it was blank—for giving artificial encouragement to absurd history, absurd metaphysics, absurd physics, absurd theology—for raising up a breed of scholars who find their scholarship an incumbrance and blemish, who live on the public while they are receiving their education, and whose education is so utterly useless to them that, when they have received it, they must either starve or live on the public all the rest of their lives. Entertaining these opinions, I am naturally desirous to decline all share in the responsibility of a body which, unless it alters its whole mode of proceedings, I must consider, not merely as useless, but as positively noxious.

T[homas] B[abington] MACAULAY

2nd February 1835.

I give my entire concurrence to the sentiments expressed in this Minute.

W[illiam] C[avendish] BENTIN

José María Morelos, *Sentiments of the Nation*

José María Morelos (1765-1815) played a prominent role in the early struggle for Mexican independence from Spain that began around 1810. Born into a poor family, Morelos became a Catholic priest, who worked in a poor parish. In 1811, he joined forces with Miguel Hidalgo, another priest who led an insurrection against the Spanish colonial government in an early bid for independence that did not succeed. Following the revolt, the Spanish captured and executed Hidalgo. Morelos then took over leadership of the independent, nationalist movement in southern Mexico. In this document, Morelos presents his plan for a new government and constitution that he hoped would be formed by the Congress of Chilpancingo, an assembly of Mexican nationalists that came together in 1813 to declare a formal break from Spain and set up an independent government. This attempt at independence, however, never came to fruition; the Spanish captured Morelos and he was executed in 1815.

Source: José María Morelos,"Sentiments of the Nation," (Chilpancingo, Mexico, 1813); reprinted in *Colonial Spanish America: A Documentary History,* eds. Kenneth Mills and William B. Taylor (Wilmington, D.E.: Scholarly Resources, 1998), 341-44.

Focus Questions:

1. What was the main purpose of this document, and what were the most important provisions for the government that was to be established?
2. What ideas and beliefs informed Morelos' ideas?
3. What kind of society and government did Morelos envision for an independent Mexico?

1. That America is free and independent of Spain and every other nation, government, or monarchy, and thus it shall be proclaimed, informing the world why.
2. That the Catholic religion shall be the only one, without tolerance for any other.
3. That the ministers of the Church shall live only from the tithes and first fruits, and the people shall not be required to pay for services, except as true offerings and expressions of their devotion.
4. That the dogma of the religion shall be upheld by the Church hierarchy, consisting of the Pope, the bishops, and the parish priests, because every plant that God did not plant should be weeded out....Matthew
5. That sovereignty flows directly from the people, and they wish it to be lodged only in the Supremo Congreso Nacional Americano, composed of representatives of the provinces in equal numbers.
6. That the legislative, executive, and judicial powers shall be divided among those bodies that are established to exercise them.
7. That the representatives shall serve for four years in rotation, the old ones leaving office so the newly elected can take their places.
8. The representatives shall be paid a sufficient but not excessive salary. For now, it shall not be more than 8,000 pesos.
9. Government posts shall be held only by Americans.
10. Foreigners shall not be allowed to enter the country unless they are artisans who can instruct others and are free of all suspicion.

11. States alter the customs of the people; therefore, the Fatherland will not be completely free and ours until the government is reformed, replacing the tyrannical with the liberal, and also expelling from our soil the enemy Spaniard who has so greatly opposed our Fatherland.

12. Since the good law is superior to any man, those [laws] that our Congreso issues shall be so, and shall promote constancy and patriotism, and moderate opulence and poverty so that the daily wage of the poor man is raised, his customs improved, and ignorance, preying upon others, and thievery removed.

13. That the general laws shall apply to everyone, including privileged corporations except as applies directly to their duties.

14. To draw up a law, there shall be a gathering of the greatest number of wise men possible, so that the deliberations may proceed with greater certainty. [These men] shall be exempt from some of the duties that might otherwise be demanded of them.

15. Slavery shall be forever forbidden, as shall caste distinctions, leaving everyone equal. One American shall be distinguished from another only by his vices and virtues.

16. That our ports may admit [the ships of] friendly foreign nations, but they cannot be based in the kingdom no matter how friendly they are. And only designated ports—ten percent of those that exist—shall be used for this purpose. Disembarkation in any other is forbidden.

17. The property of every individual shall be protected, and their homes respected as if they were a sacred asylum. Penalties shall be assigned for violators.

18. That the new legislation shall not allow torture.

19. That the new legislation shall establish by constitutional law the celebration of December 12 in every community of the land in honor of Our Most Holy Lady of Guadalupe, patroness of our liberty; and every community is to practice monthly devotions to her.

20. That foreign troops or those from any other [Spanish] kingdom shall not set foot on our soil unless it is to come to our aid, and then only with the authorization of the Suprema Junta.

21. That no expeditions outside the limits of the kingdom shall be made, especially not overseas expeditions; but others not of this kind are to be encouraged in order to propagate the faith among our brothers in the interior [tierradentro, or northern Mexico and the American Southwest].

22. That the plethora of tributes, fees, and taxes that weigh us down shall be eliminated. A five percent charge on grains and other produce, or a similarly light

tax, shall be levied on every individual. It shall not oppress us like the alcabala, the tobacco monopoly; the tribute, and others. With this light contribution and good administration of property confiscated from the enemy, the cost of the war and the salaries of employees can be paid.

Chilpancingo, 14 September 1813.

[appended Article] 23. That September 16 also shall be solemnized each year as the anniversary of the beginning of our struggle for Independence and our holy Freedom, for on that date the Nation spoke, demanding its rights with sword in hand so as to be heard. Thus the distinction of the great hero, Señor Don Miguel Hidalgo, and his companion, Don Ignacio Allende, will be remembered forever.

Karl von Clausewitz, *On War,* "Arming the Nation"

Karl von Clausewitz (1780–1831 CE) was born near Magdeburg. Clausewitz joined the Prussian army at the age of twelve. Clausewitz fought in the Rhine in 1793–1794 against the French Revolutionary Army. In 1812 he joined Russian forces against Napoleon's invasion of Russia, and served as an officer with Prussian forces at Waterloo. From 1818 until 1830 he served as chief administrator of Prussia's War College, at which time he wrote his most famous work, *On War*. Clausewitz is best known for the concept of total war, and the idea that war is a continuation of politics by other means.

Source: Karl von Clausewitz, *On War.*

Focus Questions:

1. What does Clausewitz mean by the term "people's war"?
2. According to Clausewitz, under what conditions can a people's war be effective, and how should such a war defend against a large invading army?

CHAPTER XXVI
Arming the Nation

A people's war in civilised Europe is a phenomenon of the nineteenth century. It has its advocates and its opponents: the latter either considering it in a political sense as a revolutionary means, a state of anarchy declared lawful, which is as dangerous as a foreign enemy to social order at home; or on military grounds, conceiving that the result is not commensurate with the expenditure of the nation's strength. The first point does not concern us here, for we look upon a people's war merely as a means of fighting, therefore, in its connection with the enemy; but with regard to the latter point, we must observe that a people's war in general is to be regarded as a consequence of the outburst which the military element in our day has made through its old formal limits; as an expansion and strengthening of the whole fermentation process which we call war. The requisition system, the immense increase in the size of armies by means of that system, and the general liability to military service, the utilizing militia, are all things which lie in the same direction, if we make the limited military system of former days our starting point; and the levée en masse, or arming of the people, now lies also in the same direction. If the first named of these new aids to war are the natural and necessary consequences of barriers thrown down; and if they have so enormously increased the power of those who first used them, that the enemy has been carried along in the current, and obliged to adopt them likewise, this will be the case also with people-wars. In the generality of cases, the people who make judicious use of this means, will gain a proportionate superiority over those who despise its use. If this be so, then the only question is whether this modern intensification of the military element is, upon the whole, salutary for the interests of humanity or otherwise—a question which it would be about as easy to answer as the question of war itself—we leave both to philosophers. But the opinion may be advanced, that the resources swallowed up in people's wars might be more profitably employed, if used in providing other military means; no very deep investigation, however, is necessary to be convinced that these resources are for the most part not disposable, and cannot be utilized in an arbitrary manner at pleasure. One essential part that is the moral element, is not called into existence until this kind of employment for it arises.

We therefore do not ask again: how much does the resistance which the whole nation in arms is capable of making, cost that nation? but we ask: what is the effect which such a resistance can produce? What are its conditions, and how is it to be used?

It follows from the very nature of the thing that defensive means thus widely dispersed, are not suited to great blows requiring concentrated action in time and space. Its operation, like the process of evaporation in physical nature, is according to the surface. The greater that surface and the greater the contact with the enemy's army, consequently the more that army spreads itself out, so much the greater will be the effects of arming the nation. Like a slow gradual heat, it destroys the foundations of the enemy's army. As it requires time to produce its effects, therefore whilst the hostile elements are working on each other, there is a state of tension which either gradually wears out if the people's war is extinguished at some points, and burns slowly away at others, or leads to a crisis, if the flames of this general conflagration envelop the enemy's army, and compel it to evacuate the country to save itself from utter destruction. In order that this result should be produced by a national war alone, we must suppose either a surface-extent of the dominions invaded, exceeding that of any country in Europe, except Russia, or suppose a disproportion between the strength of the invading army and the extent of the country, such as never occurs in reality. Therefore, to avoid following a phantom, we must imagine a people-war always in combination, with a war carried on by a regular army, and both carried on according to a plan embracing the operations of the whole.

The conditions under which alone the people's war can become effective are the following—

1. That the war is carried on in the heart of the country.
2. That it cannot be decided by a single catastrophe.
3. That the theatre of war embraces a considerable extent of country.
4. That the national character is favourable to the measure.
5. That the country is of a broken and difficult nature, either from being mountainous, or by reason of woods and marshes, or from the peculiar mode of cultivation in use.

Whether the population is dense or otherwise, is of little consequence, as there is less likelihood of a want of men than of anything else. Whether the inhabitants are rich or poor is also a point by no means decisive, at least it should not be; but it must be admitted that a poor population accustomed to hard work and privations usually shows itself more vigorous and better suited for war.

One peculiarity of country which greatly favors the action of war carried on by the people, is the scattered sites of the dwellings of the country people, such as is to be found in many parts of Germany. The country is thus more intersected and covered [sic]; the roads are worse, although more numerous; the lodgement of troops is attended with endless difficulties, but especially that peculiarity repeats itself on a small scale, which a people-war possesses on a great scale, namely that the principle of resistance exists everywhere, but is nowhere tangible. If the inhabitants are collected in villages, the most troublesome have troops quartered on them, or they are plundered as a punishment, and their houses burnt, etc, a system which could not be very easily carried out with a peasant community of Westphalia.

National levies and armed peasantry cannot and should not be employed against the main body of the enemy's army, or even against any considerable corps of the same, they must not attempt to crack the nut, they must only gnaw on the surface and the borders. They should rise in the provinces situated at one of the sides of the theatre of war, and in which the assailant does not appear in force, in order to withdraw these provinces entirely from his influence. Where no enemy is to be found, there is no want of courage to oppose him, and at the example thus given, the mass of the neighboring population gradually takes fire. Thus the fire spreads as it does in heather, and reaching at last that part of the surface of the soil on which the aggressor is based, it seizes his lines of communication and preys upon the vital thread by which his existence is supported. For although we entertain no exaggerated ideas of the omnipotence of a people's war, such as that it is an inexhaustible, unconquerable element, over which the mere force of an army has as little control as the human will has over the wind or the rain; in short, although our opinion is not founded on flowery ephemeral literature, still we must admit that armed peasants are not to be driven before us in the same way as a body of soldiers who keep together like a herd of cattle, and usually follow their noses. Armed peasants, on the contrary, when broken, disperse in all directions, for which no formal plan is required; through this circumstance, the march of every small body of troops in a mountainous, thickly wooded, or even broken country, becomes a service of a very dangerous character, for at any moment a combat may arise on the march; if in point of fact no armed bodies have even been seen for some time, yet the same peasants already driven off by the head of a column, may at any hour make their appearance in its rear. If it is an object to destroy roads or to block up a defile; the means which outposts or detachments from an army can apply to that purpose, bear about the same relation to those furnished by a body of insurgent peasants, as the action of an automaton does to that of a human being. The enemy has no other means to oppose to the action of national levies except that of detaching numerous parties to furnish escorts for convoys to occupy military stations, defiles, bridges, etc. In proportion as the first efforts of the national levies are small, so the detachments sent out will be weak in numbers, from the repugnance to a great dispersion of forces; it is on these weak bodies that the fire of the national war usually first properly kindles itself, they are over-powered by numbers at some points, courage rises, the love of fighting gains strength, and the intensity of this struggle increases until the crisis approaches which is to decide the issue.

According to our idea of a people's war, it should, like a kind of nebulous vapoury essence, never condense into a solid body; otherwise the enemy sends an adequate force against this core, crushes it, and makes a great many prisoners; their courage sinks; every one thinks the main question is decided, any further effort useless, and the arms fall from the hands of the people. Still, however, on the other hand, it is necessary that this mist should collect at some points into denser masses, and form threatening clouds from which now and again a formidable flash of lightning may burst forth. These points are chiefly on the flanks of the enemy's theatre of war, as already observed. There the armament of the people should be organised into greater and more systematic bodies, supported by a small force of regular troops, so as to give it the appearance of a regular force and fit it to venture upon enterprises on a larger scale. From these points, the irregular character in the organisation of these bodies should diminish in proportion as they are to be employed more in the direction of the rear of the enemy, where he is exposed to their hardest blows. These better organised masses, are for the purpose of falling upon the larger garrisons which the enemy leaves behind him. Besides, they serve to create a feeling of uneasiness and dread, and increase the moral impression of the whole, without them the total action would be wanting in force, and the situation of the enemy upon the whole would not be made sufficiently uncomfortable.

The easiest way for a general to produce this more effective form of a national armament, is to support the movement by small detachments sent from the army. Without the support of a few regular troops as an encouragement, the inhabitants generally want an impulse, and the confidence to take up arms. The stronger these detachments are, the greater will be their power of attraction, the greater will be the avalanche which is to fall down. But this has its limits; partly, first, because it would be detrimental to the army to cut it up into detachments, for this secondary object to dissolve it, as it were, into a body of irregulars, and form with it in all directions a weak defensive line, by which we may be sure both the regular army and national levies alike would become completely ruined; partly, secondly, because experience seems to tell us that when there are too many regular troops in a district, the people-war loses in vigour and efficacy; the causes of this are in the first place, that too many of the enemy's troops are thus drawn into the district, and, in the second place, that the inhabitants then rely on their own regular troops, and, thirdly, because the presence of such large bodies of troops makes too great demands on the powers of the people in other ways, that is, in providing quarters, transport, contributions, etc., etc.

Another means of preventing any serious reaction on the part of the enemy against this popular movement constitutes, at the same time, a leading principle in the method of using such levies; this is, that as a rule, with this great strategic means of defence, a tactical defence should seldom or ever take place. The character of a combat with national levies is the same as that of all combats of masses of troops of an inferior quality, great impetuosity and fiery ardour at the commencement, but little coolness or tenac-ity if the combat is prolonged. Further, the defeat and dispersion of a body of national levies is of no material consequence, as they lay their account with that, but a body of this description must not be bro-ken up by losses in killed, wounded, and prisoners; a defeat of that kind would soon cool their ardour. But both these peculiarities are entirely opposed to the nature of a tactical defensive. In the defensive combat a persistent slow systematic action is required, and great risks must be run; a mere attempt, from which we can desist as soon as we please, can never lead to results in the defensive. If, therefore, the national levies are entrusted with the defence of any particular portion of territory, care must be taken that the measure does not lead to a regular great defensive combat; for if the circumstances were ever so favourable to them, they would be sure to be defeated. They may, and should, therefore, defend the approaches to mountains, dykes, over marshes, river-passages, as long as possible; but when once they are broken, they should rather disperse, and continue their defence by sudden attacks, than concentrate and allow themselves to be shut up in some narrow last refuge in a regular defensive position. However brave a nation may be, however warlike its habits, however intense its hatred of the enemy, however favourable the nature of the country, it is an undeniable fact that a people's war cannot be kept up in an atmosphere too full of danger. If, therefore, its combustible material is to be fanned by any means into a considerable flame it must be at remote points where there is more air, and where it cannot be extinguished by one great blow.

Joseph Mazzini, *Life and Writings of Joseph Mazzini*

In the early nineteenth century the Italian peninsula was politically divided and, particularly in the northern Italian regions, dominated by Austria. In the aftermath of the French Revolutionary and Napoleonic eras, nationalist and liberal sentiments flourished in the minds of many young, idealistic Italians who dreamed of a restoration of Italian greatness. Giuseppe Mazzini (1805-1872), a committed advocate of a republican form of government, emerged as one of the most influential figures behind the drive for Italian independence and national unification in the nineteenth century. Although his republican political ideals remained largely unfulfilled, the nationalist sentiments articulated so notably by Mazzini and others contributed eventually to the successful formation of an independent and unified Italian state in the 1860s. In this excerpt Mazzini discusses his initial embrace of the ardent Italian nationalism that was to dominate much of his life and career.

Source: From Joseph Mazzini, *Life and Writings of Joseph Mazzini: Autobiographical and Political,* vol. I (London: Smith, Elder, 1890), 1-4.

Focus Questions:

1. How does Mazzini describe the specific origins of his conversion to nationalism in this excerpt?
2. What can you surmise from this excerpt about the political circumstances that created the large number of Italian refugees in Genoa in the early 1820s?
3. What was the relationship between Mazzini's nationalism and his democratic principles? From which influences did Mazzini draw his democratic ideals?

One Sunday in April 1821, while I was yet a boy, I was walking in the Strada Nuova of Genoa with my mother, and an old friend of our family named Andrea

Gambini. The Piedmontese insurrection had just been crushed; partly by Austria, partly through treachery, and partly through the weakness of its leaders.

The revolutionists, seeking safety by sea, had flocked to Genoa, and, finding themselves distressed for means, they went about seeking help to enable them to cross into Spain, where the revolution was yet triumphant. The greater number of them were crowded in S. Pier d'Arena, awaiting a chance to embark; but not a few had contrived to enter the city one by one, and I used to search them out from amongst our own people, detecting them either by their general appearance, by some peculiarity of dress, by their warlike air, or by the signs of a deep and silent sorrow on their faces.

The population were singularly moved. Some of the boldest had proposed to the leaders of the insurrection – Santarosa and Ansaldi, I think – to concentrate themselves in, and take possession of the city, and organize a new resistance; but Genoa was found to be deprived of all means of successful defence; the fortresses were without artillery, and the leaders had rejected the proposition, telling them *to preserve themselves for a better fate*.

Presently we were stopped and addressed by a tall black-bearded man, with a severe and energetic countenance, and a fiery glance that I have never since forgotten. He held out a white handkerchief towards us, merely saying, *For the refugees of Italy*. My mother and friend dropped some money into the handkerchief, and he turned from us to put the same request to others. I afterwards learned his name. He was Rini, a captain in the National Guard, which had been instituted at the commencement of the movement. He accompanied those for whom he had thus constituted himself collector, and, I believe, died – as so many of ours have perished – for the cause of liberty in Spain.

That day was the first in which a confused idea presented itself to my mind – I will not say of the country or of liberty – but an idea that we Italians *could* and therefore *ought* to struggle for the liberty of our country. I had already been unconsciously educated in the worship of equality by the democratic principles of my parents, whose bearing towards high or low was ever the same. Whatever the position of the individual, they simply regarded the *man*, and sought only the honest man. And my own natural aspirations towards liberty were fostered by constantly hearing my father and the friend already mentioned speak of the recent republican era in France; by the study of the works of Livy and Tacitus, which my Latin master had given me to translate; and by certain old French newspapers, which I discovered half-hidden behind my father's medical books. Amongst these last were some numbers of the *Chronique du Mois*, a Girondist publication belonging to the first period of the French Revolution.

But the idea of an existing wrong in my own country, against which it was a duty to struggle, and the thought that I too must bear my part in that struggle, flashed before my mind on that day for the first time, never again to leave me.

The remembrance of those refugees, many of whom became my friends in after life, pursued me where-ever I went by day, and mingled with my dreams by night. I would have given I know not what to follow them. I began collecting names and facts, and studied, as best I might, the records of that heroic struggle, seeking to fathom the causes of its failure.

They had been betrayed and abandoned by those who had sworn to concentrate every effort in the movement; the new king [Carlo Felice] had invoked the aid of Austria; part of the Piedmontese troops had even preceded the Austrians at Novara; and the leaders had allowed themselves to be overwhelmed at the first encounter, without making an effort to resist. All the details I succeeded in collecting led me to think that they *might* have conquered, if all of them had done their duty; -then why not renew the attempt?

Simon Bolívar, "Address to Second National Congress"

Simon Bolívar (1783-1830) was an instrumental figure in the independence movements in Latin America that led to the establishment of modern-day Venezuela, Columbia, Panama, Ecuador, Peru, and Bolivia. Born to wealthy noble family, his progressive education brought him into contact with the Enlightenment ideas of Locke and Rousseau. Bolívar finished his studies in Spain, and stayed in Europe for several years. When he returned to South America in 1807, he came back with the goal of liberating it from Spanish rule. Beginning in 1810, he first led forces against the Spanish in what became a long attempt to drive them out of the Americas. Bolívar's attack on the Spanish and his victory over them in New Granada (Columbia) on August 7, 1819, proved to be a major turning point in the independence movement, that finally tipped the balance in the revolutionaries favor. This excerpt comes from an address Bolívar made to the congress that assembled in Venezuela in the wake of the Spanish defeat where he describes the problems facing the Americas. Later, after the end of Spanish rule, he became the president and military dictator, of both Columbia (from 1821 to 1830) and Peru (from 1823 to 1829).

Source: Simon Bolívar, "Address Delivered at the Inauguration of the Second National Congress of Venezuela in Angostura," 15 February 1819, in *Selected Writings of Bolívar,* eds. Vincente Lecuna and Harold A. Bierch, Jr., vol. 1 (Caracas: Banco de Venezuela, 1951), 175-180.

Focus Questions:

1. What kind of government did Bolívar advocate? What arguments or ideas did he offer to support his vision of government?

2. Who was his audience? How does he try to persuade them?
3. For Bolívar, what were the legacies of Spanish rule and colonialism?

America, in separating from the Spanish monarchy, found herself in a situation similar to that of the Roman Empire when its enormous framework fell to pieces in the midst of the ancient world. Each Roman division then formed an independent nation in keeping with its location or interests; but this situation differed from America's in that those members proceeded to reestablish their former associations. We, on the contrary, do not even retain the vestiges of our original being. We are not Europeans; we are not Indians; we are but a mixed species of aborigines and Spaniards. Americans by birth and Europeans by law, we find ourselves engaged in a dual conflict: we are disputing with the natives for titles of ownership, and at the same time we are struggling to maintain ourselves in the country that gave us birth against the opposition of the invaders. Thus our position is most extraordinary and complicated. But there is more. As our role has always been strictly passive and our political existence nil, we find that our quest for liberty is now even more difficult of accomplishment; for we, having been placed in a state lower than slavery, had been robbed not only of our freedom but also of the right to exercise an active domestic tyranny. Permit me to explain this paradox.

In absolute systems, the central power is unlimited. The will of the despot is the supreme law, arbitrarily enforced by subordinates who take part in the organized oppression in proportion to the authority that they wield. They are charged with civil, political, military, and religious functions; but, in the final analysis, the satraps of Persia are Persian, the pashas of the Grand Turk are Turks, and the sultans of Tartary are Tartars. China does not seek her mandarins in the homeland of Genghis Khan, her conqueror. America, on the contrary, received everything from Spain, who, in effect, deprived her of the experience that she would have gained from the exercise of an active tyranny by not allowing her to take part in her own domestic affairs and administration. This exclusion made it impossible for us to acquaint ourselves with the management of public affairs; nor did we enjoy that personal consideration, of such great value in major revolutions, that the brilliance of power inspires in the eyes of the multitude. In brief, Gentlemen, we were deliberately kept in ignorance and cut off from the world in all matters relating to the science of government.

Subject to the threefold yoke of ignorance, tyranny, and vice, the American people have been unable to acquire knowledge, power, or [civic] virtue. The lessons we received and the models we studied, as pupils of such pernicious teachers, were most destructive. We have been ruled more by deceit than by force, and we have been degraded more by vice than by superstition. Slavery is the daughter of Darkness: an ignorant people is a blind instrument of its own destruction. Ambition and intrigue abuse the credulity and experience of men lacking all political, economic, and civic knowledge; they adopt pure illusion as reality; they take license for liberty, treachery for patriotism, and vengeance for justice. This situation is similar to that of the robust blind man who, beguiled by his strength, strides forward with all the assurance of one who can see, but, upon hitting every variety of obstacle, finds himself unable to retrace his steps.

If a people, perverted by their training, succeed in achieving their liberty, they will soon lose it, for it would be of no avail to endeavor to explain to them that happiness consists in the practice of virtue; that the rule of law is more powerful than the rule of tyrants, because, as the laws are more inflexible, everyone should submit to their beneficent austerity; that proper morals, and not force, are the bases of law; and that to practice justice is to practice liberty. Therefore, Legislators, your work is so much the more arduous, inasmuch as you have to reeducate men who have been corrupted by erroneous illusions and false incentives. Liberty, says Rousseau, is a succulent morsel, but one difficult to digest. Our weak fellow-citizens will have to strengthen their spirit greatly before they can digest the wholesome nutriment of freedom. Their limbs benumbed by chains, their sight dimmed by the darkness of dungeons, and their strength sapped by the pestilence of servitude, are they capable of marching toward the august temple of Liberty without faltering? Can they come near enough to bask in its brilliant rays and to breathe freely the pure air which reigns therein?

Legislators, mediate well before you choose. Forget not that you are to lay the political foundation for a newly born nation which can rise to the heights of greatness that Nature has marked out for it if you but proportion this foundation in keeping with the high plane that it aspires to attain. Unless your choice is based upon the peculiar tutelary experience of the Venezuelan people—a factor that should guide you in determining the nature and form of government you are about to adopt for the well-being of the people—and, I repeat, unless you happen upon the right type of government, the result of our reforms will again be slavery....

The more I admire the excellence of the federal Constitution of Venezuela, the more I am convinced of the impossibility of its application to our state. And, to my way of thinking, it is a marvel that its prototype in North America endures so successfully and has not been overthrown at the first sign of adversity or danger. Although the people of North America are a singular model of political virtue and moral rectitude; although the nation was cradled in liberty, reared on freedom, and maintained by liberty alone; and—I must reveal everything— although those people, so lacking in many respects, are unique in the history of mankind, it is a marvel, I repeat, that so weak and complicated a government as the federal system has managed to govern them in the difficult and trying circumstances of their past. But, regardless of the effectiveness of this form of government with respect to North America, I must say that it has never for a moment entered my mind to compare the position and character of two states as dissimilar as the

English-American and the Spanish-American. Would it not be most difficult to apply to Span the English system of political, civil, and religious liberty? Hence, it would be even more difficult to adapt to Venezuela the laws of North America. Does not [Montesquieu's] L'Esprit des lois state that laws should be suited to the people for whom they are made; that it would be a major coincidence if those of one nation could be adapted to another; that laws must take into account the physical conditions of the country, climate, character of the land, location, size, and mode of living of the people; that they should be in keeping with the degree of liberty that the Constitution can sanction respecting the religion of the inhabitants, their inclinations, resources, numbers, commerce, habits, and customs? This is the code we must consult, not the code of Washington!

CHAPTER 20

Industrialization in the Nineteenth Century

Andrew Ure, from *The Philosophy of Manufactures*

The factory system was not without its advocates. One of the most influential was Andrew Ure, a professor of applied science at the University of Glasgow. He was supportive of the efficiency and productive capabilities of mechanized manufacturing. Note how the major criticisms of the reformers (child labor, degrading and unhealthy work conditions, etc.) are methodically countered. Ure argued that the owners of the mills and mines were not devils, but were actually abused themselves by the demand of the workers.

Source: Andrew Ure, "A Defense of the Factory System," in The Philosophy of Manufactures (London: Charles Knight, 1835), pp. 282–284, 290, 300–301, 309–311, 398–399.

FOCUS QUESTIONS:

1. How does Andrew Ure defend the factory system?
2. What specific points does he address? Are his arguments persuasive? Why or why not?

Proud of the power of malefaction, many of the cotton-spinners, though better paid, as we have shown, than any similar set of artisans in the world, organized the machinery of strikes through all the gradations of their people, terrifying or cajoling the timid or the passive among them to join their vindictive union. They boasted of possessing a dark tribunal, by the mandates of which they could paralyze every mill whose master did not comply with their wishes, and so bring ruin on the man who had given them profitable employment for many a year. By flattery or intimidation, they levied contributions from their associates in the privileged mills, which they suffered to proceed, in order to furnish spare funds for the maintenance of the idle during the decreed suspension of labour. In this extraordinary state of things, when the inventive head and the sustaining heart of trade were held in bondage by the unruly lower members, a destructive spirit began to display itself among some partisans of the union. Acts of singular atrocity were committed, sometimes with weapons fit only for demons to wield, such as the corrosive oil of vitriol, dashed in the faces of most meritorious individuals, with the effect of disfiguring their persons, and burning their eyes out of the sockets with dreadful agony.

The true spirit of turn-outs [strikes] among the spinners is well described in the following statement made on oath to the Factory Commission, by Mr. George Royle Chappel, a manufacturer of Manchester, who employs 274 hands, and two steam-engines of sixty-four horse power.

"I have had several turn-outs, and have heard of many more, but never heard of a turn-out for short time. I will relate the circumstances of the last turn-out, which took place on the 16th October, 1830, and continued till the 17th January, 1831. The whole of our spinners, whose average (weekly) wages were 2£. 13s. 5d., turned out at the instigation, as they told us at the time, of the delegates of the union. They said they had no fault to find with their wages, their work, or their masters, but the union obliged them to turn out. The same week three delegates from the spinners' union waited upon us at our mill, and dictated certain advances in wages, and other regulations, to which, if we would not adhere, they said neither our own spinners nor any other should work for us again! Of course we declined, believing our wages to be ample, and our regulations such as were necessary for the proper conducting of the establishment. The consequences were, they set watches on every avenue to the mill, night and day, to prevent any fresh hands coming into the mill, an object which they effectually attained, by intimidating some, and promising support to others (whom I got into the mill in a caravan), if they would leave their work. Under these circumstances, I could not work the mill, and advertised it for sale, without any applications, and I also tried in vain to let it. At the end of twenty-three weeks the hands requested to be taken to the mill again on the terms that they had left it, declaring, as they had done at first, that the union alone had forced them to turn out..."

Nothing shows in a clearer point of view the credulity of mankind in general, and of the people of these islands in particular, than the ready faith which was given to the tales of cruelty exercised by proprietors of cotton-mills towards young children. The systems of calumny somewhat resembles that brought by the Pagans against the primitive Christians, of enticing children into their meetings in order to murder and devour them...

No master would wish to have any wayward children to work within the walls of his factory, who do not mind their business without beating, and he therefore usually fines or turns away any spinners who are known to maltreat their assistants. Hence, ill-usage of any kind is a very rare occurrence. I have visited many factories, both in Manchester and in the surrounding districts, during a period of several months, entering the spinning rooms, unexpectedly, and often alone, at different times of the day, and I never saw a single instance of corporal chastisement inflicted on a child, nor indeed did I ever see children in ill-humour. They seemed to be always cheerful and alert, taking pleasure in the light play of their muscles, enjoying the mobility natural to their age. The scene of industry, so far from exciting sad emotions in my mind, was always exhilarating. It was delightful to observe the nimbleness with which they pieced the broken ends, as the mule-carriage began to recede from the fixed roller-beam, and to see them at leisure, after a few seconds' exercise of their tiny fingers, to amuse themselves in any attitude they chose, till the stretch and winding-on were once more completed. The work of these lively elves seemed to resemble a sport, in which habit gave them a pleasing dexterity. Conscious of their skill, they were delighted to show it off to any stranger. As to exhaustion by the day's work, they evinced no trace of it on emerging from the mill in the evening; for they immediately began to skip about any neighbouring playground, and to commence their little amusements with the same alacrity as boys issuing from a school. It is moreover my firm conviction, that if children are not ill-used by bad parents or guardians, but receive in food and raiment the full benefit of what they earn, they would thrive better when employed in our modern factories, than if left at home in apartments too often ill-aired, damp, and cold…

Of all the common prejudices that exist with regard to factory labour, there is none more unfounded than that which ascribes to it excessive tedium and irksomeness above other occupations, owing to its being carried on in conjunction with the "unceasing motion of the steam-engine." In an establishment for spinning or weaving cotton, all the hard work is performed by the steam-engine, which leaves for the attendant no hard labour at all, and literally nothing to do in general; but at intervals to perform some delicate operation, such as joining the threads that break, taking the cops off the spindle, &c. And it is so far from being true that the work in a factory is incessant, because the motion of the steam-engine is incessant, that the fact is, that the labour is not incessant on that very count, because it is performed in conjunction with the steam-engine. Of all manufacturing employments, those are by far the most irk-some and incessant in which steam-engines are not employed, as in lace-running and stocking-weaving; and the way to prevent an employment from being incessant, is to introduce a steam-engine into it. These remarks certainly apply more especially to the labour of children in factories. Three-fourths of the children so employed are engaged in piecing at the mules. "When the carriages of these have receded a foot and a half or two feet from the rollers," says Mr. Tufnell, "nothing is to be done, not even attention is required from either spinner or piecer." Both of them stand idle for a time, and in fine spinning particularly, for three-quarters of a minute, or more. Consequently, if a child remains at this business twelve hours daily, he has nine hours of inaction. And though he attends two mules, he has still six hours of non-exertion. Spinners sometimes dedicate these intervals to the perusal of books. The scavengers, who, in Mr. Sadler's report, have been described as being "constantly in a state of grief, always in terror, and every moment they have to spare stretched all their length upon the floor in a state of perspiration," may be observed in cotton factories idle for four minutes at a time, or moving about in a sportive mood, utterly unconscious of the tragical scenes in which they were dramatized...

Mr. Hutton, who has been in practice as a surgeon at Stayley Bridge upwards of thirty-one years, and, of course, remembers the commencement, and has had occasion to trace the progress and effect, of the factory system, says that the health of the population has much improved since its introduction, and that they are much superior in point of comfort to what they were formerly. He also says that fever has become less common since the erection of factories, and that the persons employed in them were less attacked by the influenza in 1833, than other classes of work-people. Mr. Bott, a surgeon, who is employed by the operatives in Messrs. Lichfield's mills to attend them in all cases of sickness or accident, at the rate of one halfpenny a week (a sum which indicates pretty distinctly their small chances of ailment), says that the factory workmen are not so liable to epidemics as other persons; and that though he has had many cases of typhus fever in the surrounding district, nearly all the mill-hands have escaped, and not one was attacked by the cholera during its prevalence in the neighbourhood.

The Sadler Report: Child Labor in the United Kingdom 1832

By the early nineteenth century, the Industrial Revolution had spread from England and was beginning to transform Europe from a rural to an urban society. In England, this transformation often depressed the living standards of workers beneath even those of the cottage manufacturing system of an earlier era. In doing so, however, it paved the way for its own reform, for it bared to the public eye in an aggravated form conditions that had long existed but had passed relatively unnoticed. Poverty and misery could be overlooked as long as the workers remained scattered about the countryside, but once they were congregated in the hideous slums of the Midlands industrial centers, their plight became too obvious to remain unheeded. Consequently, social reform became the order of the day.

Among the most prominent of the English reformers was the seventh Earl of Shaftesbury (1801-1885), who concentrated on working conditions in the factories. At Shaftesbury's instigation, another reformer, Michael Sadler, introduced a bill in Parliament in 1831 designed to regulate the working conditions of children in textile mills. The bill was referred to a committee, with Sadler as chairman. The selection that follows is an excerpt from the evidence presented before the committee. The committee's recommendations resulted in the *Factory Act* of 1833, which limited the working hours of children and set up a system of inspection to insure that its regulations would be carried out.

The Sadler Report requires no comment; it speaks for itself. The selection included here was picked almost at random from a bulky volume of testimony provided by hundreds of witnesses. Although these witnesses were presumably selected with some care, their accounts provide a generally accurate picture of the conditions of many factory workers, children in particular, in early nineteenth-century England.

Source: *The Sadler Report: Report from the Committee on the Bill to Regulate the Labour of Children in the Mills and Factories of the United Kingdom,* (London: House of Commons, 1823).

Focus Questions:

1. Summarize conditions in the factories.
2. What effect did factory work have on other aspects of the worker's lives?

THE SADLER REPORT

VENERIS, 18° DIE MAII, 1832

Michael Thomas Sadler, Esquire, in the Chair

MR. MATTHEW CRABTREE, *called in; and Examined.*

What age are you? —Twenty-two.

What is your occupation? —A blanket manufacturer.

Have you ever been employed in a factory?-Yes.

At what age did you first go to work in one?-Eight.

How long did you continue in that occupation?-Four years.

Will you state the hours of labour at the period when you first went to the factory, in ordinary times? — From 6 in the morning to 8 at night. Fourteen hours? —Yes. With what intervals for refreshment and rest? — An hour at noon.

Then you had no resting time allowed in which to take your breakfast, or what is in Yorkshire called your "drinking"? — No.

When trade was brisk what were your hours? —From 5 in the morning to 9 in the evening.

Sixteen hours? —Yes.

With what intervals at dinner?-An hour.

How far did you live from the mill?-About two miles.

Was there any time allowed for you to get your breakfast in the mill?-No.

Did you take it before you left your home?-Generally.

During those long hours of labour could you be punctual; how did you awake? — I seldom did awake spontaneously; I was most generally awoke or lifted out of bed, sometimes asleep, by my parents.

Were you always in time?-No.

What was the consequence if you had been too late?-I was most commonly beaten.

Severely?-Very severely, I thought.

In whose factory was this?-Messrs. Hague & Cook's, of Dewsbury.

Will you state the effect that those long hours had upon the state of your health and feelings?-I was, when working those long hours, commonly very much fatigued at night, when I left my work; so much so that I sometimes should have slept as I walked if I had not stumbled and started awake again; and so sick often that I could not eat, and what I did eat I vomited.

Did this labour destroy your appetite?-It did.

In what situation were you in that mill?-I was a piecener.

Will you state to this Committee whether piecening is a very laborious employment for children, or not?-It is a very laborious employment. Pieceners are continually running to and fro, and on their feet the whole day.

The duty of the piecener is to take the cardings from one part of the machinery, and to place them on another?-Yes.

So that the labour is not only continual, but it is unabated to the last?-It is unabated to the last.

Do you not think, from your own experience, that the speed of the machinery is so calculated as to demand the utmost exertions of a child supposing the hours were moderate?-It is as much as they could do at the best; they are always upon the stretch, and it is commonly very difficult to keep up with their work.

State the condition of the children toward the latter part of the day, who have thus to keep up with the machinery.-It is as much as they do when they are not very much fatigued to keep up with their work, and toward the close of the day, when they come to be more fatigued, they cannot keep up with it very well, and the consequence is that they are beaten to spur them on.

Were you beaten under those circumstances? —Yes.

Frequently?-Very frequently.

And principally at the latter end of the day?-Yes.

And is it your belief that if you had not been so beaten, you should not have got through the work?-I should not if I had not been kept up to it by some means.

Does beating then principally occur at the latter end of the day, when the children are exceedingly fatigued?-It does at the latter end of the day, and in the morning sometimes, when they are very drowsy, and have not got rid of the fatigue of the day before.

What were you beaten with principally?-A strap.

Anything else?-Yes, a stick sometimes; and there is a kind of roller which runs on the top of the machine called a billy, perhaps two or three yards in length, and perhaps an inch and a half or more in diameter; the circumference would be four or five inches; I cannot speak exactly.

Were you beaten with that instrument?-Yes.

Have you yourself been beaten, and have you seen other children struck severely with that roller?-I have been struck very severely with it myself, so much so as to knock me down, and I have seen other children have their heads broken with it.

You think that it is a general practice to beat the children with the roller?-It is.

You do not think then that you were worse treated than other children in the mill?-No, I was not, perhaps not so bad as some were.

In those mills is chastisement towards the latter part of the day going on perpetually?-Perpetually.

So that you can hardly be in a mill without hearing constant crying?-Never an hour, I believe.

Do you think that if the over-looker were naturally a humane person it would be still found necessary for him to beat the children, in order to keep up their attention and vigilance at the termination of those extraordinary days of labour?-Yes, the machine turns off a regular quantity of cardings, and of course they must keep as regularly to their work the whole of the day; they must keep with the machine, and therefore however humane the slubber may be, as he must keep up with the machine or be found fault with, he spurs the children to keep up also by various means but that which he commonly resorts to is to strap them when they become drowsy.

At the time when you were beaten for not keeping up with your work, were you anxious to have done it if you possibly could?-Yes; the dread of being beaten if we could not keep up with our work was a sufficient impulse to keep us to it if we could.

When you got home at night after this labour, did you feel much fatigued?-Very much so.

Had you any time to be with your parents, and to receive instruction from them?-No.

What did you do?-All that we did when we got home was to get the little bit of supper that was provided for us and go to bed immediately. If the supper had not been ready directly, we should have gone to sleep while it was preparing.

Did you not, as a child, feel it a very grievous hardship to be roused so soon in the morning?-I did.

Were the rest of the children similarly circumstanced? —Yes, all of them; but they were not all of them so far from their work as I was.

And if you had been too late you were under the apprehension of being cruelly beaten?-I generally was beaten when I happened to be too late; and when I got up in the morning the apprehension of that was so great, that I used to run, and cry all the way as I went to the mill.

That was the way by which your punctual attendance was secured?-Yes.

And you do not think it could have been secured by any other means?-No.

Then it is your impression from what you have seen, and from your own experience, that those long hours of labour have the effect of rendering young persons who are subject to them exceedingly unhappy?-Yes.

You have already said it had a considerable effect upon your health?-Yes.

Do you conceive that it diminished your growth?-I did not pay much attention to that; but I have been examined by some persons who said they thought I was rather stunted, and that I should have been taller if I had not worked at the mill.

What were your wages at that time?-Three shillings [per week—Ed].

And how much a day had you for over-work when you were worked so exceedingly long?-A half— penny a day.

Did you frequently forfeit that if you were not always there to a moment?-Yes; I most frequently forfeited what was allowed for those long hours.

You took your food to the mill; was it in your mill, as is the case in cotton mills, much spoiled by being laid aside?-It was very frequently covered by flues from the wool; and in that case they had to be blown off with the mouth, and picked off with the fingers before it could be eaten.

So that not giving you a little leisure for eating your food, but obliging you to take it at the mill, spoiled your food when you did get it?-Yes, very commonly.

And that at the same time that this over-labour injured your appetite?-Yes.

Could you eat when you got home?-Not always.

What is the effect of this piecening upon the hands? —It makes them bleed; the skin is completely rubbed off, and in that case they bleed in perhaps a dozen parts.

The prominent parts of the hand?-Yes, all the prominent parts of the hand are rubbed down till they bleed; every day they are rubbed in that way.

All the time you continue at work? —All the time we are working. The hands never can be hardened in that work, for the grease keeps them soft in the first instance, and long and continual rubbing is always wearing them down, so that if they were hard they would be sure to bleed.

Is it attended with much pain? —Very much.

Do they allow you to make use of the back of the hand? —No; the work cannot be so well done with the back of the hand, or I should have made use of that.

Is the work done as well when you are so many hours engaged in it, as it would be if you were at it a less time? —I believe it is not done so well in those long hours; toward the latter end of the day the children become completely bewildered, and know not what they are doing, so that they spoil their work without knowing.

Then you do not think that the masters gain much by the continuance of the work to so great a length of time? —I believe not.

Were there girls as well as boys employed in this manner?—Yes.

Were they more tenderly treated by the overlookers, or were they worked and beaten in the same manner? —There was no difference in their treatment.

Were they beaten by the overlookers, or by the slubber?—By the slubber.

But the overlooker must have been perfectly aware of the treatment that the children endured at the mill? —Yes; and sometimes the overlooker beat them himself; but the man that they wrought under had generally the management of them.

Did he pay them their wages?—No; their wages were paid by the master.

But the overlooker of the mill was perfectly well aware that they could not have performed the duty exacted from them in the mill without being thus beaten?—I believe he was.

You seem to say that this beating is absolutely necessary, in order to keep the children up to their work; is it universal throughout all factories?—I have been in several other factories, and I have witnessed the same cruelty in them all.

Did you say that you were beaten for being too late?—Yes.

Is it not the custom in many of the factories to impose fines upon children for being too late, instead of beating them?-It was not in that factory.

What then were the fines by which you lost the money you gained by your long hours?—The spinner could not get on so fast with his work when we happened to be too late; he could not begin his work so soon, and therefore it was taken by him.

Did the slubber pay you your wages? —No, the master paid our wages.

And the slubber took your fines from you?—Yes.

Then you were fined as well as beaten?—There was nothing deducted from the ordinary scale of wages, but only from that received for over-hours, and I had only that taken when I was too late, so that the fine was not regular.

When you were not working over-hours, were you so often late as when you were working over-hours? —Yes.

You were not very often late whilst you were not working over-hours?—Yes, I was often late when I was not working over-hours; I had to go at six o'clock in the morning, and consequently had to get up at five to eat my breakfast and go to the mill, and if I failed to get up by five I was too late; and it was nine o'clock before we could get home, and then we went to bed; in the best times I could not be much above eight hours at home, reckoning dressing and eating my meals, and everything.

Was it a blanket-mill in which you worked?—Yes.

Did you ever know that the beatings to which you allude inflicted a serious injury upon the children?—I do not recollect any very serious injury, more than that they had their heads broken, if that may be called a serious injury; that has often happened; I, myself, had no more serious injury than that.

You say that the girls as well as the boys were employed as you have described, and you observed no difference in their treatment?—No difference.

The girls were beat in this unmerciful manner?—They were.

They were subject, of course, to the same bad effects from this over working?—Yes.

Could you attend an evening-school during the time you were employed in the mill?—No, that was completely impossible.

Did you attend the Sunday-school?—Not very frequently when I work at the mill.

How then were you engaged during the Sunday?-I very often slept till it was too late for school time or for divine worship, and the rest of the day I spent in walking out and taking a little fresh air.

Did your parents think that it was necessary for you to enjoy a little fresh air?—I believe they did; they never said anything against it; before I went to the mill I used to go to the Sunday-school.

Did you frequently sleep nearly the whole of the day on Sunday?—Very often.

At what age did you leave that employment?—I was about 12 years old.

Why did you leave that place?—I went very late one morning, about seven o'clock, and I got severely beaten by the spinner, and he turned me out of the mill, and I went home, and never went any more.

Was your attendance as good as the other children?—Being at rather a greater distance than some of them, I was generally one of the latest.

Where was your next work?—I worked as bobbin—winder in another part of the works of the same firm.

How long were you a bobbin—winder?—About two years, I believe.

What did you become after that?—A weaver.

How long were you a weaver?—I was a weaver till March in last year.

A weaver of what?—A blanket—weaver.

With the same firm?—With the same firm.

Did you leave them? — No; I was dismissed from my work for a reason which I am willing and anxious to explain.

Have you had opportunities of observing the way in which the children are treated in factories up to a late period?—Yes.

You conceive that their treatment still remains as you first found it, and that the system is in great want of regulation?—It does.

Children you still observe to be very much fatigued and injured by the hours of labour?—Yes.

From your own experience, what is your opinion as to the utmost labour that a child in piecening could safely undergo?—If I were appealed to from my own feelings to fix a limit, I should fix it at ten hours, or less.

And you attribute to longer hours all the cruelties that you describe?—A good deal of them.

Are the children sleepy in mills?—Very.

Are they more liable to accidents in the latter part of the day than in the other part?—I believe they are; I believe a greater number of accidents happen in the latter part of the day than in any other. I have known them so sleepy that in the short interval while the others have been going out, some of them have fallen asleep, and have been left there.

Is it an uncommon case for children to fall asleep in the mill, and remain there all night?—Not to remain there all night; but I have known a case the other day, of a child whom the overlooker found when he went to lock the door, that had been left there.

So that you think there has been no change for the better in the treatment of those children; is it your opinion that there will be none, except Parliament interfere in their behalf?—It is my decided conviction.

Have you recently seen any cruelties in mills?—Yes; not long since I was in a mill and I saw a girl severely beaten; at a mill called Hicklane Mill, in Batley; I happened to be in at the other end of the room, talking; and I heard the blows, and I looked that way, and saw the spinner beating one of the girls severely with a large stick. Hearing the sound, led me to look round, and to ask what was the matter, and they said it was "Nothing but paying [beating—Ed.] 'his ligger-on.'"

What age was the girl?—About 12 years.

Was she very violently beaten?—She was.

Was this when she was over-Fatigued?—It was in the afternoon.

Can you speak as to the effect of this labour in the mills and factories on the morals of the children, as far as you have observed?—As far as I have observed with regard to morals in the mills, there is everything about them that is disgusting to every one conscious of correct morality.

Do you find that the children, the females especially, are very early demoralized in them?—They are.

Is their language indecent?—Very indecent; and both sexes take great familiarities with each other in the mills, without at all being ashamed of their conduct.

Do you connect their immorality of language and conduct with their excessive labour?—It may be somewhat connected with it, for it is to be observed that most of that goes on toward night, when they begin to be drowsy; it is a kind of stimulus which they use to keep them awake; they say some pert thing or other to keep themselves from drowsiness, and it generally happens to be some obscene language.

Have not a considerable number of the females employed in mills illegitimate children very early in life? —I believe there are; I have known some of them have illegitimate children when they were between 16 and 17 years of age.

How many grown-up females had you in the mill?—I cannot speak to the exact number that were grown up; perhaps there might be thirty—four or so that worked in the mill at that time.

How many of those had illegitimate children? A great many of them; eighteen or nineteen of them, I think.

Did they generally marry the men by whom they had the children?—No; it sometimes happens that young women have children by married men, and I have known an instance, a few weeks since, where one of the young women had a child by a married man.

Is it your opinion that those who have the charge of mills very often avail themselves of the opportunity they have to debauch the young women?—No, not generally; most of the improper conduct takes place among the younger part of those that work in the mill.

Do you find that the children and young persons in those mills are moral in other respects, or does their want of education tend to encourage them in a breach of the law?—I believe it does, for there are very few of them that can know anything about it; few of them can either read or write.

Are criminal offences then very frequent?—Yes, theft is very common; it is practised a great deal in the mills, stealing their bits of dinner, or something of that sort. Some of them have not so much to eat as they ought to have, and if they can fall in with the dinner of some of their partners they steal it. The first day my brother and I went to the mill we had our dinner stolen, because we were not up to the tricks; we were more careful in future, but still we did not always escape.

Was there any correction going on at the mills for indecent language or improper conduct?—No, I never knew of any.

From what you have seen and known of those mills, would you prefer that the hours of labour should be so long with larger wages, or that they should be shortened with a diminution of wages?—If I were working at the mill now, I would rather have less labour and receive a trifle less, than so much labour and receive a trifle more.

Is that the general impression of individuals engaged in mills with whom you are acquainted?—I believe it is.

What is the impression in the country from which you come with respect to the effect of this Bill upon wages?—They do not anticipate that it will affect wages at all.

They think it will not lower wages?—They do.

Do you mean that it will not lower wages by the hour, or that you will receive the same wages per day? —They anticipate that it may perhaps lower their wages at a certain time of the year when they are working hard, but not at other times, so that they will have their wages more regular.

Does not their wish for this Bill mainly rest upon their anxiety to protect their children from the consequences of this excessive labour, and to have some opportunity of affording them a decent education? —Yes; such are the wishes of every humane father that I have heard speak about the thing.

Have they not some feeling of having the labour equalized?—That is the feeling of some that I have heard speak of it.

Did your parents work in the same factories?—No.

Were any of the slubbers' children working there?—Yes.

Under what slubber did you work in that mill?—Under a person of the name of Thomas Bennett, in the first place; and I was changed from him to another of the name of James Webster.

Did the treatment depend very much upon the slubber under whom you were?—No, it did not depend directly upon him, for he was obliged to do a certain quantity of work, and therefore to make us keep up with that.

Were the children of the slubbers strapped in the same way?—Yes, except that it is very natural for a father to spare his own child.

Did it depend upon the feelings of a slubber toward his children?—Very little.

Did the slubbers fine their own spinners?—I believe not.

You said that the piecening was very hard labour; what labour is there besides moving about; have you anything heavy to carry or to lift?—We have nothing heavy to carry, but we are kept upon our feet in brisk times from 5 o'clock in the morning to 9 at night.

How soon does the hand get sore in piecening?—How soon mine became sore I cannot speak to exactly; but they get a little hard on the Sunday, when we are not working, and they will get sore again very soon on the Monday.

Is it always the case in piecening that the hand bleeds, whether you work short or long hours?—They bleed more when we work more.

Do they always bleed when you are working?—Yes.

Do you think that the children would not be more competent to this task, and their hands far less hurt, if the hours were fewer every day, especially when their hands had become seasoned to the labour?—I believe it would have an effect for the longer they are worked the more their hands are worn, and the longer it takes to heal them, and they do not get hard enough after a day's rest to be long without bleeding again; if they were not so much worn down, they might heal sooner, and not bleed so often or so soon.

After a short day's work, have you found your hands hard the next morning?—They do not bleed much after we have ceased work; they then get hard; they will bleed soon in the morning when in regular work.

Do you think if the work of the children were confined to about ten hours a day, that they would not be able to perform this piecening without making their hands bleed?—I believe they would.

So that it is your opinion, from your experience, that if the hours were mitigated, their hands would not be so much worn, and would not bleed by the business of piecening?—Yes.

Do you mean to say that their hands would not bleed at all?—I cannot say exactly, for I always wrought long hours, and therefore my hands always did bleed.

Have you any experience of mills where they only work ten hours?—I have never wrought at such mills, and in most of the mills I have seen their hands bleed.

At a slack time, when you were working only a few hours, did your hands bleed?—No, they did not for three or four days, after we had been standing still for a week; the mill stood still sometimes for a week together, but when we did work we worked the common number of hours.

Were all the mills in the neighbourhood working the same number of hours in brisk times?—Yes.

So that if any parent found it necessary to send his children to the mill for the sake of being able to maintain them, and wished to take them from any mill where they were excessively worked, he could not have found any other place where they would have been less worked?—No, he could not; for myself, I had no desire to change, because I thought I was as well off as I could be at any other mill.

And if the parent, to save his child, had taken him from the mill, and had applied to the parish for relief, would the parish, knowing that he had withdrawn his child from its work, have relieved him?-No.

So that the long labour which you have described, or actual starvation, was, practically, the only alternative that was presented to the parent under such circumstances?—It was; they must either work at the mill they were at or some other, and there was no choice in the mills in that respect.

What, in your opinion, would be the effect of limiting the hours of labour upon the happiness, and the health, and the intelligence of the rising generation?—If the hours are shortened, the children may, perhaps, have a chance of attending some evening-school, and learning to read and write; and those that I know who have been to school and learned to read and write; have much more comfort than those who have not. For myself, I went to a school when I was six years old, and I learned to read and write a little then.

At a free-school?—Yes, at a free-school in Dewsbury; but I left school when I was six years old. The fact is, that my father was a small manufacturer, and in comfortable circumstances, and he got into debt with Mr. Cook for a wool bill, and as he had no other means of paying him, he came and agreed with my father, that my brother and I should go to work at his mill till that debt was paid; so that the whole of the time that we wrought at the mill we had no wages.

THOMAS BENNETT, *called in; and Examined.*

Where do you reside?—At Dewsbury.

What is your business?—A slubber.

What age are you? —About 48.

Have you had much experience regarding the working of children in factories?—Yes, about twenty-seven years.

Have you a family?—Yes, eight children.

Have any of them gone to factories?—All.

At what age?—The first went at six years of age.

To whose mill?—To Mr. Halliley's, to piece for myself.

What hours did you work at that mill?—We have wrought from 4 to 9, from 4 to 10, and from 5 to 9,

and from 5 to 10.

What sort of a mill was it?—It was a blanket-mill; we sometimes altered the time, according as the days increased and decreased.

What were your regular hours?—Our regular hours when we were not so throng, was from 6 to 7. And when you were the throngest, what were your hours then?—From 5 to 9, and from 5 to 10, and from 4 to 9.

Seventeen hours?—Yes.

What intervals for meals had the children at that period?—Two hours; an hour for breakfast, and an hour for dinner.

Did they always allow two hours for meals at Mr. Halliley's?—Yes, it was allowed, but the children did not get it, for they had business to do at that time, such as fettling and cleaning the machinery.

But they did not stop in at that time, did they?—They all had their share of the cleaning and other work to do.

That is, they were cleaning the machinery?—Cleaning the machinery at the time of dinner.

How long a time together have you known those excessive hours to continue?—I have wrought so myself very nearly two years together.

Were your children working under you then?—Yes, two of them.

State the effect upon your children.—Of a morning when they have been so fast asleep that I have had to go up stairs and lift them out of bed, and have heard them crying with the feelings of a parent; I have been much affected by it.

Were not they much fatigued at the termination of such a day's labour as that?—Yes; many a time I have seen their hands moving while they have been nodding, almost asleep; they have been doing their business almost mechanically.

While they have been almost asleep, they have attempted to work?—Yes; and they have missed the carding and spoiled the thread, when we have had to beat them for it.

Could they have done their work towards the termination of such a long day's labour, if they had not been chastised to it?—No.

You do not think that they could have kept awake or up to their work till the seventeenth hour, without being chastised?—No.

Will you state what effect it had upon your children at the end of their day's work? —At the end of their day's work, when they have come home, instead of taking their victuals, they have dropped asleep with the victuals in their hands; and sometimes when we have sent them to bed with a little bread or something to eat in their hand, I have found it in their bed the next morning.

Had it affected their health?—I cannot say much of that; they were very hearty children.

Do you live at a distance from the mill?—Half a mile.

Did your children feel a difficulty in getting home?—Yes, I have had to carry the lesser child on my back, and it has been asleep when I got home.

Did these hours of labour fatigue you?—Yes, they fatigued me to that excess, that in divine worship I have not been able to stand according to order; I have sat to worship.

So that even during the Sunday you have felt fatigue from your labour in the week?—Yes, we felt it, and always took as much rest as we could.

Were you compelled to beat your own children, in order to make them keep up with the machine? —Yes, that was forced upon us, or we could not have done the work; I have struck them often, though I felt as a parent.

If the children had not been your own, you would have chastised them still more severely?—Yes.

What did you beat them with?—A strap sometimes; and when I have seen my work spoiled, with the roller.

Was the work always worse done at the end of the day?—That was the greatest danger.

Do you conceive it possible that the children could do their work well at the end of such a day's labour as that?—No.

Matthew Crabtree, the last Witness examined by this Committee, I think mentioned you as one of the slubbers under whom he worked?—Yes.

He states that he was chastised and beaten at the mill?—Yes, I have had to chastise him.

You can confirm then what he has stated as to the length of time he had to work as a child, and the cruel treatment that he received?—Yes, I have had to chastise him in the evening, and often in the morning for being too late; when I had one out of the three wanting I could not keep up with the machine, and I was getting behindhand compared with what another man was doing; and therefore I should have been called to account on Saturday night if the work was not done.

Was he worse than others?—No.

Was it the constant practice to chastise the children?—Yes.

It was necessary in order to keep up your work?—Yes.

And you would have lost your place if you had not done so?—Yes; when I was working at Mr. Wood's mill, at Dewsbury, which at present is burnt down, but where I slubbed for him until it was, while we were taking our meals he used to come up and put the machine agoing; and I used to say, 'You do not give us time to eat"; he used to reply, "Chew it at your work"; and I often replied to him, "I have not yet become debased like a brute, I do not chew my cud." Often has that man done that, and then gone below to see if a strap were off, which would have shown if the machinery was not working, and then he would come up again.

Was this at the drinking time?—Yes, at breakfast and at drinking.

Was this where the children were working?—Yes, my own children and others.

Were your own children obliged to employ most of their time at breakfast and at the drinking in cleansing the machine, and in fettling the spindles?—I have seen at that mill, and I have experienced and mentioned it with grief, that the English children were enslaved worse than the Africans. Once when Mr. Wood was saying to the carrier who brought his work in and out, "How long has that horse of mine been at work?" and the carrier told him the time, and he said "Loose him directly, he has been in too long," I made this reply to him, 'You have more mercy and pity for your horse than you have for your men."

Did not this beating go on principally at the latter part of the day?—Yes.

Was it not also dangerous for the children to move about those mills when they became so drowsy and fatigued?—Yes, especially by lamplight.

Do the accidents principally occur at the latter end of those long days of labour?—Yes, I believe mostly so.

Do you know of any that have happened? I know of one; it was at Mr. Wood's mill; part of the machinery caught a lass who had been drowsy and asleep, and the strap which ran close by her catched her at about her middle, and bore her to the ceiling, and down she came, and her neck appeared to be broken, and the slubber ran up to her and pulled her neck, and I carried her to the doctor myself.

Did she get well?—Yes, she came about again.

What time was that?—In the evening.

You say that you have eight children who have gone to the factories?—Yes.

There has been no opportunity for you to send them to a day-school?—No; one boy had about twelve months' schooling.

Have they gone to Sunday-schools?—Yes.

Can any of them write?—Not one.

They do not teach writing at Sunday-schools?—No; it is objected to, I believe.

So that none of your children can write?—No.

What would be the effect of a proper limitation of the hours of labour upon the conduct of the rising generation?—I believe it would have a very happy effect in regard to correcting their morals; for I believe there is a deal of evil that takes place in one or other in consequence of those long hours.

Is it your opinion that they would then have an opportunity of attending night-schools?—Yes; I have often regretted, while working those long hours, that I could not get my children there.

Is it your belief that if they were better instructed, they would be happier and better members of society? —Yes, I believe so.

Karl Marx and Friedrich Engels, from *The Communist Manifesto*

Karl Marx (1818–1883 CE) was a German revolutionary philosopher and theorist. Born in Trier, Marx studied law and philosophy at major German universities. Hegel and others influenced Marx's views of dialectics, by which history develops through conflict of contradictory forces. Marx grounded this dynamic in materialism and class struggle. In 1842 he became the editor of a radical newspaper in Cologne, after which he moved to Paris, Brussels, and eventually Britain, where he would spend the rest of his life. His family lived in poverty, but was continually supported by his close and wealthy friend Friedrich Engels, with whom he wrote the *Communist Manifesto* in 1848. Marx wrote many other works, most notably Capital, and helped establish the First International in 1864.

Source: Karl Marx,"Proletarians and Communists," in *The Communist Manifesto,* trans. by Samuel Moore (1848).

Focus Questions:

1. According to Marx, when the proletariat achieves political supremacy, what will happen to private property and assets, and what will be the role of the state?
2. After the proletariat takes control, what does Marx say will happen to classes?

PART II: "PROLETARIANS AND COMMUNISTS"

We have seen above, that the first step in the revolution by the working class, is to raise the proletariat to the position of ruling as to win the battle of democracy.

The proletariat will use its political supremacy to wrest, by degrees, all capital from the bourgeoisie, to centralise all instruments of production in the hands of the State, i.e., of the proletariat organised as the ruling class; and to increase the total of productive forces as rapidly as possible.

Of course, in the beginning, this cannot be effected except by means of despotic inroads on the rights of property, and on the conditions of bourgeois production; by means of measures, therefore, which appear economically insufficient and untenable, but which, in the course of the movement, outstrip themselves, necessitate further inroads upon the old social order, and are unavoidable as a means of entirely revolutionising the mode of production.

These measures will of course be different in different countries.

Nevertheless in the most advanced countries, the following will be pretty generally applicable.

1. Abolition of property in land and application of all rents of land to public purposes.
2. A heavy progressive or graduated income tax.
3. Abolition of all right of inheritance.
4. Confiscation of the property of all emigrants and rebels.
5. Centralisation of credit in the hands of the State, by means of a national bank with State capital and an exclusive monopoly.
6. Centralisation of the means of communication and transport in the hands of the State.
7. Extension of factories and instruments of production owned by the State; the bringing into cultivation of waste-lands, and the improvement of the soil generally in accordance with a common plan.
8. Equal liability of all to labour. Establishment of industrial armies, especially for agriculture.
9. Combination of agriculture with manufacturing industries; gradual abolition of the distinction between town and country, by a more equable distribution of the population over the country.
10. Free education for all children in public schools. Abolition of children's factory labour in its present form. Combination of education with industrial production, &c., &c.

When, in the course of development, class distinctions have disappeared, and all production has been concentrated in the hands of a vast association of the whole nation, the public power will lose its political character. Political power, properly so called, is merely the organised power of one class for oppressing another. If the proletariat during its contest with the bourgeoisie is compelled, by the force of circumstances, to organise itself as a class, if, by means of a revolution, it makes itself the ruling class, and, as such, sweeps away by force the old conditions of production, then it will, along with these conditions, have swept away the conditions for the existence of class antagonisms and of classes generally, and will thereby have abolished its own supremacy as a class.

In place of the old bourgeois society, with its classes and class antagonisms, we shall have an association, in which the free development of each is the condition for the free development of all.

Edwin Chadwick, Summary from the Poor Law Commissioners

Edwin Chadwick (1803–1890) had taken an active part in the reform of the Poor Law and in factory legislation before he became secretary to a commission investigating sanitary conditions and means of improving them. The Commission's report, of which the summary is given below, is the third of the great reports of this epoch.

Source: Report...from the *Poor Law Commissioners on an Inquiry into the Sanitary Conditions of the Labouring Population of Great Britain* (London, 1842), pp. 369–372.

Focus Questions:

1. What one innovation, if implemented, would most improve the sanitary conditions of the working classes, in Chadwick's opinion?
2. How does he connect cleanliness standards and moral behavior? Why does he?
3. What does this document suggest about official concern for the poor in Industrial Britain?

After as careful an examination of the evidence collected as I have been enabled to make, I beg leave to recapitulate the chief conclusions which that evidence appears to me to establish.

First, as to the extent and operation of the evils which are the subject of this inquiry:

That the various forms of epidemic, endemic, and other disease caused, or aggravated, or propagated chiefly amongst the labouring classes by atmospheric impurities produced by decomposing animal and vegetable substances, by damp and filth, and close and overcrowded dwellings prevail amongst the population in every part of the kingdom, whether dwelling in separate houses, in rural villages, in small towns, in the larger towns— as they have been found to prevail in the lowest districts of the metropolis.

That such disease, wherever its attacks are frequent, is always found in connexion with the physical circumstances above specified, and that where those circumstances are removed by drainage, proper cleansing, better ventilation, and other means of diminishing atmospheric impurity, the frequency and intensity of such disease is abated; and where the removal of the noxious agencies appears to be complete, such disease almost entirely disappears.

Contaminated London drinking water containing various micro-organisms, refuse, and the like.

The high prosperity in respect to employment and wages, and various and abundant food, have afforded to the labouring classes no exemptions from attacks of epidemic disease, which have been as frequent and as fatal in periods of commercial and manufacturing prosperity as in any others.

That the formation of all habits of cleanliness is obstructed by defective supplies of water.

That the annual loss of life from filth and bad ventilation are greater than the loss from death or wounds in any wars in which the country has been engaged in modern times.

That of the 43,000 cases of widowhood, and 112,000 cases of destitute orphanage relieved from the poor's rates in England and Wales alone, it appears that the greatest proportion of deaths of the heads of families occurred from the above specified and other removable causes; that their ages were under 45 years; that is to say, 13 years below the natural probabilities of life as shown by the experience of the whole population of Sweden.

That the public loss from the premature deaths of the heads of families is greater than can be represented by any enumeration of the pecuniary burdens consequent upon their sickness and death.

That, measuring the loss of working ability amongst large classes by the instances of gain, even from incomplete arrangements for the removal of noxious influences from places of work or from abodes, that this loss cannot be less than eight or ten years.

That the ravages of epidemics and other diseases do not diminish but tend to increase the pressure of population.

That in the districts where the mortality is greatest the births are not only sufficient to replace the numbers removed by death, but to add to the population.

That the younger population, bred up under noxious physical agencies, is inferior in physical organization and general health to a population preserved from the presence of such agencies.

That the population so exposed is less susceptible of moral influences, and the effects of education are more transient than with a healthy population.

That these adverse circumstances tend to produce an adult population short-lived, improvident, reckless, and intemperate, and with habitual avidity for sensual gratifications.

That these habits lead to the abandonment of all the conveniences and decencies of life, and especially lead to the overcrowding of their homes, which is destructive to the morality as well as the health of large classes of both sexes.

That defective town cleansing fosters habits of the most abject degradation and tends to the demoralization of large numbers of human beings, who subsist by means of what they find amidst the noxious filth accumulated in neglected streets and bye-places.

That the expenses of local public works are in general unequally and unfairly assessed, oppressively and uneconomically collected, by separate collections, wastefully expended in separate and inefficient operations by unskilled and practically irresponsible officers.

That the existing law for the protection of the public health and the constitutional machinery for reclaiming its execution, such as the Courts Leet, have fallen into desuetude, and are in the state indicated by the prevalence of the evils they were intended to prevent.

Secondly. As to the means by which the present sanitary condition of the labouring classes may be improved:

The primary and most important measures, and at the same time the most practicable, and within the recognized province of public administration, are drainage, the removal of all refuse of habitations, streets, and roads, and the improvement of the supplies of water.

That the chief obstacles to the immediate removal of decomposing refuse of towns and habitations have been the expense and annoyance of the hand labour and cartage requisite for the purpose.

That this expense may be reduced to one-twentieth or to one-thirtieth, or rendered inconsiderable, by the use of water and self-acting means of removal by improved and cheaper sewers and drains.

That refuse when thus held in suspension in water may be most cheaply and innoxiously conveyed to any distance out of towns, and also in the best form for productive use, and that the loss and injury by the pollution of natural streams may be avoided.

That for all these purposes, as well as for domestic use, better supplies of water are absolutely necessary. That for successful and economical drainage the adoption of geological areas as the basis of operations is requisite.

That appropriate scientific arrangements for public drainage would afford important facilities for private land-drainage, which is important for the health as well as sustenance of the labouring classes.

That the expense of public drainage, of supplies of water laid on in houses, and of means of improved cleansing would be a pecuniary gain, by diminishing the existing charges attendant on sickness and pre-mature mortality.

That for the protection of the labouring classes and of the ratepayers against inefficiency and waste in all new structural arrangements for the protection of the public health, and to ensure public confidence that the expenditure will be beneficial, securities should be taken that all new local public works are devised and conducted by responsible officers qualified by the possession of the science and skill of civil engineers.

That the oppressiveness and injustice of levies for the whole immediate outlay on such works upon persons who have only short interests in the benefits may be avoided by care in spreading the expense over periods coincident with the benefits.

That by appropriate arrangements, 10 or 15 per cent. on the ordinary outlay for drainage might be saved, which on an estimate of the expense of the necessary structural alterations of one-third only of the existing tenements would be a saving of one million and a half sterling, besides the reduction of the future expenses of management.

That for the prevention of the disease occasioned by defective ventilation and other causes of impurity in places of work and other places where large numbers are assembled, and for the general promotion of the means necessary to prevent disease, that it would be good economy to appoint a district medical officer independent of private practice, and with the securities of special qualifications and responsibilities to initiate sanitary measures and reclaim the execution of the law.

That by the combinations of all these arrangements, it is probable that the full ensurable period of life indicated by the Swedish tables; that is, an increase of 13 years at least, may be extended to the whole of the labouring classes.

That the attainment of these and the other collateral advantages of reducing existing charges and expenditure are within the power of the legislature, and are dependent mainly on the securities taken for the application of practical science, skill, and economy in the direction of local public works.

And that the removal of noxious physical circumstances, and the promotion of civic, household, and personal cleanliness, are necessary to the improvement of the moral condition of the population; for that sound morality and refinement in manners and health are not long found co-existent with filthy habits amongst any class of the community.

Chartist Movement: The People's Petition of 1838

Although the Factory Act of 1833 resulted in an improvement in factory working conditions and in restrictions on child labor, many critics favored more radical reform. The Chartist movement in Great Britain, which was popular in the 1840s, sought political participation and especially universal man-hood suffrage as means of improving the living conditions of the working poor. The following is an excerpt from the People's Petition of 1838, which articulated Chartist demands to the British House of Commons.

Source: "The Chartist Demands," in *The Life and Struggles of William Lovett* (New York: Knopf, 1920), pp. 478–481.

FOCUS QUESTION:

1. Who were the Chartists and what were their demands for reform? Was this a political or social reform program?

We, your petitioners, dwell in a land whose merchants are noted for enterprise, whose manufacturers are very skillful, and whose workmen are proverbial for their industry.

The land itself is goodly, the soil rich, and the temperature wholesome; it is abundantly furnished with the materials of commerce and trade; it has numerous and convenient harbours; in facility of internal communication it exceeds all others. For three-and-twenty years we have enjoyed a profound peace.

Yet, with all these elements of national prosperity, and with every disposition and capacity to take advantage of them, we find ourselves overwhelmed with public and private suffering.

We are bowed down under a load of taxes; which, notwithstanding, fall greatly short of the wants of our rulers; our traders are trembling on the verge of bankruptcy; our workmen are starving; capital brings no profit, and labour no remuneration; the home of the artificer is desolate, and the warehouse of the pawnbroker is full; the workhouse is crowded, and the manufactory is deserted…

It was the found expectation of the people that a remedy for the greater part, if not for the whole, of their grievances, would be found in the Reform Act of 1832.

They were taught to regard that Act as a wise means to a worthy end; as the machinery of an improved legislation, when the will of the masses would be at length potential.

They have been bitterly and basely deceived.

The fruit which looked so fair to the eye has turned to dust and ashes when gathered.

The Reform Act has effected a transfer of power from one domineering faction to another, and left the people as helpless as before…

Required as we are, universally, to support and obey the laws, nature and reason entitle us to demand, that in the making of the laws, the universal voice shall be implicitly listened to. We perform the duties of freemen; we must have the privileges of freemen. WE DEMAND UNIVERSAL SUFFRAGE The suffrage to be exempt from the corruption of the wealthy, and the violence of the powerful, must be secret…

WE DEMAND THE BALLOT

The connection between the representatives and the people, to be beneficial must be intimate…To public safety as well as public confidence, frequent elections are essential.

WE DEMAND ANNUAL PARLIAMENTS

With power to choose, and freedom in choosing, the range of our choice must be unrestricted.

We are compelled, by the existing laws, to take for our representatives, men who are incapable of appreciating our difficulties, or who have little sympathy with them; merchants who have retired from trade, and no longer feel its harassings; proprietors of land who are alike ignorant of its evils and their cure; lawyers, by whom the honours of the senate are sought after only as means of obtaining notice in the courts…

We demand that in the future election of members of your Honourable House, the approbation of the constituency shall be the sole qualification; and that to every representative so chosen shall be assigned, out of the public taxes, a fair and adequate remuneration for the time which he is called upon to devote to the public service.

Finally, we would most earnestly impress on your Honourable House, that this petition has not been dictated by an idle love of change; that it springs out of no inconsiderate attachment to fanciful theories; but that it is the result of much and long deliberation, and of convictions, which the events of each succeeding year tend more and more to strengthen.

British Parliament, "Inquiry: Labor in Mines"

As a result of innovations in the early nineteenth century, by mid-century steam had become the primary power source for machines and industry. The new transportation networks connecting European regions by railroads, with steam locomotives, also depended on steam power. Massive amounts of coal, pitched into roaring furnaces, created steam power. As a result of the demand for coal brought by steam power, mines then became an integral and vital part of the industrialized economy. As with factory work, the mines employed men, women and children. Both boys and girls labored along side adults in these hazardous work environments. The work was physically demanding, very dangerous, and caused an array of health problems in those who worked in the mines. In this passage, taken from Parliament inquires in 1842 regarding labor in coal mines, we see a glimpse of what the work conditions were like for female mine workers in Wales.

Source: Great Britain, *Parliament Papers, 1842,* vol. 16: 24, 196, vol. 15: 84, and vol. 17:108; reprinted in *The Western Heritage: Documents Set,* eds. Donald Kagan, Steven Ozment, Frank M. Turner, vol. 2, 6th ed., (Upper Saddle River, N.J.: Prentice Hall, 1998), 204-205.

Focus Questions:

1. Why would so many women miners prefer to work in the mines without clothing? Why did the women need the heavy belts around their waists and chains between their legs?
2. What was the average workday of these female miners? What was their daily diet? What would be the social and familial cost for these female miners?
3. Karl Marx and Friedrich Engels argue that capitalism and industrialism are inherently exploitive of women so that "The bourgeois sees in his wife only an instrument of production." Based upon an analysis of this document, how would you respond to Marx and Engels's argument?

England, exclusive of Wales, it is only in some of the colliery districts of Yorkshire and Lancashire that female Children of tender age and young and adult women are allowed to descend into the coal mines and regularly to perform the same kinds of underground work, and to work for the same number of hours, as boys and men; but in the East of Scotland their employment in the pits is general; and in South Wales it is not uncommon.

West Riding of Yorkshire: Southern Part—In many of the collieries in this district, as far as relates to the underground employment, there is no distinction of sex, but the labour is distributed indifferently among both sexes, except that it is comparatively rare for the women to hew or get the coals, although there are numerous instances in which they regularly perform even this work. In great numbers of the coalpits in this district the men work in a state of perfect nakedness, and are in this state assisted in their labour by females of all ages, from girls of six years old to women of twenty-one, these females being themselves quite naked down to the waist.

"Girls," says the Sub-Commissioner [J. C. Symons], "regularly perform all the various offices of trapping, hurrying [Yorkshire terms for drawing the loaded coal corves],[1] filling, riddling,[2] tipping, and occasionally getting, just as they are performed by boys. One of the most disgusting sights I have ever seen was that of young females, dressed like boys in trousers, crawling on all fours, with belts round their waists and chains passing between their legs, at day pits at Hunshelf Bank, and in many small pits near Holmfirth and New Mills: it exists also in several other places. I visited the Hunshelf Colliery on the 18th of January: it is a day pit; that is, there is no shaft or descent; the gate or entrance is at the side of a bank, and nearly horizontal. The gate was not more than a yard high, and in some places not above 2 feet.

"When I arrived at the board or workings of the pit I found at one of the sideboards down a narrow passage a girl of fourteen years of age in boy's clothes, picking down the coal with the regular pick used by the men. She was half sitting half lying at her work, and said she found it tired her very much, and 'of course she didn't like it.' The place where she was at work was not 2 feet high. Further on were men lying on their sides and getting. No less than six girls out of eighteen men and children are employed in this pit. "Whilst I was in the pit the Rev. Mr Bruce, of Wadsley, and the Rev. Mr Nelson, of Rotherham, who accompanied me, and remained outside, saw another girl of ten years of age, also dressed in boy's clothes, who was employed in hurrying, and these gentlemen saw her at work. She was a nice-looking little child, but of course as black as a tinker, and with a little necklace round her throat.

1 These were baskets to carry the hewn coal.
2 Sifting and separating of the coal.

"In two other pits in the Huddersfield Union I have seen the same sight. In one near New Mills, the chain, passing high up between the legs of two of these girls, had worn large holes in their trousers; and any sight more disgustingly indecent or revolting can scarcely be imagined than these girls at work—no brothel can beat it.

"On descending Messrs Hopwood's pit at Barnsley, I found assembled round a fire a group of men, boys, and girls, some of whom were of the age of puberty; the girls as well as the boys *stark naked* down to the waist, their hair bound up with a tight cap, and trousers supported by their hips. (At Silkstone and at Flockton they work in their shifts and trousers.) Their sex was recognizable only by their breasts, and some little difficulty occasionally arose in pointing out to me which were girls and which were boys, and which caused a good deal of laughing and joking. In the Flockton and Thornhill pits the system is even more indecent; for though the girls are clothed, at least three-fourths of the men for whom they "hurry" work stark naked, or with a flannel waistcoat only, and in this state they assist one another to fill the corves 18 or 20 times a day: I have seen this done myself frequently.

"When it is remembered that these girls hurry chiefly for men who are *not* their parents; that they go from 15 to 20 times a day into a dark chamber (the bank face), which is often 50 yards apart from any one, to a man working naked, or next to naked, it is not to be supposed but that where opportunity thus prevails sexual vices are of common occurrence. Add to this the free intercourse, and the rendezvous at the shaft or bullstake, where the corves are brought, and consider the language to which the young ear is habituated, the absence of religious instruction, and the early age at which contamination begins, and you will have before you, in the coal-pits where females are employed, the picture of a nursery for juvenile vice which you will go far and wide above ground to equal."

TWO WOMEN MINERS[3]

Betty Harris, age 37: I was married at 23, and went into a colliery when I was married. I used to weave when about 12 years old; can neither read nor write. I work for Andrew Knowles, of Little Bolton (Lancs), and make sometimes 7s a week, sometimes not so much. I am a drawer, and work from 6 in the morning to 6 at night. Stop about an hour at noon to eat my dinner; have bread and butter for dinner; I get no drink. I have two children, but they are too young to work. I worked at drawing when I was in the family way. I know a woman who has gone home and washed herself, taken to her bed, been delivered of a child, and gone to work again under the week.

3 From Great Britan, Parliamentary Papers, 1842, Vol. XV, p. 84, and ibid., Vol. XVII, p. 108

I have a belt round my waist, and a chain passing between my legs, and I go on my hands and feet. The road is very steep, and we have to hold by a rope; and when there is no rope, by anything we can catch hold of. There are six women and about six boys and girls in the pit I work in; it is very hard work for a woman. The pit is very wet where I work, and the water comes over our clog-tops always, and I have seen it up to my thighs; it rains in at the roof terribly. My clothes are wet through almost all day long. I never was ill in my life, but when I was lying in.

My cousin looks after my children in the day time. I am very tired when I get home at night; I fall asleep sometimes before I get washed. I am not so strong as I was, and cannot stand my work so well as I used to. I have drawn till I have had the skin off me; the belt and chain is worse when we are in the family way. My feller (husband) has beaten me many a time for not being ready. I were not used to it at first, and he had little patience.

I have known many a man beat his drawer. I have known men take liberties with the drawers, and some of the women have bastards.

Patience Kershaw, age 17, Halifax: I go to pit at 5 o'clock in the morning and come out at 5 in the evening; I get my breakfast, porridge and milk, first; I take my dinner with me, a cake, and eat it as I go; I do not stop or rest at any time for the purpose, I get nothing else until I get home, and then have potatoes and meat, not every day meat.

I hurry in the clothes I have now got on—trousers and a ragged jacket; the bald place upon my head is made by thrusting the corves; I hurry the corves a mile and more under ground and back; they weigh 3 cwt. I hurry eleven a day. I wear a belt and chain at the workings to get the corves out. The getters that I work for are naked except their caps; they pull off all their clothes; I see them at work when I go up.

Sometimes they beat me if I am not quick enough, with their hands; they strike me upon my back. The boys take liberties with me sometimes; they pull me about. I am the only girl in the pit; there are about 20 boys and 15 men; all the men are naked. I would rather work in mill than in coal-pit.

Note by Sub-Commissioner Scriven: This girl is an ignorant, filthy, ragged, and deplorable looking object, and such a one as the uncivilized natives of the prairies would be shocked to look upon.

British Parliament, "Inquiry: Child Labor"

Work in the early factories of the industrial revolution was not regulated by governments. Hours, wages, and conditions were set by owners, managers and investors, often with little concern for the interests and health of workers. Along with men and women, children were a part of the factory work force, just as they had been part of the economy of earlier eras, when children provided labor in the agricultural fields and in artisan workshops. The factory environment, however, created new patterns of child labor. In factories, managers now supervised children's work, rather than their parents or a family member, as before. Also, children worked much longer hours than they had in previous eras. In the early 1800s, the British Parliament began investigations into child labor practices. In 1833, the Parliament passed some initial laws designed to regulate child labor, but these measures were quite limited and not fully enforced. For example, the laws only banned work for children under nine years old, and allowed young children to work as long as nine hours per day.

Source: British Sessional Papers 1831–1832, House of Commons vol. XV, pp. 17–19; reprinted in *Documents in World History,vol. 2: The Modern Centuries: From 1500 to the Present* ,ed. Peter N. Steams, et al., (NewYork: Harper Collins Publishers, 1988), pp. 26–27.

Focus Questions:

1. Based on this interview, what were the work conditions for children in factories? What affects did these conditions have on them?
2. Based on the questions, what were the main concerns of the middle class interviewers examining the issue? How did they view this problem and its possible solutions?
3. What does this passage tell us about debates and problems regarding labor in Great Britain during the period of industrialization?

Mr. Abraham Whitehead

431. What is your business?—A clothier.

432. Where do you reside?—At Scholes, near Holmfirth.

433. Is not that in the centre of very considerable woolen mills? Yes, for a space of three of four miles; I live nearly in the centre of thirty or forty woollen mills....

436. Are the children and young persons of both sexes employed in these mills?—Yes.

437. At how early an age are children employed?—The youngest age at which children are employed is never under five, but some are employed between five and six in woollen mills at piecing.

438. How early have you observed these young children going to their work, speaking for the present in the summer time?—In the summer time I have frequently seen them going to work between five and six in the morning, and I know the general practice is for them to go as early to all the mills....

439. How late in the evening have you seen them at work, or remarked them returning to their homes?—I have seen them at work in the summer season between nine and ten in the evening; they continue to work as long as they can see, and they can see to work in these mills as long as you could see to read....

* * *

441. You say that on your own personal knowledge?—I live near to parents who have been sending their children to mills for a great number of years, and I know positively that these children are every morning in the winter seasons called out of bed between five and six, and in some instances between four and five.

442. Your business as a clothier has often led you into these mills?—Frequently;...

* * *

460. What has been the treatment which you have observed that these children received at the mills, to keep them attentive for so many hours at such early ages?—They are generally cruelly treated; so cruelly treated, that they dare not hardly for their lives be too late at their work in a morning.... My heart has been ready to bleed for them when I have seen them so fatigued, for they appear in such a state of apathy and insensibility as really not to know whether they are doing their work or not;...

461. Do they frequently fall into errors and mistakes in piecing when thus fatigued?—Yes; the errors they make when thus fatigued are, that instead of placing the cording in this way [describing it], they are apt to place them obliquely, and that causes a flying, which makes bad yarn; and when the billy-spinner sees that, he takes his strap or the billy-roller, and says, "Damn thee, close it-little devil, close it," and they smite the child with the strap or the billy-roller....

* * *

510. You say that the morals of the children are very bad when confined in these mills; what do you consider to be the situation of children who have nothing to do, and are running about such towns as Leeds, with no employment to

keep them out of mischief?—Children that are not employed in mills are generally more moral and better behaved than children who are employed in mills.

511. Those in perfect idleness are better behaved than those that are employed?—That is not a common thing; they either employ them in some kind of business at home, or send them to school.

512. Are there no day-schools to which these factory children go?—They have no opportunity of going to school when they are thus employed at the mill

Michael Bakunin, "Principles and Organization of the International Brotherhood"

As an outgrowth of socialism, the anarchist ideas of Michael Bakunin (1814-1876) influenced politics in Russia and Western Europe. Bakunin was born into an aristocratic Russian family, but despite his background became active in radical politics. As a result of his participation in the revolutions that swept through Europe in the 1840s, especially for his prominent role in the insurrections in Dresden, he was arrested, sent back to Russia, and later exiled to Siberia. In 1861, he escaped, fleeing first to Japan, then to the US, and finally to London. In the next years, he traveled throughout Western Europe, continued to write and publish, and became an influential figure in socialist politics. Bakunin believed the working class should achieve liberty through revolution, but his belief in radical individualism brought him into conflict with Karl Marx. In this document, Bakunin outlines the political and social principles for a revolutionary society.

Source: Michael Bakunin, "Principles and Organization of the International Brotherhood," in *Michael Bakunin Selected Writings*, ed. Arthur Lehning (New York: Grove Press, 1974), 64-69, 76-78, 82-85, 87, 90-92.

Focus Questions:

1. What were Bakunin's ideas regarding equality and liberty? How did he view revolution?
2. What groups did Bakunin target for membership for his society? What groups would find his ideas appealing? Why?
3. How were Bakunin's ideas related to socialism? How were they different?

I. AIM OF THE SOCIETY

1. The aim of this society is the triumph of the principle of revolution in the world, and consequently the radical overthrow of all presently existing reli-

gious, political, economic and social organizations and institutions and the reconstitution first of European and subsequently of world society on the basis of liberty, *reason, justice* and *work.*

2. This kind of task cannot be achieved overnight. The association is therefore constituted for an indefinite period, and will cease to exist only on the day when the triumph of its principle throughout the world removes its *raison de être*[1].

II. REVOLUTIONARY CATECHISM

1. Denial of the existence of a real, extra-terrestrial, individual God, and consequently also of any revelation and any divine intervention in the affairs of the human world. *Abolition of the service and worship of divinity.*

2. In replacing the worship of God by *respect* and *love for humanity,* we assert *human reason* as the one criterion of truth; human conscience as the basis of justice; *individual and collective liberty* as the only creator of order for mankind.

3. *Liberty* is the absolute right of all adult men and women to seek no sanction for their actions except their own conscience and their own reason, to determine them only of their own free will, and consequently to be responsible for them to themselves first of all, and then to the society of which they are a part, but only in so far as they freely consent to be a part of it.

4. It is quite untrue that the freedom of the individual is bounded by that of every other individual. Man is truly free only to the extent that his own freedom, freely acknowledged and reflected as in a mirror by the free conscience of all other men, finds in their freedom the confirmation of its infinite scope. Man is truly free only among other equally free men, and since he is free only in terms of mankind, the enslavement of any one man on earth, being an offense against the very principle of humanity, is a denial of the liberty of all.

5. Every man's *liberty* can be realized, therefore, only by the equality of all. The realization of liberty in legal and actual *equality* is *justice.*

6. There is only one dogma, one law, one moral basis for men, and *that is liberty.* To respect your neighbor's liberty *is duty;* to love, help and serve him, *is virtue.*

7. *Absolute rejection of any principle of authority and of raison d'État.*[2] *Human society,* which was originally a natural fact, prior to liberty and the awakening of the human mind, and which later became a religious fact, organized on the principle of divine and human authority, must now be reconstituted on the basis of liberty, henceforward to be the sole determinant of its organization,

1 French: reason for being.

2 French: reason of State; a measure taken by a government for the continuance of the state.

both political and economic. *Order in society must be the outcome of the greatest possible development of all local, collective and individual liberties...*

* * *

9. Political organization. It is impossible to determine a concrete, universal and compulsory norm for the internal development and political organization of nations, since the existence of each is subordinate to a host of variable historical, geographical and economic factors which never permit of the establishment of an organizational model equally applicable and acceptable to all. Furthermore, any undertaking of this nature, being utterly devoid of practical utility, would militate against the richness and spontaneity of life, which delights in infinite diversity, and would in addition be contrary to the very principle of liberty. Nevertheless, there do exist essential, absolute conditions without which the practical realization and organization of liberty will always be impossible. These conditions are:

9(a). The radical abolition of all official religion and every privileged or state-protected, -financed or maintained church. Absolute freedom of conscience and propaganda for all, each man having the unlimited option of building as many temples as he pleases to his gods, whatever their denomination, and of paying and maintaining the priests of his religion.

9(b). Seen as religious corporations, churches shall enjoy none of the political rights which will belong to productive associations, shall be unable to inherit or possess wealth in common, excepting their houses or establishments of prayer, and shall never be allowed to participate in the upbringing of children, since their sole aim in life is the systematic negation of morality and liberty, and the practice of sorcery for profit.

9(c). Abolition of monarchy, republic.

9(d). Abolition of class, rank, privilege and distinction in all its forms. Complete equality of political rights for all men and all women; universal suffrage.

9(e). Abolition, dissolution, and moral, political, legal, bureaucratic and social bankruptcy of the *custodial, transcendental,* centralist *state,* lackey and alter ego of the church, and as such the permanent source of poverty, degradation and subjugation among the people. As a natural consequence, *abolition of all state universities— public* education must be the exclusive prerogative of the free communes and associations; *abolition of state magistracy—all judges* to be elected by the people; *abolition* of the *criminal and civil codes currently in force in Europe—because* all of these, being equally inspired by the worship of God, state, family as a religious and political entity, and property, are contrary to human rights, and because *only by liberty* can the code of liberty be created. *Abolition of banks, and all other state credit institutions. Abolition of all central administration, bureaucracies, standing armies and state police.*

9(f). Immediate and direct election of all public officials, both civil and judicial, as well of all national, provincial and communal councilors or representatives, by popular vote, which is to say by the universal suffrage of all adult men and women.

9(g). Reorganization of each region, taking as its basis and starting point *the absolute freedom of individual, productive association and commune.*

9(h). Individual rights.

(i). The right of every man or woman to be completely supported, cared for, protected, brought up and educated from birth to coming of age in all public, primary, secondary, higher, industrial, artistic and scientific schools at the expense of society.

(ii). The equal right of each to be advised and assisted by the latter, as far as possible, at the outset of the career which each new adult will freely choose, after which the society which has declared him completely free will exercise no further supervision or authority over him, decline all responsibility toward him, and owe him nothing more than respect and if necessary protection for his liberty.

(iii). The liberty of every adult man and woman must be absolute and complete freedom to come and go, openly to profess any shade of opinion, to be idle or active, immoral or moral, in other words to dispose of his own person and his own belongings as he pleases and to be answerable to no one; freedom either to live honestly, by their own labor, or shamefully, by exploiting charity or individual trust, given that such charity and trust be voluntary and be proffered by adults only.

(iv). Unconditional freedom for every variety of propaganda, whether through conversation, the press or in public or private meetings, without any constraint but the natural corrective power of public opinion. Absolute liberty of associations, not excepting those whose aims may be or seem to be immoral, and even including those whose aim is the corruption and [destruction] of individual and public liberty....

(ix). Absolute abolition of all cruel and degrading sentences, corporal punishment and the death penalty as sanctioned and enforced by the law. Abolition of all those indefinite or protracted punishments which leave no hope and no real possibility of rehabilitation, since crime ought to be considered as sickness, and punishment as cure rather than social retaliation.

(x). Any individual condemned by the laws of any society, commune, province or nation shall retain the right not to submit to the sentence imposed on him, by declaring that he no longer wishes to be part of that society. But in such a case the society in question shall have the concomitant right to expel him from its midst and to declare him outside its warrant and protection. (xi). Having thus reverted to the natural law of an eye for an eye, a tooth for a tooth, at least inside the territory occupied by that society, the individual shall be liable to robbery, ill-treatment and even death without any cause for alarm. Any person will be able to dispose of him like a dangerous animal, although never to subject him or use him as a slave.

10. *Social organization.* Without political equality there is no true political liberty, but political equality will only become possible when there is *economic and social equality.*

10(a). Equality does not mean the leveling down of individual differences, nor intellectual, moral and physical uniformity among individuals.... Nor do economic and social equality mean the leveling down of individual fortunes, in so far as these are products of the ability, productive energy and thrift of an individual....

10(c). Justice, as well as human dignity, demands that *each individual should be the child of his own achievements,* and only those achievements. We hotly reject the doctrine of hereditary sin, disgrace and responsibility. By the same token, we must reject the illusory heredity of virtue, honors and rights—*and of wealth also.* The heir to any kind of wealth is no longer the complete child of his own achievements, and in terms of initial circumstance he is privileged.

10(d). Abolition of the right of inheritance. As long as this right continues, hereditary differences of class, rank and wealth—in other words, social inequality and privilege—will survive in fact, if not in law. But it is an inescapable social law that *defacto* in equality always produces inequality of rights: social inequality necessarily becomes political....

10(g). Once the inequality produced by the right of inheritance has been abolished, there will still remain (but to a far lesser degree) the inequality that arises from differences in individual ability, strength and productive capacity— a difference which, while never disappearing altogether, will be of diminishing importance under the influence of an egalitarian upbringing and social system, and which in addition will never weigh upon future generations once there is no more right of inheritance.

10(h). Labor is the sole producer of wealth. Everybody is free, of course, either to die of starvation or to dwell among the wild beasts of the desert or the forest, but anybody who wants to live within society should earn his living by his own work, or run the risk of being considered a parasite, an exploiter of the wealth (that is, the labor) of others, and a thief.

10(i). Labor is the fundamental basis of dignity and human rights, for it is only by means of his own free, intelligent work that man becomes a creator in his turn, wins from the surrounding world and his own animal nature his humanity and rights, and creates the world of civilization....

10(l). The land, with all its natural resources, belongs to all, but will be held only by those who work it.

10(m). Woman, differing from man but not inferior to him, intelligent, industrious and free like him, is declared his equal both in rights and in all political and social functions and duties.

10(n). Abolition not of the natural but of the *legal* family, based on civil law and ownership. Religious and civil marriage are replaced by *free marriage.* Two *adult* individuals of opposite sex have the right to unite and separate in accordance with their desires and mutual interests and the promptings of their hearts, nor does society have any right either to prevent their union or to hold them to it against their will....

10(o). From the moment of conception until her child is born, a woman is entitled to a social subvention paid not for her benefit but for her child's. Any mother wishing to feed and rear her children will also receive all the costs of their maintenance and care from society....

10(q). Children belong neither to their parents nor to society but to themselves and their future liberty....It is true that their parents are their natural protectors, but *the legal and ultimate protector is society,* which has the right and duty to tend them because its own future depends on the intellectual and moral guidance they receive. Society can only give liberty to adults provided it supervises the upbringing of minors.

10(r). School must take the place of church, with the immense difference that the religious education provided by the latter has no other purpose than to perpetuate the rule of human ignorance or so-called divine authority, whereas school upbringing and education will have no other purpose than the true emancipation of the children upon reaching the age of majority, and will consist of nothing less than their progressive initiation into liberty by the threefold development of their physical and mental powers and their will. Reason, truth, justice, human respect, awareness of personal dignity (inseparable from the human dignity of another), love of liberty for one's own sake and for others belief in work as the basis and condition of all rights; contempt for unreason, falsehood, injustice, cowardice, slavery and idleness—these must be the keystones of public education....

10(s). As soon as he comes of age, the adolescent will be declared a free citizen and absolute master of his actions. In exchange for the care it has exercised during his infancy, society will ask for three things: that he remain free, that he *live by his own labor,* and that he *respect the liberty of others.* And because the crimes and vices by which present—day society is afflicted are the sole outcome of defective social organization, we may be sure that given a form of organization and upbringing based on reason, justice, liberty, human respect and complete equality, good will become the rule and evil a morbid exception, ever decreasing under the all-powerful influence of moralized public opinion.

10(t). The old, the disabled and the sick will be cared for and respected, enjoy all public and social rights, and be generously maintained at the common expense....

III. REQUISITE EQUALITIES FOR MEMBERSHIP OF THE INTERNATIONAL FAMILY

He must be an atheist....

He must, like ourselves, be the adversary of the principle of authority....

He must be a revolutionary. He must understand that such a complete and radical transformation of society, which must necessarily involve the downfall of all privilege, monopoly and constituted power, will naturally not occur by peaceful means....

He must understand that the sole and final purpose of this revolution is the true political, economic and social emancipation of the people....

He will therefore despise any secondary movement whose immediate, direct aim is other than the political and social emancipation of the working classes, in other words the people, and will see it either as a fatal error or a shabby trick. Hostile to all compromise and conciliation—henceforward impossible—and to any false coalition with those whose interests make them the natural enemies of the people, *he must see that the only salvation for his own country and for the entire world lies in social revolution.*

.... He must understand that the social revolution will necessarily become a European and worldwide revolution.

That the world will inevitably split into two camps, that of the new life and of the old privileges, and that between these two opposing camps, created as in the time of the wars of religion not by national sympathies but by community of ideas and interests, a war of extermination is bound to erupt, with no quarter and no respite....

That this will not be a war of conquest, but of emancipation....

That even in the most apparently hostile countries, once the social revolution breaks out at one point it will find keen and tenacious allies in the popular masses, who will be unable to do other than rally to its banner as soon as they understand and come in contact with its activities and purpose. That it will consequently be necessary to choose the most fertile soil for its beginning, where it has only to withstand the first assault of reaction before expanding to overwhelm the frenzies of its enemies, federalizing all the lands it has absorbed and welding them into a single indomitable revolutionary alliance.

CHAPTER 21

Society and Social Change in the Nineteenth Century

John Stuart Mill, Excerpts from *On Liberty*

John Stuart Mill (1860–1873 CE), a son of the philosopher James Mill, had already learned Greek and Latin by age twelve, as well as received a rigorous education in mathematics, economics, and philosophy. He published works on politics, society, and economics, including *On Liberty* (1859), *Considerations on Representative Government* (1861), *Utilitarianism* (1861), and *The Subjection of Women* (1869). Many of his ideas were deemed radical during his day, but have since become established ideas in liberal thought. He authored works with his wife Harriet Taylor and advocated the right to vote and equal rights for women.

Source: John Stuart Mill, *On Liberty* (P. F. Collier and Son, 1909).

Focus Questions:

1. Under what conditions does Mill consider it acceptable to exercise control over an individual?
2. According to Mill, does the individual owe anything to society? If so, what?

CHAPTER I
INTRODUCTORY

The object of this Essay is to assert one very simple principle, as entitled to govern absolutely the dealings of society with the individual in the way of compulsion and control, whether the means used be physical force in the form of legal penalties, or the moral coercion of public opinion. That principle is, that the sole end for which mankind are warranted, individually or collectively in interfering with the liberty of action of any of their number, is self-protection. That the only purpose for which power can be rightfully exercised over any member of a civilized community, against his will, is to prevent harm to others. His own good, either physical or moral, is not a sufficient warrant. He cannot rightfully be compelled to do or forbear because it will be better for him to do so, because it will make him happier, because, in the opinions of others, to do so would be wise, or even right. These are good reasons for remonstrating with him, or reasoning with him, or persuading him, or entreating him, but not for compelling him, or visiting him with any evil, in case he do otherwise. To justify that, the conduct from which it is desired to deter him must be calculated to produce evil to some one else. The only part of the conduct of any one, for which he is amenable to society, is that which concerns others. In the part which merely concerns himself, his independence is, of right, absolute. Over himself, over his own body and mind, the individual is sovereign.

It is, perhaps, hardly necessary to say that this doctrine is meant to apply only to human beings in the maturity of their faculties. We are not speaking of children, or of young persons below the age which the law may fix as that of manhood or womanhood. Those who are still in a state to require being taken care of by others, must be protected against their own actions as well as against external injury. For the same reason, we may leave out of consideration those backward states of society in which the race itself may be considered as in its nonage. The early difficulties in the way of spontaneous progress are so great, that there is seldom any choice of means for overcoming them; and a ruler full of the spirit of improvement is warranted in the use of any expedients that will attain an end, perhaps otherwise unattainable. Despotism is a legitimate mode of government in dealing with barbarians, provided the end be their improvement, and the means justified by actually effecting that end. Liberty, as a principle, has no application to any state of things anterior to the time when mankind have become capable of being improved by free and equal discussion. Until then, there is nothing for them but implicit obedience to an Akbar or a Charlemagne, if they are so fortunate as to find one. But as soon as mankind have attained the capacity of being guided to their own improvement by conviction or persuasion (a period long since reached in all nations with whom we need here concern ourselves), compulsion, either in the direct form or in that of pains and penalties for non-compliance, is no longer admissible as a means to their own good, and justifiable only for the security of others.

* * *

CHAPTER IV

OF THE LIMITS TO THE AUTHORITY OF SOCIETY OVER THE INDIVIDUAL

What, then, is the rightful limit to the sovereignty of the individual over himself? Where does the authority of society begin? How much of human life should be assigned to individuality, and how much to society?

Each will receive its proper share, if each has that which more particularly concerns it. To individuality should belong the part of life in which it is chiefly the individual that is interested; to society, the part which chiefly interests society.

Though society is not founded on a contract, and though no good purpose is answered by inventing a contract in order to deduce social obligations from it, every one who receives the protection of society owes a return for the benefit, and the fact of living in society renders it indispensable that each should be bound to observe a certain line of conduct towards the rest. This conduct consists, first, in not injuring the interests of one another; or rather certain interests, which, either by express legal provision or by tacit understanding, ought to be considered as rights; and secondly, in each person's bearing his share (to be fixed on some equitable principle) of the labors and sacrifices incurred for defending the society or its members from injury and molestation. These conditions society is justified in enforcing, at all costs to those who endeavor to withhold fulfilment. Nor is this all that society may do. The acts of an individual may be hurtful to others, or wanting in due consideration for their welfare, without going the length of violating any of their constituted rights. The offender may then be justly punished by opinion, though not by law. As soon as any part of a person's conduct affects prejudicially the interests of others, society has jurisdiction over it, and the question whether the general welfare will or will not be promoted by interfering with it, becomes open to discussion. But there is no room for entertaining any such question when a person's conduct affects the interests of no persons besides himself, or needs not affect them unless they like (all the persons concerned being of full age, and the ordinary amount of understanding). In all such cases there should be perfect freedom, legal and social, to do the action and stand the consequences.

W.E.B. Du Bois, *Souls of Black Folk,* "Of Mr. Booker T. Washington and Others"

W.E.B. Du Bois (1868–1963) grew up in Great Barrington, Massachusetts, the descendent of several generations of free African Americans. In 1896 he became the first African American to receive a Doctorate from Harvard University. Du Bois' work as a scholar demonstrated the central role of African Americans in the history of America in the second half of the nineteenth century. As a civil rights activist, Du Bois founded the National Association for the Advancement of Colored People. His debates with Booker T. Washington centered on the place of civil and political rights in the struggle for greater opportunities for African Americans.

Source: W.E.B. Du Bois, "Of Mr. Booker T. Washington and Others," in Du Bois, *Souls of Black Folk* (Chicago: A. C. McClurg, 1903), pp. 42–54.

Focus Questions:

1. Did Du Bois accurately depict Booker T. Washington's position? How might Washington have responded to Du Bois' critique?
2. Why did Du Bois think civil and political rights were so crucial to the advancement of African Americans? What critique might Washington have offered of this position?

Easily the most striking thing in the history of the American Negro since 1876 is the ascendancy of Mr. Booker T. Washington. It began at the time when war memories and ideals were rapidly passing; a day of astonishing commercial development was dawning; a sense of doubt and hesitation overtook the freedmen's sons, then it was that his leading began. Mr. Washington came, with a single definite programme, at the psychological moment when the nation was a little ashamed of having bestowed so much sentiment on Negroes, and was concentrating its energies on Dollars. His programme of industrial education, conciliation of the South, and submission and silence as to civil and political rights, was not wholly original; the Free Negroes from 1830 up to war-time had striven to build industrial schools, and the American Missionary Association had from the first taught various trades; and Price and others had sought a way of honorable alliance with the best of the Southerners. But Mr. Washington first indissolubly linked these things; he put enthusiasm, unlimited energy, and perfect faith into this programme, and changed it from a by-path into a veritable Way of Life. And the tale of the methods by which he did this is a fascinating study of human life.

It startled the nation to hear a Negro advocating such a programme after many decades of bitter complaint; it startled and won the applause of the South, it interested and won the admiration of the North; and after a confused murmur of protest, it silenced if it did not convert the Negroes themselves.

To gain the sympathy and cooperation of the various elements comprising the white South was Mr. Washington's first task; and this, at the time Tuskegee was founded, seemed, for a black man, well-nigh impossible. And yet ten years later it was done in the word spoken at Atlanta: "In all things purely social we can be as separate as the five fingers, and yet one as the hand in all things essential to mutual progress." This "Atlanta Compromise" is by all odds the most notable thing in Mr. Washington's career. The South interpreted it in different ways: the radicals received it as a complete surrender of the demand for civil and political equality; the conservatives, as a generously conceived working basis for mutual understanding. So both approved it, and today its author is certainly the most distinguished Southerner since Jefferson Davis, and the one with the largest personal following.

Next to this achievement comes Mr. Washington's work in gaining place and consideration in the North. Others less shrewd and tactful had formerly essayed to sit on these two stools and had fallen between them; but as Mr. Washington knew the heart of the South from birth and training, so by singular insight he intuitively grasped the spirit of the age which was dominating the North. And so thoroughly did he learn the speech and thought of triumphant commercialism, and the ideals of material prosperity, that the picture of a lone black boy poring over a French grammar amid the weeds and dirt of a neglected home soon seemed to him the acme of absurdities. One wonders what Socrates and St. Francis of Assisi would say to this.

And yet this very singleness of vision and thorough oneness with his age is a mark of the successful man. It is as though Nature must needs make men narrow in order to give them force. So Mr. Washington's cult has gained unquestioning followers, his work has wonderfully prospered, his friends are legion, and his enemies are confounded. Today he stands as the one recognized spokesman of his ten million fellows, and one of the most notable figures in a nation of seventy millions, One hesitates, therefore, to criticize a life which, beginning with so little, has done so much. And yet the time is come when one may speak in all sincerity and utter courtesy of the mistakes and shortcomings of Mr. Washington's career, as well as of his triumphs, without being thought captious or envious, and without forgetting that it is easier to do ill than well in the world.

The criticism that has hitherto met Mr. Washington has not always been of this broad character. In the South especially has he had to walk warily to avoid the harshest judgments—and naturally so, for he is dealing with the one subject of deepest sensitiveness to that section. Twice—once when at the Chicago celebration of the Spanish-American War he alluded to the color-prejudice that is "eating away the vitals of the South," and once when he dined with President Roosevelt—has the resulting Southern criticism been violent enough to threaten seriously his popularity. In the North the feeling has several times forced itself into words, that Mr. Washington's counsels of submission overlooked certain elements of true manhood, and that his educational programme was unnecessarily narrow. Usually, however, such criticism has not found open expression, although, too, the spiritual sons of the Abolitionists have not been pre-pared to acknowledge that the schools founded before Tuskegee, by men of broad ideals and self-sacrificing spirit, were wholly failures or worthy of ridicule. While, then, criticism has not failed to follow Mr. Washington, yet the prevailing public opinion of the and has been but too willing to deliver the solution of a wearisome problem into his hands, and say, "If that is all you and your race ask, take it."

Among his own people, however, Mr. Washington has encountered the strongest and most lasting opposition, amounting at times to bitterness, and even to-day continuing strong and insistent even though largely silenced in outward expression by the public opinion of the nation. Some of this opposition is, of course, mere envy; the disappointment of displaced demagogues and the spite of narrow minds. But aside from this, there is among educated and thoughtful colored-men in all parts of the land a feeling of deep regret, sorrow, and apprehension at the wide currency and ascendancy which some of Mr. Washington's theories have gained. These same men admire his sincerity of purpose, and are willing to forgive much to honest endeavor which is doing something worth s the doing. They cooperate with Mr. Washington as far as they conscientiously can; and, indeed, it is no ordinary tribute to this man's tact and power that, steering as he must between so many diverse interests and opinions, he so largely retains the respect of all.

But the hushing of the criticism of honest opponents is a dangerous thing. It leads some of the best of the critics to unfortunate silence and paralysis of effort, and others to burst into speech so passionately and intemperately as to lose listeners. Honest and earnest criticism from those whose interests are most nearly touched—criticism of writers by readers, of government by those governed, of leaders by those led—this is the soul of democracy and the safeguard of modern society. If the best of the American Negroes receive by outer pressure a leader whom they had not recognized before, manifestly there is here a certain palpable gain. Yet there is also irreparable loss—a loss of that peculiarly valuable education which a group receives when by search and criticism it finds and commissions its own leaders. The way in which this is done is at once the most elementary and the nicest problem of social growth. History is but the record of such group-leadership: and yet how infinitely changeful is its type and character! And of all types and kinds, what can be more instructive than the leadership of a group within a group?— that curious double movement where real progress may be negative and actual advance be relative retrogression. All this is the social student's inspiration and despair.

Now in the past the American Negro has had instructive experience in the choosing of group leaders, founding thus a peculiar dynasty which in the light of present condition is worth while studying. When sticks and stones and beasts form the sole environment of a people, their attitude is largely one of determined opposition to and conquest of natural forces. But when to earth and brute is added an environment of men and ideas, then the attitude of the imprisoned group may take three main forms—a feeling of revolt and revenge: an attempt to adjust all thought and action to the will of the greater group: or, finally a determined effort at self-realization and self-development despite environing opinion. The influence of all of these attitudes at various times can be traced in the history of the American Negro, and in the evolution of his successive leaders.

Before 1750, while the fire of American freedom still burned in the veins of the slaves, there was in all leadership or attempted leadership but the one motive of revolt and revenge—typified in the terrible Marrons, the Danish blacks, and Cato of Stono, and veiling all the Americas in fear of insurrection. The liberalizing tendencies of the latter half of the eighteenth century brought, along with kindlier relation between black and white, thoughts of ultimate adjustment and assimilation. Such aspiration was especially voiced in the earnest songs of Phyllis, in the martyrdom of Attucks, the fighting of Salem and Poor, the intellectual accomplishments of Banneker and Derham, and the political demands of the Cuffes.

Stern financial and social stress after the war cooled much of the previous humanitarian ardor. The disappointment and impatience of the Negroes at the persistence of slavery and serfdom voiced itself in two movements. The slaves in the South, aroused undoubtedly by vague rumors of the Haytian revolt, made three fierce attempts at insurrection—in 1800 under Gabriel in Virginia, in 1822 under Vesey in Carolina, and in 1831 again in Virginia under the terrible Nat Turner. In the Free States, on the other hand, a new and curious attempt at self-development was made. In Philadelphia and New York color-prescription led to a withdrawal of Negro communicants from white churches and the formation of a peculiar socio-religious institution among the Negroes known as the African Church—an organization still living and controlling in its various branches over a million of men.

Walker's wild appeal against the trend of the times showed how the world was changing after the coming of the cotton-gin. By 1830 slavery seemed hopelessly fastened on the South, and the slaves thoroughly cowed into submission. The free Negroes of the North, inspired by the mulatto immigrants from the West Indies, began to change the basis of their demands; they recognized the slavery of slaves, but insisted that they themselves were freemen, and sought assimilation and amalgamation with the nation on the same terms with other men. Thus, Forten and Purvis of Philadelphia, Shad of Wilmington, Du Bois of New Haven, Barbadoes of Boston, and others, strove singly and together as men, they said, not as slaves; as "people of color," not as "Negroes." The trend of the times, however, refused them recognition save in individual and exceptional cases, considered them as one with all the despised blacks, and they soon found themselves striving to keep even the rights they formerly had of voting and working and moving as freemen. Schemes of migration and colonization arose among them; but these they refused to entertain, and they eventually turned to the Abolition movement as a final refuge.

Here, led by Remond, Nell, Wells-Brown, and Douglass, a new period of self-assertion and self-development dawned. To be sure, ultimate freedom and assimilation was the ideal before the leaders, but the assertion of the manhood rights of the Negro by himself was the main reliance, and John Brown's raid was the extreme of its logic. After the war and emancipation, the great form of Frederick Douglass, the greatest of American Negro leaders, still led the host. Self-assertion, especially in political lines, was the main programme, and behind Douglass came Elliot, Bruce, and Langston, and the Reconstruction politicians, and, less conspicuous but of greater social significance Alexander Crummell and Bishop Daniel Payne.

Then came the Revolution of 1876, the suppression of the Negro votes, the changing and shifting of ideals, and the seeking of new lights in the great night. Douglass, in his old age, still bravely stood for the ideals of his early manhood—ultimate assimilation through self-assertion, and on no other terms. For a time Price arose as a new leader, destined, it seemed, not to give up, but to restate the old ideals in a form less repugnant to the white South. But he passed away in his prime. Then came the new leader. Nearly all the former ones had become leaders by the silent suffrage of their fellows, had sought to lead their own people alone, and were usually, save Douglass, little known outside their race. But Booker T. Washington arose as essentially the leader not of one race but of two—a compromiser between the South, the North, and the Negro. Naturally the Negroes resented, at first bitterly, signs of compromise which surrendered their civil and political rights, even though this was to be exchanged for larger chances of economic development. The rich and dominating North, however, was not only weary of the race problem, but was investing largely in Southern enterprises, and welcomed any method of peaceful coöperation. Thus, by national opinion, the Negroes began to recognize Mr. Washington's leadership; and the voice of criticism was hushed.

Mr. Washington represents in Negro thought the old attitude of adjustment and submission; but adjustment at such a peculiar time as to make his programme unique. This is an age of unusual economic development, and Mr. Washington's programme naturally takes an economic cast, becoming a gospel of Work and Money to such an extent as apparently almost completely to overshadow the higher aims of life. Moreover, this is an age when the more advanced races are coming in closer contact with the less developed races, and the race-feeling is therefore intensified; and Mr. Washington's programme practically accepts the alleged inferiority of the Negro races. Again, in our own land, the reaction from the sentiment of war time has given impetus to race-prejudice against Negroes, and Mr. Washington withdraws many of the high demands of Negroes as men and American citizens. In other periods of intensified prejudice all the Negro's tendency to self-assertion has been called forth; at this period a policy of submission is advocated. In the history of nearly all other races and peoples the doctrine preached at such crises has been that manly self-respect is worth more than lands and houses, and that a people who voluntarily surrender such respect, or cease striving for it, are not worth civilizing.

In answer to this, it has been claimed that the Negro can survive only through submission. Mr. Washington distinctly asks that black people give up, at least for the present, three things—

First, political power,

Second, insistence on civil rights,

Third, higher education of Negro youth—

and concentrate all their energies on industrial education, the accumulation of wealth, and the conciliation of the South. This policy has been courageously and insistently advocated for over fifteen years, and has been triumphant for perhaps ten years. As a result of this tender of the palm-branch, what has been the return? In these years there have occurred:

1. The disfranchisement of the Negro.
2. The legal creation of a distinct status of civil inferiority for the Negro.
3. The steady withdrawal of aid from institutions for the higher training of the Negro.

These movements are not, to be sure, direct results of Mr. Washington's teachings; but his propaganda has, without a shadow of doubt, helped their speedier accomplishment. The question then comes: Is it possible, and probable, that nine millions of men can make effective progress in economic lines if they are deprived of political rights, made a servile caste, and allowed only the most meagre chance for developing their exceptional men? If history and reason give any distinct answer to these questions, it is an emphatic No. And Mr. Washington thus faces the triple paradox of his career:

1. He is striving nobly to make Negro artisans business men and property-owners; but it is utterly impossible, under modern competitive methods, for workingmen and property-owners to defend their rights and exist without the right of suffrage.
2. He insists on thrift and self-respect, but at the same time counsels a silent submission to civic inferiority such as is bound to sap the manhood of any race in the long run.
3. He advocates common-school and industrial training, and depreciates institutions of higher learning; but neither the Negro common-schools, nor Tuskegee itself, could remain open a day were it not for teachers trained in Negro colleges, or trained by their graduates.

This triple paradox in Mr. Washington's position is the object of criticism by two classes of colored Americans. One class is spiritually descended from Toussaint the Savior, through Gabriel, Vesey, and Turner, and they represent the attitude of revolt and revenge; they hate the white South blindly and distrust the white race generally, and so far as they agree on definite action, think that the Negro's only hope lies in emigration beyond the borders of the United States. And yet, by the irony of fate, nothing has more effectually made this programme seem hopeless than the recent course of the United States toward weaker and darker peoples in the West Indies, Hawaii, and the Philippines—for where in the world may we go and be safe from lying and brute force?

The other class of Negroes who cannot agree with Mr. Washington has hitherto said little aloud. They deprecate the sight of scattered counsels, of internal disagreement; and especially they dislike making their just criticism of a useful and earnest man an excuse for a general discharge of venom from small-minded opponents. Nevertheless, the questions involved are so fundamental and serious that it is difficult to see how men like the Grimkes, Kelly Miller, J. W. E. Bowen, and other representatives of this group, can much longer be silent. Such men feel in conscience bound to ask of this nation three things:

1 The right to vote.

2 Civic equality

3 The education of youth according to ability.

They acknowledge Mr. Washington's invaluable service in counselling patience and courtesy in such demands; they do not ask that ignorant black men vote when ignorant whites are debarred, or that any reasonable restrictions in the suffrage should not be applied; they know that the low social level of the mass of the race is responsible for much discrimination against it, but they also know, and the nation knows, that relentless color-prejudice is more often a cause than a result of the Negro's degradation; they seek the abatement of this relic of barbarism, and not its systematic encouragement and pampering by all agencies of social power from the Associated Press to the Church of Christ. They advocate, with Mr. Washington, a broad system of Negro common schools supplemented by thorough industrial training; but they are surprised that a man of Mr. Washington's insight cannot see that no such educational system ever has rested or can rest on any other basis than that of the well-equipped college and university, and they insist that there is a demand for a few such institutions throughout the South to train the best of the Negro youth as teachers, professional men, and leaders.

This group of men honor Mr. Washington for his attitude of conciliation toward the white South; they accept the "Atlanta Compromise" in its broadest interpretation; they recognize, with him, many signs of promise, many men of high purpose and fair judgment, in this section; they know that no easy task has been laid upon a region already tottering under heavy burdens. But, nevertheless, they insist that the way to truth and right lies in straightforward honesty, not in indiscriminate flattery; in praising those of the South who do well and criticising uncompromisingly those who do ill; in taking advantage of the opportunities at hand and urging their fellows to do the same, but at the same time in remembering that only a firm adherence to their higher ideals and aspirations will ever keep those ideals within the realm of possibility. They do not expect that the free right to vote, to enjoy civic rights, and to be educated, will come in a moment; they do not expect to see the bias and prejudices of years disappear at the blast of a trumpet; but they are absolutely certain that the way for a people to gain their reasonable rights is not by voluntarily throwing them away and insisting that they do not want them; that the way for a people to gain respect is not by continually belittling and ridiculing themselves; that, on the contrary, Negroes must insist continually, in season and out of season, that voting is necessary to modern man-hood, that color discrimination is barbarism, and that black boys need education as well as white boys.

In failing thus to state plainly and unequivocally the legitimate demands of their people, even at the cost of opposing an honored leader, the thinking classes of American Negroes would shirk a heavy responsibility—a responsibility to themselves, a responsibility to the struggling masses, a responsibility to the darker races of men whose future depends so largely on this American experiment, but especially a responsibility to this nation— this common Fatherland. It is wrong to encourage a man or a people in evildoing; it is wrong to aid and abet a national crime simply because it is unpopular not to do so. The growing spirit of kindliness and reconciliation between the North and South after the frightful difference of a generation ago ought to be a source of deep congratulation to all, and especially to those whose mistreatment caused the war; but if that reconciliation is to be marked, by the industrial slavery and civic death of those same black men, with permanent legislation into a position of inferiority, then those black men, if they are really men, are called upon by every consideration of patriotism and loyalty to oppose such a course by all civilized methods, even though such opposition involves disagreement with Mr. Booker T. Washington. We have no right to sit silently by while the inevitable seeds are sown for a harvest of disaster to our children, black and white.

First, it is the duty of black men to judge the South discriminatingly. The present generation of Southerners are not responsible for the past, and they should not be blindly hated or blamed for it. Furthermore, to no class is the indiscriminate endorsement of the recent course of the South toward negroes more nauseating than to the best thought of the South. The South is not "solid"; it is a land in the ferment of social change, wherein forces of all kinds are fighting for supremacy; and to praise the ill the South is to-day perpetrating is just as wrong as to condemn the good. Discriminating and broad-minded criticism is what the South needs—needs it for the sake of her own white sons and daughters, and for the insurance of robust, healthy mental and moral development.

Today even the attitude of the Southern whites toward the blacks is not, as so many assume, in all cases the same; the ignorant Southerner hates the Negro, the workingmen fear his competition, the money-makers wish to use him as a laborer, some of the educated see a menace in his upward development, while others—usually the sons of the masters—wish to help him to rise. National opinion has enabled this last class to maintain the Negro common schools, and to protect the Negro partially in property, life, and limb. Through the pressure of the moneymakers, the Negro is in danger of being reduced to semi-slavery, especially in the country districts; the workingmen, and those of the educated who fear the Negro, have united to disfranchise him, and some have urged his deportation; while the passions of the ignorant are easily aroused to lynch and abuse any black man. To praise this intricate whirl of thought and prejudice is nonsense; to inveigh indiscriminately against "the South" is unjust; but to use the same breath in praising Governor Aycock, exposing Senator Morgan, arguing with Mr. Thomas Nelson Page, and denouncing Senator Ben Tillman, is not only sane, but the imperative duty of thinking black men.

It would be unjust to Mr. Washington not to acknowledge that in several instances he has opposed movements in the South which were unjust to the Negro; he sent memorials to the Louisiana and Alabama constitutional conventions, he has spoken against lynching, and in other ways has openly or silently set his influence against sinister schemes and unfortunate happenings. Notwithstanding this, it is equally true to assert that on the whole the distinct impression left by Mr. Washington's propaganda is, first, that the South is justified in its present attitude toward the Negro because of the Negro's degradation; secondly, that the prime cause of the Negro's failure to rise more quickly is his wrong education in the past; and, thirdly, that his future rise depends primarily on his own efforts. Each of these propositions is a dangerous halftruth. The supplementary truths must never be lost sight of: first, slavery and race-prejudice are potent if not sufficient causes of the Negro's position; second, industrial and common-school training were necessarily slow in planting because they had to await the black teachers trained by higher institutions—it being extremely doubtful if any essentially different development was possible, and certainly a Tuskegee was unthinkable before 1880; and, third, while it is a great truth to say that the Negro must strive and strive mightily to help himself, it is equally true that unless his striving be not simply seconded, but rather aroused and encouraged, by the initiative of the richer and wiser environing group, he can not hope for great success.

In his failure to realize and impress this last point, Mr. Washington is especially to be criticized. His doctrine has tended to make the whites, North and South, shift the burden of the Negro problem to the Negro's shoulders and stand aside as critical and rather pessimistic spectators; when in fact the burden belongs to the nation, and the hands of none of us are clean if we bend not our energies to righting these great wrongs.

The South ought to be led, by candid and honest criticism, to assert her better self and do her full duty to the race she has cruelly wronged and is still wronging. The North—her co-partner in guilt—cannot salve her conscience by plastering it with gold. We cannot settle this problem by diplomacy and suaveness, by "policy" alone. If worse come to worst, can the moral fibre of this country survive the slow throttling and murder of nine millions of men?

The black men of America have a duty to perform, a duty stern and delicate—a forward movement to oppose a part of the work of their greatest leader. So far as Mr. Washington preaches Thrift, Patience, and Industrial Training for the masses, we must hold up his hands and strive with him, rejoicing in his honors and glorying in the strength of this Joshua called of God and of man to lead the headless host. But so far as Mr. Washington apologizes for injustice, North or South, does not tightly value the privilege and duty of voting, belittles the emasculating effects of caste distinctions, and opposes the higher training and ambition of our brighter minds— so far as he, the South, or the Nation, does this—we must unceasingly and firmly oppose them. By every civilized and peaceful method we must strive for the rights which the world accords to men, clinging unwaveringly to those great words which the sons of the Fathers would fain forget: "We hold these truths to be self-evident: That all men are created equal; that they are endowed by their Creator with certain unalienable rights; that among these are life, liberty, and the pursuit of happiness."

George Bernard Shaw, *Mrs. Warren's Profession*

George Bernard Shaw's (1856-1950) successful career as a playwright spanned several decades from the 1890s through the 1920s. Shaw got his start as a theater and music critic for periodicals and reviews when he moved from Dublin to London in the 1870s. As a critic, he supported artists whose unconventional approaches challenged tradition, such as Norwegian playwright Henrik Ibsen (1828-1906) and German musical composer Richard Wagner (1813-1883). Shaw's plays, like Ibsen's, centered on moral dilemmas which Shaw presented in all their complexity. Through his plays, he hoped to affect social change by forcing theater goers to confront hypocrisy and wrestle with accepted values that perpetuated social problems. His many plays addressed social problems such as the creation of slums, the inequalities of the English class system, and prostitution. The following excerpt is from Act II of Shaw's play, *Mrs. Warren's Profession*, which he wrote in 1893. The British government banned public performance of it because it dealt openly with the issues of prostitution, and the play wasn't legally performed in Britain until 1926.

Source: M.H. Abrams, ed., *The Norton Anthology of English Literature* (New York: W.W. Norton and Company, 1993), 1780-1797.

FOCUS QUESTIONS:

1. What beliefs and attitudes about prostitution does Shaw question in this passage?
2. What criticism does Shaw make about the inequalities of class and education in Britain?
3. What does Shaw's work tell us about women's roles and status in Victorian society?

FRANK. [to Vivie] Kissums?

VIVIE. [fiercely] No. I hate you. [She takes a couple of books and some paper from the writing-table, and sits down with them at the middle table, at the end next to the fireplace]

FRANK. [grimacing] Sorry. [He goes for his cap and rifle. Mrs. Warren returns. He takes her hand] Goodnight, d e a r Mrs. Warren. [He kisses her hand. She snatches it away, her lips tightening, and looks more than half disposed to box his ears. He laughs mischievously and runs off, clapping-to the door behind him]

MRS WARREN. [resigning herself to an evening of boredom now that the men are gone] Did you ever in your life hear anyone rattle on so? Isn't he a tease? [She sits at the table] Now that I think of it, dearie, don't you go on encouraging him. I'm sure he's a regular good-for-nothing.

VIVIE. [rising to fetch more books] I'm afraid so. Poor Frank! I shall have to get rid of him; but I shall feel sorry for him, though he's not worth it. That man Crofts does not seem to me to be good for much either: is he? [She throws the books on the table rather roughly]

MRS WARREN. [galled by Vivie's indifference] What do you know of men, child, to talk that way about them? You'll have to make up your mind to see a good deal of Sir George Crofts, as he's a friend of mine.

VIVIE. [quite unmoved] Why? [She sits down and opens a book]. Do you expect that we shall be much together? You and I, I mean?

MRS WARREN. [staring at her] Of course: until you're married. Your not going back to college again.

VIVIE. Do you think my way of life would suit you? I doubt it.

MRS WARREN. Y o u r way of life! What do you mean?

VIVIE. [cutting a page of her book with the paper knife on her chatelaine]

Has it really never occurred to you, mother, that I have a way of life like other people?

MRS WARREN. What nonsense is this you're trying to talk? Do you want to show your independence, now that you're a great little person at school? Don't be a fool, child.

VIVIE. [indulgently] That all you have to say on the subject, is it, mother?

MRS WARREN. [puzzled, then angry] Don't you keep on asking me questions like that. [Violently] Hold your tongue. [Vivie works on, losing no time, and saying nothing] You and your way of life, indeed! What next? [She looks at Vivie again. No reply] Your way of life will be what I please, so it will. [Another pause] I've been noticing these airs in you ever since you got that tripos or whatever you call it. If you think I'm going to put up with them you're mistaken; and the sooner you find it out, the better. [Muttering] All I have to say on the subject, indeed! [Again raising her voice angrily] Do you know who you're speaking to, Miss?

VIVIE. [looking across at her without raising her head from her book] No. Who are you? What are you?

MRS WARREN. [rising breathless] You young imp!

VIVIE. Everybody knows my reputation, my social standing, and the profession I intended to pursue. I know nothing about you. What is that way of life which you invite me to share with you and Sir George Crofts, pray?

MRS WARREN. Take care. I shall do something I'll be sorry for after, and you too.

VIVIE. [putting aside her books with cool decision] Well, let us drop the subject until you are better able to face it. [Looking critically at her mother] You want some good walks and a little lawn tennis to set you up. You are shockingly out of condition: you were not able to manage twenty yards uphill today without stopping to pant; and your wrists are mere rolls of fat. Look at mine. [She holds out her wrists]

MRS WARREN. [after looking at her helplessly, begins to whimper] Vivie—

VIVIE. [springing up sharply] Now pray don't begin to cry. Anything but that. I really cannot stand whimpering. I will go out of the room if you do.

MRS WARREN. [piteously] Oh, my darling, how can you be so hard on me? Have I no rights over you as your mother?

VIVIE. Are you my mother?

MRS WARREN. [appalled] Am I your mother! Oh, Vivie!

VIVIE. Then where are our relatives? my father? our family friends? You claim the rights of a mother: the right to call me fool and child; to speak to me as no woman in authority over me at college dare speak to me; to dictate my way of life; and to force on me the acquaintance of a brute whom anyone can see to be the most vicious sort of London man about town. Before I give myself the trouble to resist such claims, I may as well find out whether they have any real existence.

MRS WARREN. [distracted, throwing herself on her knees] Oh no, no. Stop, stop. I am your mother: I swear it. Oh, you can't mean to turn on me—my own child! It's not natural. You believe me, don't you? Say you believe me.

VIVIE. Who was my father?

MRS WARREN. You don't know what you're asking. I cant tell you.

VIVIE. [determinedly] Oh yes you can, if you like. I have a right to know and you know very well that I have that right. You can refuse to tell me, if you please; but if you do, you will see the last of me tomorrow morning.

MRS WARREN. Oh, it's too horrible to hear you talk like that. You wouldn't—you c o u l d n t leave me.

VIVIE. [ruthlessly] Yes, without a moment's hesitation, if you trifle with me about this. [Shivering with disgust] How can I feel sure that I may not have the contaminated blood of that brutal waster in my veins?

MRS WARREN. No, no. On my oath it's not he, nor any of the rest that you have ever met. I'm certain of that, at least. Vivie's eyes fasten sternly on her mother as the significance of this flashes on her.

VIVIE. [slowly] You are certain of that, a t l e a s t. Ah! You mean that that is all you are certain of. [Thoughtfully] I see. [Mrs. Warren buries her face in her hands] Don't do that, mother: you know you dont feel it a bit. [Mrs. Warren takes down her hands and looks up deplorably at Vivie, who takes out her watch and says] Well, that is enough for tonight. At what hour would you like breakfast? Is half-past eight too early for you?

MRS WARREN. [wildly] My God, what sort of woman are you?

VIVIE. [coolly] The sort the world is mostly made of, I should hope. Otherwise I don't understand how it gets its business done. Come [taking her mother by the wrist, and pulling her up pretty resolutely]; pull yourself together. That's right.

MRS WARREN. [querulously] You're very rough with me, Vivie.

VIVIE. Nonsense. What about bed? It's past ten.

MRS WARREN. [passionately] What the use of my going to bed? Do you think I could sleep?

VIVIE. Why not? I shall.

MRS WARREN. You! youve no heart. [She suddenly breaks out vehemently in her natural tongue—the dialect of a woman of the people—with all her affections of maternal authority and conventional manners gone and an overwhelming inspiration of true conviction and scorn in her.] Oh, I wont bear it: I wont put up with the injustice of it. What right have you to set yourself up above me like this? You boast of what you are to me—to m e, who gave you the chance of being what you are. What chance had I! Shame on you for a bad daughter and a stuck-up prude!

VIVIE. [sitting down with a shrug, no longer confident; for her replies, which have sounded sensible and strong to her so far, now begin to ring rather woodenly and even priggishly against the new tone of her mother] Don't think for a moment I set myself above you in any way. You attacked me with the conventional authority of a mother: I defended myself with the conventional superiority of a respectable woman. Frankly, I am not going to stand any of your nonsense; and when you drop it I shall not expect you to stand any of mine. I shall always respect your right to your own opinions and your own way of life.

MRS WARREN. My own opinions and my own way of life! Listen to her talking? Do you think I was brought up like you? Able to pick and choose my own way of life? Do you think I did what I did because I liked it, or thought it right, or wouldn't rather have gone to college and been a lady if I'd had the chance?

VIVIE. Everybody has some choice, mother. The poorest girl alive may not be able to choose between being Queen of England or Principal of Newnham; but she can choose between ragpicking and flower-selling, according to her taste. People are always blaming their circumstances for what they are. I don't believe in circumstances. The people who get on in this world are the people who get up and look for the circumstances they want, and, if they cant find them, make them.

MRS WARREN. Oh, it's easy to talk, very easy, isnt it? Here! Would you like to know what my circumstances were?

VIVIE. Yes: you had better tell me. Wont you sit down?

MRS WARREN. Oh, I'll sit down: don't you be afraid. [She plants her chair farther forward with brazen energy, and sits down. Vivie is impressed in spite of herself] D'you know what your gran'mother was?

VIVIE. No.

MRS WARREN. No you dont. I do. She called herself a widow and had a fried-fish shop down by the Mint, and kept herself and four daughters out of it. Two of us were sisters: that was me and Liz; and we were both good-looking and well made. I suppose our father was a well-fed man: mother pretended he was a gentleman; but I don't know. The other two were only half sisters: undersized, ugly, starved looking, hard working, honest poor creatures: Liz and I would have half-murdered them if mother hadn't half-murdered us to keep our hands off them. They were the respectable ones. Well, what did they get by their respectability? I'll tell you. One of them worked in a whitelead factory twelve hours a day for nine shillings a week until she died of lead poisoning. She only expected to get her hands a little paralyzed; but she died. The other was always held up to us as a model because she married a Government laborer in the Deptford victualling yard, and kept his room and the three children neat and tidy on eighteen shillings a week—until he took to drink. That was worth being respectable for, wasn't it?

VIVIE. [now thoughtfully attentive] Did you and your sister think so?

MRS WARREN. Liz didn't, I can tell you: she had more spirit. We both went to a church school—that was part of the ladylike airs we got ourselves to be superior to the children that knew nothing and went nowhere—and we stayed there until Liz went out one night and never came back. I know the school-mistress thought I'd soon follow her example; for the clergyman was always warning me that Lizzie'd died by jumping off Waterloo Bridge. Poor fool: that was all he knew about it! But I was more afraid of the whitelead factory than I was of the river; and so would you have been in my place. That clergyman got me a situation as a scullery maid in a temperance restaurant where they sent out for anything you liked. Then I was waitress; and then I went to the bar at Waterloo station: fourteen hours a day serving drinks and washing glasses for four shillings a week and my board. That was considered a great promotion for me. Well, one cold, wretched night when I was so tired I could hardly keep myself awake, who should come up for a half of Scotch but Lizzie, in a long fur cloak, elegant and comfortable, with a lot of sovereigns in her purse.

VIVIE. [grimly] My aunt Lizzie!

MRS WARREN. Yes; and a very good aunt to have, too. She's living down at Winchester now, close to the cathedral, one of the most respectable ladies there. Chaperones girls at the county ball, if you please. No river for Liz, thank you! You remind me of Liz a little: she was a first rate business woman—saved money from the beginning—never let herself look too like what she was—never lost her head or threw away a chance. When she saw I'd grown up good-looking she said to me across the bar "What are you doing there, you little fool? Wearing out your health and your appearance for other people's profit!" Liz was saving money then to take a house for herself in Brussels; and she thought we two could save faster than one. So she lent me some money and gave me a start; and I saved steadily and first paid her back, and then went into business with her as her partner. Why shouldn't I have done it? The house in Brussels was real high class: a much better place for a woman to be in than the factory where Anne Jane got poisoned.

None of our girls were ever treated as I was treated in the scullery of that temperance place, or at the Waterloo bar, or at home. Would you have had me stay in them and become a worn out old drudge before I was forty?

VIVIE. [intensely interested by this time] No; but why did you choose that business? Saving money and good management will succeed in any business.

MRS WARREN. Yes, saving money. But where can a woman get the money to save in any other business? Could you save out of four shillings a week, and keep yourself dressed as well? Not you. Of course, if you're a plain woman and cant earn anything more; or if you have a turn for music, or the stage, or newspaper writing; that's different. But neither Liz nor I had any turn for such things: all we had was our appearance and our turn for pleasing men. Do you think we were such fools as to let other people trade in our good looks by employing us as showgirls, or barmaids, or waitresses, when we could trade in them ourselves and get all the profits instead of starvation wages? Not likely.

VIVIE. You were certainly quite justified—from the business point of view.

MRS WARREN. Yes; or any other point of view. What is any respectable girl brought up to do but to catch some rich man's fancy and get the benefit of his money by marrying him?—as if a marriage ceremony could make any difference in the right or wrong of the thing! Oh! the hypocrisy of the world makes me sick! Liz and I had to work and save and calculate just like other people; elseways we should be as poor as any good-fornothing drunken waster of a woman that thinks her luck will last for ever. [With great energy] I despise such people: they've no character; and if there's a thing I hate in a woman, it's want of character.

VIVIE. Come now, mother: frankly! Isn't it part of what you call character in a woman that she should greatly dislike such a way of making money?

MRS WARREN. Why, of course. Everybody dislikes having to work and make money; but they have to do it all the same. I'm sure I've often pitied a poor girl; tired out and in low spirits, having to try to please some man that doesn't care two straws for—some half-drunken fool that thinks he's making himself agreeable when he's teasing and worrying and disgusting a woman so that hardly any money could pay her for putting up with it. But she has to bear with disagreeables and take the rough with the smooth, just like a nurse in a hospital or anyone else. It's not work that any woman would do for pleasure, goodness knows; though to hear the pious people talk you would suppose it was a bed of roses.

VIVIE. Still, you consider it worth while. It pays.

MRS WARREN. Of course it's worth while to a poor girl, if she can resist temptation and is good-looking and well conducted and sensible. It's far better than any other employment open to her. I always thought that oughtnt to be. It c a n t be right, Vivie, that there shouldn't be better opportunities for women. I stick to that: it's wrong. But it's so, right or wrong; and a girl must make the best of it. But of course it's not worth while for a lady. If you took to it you'd be a fool; but I should have been a fool if I'd taken to anything else.

VIVIE. [more and more deeply moved] Mother; suppose we were both as poor as you were in those wretched old days, are you quite sure that you wouldn't advise me to try the Waterloo bar, or marry a laborer, or even go into the factory?

MRS WARREN. [indignantly] Of course not. What sort of mother do you take me for! How could you keep your self-respect in such starvation and slavery? And what's a woman worth? What's life worth? without selfrespect! Why am I independent and able to give my daughter a first-rate education, when other women that had just as good opportunities are in the gutter? Because I always knew how to respect myself and control myself. Why is Liz looked up to in a cathedral town? The same reason. Where would we be now if we'd minded the clergyman's foolishness? Scrubbing floors for one and sixpence a day and nothing to look forward to but the workhouse infirmary. Dont you be led astray by people who dont know the world, my girl. The only way for a woman to provide for herself decently is for her to be good to some man that can afford to be good to her. If she's in his own station of life, let her make him marry her; but if she's far beneath him she cant expect it: why should she? it wouldn't be for her own happiness. Ask any lady in London society that has daughters; and she'll tell you the same, except that I tell you straight and she'll tell you crooked. Thats all the difference.

VIVIE. [fascinated, gazing at her] My dear mother; you are a wonderful woman: you are stronger than all England. And you are really a truly not one wee bit doubtful—or—or—ashamed?

MRS WARREN. Well, of course, dearie, it's only good manners to be ashamed of it; it's expected from a woman. Women have to pretend to feel a great deal that they don't feel. Liz used to be angry with me for plumping out the truth about it. She used to say that when every woman could learn enough from what was going on in the world before her eyes, there was no need to talk about it to her. But this Liz was such a perfect lady! She had the true instinct of it; while I was always a bit of a vulgarian. I used to be so pleased when you sent us your photos to see that you were growing up like Liz: you've just her ladylike, determined way. But I cant stand saying one thing when everyone knows I mean another. What's the use in such hypocrisy? people arrange the world that way for women, there's no good pretending its arranged the other way. No: I never was a bit ashamed really. I consider I had a right to be proud of how we managed everything so respectably, and never had a word against us, and how the girls were so well taken care of. Some of them did very well: one of them married an ambassador. But of course now I daren't talk about such things: whatever would they think of us! [She yawns] Oh dear, I do believe I'm getting sleepy after all. [She stretches herself lazily, thoroughly relieved by her explosion, and placidly ready for her night's rest.]

VIVIE. I believe it is I who will not be able to sleep now. [She goes to the dresser and lights the candle. Then she extinguishes the lamp, darkening the room a good deal] Better let in some fresh air before locking up. [She opens the cottage door, and finds that it is broad moonlight.] What a beautiful night! Look! [She draws aside the curtains of the window. The landscape is seen bathed in the radiance of the harvest moon rising over Blackdown]

VIVIE. [with a perfunctory glance at the scene] Yes, dear; but take care you don't catch your death of cold from the night air.

VIVIE. [contemptuously] Nonsense.

MRS WARREN. [querulously] Oh yes: everything I say is nonsense, according to you.

VIVIE. [turning to her quickly] No: really that is not so, mother. You have got completely the better of me tonight, though I intended it to be the other way. Let us be good friends now.

MRS WARREN. [shaking her head a little ruefully] So it has been the other way. But I suppose I must give in to it. I always got the worst of it from Liz; and now I suppose it'll be the same with you.

VIVIE. Well, never mind. Come: goodnight, dear old mother. [She takes her mother in her arms]

MRS WARREN. [fondly] I brought you up well, didn't I, dearie?

VIVIE. You did.

MRS WARREN. And you'll be good to your poor old mother for it, wont you?

VIVIE. I will, dear. [Kissing her] Goodnight.

MRS WARREN. [with unction] Blessings on my own dearie darling, a mother's blessing! She embraces her daughter protectingly, instinctively looking upward for divine sanction.

Seneca Falls Convention, "Declaration of Sentiments"

In the nineteenth century, the "woman question" emerged on several fronts in Europe and the US as a lively debate on a wide array of issues regarding women's roles and status in society, the economy, and politics. This document reflects some of the issues debated in the period. It results from a meeting of women in Seneca Falls, New York, held in July of 1848. Many of the women who met in Seneca Falls had also been involved in the antislavery movement and were members of the religious group, the Quakers. They met in Seneca Falls, in part, as a result of a group of American women being barred from an earlier meeting, in London, in 1840, where they had traveled to attend and participate in the London Antislavery Convention. Although women had participated along with men in the anti-slavery movement, they were not always treated equally. As a result of this incident and other similar experiences, a group of women met in Seneca Falls, where they drafted and proclaimed this "Declaration of Sentiments."

Source: Seneca Falls Convention, "Declaration of Sentiments" and "Resolutions" in *History of Woman Suffrage,* eds., Elizabeth Cady Stanton, Susan B. Anthony, and Matilda Joslyn Gage, vol. 1, (New York: Fowler and Wells, 1881), 70-73; reprinted in *Women, the Family, and Freedom: The Debate in Documents,* ed. Susan Groag Bell and Karen M. Offen, vol. 1 (Stanford: Stanford University Press, 1983), 252-255.

Focus Questions:

1. What rights and reforms does this document call for?
2. What ideas, beliefs and principles provide the basis for their proclamation of women's equality?
3. Who was the main audience, and what were the primary goals of the document?

When, in the course of human events, it becomes necessary for one portion of the family of man to assume among the people of the earth a position different from that which they have hitherto occupied, but one to which the laws of nature and of nature's God entitle them, a decent respect to the opinions of mankind requires that they should declare the causes that impel them to such a course.

We hold these truths to be self-evident: that all men and women are created equal; that they are endowed by their Creator with certain inalienable rights; that among these are life, liberty, and the pursuit of happiness; that to secure these rights governments are instituted, deriving their just powers from the consent of the governed. Whenever any form of government becomes destructive of these ends, it is the right of those who suffer from it to refuse allegiance to it, and to insist upon the institution of a new government, laying its foundation on such principles, and organizing its powers in such form, as to them shall seem most likely to effect their safety and happiness. Prudence indeed, will dictate that governments long established should not be changed for light and transient causes; and accordingly all experience hath shown that mankind are more disposed to suffer, while evils are sufferable, than to right themselves by abolishing the forms to which they were accustomed. But when a long train of abuses and usurpations, pursuing invariably the same object evinces a design to reduce them under absolute despotism, it is their duty to throw off such government, and to provide new guards for their future security. Such has been the patient sufferance of the women under this government, and such is now the necessity which constrains them to demand the equal station to which they are entitled.

The history of mankind is a history of repeated injuries and usurpations on the part of man toward woman, having in direct object the establishment of an absolute tyranny over her. To prove this, let facts be submitted to a candid world.

He has never permitted her to exercise her inalienable right to the elective franchise.

He has compelled her to submit to laws, in the formation of which she had no voice.

He has withheld from her rights which are given to the most ignorant and degraded men—both natives and foreigners.

Having deprived her of this first right of a citizen, the elective franchise, thereby leaving her without representation in the halls of legislation, he has oppressed her on all sides.

He has made her, if married, in the eye of the law, civilly dead.

He has taken from her all right in property, even to the wages she earns.

He has made her, morally, an irresponsible being, as she can commit many crimes with impunity, provided they be done in the presence of her husband. In the covenant of marriage, she is compelled to promise obedience to her husband, he becoming, to all intents and purposes, her master—the law giving him power to deprive her of her liberty, and to administer chastisement.

He has so framed the laws of divorce, as to what shall be the proper causes, and in case of separation, to whom the guardianship of the children shall be given, as to be wholly regardless of the happiness of women—the law, in all cases, going upon a false supposition of the supremacy of man, and giving all power into his hands.

After depriving her of all rights as a married woman, if single, and the owner of property, he has taxed her to support a government which recognizes her only when her property can be made profitable to it.

He has monopolized nearly all the profitable employments, and from those she is permitted to follow, she receives but a scanty remuneration. He closes against her all the avenues to wealth and distinction which he considers most honorable to himself. As a teacher of theology, medicine, or law, she is not known.

He has denied her the facilities for obtaining a thorough education, all colleges being closed against her.

He allows her in Church, as well as State, but a subordinate position, claiming Apostolic authority for her exclusion from the ministry, and, with some exceptions, from any public participation in the affairs of the Church.

He has created a false public sentiment by giving to the world a different code of morals for men and women, by which moral delinquencies which exclude women from society, are not only tolerated, but deemed of little account in man.

He has usurped the prerogative of Jehovah himself, claiming it as his right to assign for her a sphere of action, when that belongs to her conscience and to her God.

He has endeavored, in every way that he could, to destroy her confidence in her own powers, to lessen her self-respect, and to make her willing to lead a dependent and abject life.

Now, in view of this entire disfranchisement of one-half the people of this country, their social and religious degradation—in view of the unjust laws above mentioned, and because women do feel themselves aggrieved, oppressed, and fraudulently deprived of their most sacred rights, we insist that they have immediate admission to all the rights and privileges which belong to them as citizens of the United States.

In entering upon the great work before us, we anticipate no small amount of misconception, misrepresentation, and ridicule; but we shall use every instrumentality within our power to effect our object. We shall employ agents, circulate tracts, petition the State and National legislatures, and endeavor to enlist the pulpit and the press in our behalf. We hope this Convention will be followed by a series of Conventions embracing every part of the country.

The following resolutions were discussed by Lucretia Mott, Thomas and Mary Ann McClintock, Amy Post,

Catharine A. F. Stebbins, and others, and were adopted:

WHEREAS, The great precept of nature is conceded to be, that "man shall pursue his own true and substantial happiness." Blackstone in his Commentaries remarks, that this law of Nature being coeval with man-kind, and dictated by God himself, is of course superior in obligation to any other. It is binding over all the globe, in all countries, and at all times; no human laws are of any validity if contrary to this, and such of them as are valid, derive all their force, and all their validity, and all their authority, mediately and immediately, from this original; therefore;

Resolved, That such laws as conflict, in any way, with the true and substantial happiness of woman, are contrary to the great precept of nature and of no validity, for this is "superior in obligation to any other."

Resolved , That all laws which prevent woman from occupying such a station in society as her conscience shall dictate, or which place her in a position inferior to that of man, are contrary to the great precept of nature, and therefore of no force or authority.

Resolved , That woman is man's equal—was intended to be so by the Creator, and the highest good of the race demands that she should be recognized as such.

Resolved , That the women of this country ought to be enlightened in regard to the laws under which they live, that they may no longer publish their degradation by declaring themselves satisfied with their present position, nor their ignorance by asserting that they have all the rights they want.

Resolved , That inasmuch as man, while claiming for himself intellectual superiority, does accord to woman moral superiority, it is preeminently his duty to encourage her to speak and teach, as she has an opportunity, in all religious assemblies.

Resolved , That the same amount of virtue, delicacy, and refinement of behavior that is required of woman in the social state, should also be required of man, and the same transgressions should be visited with equal severity on both man and woman.

Resolved , That the objection of indelicacy and impropriety, which is so often brought against woman when she addresses a public audience, comes with a very ill-grace from those who encourage, by their attendance, her appearance on the stage, in the concert, or in feats of the circus.

Resolved , That woman has too long rested satisfied in the circumscribed limits which corrupt customs and a perverted application of the Scriptures have marked out for her, and that it is time she should move in the enlarged sphere which her great Creator has assigned her.

Resolved , That it is the duty of the women of this country to secure to themselves their sacred right to the elective franchise.

Resolved , That the equality of human rights results necessarily from the fact of the identity of the race in capabilities and responsibilities.

Resolved , therefore, That being invested by the Creator with the same capabilities, and the same consciousness of responsibility for their exercise, it is demonstrably the right and duty of woman, equally with man, to promote every righteous cause by every righteous means; and especially in regard to the great subjects of morals and religion, it is self-evidently her right to participate with her brother in teaching them, both in private and in public, by writing and by speaking, by any instrumentalities proper to be used, and in any assemblies proper to be held; and this being a self-evident truth growing out of the divinely implanted principles of human nature, any custom or authority adverse to it, whether modern or wearing the hoary sanction of antiquity, is to be regarded as a self-evident falsehood, and at war with mankind.

At the last session Lucretia Mott offered and spoke to the following resolution:

Resolved , That the speedy success of our cause depends upon the zealous and untiring efforts of both men and women, for the overthrow of the monopoly of the pulpit, and for the securing to woman an equal participation with men in the various trades, professions, and commerce.

Adelheid Popp, "Finding Work: Women Factory Workers"

Adelheid Popp (1869-1939) came from a poor family. Her father, a weaver by trade, died when she was a small girl, leaving her mother alone to raise Popp and her fourteen brothers and sisters. Popp entered the work force while still a young child. She was employed in a variety of jobs in Vienna including as a maid, a seamstress, and in factories. At sixteen years old, she became involved in the Social Democratic party in Austria, a group that advocated social and political reforms for workers. She eventually became the editor of the party affiliated newspaper, Working Women's News (Arbeiterinnen Zeitung). After World War I, she became an elected member of the Austrian parliament. This excerpt comes from her autobiography which a large reading audience enthusiastically received after its publication in Germany in 1909. A few years after it appeared in German, it was translated into English and published in Britain.

Source: Adelheid Popp, *Die Jugendgeschichte einer Arbeiterin*, ed. Hans J. Schutz (Munich: Ernst Reinhardt Verlag, 1909), 48-60; reprinted in *The German Worker: Working-Class Autobiographies from the Age of Industrialization*, trans. Alfred Kelly (Berkeley: University of California Press, 1987), 122-126, 130, 132, 134.

FOCUS QUESTIONS:

1. What conditions does Popp describe for working women (pay, work environment, health job security, etc.)?
2. What reading audience did Popp target for her account? What did she hope to accomplish by having her story published?
3. What stereotypes and ideas about women who worked in factories was she working against?

FINDING WORK

It was a cold, severe winter, and the wind and snow could come unhindered into our room. In the morning when we opened the door we first had to hack away the ice on it in order to get out, because the entrance to our room was directly on the courtyard, and we had only a single glass door. My mother left the house at five-thirty because she had to start work at six. An hour later I went out to look for work. "Please, I need a job"—it had to be repeated countless times. I used to be on the street for almost the whole day. We couldn't heat our room—that would have been extravagant—so I wandered around the streets, into churches, and to the cemetery. I took along a piece of bread and a few kreuzers to buy myself something at noon. I always had to hold back the tears forcibly when my request for work was denied and I had to leave the warm room. How gladly I would have done any work, just so I wouldn't have to freeze. My clothes got wet in the snow, and my limbs were stiff from the hours of walking around. What's more, my mother was getting more and more resentful. My brother had found work; snow had fallen, so he was busy*—of course the pay was so low that he could hardly support himself. I was the only one still without work.

I couldn't even get work in the candy factories, where I had assumed they would need more help at Christmas-time. Today I know that almost all of the Christmas work is done several weeks before the holidays; the factory women have to work day and night for weeks, and then right before the holidays they are dismissed without consideration. At that time I still had no idea how the production process was carried out. How piously and faithfully I used to pray for work in church. I sought out the most celebrated saints. I went from altar to altar, kneeled down on the cold stones, and prayed to the Virgin Mary, the Mother of God, the Queen of Heaven, and many other saints who were said to have special power and compassion.

* * *

My new workplace was on the third floor of a building that was used exclusively for industrial purposes. Not having known the bustle of a factory, I had never felt so uncomfortable. Everything displeased me—the dirty, sticky work; the unpleasant glass dust; the crowd of people; the crude tone; and the whole way that the girls and even married women behaved.

The owner's wife—the "gracious lady," as she was called—was the actual manager of the factory, and she talked just like the girls. She was a nice-looking woman, but she drank brandy, took snuff, and made unseemly rude jokes with the workmen. The owner was very ill, and when he came himself, there was always a violent scene. I pitied him. He seemed to me to be so good and noble, and I gathered from the behavior and whole manner of his wife that he must be unhappy. At his instructions I received a different, much more pleasant job. Up to then my job had been to hang the papers, which were smeared with glue and sprinkled with glass, onto lines strung rather high across the workroom. This work exhausted me greatly, and the owner must have noticed that it wasn't suitable for me, because he instructed that from then on I was to keep count of the papers that were ready for processing. This work was clean and I liked it a lot better. Of course when there wasn't anything to count, I had to do other kinds of work.

* * *

They often spoke of a Herr Berger, who was the company's traveling representative and was expected back about then. All the women raved about him, so I was curious to see the man. I had been there for two weeks when he came. Everything was in a dither, and the only talk was of the looks of the traveler they so admired. Accompanied by the owner's wife, he came into the room where I worked. I didn't like him at all. That afternoon I was called into his office; Herr Berger sent me on an errand and made a silly remark about my "beautiful hands." It was already dark when I returned; I had to pass through an empty anteroom that wasn't lighted; it was half-dark since it got light only through the glass door leading into the workroom. Herr Berger was in the anteroom when I came. He took me by the hand and inquired sympathetically about my circumstances. I answered him truthfully and told of our poverty. He spoke a few words, taking pity on me and promising to use his influence to get me higher wages. Of course I was delighted with the prospect opening up to me, for I was getting only two and a half guilders a week, for which I had to work twelve hours a day. I stammered a few words of thanks and assured him that I would prove myself worthy of his solicitude. Before I even knew what was happening, Herr Berger had kissed me. He tried to calm my fright with the words, "It was just a fatherly kiss." He was twenty-six years old, and I was almost fifteen, so fatherliness was out of the question.

Beside myself, I hurried back to my work. I didn't know how I should interpret the incident; I thought the kiss was disgraceful, but Herr Berger had spoken so sympathetically and had held out the prospect of higher wages! At home I did tell of the promise, but I said nothing about the kiss because I was ashamed to talk about it in front of my brother. But my mother and brother were happy that I had found such an influential protector.

The next day I was overwhelmed with reproaches from one of my coworkers, a young blond girl whom I liked most of all. She reproached me for having taken her place with the traveler; up to now, if he had something to do or an errand to run, she had done it; he loved her, she protested through tears and sobs, and now I'd put an end to everything. The other girls joined in too; they called me a hypocrite, and the gracious lady herself asked me how I'd liked the kisses of the"handsome traveler."The incident of the previous evening had been observed through the glass door, and they interpreted it in a way very insulting to me.

I was defenseless against their taunts and sneers and longed for the hour when I could go home. It was Saturday, and when I received my wages, I went home with the intention of not returning on Monday.

When I spoke of the matter at home, I was severely scolded. It was strange. My mother, who was always so intent on raising me to be a respectable girl, who always gave me instructions and warnings not to talk to men ("You should only allow yourself to be kissed by the man you're going to marry,"she used to impress upon me)—in this instance my mother was against me. She said I was going too far. A kiss was nothing bad, and if I was getting more wages as a result, then it would be silly to give up my job. In the end she held my books responsible for my"overexcitement." My mother got so mad about my"pigheadedness" that all the splendid things I'd been lent—The Book for Everyone [Das Buch für Alle], Over Landand Sea [Über Land und Meer], and Chronicle of the Times [Chronik der Zeit] (that's how far advanced I was in literature)—were thrown out the door.* I collected them all again, but I didn't dare read in the evening, although I'd usually been allowed to read longer on Saturdays.

That was a sad Sunday! I was depressed, and what's more I was scolded the whole day. On Monday my mother awakened me as usual and impressed upon me as she left for work not to do anything stupid, but rather to remember that in a few days it would be Christmas.

I went out intending to control myself and go to the factory; I got as far as the door and then I turned around. I had such a dreadful fear of unknown dangers that I preferred to go hungry than to suffer disgrace. Everything that had happened -the kiss and the reproaches of my coworkers -seemed a disgrace to me. Besides, I had been told that one of the girls always enjoyed the traveler's special favor. But he was changeable; if a new girl came who pleased him more, then she would take the place of the previous one. All indications were that I had been chosen as the new favorite. That scared me a lot. I'd read so much in books about seduction and fallen virtue that I imagined the most hideous things happening. So I didn't go in.

* * *

[She eventually found a factory job paying 4 guilders a week. After six months, pay was raised to 5 guilders.]

It seemed to me that I was almost rich. I figured out how much I'd be able to save over a few years, and I built castles in the air. Since I was used to extraordinary deprivations, I would have considered it extravagant to spend more now on food. As long as I didn't feel hungry I didn't take into account what I was eating. All I wanted was to dress nicely. When I went to church on Sunday no one should recognize me as a factory girl; I was ashamed of my work. Working in a factory always seemed to me to be degrading. When I was still an apprentice, I'd often heard it said that factory girls were bad, loose, and spoiled.* They were spoken of in the most insulting words, and I too had picked up this false notion. Now I myself was employed in a factory where there were so many girls.

The girls were friendly; they instructed me in my work in the most amiable manner, and they introduced me to the customs of the business. The girls in the sorting room were considered the elite of the personnel. The owner himself chose them, whereas the hiring for the machine room was left to the foremen. Men and women were together in the other rooms; but in my room there were only female employees. Men were used as extra help only when the heavy packages of sorted, counted, and labeled goods were moved to the courtyard.

* * *

In general, the only girls who ate well were those supported by their families. But there were only a few of them. More often the working girls had to support their parents or pay for baby-sitting for their children. How self-sacrificing these mothers were! They saved kreuzer after kreuzer to better the lot of their children and to enable them to make gifts to the baby-sitter so that she would take good care of the children. Many women often had to provide for their unemployed husbands; they underwent double deprivation because they had to meet the household expenses alone. I also got to know the much-maligned frivolousness of factory girls. To be sure, the girls went dancing and they had love affairs; others stood in line at a theater at three o'clock in the afternoon so that they could see an evening performance for thirty kreuzers. In the summer they went on outings and walked for hours in order to save a couple of kreuzers of tram fare. For a few breaths of country air they had to pay with days of tired feet. If you want you can call all that frivolity, or even pleasure-seeking or debauchery, but who would dare to?

I saw among my coworkers—the despised factory women-examples of the most extraordinary sacrifices for others. If there was a special emergency in one family, then they chipped in their kreuzers to help. Even though they had worked twelve hours in the factory and many still had an hour's walk home, they mended their own clothes, without ever having been taught how. They took apart their old dresses to fashion new ones from the separate pieces, which they sewed at night and on Sundays.

* * *

"A good boss"—that was the general opinion of our employer. But in the case of this very factory owner, one can see how profitable is the exploitation of human labor. He, who really did grant his workers more than most other entrepreneurs; he, who would continue for weeks to pay the wages of men and women who were sick; he, who in case of a death made a considerable contribution to the survivors; and he, who almost never rejected a request if someone turned to him in need— despite all this, he had gotten rich through the productive labor of the men and women working in his factory.

Pope Leo XIII, *Rerum Novarum* (Of New Things)

In response to the many social and economic changes brought about by industrialization, Pope Leo XIII (pope from 1878 to 1903) issued the papal encyclical *Rerum Novarum (Of New Things)*. In the Catholic Church tradition, popes issues encyclicals as official declarations of the Church's policy on an issue. Encyclicals are specifically addressed to all Catholic bishops, but are also to be read and heard by all members of the Catholic Church, as well as the public at large. *Rerum Novarum (Of New Things)* was a very progressive statement for its time. In it, the Pope committed the Catholic Church to supporting policies and movements that would bring improved conditions and social justice, for the poor and workers. It also set the standard for the Catholic Church to make public, moral assessments of social issues and conditions.

Source: Henry Bettenson, ed., *Documents of the Christian Church* (New York: Oxford University Press, 1967), 275-281; reprinted in *The Western Heritage: Documents Set*, eds. Donald Kagan, Steven Ozment, Frank M. Turner, 6th ed., vol. 2 (Upper Saddle River, N.J.: Prentice Hall, 1998), 250-251.

Focus Questions:

1. How does this document define rights in relation to private property, and why are they defined in this way?

2. What was the Church's stance on wages and trade unions? How was this in direct response to workers' conditions in the period when this encyclical was issued?
3. What did the Pope and Catholic Church hope to accomplish by addressing social problems in this way?

PROPERTY

The possession of private property is a right given to man by nature.... There is no reason why the directing power of the state should be brought in; for man is prior to the state, and therefore he must have had by nature the right to preserve his life and person before any community was organized.... The necessary materials for the preservation of life are lavishly supplied by the earth; but the earth could not supply them by itself without man's cultivation, and since man applies the activity of his mind and the strength of his body in the production of the good things of nature, it follows that he claims for himself the portion of physical nature which he has himself tended, which he has in a sense stamped with his own personal impress. And so it should be altogether right for that portion to be possessed by him as his personal property; nor should anyone be allowed to violate that right in any way.... The force of these arguments is so obvious that it seems strange that they are opposed by some people who seek to re-establish worn-out doctrines; who allow individuals the use of the soil and the different products of lands, but say that it is not right that a man should possess, as an owner, the land on which he has built, or the estate which he has cultivated....

WAGES

Man's labour has two inherent natural characteristics; it is personal, since the active force is attached to a person, and is completely the personal possession of the man by whom it is exercised, and is by nature designed for his advantage: and secondly, it is necessary, for this reason, that man requires the fruit of his labour for the preservation of his life, and the duty of self-preservation is grounded in the natural order. It follows that if we consider merely the personal aspect there is no doubt that it is open to the worker to reduce the agreed wage to narrow dimensions. He gives his services of his free will, and he can, of free will, content himself with a slender reward, or even with none at all. But a very different conclusion is reached when we combined the necessary with the personal element, and indeed they are only separable in thought, not in reality. To remain alive is a duty incumbent on all alike, in fact, and to fail in this duty is a crime. Hence arises of necessity the right of acquiring the materials for the support of life; and it is only by the wage earned with their labour that the lower orders are supplied with these means. Therefore the worker and the employer should freely come to agreement, especially in regard to the level of wages.... But there is an underlying condition which arises from natural laws, namely that the wage should be sufficient to support the worker, provided he is thrifty and well behaved. If the worker is compelled to accept harsher terms, or is induced to do so by fear of worse hardships, and these have to be accepted because they are imposed by a master or employer, this is submission to force and therefore repugnant to justice.... If the worker receives sufficient payment to maintain himself, his wife, and his children, in comfort, he will be ready to practise thrift, if he is sensible, and will follow the prompting of nature by reducing his expenditure to ensure some surplus by means of which he may attain a modest property.... The right of private property ought to be inviolate.... For the attainment of these advantages it is an essential condition that private property should not be exhausted by inordinate taxation. The right of personal possessions is not based on human law; it is given by nature. Therefore public authority cannot abolish it; it can only control its use and adjust it to the common good.

TRADES UNIONS

That men should commonly unite in associations of this kind [trades unions and the like], whether made up wholly of workers or of both classes together, is to be welcomed.... Natural law grants man the right to join particular associations, and the state is appointed to support natural law, not to destroy it... and the state arises from the same principle which produces particular societies, the fact that men are by nature gregarious. But circumstances sometimes arise when it is right for the laws to check associations of this kind; this happens if ever these associations deliberately adopt aims which are in open conflict with honesty, with justice, and with the well-being of the community.

John Stuart Mill, *The Subjection of Women*

John Stuart Mill (1806-1873), an advocate of social and political reform, drew on the theory of utilitarianism, in his philosophical works. Mill wrote several essays, articles, and longer works, including his well-known treatise of political philosophy, *On Liberty* (1859). In this work, *The Subjection of Women*, published in 1869, Mill called for the extension of full legal and political rights to women. As a member of the British Parliament in the House of Commons, Mill also introduced measures that would grant women the right to vote in Britain. These initiatives ultimately failed, but they did serve as an early basis for the women's suffrage movement in Britain. His friendships and collaboration with Harriet Hardy, whom he married in 1851, influenced his ideas about the women and inspired his support for full political rights for women.

Source: John Stuart Mill, *The Subjection of Women* (Amherst: Prometheus Books, 1991), 7-13.

Focus Questions:

1. What arguments does Mill make in support of extending full rights to women? What examples and evidence does he use to support his arguments?
2. What groups were the main audience for this work? How does Mill tailor his arguments to this audience in an effort to persuade them?
3. What contributions does Mill make to nineteenth century debates on the woman question?

11..The object of this Essay is to explain, as clearly as I am able, the grounds of an opinion which I have held from the very earliest period when I had formed any opinions at all on social or political matters, and which, instead of being weakened or modified, has been constantly growing stronger by the progress of reflection and the experience of life : That the principle which regulates the existing social relations between the two sexes—the legal subordination of one sex to the other—is wrong in itself, and now one of the chief hindrances to human improvement; and that it ought to be replaced by a principle of perfect equality, admitting no power or privilege on the one side, nor disability on the other.

22..The very words necessary to express the task I have undertaken, show how arduous it is. But it would be a mistake to suppose that the difficulty of the case must lie in the insufficiency or obscurity of the grounds of reason on which my conviction rests. The difficulty is that which exists in all cases in which there is a mass of feeling to be contended against. So long as an opinion is strongly rooted in the feelings, it gains rather than loses in stability by leaving a preponderating weight of argument against it. For if it were accepted as a result of argument, the refutation of the argument might shake the solidity of the conviction; but when it rests solely on feeling, the worse it fares in argumentative contest, the more persuaded its adherents are that their feeling must have some deeper ground, which the arguments do not reach; and why the feeling remains, it is always throwing up fresh entrenchments of argument to repair any breach made in the old. And there are so many causes tending to make the feelings connected with this subject the most intense and most deeply-rooted of all those which gather round and protect old institutions and customs, that we need not wonder to find them as yet less undermined and loosened than any of the rest by the progress the great modern spiritual and social transition; nor suppose that the barbarisms to which men cling longes must be less barbarisms than those which they earlier shake off.

33..In every respect the burthen is hard on those who attack an almost universal opinion. They must be very fortunate as well as unusually capable if they obtain a hearing at all. They have more difficulty in obtaining a trial, than any other litigants have in getting a verdict. If they do extort a hearing, they are subjected to a set of logical requirements totally different from those exacted from other people. In all other cases, the burthen of proof is supposed to lie with the affirmative. If a person is charged with a murder, it rests with those who accuse him to give proof of his guilt, not with himself to prove his innocence. If there is a difference of opinion about the reality of any alleged historical event, in which the feelings of men in general are not much interested, as the Siege of Troy for example, those who maintain that the event took place are expected to produce their proofs, before those who take the other side can be required to say anything; and at no time are these required to do more than show that the evidence produced by the others of no value. Again, in practical matters, the burthen of proof is supposed to be with those who are against liberty; who contend for any restriction or prohibition; either any limitation of the general freedom of hum action, or any disqualification or disparity of privilege affecting one person or kind of persons, as compare with others. The a prioripresumption is in favour of freedom and impartiality. It is held that there should be no restraint not required by the general good, and that the law should be no respecter of persons, but should treat all alike, save where dissimilarity of treatment is required by positive reasons, either of justice or of policy. But of none of these rules of evidence will them benefit be allowed to those who maintain the opinion I profess. It is useless for me to say that those who maintain the doctrine that men have a right to command and women are under an obligation to obey, or that men are fit for government and women unfit are on the affirmative side of the question, and that they are bound to show positive evidence for the assertions, or submit to their rejection. It is equally unavailing for me to say that those who deny to women any freedom or privilege rightly allowed to men, having the double presumption against them that they are opposing freedom and recommending partiality, must be held to the strictest proof of their case, and unless their success be such as to exclude all doubt, the judgment ought to go against them. These would be thought good pleas in any common case; but they will not be thought so in this instance. Before I could hope to make any impression, I should be expected not only to answer all that has ever been said by those who take the other side of the question, but to imagine all that could be said by them—to find them in reasons, as well as answer all I find: and besides refuting all arguments for the affirmative, I shall be called upon for invincible positive arguments to prove a negative. And even if I could do all this, and leave the opposite party with a host of unanswered arguments against them, and not a single unrefuted one on their side, I should be thought to have done little; for a cause supported on the one hand by universal usage, and on the other by so great a preponderance of popular sentiment, is supposed to have a presumption in its favour, superior to any conviction which an appeal to reason has power to produce in any intellects but those of a high class.

44..I do not mention these difficulties to complain of them; first, because it would be useless; they are inseparable from having to contend through people's understandings against the hostility of their feelings and practical tendencies: and truly the understanding of the majority of mankind would need to be much better cultivated than has ever yet been the case, before they can be asked to place such reliance in their own power of estimating arguments, as to give up practical principles in which they have been born and bred, and which are the basis of much of the existing order of the world, at the first argumentative attack which they are not capable of logically resisting. I do not therefore quarrel with them for having too little faith in argument, but for having too much faith in custom and the general feeling. It is one of the characteristic prejudices of the reaction of the nineteenth century against the eighteenth, to accord to the unreasoning elements in human nature the infallibility which the eighteenth century is supposed to have ascribed to the reasoning elements. For the apotheosis of Reason we have substituted that of Instinct; and we call everything instinct which we find in ourselves and for which we cannot trace any rational foundation. This idolatry, infinitely more degrading than the other, and the most pernicious of the false worships of the present day, of all of which it is now the main support, will probably hold its ground until it gives way before a sound psychology, laying bare the real root of much that is bowed down to as the intention of Nature and the ordinance of God. As regards the present question, I am willing to accept the unfavourable conditions which the prejudice assigns to me. I consent that established custom, and the general feeling, should be deemed conclusive against me, unless that custom and feeling from age to age can be shown to have owed their existence to other causes than their soundness, and to have derived their power from the worse rather than the better parts of human nature. I am willing that judgment should go against me, unless can show that my judge has been tampered with. The concession is not so great as it might appear; for to prove this is by far the easiest portion of my task.

55..The generality of a practice is in some cases a strong presumption that it is, or at all events once was, conducive to laudable ends. This is the case, when the practice was first adopted, or afterwards kept up, as means to such ends, and was grounded on experience of the mode in which they could be most effectually attained. If the authority of men over women, when first established, had been the result of a conscientious comparison between different modes of constituting the government of society; if, after trying various other modes of social organization—the government of women over men, equality between the two, and such mixed and divided modes of government as might be invented—it had been decided, on the testimony of experience, that the mode in which women are wholly under the rule of men, having no share at all in public concerns, and each in private being under the legal obligation of obedience to the man with whom she has associated her destiny, was the arrangement most conducive to the happiness and well-being of both; its general adoption might then be fairly thought to be some evidence that, at the time when it was adopted, it was the best: though even then the considerations which recommended it may, like so many other primeva social facts of the greatest importance, have subsequently, in the course of ages, ceased to exist. But the state of the case is in every respect the reverse of this. In the first place, the opinion in favour of the present system, which entirely subordinates the weaker sex to the stronger, rests upon theory only; for there never has been trial made of any other: so that experience, in the sense in which it is vulgarity opposed to theory, cannot be pretended to have pronounced any verdict. And in the second place, the adoption of this system inequality never was the result of deliberation, or forethought, or any social ideas, or any notion whatever what conduced to the benefit of humanity or the good order of society. It arose simply from the fact that from the very earliest twilight of human society, every woman (owing to the value attached to her by men, combined with her inferiority in muscular strength) was found in a state of bondage to some man. Laws and systems of polity always beg recognizing the relations they find already existing between individuals. The convert what was a mere physical fact into a legal right, give it the sanction of society, and principally aim at the substitution of public and organized means of asserting and protecting these rights, instead of the irregular and lawless conflict of physical strength. Those who had already been compelled to obedience became in this manner legally bound to it. Slavery, from being a mere affair of force between the master a the slave, became regularized and a matter of compact among the masters, who, binding themselves to one another for common protection, guaranteed by their collective strength the private possessions of each, including his slaves. In early times, the great majority of the male sex were slaves, as well as the whole of the female. And many ages elapsed, some of them ages of high cultivation, before any thinker was bold enough to question the rightfulness, and the absolute social necessity, either of the one slavery or of the other. By degrees such thinkers did arise: and (the general progress of society assisting) the slavery of the male sex has, in all the countries of Christian Europe at least (the general in one of them, only within the la few years), been at length abolished, and that of the female sex has been gradually changed into a milder form of dependence. But this dependence, as it exists at present, is not an original institution, taking a fresh start from considerations of justice and social expediency—it is the primitive state of slavery lasting on, through successive mitigations and modifications occasioned by the same causes which have softened the general manners, and brought all human relations more under the control of justice and the influence of humanity. It has not lost the taint of its brutal origin. No presumption in its favour, therefore, can be drawn from the fact of its existence. The only such presumption which it could be supposed to have, must be grounded on its having lasted till now, when so many other things which came down from the same odious source have been done away with. And this, indeed, is what makes it strange to ordinary ears, to hear it asserted that the inequality of rights between men and women has no other source than the law of the strongest.

66..That this statement should have the effect of a paradox is in some respects creditable to the progress of civilization, and the improvement of the moral sentiments of mankind. We now live—that is to say, one or two of the most advanced nations of the world now live—in a state in which the law of the strongest seems to be entirely abandoned as the regulating principle of the world's affairs: nobody professes it, and, as regards most of the relations between human beings, nobody is permitted to practise it. When anyone succeeds in doing so, it is under cover of some pretext which gives him the semblance of having some general social interest on his side. This being the ostensible state of things, people flatter themselves that the rule of mere force is ended; that the law of the strongest cannot be the reason of existence of anything which has remained in full operation down to the present time. However any of our present institutions may have begun, it can only, they think, have been preserved to this period of advanced civilization by a well-grounded feeling of its adaptation to human nature, and conduciveness to the general good. They do not understand the great vitality and durability of institutions which place right on the side of might; how intensely they are clung to; how the good as well as the bad propensities and sentiments of those who have power in their hands, become identified with retaining it; how slowly these bad institutions give way, one a time, the weakest first, beginning with those which are least interwoven with the daily habits of life; and how very rarely those who have obtained legal power because they first had physical, have ever lost their hold of the former until the physical power had passed over to the other side. Such shifting of the physical force not having taken place in the case of women; this fact, combined with all the peculiar and characteristic features of the particular case, made it certain from the first that this branch of the system of right founded on might, though softened in its most atrocious features at an earlier period than several of the others, would be the very last to disappear. It was inevitable that this one case of a social relation grounded on force would survive through generations of institutions grounded on equal justice, an almost solitary exception to the general character of their laws and customs; but which, so long as it does not proclaim its own origin, and as discussion has not brought out its true character, is not felt to jar with modern civilization, any more than domestic slavery among the Greeks jarred with their notion of themselves as a free people.

George Eliot
"Review: Margaret Fuller and Mary Wollstonecraft"

Marian Evans (1819-1880) wrote under the pen name George Eliot. She grew up in the English Midlands, the daughter of a land agent. Later in her life, she drew on her experiences growing up in the Warwickshire countryside for many of her fictional works. When she was sixteen, her mother died, so she left boarding school to return home and care for her father. In Coventry, where her father then lived, she came into a circle of freethinkers whose ideas greatly influenced her intellectual development. After her father's death in 1849, she moved to London and worked as an assistant editor of a well-regarded journal, the *Westminster Review*. She also wrote freelance articles for other publications, including the following book review she published in *The Leader*, another periodical, in 1855. She published her first novel, *Adam Bede* (1859) when she was forty years old, and went on to write several others including *Silas Marner* (1861) and *Middlemarch* (1871-1872). In this essay, Eliot reviews two important early authors whose ideas contributed to debates on the role of women in the nineteenth century. In this review, she compares the ideas of Margaret Fuller (1810-1850), an American author, with those of Mary Wollstonecraft (1759-1797), an eighteenth-century British author and philosopher.

Source: George Eliot, "Margaret Fuller and Mary Wollstonecraft" in *The Norton Anthology of English Literature*, ed. M. H. Abrams, vol. 2 (New York: W.W. Norton, 1993), 1314-1319.

Focus Questions:

1. Why did Eliot choose to review Wollstonecraft and Fuller's works?
2. What does Eliot say about their ideas and arguments? How are they similar? Different?
3. What does this review tell us about debates regarding women's roles in nineteenth century Europe and the U.S.?

The dearth of new books just now gives us time to recur to less recent ones which we have hitherto noticed but slightly; and among these we choose the late edition of Margaret Fuller's *Woman in the Nineteenth Century,* because we think it has been unduly thrust into the background by less comprehensive and candid productions on the same subject. Notwithstanding certain defects of taste and a sort of vague spiritualism and grandiloquence which belong to all but the very best American writers, the book is a valuable one; it has the enthusiasm of a noble and sympathetic nature, with the moderation and breadth and large allowance of a vigorous and cultivated understanding. There is no exaggeration of woman's moral excellence or intellectual capabilities; no injudicious insistence on her fitness for this or that function hitherto engrossed by men; but a calm plea for the removal of unjust laws and artificial restrictions, so that the possibilities of her nature may have room for full development, a wisely stated demand to disencumber her of the

> Parasitic forms
> That seem to keep her up, but drag her down—
> And leave her field to burgeon and to bloom
> From all within her, make herself her own
> To give or keep, to live and learn and be
> All that not harms distinctive womanhood.[1]

It is interesting to compare this essay of Margaret Fuller's published in its earliest form in 1843, with a work on the position of woman, written between sixty and seventy years ago—we mean Mary Wollstonecraft's *Rights of Woman*. The latter work was not continued beyond the first volume; but so far as this carries the subject, the comparison, at least in relation to strong sense and loftiness of moral tone, is not at all disadvantageous to the woman of the last century. There is in some quarters a vague prejudice against the *Rights of Woman* as in some way or other a reprehensible book, but readers who go to it with this impression will be surprised to find it eminently serious, severely moral, and withal rather heavy—the true reason, perhaps, that no edition has been published since 1796, and that it is now rather scarce. There are several points of resemblance, as well as of striking difference, between the two books. A strong understanding is present in both; but Margaret Fuller's mind was like some regions of her own American continent, where you are constantly stepping from the sunny"clearings"into the mysterious twilight of the tangled forest—she often passes in one breath from forcible reasoning to dreamy vagueness; moreover, her unusually varied culture gives her great command of illustration, Mary Wollstonecraft, on the other hand, is nothing if not rational; she has no erudition, and her grave pages are lit up by no ray of fancy. In both writers we discern, under the brave bearing of a strong and truthful nature, the beating of a loving woman's heart, which teaches them not to undervalue the smallest offices of domestic care or kindliness. But Margaret Fuller, with all her passionate sensibility, is more of the literary woman, who would not have been satisfied without intellectual production; Mary Wollstonecraft, we imagine, wrote not at all for writing's sake, but from the pressure of other motives. So far as the difference of date allows, there is a striking coincidence in their trains of thought; indeed, every important idea in the *Rights of Woman*, except the combination of home

1 These lines are from Alfred Lord Tennyson, The Princess, 7.253–258.

education with a common day-school for boys and girls, reappears in Margaret Fuller's essay....

There is a notion commonly entertained among men that an instructed woman, capable of having opinions, is likely to prove an unpracticable yoke-fellow, always pulling one way when her husband wants to go the other, oracular in tone, and prone to give curtain lectures[2] on metaphysics. But surely, so far as obstinacy is concerned, your unreasoning animal is the most unmanageable of creatures, where you are not allowed to settle the question by a cudgel, a whip and bridle, or even a string to the leg. For our own parts, we see no consistent or commodious medium between the old plan of corporal discipline and that thorough education of women which will make them rational beings in the highest sense of the word. Wherever weakness is not harshly controlled it must *govern,* as you may see when a strong man holds a little child by the hand, how he is pulled hither and thither, and wearied in his walk by his submission to the whims and feeble movements of his companion. A really cultured woman, like a really cultured man, will be ready to yield in trifles. So far as we see, there is no indissoluble connection between infirmity of logic and infirmity of will, and a woman quite innocent of an opinion in philosophy, is as likely as not to have an indomitable opinion about the kitchen. As to airs of superiority, no woman ever had them in consequence of true culture, but only because her culture was shallow or unreal, only as a result of what Mrs. Malaprop well calls "the ineffectual qualities in a woman"[3]—mere acquisitions carried about, and not knowledge thoroughly assimilated so as to enter into the growth of the character.

To return to Margaret Fuller, some of the best things she says are on the folly of absolute definitions of woman's nature and absolute demarcations of woman's mission. "Nature," she says, "seems to delight in varying the arrangements, as if to show that she will be fettered by no rule; and we must admit the same varieties that she admits." Again: "If nature is never bound down, nor the voice of inspiration stifled, that is enough. We are pleased that women should write and speak, if they feel need of it, from having something to tell; but silence for ages would be no misfortune, if that silence be from divine command, and not from man's tradition." And here is a passage, the beginning of which has been often quoted:

> If you ask me what offices they [women] may fill, I reply any I do not care what case you put; let them be sea-captains if you will. I do not doubt there are women well fitted for such an office, and, if so, I should be as glad as to welcome the Maid of Saragossa, or the Maid of Missolonghi, or the Suliote

2 In Mrs. Caudle's Curtain Lectures, written in 1846 by Douglas Jerrold, there is a comic sketch of a wife who delivers nightly lectures to her husband from behind their bed curtains. * Her subsequent novels include The Mill on the Floss (1860) and Middlemarch (1871–2).

3 Mrs. Malaprop is a character in The Rivals, by Richard Brinsley Sheridan, 1775. In response to compliments about her "intellectual accomplishment," Mrs. Malaprop exclaims, "Ah! Few gentlemen, nowadays, know how to value the ineffectual qualities in a woman!"

> heroine, or Emily Plater.[4] I think women need, especially at this juncture, a much greater range of occupation than they have, to rouse their latent powers.... In families that I know, some little girls like to saw wood, others to use carpenter's tools. Where these tastes are indulged, cheerfulness and good-humor are promoted. Where they are forbidden, because "such things are not proper for girls," they grow sullen and mischievous Fourier had observed these wants of women, as no one can fail to do who watches the desires of little girls, or knows the *ennui* that haunts grown women, except where they make to themselves a serene little world by art of some kind. He, therefore, in proposing a great variety of employments in manufactures or the care of plants and animals, allows for one-third of women as likely to have a taste for masculine pursuits, one-third of men for feminine.... I have no doubt, however, that a large proportion of women would give themselves to the same employments as now, because there are circumstances that must lead them. Mothers will delight to make the nest soft and warm. Nature would take care of that; no need to clip the wings of any bird that wants to soar and sing, or finds in itself the strength of pinion for a migratory flight unusual to its kind. The difference would be that all need not he constrained to employments for which *some* are unfit.

Apropos of the same subject, we find Mary Wollstonecraft offering a suggestion which the women of the United States have already began to carry out.

She says:

> Women in particular, all want to be ladies, which is simply to have nothing to do, but listlessly to go they scarcely care where, for they cannot tell what. But what have women to do in society? I may be asked, but to loiter with easy grace; surely you would not condemn them all to suckle fools and chronicle small beer. No. *Women might certainly study the art of healing, and be physicians as well as nurses. . . .* Business of various kinds they might likewise pursue, if they were educated in a more orderly manner.... Women would not then marry for a support, as men accept of places under government and neglect the implied duties.

Men pay a heavy price for their reluctance to encourage self-help and independent resources in women. The precious meridian years of many a man of genius have to be spent in the toil of routine, that an "establishment" may be kept up for a woman who can understand none of his secret yearnings, who is fit for nothing but to sit in her drawing-room like a doll-Madonna in her shrine. No matter. Anything is more endurable than to change our established formulae

4 These are all heroines who distinguished themselves in war, the most obvious masculine field of activity. Maria Agustin was the Maid of Saragossa who fought against the French at the siege of Saragossa, Spain in 1808. The Maid of Misslonghi was an unidentified Greek girl at the Turkish sieges of that town in 1822 or 1826. The Suliote heroine was probably Moscha, who led a band of 300 women against the Turks during the siege of Souli in Albania, 1803. Emily Plater, a Polish patriot, became a captain in command of a company in the insurgent army fighting the Russians in 1831.

about women, or to run the risk of looking up to our wives instead of looking down on them. Sit divus, dummodo non sit vivus (let him be a god, provided he be not living), said the Roman magnates of Romulus, and so men say of women, let them be idols, useless absorbents of previous things, provided we are not obliged to admit them to be strictly fellow-beings, to be treated, one and all, with justice and sober reverence.

On one side we hear that woman's position can never be improved until women themselves are better; and, on the other, that women can never become better until their position is improved-until the laws are made more just, and a wider field opened to feminine activity. But we constantly hear the same difficulty stated about the human race in general. There is a perpetual action and reaction between individuals and institutions; we must try and mend both by little and little—the only way in which human things can be mended. Unfortunately, many over-zealous champions of women assert their actual equality with men—nay, even their moral superiority to men—as a ground for their release from oppressive laws and restrictions. They lose strength immensely by this false position. If it were true, then there would be a case in which slavery and ignorance nourished virtue, and so far we should have an argument for the continuance of bondage. But we want freedom and culture for woman, because subjection and ignorance have debased her, and with her, Man; for—

> If she be small, slight-natured, miserable, How shall men grow?

Both Margaret Fuller and Mary Wollstonecraft have too much sagacity to fall into this sentimental exaggeration. Their ardent hopes of what women may become do not prevent them from seeing and painting women as they are. On the relative moral excellence of men and women Mary Wollstonecraft speaks with the most decision:

> Women are supposed to possess more sensibility, and even humanity, than men, and their strong attachments and instantaneous emotions of compassion are given as proofs; but the clinging affection of ignorance has seldom anything noble in it, and may mostly be resolved into selfishness, as well as the affection of children and brutes. I have known many weak women whose sensibility was entirely engrossed by their husbands; and as for their humanity, it was very faint indeed, or rather it was only a transient emotion of compassion. Humanity does not consist "in a squeamish ear," says an eminent orator. "It belongs to the mind as well as to the nerves." But this kind of exclusive affection, though it degrades the individual, should not be brought forward as a proof of the inferiority of the sex, because it is the natural consequence of confined views; for even women of superior sense, having their attention turned to little employments and private plans, rarely rise to heroism, unless when spurred on by love! and love, as an heroic passion, like genius, appears but once in an age. I therefore agree with the moralist who asserts "that women have seldom so much generosity as men"; and that

their narrow affections, to which justice and humanity are often sacrificed, render the sex apparently inferior, especially as they are commonly inspired by men; but I contend that the heart would expand as the understanding gained strength, if women were not depressed from their cradles.

We had marked several other passages of Margaret Fuller's for extract, but as we do not aim at an exhaustive treatment of our subject, and are only touching a few of its points, we have, perhaps, already claimed as much of the reader's attention as he will be willing to give to such desultory material.

Booker T. Washington, "Industrial Education for the Negro"

Born in 1856 in Franklin County, Virginia, Booker T. Washington was freed from slavery at age nine. When he was sixteen he began his training to become a teacher. In 1881 he became the first leader of the Tuskegee Institute in Alabama, an institution dedicated to the industrial education of African Americans. Washington came to national attention after his famous Atlanta address of 1895, calling for economic cooperation between whites and blacks. His message was well received by white America and he received an honorary Masters degree from Harvard in 1896 and an honorary Doctorate from Dartmouth in 1901.

Source: Booker T. Washington, "Industrial Education for the Negro." *The Negro Problem: A Series of Articles by Representative American Negroes of Today* (New York: James Pott and Company, 1903), pp. 7–30.

Focus Questions:

1. What assumptions did Washington make about race and about racial progress? What did he mean by "civilization"? How, in his view, did a race become "civilized"?
2. How might you explain Washington's appeal to white America?

One of the most fundamental and far-reaching deeds that has been accomplished during the last quarter of a century has been that by which the Negro has been helped to find himself and to learn the secrets of civilization—to learn that there are a few simple, cardinal principles upon which a race must start its upward course, unless it would fail, and its last estate be worse than its first.

It has been necessary for the Negro to learn the difference between being worked and working—to learn that being worked meant degradation, while working means civilization; that all forms of labor are honorable, and all forms of idleness disgraceful. It has been necessary for him to learn that all races that have got upon their feet have done so largely by laying an economic foundation, and, in general, by beginning in a proper cultivation and ownership of the soil.

Forty years ago my race emerged from slavery into freedom. If, in too many cases, the Negro race began development at the wrong end, it was largely because neither white nor black properly understood the case. Nor is it any wonder that this was so, for never before in the history of the world had just such a problem been presented as that of the two races at the coming of freedom in this country.

For two hundred and fifty years, I believe the way for the redemption of the Negro was being prepared through industrial development. Through all those years the Southern white man did business with the Negro in a way that no one else has done business with him. In most cases if a Southern white man wanted a house built he consulted a Negro mechanic about the plan and about the actual building of the structure. If he wanted a suit of clothes made he went to a Negro tailor, and for shoes he went to a shoemaker of the same race. In a certain way every slave plantation in the South was an industrial school. On these plantations young colored men and women were constantly being trained not only as farmers but as carpenters, blacksmiths, wheel-wrights, brick masons, engineers, cooks, laundresses, sewing women and housekeepers.

I do not mean in any way to apologize for the curse of slavery, which was a curse to both races, but in what I say about industrial training in slavery I am simply stating facts. This training was crude, and was given for selfish purposes. It did not answer the highest ends, because there was an absence of mental training in connection with the training of the hand. To a large degree, though, this business contact with the Southern white man, and the industrial training on the plantations, left the Negro at the close of the war in possession of nearly all the common and skilled labor in the South. The industries that gave the South its power, prominence and wealth prior to the Civil War were mainly the raising of cotton, sugar cane, rice and tobacco. Before the way could be prepared for the proper growing and marketing of these crops forests had to be cleared, houses to be built, public roads and railroads constructed. In all these works the Negro did most of the heavy work. In the planting, cultivating and marketing of the crops not only was the Negro the chief dependence, but in the manufacture of tobacco he became a skilled and proficient workman, and in this, up to the present time, in the South, holds the lead in the large tobacco manufactories.

In most of the industries, though, what happened? For nearly twenty years after the war, except in a few instances, the value of the industrial training given by the plantations was overlooked. Negro men and women were educated in literature, in mathematics and in the sciences, with little thought of what had been taking place during the preceding two hundred and fifty years, except, perhaps, as something to be escaped, to be got as far away from as possible. As a generation began to pass, those who had been trained as mechanics in slavery began to disappear by death, and gradually it began to be realized that there were few to take their places. There were young men educated in foreign tongues, but few in carpentry or in mechanical or architectural drawing. Many were trained in Latin, but few as engineers and blacksmiths. Too many were taken from the farm and educated, but educated in everything but farming. For this reason they had no interest in farming and did not return to it. And yet eighty-five percent. of the Negro population of the Southern states lives and for a considerable time will continue to live in the country districts. The charge is often brought against the members of my race—and too often justly, I confess—that they are found leaving the country districts and flocking into the great cities where temptations are more frequent and harder to resist, and where the Negro people too often become demoralized. Think, though, how frequently it is the case that from the first day that a pupil begins to go to school his books teach him much about the cities of the world and city life, and almost nothing about the country. How natural it is, then, that when he has the ordering of his life he wants to live it in the city.

Only a short time before his death the late Mr. C. P. Huntington, to whose memory a magnificent library has just been given by his widow to the Hampton Institute for Negroes, in Virginia, said in a public address some words which seem to me so wise that I want to quote them here:

"Our schools teach everybody a little of almost everything, but, in my opinion, they teach very few children just what they ought to know in order to make their way successfully in life. They do not put into their hands the tools they are best fitted to use, and hence so many failures. Many a mother and sister have worked and slaved, living upon scanty food, in order to give a son and brother a "liberal education," and in doing this have built up a barrier between the boy and the work he was fitted to do. Let me say to you that all honest work is honorable work. If the labor is manual, and seems common, you will have all the more chance to be thinking of other things, or of work that is higher and brings better pay, and to work out in your minds better and higher duties and responsibilities for yourselves, and for thinking of ways by which you can help others as well as yourselves, and bring them up to your own higher level."

Some years ago, when we decided to make tailoring a part of our training at the Tuskegee Institute, I was amazed to find that it was almost impossible to find in the whole country an educated colored man who could teach the making of clothing. We could find numbers of them who could teach astronomy, theology, Latin or grammar, but almost none who could instruct in the making of clothing, something that has to be used by every one of us every day in the year. How often have I been discouraged as I have gone through the South, and into the homes of the people of my race, and have found women who could converse intelligently upon abstruse subjects, and yet could not tell how to improve the condition of the poorly cooked and still more poorly served bread and meat which they and their families were eating three times a day. It is discouraging to find a girl who can tell you the geographical location of any country on the globe and who does not know where to place the dishes upon a common dinner table. It is discouraging to find a woman who knows much about theoretical chemistry, and who cannot properly wash and iron a shirt. In what I say here I would not by any means have it understood that I would limit or circumscribe the mental development of the Negro student. No race can be lifted until its mind is awakened and strengthened. By the side of industrial training should always go mental and moral training, but the pushing of mere abstract knowledge into the head means little. We want more than the mere performance of mental gymnastics. Our knowledge must be harnessed to the things of real life. I would encourage the Negro to secure all the mental strength, all the mental culture—whether gleaned from science, mathematics, history, language or literature that his circumstances will allow, but I believe most earnestly that for years to come the education of the people of my race should be so directed that the greatest proportion of the mental strength of the masses will be brought to bear upon the everyday practical things of life, upon something that is needed to be done, and something which they will be permitted to do in the community in which they reside. And just the same with the professional class which the race needs and must have, I would say give the men and women of that class, too, the training which will best fit them to perform in the most successful manner the service which the race demands.

I would not confine the race to industrial life, not even to agriculture, for example, although I believe that by far the greater part of the Negro race is best off in the country districts and must and should continue to live there, but I would teach the race that in industry the foundation must be laid—that the very best service which any one can render to what is called the higher education is to teach the present generation to provide a material or industrial foundation. On such a foundation as this will grow habits of thrift, a love of work, economy, ownership of property, bank accounts. Out of it in the future will grow practical education, professional education, positions of public responsibility. Out of it will grow moral and religious strength. Out of it will grow wealth from which alone can come leisure and the opportunity for the enjoyment of literature and the fine arts.

In the words of the late beloved Frederick Douglass: "Every blow of the sledge hammer wielded by a sable arm is a powerful blow in support of our cause. Every colored mechanic is by virtue of circumstances an elevator of his race. Every house built by a black man is a strong tower against the allied hosts of prejudice. It is impossible for us to attach too much importance to this aspect of the subject. Without industrial development there can be no wealth; without wealth there can be no leisure; without leisure no opportunity for thoughtful reflection and the cultivation of the higher arts."

I would set no limits to the attainments of the Negro in arts, in letters or statesmanship, but I believe the surest way to reach those ends is by laying the foundation in the little things of life that lie immediately about one's door. I plead for industrial education and development for the Negro not because I want to cramp him, but because I want to free him. I want to see him enter the all-powerful business and commercial world. It was such combined mental, moral and industrial education which the late General Armstrong set out to give at the Hampton Institute when he established that school thirty years ago. The Hampton Institute has continued along the lines laid down by its great founder, and now each year an increasing number of similar schools are being established in the South, for the people of both races.

Early in the history of the Tuskegee Institute we began to combine industrial training with mental and moral culture. Our first efforts were in the direction of agriculture, and we began teaching this with no appliances except one hoe and a blind mule. From this small beginning we have grown until now the Institute owns two thousand acres of land, eight hundred of which are cultivated each year by the young men of the school. We began teaching wheelwrighting and blacksmithing in a small way to the men, and laundry work, cooking and sewing and housekeeping to the young women. The fourteen hundred and over young men and women who attended the school during the last school year received instruction— in addition to academic and religious training—in thirty-three trades and industries, including carpentry, blacksmithing, printing, wheelwrighting, harnessmaking, painting, machinery, founding, shoemaking, brickmasonry and brickmaking, plastering, sawmilling, tinsmithing, tailoring, mechanical and architectural drawing, electrical and steam engineering, canning, sewing, dressmaking, millinery, cooking, laundering, housekeeping, mattress making, basketry, nursing, agriculture, dairying and stock raising, horticulture.

Not only do the students receive instruction in these trades, but they do actual work, by means of which more than half of them pay some part or all of their expenses while remaining at the school. Of the sixty buildings belonging to the school all but four were almost wholly erected by the students as a part of their industrial education. Even the bricks which go into the walls are made by students in the school's brick yard, in which, last year, they manufactured two million bricks.

When we first began this work at Tuskegee, and the idea got spread among the people of my race that the students who came to the Tuskegee school were to be taught industries in connection with their academic studies, were, in other words, to be taught to work, I received a great many verbal messages and letters from parents informing me that they wanted their children taught books, but not how to work. This protest went on for three or four years, but I am glad to be able to say now that our people have very generally been educated to a point where they see their own needs and conditions so clearly that it has been several years since we have had a single protest from parents against the teaching of industries, and there is now a positive enthusiasm for it. In fact, public sentiment among the students at Tuskegee is now so strong for industrial training that it would hardly permit a student to remain on the grounds who was unwilling to labor.

It seems to me that too often mere book education leaves the Negro young man or woman in a weak position. For example, I have seen a Negro girl taught by her mother to help her in doing laundry work at home. Later, when this same girl was graduated from the public schools or a high school and returned home she finds herself educated out of sympathy with laundry work, and yet not able to find anything to do which seems in keeping with the cost and character of her education. Under these circumstances we cannot be surprised if she does not fulfill the expectations made for her. What should have been done for her, it seems to me, was to give her along with her academic education thorough training in the latest and best methods of laundry work, so that she could have put so much skill and intelligence into it that the work would have been lifted out from the plane of drudgery. The home which she would then have been able to found by the results of her work would have enabled her to help her children to take a still more responsible position in life.

Almost from the first Tuskegee has kept in mind—and this I think should be the policy of all industrial schools—fitting students for occupations which would be open to them in their home communities. Some years ago we noted the fact that there was beginning to be a demand in the South for men to operate dairies in a skillful, modern manner. We opened a dairy department in connection with the school, where a number of young men could have instruction in the latest and most scientific methods of dairy work. At present we have calls—mainly from Southern white men—for twice as many dairymen as we are able to supply. What is equally satisfactory, the reports which come to us indicate that our young men are giving the highest satisfaction and are fast changing and improving the dairy product in the communities into which they go. I use the dairy here as an example. What I have said of this is equally true of many of the other industries which we teach. Aside from the economic value of this work I can-not but believe, and my observation confirms me in my belief, that as we continue to place Negro men and women of intelligence, religion, modesty, conscience and skill in every community in the South, who will prove by actual results their value to the community, I cannot but believe, I say, that this will constitute a solution to many of the present political and social difficulties.

Many seem to think that industrial education is meant to make the Negro work as he worked in the days of slavery. This is far from my conception of industrial education. If this training is worth anything to the Negro, it consists in teaching him how not to work, but how to make the forces of nature—air, steam, water, horse-power and electricity—work for him. If it has any value it is in lifting labor up out of toil and drudgery into the plane of the dignified and the beautiful. The Negro in the South works and works hard; but too often his ignorance and lack of skill causes him to do his work in the most costly and shiftless manner, and this keeps him near the bottom of the ladder in the economic world.

I have not emphasized particularly in these pages the great need of training the Negro in agriculture, but I believe that this branch of industrial education does need very great emphasis. In this connection I want to quote some words which Mr. Edgar Gardner Murphy, of Montgomery, Alabama, has recently written upon this subject:

"We must incorporate into our public school system a larger recognition of the practical and industrial elements in educational training. Ours is an agricultural population. The school must be brought more closely to the soil. The teaching of history, for example, is all very well, but nobody can really know anything of history unless he has been taught to see things grow—has so seen things not only with the outward eye, but with the eyes of his intelligence and conscience. The actual things of the present are more important, however, than the institutions of the past. Even to young children can be shown the simpler conditions and processes of growth—how corn is put into the ground—how cotton and potatoes should be planted—how to choose the soil best adapted to a particular plant, how to improve that soil, how to care for the plant while it grows, how to get the most value out of it, how to use the elements of waste for the fertilization of other crops; how, through the alternation of crops, the land may be made to increase the annual value of its products—these things, upon their elementary side are absolutely vital to the worth and success of hundreds of thousands of these people of the Negro race, and yet our whole educational system has practically ignored them.

..."Such work will mean not only an education in agriculture, but an education through agriculture and education, through natural symbols and practical forms, which will educate as deeply, as broadly and as truly as any other system which the world has known. Such changes will bring far larger results than the mere improvement of our Negroes. They will give us an agricultural class, a class of tenants or small land owners, trained not away from the soil, but in relation to the soil and in intelligent dependence upon its resources."

I close, then, as I began, by saying that as a slave the Negro was worked, and that as a freeman he must learn to work. There is still doubt in many quarters as to the ability of the Negro unguided, unsupported, to hew his own path and put into visible, tangible, indisputable form, products and signs of civilization. This doubt cannot be much affected by abstract arguments, no matter how delicately and convincingly woven together. Patiently, quietly, doggedly, persistently, through summer and winter, sunshine and shadow, by self-sacrifice, by foresight, by honesty and industry, we must re-enforce argument with results. One farm bought, one house built, one home sweetly and intelligently kept, one man who is the largest tax payer or has the largest bank account, one school or church maintained, one factory running successfully, one truck garden profitably cultivated, one patient cured by a Negro doctor, one sermon well preached, one office well filled, one life cleanly lived—these will tell more in our favor than all the abstract eloquence that can be summoned to plead our cause. Our pathway must be up through the soil, up through swamps, up through forests, up through the streams, the rocks, up through commerce, education and religion!

CHAPTER 22

Nineteenth-Century Culture and Thought

William James, from *Pragmatism*

William James (1842–1910) was born into a wealthy and highly intellectual family. His father, Henry Sr., was a Swedenborgian theologian, and his brother Henry Jr. became a famous novelist in his own right. James graduated from Harvard University in 1869, later returning as a faculty member, where he would teach anatomy, physiology, psychology, and philosophy for more than three decades. His works include The Principles of Psychology (1890), which exhibited the transformation of this discipline into its modern methods, and The Varieties of Religious Experience (1902). In his writings on philosophy, religion, pragmatism, and truth, James helped to develop the idea of the individual's "stream of consciousness."

Source: William James, *Pragmatism* (New York: Longman Green and Company, 1907).

Focus Questions:

1. According to James, how is true dogma or religion established?
2. Why does James see value in a synthesis of religions?

PRAGMATISM

A New Name for Some Old Ways of Thinking

* * *

I fear that my previous lectures, confined as they have been to human and humanistic aspects, may have left the impression on many of you that pragmatism means methodically to leave the superhuman out. I have shown small respect indeed for the Absolute, and I have until this moment spoken of no other superhuman hypothesis but that. But I trust that you see sufficiently that the Absolute has nothing but its superhumanness in common with the theistic God. On pragmatistic principles, if the hypothesis of God works satisfactorily in the widest sense of the word, it is true. Now whatever its residual difficulties may be, experience shows that it certainly does work, and that the problem is to build it out and determine it, so that it will combine satisfactorily with all the other working truths. I cannot start upon a whole theology at the end of this last lecture; but when I tell you that I have written a book on men's religious experience, which on the whole has been regarded as making for the reality of God, you will perhaps exempt my own pragmatism from the charge of being an atheistic system. I firmly disbelieve, myself, that our human experience is the highest form of experience extant in the universe. I believe rather that we stand in much the same relation to the whole of the universe as our canine and feline pets do to the whole of human life. They inhabit our drawing-rooms and libraries. They take part in scenes of whose significance they have no inkling. They are merely tangent to curves of history the beginnings and ends and forms of which pass wholly beyond their ken. So we are tangents to the wider life of things. But, just as many of the dog's and cat's ideals coincide with our ideals, and the dogs and cats have daily living proof of the fact, so we may well believe, on the proofs that religious experience affords, that higher powers exist and are at work to save the world on ideal lines similar to our own.

You see that pragmatism can be called religious, if you allow that religion can be pluralistic or merely melioristic in type. But whether you will finally put up with that type of religion or not is a question that only you yourself can decide. Pragmatism has to postpone dogmatic answer, for we do not yet know certainly which type of religion is going to work best in the long run. The various overbeliefs of men, their several faith-ventures, are in fact what are needed to bring the evidence in. You will probably make your own ventures severally. If radically tough, the hurly-burly of the sensible facts of nature will be enough for you, and you will need no religion at all. If radically tender, you will take up with the more monistic form of religion: the pluralistic form, with its reliance on possibilities that are not necessities, will not seem to afford you security enough.

But if you are neither tough nor tender in an extreme and radical sense, but mixed as most of us are, it may seem to you that the type of pluralistic and moralistic religion that I have offered is as good a religious synthesis as you are likely to find. Between the two extremes of crude naturalism on the one hand and transcendental absolutism on the other, you may find that what I take the liberty of calling the pragmatistic or melioristic type of theism is exactly what you require.

Thorstein Veblen, Excerpt from *The Theory of the Leisure Class*

Thorstein Veblen (1857–1929) was an economist and social critic. Born to Norwegian immigrants and raised in rural Minnesota, Veblen attended Carleton College and received a Ph.D. in philosophy from Yale University. His eccentric personality and personal scandals did not serve him well professionally, yet over the course of his career he taught at the University of Chicago, Stanford University, University of Missouri, and the New School for Social Research. His most famous work, The Theory of the Leisure Class (1899), introduced the concepts of "conspicuous consumption" and "pecuniary emulation." The latter term describes the working class's desire to ascend to the upper class, rather than overthrow it.

Source: Thorstein Veblen, "Industrial Exemption and Conservatism," in *The Theory of the Leisure Class*, Ch. 8, (1899).

Focus Questions:

1. According to Veblen, what is it that truly can change people's views and behavior?
2. What is Veblen's attitude toward the influence of the leisure class, and how does this influence affect social attitudes about conservatism and innovation?

CHAPTER 8: INDUSTRIAL EXEMPTION AND CONSERVATISM

Any one who is required to change his habits of life and his habitual relations to his fellow men will feel the discrepancy between the method of life required of him by the newly arisen exigencies, and the traditional scheme of life to which he is accustomed. It is the individuals placed in this position who have the liveliest incentive to reconstruct the received scheme of life and are most readily persuaded to accept new standards; and it is through the need of the means of livelihood that men are placed in such a position. The pressure exerted by the environment upon the group, and making for a readjustment of the group's scheme of life, impinges upon the members of the group in the form of pecuniary exigencies; and it is owing to this fact—that external forces are in great part translated into the form of pecuniary or economic exigencies— it is owing to this fact that we can say that the forces which count toward a readjustment of institutions in any modern industrial community are chiefly economic forces; or more specifically, these forces take the form of pecuniary pressure. Such a readjustment as is here contemplated is substantially a change in men's views as to what is good and right, and the means through which a change is wrought in men's apprehension of what is good and right is in large part the pressure of pecuniary exigencies.

Any change in men's views as to what is good and right in human life make its way but tardily at the best. Especially is this true of any change in the direction of what is called progress; that is to say, in the direction of divergence from the archaic position—from the position which may be accounted the point of departure at any step in the social evolution of the community. Retrogression, reapproach to a stand-point to which the race has been long habituated in the past, is easier. This is especially true in case the development away from this past standpoint has not been due chiefly to a substitution of an ethnic type whose temperament is alien to the earlier standpoint.

* * *

It is a matter of common notoriety that when individuals, or even considerable groups of men, are segregated from a higher industrial culture and exposed to a lower cultural environment, or to an economic situation of a more primitive character, they quickly show evidence of reversion toward the spiritual features which characterize the predatory type; and it seems probable that the dolicho-blond type of European man is possessed of a greater facility for such reversion to barbarism than the other ethnic elements with which that type is associated in the Western culture. Examples of such a reversion on a small scale abound in the later history of migration and colonization. Except for the fear of offending that chauvinistic patriotism which is so characteristic a feature of the predatory culture, and the presence of which is frequently the most striking mark of reversion in modern communities, the case of the American colonies might be cited as an example of such a reversion on an unusually large scale, though it was not a reversion of very large scope.

The leisure class is in great measure sheltered from the stress of those economic exigencies which prevail in any modern, highly organized industrial community. The exigencies of the struggle for the means of life are less exacting for this class than for any other; and as a consequence of this privileged position we should expect to find it one of the least responsive of the classes of society to the demands which the situation makes for a further growth of institutions and a readjustment to an altered industrial situation. The leisure class is the conservative class. The exigencies of the general economic situation of the community do not freely or directly impinge upon the members of this class. They are not required under penalty of forfeiture to change their habits of life and their theoretical views of the external world to suit the demands of an altered industrial technique, since they are not in the full sense an organic part of the industrial community. Therefore these exigencies do not readily produce, in the members of this class, that degree of uneasiness with the existing order which alone can lead any body of men to give up views and methods of life that have become habitual to them. The office of the leisure class in social evolution is to retard the movement and to conserve what is obsolescent. This proposition is by no means novel; it has long been one of the commonplaces of popular opinion.

The prevalent conviction that the wealthy class is by nature conservative has been popularly accepted without much aid from any theoretical view as to the place and relation of that class in the cultural development. When an explanation of this class conservatism is offered, it is commonly the invidious one that the wealthy class opposes innovation because it has a vested interest, of an unworthy sort, in maintaining the present conditions. The explanation here put forward imputes no unworthy motive. The opposition of the class to changes in the cultural scheme is instinctive, and does not rest primarily on an interested calculation of material advantages; it is an instinctive revulsion at any departure from the accepted way of doing and of looking at things—a revulsion common to all men and only to be over-come by stress of circumstances. All change in habits of life and of thought is irksome. The difference in this respect between the wealthy and the common run of mankind lies not so much in the motive which prompts to conservatism as in the degree of exposure to the economic forces that urge a change. The members of the wealthy class do not yield to the demand for innovation as readily as other men because they are not constrained to do so.

This conservatism of the wealthy class is so obvious a feature that it has even come to be recognized as a mark of respectability. Since conservatism is a characteristic of the wealthier and therefore more reputable portion of the community, it has acquired a certain honorific or decorative value. It has become prescriptive to such an extent that an adherence to conservative views is comprised as a matter of course in our notions of respectability; and it is imperatively incumbent on all who would lead a blameless life in point of social repute.

Conservatism, being an upper-class characteristic, is decorous; and conversely, innovation, being a lower-class phenomenon, is vulgar. The first and most unreflected element in that instinctive revulsion and reprobation with which we turn from all social innovators is this sense of the essential vulgarity of the thing. So that even in cases where one recognizes the substantial merits of the case for which the innovator is spokesman—as may easily happen if the evils which he seeks to remedy are sufficiently remote in point of time or space or personal contact—still one cannot but be sensible of the fact that the innovator is a person with whom it is at least distasteful to be associated, and from whose social contact one must shrink. Innovation is bad form.

The fact that the usages, actions, and views of the well-to-do leisure class acquire the character of a prescriptive canon of conduct for the rest of society, gives added weight and reach to the conservative influence of that class. It makes it incumbent upon all reputable people to follow their lead. So that, by virtue of its high position as the avatar of good form, the wealthier class comes to exert a retarding influence upon social development far in excess of that which the simple numerical strength of the class would assign it. Its prescriptive example acts to greatly stiffen the resistance of all other classes against any innovation, and to fix men's affections upon the good institutions handed down from an earlier generation. There is a second way in which the influence of the leisure class acts in the same direction, so far as concerns hindrance to the adoption of a conventional scheme of life more in accord with the exigencies of the time. This second method of upper-class guidance is not in strict consistency to be brought under the same category as the instinctive conservatism and aversion to new modes of thought just spoken of; but it may as well be dealt with here, since it has at least this much in common with the conservative habit of mind that it acts to retard innovation and the growth of social structure. The code of proprieties, conventionalities, and usages in vogue at any given time and among any given people has more or less of the character of an organic whole; so that any appreciable change in one point of the scheme involves some-thing of a change or readjustment at other points also, if not a reorganization all along the line. When a change is made which immediately touches only a minor point in the scheme, the consequent derangement of the structure of conventionalities may be inconspicuous; but even in such a case it is safe to say that some derangement of the general scheme, more or less far-reaching, will follow. On the other hand, when an attempted reform involves the suppression or thorough-going remodelling of an institution of first-rate importance in the conventional scheme, it is immediately felt that a serious derangement of the entire scheme would result; it is felt that a readjustment of the structure to the new form taken on by one of its chief elements would be a painful and tedious, if not a doubtful process.

Friedrich Nietzsche, *Beyond Good and Evil*

Collectively, Friedrich Nietzsche's (1844-1900) writings are a fierce rejection of western civilization. His ideas influenced scientists, intellectuals, authors, and philosophers well into the twentieth century. Raised the son of a Lutheran minister in the Prussian region, as an adult he rejected middle-class Christian morality. He became a professor of classics in his early twenties at the university in Basel, Switzerland in 1869. He also served for a short time as a medical orderly during the Franco-Prussian War (1870-1871). Throughout his life, he suffered from mental and physical frailty, and his illnesses forced him to resign his post at the university in 1879. After this early retirement from his professional duties, he became interested in philosophy and natural sciences. For the next two years, he wrote scathing critiques of traditional approaches to philosophy and the study of the human psyche. He published this work, *Beyond Good and Evil,* in German, in1886. Nietzsche had a breakdown in 1889, and retreated for a year to a mental institution. He never fully recovered and spent the rest of his life being taken care of by his mother and sister.

Source: *Beyond Good and Evil,* trans. Helen Zimmern (Edinburgh: Darien Press, 1907), 5-12, 20-34.

Focus Questions:

1. What main ideas does Nietzsche explain in this passage?
2. What ideas and beliefs does Nietzsche challenge? How and why?
3. Why did his ideas resonate? What trends and movements in this period help to explain the adoption of Nietzsche's theories and outlook?

[1. The Will to Truth, which is to tempt us to many a hazardous enterprise, the famous Truthfulness of which all philosophers have hitherto spoken with respect, what questions has this Will to Truth not laid before us! What strange, perplexing, questionable questions! It is already a long story; yet it seems as if it were hardly commenced. Is it any wonder if we at last grow distrustful, lose patience, and turn impatiently away? That this Sphinx teaches us at last to ask questions ourselves? *Who* is it really that puts questions to us here? *What* really is this "Will to Truth" in us? In fact we made a long halt at the question as to the origin of this Will—until at last we came to an absolute standstill before a yet more fundamental question. We inquired about the *value* of this Will. Granted that we want the truth: *why not rather* untruth? And uncertainty? Even ignorance? The problem of the value of truth presented itself before us—or was it we who presented ourselves before the problem? Which of us is the Oedipus here? Which the Sphinx? It would seem to be a rendezvous of questions and notes of interrogation. And could it be believed that it at last seems to us as if the problem had never been propounded before, as if we were the first to discern it, get a sight of it, and risk raising it. For there is risk in raising it, perhaps there is no greater risk.

2. "*How could* anything originate out of its opposite? For example, truth out of error? or the Will to Truth out of the will to deception? or the generous deed out of selfishness? or the pure sun-bright vision of the wise man out of covetousness? Such genesis is impossible; whoever dreams of it is a fool, nay, worse than a fool; things of the highest value must have a different origin, an origin of *their own*—in this transitory, seductive, illusory, paltry world, in this turmoil of delusion and cupidity, they cannot have their source. But rather in the lap of Being, in the intransitory, in the concealed God, in the 'Thing-in-itself'—*there* must be their source, and nowhere else!"—This mode of reasoning discloses the typical prejudice by which metaphysicians of all times can be recognised, this mode of valuation is at the back of all their logical procedure; through this "belief" of theirs, they exert themselves for their "knowledge," for

something that is in the end solemnly christened "the Truth." The fundamental belief of metaphysicians is *the belief in antitheses of values*. It never occurred even to the wariest of them to doubt here on the very threshold (where doubt, however, was most necessary); though they had made a solemn vow, "*de omnibus dubitandum*." For it may be doubted, firstly, whether antitheses exist at all; and secondly, whether the popular valuations and antitheses of value upon which metaphysicians have set their seal, are not perhaps merely superficial estimates, merely provisional perspectives, besides being probably made from some corner, perhaps from below—"frog perspectives," as it were, to borrow an expression current among painters. In spite of all the value which may belong to the true, the positive, and the unselfish, it might be possible that a higher and more fundamental value for life generally should be assigned to pretence, to the will to delusion, to selfishness, and cupidity. It might even be possible that *what* constitutes the value of those good and respected things, consists precisely in their being insidiously related, knotted, and crocheted to these evil and apparently opposed things—perhaps even in being essentially identical with them. Perhaps! But who wishes to concern himself with such dangerous "Perhapses"! For that investigation one must await the advent of a new order of philosophers, such as will have other tastes and inclinations, the reverse of those hitherto prevalent—philosophers of the dangerous "Perhaps" in every sense of the term. And to speak in all seriousness, I see such new philosophers beginning to appear.

3. Having kept a sharp eye on philosophers, and having read between their lines long enough, I now say to myself that the greater part of conscious thinking must be counted amongst the instinctive functions, and it is so even in the case of philosophical thinking; one has here to learn anew, as one learned anew about heredity and "ineptness." As little as the act of birth comes into consideration in the whole process and continuation of heredity, just as little is "being-conscious" *opposed* to the instinctive in any decisive sense; the greater part of the conscious thinking of a philosopher is secretly influenced by his instincts, and forced into definite channels. And behind all logic and its seeming sovereignty of movement, there are valuations, or to speak more plainly, physiological demands, for the maintenance of a definite mode of life....

4. The falseness of an opinion is not for us any objection to it: it is here, perhaps, that our new language sounds most strangely. The question is, how far an opinion is life-furthering, life-preserving, species-preserving, perhaps species-rearing; and we are fundamentally inclined to maintain that the falsest opinions (to which the synthetic judgments *a priori* belong), are the most indispensable to us; that without a recognition of logical fictions, without a comparison of reality with the purely imagined world of the absolute and immutable, without a constant counterfeiting of the world by means of

numbers, man could not live—that the renunciation of false opinions would be a renunciation of life, a negation of life. *To recognise untruth as a condition of life*: that is certainly to impugn the traditional ideas of value in a dangerous manner, and a philosophy which ventures to do so, has thereby alone placed itself beyond good and evil.

5. That which causes philosophers to be regarded half-distrustfully and half-mockingly, is not the oft-repeated discover how innocent they are—how often and easily they make mistakes and lose their way, in short, how childish and childlike they are,—but that there is not enough honest dealing with them, whereas they all raise a loud and virtuous outcry when the problem of truthfulness is even hinted at in the remotest manner. They all pose as though their real opinions had been discovered and attained through the self-evolving of a cold, pure, divinely indifferent dialectic (in contrast to all sorts of mystics, who, fairer and foolisher, talk of "inspiration"); whereas, in fact, a prejudiced proposition, idea, or "suggestion," which is generally their heart's desire abstracted and refined, is defended by them with arguments sought out after the event. They are all advocates who do not wish to be regarded as such, generally astute defenders, also, of their prejudices, which they dub "truths,"—and *very* far from having the conscience' which bravely admits this to itself; very far from having the good taste or the courage which goes so far as to let this be understood, perhaps to warn friend or foe, or in cheerful confidence and self-ridicule. The spectacle of the Tartuffery of old Kant, equally stiff and decent, with which he entices us into the dialectic by-ways that lead (more correctly mislead) to his "categorical imperative"—makes us fastidious ones smile, we who find no small amusement in spying out the subtle tricks of old moralists and ethical preachers. Or, stiff more so, the hocus-pocus of mathematical form, by means of which Spinoza has as it were clad his philosophy in mail and mask—in fact, the "love of *his* wisdom," to translate the term fairly and squarely—in order thereby to strike terror at once into the heart of the assailant who should dare to cast a glance on that invincible maiden, that Pallas Athene:—how much of personal timidity and vulnerability does this masquerade of a sickly recluse betray!

6. It has gradually become clear to me what every great philosophy up till now has consisted of—namely, the confession of its originator, and a species of involuntary and unconscious autobiography: and moreover that the moral (or immoral) purpose in every philosophy has constituted the true vital germ out of which the entire plant has always grown. Indeed, to understand how the abstrusest metaphysical assertions of a philosopher have been arrived at, it is always well (and wise) to first ask oneself: "What morality do they (or does he) aim at?" Accordingly, I do not believe that an "impulse to knowledge" is the father of philosophy; but that another impulse, here as elsewhere, has only made use of knowledge (and mistaken knowledge!) as an instrument. But

whoever considers the fundamental impulses of man with a view to determining how far they may have here acted as *inspiring* genii (or as demons and cobolds), will find that they have all practised philosophy at one time or another, and that each one of them would have been only too glad to look upon itself as the ultimate end of existence and the legitimate *lord* over all the other impulses. For every impulse is imperious, and as *such*, attempts to philosophise. To be sure, in the case of scholars, in the case of really scientific men, it may be otherwise— better," if you will; there may really be such a thing as an "impulse to knowledge," some kind of small, independent clockwork, which, when well wound up, works away industriously to that end, *without* the rest of the scholarly impulses taking any material part therein. The actual "interests" of the scholar, therefore, are generally in quite another direction— in the family, perhaps, or in money-making, or in politics; it is, in fact, almost indifferent at what point of research his little machine is placed, and whether the hopeful young worker becomes a good philologist, a mushroom specialist, or a chemist; he is not *characterised* by becoming this or that. In the philosopher, on the contrary, there is absolutely nothing impersonal; and above all, his morality furnishes a decided and decisive testimony as to *who he is*,—that is to say, in what order the deepest impulses of his nature stand to each other.

13. Psychologists should bethink themselves before putting down the instinct of self-preservation as the cardinal instinct of an organic being. A living thing seeks above all to *discharge* its strength—life itself is *Will to Power*; self-preservation is only one of the indirect and most frequent *results* thereof. In short, here, as everywhere else, let us beware of *superfluous* teleological principles!—one of which is the instinct of self-preservation (we owe it to Spinoza's inconsistency). It is thus, in effect, that method ordains, which must be essentially economy of principles.

16. There are still harmless self-observers who believe that there are "immediate certainties"; for instance or as the superstition of Schoperihauer puts it, "I will"; as though cognition here got hold of its object purely and simply as "the thing in itself," without any falsification taking place either on the part of the subject or the object. I would repeat it, however, a hundred times, that "immediate certainty," as well as "absolute knowledge" and the "thing in itself," involve a contradictio *in adjecto*; we really ought to free ourselves from the misleading significance of words! The people on their part may think that cognition is knowing all about things, but the philosopher must say to himself: "When I analyse the process that is expressed in the sentence, 'I think,' I find a whole series of daring assertions, the argumentative proof of which would be difficult, perhaps impossible: for instance, that it is I who think, that there must necessarily be something that thinks, that thinking is an activity and operation on the part of a being who is thought of as a cause, that there

is an 'ego,' and finally, that it is already determined what is to be designated by thinking—that *I know* what thinking is. For if I had not already decided within myself what it is, by what standard could I determine whether that which is just happening is not perhaps 'willing' or 'feeling'? In short, the assertion 'I think,' assumes that *I compare* my state at the present moment with other states of myself which I know, in order to determine what it is; on account of this retrospective connection with further 'knowledge,' it has at any rate no immediate certainty for me."—In place of the "immediate certainty" in which the people may believe in the special case, the philosopher thus finds a series of metaphysical questions presented to him, veritable conscience questions of the intellect, to wit: "From whence did I get the notion of 'thinking'? Why do I believe in cause and effect? What gives me the right to speak of an 'ego,' and even of an 'ego' as cause, and finally of an 'ego' as cause of thought?" He who ventures to answer these metaphysical questions at once by an appeal to a sort of intuitive perception, like the person who says, "I think, and know that this, at least, is true, actual, and certain"—will encounter a smile and two notes of interrogation in a philosopher nowadays. "Sir," the philosopher will perhaps give him to understand, "it is improbable that you are not mistaken, but why should it be the truth?"

17. With regard to the superstitions of logicians, I shall never tire of emphasising, a small, terse fact, which is unwillingly recognised by these credulous minds—namely, that a thought comes when "it" wishes, and not when "I" wish; so that it is a *perversion* of the facts of the case to say that the subject "I" is the condition of the predicate "think." One thinks; but that this "one" is precisely the famous old "ego," is, to put it mildly, only a supposition, an assertion, and assuredly not an "immediate certainty." After all, one has even gone too far with this one thinks"—even the "one" contains an *interpretation* of the process, and does not belong to the process itself. One infers here according to the usual grammatical formula—"To think is an activity; every activity requires an agency that is active; consequently" . . . It was pretty much on the same lines that the older atomism sought, besides the operating "power," the material particle wherein it resides and out of which it operates—the atom. More rigorous minds, however, learnt at last to get along without this "earth-residuum," and perhaps some day we shall accustom ourselves, even from the logician's point of view, to get along without the little "one" (to which the worthy old "ego" has refined itself).

18. It is certainly not the least charm of a theory that it is refutable; it is precisely thereby that it attracts the more subtle minds. It seems that the hundred-times-refuted theory of the "free will" owes its persistence to this charm alone; someone is always appearing who feels himself strong enough to refute it.

19. Philosophers are accustomed to speak of the will as though it were the best-known thing in the world; indeed, Schopenhauer has given us to understand

that the will alone is really known to us, absolutely and completely known, without deduction or addition. But it again and again seems to me that in this case Schopenhauer also only did what philosophers are in the habit of doing—he seems to have adopted a *popular prejudice* and exaggerated it. Willing—seems to me to be above all something *complicated*, something that is a unity only in name—and it is precisely in a name that popular prejudice lurks, which has got the mastery over the inadequate precautions of philosophers in all ages. So let us for once be more cautious, let us be "unphilosophical": let us say that in all willing there is firstly a plurality of sensations, namely, the sensation of the condition "*away from which we go,*" the sensation of the condition "*towards which we go,*" the sensation of this "*from*" and "*towards*" itself, and then besides, an accompanying muscular sensation, which, even without our putting in motion "arms and legs," commences its action by force of habit, directly we "will" anything. Therefore, just as sensations (and indeed many kinds of sensations) are to be recognised as ingredients of the will, so, in the second place, thinking is also to be recognised; in every act of the will there is a ruling thought;—and let us not imagine it possible to sever this thought from the "willing," as if the will would then remain over! In the third place, the will is not only a complex of sensation and thinking, but it is above all an emotion, and in fact the *emotion* of the command. That which is termed "freedom of the will" is essentially the emotion of supremacy in respect to him who must obey: "I am free, 'he' must obey"—this consciousness is inherent in every will; and equally so the straining of the attention, the straight look which fixes itself exclusively on one thing, the unconditional judgment that "this and nothing else is necessary now," the inward certainty that obedience will be rendered—and whatever else pertains to the position of the commander. A man who *wills* commands something within himself which renders obedience, or which he believes renders obedience. But now let us notice what is the strangest thing about the will,—this affair so extremely complex, for which the people have only one name. Inasmuch as in the given circumstances we are at the same time the commanding *and* the obeying parties, and as the obeying party we know the sensations of constraint, impulsion, pressure, resistance, and motion, which usually commence immediately after the act of will; inasmuch as, on the other hand, we are accustomed to disregard this duality, and to deceive ourselves about it by means of the synthetic term "I": a whole series of erroneous conclusions, and consequently of false judgments about the will itself, has become attached to the act of willing—to such a degree that he who wills believes firmly that willing *suffices* for action. Since in the majority of cases there has only been exercise of will when the effect of the command—consequently obedience, and therefore action—was to be *expected*, the *appearance* has translated itself into the sentiment, as if there were there a *necessity of effect*; in a word, he who wills believes with a fair amount of certainty that will and action are somehow one; he ascribes the success, the carrying out of the willing, to the will itself, and thereby enjoys an increase of the sensation of power which accompanies all success."Freedom of Will"— that is the expression for the complex state of delight of the person exercising volition, who commands and at the same time identifies himself with the executor of the order—who, as such, enjoys also the triumph over obstacles, but thinks within himself that it was really his own will that overcame them.

21. The *causa sui* is the best self-contradiction that has yet been conceived, it is a sort of logical violation and unnaturalness; but the extravagant pride of man has managed to entangle itself profoundly and frightfully with this very folly. The desire for"freedom of will"in the superlative, metaphysical sense, such as still holds sway, unfortunately, in the minds of the half-educated, the desire to bear the entire and ultimate responsibility for one's actions oneself, and to absolve God, the world, ancestors, chance, and society therefrom, involves nothing less than to be precisely this *causa sui,* and, with more than Munchausen daring, to pull oneself up into existence by the hair, out of the slough of nothingness. If any one should find out in this manner the crass stupidity of the celebrated conception of"free will"and put it out of his head altogether, I beg of him to carry his"enlightenment" a step further, and also put out of his head the contrary of this monstrous conception of"free will": I mean "non-free will," which is tantamount to a misuse of cause and effect. One should not wrongly *materialise* "cause" and "effect," as the natural philosophers do (and whoever like them naturalise in thinking at present), according to the prevailing mechanical doltishness which makes the cause press and push until it "effects" its end; one should use "cause" and "effect" only as pure *conceptions,* that is to say, as conventional fictions for the purpose of designation and mutual understanding,—not for explanation. In"beingin-itself"there is nothing of"causal-connection,"of"necessity,"or of"psychological non-freedom"; there the effect does *not* follow the cause, there"law"does not obtain. It is we alone who have devised cause, sequence, reciprocity, relativity, constraint, number, law, freedom, motive, and purpose; and when we interpret and intermix this symbol-world, as"being in itself,"with things, we act once more as we have always acted— *mythologically*. The"non-free will" is mythology; in real life it is only a question of *strong* and *weak* wills.—It is almost always a symptom of what is lacking in himself, when a thinker, in every"causal-connection"and"psychological necessity,"manifests something of compulsion, indigence, obsequiousness, oppression, and non-freedom; it is suspicious to have such feelings—the person betrays himself. And in general, if I have observed correctly, the "non-freedom of the will" is regarded as a problem from two entirely opposite standpoints, but always in a profoundly *personal* manner: some will not give up their "responsibility," their belief in *themselves,* the personal right to *their* merits, at any price (the vain races belong to this class); others on the contrary, do not wish to be answerable for

anything, or blamed for anything, and owing to an inward self-contempt, seek *to get out of the business,* no matter how. The latter, when they write books, are in the habit at present of taking the side of criminals; a sort of socialistic sympathy is their favourite disguise. And as a matter of fact, the fatalism of the weak-willed embellishes itself surprisingly when it can pose as *"la religion de la sufferance humaine"*; that is its "good taste."

22. Let me be pardoned, as an old philologist who cannot desist from the mischief of putting his finger on bad modes of interpretation, but "Nature's conformity to law," of which you physicists talk so proudly, as though— why, it exists only owing to your interpretation and bad "philology." It is no matter of fact, no "text," but rather just a naïvely humanitarian adjustment perversion of meaning, with which you make abundant concessions to the democratic instincts of the modern soul! "Everywhere equality before the law—Nature is not different in that respect, nor better than we": a fine instance of secret motive, in which the vulgar antagonism to everything privileged and autocratic—likewise a second and more refined antheism—is once more distinguished. *"Ni dieu, ni maître"*—that, also, is what you want; and therefore "Cheers for natural law!"—is it not so? But, as has been said, that is interpretation, not text; and somebody might come along, who, with opposite intentions and modes of interpretation could read out of the same "Nature," and with regard to the same phenomena, just the tyrannically inconsiderate and relentless enforcement of the claims of power—an interpreter who should so place the unexceptionalness and unconditionalness of all "Will to Power" before your eyes, that almost every word, and the word "tyranny" itself, would eventually seem unsuitable or like a weakening and softening metaphor—as being too human; and who should, nevertheless, end by asserting the same about this world as you do, namely, that it has a "necessary" and "calculable" course, *not,* however, because laws obtain in it, because they are absolutely *lacking,* and every power effects its ultimate consequences every moment. Granted that this also is only interpretation—and you will be eager enough to make this objection?—well, so much the better.

23. All psychology hitherto has run around on moral prejudices and timidities, it has not dared to launch out into the depths. In so far as it is allowable to recognise in that which has hitherto been written, evidence of that which has hitherto been kept silent, it seems as if nobody had yet harboured the notion of psychology as the Morephology and *Development-doctrine of the Will to Power,* as I conceive of it. The power of moral prejudices has penetrated deeply into the most intellectual world, the world apparently most indifferent and unprejudiced, and has obviously operated in an injurious, obstructive, blinding, and distorting manner. A proper physio-psychology has to contend with unconscious antagonism in the heart of the investigator, it has "the heart" against it: even a doctrine of the reciprocal conditionalness of the

"good" and the "bad" impulses, causes (as refined immorality) distress and aversion in a still strong and manly conscience—still more so, a doctrine of the derivation of all good impulses from bad ones. If, however, a person should regard even the emotions of hatred, envy, covetousness, and imperiousness as life-conditioning emotions, as factors which must be present, fundamentally and essentially, in the general economy of life (which must, therefore, be further developed if life is to be further developed), he will suffer from such a view of things as from sea-sickness. And yet this hypothesis is far from being the strangest and most painful in this immense and almost new domain of dangerous knowledge; and there are in fact a hundred good reasons why everyone should keep away from it who can do so! On the other hand, if one has once drifted hither with one's bark, well! very good! now let us set our teeth firmly! let us open our eyes and keep our hand fast on the helm! We sail away right over morality, we crush out, we destroy perhaps the remains of our own morality by daring to make our voyage thither—but what do we matter! Never yet did a *profounder* world of insight reveal itself to daring travellers and adventurers, and the psychologist who thus "makes a sacrifice"—it is not the *sacrifizio dell'intelletto,* on the contrary!—will at least be entitled to demand in return that psychology shall once more be recognised as the queen of the sciences for whose service and equipment the other sciences exist. For psychology is once more the path to the fundamental problems.]

Frederick Winslow Taylor, "A Piece-Rate System," 1896

As industrialization matured, attention focused on improving efficiency. Scientific management emerged as a means of ordering the industrial and business world. In a sense, scientific management was related to the Progressive idea of ordering the world. Frederick Winslow Taylor was perhaps the most famous advocate of applying science to industry.

Source: Frederick Winslow Taylor, "A Piece-Rate System," 1896.

Focus Questions:

1. What were the benefits of Taylor's system over the ordinary piece-rate system?
2. What distinguished a modern manager from his old-school counterpart?

The ordinary piece-work system involves a permanent antagonism between employers and men, and a certainty of punishment for each workman who reaches a high rate of efficiency. The demoralizing effect of this system is most serious. Under it, even the best workmen are forced continually to act the part of hypocrites, to hold their own in the struggle against the encroachments of their employers.

The system introduced by the writer, however, is directly the opposite, both in theory and in its results. It takes each workman's interests the same as that of his employer, pays a premium for high efficiency, and soon convinces each man that it is for his permanent advantage to turn out each day the best quality and maximum quantity of work…Elementary rate-fixing differs from other methods of making piece-work prices in that a careful study is made of the time required to do each of the many elementary operations into which the manufacturing of an establishment may be analyzed or divided. These elementary operations are then classified, recorded, and indexed and when a piece-work price is wanted for work the job is first divided into its elementary operations, the time required to do each elementary operation is found from the records, and the total time for the job is summed up from these data.

While this method seems complicated at the first glance, it is, in fact, far simpler and more effective than the old method of recording the time required to do whole jobs of work, and then, after looking over the records of similar jobs, guessing at the time required for any new piece of work. The differential rate system of piece-work consists briefly, in offering two different rates for the same job, a high price per piece in case the work is finished in the shortest possible time and in perfect condition, and a low price if it takes a longer time to do the job, of if there are any imperfections in the work. (The high rate should be such that the workman can earn more per day than is usually paid in similar establishments.) This is directly the opposite of the ordinary plan of piece-work in which the wages of the workmen are reduced when they increase their productivity. The system by which the writer proposes managing the men who are on day-work consists in paying men and not positions. Each man's wages, as far as possible, are fixed according to the skill and energy with which he performs his work, and not according to the position which he fills. Every endeavor is made to stimulate each man's personal ambition. This involves keeping systematic and careful records of the performance of each man, as to his punctuality, attendance, integrity, rapidity, skill, and accuracy, and a readjustment from time to time of the wages paid him, in accordance with this record.

The advantages of this system of management are:

First. That the manufactures are produced cheaper under it, while at the same time the workmen earn higher wages than are usually paid.

Second. Since the rate-fixing is done from accurate knowledge instead of more or less by guess-work, the motive for holding back on work, or"soldiering," and endeavoring to deceive the employers as to the time required to do work, is entirely removed, and with it the greatest cause for hard feelings and war between the management and the men.

Third. Since the basis from which piece-work as well as day rates are fixed is that of exact observation, instead of being founded upon accident or deception, as is too frequently the case under ordinary systems, the men are treated with greater uniformity and justice, and respond by doing more and better work.

Fourth. It is for the common interest of both the management and the men to cooperate in every way, so as to turn out each day the maximum quantity and best quality of work.

Fifth. The system is rapid, while other systems are slow, in attaining the maximum productivity of each machine and man; and when this maximum is once reached, it is automatically maintained by the differential rate.

Sixth. It automatically selects and attracts the best men for each class of work, and it develops many first class men who would otherwise remain slow or inaccurate, while at the same time it discourages and sifts out men who are incurably lazy or inferior.

Finally. One of the chief advantages derived from the above effects of the system is, that it promotes a most friendly feeling between the men and their employers and so renders labor unions and strikes unnecessary…

It is not unusual for the manager of a manufacturing business to go most minutely into every detail of the buying and selling and financiering, and arrange every element of these branches in the most systematic manner and according to principles that have been carefully planned to insure the business against almost any contingency which may arise, while the manufacturing is turned over to a superintendent or foreman, with little or no restrictions as to the principles and methods which he is to pursue, either in the management of his men or the care of the company's plant…

Such managers belong distinctly to the old school of manufacturers; and among them are to be found, in spite of their lack of system, many of the best and most successful men of the country. They believe in men, not in methods, in the management of their shops; and what they would call system in the office and sales departments, would be called red tape by them in the factory. Through their keen insight and knowledge of character they are able to select and train good superintendents, who in turn secure good workmen; and frequently the business prospers under this system (or rather, lack of system) for a term of years. The modern manufacturer, however, seeks not only to secure the best superintendents and work-men, but to surround each department of his manufacture with the most carefully woven net-work of system and method, which should render the business, for a considerable period at least, independent of the loss of any one man, and frequently of any combination of men. It is the lack of this system and method which, in the judgment of the writer, constitutes the greatest risk to manufacturing; placing, as it frequently does, the success of the business at the hazard of the health of whims of a few employees.

Charles Darwin, *Autobiography*

Charles Darwin (1809-1882), a British naturalist, traveled on board the HMS Beagle, that sailed to the west coast of South America and the Pacific islands on a five year voyage beginning in 1831. Darwin joined the voyage specifically to study wildlife in those regions that were relatively unfamiliar to Europeans at that time. During that trip, based on his observations and comparisons of animals in the different locales he visited, he formulated the theory of evolution. Afraid of how his ideas would be received by the public, he waited over twenty years before publishing his theory. He finally published *The Origin of the Species* in 1859. In the following excerpts from his autobiography, Darwin discusses his education which was very typical for a middle or upper class boy at that time in Great Britain. Traditional educational curriculum in Europe still emphasized the study of classical and ancient authors, with little attention paid to the sciences or the scientific method. In his excerpt, Darwin discusses his early interest in science and how he obtained the knowledge and skills he needed to embark on his later scientific endeavors.

Source: Charles Darwin, *The Autobiography of Charles Darwin*, ed. Nora Barlow (New York: W.W. Norton, 1969), 27-28, 44-46, 58, 60, 62, 71, 76-79, 80-82.

Focus Questions:

1. How does Darwin describe his education at schools and universities? What were his main criticisms of the educational system in Britain at this time?
2. How was Darwin able to study the sciences? How did he acquire the skills and knowledge he needed?
3. What does this tell us about the field and study of science in the late nineteenth century?

Nothing could have been worse for the development of my mind than Dr. Butler's school, as it was strictly classical, nothing else being taught except a little ancient geography and history. The school as a means of education to me was simply a blank. During my whole life I have been singularly incapable of mastering any language. Special attention was paid to verse-making, and this I could never do well. I had many friends, and got together a grand collection of old verses, which by patching together, sometimes aided by other boys, I could work into any subject. Much attention was paid to learning by heart the lessons of the previous day; this I could effect with great facility learning forty or fifty lines of Virgil or Homer, whilst I was in morning chapel; but this exercise was utterly useless, for every verse was forgotten in forty-eight hours.

* * *

Early in my school-days a boy had a copy of the Wonders of the World, which I often read and disputed with other boys about the veracity of some of the statements; and I believe this book first gave me a wish to travel in remote countries, which was ultimately fulfilled by the voyage of the Beagle. In the latter part of my school life I became passionately fond of shooting, and I do not believe that anyone could have shown more zeal for the most holy cause than I did for shooting birds.

* * *

With respect to science, I continued collecting minerals with much zeal, but quite unscientifically—all that I cared for was a new named mineral, and I hardly attempted to classify them.

* * *

Towards the close of my school life, my brother worked hard at chemistry and made a fair laboratory with proper apparatus in the tool-house in the garden, and I was allowed to aid him as a servant in most of his experiments. He made all the gases and many compounds, and I read with care several books on chemistry, such as Henry and Parkes' Chemical Catechism. The subject interested me greatly, and we often used to go on working till rather late at night. This was the best part of my education at school, for it showed me practically the meaning of experimental science. The fact that we worked at chemistry somehow got known at school, and as it was an unprecedented fact, I was nicknamed "Gas." I was also once publicly rebuked by the head-master, Dr. Butler, for thus wasting my time over such useless subjects.

* * *

During the three years which I spent at Cambridge my time was wasted, as far as the academical studies were concerned, as completely as at Edinburgh and at school.

* * *

Although as we shall presently see there were some redeeming features in my life at Cambridge, my time was sadly wasted there and worse than wasted. From my passion for shooting and for hunting and when this failed, for riding across country I got into a sporting set, including some dissipated low-minded young men. We used often to dine together in the evening, though these dinners often included men of a higher stamp, and we sometimes drank too much, with jolly singing and playing at cards afterwards. I know that I ought to feel ashamed of days and evenings thus spent, but as some of my friends were very pleasant and we were all in the highest spirits, I cannot help looking back to these times with much pleasure.

* * *

But no pursuit at Cambridge was followed with nearly so much eagerness or gave me so much pleasure as collecting beetles. It was the mere passion for collecting, for I did not dissect them and rarely compared their external characters with published descriptions, but got them named anyhow.

* * *

I was very successful in collecting and invented two new methods; I employed a labourer to scrape during the winter, moss off old trees and place [it] in a large bag, and likewise to collect the rubbish at the bottom of the barges in which reeds are brought from the fens, and thus I got some very rare species. No poet ever felt more delight at seeing his first poem published than I did at seeing in Stephen's Illustrations of British Insectsthe magic words, "captured by C. Darwin, Esq."

* * *

On returning home from my short geological tour in N. Wales, I found a letter from Henslow, informing me that Captain Fitz-Roy was willing to give up part of his own cabin to any young man who would volunteer to go with him without pay as naturalist to the Voyage of the Beagle. I have given as I believe in my M.S. Journal an account of all the circumstances which then occurred; I will here only say that I was instantly eager to accept the offer, but my father strongly objected, adding the words fortunate for me,—"If you can find any man of common sense, who advises you to go, I will give my consent." So I wrote that evening and refused the offer.

[His uncle then argued he should go, and his father consented.]

* * *

The voyage of the Beagle has been by far the most important event in my life and has determined my whole career; yet it depended on so small a circumstance as my uncle offering to drive me 30 miles to Shrewsbury, which few uncles would have done, and on such a trifle as the shape of my nose. I have always felt that I owe to the voyage the first real training or education of my mind. I was led to attend closely to several branches of natural history, and thus my powers of observation were improved, though they were already fairly developed.

The investigation of the geology of all the places visited was far more important, as reasoning here comes into play. On first examining a new district nothing can appear more hopeless than the chaos of rocks; but by recording the stratification and nature of the rocks and fossils at many points, always reasoning and predicting what will be found elsewhere, light soon begins to dawn on the district, and the structure of the whole becomes more or less intelligible. I had brought with me the first volume of Lyell's Principles of Geology, which I studied attentively; and this book was of the highest service to me in many ways. The very first place which I examined, namely St. Jago in the Cape Verde islands, showed me clearly the wonderful superiority of Lyell's manner of treating geology, compared with that of any other author, whose works I had with me or ever afterwards read.

Another of my occupations was collecting animals of all classes, briefly describing and roughly dissecting many of the marine ones; but from not being able to draw and from not having sufficient anatomical knowledge a great pile of MS. which I made during the voyage has proved almost useless. I thus lost much time, with the exception of that spent in acquiring some knowledge of the Crustaceans, as this was of service when in after years I undertook a monograph of the Cirripedia.

During some part of the day I wrote my Journal, and took much pains in describing carefully and vividly all that I had seen; and this was good practice. My Journal served, also, in part as letters to my home, and portions were sent to England, whenever there was an opportunity.

The above various special studies were, however, of no importance compared with the habit of energetic industry and of concentrated attention to whatever I was engaged in, which I then acquired. Everything about which I thought or read was made to bear directly on what I had seen and was likely to see; and this habit of mind was continued during the five years of the voyage. I feel sure that it was this training which has enabled me to do whatever I have done in science.

Looking backwards, I can now perceive how my love for science gradually preponderated over every other taste. During the first two years my old passion for shooting survived in nearly full force, and I shot myself all the birds and animals for my collection; but gradually I gave up my gun more and more, and finally altogether to my servant, as shooting interfered with my work, more especially with making out the geological structure of a country. I discovered, though unconsciously and insensibly, that the pleasure of observing and reasoning was a much higher one than that of skill and sport. The primeval instincts of the barbarian slowly yielded to the acquired tastes of the civilized man. That my mind became developed through my pursuits during the voyage, is rendered probable by a remark made by my father, who was the most acute observer whom I ever saw, of a sceptical disposition, and far from being a believer in phrenology; for on first seeing me after the voyage, he turned round to my sisters and exclaimed, "Why, the shape of his head is quite altered."

* * *

As far as I can judge of myself I worked to the utmost during the voyage from the mere pleasure of investigation, and from my strong desire to add a few facts to the great mass of facts in natural science. But I was also ambitious to take a fair place among scientific men,—whether more ambitious or less so than most of my fellow-workers I can form no opinion.

* * *

Towards the close of our voyage I received a letter whilst at Ascension, in which my sisters told me that Sedgwick had called on my father and said that I should take a place among the leading scientific men. I could not at the time understand how he could have learnt anything of my proceedings, but I heard (I believe afterwards) that Henslow had read some of the letters which I wrote to him before the Philosophical Soc. of Cambridge and had printed them for private distribution. My collection of fossil bones, which had been sent to Henslow, also excited considerable attention amongst palaeontologists. After reading this letter I clambered over the mountains of Ascension with a bounding step and made the volcanic rocks resound under my geological hammer! All this shows how ambitious I was; but I think that I can say with truth that in after years, though I cared in the highest degree for the approbation of such men as Lyell and Hooker, who were my friends, I did not care much about the general public. I do not mean to say that a favourable review or a large sale of my books did not please me greatly; but the pleasure was a fleeting one, and I am sure that I have never turned one inch out of my course to gain fame.

CHAPTER 23

European Imperialism

Cecil Rhodes, "Confessions of Faith"

In the late nineteenth and early twentieth century, European nations began the drive to establish profitable colonies in Africa and Asia. Fueled by extreme nationalism and a sense of cultural and social superiority, Europeans conquered vast territories bringing the people who lived there under the authority of colonial administrations. European industrialization provided the tools for empire building. Resistance efforts on the part of local populations proved to be no match for superior, industrialized, European weaponry. Novel modes of transportation resulting from industrialization, such as the steam engine, gave the Europeans the means by which they could penetrate the interior of these vast continents, as they never had been able to do before. As the colonial empires grew, Europeans defended and justified imperialism drawing on many different ideas, beliefs, and arguments. Justifications for European imperialism included the notion of racial superiority, nationalism and patriotism, the quest for converts to Christianity, and the promise of economic growth. Cecil Rhodes (1853-1902), was one of Britain's strongest promoters of imperialism. Born in England, Rhodes made his fortune as one of the founders of the De Beers diamond mining company in South Africa. After establishing successful economic ventures in colonial Africa, Rhodes entered politics in 1881. He became a member of the parliament of the Cape Colony in British South Africa and, in 1890, became the prime minister of the colony. He outlined his views on British imperialism in this tract, published in 1877.

Source: John Flint, *Cecil Rhodes* (Boston: Little, Brown and Company, 1974), 248-250.

Focus Questions:

1. What were Rhodes' views regarding the British empire in the past, and how did he use this history as arguments for expanding the empire?

2. What were Rhodes' plans for expanding the British empire? What actions does he propose?
3. How did Rhodes define "civilization"? What ideas and beliefs informed his perceptions of who was "civilized," and who was not?

It often strikes a man to inquire what is the chief good in life; to one the thought comes that it is a happy marriage, to another great wealth, and as each seizes on his idea, for that he more or less works for the rest of his existence. To myself thinking over the same question the wish came to render myself useful to my country. I then asked myself how could I and after reviewing the various methods I have felt that at the present day we are actually limiting our children and perhaps bringing into the world half the human beings we might owing to the lack of country for them to inhabit that if we had retained America there would at this moment be millions more of English living. I contend that we are the finest race in the world and that the more of the world we inhabit the better it is for the human race. Just fancy those parts that are at present inhabited by the most despicable specimens of human beings what an alteration there would be if they were brought under Anglo-Saxon influence, look again at the extra employment a new country added to our dominions gives. I contend that every acre added to our territory means in the future birth to some more of the English race who otherwise would not be brought into existence. Added to this the absorption of the greater portion of the world under our rule simply means the end of all wars, at this moment had we not lost America I believe we could have stopped the Russian-Turkish war by merely refusing money and supplies. Having these ideas what scheme could we think of to forward this object. I look into history and I read the story of the Jesuits I see what they were able to do in a bad cause and I might say under bad leaders.

In the present day I become a member in the Masonic order I see the wealth and power they possess the influence they hold and I think over their ceremonies and I wonder that a large body of men can devote themselves to what at times appear the most ridiculous and absurd rites without an object and without an end.

The idea gleaming and dancing before ones eyes like a will-of-the-wisp at last frames itself into a plan. Why should we not form a secret society with but one object the furtherance of the British Empire and the bringing of the whole uncivilised world under British rule for the recovery of the United States for the making the Anglo-Saxon race but one Empire. What a dream, but yet it is probable, it is possible. I once heard it argued by a fellow in my own college, I am sorry to own it by an Englishman, that it was a good thing for us that we have lost the United States. There are some subjects on which there can be no arguments, and to an Englishman this is one of them, but even from an American's point of view just picture what they have lost, look at their government, are not the frauds that yearly come before the public view a disgrace to any country and especially theirs which is the finest in the world. Would they have occurred had they remained under English rule great as they have become how infinitely greater they would have been with the softening and elevating influences of English rule, think of those countless 000's of Englishmen that during the last 100 years would have crossed the Atlantic and settled and populated the United States. Would they have not made without any prejudice a finer country of it than the low class Irish and German emigrants? All this we have lost and that country loses owing to whom? Owing to two or three ignorant pig-headed statesmen of the last century, at their door lies the blame. Do you ever feel mad? do you ever feel murderous? I think I do with those men. I bring facts to prove my assertion. Does an English father when his sons wish to emigrate ever think of suggesting emigration to a country under another flag, never—it would seem a disgrace to suggest such a thing I think that we all think that poverty is better under our own flag than wealth under a foreign one.

Put your mind into another train of thought. Fancy Australia discovered and colonised under the French flag, what would it mean merely several millions of English unborn that at present exist we learn from the past and to form our future. We learn from having lost to cling to what we possess. We know the size of the world we know the total extent. Africa is still lying ready for us it is our duty to take it. It is our duty to seize every opportunity of acquiring more territory and we should keep this one idea steadily before our eyes that more territory simply means more of the Anglo-Saxon race more of the best the most human, most honourable race the world possesses.

To forward such a scheme what a splendid help a secret society would be a society not openly acknowledged but who would work in secret for such an object.

I contend that there are at the present moment numbers of the ablest men in the world who would devote their whole lives to it. I often think what a loss to the English nation in some respects the abolition of the Rotten Borough System has been. What thought strikes a man entering the house of commons, the assembly that rules the whole world? I think it is the mediocrity of the men but what is the cause. It is simply—an assembly of wealth of men whose lives have been spent in the accumulation of money and whose time has been too much engaged to be able to spare any for the study of past history. And yet in the hands of such men rest our destinies. Do men like the great Pitt, and Burke and Sheridan not now exist. I contend they do.... They live and die unused unemployed. What has been the main cause of the success of the Romish Church? The fact that every enthusiast, call it if you like every madman finds employment in it. Let us form the same kind of society—a Church for the extension of the British

Empire. A society which should have its members in every part of the British Empire working with one object and one idea we should have its members placed at our universities and our schools and should watch the English youth passing through their hands just one perhaps in every thousand would have the mind and feelings for such an object, he should be tried in every way, he should be tested whether he is endurant, possessed of eloquence, disregardful of the petty details of life, and if found to be such, then elected and bound by oath to serve for the rest of his life in his Country. He should then be supported if without means by the Society and sent to that part of the Empire where it was felt he was needed.

Take another case,... of the younger son with high thoughts, high aspirations, endowed by nature with all the faculties to make a great man, and with the sole wish in life to serve his Country but he lacks two things the means and the opportunity, ever troubled by a sort of inward deity urging him on to high and noble deeds, he is compelled to pass his time in some occupation which furnishes him with mere existence, he lives unhappily and dies miserably. Such men as these the Society should search out and use for the furtherance of their object.

(In every Colonial legislature the Society should attempt to have its members prepared at all times to vote or speak and advocate the closer union of England and the colonies, to crush all disloyalty and every movement for the severance of our Empire. The Society should inspire and even own portions of the press for the press rules the mind of the people. The Society should always be searching for members who might by their position in the world by their energies or character forward the object but the ballot and test for admittance should be severe.)

Once make [the society] common and it fails. Take a man of great wealth who is bereft of his children perhaps having his mind soured by some bitter disappointment who shuts himself up separate from his neighbours and makes up his mind to a miserable existence. To such men as these the society should go gradually disclose the greatness of their scheme and entreat him to throw in his life and property with them for this object. I think that there are thousands now existing who would eagerly grasp at the opportunity. Such are the heads of my scheme.

Carl Peters, "A Manifesto for German Colonization"

Newly unified, Germany entered the nineteenth-century competition for colonies late, long after Britain and France had already amassed substantial territories. In the 1880s and 1890s, however, Germany did establish colonies in Southwest and Eastern Africa, taking part in the European partition of Africa. Carl Peters (18561918) played a major role in Germany's empire-building on that continent. Peters founded the Society for German Colonization, in 1884, an organization that supported German colonial expansion in Africa. Peters played a major role in establishing a German colonial foothold in East Africa. Months after the establishment of the society in 1884, he seized land in the region of Tanganyika (now a part of Tanzania). Named to a high-ranking colonial post in 1891, he was forced to step down in 1897 as a result of charges of mistreating Africans and abusing his position for personal gain. He remained in Africa, and in the late 1890s he voyaged down the Zambezi River, with a view to colonizing it, and published an account of the old cities and gold mines he saw along the coasts entitled *The Eldorado of the Ancients* (1902). This excerpt comes from documents establishing the Society for German Colonization in 1884.

Source: Carl Peters, Die Grundung von Deutsch-Ostafrika (Berlin: Schwetschke, 1906), 43-45, in *Modern Imperialism: Western Overseas Expansion and its Aftermath, 1775-1996,* ed. Ralph A. Austen (Lexington: D.C. Health, 1969), 62-63.

Focus Questions:

1. What were the functions and goals of this society?
2. What arguments does Peters make about Germany's quest for colonies? Why did he think it was important?
3. What was the relationship between nationalism and the quest for colonial empires?

APRIL, 1884

In the partition of the earth, as it has proceeded from the beginning of the fifteenth century up to our times, the German nation received nothing. All the remaining European culture-bearing peoples possess areas outside our continent where their languages and customs can take firm root and flourish. The moment that the German emigrant leaves the borders of the Reich behind him, he is a stranger sojourning on foreign soil. The German Reich, great in size and strength through its bloodily achieved unity, stands in the leading position among the continental European powers: her sons abroad must adapt themselves to nations which look upon us with either indifference or even hostility. For centuries the great stream of German emigration has been plunging down into foreign races where it is lost sight of. Germandom outside Europe has been undergoing a perpetual national decline.

This fact, so painful to national pride, also represents a great economic disadvantage for our Volk. Every year our Fatherland loses the capacity of approximately 200,000 Germans. The greatest amount of this capacity flows directly into the camp of our economic competitors and increases the strength of our rivals. Germany's imports of products from tropical zones originate in foreign settlements whereby many millions of German capital are lost every year to alien nations. German exports are dependent upon the discretion of foreign tariff policies. Our industry lacks an absolutely safe market for its goods because our Volklacks colonies of its own.

The alleviation of this national grievance requires taking practical steps and strong action. In recognition of this point of view, a society has been organized in Berlin with the goal of mobilizing itself for such steps and such action. The Society for German Colonization aims to undertake on its own, in a resolute and sweeping manner, carefully chosen colonization projects and thereby supplement the ranks of organizations with similar tendencies.

Its particular tasks will be:

1. to provide necessary sums of capital for colonization;
2. to seek out and lay claim to suitable districts for colonization;
3. to direct German emigrants to these regions.

Imbued as we are with the conviction that it is no longer permissible to hesitate in energetically mobilizing ourselves for this great national task, we venture to come before the German Volk with a plea for active support of the endeavors of our Society! The German nation has proven time and again its willingness to make sacrifices for general patriotic undertakings: may she also bring her full energies to play in the solution of this great historical task.

Every German whose heart beats for the greatness and the honor of our nation is entreated to come to the side of our Society. What is at stake is compensation for centuries of deprivation: to prove to the world that, along with the splendor of the Reich, the German Volk has inherited the old German national spirit of its forefathers!

Edward D. Morel, *The Black Man's Burden*

Edward Morel was a British journalist who was interested in the economic and social impact of imperialism on Africa. *The Black Man's Burden* was a direct response to Rudyard Kipling's *The White Man's Burden*, a defense of western imperialism in Africa. Morel's work contributed to the emergence of an anti-imperialist movement in Europe.

Source: Edward D. Morel, *The Black Man's Burden* (London: The National Labor Press, 1920), pp. 7–11.

Focus Questions:

1. What role did Morel think capitalism played in the oppression of Africans? Why did he think capitalism in Africa was uniquely pernicious?
2. Why was Morel so pessimistic about the potential for Africans to resist the combined forces of imperialism, capitalism, and militarism? What future did he envision for the continent?

It is with the peoples of Africa, then, that our inquiry is concerned. It is they who carry the "Black man's" burden. They have not withered away before the white man's *occupation*. Indeed, if the scope of this volume permitted, there would be no difficulty in showing that Africa has ultimately absorbed within itself every Caucasian and, for that matter, every Semitic invader too. In hewing out for himself a fixed abode in Africa, the white man has massacred the African in heaps. The African has survived, and it is well for the white settlers that he has.

In the process of imposing his political dominion over the African, the white man has carved broad and bloody avenues from one end of Africa to the other. The African has resisted, and persisted.

For three centuries the white man seized end enslaved millions of Africans and transported them, with every circumstance of ferocious cruelty, across the seas. Still the African survived and, in his land of exile, multiplied exceedingly.

But what the partial occupation of his soil by the white man has failed to do; what the mapping out of European political "spheres of influence" has failed to do; what the maxim and the rifle; the slave gang, labor in the bowels of the earth and the lash, have failed to do; what imported measles, smallpox and syphilis have failed to do; what even the oversea slave trade failed to do, the flower of modern capitalistic exploitation, assisted by modern engines of destruction, may yet succeed in accomplishing.

For from the evils of the latter, scientifically applied and enforced, there is no escape for the African. Its destructive effects are not spasmodic: they are permanent. In its permanence resides its fatal consequences. It kills not the body merely, but the soul. It breaks the spirit. It attacks the African at every turn, from every point of vantage. It wrecks his polity, uproots him from the land, invades his family life, destroys his natural pursuits and occupations, claims his whole time, enslaves him in his own home.

Economic bondage and wage slavery, the grinding pressure of a life of toil, the incessant demands of industrial capitalism—these things a landless European proletariat physically endures, though hardly. […] The recuperative forces of a temperate climate are there to arrest the ravages, which alleviating influences in the shape of prophylactic and curative remedies will still further circumscribe. But in Africa, especially in tropical Africa, which a capitalistic imperialism threatens and has, in part, already devastated, man is incapable of reacting against unnatural conditions. In those regions man is engaged in a perpetual struggle against disease and an exhausting climate, which tells heavily on child-bearing; and there is no scientific machinery for salving the weaker members of the community. The African of the tropics is capable of tremendous physical labours. But he cannot accommodate himself to the European system of monotonous, uninterrupted labour, with its long and regular hours, involving, moreover, as it frequently does, severance from natural surroundings and nostalgia, the condition of melancholy resulting from separation from home, a malady to which the African is prone. Climatic conditions forbid it. When the system is forced upon him, the tropical African droops and dies.

Nor is violent physical opposition to abuse and injustice henceforth possible for the African in any part of Africa. His chances of effective resistance have been steadily dwindling with the increasing perfectibility in the killing power of modern armament. Gunpowder broke the effectiveness of his resistance to the slave trade, although he continued to struggle. He has forced and, on rare occasions and in exceptional circumstances beaten, in turn the old-fashioned musket, the elephant gun, the seven-pounder, and even the repeating rifle and the gatling gun. He has been known to charge right down repeatedly, foot and horse, upon the square, swept on all sides with the pitiless and continuous hail of maxims. But against the latest inventions, physical bravery, though associated with a perfect knowledge of the country, can do nothing. The African cannot face the high-explosive shell and the bomb-dropping aeroplane. He has inflicted sanguinary reverses upon picked European troops, hampered by the climate and by commissariat difficulties. He cannot successfully oppose members of his own race free from these impediments, employed by his white adversaries, and trained in all the diabolical devices of scientific massacre. And although the conscripting of African armies for use in Europe or in Africa as agencies for the liquidation of white man's quarrels must bring in its train evils from which the white man will be the first to suffer, both in Africa and in Europe; the African himself must eventually disappear in the process. Winter in Europe, or even in Northern Africa, is fatal to the tropical or subtropical African, while in the very nature of the case anything approaching real European control of Africa, of hordes of African soldiery armed with weapons of precisions is not a feasible proposition. The Black man converted by the European into a scientifically-equipped machine for the slaughter of his kind, is certainly not more merciful than the white man similarly equipped for like purposes in dealing with unarmed communities. And the experiences of the civilian population of Belgium, East Prussia, Galicia and Poland [First World War] is indicative of the sort of visitation involved for peaceable and powerless African communities if the white man determines to add to his appalling catalogue of past misdeeds toward the African, the crowning wickedness of once again, as in the day of the slave trade, supplying him with the means of encompassing his own destruction.

Thus the African is really helpless against the material gods of the white man, as embodied in the trinity of imperialism, capitalistic-exploitation, and militarism. If the white man retains these goes [sic] and if he insists upon making the African worship them as assiduously as he has done himself, the African will go the way of the Red Indian, the Amerindian, the Carib, the Guanche, the aboriginal Australian, and many more. And this would be at once a crime of enormous magnitude, and a world disaster.

An endeavor will now be made to describe the nature, and the changing form, which the burden inflicted by the white man in modern times upon the black has assumed. It can only be sketched here in the broadest outline, but in such a way as will, it is hoped, explain the differing causes and motives which have inspired white activities in Africa and illustrate, by specific and notable examples, their resultant effects upon African peoples. It is important that these differing causes and motives should be understood, and that we should distinguish between them in order that we may hew our way later on through the jungle of error which impedes the pathway to reform. Diffused generalities and sweeping judgments generate confusion of thought and hamper the evolution of a constructive policy based upon clear apprehension of the problem to be solved.

The history of contact between the white and black peoples in modern times is divisible into two distinct and separate periods: the period of the slave trade and the period of invasion, political control, capitalistic exploitation, and, the latest development, militarism. Following the slave trade period and preceding the period of invasion, occurs the trade interlude which, indeed, has priority of both periods, as when the Carthagenians bartered salt and iron implements for gold dust on the West Coast. But this interlude concerns our investigations only when we pass from destructive exposure to constructive demonstration.

The first period needs recalling, in order to impress once more upon our memories the full extent of the African's claim upon us, the white imperial peoples, for tardy justice, for considerate and honest conduct.

Our examination of the second period will call for sectional treatment. The history of contact and is consequences during this period may be roughly subdivided thus:

a. The struggle for supremacy between the European invading *Settlers* and the resident African peoples in those portions of Africa where the climate and other circumstances permit of European rearing families of white children.

b. Political action by European Governments aimed at the assertion of sovereign rights over particular areas of African territory.

c. Administrative policy, sanctioned by European Governments, and applied by their local representatives in particular areas, subsequent to the successful assertion of sovereign rights.

These sub-divisions are, perhaps, somewhat arbitrary. The distinctiveness here given to them cannot be absolutely preserved. There is, for instance, a natural tendency for both a and b to merge into c as, though efflux of time, the originating cause and motive of contact is obscured by developments to which contact has given rise.

Thus racial contention for actual possession of the soil, and political action often resulting in so-called treaties of Protectorate thoroughly unintelligible to the African signees, are both landmarks upon the road leading to eventual administrative policy: i.e., to direct government of the black man by the white.

Lin Zexu, *Letter to Queen Victoria,* 1839

Lin Zexu (1785-1850 CE). Although the English East India Company's trade with China was profitable, the overall balance of trade had remained in China's favor until the early decades of the nineteenth century. European traders bought tea, silk, rhubarb, and other goods from China, but the Chinese found little need for Western goods. A reversal in the trade balance came in the 1830s, and opium importation was one of the most important factors. Opium, forbidden in China, was smuggled into the country from India in ever-increasing quantities, primarily by English East India Company ships through the port of Canton [Guanzhou]. During the years of 1838–1839 alone, more than five million pounds of opium were imported illegally by East India Company ships.

The effects of the illicit trade on Chinese morality and health, as well as on the economy, were so deleterious that Emperor Tao-kuang [Daoguang] (r. 1821–1850) was gravely concerned. He searched for an official who would be able to deal with the opium menace effectively and resolutely. In Lin Tse-hsü [Lin Zexu] he found such a person. A high official in the Imperial government, Lin had enjoyed a wide reputation for his competence and integrity and for his hard-line approach toward the proliferation of opium. In December 1838, he was appointed imperial commissioner at Canton, with full power to stop the Canton opium traffic.

Lin Tse-hsü arrived in Canton in March 1839 and immediately began to stamp out the opium traffic; however, it became clear to him that the solution was to stop the supply at its source. The following selection is his letter to Queen Victoria, appealing to the British conscience and demanding an end to the opium trade. The letter was written in the summer of 1839, only a few months before the outbreak of the Opium War in November 1839. The fact that Lin Tse-hsü refers to Queen Victoria as "king" might suggest how knowledgeable the Chinese government was of English politics.

Source: Lin Zexu, *Letter to Queen Victoria,* 1839.

Focus Questions:

1. What moral arguments did Commissioner Lin present against the British importation of opium into China?
2. On the basis of Lin's letter to Queen Victoria and Emperor Ch'ien-lung's letter to King George III, describe China's view of the West, especially of Great Britain. Contrast these views with those expressed by Rudyard Kipling in "The White Man's Burden".

Lin, high imperial commissioner, a president of the Board of War, viceroy of the two Keang provinces, &c., Tang, a president of the Board of War, viceroy of the two Kwang provinces, &c., and E., a vice-president of the Board of War, lieut.-governor of Kwangtung, &c., hereby conjointly address this public dispatch to the queen of England for the purpose of giving her clear and distinct information (on the state of affairs) &c. It is only our high and mighty emperor, who alike supports and cherishes those of the Inner Land, and those from beyond the seas–who looks upon all mankind with equal benevolence–who, if a source of profit exists anywhere, diffuses it over the whole world–who, if the tree of evil takes root anywhere, plucks it up for the benefit of all nations–who, in a word, hath implanted in his breast that heart (by which beneficent nature herself) governs the heavens and the earth! You, the queen of your honorable nation, sit upon a throne occupied through successive generations by predecessors, all of whom have been styled respectful and obedient. Looking over the public documents accompanying the tribute sent (by your predecessors) on various occasions, we find the following: "All the people of my country, arriving at the Central Land for purposes of trade, have to feel grateful to the great emperor for the most perfect justice, for the kindest treatment," and other words to that effect. Delighted did we feel that the kings of your honorable nation so clearly understood the great principles of propriety, and were so deeply grateful for the heavenly goodness (of our emperor)–therefore, it was that we of the heavenly dynasty nourished and cherished your people from afar, and bestowed upon them redoubled proofs of our urbanity and kindness. It is merely from these circumstances, that your country–deriving immense advantage from its commercial intercourse with us, which has endured now two hundred years–has become the rich and flourishing kingdom that it is said to be!

But, during the commercial intercourse which has existed so long, among the numerous foreign merchants resorting hither, are wheat and tares, good and bad; and of these latter are some, who, by means of introducing opium by stealth, have seduced our Chinese people, and caused every province of the land to overflow with that poison. These then know merely to advantage themselves, they care not about injuring others! This is a principle which heaven's Providence repugnates; and which mankind conjointly look upon with abhorrence! Moreover, the great emperor hearing of it, actually quivered with indignation, and especially dispatched me, the commissioner, to Canton, that in conjunction with the viceroy and lieut.-governor of the province, means might be taken for its suppression!

Every native of the Inner Land who sells opium, as also all who smoke it, are alike adjudged to death. Were we then to go back and take up the crimes of the foreigners, who, by selling it for many years have induced dreadful calamity and robbed us of enormous wealth, and punish them with equal severity, our laws could not but award to them absolute annihilation! But, considering that these said foreigners did yet repent of their crime, and with a sincere heart beg for mercy; that they took 20,283 chests of opium piled up in their store-ships, and through Elliot, the superintendent of the trade of your said country, petitioned that they might be delivered up to us, when the same were all utterly destroyed, of which we, the imperial commissioner and colleagues, made a duly prepared memorial to his majesty–considering these circumstances, we have happily received a fresh proof of the extraordinary goodness of the great emperor, inasmuch as he who voluntarily comes forward, may yet be deemed a fit subject for mercy, and his crimes be graciously remitted him. But as for him who again knowingly violates the laws, difficult indeed will it be thus to go on repeatedly pardoning! He or they shall alike be doomed to the penalties of the new statute. We presume that you, the sovereign of your honorable nation, on pouring out your heart before the altar of eternal justice, cannot but command all foreigners with the deepest respect to reverence our laws! If we only lay clearly before your eyes, what is profitable and what is destructive, you will then know that the statutes of the heavenly dynasty cannot but be obeyed with fear and trembling! We find that your country is distant from us about sixty or seventy thousand miles, that your foreign ships come hither striving the one with the other for our trade, and for the simple reason of their strong desire to reap a profit. Now, out of the wealth of our Inner Land, if we take a part to bestow upon foreigners from afar, it follows, that the immense wealth which the said foreigners amass, ought properly speaking to be portion of our own native Chinese people. By what principle of reason then, should these foreigners send in return a poisonous drug, which involves in destruction those very natives of China? Without meaning to say that the foreigners harbor such destructive intentions in their hearts, we yet positively assert that from their inordinate thirst after gain, they are perfectly careless about the injuries they inflict upon us! And such being the case, we should like to ask what has become of that conscience which heaven has implanted in the breasts of all men?

We have heard that in your own country opium is prohibited with the utmost strictness and severity–this is a strong proof that you know full well how hurtful it is to mankind. Since then you do not permit it to injure your own country, you ought not to have the injurious drug transferred to another country, and above all others, how much less to the Inner Land! Of the products which China exports to your foreign countries, there is not one which is not beneficial to mankind in some shape or other. There are those which serve for food, those which are useful, and those which are calculated for re-sale; but all are beneficial. Has China (we should like to ask) ever yet sent forth a noxious article from its soil? Not to speak of our tea and rhubarb, things which your foreign countries could not exist a single day without, if we of the Central Land were to grudge you what is beneficial, and not to compassionate your wants, then wherewithal could you foreigners manage to exist? And further, as regards your woolens, camlets, and longells, were it not that you get supplied with our native raw silk, you could not get these manufactured! If China were to grudge you those things which yield a profit, how could you foreigners scheme after any profit at all? Our other articles of food, such as sugar, ginger, cinnamon, &c., and our other articles for use, such as silk piece-goods, chinaware, &c., are all so many necessaries of life to you; how can we reckon up their number! On the other hand, the things that come from your foreign countries are only calculated to make presents of, or serve for mere amusement. It is quite the same to us if we have them, or if we have them not. If then these are of no material consequence to us of the Inner Land, what difficulty would there be in prohibiting and shutting our market against them? It is only that our heavenly dynasty most freely permits you to take off her tea, silk, and other commodities, and convey them for consumption everywhere, without the slightest stint or grudge, for no other reason, but that where a profit exists, we wish that it be diffused abroad for the benefit of all the earth! Your honorable nation takes away the products of our central land, and not only do you thereby obtain food and support for yourselves, but moreover, by re-selling these products to other countries you reap a threefold profit. Now if you would only not sell opium, this threefold profit would be secured to you: how can you possibly consent to forgo it for a drug that is hurtful to men, and an unbridled craving after gain that seems to know no bounds! Let us suppose that foreigners came from another country, and brought opium into England, and seduced the people of your country to smoke it, would not you, the sovereign of the said country, look upon such a procedure with anger, and in your just indignation endeavor to get rid of it? Now we have always heard that your highness possesses a most kind and benevolent heart, surely then you are incapable of doing or causing to be done unto another, that which you should not wish another to do unto you! We have at the same time heard that your ships which come to Canton do each and every of them carry a document granted by your highness' self, on which are written these words "you shall not be permitted to carry contraband goods;" this shows that the laws of your highness are in their origin both distinct and severe, and we can only suppose that because the ships coming here have been very numerous, due attention has not been given to search and examine; and for this reason it is that we now address you this public document, that you may clearly know how stern and severe are the laws of the central dynasty, and most certainly you will cause that they be not again rashly violated!

Moreover, we have heard that in London the metropolis where you dwell, as also in Scotland, Ireland, and other such places, no opium whatever is produced. It is only in sundry parts of your colonial kingdom of Hindostan, such as Bengal, Madras, Bombay, Patna, Malwa, Benares, Malacca, and other places where the very hills are covered with the opium plant, where tanks are made for the preparing of the drug; month by month, and year by year, the volume of the poison increases, its unclean stench ascends upwards, until heaven itself grows angry, and the very gods thereat get indignant! You, the queen of the said honorable nation, ought immediately to have the plant in those parts plucked up by the very root! Cause the land there to be hoed up afresh, sow in its stead the five grains, and if any man dare again to plant in these grounds a single poppy, visit his crime with the most severe punishment. By a truly benevolent system of government such as this, will you indeed reap advantage, and do away with a source of evil. Heaven must support you, and the gods will crown you with felicity! This will get for yourself the blessing of long life, and from this will proceed the security and stability of your descendants!

In reference to the foreign merchants who come to this our central land, the food that they eat, and the dwellings that they abide in, proceed entirely from the goodness of our heavenly dynasty: the profits which they reap, and the fortunes which they amass, have their origin only in that portion of benefit which our heavenly dynasty kindly allots them: and as these pass but little of their time in your country, and the greater part of their time in our's, it is a generally received maxim of old and of modern times, that we should conjointly admonish, and clearly make known the punishment that awaits them. Suppose the subject of another country were to come to England to trade, he would certainly be required to comply with the laws of England, then how much more does this apply to us of the celestial empire! Now it is a fixed statute of this empire, that any native Chinese who sells opium is punishable with death, and even he who merely smokes it, must not less die. Pause and reflect for a moment: if you foreigners did not bring the opium hither, where should our Chinese people get it to re-sell? It is you foreigners who involve our simple natives in the pit of death, and are they alone to be permitted to escape alive? If so much as one of those deprive one of our people of his life, he must forfeit his life in requital for that which he has taken: how much more does this apply to him who by means of opium destroys his fellow-men? Does the havoc which he commits stop with a single life? Therefore it is that those foreigners who now import opium into the Central Land are condemned to be beheaded and strangled by the new statute, and this explains what we said at the beginning about plucking up the tree of evil, wherever it takes root, for the benefit of all nations.

We further find that during the second month of this present year, the superintendent of your honorable country, Elliot, viewing the law in relation to the prohibiting of opium as excessively severe, duly petitioned us, begging for"an extension of the term already limited, say five months for Hindostan and the different parts of India, and ten for England, after which they would obey and act in conformity with the new statute," and other words to the same effect. Now we, the high commissioner and colleagues, upon making a duly prepared memorial to the great emperor, have to feel grateful for his extraordinary goodness, for his redoubled compassion. Any one who within the next year and a half may by mistake bring opium to this country, if he will but voluntarily come forward, and deliver up the entire quantity, he shall be absolved from all punishment for his crime. If, however, the appointed term shall have expired, and there are still persons who continue to bring it, then such shall be accounted as knowingly violating the laws, and shall most assuredly be put to death! On no account shall we show mercy or clemency! This then may be called truly the extreme of benevolence, and the very perfection of justice!

Our celestial empire rules over ten thousand kingdoms! Most surely do we possess a measure of godlike majesty which ye cannot fathom! Still we cannot bear to slay or exterminate without previous warning, and it is for this reason that we now clearly make known to you the fixed laws of our land. If the foreign merchants of your said honorable nation desire to continue their commercial intercourse, they then must tremblingly obey our recorded statutes, they must cut off for ever the source from which the opium flows, and on no account make an experiment of our laws in their own persons!

Let then your highness punish those of your subjects who may be criminal, do not endeavor to screen or conceal them, and thus you will secure peace and quietness to your possessions, thus will you more than ever display a proper sense of respect and obedience, and thus may we unitedly enjoy the common blessings of peace and happiness. What greater joy! What more complete felicity than this!

Let your highness immediately, upon the receipt of this communication, inform us promptly of the state of matters, and of the measure you are pursuing utterly to put a stop to the opium evil. Please let your reply be speedy. Do not on any account make excuses or procrastinate. A most important communication.

P. S. We annex an abstract of the new law, now about to be put in force.

"Any foreigner or foreigners bringing opium to the Central Land, with design to sell the same, the principals shall most assuredly be decapitated, and the accessories strangled; and all property (found on board the same ship) shall be confiscated. The space of a year and a half is granted, within the which, if any one bringing opium by mistake, shall voluntarily step forward and deliver it up, he shall be absolved from all consequences of his crime."

This said imperial edict was received on the 9th day of the 6th month of the 19th year of Taoukwang, at which the period of grace begins, and runs on to the 9th day of the 12th month of the 20th year of Taoukwang, when it is completed.

Mary Kingsley, *Travels in West Africa*

Mary Kingsley (1862-1900) traveled to areas in Central and West Africa in the 1890s. While a young girl, she grew up hearing the travel stories of her father and elder brother, both of whom voyaged to regions considered "exotic" by Europeans at the time. A small inheritance she received from her parents' after their deaths, allowed her to make two voyages to Africa in 1893 and 1895. Influenced by her uncle, Charles, a celebrated scientist, she collected specimens of African fish from the Niger and Congo rivers, previously unknown to Europeans, to bring back to Britain for scientific study. For her journey, she relied heavily on the African guides who accompanied her, but she did seek opportunities for direct encounters with Africans so as to learn about their customs and way of life. Along the way, she often stayed with European missionaries. She published her account of these voyages in Britain in 1897, based on the notebooks she compiled during the two trips. At the turn of the century, Kingsley went back to Africa as a nurse in the South Africa Boer War. During the war, she fell ill and died. In these excerpts, she discusses the region around the French colony of Lembarene and then, more generally, the region of Western Africa.

Source: Mary Kingsley, *Travels in West Africa* (London: Macmillan and Company, 1897), 101-123; and Mary Kingsley, "Life in West Africa" lecture in the Sunday Afternoon Course at the South Place Institute, Finsbury, between 1895-1898 in *British Empire Series II*, 366-380; reprinted in *Women's Voices on Africa: A Century of Travel Writings*, ed. Patricia W. Romero (New York: Markus Wiener Publishing, 1992), 56-67, 60, 65-70.

Focus Questions:

1. What African customs and traditions does Kingsley discuss? What does she say about them? How does her own background and perspective inform her views?
2. How does Kingsley view the efforts and goals of European missionaries in the region?
3. To what extent does Kingsley question imperial views, and to what extent does she embrace them?

Then in addition to the store work, a fruitful source of work and worry are the schools, for both boys and girls. It is regarded as futile to attempt to get any real hold over the children unless they are removed from the influence of the country fashions that surround them in their village homes; therefore the schools are boarding; hence the entire care of the children, including feeding and clothing, falls on the missionary.

The French government has made things harder by decreeing that the children should be taught French. It does not require that evangelistic work should be carried on in French, but that if foreign languages are taught, that language shall be French first. The general feeling of the missionaries is against this, because of the great difficulty in teaching the native this delicate and highly complex language. English, the Africans pick up sooner than any foreign language. I do not like to think that my esteemed friend Donna Maria de Sousa Coutinho is right in saying "because it is so much more like their own savage tongue," but regard this facility in acquiring it to the universal use of it in the form of trade English in the villages round them. Indeed, I believe that if the missionary was left alone he would not teach any European language, but confine himself to using the native languages in his phonetically written-down form; because the Africans learn to read this very quickly, and the missionary can confine their reading to those books he thinks suitable for perusal by his flock— namely, the Bible, hymn-book, and Bunyan's Holy War.

The native does not see things in this light, and half the time comes to the schools only to learn, what he calls "sense" i.e., white man's ways and language, which will enable him to trade with greater advantage. Still, I think the French government is right, from what I have seen in our own possessions of the disadvantage, expense and inconvenience of the bulk of the governed not knowing the language of their governors, both parties having therefore frequently to depend on native interpreters: and native interpreters are "deceitful above all things and desperately wicked" occasionally, and the just administration of the country under these conditions is almost impossible....

But to return to the Mission Évangélique schools. This mission does not undertake technical instruction. All the training the boys get is religious and scholastic. The girls fare somewhat better, for they get in addition instruction from the mission ladies in sewing, washing, and ironing, and for the rest of it they have an uncommonly pleasant and easy time which they most bitterly regret as past when they go to their husbands, for husbands they each of them have.

The teaching even of sewing, washing, and ironing is a little previous. Good Mme. Jacot will weary herself for months to teach a Fan girl how to make herself a dress, and the girl will learn eagerly, and so keenly enjoy the dress when it is made that it breaks one's heart when one knows that this same girl, when her husband takes her to his village soon, in spite of the two dresses the mission gave her, will be reduced to a bit of filthy rag, which will serve her for dress, sheet, towel and dish cloth: for even were her husband willing to get her more cloth to exercise her dressmaking accomplishments on, he dare not. Men are men, and women are women all the world over; and what would his other wives, and his mother and sisters say? Then the washing and ironing are quite parlour accomplishments when your husband does not wear a shirt, and household linen is non-existent as is the case among the Fans and many other African tribes. There are other things that the women might be taught with greater advantage to them and those round them.

It is strange that all the cooks employed by the Europeans should be men, yet all the cooking among the natives themselves is done by women, and done abominably badly in all the Bantu tribes I have ever come across; and the Bantu are in this particular, and indeed in most particulars, far inferior to the true Negro; though I must say this is not the orthodox view. The Negroes cook uniformly very well, and at moments are inspired in the direction of palm-oil chop and fish cooking. Not so the Bantu, whose methods cry aloud for improvement, they having just the very easiest and laziest way possible of dealing with food.

* * *

Now polygamy is, like most other subjects, a difficult thing to form an opinion on, if, before forming that opinion, you go and make a study of the facts and bearings of the case. It is therefore advisable to follow the usual method employed by the majority of people. Just take a prejudice of your own, and fix it up with the so-called opinions of people who go in for that sort of prejudice too.

This method is absolutely essential to the forming of an opinion on the subject of polygamy among African tribes, that will be acceptable in enlightened circles. Polygamy is the institution which above all others governs the daily life of the native; and it is therefore the one which the missionaries who enter into this daily life, and not merely into the mercantile and legal, as do the trader and the government official, are constantly confronted with and hindered by. All the missionaries have set their faces against it and deny Church membership to those men who practise it; whereby it falls out that many men are excluded from the fold who would make quite as good Christians as those within it.

* * *

briefly I will say that I consider the African fails in enthusiasm, in power of combination, and in that restless desire for wealth and conquest, not conquest over the next-door tribe only, but conquest over the very powers of Nature themselves that characterise our race. He looks at things white men do, not with that awe usually credited to him; he thinks our things are queer, possibly dangerous, not necessarily desirable in every case, he soon gets used to them, and learns how to manage them, but he does not bother his head to make himself some like them; his imitation of white men's way is founded on a feeling that white men are big men, and he would like to be a big man too in a way, but it is a feeling more akin to vanity than akin to emulation; that it has not been a sound ground to build on has been amply shown by the effects of the treatment of Africans by the white man, a subject I will next briefly mention by saying I think we may safely assume both sides have been to blame. There are two things that the white is most virulently abused for by moralists, the slave trade and the liquor traffic, while the most common forms of criticism on the black is that he is an indolent brute, a fiendish savage or a child—irresponsible, ungrateful, lying, thievish, and so on, are thrown in on top as remarks by the way on his character.

* * *

If the African were a flighty-minded fiend, a lazy brute, or a child, the methods now in force, and that have been in force all these years, would have succeeded. In spite of all the noble and devoted lives laid down, in spite of all the blood and money, they have not. That he is not a fiend the African has shown by his treatment of Livingstone, Thompson. Barth, and a hundred others, least amongst whom am I; that he is not a child he has shown clearly to those who have traded with him, and by the individual Africans who have risen to a higher culture level under European and Asiatic education. I am aware that the educated African is said to invariably go fanttee, as it is called up here, and this picturesque and thrilling conduct of the educated African is supported by a few instances. But I need hardly assure you it is not the invariable custom; and there have been in the past and there are now living dozens of Europeanised Africans in West Africa, ministers, lawyers, and doctors, who would no more want to take off their store clothing and go cannibalising and howling about the bush than you would. Nevertheless, the African who turns into a Europeanised man is the exception that proves the rule, and whose isolated conduct misleads the white man, inducing him to go on on this old line, dazzled by the performance of one in a hundred thousand; we seem blind to the inertia of the great mass, that great mass that we have to deal with today in a state practically unaltered by the white work of four hundred years' duration.

Now I have said I would give a suggestion for the solution of this problem, and I humbly give it—it is, understand the nature of the African. If any of you want to make a great piece of machinery, or build a bridge, or a house, you succeed in your endeavour primarily from a knowledge of the nature of the materials you employ, and so you may succeed in dealing with the African if you will clear your mind of all prejudice and study what is the nature of man. Take him at his lowest. To my mind he is the most magnificent mass of labour material in the world, and he is, taken as a whole, one of the most generous, kindly, good-tempered races of men on earth: intellectually he is at any rate shrewd, and, strange to say, possessed of an immense wealth of practical common sense. Surely that is good stuff to go on, surely something ought to be done with it more economically and more humanely than is being done; . . . .

The nature of the African thought-form in the region, therefore, between the Niger and the Congo, is the thing I have devoted my time to, recognising that with him his religion—his conception of the status of Man in Nature, is the ruling thing of his life and action; for whether he be altered by outside influence or no, the African can never say, "Oh, one must be practical, you know! That's all right from a religious point of view, but one must be practical." To be practical, to get on in this world, the African must be right from his religious point of view all the time, therefore to understand him you must understand that religious point of view to its very root, and go and study it in an unadulterated form.

The thing is worth taking up alike for humane as well as scientific reasons; though it is difficult, one has no right to dwell on its danger. No one need go out to West Africa without knowing the chances are they go out there to stay, and even if they should go out in ignorance, on landing they will be enlightened, and can take the next boat home. I remember on my first landing at a place where there are three small factories only, but which I had seen marked large on a map, asking a resident white if this was all the settlement. "Oh no," said he, "this is only the porter's lodge, I'll show you the settlement," and he took me to the cemetery; that cemetery justified the large lettering on the map. But settlements, even with the best of cemetery accommodation, are not the ethnologist's place: he must go right away into the fastnesses of the forest, sit and gossip at village fires, become the confidential friend of witch doctors and old ladies, and he must go alone without an armed expedition which will wall him off from the residential African. This sort of life he can comparatively easily lead, if he will learn the trade details of the locality sufficiently to enable him to pass as a trader; in the wildest districts he is reasonable to the African mind if he appears in this guise, and he is safer than he has any right to expect to be under the circumstances, and the amount of information he can pick up is immense, only, alas! that information is not arranged in a manner suitable for use in schools. Nevertheless, it is worth having. In past days, when Africa was left to the Europeans out there and the natives, the collection of ethnological information had merely a scientific and philosophic interest; now it has a greater one, for now European governments are undertaking to legislate domestically for the African from European offices. They cannot do this thing successfully unless they have in their possession a full knowledge of the nature of the people they are legislating for; without this, let their intentions be of the best, they will waste a grievous mass of blood and money, and fail in the end.

Raden Ayu Kartini, *Letters of a Javanese Princess*

The Dutch colonized the island of Java (now a part of Indonesia), beginning in the late sixteenth century, claiming a series of islands in the Pacific Ocean, as the Dutch East Indies. Raden Ayu Kartini (1879-1904), a Javanese aristocrat, grew up exposed to both Javanese Muslim traditions as well as European cultural influences. Her father served as a regent (regional governor) working with the Dutch colonial government in the city of Japara, he was an educated man who spoke Dutch fluently. Kartini received a primary education based on Javanese and Western intellectual traditions. She then secured a scholarship to continue her education in Holland, but her parents opposed the plan. During this period, in 1899, Kartini started writing letters to several different correspondents in Europe. The exchange of letters eased her sense of isolation, as in Javanese culture, it was improper for her, as an upper-class single woman, to venture out alone in public. She wrote regularly to Rosa Abendanon-Maudri, the wife of a high level Dutch colonial official who had been Kartini's tutor and mentor while she and her husband were stationed in Japara. Kartini also wrote to Stella Zeehandelaar, a Dutch feminist and reformer, whom Kartini found through an announcement, advertising for a "pen-pal" that she placed in a Dutch newspaper. By 1903, Kartini decided to abandon her plans to study in Holland and to stay in Java. She agreed to a marriage, which according to tradition her parents arranged, with a Javanese man who was the regent in Rembang. As a married woman, she was allowed more freedom to pursue many of her goals, including founding a vocational school for Javanese girls. Kartini died prematurely in 1904, from complications during childbirth. Her letters, which spanned from 1899 to 1904, were first published in Europe, in

Dutch, in 1911. In 1920, a new, expanded English language edition was published in London, with the title *Letters of a Javanese Princess*. The following is an excerpt from Kartini's letter, dated January, 12 1900, to Stella Zeehandelaar.

Source: Raden Ajeng Kartini, *Letters of a Javanese Princess*, trans. Agnes Louise Symmers (New York: Alfred A. Knopf, 1920), 39-44; reprinted in *The Global Experience: Readings in World History*, eds. Stuart B. Schwartz, et al., (New York: Addison Wesley Longman, 1997), 193-194.

FOCUS QUESTIONS:

1. What does this passage tell us about the relationship between education and imperialism? About language and imperialism?
2. What ideas and perspectives inform Kartini's views? How does her background affect her perceptions of colonial society in Java?
3. What does Kartini tell us about Dutch relations with and views of the Javanese, and about colonial societies in general?

I shall relate to you the history of a gifted and educated Javanese. The boy had passed his examinations, and was number one in one of three principal high schools of Java. Both at Semarang, where he went to school, and at Batavia, where he stood his examinations, time doors of the best houses were open to the amiable school-boy, with his agreeable and cultivated manners and great modesty.

Every one spoke Dutch to him, and he could express himself in that language with distinction. Fresh from this environment, he went back to the house of his parents. He thought it would be proper to pay his respects to the authorities of the place and he found himself in the presence of the Resident who had heard of him, and here it was that my friend made a mistake. He dared to address the great man in Dutch.

The following morning notice of an appointment as clerk to a comptroller in the mountains was sent to him. There the young man must remain to think over his "misdeeds" and forget all that he had learned at the schools. After some years a new comptroller or possibly assistant comptroller came; then the measure of his misfortunes was made to overflow. The new chief was a former school-fellow, one who had never shone through his abilities. The young man who had led his classes in everything must now creep upon the ground before the onetime dunce, and speak always high Javanese to him, while he himself was answered in bad Malay. Can you understand the misery of a proud and independent spirit so humbled? And how much strength of character it must have taken to endure that petty and annoying oppression?

But at last he could stand it no longer, he betook himself to Batavia and asked his excellency the Governor General for an audience; it was granted him. The result was that he was sent to Preanger, with a commission to make a study of the rice culture there. He made himself of service through the translation of a pamphlet on the cultivation of water crops from Dutch into Javanese and Sudanese. The government presented him in acknowledgement with several hundred guilders. In the comptroller's school at Batavia, a teacher's place was vacant—a teacher of the Javanese language be it understood—and his friends (among the Javanese) did all in their power to secure this position for him, but without result. It was an absurd idea for a Native to have European pupils who later might become ruling government officials. Perish the thought! I should like to ask who could teach Javanese better than a born Javanese?

The young man went back to his dwelling place; in the meantime another Resident had come, and the talented son of the brown race might at last become an assistant wedono.* Not for nothing had he been banished for years to that distant place. He had learned wisdom there; namely, that one cannot serve a European official better than by creeping in the dust before him, and by never speaking a single word of Dutch in his presence. Others have now come into power, and lately when the position of translator of the Javanese language became vacant it was offered to our friend (truly opportunely) now that he does not stand in any one's way!

Stella, I know an Assistant Resident, who speaks Malay with a Regent, although he knows that the latter speaks good Dutch. Every one else converses confidentially with this native ruler but the Assistant Resident—never.

My brothers speak in high Javanese to their superiors, who answer them in Dutch or in Malay. Those who speak Dutch to them are our personal friends; several of whom have asked my brothers to speak to them in the Dutch language, but they prefer not to do it, and Father also never does. The boys and Father know all too well why they must hold to the general usage.

There is too much idle talk about the word "prestige," through the imaginary dignity of the under officials. I do not bother about prestige. I am only amused at the manner in which they preserve their prestige over us Javanese.

Sometimes I cannot suppress a smile. It is distinctly diverting to see the great men try to inspire us with awe. I had to bite my lips to keep from laughing outright when I was on a journey not long ago, and saw an Assistant Resident go from his office to his house under the shade of a gold umbrella, which a servant held spread above his noble head. It was such a ridiculous spectacle! Heavens! If he only knew how the humble crowds who respectfully retreated to one side before the glittering sunshade, immediately his back was turned, burst out laughing.

There are many, yes very many Government officials, who allow the native rulers to kiss their feet, and their knees. Kissing the foot is the highest token of respect that we Javanese can show to our parents, or elderly blood relatives, and to our own rulers. We do not find it pleasant to do this for strangers; no, the European makes himself ridiculous in our eyes whenever he demands from us those tokens of respect to which our own rulers alone have the right.

It is a matter of indifference when Residents and Assistant Residents allow themselves to be called "Kandjeng," but when overseers, railroad engineers (and perhaps tomorrow, station-masters too) allow themselves to be thus addressed by their servants, it is absurdly funny. Do these people really know what Kandjeng means?

It is a title that the natives give to their hereditary rulers. I used to think that it was only natural for the stupid Javanese to love all this flim-flam, but now I see that the civilized, enlightened Westerner is not averse to it, that he is daft about it.

I never allow women older than I to show all the prescribed ceremonies to me, even though I know they would gladly, for though I am so young, I am a scion of what they consider an ancient, noble and honoured house; for which in the past, they have poured out both blood and gold in large measure. It is strange how attached inferiors are to those above them. But to me, it goes against the grain when people older than I creep in the dust before me.

With heavy hearts, many Europeans here see how the Javanese, whom, they regard as their inferiors, are slowly awakening, but at every turn a brown man comes up, who shows that he has just as good brains in his head, and a just as good heart in his body, as the white man.

But we are going forward, and they cannot hold back the current of time. I love the Hollanders very, very much, and I am grateful for everything that we have gained through them. Many of them are among our best friends, but there are also others who dislike us, for no other reason than we are bold enough to emulate them in education and culture.

In many subtle ways they make us feel their dislike. "I am a European, you are a Javanese," they seem to say, or "I am the master, you the governed." Not once, but many times, they speak to us in broken Malay; although they know very well that we understand the Dutch language. It would be a matter of indifference to me in what language they addressed us, if the tone were only polite. Not long ago, a Raden Ajoe was talking to a gentleman, and impulsively she said, "Sir, excuse me, but may I make a friendly request, please, speak to me in your own language. I understand and speak Malay very well, but alas, only high Malay. I do not understand this passer-Malay." How our gentleman hung his head!

Why do many Hollanders find it unpleasant to converse with us in their own language? Oh yes, now I understand; Dutch is too beautiful to be spoken by a brown mouth.

A few days ago we paid a visit to Totokkers (Europeans who are new-comers in Java). Their domestics were old servants of ours, and we knew that they could speak and understand Dutch very well. I told the host this, and what answer did I receive from my gentleman? "No, they must not speak Dutch." "No, why?" I asked. "Because natives ought not to know Dutch." I looked at him in amazement, and a satirical smile quivered at the corners of my mouth. The gentleman grew fiery red, mumbled something into his beard, and discovered something interesting in his boots, at least he devoted all of his attention to them.

Jules Ferry, from *Le Tonkin et la Mere-Patrie*

Jules Ferry (1832–1893) was a French statesman, holding at different times several ministerial positions and the premiership in the Republican governments of 1879–1885. He is best known for removing the Catholic Church from any significant role in French education, and for initiating the most aggressive period of French colonialist expansion in the 19th century. France established possessions in Africa and above all in Indochina (Tonkin was the northernmost part of Vietnam, gained as a French colony by treaty with the Qing Empire in 1885). Colonialism met some opposition, and the passages below from Ferry's book *Le Tonkin et la Mere-Patrie* defend the policy.

Source: J. Megan Greene, trans., Jules Ferry, *Le Tonkin et la Mere-Patrie* (Paris: Victor-Havard, 1890), pp. 40– 43.

Focus Questions:

1. What are Ferry's chief reasons for promoting colonial expansion? What does his analysis assume about the state of world economics?
2. What consequences does Ferry predict for European countries should they not expand their markets through colonialism? What political views might he be influenced by in making this prediction?
3. Note the phrases "where the culture of the land is condemned to support industrialization" and "the industrial life, has sent the entire Occident...on a slope that cannot be climbed back up." Does Ferry seem happy about industrialization? Why might he view it as a problem demanding rational policy reactions rather than as "progress"?

Colonial policy is the daughter of industrial policy. For rich states, where capital abounds and accumulates rapidly, where the manufacturing regime is on the path of continual growth, attracting to itself if not the majority, at least the most awake and lively among the population of manual workers, where the culture of the land is condemned to support industrialization, exports are an essential factor in public prosperity, and the use of capital, like the demand for work, is measured by the size of foreign markets. If there could be established among manufacturing nations something along the lines of a division of industrial labor, a methodical and rational allocation of industry according to ability and the economic, natural, and social conditions of the different producing countries—placing here the cotton and metallurgy industries, reserving for one alcohol and sugar, and for another wool and silk—Europe would not have to look beyond its own borders for outlets for its products. It was with this ideal in mind that they made the treaties of 1860. But today, everyone wants to spin and weave, forge and distill. All of Europe manufactures sugar in excess and wishes to export it. The arrival on the scene of the latest comers to industrialism—the US on the one hand, Germany on the other, the advent of the small states, of sleepy and lazy people, of the regenerated Italy, of Spain enriched by French capital, and of Switzerland, so enterprising and informed—to the industrial life, has sent the entire Occident, except for Russia, which is still preparing and growing, on a slope that cannot be climbed back up.

From the other side of the Vosges, as from beyond the Atlantic, the protection system has multiplied manufactures, suppressed old outlets, and thrust on the European market a formidable competition. To defend one's perimeters by raising barriers is something, but it is not enough. Mister Torrens has well demonstrated, in his good book on the colonization of Australia, that a growth in manufacturing capital, if it is not accompanied by a proportional expansion of outlets abroad, will produce, simply through domestic competition, a general lowering of prices, profits, and wages. (Torrens, Colonisation of South Australia).

The protection system is a steam engine without a safety valve if it doesn't have as a corrective and a back up a healthy and serious colonial policy. An excess of capital committed to industry tends not only to diminish the profits of capital, it stops the rise of wages, even though that [rising wages] is a natural law and beneficial to modern societies. And that is not an abstract law, but a phenomenon made of flesh and blood, of passion and will, that moves, complains, and defends itself. Preservation of social harmony is, in humanity's industrial age, a question of outlets. The economic crisis that has weighed so heavily on the European working class since 1876 or 1877, the malaise that has followed it, of which frequent, long, and often ill advised, but always formidable strikes are the most painful symptoms, coincided in France, Germany, and England with a notable and persistent reduction in exports. Europe is like a busi-ness that wants, after a certain number of years, to diminish its sales revenue. European consumption is saturated and it [Europe] must now conjure up from other parts of the globe new groups of consumers or suffer the penalty of bankrupting modern society and preparing for the dawn of the twentieth century a social cataclysm of which we cannot know how to calculate the consequences.

PART 6

The Modern World
(1914 – Present)

CHAPTER 24

World War I

The Balfour Declaration

To enlist Jewish support for the war, British Foreign Secretary Arthur James Balfour wrote the following letter to Lord Rothschild, a prominent Jewish leader, and had it printed in *The Times*. The letter contains the official statement that soon became known as the Balfour Declaration.

Source: From *The Times* (London), November 9, 1917.

FOCUS QUESTIONS:

1. Why did the British government wait until 1917 to publicly support the desire of the Jewish people for a state?
2. What are the contemporary implications of Lord Balfour's statement: "...it being clearly understood that nothing shall be done which may prejudice the civil and religious rights of existing non-Jewish communities in Palestine"?

Foreign Office
November 2nd, 1917

Dear Lord Rothschild:

I have much pleasure in conveying to you, on behalf of His Majesty's Government, the following declaration of sympathy with Jewish Zionist aspirations which has been submitted to, and approved by, the Cabinet:

His Majesty's Government view with favor the establishment in Palestine of a national home for the Jewish people, and will use their best endeavors to facilitate the achievement of this object, it being clearly understood that nothing shall be done which may prejudice the civil and religious rights of existing non-Jewish communities in Palestine, or the rights and political status enjoyed by Jews in any other country.

I should be grateful if you would bring this declaration to the knowledge of the Zionist Federation.

Yours,
Arthur James Balfour

Sir Henry McMahon, Letter to Ali Ibn Husain 1915

Sir Henry McMahon, the British high commissioner in Egypt, and Ali Ibn Husain, the sherif of Mecca, exchanged ten letters from 1915 to 1916. The following excerpt from a letter written October 24, 1915, shows Britain's aim—to enlist Arab support against Britain's enemy Turkey in return for hints of British support of an independent Arab state.

Source: From Great Britain, *Parliamentary Papers,* 1939, Misc. No. 3, Cmd. 5957.

Focus Questions:

1. Do the suggestions made in the McMahon letter provide a perspective on the contemporary political problems in the Middle East?
2. Did the British government have the legal and moral authority to promise the birth of an Arab state?

As for those regions lying within those frontiers wherein Great Britain is free to act without detriment to the interests of her ally, France, I am empowered in the name of the Government of Great Britain to give the following assurances and make the following reply to your letter:

1. Subject to the above modifications, Great Britain is prepared to recognise and support the independence of the Arabs in all the regions within the limits demanded by the Sherif of Mecca.
2. Great Britain will guarantee the Holy Places against all external aggression and will recognise their inviolability.
3. When the situation admits, Great Britain will give to the Arabs her advice and will assist them to establish what may appear to be the most suitable forms of government in those various territories.

4. On the other hand, it is understood that the Arabs have decided to seek the advice and guidance of Great Britain only, and that such European advisers and officials as may be required for the formation of a sound form of administration will be British.

5. With regard to the vilayets [provinces] of Bagdad and Basra, the Arabs will recognise that the established position and interests of Great Britain necessitate special administrative arrangements in order to secure these territories from foreign aggression, to promote the welfare of the local populations and to safeguard our mutual economic interests.

I am convinced that this declaration will assure you beyond all possible doubt of the sympathy of Great Britain towards the aspirations of her friends the Arabs and will result in a firm and lasting alliance, the immediate results of which will be the expulsion of the Turks from the Arab countries and the freeing of the Arab peoples from the Turkish yoke, which for so many years has pressed heavily upon them.

Siegfried Sassoon, "They"

Siegfried Sasson (1886-1967) grew up in Britain and attended Clare College in Cambridge before moving to London where he frequented literary circles. In 1914 with the start of the war, he became a British infantry officer, fighting in the trenches of the western front. His almost reckless fearlessness in early battles earned him the nickname "Mad Jack." His view of the war began to shift, however, after he was shot and wounded in battle. He began to view the war as one of aggression and conquest, rather than defensive. His writings describe in stark detail the brutality and ravages of war. Sassoon survived the war and later published two memoirs based on his experiences. His poem "They" presents two very opposing visions of the nature and impact of war.

Source: Siegfried Sasson,"They" *The Norton Anthology of English Literature,* ed. M. H. Abrams, vol. 2 (New York: Oxford University Press, 1993), 1832.

Focus Questions:

1. Who and what does Sassoon criticize in this poem?
2. According to this poem what was the impact of the war for soldiers who survived it?
3. What does the poem tell us about attitudes and debates regarding World War I and its aftermath?

They

The Bishop tells us: "when the boys come back
They will not be the same; for they'll have fought
In a just cause: they lead the last attack
On Anti-Christ; their comrades' blood has bought
New right to breed an honourable race,
They have challenged Death and dared him face to face."

"We're none of us the same!" the boys reply.
"For George lost both his legs; and Bill's stone blind;
Poor Jim's shot through the lungs and like to die;
And Bert's gone syphilitic: you'll not find
A chap who's served that hasn't found *some* change."
And the Bishop said: "The ways of God are strange!"
Oct. 31, 1916

Isaac Rosenberg, "Dead Man's Dump"

Isaac Rosenberg (1890-1918) grew up first in Bristol, and then in London. At fourteen years old he became an apprentice in an engraving and art publishing firm. Working during the day, he attended art school in the evenings with the goal of becoming a painter. In this same period, he also began to write poetry. In 1912, he published the first his several short collections poetry *Night and Day*. After the war broke out, he enlisted in the army. In April of 1918, he died in battle. After his death, the poems he wrote about the war gained popular and critical acclaim with his clear, direct language and haunting imagery. His poem "Dead Man's Dump" depicts the carnage of a World War I battlefield.

Source: Isaac Rosenberg "Dead Man's Dump," *The Norton Anthology of English Literature*, ed. M. H. Abrams, vol. 2 (New York: Oxford University Press, 1993), 1907.

Focus Questions:

1. How does Rosenberg describe war and the affects of war? What is the significance of the title of the poem?
2. How did Rosenberg's view and portrayal of war different from the previous authors (27.3 and 27.4)?
3. What does this poem tell us about World War I?

The plunging limbers[1] over the shattered track
Racketed with their rusty freight,
Stuck out like many crowns of thorns,
And the rusty stakes like scepters old
To stay the flood of brutish men
Upon our brothers dear.

The wheels lurched over sprawled dead
But pained them not, though their bones crunched,
Their shut mouths made no moan.
They lie there huddled, friend and foeman
Man born of man, and born of woman,
And shells go crying over them
From night till night and now.

Earth has waited for them,
All the time of their growth
Fretting for their decay:
Now she has them at last!
In the strength of their strength
Suspended-stopped and held.

What fierce imaginings their dark souls lit?
Earth! have they gone into you?
Somewhere they must have gone,
And flung on your hard back
Is their soul's sack,

Emptied of God-ancestralled essences.
Who hurled them out? Who hurled?

None saw their spirits' shadow shake the grass,
Or stood aside for the half-used life to pass
Out of those doomed nostrils and the doomed mouth,
When the swift iron burning bee
Drained the wild honey of their youth.

What of us who, flung on the shrieking pyre,
Walk, our usual thoughts untouched,
Our lucky limbs as on ichor[2] fed,
Immortal seeming ever?

1 Two-wheeled vehicles for pulling guns or caissons.
2 In Greek mythology, the ethereal fluid that flowed in the veins of the gods.

Perhaps when the flames beat loud on us,
A fear may choke in our veins
And the startled blood may stop.

The air is loud with death,
The dark air spurts with fire,
The explosions ceaseless are.
Timelessly now, some minutes past,
These dead strode time with vigorous life,
Till the shrapnel called "An end!"
But not to all. In bleeding pangs
Some borne on stretchers dreamed of home,
Dear things, war-blotted from their hearts.

A man's brains splattered on
A stretcher-bearer's face;
His shook shoulders slipped their load,
But when they bent to look again
The drowning soul was sunk too deep
For human tenderness.

They left this dead with the older dead,
Stretched at the crossroads.

Burnt black by strange decay
Their sinister faces like;
The lid over each eye,
The grass and coloured clay
More motion have than they,
Joined to the great sunk silences.

Here is one not long dead;
His dark hearing caught our far wheels,
And the choked soul stretched weak hands
To reach the living word the far wheels said,
The blood-dazed intelligence beating for light,
Crying through the suspense of the far torturing wheels
Swift for the end to break.

Or the wheels to break,
Cried as the tide of the world broke over his sight.
Will they come? Will they ever come?

Even as the mixed hoofs of the mules,
The quivering-bellied mules,
And the rushing wheels all mixed
With his tortured upturned sight.
So we crashed round the bend,
We heard his weak scream,
We heard his very last sound,
And our wheels grazed his dead face.
1917 1922

Woodrow Wilson, *"Speech on the Fourteen Points,"* 1918

On January 8, 1918, U.S. President Woodrow Wilson, speaking before a joint session of Congress, put forth his Fourteen Points proposal for ending the war. In this speech, he established the basis of a peace treaty and the foundation of a League of Nations.

Source: Fourteen Points Speech, by Woodrow Wilson, 1918 (National Archives and Records Administration).

Focus Questions:

1. What was the political impact of the Fourteen Points on the peoples living under colonial rule? Was Wilson's idea of self-determination for colonial peoples to decide their own fate?
2. An underlying assumption of the Fourteen Points is that America should use its power to ensure that the world "be made fit and safe to live in." Is this the proper policy of the United States? Why? Why not?

We entered this war because violations of right had occurred which touched us to the quick and made the life of our own people impossible unless they were corrected and the world secured once and for all against their recurrence. What we demand in this war, therefore, is nothing peculiar to ourselves. It is that the world be made fit and safe to live in; and particularly that it be made safe for every peace-loving nation which, like our own, wishes to live its own life, determine its own institutions, be assured of justice and fair dealing by the other peoples of the world as against force and selfish aggression. All the peoples of the world are in effect partners in this interest, and for our own part we see very clearly that unless justice be done to others it will not be done to us. The programme of the world's peace, therefore, is our programme; and that programme, the only possible programme, as we see it, is this:

I. Open covenants of peace, openly arrived at, after which there shall be no private international understanding of any kind but diplomacy shall proceed always frankly and in the public view.

II. Absolute freedom of navigation upon the seas, outside territorial waters, alike in peace and in war, except as the seas may be closed in whole or in part by international action for the enforcement of international covenants.

III. The removal, so far as possible, of all economic barriers and the establishment of an equality of trade conditions among all the nations consenting to the peace and associating themselves for its maintenance.

IV. Adequate guarantees given and taken that national armaments will be reduced to the lowest point consistent with domestic safety.

V. A free, open-minded, and absolutely impartial adjustment of all colonial claims, based upon a strict observance of the principle that in determining all such questions of sovereignty the interests of the populations concerned must have equal weight with the equitable claims of the government whose title is to be determined.

VI. The evacuation of all Russian territory and such a settlement of all questions affecting Russia as will secure the best and freest cooperation of the other nations of the world in obtaining for her an unhampered and unembarrassed opportunity for the independent determination of her own political development and national policy and assure her a sincere welcome into the society of free nations under institutions of her own choosing; and, more than a welcome, assistance also of every kind that she may need and may herself desire. The treatment accorded Russia by her sister nations in the months to come will be the acid test of their good will, of their comprehension of her needs as distinguished from their own interests, and of their intelligent and unselfish sympathy.

VII. Belgium, the whole world will agree, must be evacuated and restored, without any attempt to limit the sovereignty which she enjoys in common with all other free nations. No other single act will serve as this will serve to restore confidence among the nations in the laws which they have themselves set and determined for the government of their relations with one another. Without this healing act the whole structure and validity of international law is forever impaired.

VIII. All French territory should be freed and the invaded portions restored, and the wrong done to France by Prussia in 1871 in the matter of Alsace-Lorraine, which has unsettled the peace of the world for nearly fifty years, should be righted, in order that peace may once more be made secure in the interest of all.

IX. A readjustment of the frontiers of Italy should be effected along clearly recognizable lines of nationality.

X. The peoples of Austria-Hungary, whose place among the nations we wish to see safeguarded and assured, should be accorded the freest opportunity of autonomous development.

XI. Rumania, Serbia, and Montenegro should be evacuated; occupied territories restored; Serbia accorded free and secure access to the sea; and the relations of the several Balkan states to one another determined by friendly counsel along historically established lines of allegiance and nationality; and international guarantees of the political and economic independence and territorial integrity of the several Balkan states should be entered into.

XII. The Turkish portions of the present Ottoman Empire should be assured a secure sovereignty, but the other nationalities which are now under Turkish rule should be assured an undoubted security of life and an absolutely unmolested opportunity of autonomous development, and the Dardanelles should be permanently opened as a free passage to the ships and commerce of all nations under international guarantees.

XIII. An independent Polish state should be erected which should include the territories inhabited by indisputably Polish populations, which should be assured a free and secure access to the sea, and whose political and economic independence and territorial integrity should be guaranteed by international covenant.

XIV. A general association of nations must be formed under specific covenants for the purpose of affording mutual guarantees of political independence and territorial integrity to great and small states alike.

International Congress of Women, "Manifesto"

When World War I began, most of the women's associations involved in the women's suffrage and rights movements, put their efforts on hold and redirected their energies to supporting their countries in the war effort. As the war dragged on, however, a small yet vocal minority of women actively worked, both individually and through larger organizations, for peace. In 1915, a group of women from European countries as well as the United States, toured through Europe as representatives of the International Congress of Women. The tour of Europe resulted from an earlier meeting, held in the Netherlands (The Hague), some months before their tour began. Jane Addams (1860-1935), an American, was the head of the organization in this period. During their tour of Europe, the women met with political leaders to discuss peace initiatives and push for an end to the war. After their tour, the representatives traveled to the US and drafted a manifesto for peace, which is excerpted below.

Source: "Manifesto by the Envoys of the International Congress of Women at The Hague to the Governments of Europe and the President of the United States," in Jane Addams, Emily G. Balch, and Alice Hamilton *Women at the Hague: The International Congress of Women and Its Results, by* (New York: Macmillian, 1915), 160-166; reprinted in *Women, The Family, and Freedom: The Debate in Documents, vol. I: 1750-1880,* ed. Susan Groag Bell and Karen M. Offen (Stanford: Stanford University Press, 1983), 267-269.

Focus Questions:

1. What strategies and arguments did these women employ in an effort to further peace?
2. What was the relationship between the movements for expanded rights for women and this peace movement, led by women?
3. What ideas, beliefs, and events provide a context for this appeal for peace?

Here in America, on neutral soil, far removed from the stress of the conflict we, the envoys to the Governments from the International Congress of Women at The Hague, have come together to canvass the results of our missions. We put forth this statement as our united and deliberate conclusions.

At a time when the foreign offices of the great belligerents have been barred to each other, and the public mind of Europe has been fixed on the war offices for leadership, we have gone from capital to capital and conferred with the civil governments.

Our mission was to place before belligerent and neutral alike the resolutions of the International Congress of Women held at The Hague in April; especially to place before them the definite method of a conference of neutral nations as an agency of continuous mediation for the settlement of the war.

To carry out this mission two delegations were appointed, which included women of Great Britain, Hungary, Italy, the Netherlands, Sweden, and the United States. One or other of these delegations were received by the governments in fourteen capitals, Berlin, Berne, Budapest, Christiania, Copenhagen, The Hague, Havre (Belgian Government), London, Paris, Petrograd, Rome, Stockholm, Vienna, and Washington. We were received by the Prime Ministers and Foreign Ministers of the Powers, by the King of Norway, by the Presidents of Switzerland and of the United States, by the Pope and the Cardinal Secretary of State. In many capitals more than one audience was given, not merely to present our resolutions, but for a thorough discussion. In addition to the thirty-five governmental visits we met—everywhere—members of parliaments and other leaders of public opinion.

We heard much the same words spoken in Downing Street as those spoken in Wilhelmstrasse, in Vienna, as in Petrograd, in Budapest, as in the Havre, where the Belgians have their temporary government.

Our visits to the war capitals convinced us that the belligerent Governments would not be opposed to a conference of neutral nations; that while the belligerents have rejected offers of mediation by single neutral nations, and while no belligerent could ask for mediation, the creation of a continuous conference of neutral nations might provide the machinery which would lead to peace. We found that the neutrals on the other hand were concerned, lest calling such a conference might be considered inopportune by one or other of the belligerents. Here our information from the belligerents themselves gave assurance that such initiative would not be resented. "My country would not find anything unfriendly in such action by the neutrals," was the assurance given us by the foreign Minister of one of the great belligerents. "My Government would place no obstacle in the way of its institution," said the Minister of an opposing nation. "What are the neutrals waiting for?" said a third, whose name ranks high not only in his own country, but all over the world.

It remained to put this clarifying intelligence before the neutral countries. As a result the plan of starting mediation through the agency of a continuous conference of the neutral nations is to-day being seriously discussed alike in the Cabinets of the belligerent and neutral countries of Europe and in the press of both.

We are in a position to quote some of the expressions of men high in the councils of the great nations as to the feasibility of the plan. "You are right," said one Minister, "that it would be of the greatest importance to finish the fight by early negotiation rather than by further military efforts, which would result in more and more destruction and irreparable loss." "Yours is the sanest proposal that has been brought to this office in the last six months," said the Prime Minister of one of the larger countries.

We were also in position to canvass the objections that have been made to the proposal, testing it out severely in the judgment of those in the midst of the European conflict. It has been argued that it is not the time at present to start such a process of negotiations, and that no step should be taken until one or other party has a victory, or at least until some new military balance is struck. The answer we bring is that every delay makes more difficult the beginnings of negotiations, more nations become involved, and the situation becomes more complicated; that when at times in the course of the war such a balance was struck, the neutrals were unprepared to act. The opportunity passed. For the forces of peace to be unprepared when the hour comes, is as irretrievable as for a military leader to be unready.

It has been argued that for such a conference to be called at any time when one side has met with some military advantage, would be to favor that side. The answer we bring is that the proposed conference would start mediation at a higher level than that of military advantage. As to the actual military situation, however, we quote a remark made to us by a foreign Minister of one of the belligerent Powers. "Neither side is to-day strong enough to dictate terms, and neither side is so weakened that it has to accept humiliating terms."

It has been suggested that such a conference would bind the neutral governments cooperating in it. The answer we bring is that, as proposed, such a conference should consist of the ablest persons of the neutral countries, assigned not to problems of their own governments, but to the common service of a supreme crisis. The situation calls for a conference cast in a new and larger mould than those of conventional diplomacy...

CHAPTER 25

The West Between the Wars

Soviet Union "Law Code on Marriage" and "Law Code on Motherhood"

Under Lenin's leadership, the new soviet government promised women more prominent roles in government, greater economic equality, expanded legal rights in marriage, and more educational opportunities. Under Joseph Stalin, however, these earlier socialist initiatives redefining women's rights shifted back to policies based on more traditional values that excluded women from the political sphere. Stalin placed more emphasis on women's roles as wives and mothers. The following law code from 1926 outlines the legal rights and responsibilities in marriage for both men and women in the USSR. The next document outlines soviet law in respect to state aid to women with children in 1944. Russia was not alone in granting medals for motherhood in the interwar period; the governments of Germany, Italy, and France did so as well.

Source: "The Soviet Code on Marriage and Divorce, the Family, and Guardianship, decrees of the All-Russian Central Executive Committee, 19 November 1926" and "The Soviet Family Law of 8 July 1944, decree of the Presidium of the Supreme Soviet of the USSR" in *The Family in the U.S.S.R*, ed. Rudolf Schlesinger (London: Rutledge, 1949); reprinted in *Women, the Family, and Freedom: The Debate in Documents: 1880-1950*, vol. 2, ed. Susan Groag Bell and Karen M. Offen (Stanford: Stanford University Press, 1983), 400-401, 407-411.

Focus Questions:

1. What were the rights and responsibilities of women in soviet Russia as outlined by these codes?
2. What did the soviet government hope to accomplish by passing these law codes? What concerns did they hope to address, what goals did they hope to accomplish?

3. Compare the legal status and political role of women in the USSR with the status of women in Western Europe and the US in the same period. How and why are they similar? Different?

RIGHTS AND DUITIES OF HUSBAND AND WIFE

7. On registering a marriage the contracting parties may declare it to be their wish to have a common surname, either that of the husband or of the wife, or to retain their antenuptial surnames.

8. On the registration of a marriage between a person who is a citizen of the R.S.F.S.R. and a person who is a foreign citizen, each party retains his or her respective citizenship. Change in citizenship of such persons may be effected in the simplified manner provided for by the Union laws....

9. Both husband and wife enjoy full liberty in the choice of their respective trades and occupations. The manner in which their joint household is conducted is determined by the mutual agreement of the two contracting parties. A change of residence by either husband or wife does not oblige the other marriage partner to follow the former.

10. Property which belonged to either husband or wife prior to their marriage remains the separate property of each of them. Property acquired by husband and wife during continuance of their marriage is regarded as their joint property. The share belonging to either husband or wife shall, in case of dispute, be determined by the court.

Note.—The rights of either husband or wife in regard to the use of land and in regard to property used in common and forming part of a peasant household are defined by Sections 66 and 67 of the Land Code and by the enactments published to supplement the same.

11. Section 10 of the present code extends also to the property of persons married *de facto* though not registered, provided such persons recognize their mutual status of husband and wife, or their marital relationship is established as a fact by a court on the basis of the actual conditions under which they live.

12. Proof of joint cohabitation is sufficient for the court to establish marital cohabitation in cases where the marriage has not been registered, provided that in addition to proof of joint cohabitation proof of a common household be adduced and that statements have been made to third persons either in personal correspondence or in other documents tending to prove the existence of marital relations, taking also into consideration such circumstances as the presence or absence of mutual material support, joint raising of children, and the like.

13. The husband and wife may enter into any contractual relations with each other regarding property provided they are lawful. Agreements between hus-

band and wife intended to restrict the property rights of the wife or of the husband are invalid and are not binding on third parties or on the husband or wife, who may at any time refuse to carry them out.

14. When either husband or wife is in need and unable to work he or she is entitled to receive alimony from the other conjugal partner, if the court finds that the latter is able to support the former. A husband or wife in need of support but able to work is likewise entitled to alimony during the period of his or her unemployment.

15. The right of a husband or wife in need and unable to work to receive alimony from the other conjugal partner continues even after the dissolution of the marriage until there has been a change in the conditions which according to Section 14 of the present code serve as a basis for the receipt of alimony, but not for a period exceeding one year from the time of the dissolution of the marriage. The amount of alimony to be paid to a needy unemployed husband or wife in case of dissolution of the marriage is fixed by the court for a period not exceeding six months and shall not exceed the corresponding amount of Social Insurance relief.

16. The right to receive alimony both during marriage and after its dissolution extends also to persons who are married *de facto,* though not registered, provided they fall within the purview of Sections 11 and 12 of the present code.

17. A marriage is dissolved by the death of one of the parties to it or by a declaration of the presumptive death of either the husband or the wife through a notary public or court....

18. During the lifetime of both parties to a marriage the marriage may be dissolved either by the mutual consent of both parties to it or upon the *ex parte* application of either of them.

19. During the lifetime of both parties, the dissolution of a marriage (divorce) may be registered at the Civil Registrar's Office, whether the marriage was registered or unregistered, provided that in the latter case it had been established as a fact by the court in accordance with Section 12 of the present code.

20. The fact that a marriage has been dissolved may also be established by a court, if the divorce was not registered.

Motherhood for the Fatherland

Source: "The Soviet Family Law of 8 July 1944, decree of the Praesidium of the Supreme Soviet of the U.S.S.R."; reprinted and trans. in The Family in the U.S.S.R.,pp. 367–72; reprinted in Women, the Family, and Freedom:

The Debate in Documents,ed. Susan Groag Bell and Karen M. Offen, (Stanford, CA: Stanford University Press, 1983), vol. 1, 1750–1880, pp. 407–11.

Decree of the Presidium of the Supreme Soviet of the U.S.S.R. on increase of State aid to pregnant women, mothers with many children and unmarried mothers; on strengthening measures for the protection of motherhood and childhood; on the establishment of the title"Heroine Mother"; and on the institution of the order"Motherhood Glory"and the"Motherhood Medal"

Care for children and mothers and the strengthening of the family have always been among the most important tasks of the Soviet State. In safeguarding the interests of mother and child, the State is rendering great material aid to pregnant women and mothers for the support and upbringing of their children. During and after the War, when many families face more considerable material difficulties, a further extension of State aid measures is necessary.

With a view to increasing the material assistance to pregnant women, mothers with many children, and unmarried mothers, and to encouraging large families and providing increased protection for motherhood and childhood the Presidium of the Supreme Soviet of the U.S.S.R. Decrees:

SECTION I

ON THE INCREASE OF STATE AID TO MOTHERS WITH MANY CHILDREN AND UNMARRIED MOTHERS

It is Decreed:

Article 1

That in place of the existing regulation which gives State aid to mothers with six children at the birth of the seventh and of each subsequent child, State assistance shall be given to mothers (either with husbands or widowed) who have two children, on the birth of the third and of each subsequent child.

Article 2

In assessing the amount of State assistance to mothers with many children, those children who perished or disappeared without trace on the fronts of the Patriotic War are included.

Article 3

To establish State assistance to single (unmarried) mothers for support and upbringing of children born after the publication of the present Decree, in the following amounts:

100 rubles monthly for	1 child
150" "	for 2 children
200" "	for 3 or more children

State assistance to unmarried mothers is paid until the children reach 12 years of age.

Unmarried mothers with 3 or more children receive the State assistance laid down in the present article, in addition to the regular assistance to mothers with many children which is received in accordance with article 2 of the present Decree.

When an unmarried mother marries, the right to assistance laid down in the present article is retained by her. ....

Article 4

If an unmarried mother wishes to place a child to which she has given birth in a children's institution for its upbringing, the children's institution is obliged to accept the child, to support and bring it up entirely at the expense of the State.

The mother of the child has the right to remove her child from the children's institution and to bring it up herself. While the child is in the children's institution, State assistance for the child is not paid.

* * *

SECTION II

ON THE INCREASE OF PRIVILEGES FOR PREGNANT WOMEN AND MOTHERS AND ON MEASURES TO EXTEND THE NETWORK OF INSTITUTIONS FOR THE PROTECTION OF MOTHERHOOD AND CHILDHOOD

Article 6

To increase the leave of absence for pregnancy and childbirth for women workers and women office employees from 63 calendar days to 77 calendar days, establishing the length of the leave of absence at 35 calendar days before the birth and 42 calendar days after the birth, assistance to be given during this period at the expense of the State to the amount previously laid down. In cases of difficult births or the birth of twins, leave of absence after birth is increased to 56 calendar days.

To instruct the directors of factories and offices to provide pregnant women with their regular leave of absence, at a suitable time in relation to the leave of absence for pregnancy and birth.

Article 7

Pregnant women from the 4th month of pregnancy not to be put on overtime work in factories and offices, and women with children at the breast not to be put on nightwork during the period the child is breast-fed.

Article 8

To double the normal ration of supplementary food for pregnant women, beginning with the 6th month of pregnancy, and for nursing mothers for four months of the nursing period.

Article 9

To instruct the directors of factories and offices to give aid to pregnant women and nursing mothers in the form of supplementary foodstuffs from their auxiliary farms.

Article 10

To reduce by 50 per cent the fees for places in créches and kindergartens for:

Parents with 3 children and earning up to 400 rubles a month.

Parents with 4 children and earning up to 600 rubles a month.

Parents with 5 or more children irrespective of earnings.

Article 11

To instruct the Council of People's Commissars of the U.S.S.R.:

(a) To confirm the plan for the organization in Republics and Regions of additional Homes for Mother and Child and also of special rest homes for unmarried women needing them and for weakened nursing mothers, the women resting there to be given work in them according to their strength.

(b) To confirm the plan for extending the network of children's institutions under the People's Commissariats and departments, with a view to covering fully all children needing such institutions; to provide for extension of the network of children's consulting centres and milk kitchens, organization of crèches for breast-fed children, of evening groups in the kindergartens and maternity institutions in the districts liberated from the German invaders.

(c) To provide for the compulsory organization in factories and offices employing women on a mass scale of crèches, kindergartens, rooms for the feeding of breast-fed children, and personal hygiene rooms for women.

(d) To instruct the People's Commissariats to include in their plans of industrial construction the building of children's institutions (crèches, kindergartens, Mother and Child Rooms), calculated to cover fully all the children of the women workers and office employees of the given enterprise who require such services.

(e) To confirm measures for the considerable expansion of the production of children's clothing, footwear, sanitary and hygienic articles for children, and other articles required by children both for children's institutions and for sale to the population, and measures also for the extension of the network of children's clothing factories and of the network of Mother and Child shops.

SECTION III

ON THE INSTITUTION OF THE "MOTHERHOOD MEDAL" AND THE ORDER "MOTHERHOOD GLORY." AND ESTABLISHMENT OF THE TITLE OF HONOUR "HEROINE MOTHER"

Article 12

To institute a"Motherhood Medal"—1st and 2nd class—for award to mothers who have given birth to and brought up:

5 children	2nd class medal
6 children	1st class medal

Article 13

To establish the Order "Motherhood Glory"—1st, 2nd and 3rd class—for award to mothers who have given birth to and brought up:

7 children	3rd class
8 children	2nd class
9 children	1st class

Article 14

To establish that mothers who have given birth to and brought up 10 children shall receive the title of honour"Heroine Mother"with award of the Order Heroine Mother and certificate of the Presidium of the Supreme Soviet of the U.S.S.R.

SECTION IV
ON TAXES ON BACHELORS, SINGLE CITIZENS, AND CITIZENS OF THE U.S.S.R WITH SMALL FAMILIES

Article 16

As a modification of the Decree of the Presidium of the Supreme Soviet of the U.S.S.R. dated November 21, 1941, "On taxes on bachelors, single and childless citizens of the U.S.S.R.," to establish that a tax is paid by citizens—men between the ages of 20 and 50 years, and women between the ages of 20 and 45 years—having no children and citizens having 1 or 2 children.

Joseph Stalin, Five Year Plan

From the standpoint of political ideology, the fascist movements in Italy and Germany were in complete opposition to the communist principles that provided the basis for government in the Soviet Union. Despite this very important difference, however, some of the authoritarian methods employed by these governments were quite similar. For example, Italy, Germany and the USSR were all ruled by dictators and one-party states, and their governments all used violence and coercion to suppress political opposition. After the Russian Revolution of 1917, and the civil war (1917-1921), Lenin had little time to fully establish a government before his stroke in 1922. He remained weak and ill throughout the next two years and died in 1924. After Lenin's death, Joseph Stalin (1879-1953) cunningly marginalized Leon Trotsky (1879-1940), to succeed Lenin, emerging as the next leader of Soviet Russia by the 1920s. As a leader, Stalin sought greater political and cultural centralization by forming a dictatorship. In 1929, in an effort to realize rapid industrialization, Stalin initiated a plan to build heavy industry funded by the state, called the Five Year Plan. Under the plan, the government forced peasants into collectivized farms in order to increase agricultural yields. The surplus revenue from agricultural then financed industrialization, by paying for the creation of government owned factories and industries. In this excerpt, from 1933, Stalin addresses the Central Communist Party, speaking about the objectives and results of the first Five Year Plan.

Source: "The First Five Year Plan: Stalin's Speech to the Central Communist Party, January 1933" in *Primary Source Document Workbook to Accompany World Civilizations*, by Philip J. Adier, ed. Robert Weborn (New York: West Publishing Company, 1996), 92-93.

Focus Questions:

1. What were the primary goals of the Five Year Plan, as described here by Stalin, and what were the methods used to implement the plan?
2. In his estimation, how successful had the plan been? In what ways?

3. How did this path to industrialization differ from the patterns of industrialization in Western Europe? Why?

What was the fundamental task of the five-year plan?

The fundamental task of the five-year plan was to transfer our country, with its backward, and in part medieval, technology, on to the lines of new, modern technology.

The fundamental task of the five-year plan was to convert the U.S.S.R. from an agrarian and weak country, dependent upon the caprices of the capitalist countries, into an industrial and powerful country, fully self-reliant and independent of the caprices of world capitalism.

The fundamental task of the five-year plan was, in converting the U.S.S.R. into an industrial country, to completely oust the capitalist elements, to widen the front of socialist forms of economy, and to create the economic basis for the abolition of classes in the U.S.S.R., for the building of a socialist society....

The fundamental task of the five-year plan was to transfer small and scattered agriculture on to the lines of large-scale collective farming, so as to ensure the economic basis of socialism in the countryside and thus to eliminate the possibility of the restoration of capitalism in the U.S.S.R.

Finally, the task of the five-year plan was to create all the necessary technical and economic prerequisites for increasing to the utmost the defense capacity of the country, enabling it to organize determined resistance to any attempt at military intervention from abroad, to any attempt at military attack from abroad....

The main link in the five-year plan was heavy industry, with machine building as its core. For only heavy industry is capable of reconstructing both industry as a whole, transport and agriculture, and of putting them on their feet. It was necessary to begin the fulfillment of the five-year plan with heavy industry. Consequently, the restoration of heavy industry had to be made the basis of the fulfillment of the five-year plan....

But the restoration and development of heavy industry, particularly in such a backward and poor country as ours was at the beginning of the five-year plan period, is an extremely difficult task; for, as is well known, heavy industry calls for enormous financial expenditure and the existence of a certain minimum of experienced technical forces.... Did the Party know this, and did it take this into account? Yes, it did. Not only did the Party know this, but it announced it for all to hear. The Party knew how heavy industry had been built in Britain, Germany, and America. It knew that in those countries heavy industry had been built either with the aid of big loans, plundering other countries, or by both methods simultaneously. The Party knew that those paths were closed to our country. What, then, did it count on? It counted on our country's own resources. It counted on the fact that, with a Soviet government at the helm, and the land, industry, transport, the banks and trade nationalized, we could pursue a regime of the strictest economy in order to accumulate sufficient resources for the restoration and development of heavy industry. The Party declared frankly that this would call for serious sacrifices, and that it was our duty openly and consciously to make these sacrifices if we wanted to achieve our goal....

What are the results of the five-year plan in four years in the sphere of industry?

We did not have an iron and steel industry, the basis for the industrialization of the country.

Now we have one.

We did not have a tractor industry. Now we have one.

We did not have an automobile industry. Now we have one.

We did not have a machine-tool industry. Now we have one.

We did not have a big and modern chemical industry. Now we have one.

We did not have a real and big industry for the production of modern agricultural machinery. Now we have one.

We did not have an aircraft industry. Now we have one.

In output of electrical power we were last on the list. Now we rank among the first.

In output of oil products and coal we were last on the list. Now we rank among the first....

Finally, as a result of all this the Soviet Union has been converted from a weak country, unprepared for defense, into a country mighty in defense, a country prepared for every contingency, a country capable of producing on a mass scale all modern means of defense and of equipping its army with them in the event of an attack from abroad....

Chicago Commission on Race Relations, The Negro in Chicago: A Study of Race Relations and a Race Riot

In the aftermath of World War I, America faced significant economic and labor problems. These problems contributed to rising racial tension. The Chicago riot described below left 38 people dead and 537 injured. The riot was not an isolated incident. At about the same time, riots occurred in a number of Midwestern and Northern cities.

Source: "The Negro in Chicago: A Study of Race Relations and a Race Riot," in The Chicago Commission on Race Relations (Chicago: University of Chicago Press, 1922).

Focus Questions:

1. What role did rumor and racial mistrust play in the riot?
2. How did the press cover the riot? What significance do you attach to the discrepancies between press accounts and the commission's report?

BACKGROUND

In July, 1919, a race riot involving whites and Negroes occurred in Chicago. For some time thoughtful citizens, white and Negro, had sensed increasing tension, but, having no local precedent of riot and wholesale bloodshed, had neither prepared themselves for it nor taken steps to prevent it. The collecting of arms by members of both races was known to the authorities, and it was evident that this was in preparation for aggression as well as for self-defense.

Several minor clashes preceded the riot. On July 3, 1917, a white saloonkeeper who, according to the coroner's physician, died of heart trouble, was incorrectly reported in the press to have been killed by a Negro. That evening a party of young white men riding in an automobile fired upon a group of Negroes at Fifty-third and Federal streets. In July and August of the same year recruits from the Great Lakes Naval Training Station clashed frequently with Negroes, each side accusing the other of being the aggressor.

Gangs of white "toughs," made up largely of the membership of so-called athletic clubs from the neighborhood between Roosevelt Road and Sixty-third Street, Wentworth Avenue and the city limits—a district contiguous to the neighborhood of the largest Negro settlement—were a constant menace to Negroes who traversed sections of the territory going to and returning from work. The activities of these gangs and athletic clubs became bolder in the spring of 1919, and on the night of June 21, five weeks before the riot, two wanton murders of

Negroes occurred, those of Sanford Harris and Joseph Robinson. Harris, returning to his home on Dearborn Street at about 11:30 at night, passed a group of young white men. They threatened him and he ran. He had gone but a short distance when one of the group shot him. He died soon afterward. Policemen who came on the scene made no arrests, even when the assailant was pointed out by a white woman witness of the murder. On the same evening Robinson, a Negro laborer, forty-seven years of age, was attacked while returning from work by a gang of white "toughs" at Fifty-fifth Street and Princeton Avenue, apparently without provocation, and stabbed to death.

Negroes were greatly incensed over these murders, but their leaders, joined by many friendly whites, tried to allay their fears and counseled patience.

After the killing of Harris and Robinson, notices were conspicuously posted on the South Side that an effort would be made to "get all the niggers on July 4th." The notices called for help from sympathizers. Negroes, in turn, whispered around the warning to prepare for a riot; and they did prepare.

Since the riot in East St. Louis, July 4, 1917, there had been others in different parts of the country which evidenced a widespread lack of restraint in mutual antipathies and suggested further resorts to lawlessness. Riots and race clashes occurred in Chester, Pennsylvania; Longview, Texas; Coatesville, Pennsylvania; Washington, D. C.; and Norfolk, Virginia, before the Chicago riot.

Aside from general lawlessness and disastrous riots that preceded the riot here discussed, there were other factors which may be mentioned briefly here. In Chicago considerable unrest had been occasioned in industry by increasing competition between white and Negro laborers following a sudden increase in the Negro population due to the migration of Negroes from the South. This increase developed a housing crisis. The Negroes overran the hitherto recognized area of Negro residence, and when they took houses in adjoining neighborhoods friction ensued. In the two years just preceding the riot, twenty-seven Negro dwellings were wrecked by bombs thrown by unidentified persons.

STORY OF THE RIOT

Sunday afternoon, July 27, 1919, hundreds of white and Negro bathers crowded the lake-front beaches at Twenty-sixth and Twenty-ninth streets. This is the eastern boundary of the thickest Negro residence area. At Twenty-sixth Street Negroes were in great majority; at Twenty-ninth Street there were more whites. An imaginary line in the water separating the two beaches had been generally observed by the two races. Under the prevailing relations, aided by wild rumors and reports, this line served virtually as a challenge to either side to cross it. Four Negroes who attempted to enter the water from the "white" side were driven away by the whites. They returned with more Negroes, and there followed a series of attacks with stones, first one side gaining the advantage, then the other.

Eugene Williams, a Negro boy of seventeen, entered the water from the side used by Negroes and drifted across the line supported by a railroad tie. He was observed by the crowd on the beach and promptly became a target for stones. He suddenly released the tie, went down and was drowned. Guilt was immediately placed on Stauber, a young white man, by Negro witnesses who declared that he threw the fatal stone.[1]

White and Negro men dived for the boy without result. Negroes demanded that the policeman present arrest Stauber. He refused; and at this crucial moment arrested a Negro on a white man's complaint. Negroes then attacked the officer. These two facts, the drowning and the refusal of the policeman to arrest Stauber, together marked the beginning of the riot. Two hours after the drowning, a Negro, James Crawford, fired into a group of officers summoned by the policeman at the beach and was killed by a Negro policeman. Reports and rumors circulated rapidly, and new crowds began to gather. Five white men were injured in clashes near the beach. As darkness came, Negroes in white districts to the west suffered severely. Between 9:00 p.m. and 3:00 a.m. twenty-seven Negroes were beaten, seven stabbed, and four shot. Monday morning was quiet, and Negroes went to work as usual.

Returning from work in the afternoon, many Negroes were attacked by white ruffians. Streetcar routes, especially at transfer points, were the centers of lawlessness. Trolleys were pulled from the wires, and Negro passengers were dragged into the street, beaten, stabbed, and shot. The police were powerless to cope with these numerous assaults. During Monday, four Negro men and one white assailant were killed, and thirty Negroes were severely beaten in streetcar clashes. Four white men were killed, six stabbed, five shot, and nine severely beaten. It was rumored that the white occupants of the Angelus Building at Thirty-fifth Street and Wabash Avenue had shot a Negro. Negroes gathered about the building. The white tenants sought police protection, and one hundred policemen, mounted and on foot, responded. In a clash with the mob, the police killed four Negroes and injured many.

Raids into the Negro residence area then began. Automobiles sped through the streets, the occupants shooting at random. Negroes retaliated by "sniping" from ambush. At midnight surface and elevated car service was discontinued because of a strike for wage increases, and thousands of employees were cut off from work.

On Tuesday, July 29, Negro men en route on foot to their jobs through hostile territory were killed. White soldiers and sailors in uniform, aided by civilians, raided the "Loop" business section, killing two Negroes and beating and robbing several others. Negroes living among white neighbors in Englewood, far to the south, were driven from their homes, their household goods were stolen, and

1 The coroner's jury found that Williams had drowned from fear of stone-throwing which kept him from the shore.

their houses were burned or wrecked. On the West Side an Italian mob, excited by a false rumor that an Italian girl had been shot by a Negro, killed Joseph Lovings, a Negro.

Wednesday night at 10:30 Mayor Thompson yielded to pressure and asked the help of the three regiments of militia which had been stationed in nearby armories during the most severe rioting, awaiting the call. They immediately took up positions throughout the South Side. A rainfall Wednesday night and Thursday kept many people in their homes, and by Friday the rioting had abated. On Saturday incendiary fires burned forty-nine houses in the immigrant neighborhood west of the Stock Yards. Nine hundred and forty-eight people, mostly Lithuanians, were made homeless, and the property loss was about $250,000. Responsibility for the fires was never fixed.

The total casualties of this reign of terror were thirty-eight deaths—fifteen white, twenty-three Negro— and 537 people injured. Forty-one per cent of the reported clashes occurred in the white neighborhood near the Stock Yards between the south branch of the Chicago River and Fifty-fifth Street, Wentworth Avenue and the city-limits, and 34 per cent in the "Black Belt" between Twenty-second and Thirty-ninth streets, Wentworth Avenue and Lake Michigan. Others were scattered.

Responsibility for many attacks was definitely placed by many witnesses upon the "athletic clubs," including "Ragen's Colts," the "Hamburgers," "Aylwards," "Our Flag," the "Standard," the "Sparklers," and several others. The mobs were made up for the most part of boys between fifteen and twenty-two. Older persons participated but the youth of the rioters was conspicuous in every clash. Little children witnessed the brutalities and frequently pointed out the injured when the police arrived.

RUMORS AND THE RIOT

Wild rumors were in circulation by word of mouth and in the press throughout the riot and provoked many clashes. These included stories of atrocities committed by one race against the other. Reports of the numbers of white and Negro dead tended to produce a feeling that the score must be kept even. Newspaper reports, for example, showed 6 percent more whites injured than Negroes. As a matter of fact, there were 28 per cent more Negroes injured than whites. The Chicago Tribune on July 29 reported twenty persons killed, of whom thirteen were white and seven colored. The true figures were exactly the opposite.

Among the rumors provoking fear were numerous references to the arming of Negroes. In the Daily News of July 30, for example, appeared the subheadline: "Alderman Jos. McDonough tells how he was shot at on South Side visit. Says enough ammunition in section to last for years of guerrilla warfare." In the article following, the reference to ammunition was repeated but not elaborated or explained.

The alderman was quoted as saying that the mayor contemplated opening up Thirty-fifth and Forty-seventh streets in order that colored people might get to their work. He thought this would be most unwise for, he stated, "They are armed and white people are not. We must defend ourselves if the city authorities won't protect us." Continuing his story, he described bombs going off: "I saw white men and women running through the streets dragging children by the hands and carrying babies in their arms. Frightened white men told me the police captains had just rushed through the district crying, 'For God's sake, arm; they are coming; we cannot hold them.'"

Whether or not the alderman was correctly quoted, the effect of such statements on the public was the same. There is no record in any of the riot testimony in the coroner's office or state's attorney's office of any bombs going off during the riot, nor of police captains warning the white people to arm, nor of any fear by whites of a Negro invasion. In the Berger Odman case before a coroner's jury, there was a state-ment to the effect that a sergeant of police warned the Negroes of Ogden Park to arm and to shoot at the feet of rioters if they attempted to invade the few blocks marked off for Negroes by the police. Negroes were warned, not whites.

CONDUCT OF THE POLICE

Chief of Police John J. Garrity, in explaining the inability of the police to curb the rioters, said that there was not a sufficient force to police one-third of the city. Aside from this, Negroes distrusted the white police officers, and it was implied by the chief and stated by State's Attorney Hoyne, that many of the police were "grossly unfair in making arrests." There were instances of actual police participation in the rioting as well as neglect of duty. Of 229 persons arrested and accused of various criminal activities during the riot, 154 were Negroes and seventy-five were whites. Of those indicted, eighty-one were Negroes and forty-seven were whites. Although this, on its face, would indicate great riot activity on the part of Negroes, further reports of clashes show that of 520 persons injured. 342 were Negroes and 178 were whites. The fact that twice as many Negroes appeared as defendants and twice as many Negroes as whites were injured leads to the conclusion that whites were not apprehended as readily as Negroes.

Many of the depredations outside the "Black Belt" were encouraged by the absence of policemen. Out of a force of 3,000 police, 2,800 were massed in the "Black Belt" during the height of the rioting. In the "Loop" district, where two Negroes were killed and several others wounded, there were only three policemen and one sergeant. The Stock Yards district, where the greatest number of injuries occurred, was also weakly protected.

THE MILITIA

Although Governor Lowden had ordered the militia into the city promptly and they were on hand on the second day of the rioting, their services were not requested by the mayor and chief of police until the evening of the fourth day. The reason expressed by the chief for this delay was a belief that inexperienced militiamen would add to the deaths and disorder. But the troops, when called, proved to be clearly of high character, and their discipline was good, not a case of breach of discipline being reported during their occupation. They were distributed more proportionately through all the riotous areas than the police and, although they reported some hostility from members of "athletic clubs," the rioting soon ceased.

RESTORATION OF ORDER

Throughout the rioting, various social organizations and many citizens were at work trying to hold hostilities in check and to restore order. The Chicago Urban League, Wabash Avenue Y.M.C.A., American Red Cross, and various other social organizations and the churches of the Negro community gave attention to caring for stranded Negroes, advising them of dangers, keeping them off the streets and, in such ways as were possible, co-operating with the police. The packing companies took their pay to Negro employees, and various banks made loans. Local newspapers in their editorial columns insistently condemned the disorder and counseled calmness.

THE AFTERMATH

Of the thirty-eight persons killed in the riot:

Fifteen met death at the hands of mobs. Coroner's juries recommended that the members of the unknown mobs be apprehended. They were never found.

Six were killed in circumstances fixing no criminal responsibility: three white men were killed by Negroes in self-defense, and three Negroes were shot by policemen in the discharge of their duty.

Four Negroes were killed in the Angelus riot. The coroner made no recommendations, and the cases were not carried farther.

Four cases, two Negro and two white, resulted in recommendations from coroner's juries for further investigation of certain persons. Sufficient evidence was lacking for indictments against them.

Nine cases led to indictments. Of this number four cases resulted in convictions.

	Negro		White	
	Cases	**Persons**	**Cases**	**Persons**
Indictments	6	17	3	4
Convictions	2	3	2	2

Thus in only four cases of death was criminal responsibility fixed and punishment meted out. Indictments and convictions, divided according to the race of the persons criminally involved, were as Despite the community's failure to deal firmly with those who disturbed its peace and contributed to the reign of lawlessness that shamed Chicago before the world, there is evidence that the riot aroused many citizens of both races to a quickened sense of the suffering and disgrace which had come and might again come to the city, and developed a determination to prevent a recurrence of so disastrous an outbreak of race hatred. This was manifest on at least three occasions in 1920 when, confronted suddenly with events out of which serious riots might easily have grown, people of both races acted with such courage and promptness as to end the trouble early. One of these was the murder of two innocent white men and the wounding of a Negro policeman by a band of Negro fanatics who styled themselves "Abyssinians"; another was the killing of a white man by a Negro whom he had attacked while returning from work; and still another was the riotous attacks of sailors from the Great Lakes Naval Training Station on Negroes in Waukegan, Illinois.

OUTSTANDING FEATURES OF THE RIOT

This study of the facts of the riot of 1919, the events as they happened hour by hour, the neighborhoods involved, the movements of mobs, the part played by rumors, and the handling of the emergency by the various authorities, shows certain outstanding features which may be listed as follows:

a. The riot violence was not continuous hour by hour, but was intermittent.

b. The greatest number of injuries occurred in the district west and inclusive of Wentworth Avenue, and south of the south branch of the Chicago River to Fifty-fifth Street, or in the Stock Yards district. The next greatest number occurred in the so-called Black Belt: Twenty-second to Thirty-ninth streets, inclusive, and Wentworth Avenue to the lake, exclusive of Wentworth Avenue; Thirty-ninth to Fifty-fifth streets, inclusive, and Clark Street to Michigan Avenue, exclusive of Michigan Avenue.

c. Organized raids occurred only after a period of sporadic clashes and spontaneous mob outbreaks.

d. Main thoroughfares witnessed 76 per cent of the injuries on the South Side. The streets which suffered most severely were State, Halsted, Thirty-first, Thirty-fifth, and Forty-seventh. Transfer corners were always centers of disturbances.

e. Most of the rioting occurred after work hours among idle crowds on the streets. This was particularly true after the streetcar strike began.

f. Gangs, particularly of young whites, formed definite nuclei for crowd and mob formation. "Athletic clubs" supplied the leaders of many gangs.

g. Crowds and mobs engaged in rioting were generally composed of a small nucleus of leaders and an acquiescing mass of spectators. The leaders were mostly young men, usually between the ages of sixteen and twenty-one. Dispersal was most effectively accomplished by sudden, unexpected gun fire.

h. Rumor kept the crowds in an excited, potential mob state. The press was responsible for giving wide dissemination to much of the inflammatory matter in spoken rumors, though editorials calculated to allay race hatred and help the forces of order were factors in the restoration of peace.

i. The police lacked sufficient forces for handling the riot; they were hampered by the Negroes' distrust of them; routing orders and records were not handled with proper care; certain officers were undoubtedly unsuited to police or riot duty.

j. The militiamen employed in this riot were of an unusually high type. This unquestionably accounts for the confidence placed in them by both races. Riot training, definite orders, and good staff work contributed to their efficiency.

k. There was a lack of energetic co-operation between the police department and the state's attorney's office in the discovery and conviction of rioters.

The riot was merely a symptom of serious and profound disorders lying beneath the surface of race relations in Chicago. The study of the riot, therefore, as to its interlocking provocations and causes, required a study of general race relations that made possible so serious and sudden an outbreak. Thus to understand the riot and guard against another, the Commission probed systematically into the principal phases of race contact and sought accurate information on matters which in the past have been influenced by dangerous speculation; and on the basis of its discoveries certain suggestions to the community are made.

Transcript of the Rape of Nanjing Sentencing, 1947

On December 13, 1937, Nanjing, the capital city of Nationalist China, fell to the onslaught of the invading Japanese army. For the Chinese forces of Jiang Jieshi, which had fought to defend the Yangtze Valley, this was a bitter defeat. The ancient walled city of Nanjing lay open to the fury of the Japanese who, for the next six weeks, pillaged and burned the town, executed tens of thousands of Chinese soldiers, slaughtered civilian men, and raped the women and children. This was no temporary lapse of military discipline in the Japanese ranks, but a methodical and horrific act of terror that resulted in the death of nearly 300,000 Chinese. The Rape of Nanjing, as it was immediately called, was not publicized after the war and has been termed by some historians, the "forgotten Holocaust." But its lingering memory has poisoned Chinese-Japanese relations for over sixty years. The following transcript of the 1947 sentencing of a convicted Japanese war criminal testifies to the savagery and tragedy of the Rape of Nanjing.

Source: "The Rape of Nanjing," in Military Tribunal for the Trial of War Criminals (March 10, 1947), in Dun J. Li, The Road to Communism (New York: Van Nostrand Reinhold Company).

Focus Questions:

1. What motivated the Japanese to commit such acts?
2. Until recently, why did the Japanese brutality in Nanjing go relatively unnoticed? Why has Nanjing been called the "forgotten Holocaust"?
3. The poet W. H. Auden reflected on the holocaust of World War II: "And maps can really point to places/Where life is evil now: Nanjing; Dachau." What do you think? Can evil be defined by the atrocities conducted on these sites? Or is evil such a relative concept that it defies definition? Was Hitler evil?

FILE NUMBER: SHEN1, 1947

Defendant: Tani Hsiao, male, age 66, native of Japan; a former lieutenant general and division commander of the Japanese army. The above defendant was accused by the public prosecutor of this Tribunal as a war criminal. The trial has been duly conducted. The decision is as follows:

Decision: During the period of war, Tani Hsiao, the defendant, condoned and encouraged the soldiers under his command to commit mass murder against prisoners of war as well as civilians, in addition to rape, looting, and deliberate destruction of properties. The defendant is hereby sentenced to death.

Facts: The defendant is regarded as one of the most ferocious and ablest generals among the Japanese militarists. He joined the Japanese army as early as the Russo-Japanese War [1905] and distinguished himself repeatedly on the battlefield. He was the commander of the Japanese Sixth Division when the Sino-Japanese War began in 1937; in August of that year, he came to China with his command and participated in the war of aggression...Since Nanjing was the capital of our country and the center of resistance against the Japanese aggression, the Japanese militarists mobilized their best and most ferocious military units, including the Sixth Division headed by the defendant...to launch an all-out attack under the overall supervision of General Matsu Iwane. Because of the fact that the defenders of the city had continued to resist and refused to surrender, the Japanese army, after capturing the city, conducted a systematic campaign of murder to show its revenge, hatred, and frustration.

On the afternoon of December 12, the invaders, led by the Sixth Division under the command of the defendant, captured the Zhonghua Gate. Massacre began the moment they roped over the city wall and descended upon the civilians...The massacre was followed by looting, rape, and arson. The worst slaughter occurred between December 12 and 21, the time when the defendant's troops were stationed inside the city...The total number of captured soldiers and civilians who were collectively machine-gunned and then burned into ashes amounted to more than 190,000. The total number of victims who were murdered on an individual basis and whose bodies were later buried by philanthropic organizations were more than 150,000. Thus, the grand total of civilians and prisoners of war who fell victim to this campaign of mass murder was well beyond 300,000. Dead bodies were piled from one street corner to another, and no words, however eloquent, were adequate enough to describe this atrocity of unprecedented scale...

On December 12, Mrs. Wang of Xu, a peasant woman, was beheaded on the harbor outside of the Zhonghua Gate...On December 14, Yao Qialong, a native of Nanjing, was ordered to watch the performance when Japanese soldiers took turns raping his wife. When his eight-year-old son and three-year-old daughter pleaded for mercy on behalf of their mother, the rapists picked them up with their bayonets and roasted them to death over a camp fire...In another case, two Japanese officers entered a murder contest; later, the one who had killed 106 persons was declared the winner over the other who had killed 105. On December 19, Xie Shanzhen, a peasant woman more than sixty years old, was cut into pieces after a Japanese soldier had pierced her vagina with a bamboo stick. In each and every case, the atrocities committed by the Japanese army were brutal to the greatest extreme. From December 12 to 21, the total number of atrocity cases that can be documented amounts to 886.

Adolf Hitler, The Obersalzberg Speech, 1939

On August 22, 1939, Adolf Hitler invited his chief military commanders and commanding generals, including Air Marshall Hermann Göring, to his Bavarian retreat high in the Obersalzberg. Here in the rarified mountain air, he informed his military commanders of his plans for war. No complete text of this speech survives, so what we have here is a collation of notes of the generals who were in attendance. Although no one disputes the overall outline and argument of this speech, some historians caution that the graphic language attributed to Hitler in this speech, for example, his identification with Genghis Khan and such phrases as "Chamberlain or some other such pig of a fellow," might have been inserted afterward by his dissident generals, who wanted to portray Hitler as brutally as possible. This florid language, if inserted by a dissident, could have been used to alert his adversaries, such as British Prime Minister Neville Chamberlain, or the French Premier Édouard Daladier, that by August 1939, Hitler was determined to go to war immediately. Yet, one cannot dismiss entirely the authenticity of this speech. Hitler was quite unpredictable, and the sensational and vulgar rhetoric of this text can be found in many of his other speeches. Despite the emotional character and questions of attribution, the Obersalzberg speech remains important because it provides a good insight into Hitler's grasp of history and his strategic thinking just on the eve of his September 1, 1939, attack on Poland. Similar versions of this speech have been printed in the principal documents of the Nuremberg War Trials (1945–1946), as well as in the official U.S. and British government documents on Hitler and the coming of World War II.

Source: E.L. Woodward and Rohan Butler, ed., *Documents on British Foreign Policy, 1919–1939,* 3rd series (London: HMSO, 1954), 7:258–60.

Focus Questions:

1. What does Hitler think of Stalin, his Italian and Japanese allies, and the leaders of Britain, France, and Turkey?
2. Hitler asks, "Who after all is today speaking about the destruction of the Armenians?" What does this suggest about his views of the twentieth century's first large-scale genocide?
3. How does Hitler view the coming war? What does he plan for Poland and the Polish people? How closely did he follow these plans?

Decision to attack Poland was arrived at in spring. Originally there was fear that because of the political constellation we would have to strike at the same time against England, France, Russia and Poland. This risk too we should have had to take. Göring had demonstrated to us that his Four-Year Plan is a failure and that we are at the end of our strength, if we do not achieve victory in a coming war.

Since the autumn of 1938 and since I have realised that Japan will not go with us unconditionally and that Mussolini is endangered by that nitwit of a King and the treacherous scoundrel of a Crown Prince, I decided to go with Stalin. After all there are only three great statesmen in the world, Stalin, I and Mussolini. Mussolini is the weakest, for he has been able to break the power neither of the crown nor of the Church. Stalin and I are the only ones who visualise the future. So in a few weeks hence I shall stretch out my hand to Stalin at the common German-Russian frontier and with him undertake to redistribute the world.

Our strength lies in our quickness and in our brutality; Genghis Khan has sent millions of women and children into death knowingly and with a light heart. History sees in him only the great founder of States. As to what the weak Western European civilisation asserts about me, that is of no account. I have given the command and I shall shoot everyone who utters one word of criticism, for the goal to be obtained in the war is not that of reaching certain lines but of physically demolishing the opponent. And so for the present only in the East I have put my death-head formations[1] in place with the command relentlessly and without compassion to send into death many women and children of Polish origin and language. Only thus we can gain the living space that we need. Who after all is today speaking about the destruction of the Armenians?

Colonel-General von Brauchitsch has promised me to bring the war against Poland to a close within a few weeks. Had he reported to me that he needs two years or even only one year, I should not have given the command to march and should have allied myself temporarily with England instead of Russia for we cannot conduct a long war. To be sure a new situation has arisen. I experienced those poor worms Daladier and Chamberlain in Munich. They will be too cowardly to attack. They won't go beyond a blockade. Against that we have our autarchy and the Russian raw materials.

Poland will be depopulated and settled with Germans. My pact with the Poles was merely conceived of as a gaining of time. As for the rest, gentlemen, the fate of Russia will be exactly the same as I am now going through with in the case of Poland. After Stalin's death—he is a very sick man—we will break the Soviet Union. Then there will begin the dawn of the German rule of the earth.

The little States cannot scare me. After Kemal's death Turkey is governed by "cretins" and half idiots. Carol of Roumania is through and through the corrupt slave of his sexual instincts. The King of Belgium and the Nordic kings are soft jumping jacks who are dependent upon the good digestions of their overeating and tired peoples.

1 The S.S. Death's Head formations were principally employed in peacetime in guarding concentration camps. With the S.S. Verfüngstruppen, they formed the nucleus of the Waffen S.S.

We shall have to take into the bargain the defection of Japan. I gave Japan a full year's time. The Emperor is a counterpart to the last Czar—weak, cowardly, undecided. May he become a victim of the revolution. My going together with Japan never was popular. We shall continue to create disturbances in the Far East and in Arabia. Let us think as "gentlemen" and let us see in these peoples at best lacquered half maniacs who are anxious to experience the whip.

The opportunity is as favourable as never before. I have but one worry, namely that Chamberlain or some other such pig of a fellow ("Saukerl") will come at the last moment with proposals or with ratting ("Umfall"). He will fly down the stairs, even if I shall personally have to trample on his belly in the eyes of the photographers.

No, it is too late for this. The attack upon and the destruction of Poland begins Saturday early. I shall let a few companies in Polish uniform attack in Upper Silesia or in the Protectorate. Whether the world believes it is quite indifferent ("scheissegal"). The world believes only in success.

For you, gentlemen, fame and honour are beginning as they have not since centuries. Be hard, be without mercy, act more quickly and brutally than the others. The citizens of Western Europe must tremble with horror. That is the most human way of conducting a war. For it scares the others off.

The new method of conducting war corresponds to the new drawing of the frontiers. A war extending from Reval, Lublin, Kaschau to the mouth of the Danube. The rest will be given to the Russians. Ribbentrop has orders to make every offer and to accept every demand. In the West I reserve to myself the right to determine the strategically best line. Here one will be able to work with Protectorate regions, such as Holland, Belgium and French Lorraine.

And now, on to the enemy, in Warsaw we will celebrate our reunion.

The speech was received with enthusiasm. Göring jumped on a table, thanked blood-thirstily and made bloodthirsty promises. He danced like a wild man. The few that had misgivings remained quiet. (Here a line of the memorandum is missing in order no doubt to protect the source of information.)

CHAPTER 26

World War II

Winston Churchill, "Their Finest Hour"

As Prime Minister of Britain during World War II, Winston Churchill (1874-1965) played a crucial role in maintaining morale at home and in building allies to aid with Britain's defense. When World War II began in 1939, it initially pitted the French and British allied forces against the Germans who invaded France on their Northeastern border after a successful sweep through Belgium. When Churchill gave this speech on June 18, 1940, the German army had overrun France and driven the British expeditionary force back across the English Channel. In this speech to the House of Commons of the British Parliament, Churchill explained the situation in France particularly in relation to the involvement of the British military in the battles. With the Germans poised to occupy all of France, Churchill sought to rally British support for the war, to ready all needed military forces, and to outline future strategies for combating Hitler and his allies.

Source: David Cannadine ed., *Blood, Toil, Tears, and Sweat: The Speeches of Winston Churchill* (Boston: Houghton Mifflin, 1989), 166-178.

Focus Questions:

1. Who was the audience for this speech, and what did Churchill hope to accomplish by delivering it?
2. What does this speech tell us about changes in warfare and strategy during this war? How was it different from World War I?
3. According to Churchill, what advantages and strengths could the British draw on for their defense?

I spoke the other day of the colossal military disaster which occurred when the French High Command failed to withdraw the Northern Armies from

Belgium at the moment when they knew that the French front was decisively broken at Sedan and on the Meuse. This delay entailed the loss of fifteen or sixteen French divisions and threw out of action for the critical period the whole of the British Expeditionary Force. Our Army and 120,000 French troops were indeed rescued by the British Navy from Dunkirk but only with the loss of their cannon, vehicles and modern equipment. This loss inevitably took some weeks to repair, and in the first two of those weeks the battle in France has been lost. When we consider the heroic resistance made by the French Army against heavy odds in this battle, the enormous losses inflicted upon the enemy and the evident exhaustion of the enemy, it may well be thought that these twenty-five divisions of the best-trained and best-equipped troops might have turned the scale. However, General Weygand had to fight without them. Only three British divisions or their equivalent were able to stand in the line with their French comrades. They had suffered severely, but they had fought well. We sent every man we could to France as fast as we could re-equip and transport their formations.

I am not reciting these facts for the purpose of recrimination. That I judge to be utterly futile and even harmful. We cannot afford it. I recite them in order to explain why it was we did not have, as we could have had, between twelve and fourteen British divisions fighting in the line in this great battle instead of only three. Now I put all this aside. I put it on the shelf, from which the historians, when they have time, will select their documents to tell their stories. We have to think of the future and not of the past. This also applies in a small way to our own affairs at home. There are many who would hold an inquest in the House of Commons on the conduct of the Governments—and of Parliaments, for they are in it, too—during the years which led up to this catastrophe. They seek to indict those who were responsible for the guidance of our affairs. This also would be a foolish and pernicious process. There are too many in it. Let each man search his conscience and search his speeches. I frequently search mine.

Of this I am quite sure, that if we open a quarrel between the past and the present, we shall find that we have lost the future. Therefore, I cannot accept the drawing of any distinctions between Members of the present Government. It was formed at a moment of crisis in order to unite all the parties and all sections of opinion. It has received the almost unanimous support of both Houses of Parliament. Its Members are going to stand together, and, subject to the authority of the House of Commons, we are going to govern the country and fight the war. It is absolutely necessary at a time like this that every Minister who tries each day to do his duty shall be respected; and their subordinates must know that their chiefs are not threatened men, men who are here today and gone tomorrow, but that their directions must be punctually and faithfully obeyed. Without this concentrated power we cannot face what lies before us. I should not think it would be very advantageous for the House to prolong this Debate this afternoon under conditions of public stress. Many facts are not clear that will be clear in a short time. We are to have a Secret Session on Thursday, and I should think that would be a better opportunity for the many earnest expressions of opinion which Members will desire to make and for the House to discuss vital matters without having everything read the next morning by our dangerous foes.

The disastrous military events which have happened during, the past fortnight have not come to me with any sense of surprise. Indeed, I indicated a fortnight ago as clearly as I could to the House that the worst possibilities were open; and I made it perfectly clear then that whatever happened in France would make no difference to the resolve of Britain and the British Empire to fight on, 'if necessary for years, if necessary alone.' During the last few days we have successfully brought off the great majority of the troops we had on the lines of communication in France; and seven-eighths of the troops we have sent to France since the beginning of the war—that is to say, about 350,000 out Of 400,000 men—are safely back in this country. Others are still fighting with the French, and fighting with considerable success in their local encounters against the enemy. We have also brought back a great mass of stores, rifles and munitions of all kinds which had been accumulated in France during the last nine months.

We have, therefore, in this island today a very large and powerful military force. This force comprises all our best-trained and our finest troops, including scores of thousands of those who have already measured their quality against the Germans and found themselves at no disadvantage. We have under arms at the present time in this island over a million and a quarter men. Behind these we have the Local Defence Volunteers, numbering half a million, only a portion of whom, however, are yet armed with rifles or other firearms. We have incorporated into our Defence Forces every man for whom we have a weapon. We expect very large additions to our weapons in the near future, and in preparation for this we intend forthwith to call up, drill and train further large numbers. Those who are not called up, or else are employed upon the vast business of munitions production in all its branches—and their ramifications are innumerable—will serve their country best by remaining at their ordinary work until they receive their summons. We have also over here Dominions armies. The Canadians had actually landed in France, but have now been safely withdrawn, much disappointed, but in perfect order, with all their artillery and equipment. And these very high-class forces from the Dominions will now take part in the defence of the Mother Country.

Lest the account which I have given of these large forces should raise the question: Why did they not take part in the great battle in France? I must make it clear that, apart from the divisions training and organizing at home, only twelve divisions were equipped to fight upon a scale which justified their being sent abroad. And this was fully up to the number which the French had been led to expect would be available in France at the ninth month of the war. The rest of our forces at home have fighting value for home defence which will, of course, steadily increase every week that passes. Thus, the invasion of Great Britain would at this time require the transportation across the sea of hostile armies on a very large scale, and after they been so transported they would have to be continually maintained with all the masses of munitions and supplies which are required for continuous battle— as continuous battle it will surely be.

Here is where we come to the Navy—and after all, we have a Navy. Some people seem to forget that we have a Navy. We must remind them. For the last thirty years I have been concerned in discussions about the possibilities of overseas invasion, and I took the responsibility on behalf of the Admiralty, at the beginning of the last war, of allowing all regular troops to be sent out of the country. That was a very serious step to take, because our Territorials had only just been called up and were quite untrained. Therefore, this island was for several months practically denuded of fighting troops. The Admiralty had confidence at that time in their ability to prevent a mass invasion even though at that time the Germans had a magnificent battle fleet the proportion of ten to sixteen, even though they were capable of fighting a general engagement every day and any day, whereas now they have only a couple of heavy ships worth speaking of—the Scharnhorstand the Gneisenau. We are also told that the Italian Navy is to come out and gain sea superiority in these waters. If they seriously intend it, I shall only say that we shall be delighted to offer Signor Mussolini a free and safeguarded passage through the Straits of Gibraltar in order that he may play the part to which he aspires. There is a general curiosity in the British Fleet to find out whether the Italians are up to the level they were at in the last war or whether they have fallen off at all.

Therefore, it seems to me that as far as seaborne invasion on a great scale is concerned, we are far more capable of meeting it today than we were at many periods in the last war and during the early months of this war, before our other troops were trained, and while the BEF had proceeded abroad. Now, the Navy have never pretended to be able to prevent raids by bodies of 5,000 or 10,000 men flung suddenly across and thrown ashore at several points on the coast some dark night or foggy morning. The efficacy of sea-power, especially under modern conditions, depends upon the invading force being of large size. It has to be of large size, in view of our military strength, to be of any use. If it is of large size, then the Navy have something they can find and meet and, as it were, bite on. Now we must remember that even five divisions, however lightly equipped, would require 200 to 250 ships, and with modern air reconnaissance and photography it would not be easy to collect such an armada, marshal it and conduct it across the sea without any powerful naval forces to escort it; and there would be very great possibilities, to put it mildly, that this armada would be intercepted long before it reached the coast, and all the men drowned in the sea or, at the worst, blown to pieces with their equipment while they were trying to land. We also have a great system of minefields, recently strongly reinforced, through which we alone know the channels. If the enemy tries to sweep passages through these minefields, it will be the task of the Navy to destroy the minesweepers and any other forces employed to protect them. There should be no difficulty in this, owing to our great superiority at sea.

Those are the regular, well-tested, well-proved arguments on which we have relied during many years in peace and war. But the question is whether there are any new methods by which those solid assurances can be circumvented. Odd as it may seem, some attention has been given to this by the Admiralty, whose prime duty and responsibility it is to destroy any large seaborne expedition before it reaches, or at the moment when it reaches these shores. It would not be a good thing for me to go into details of this. It might suggest ideas to other people which they have not thought of, and they would not be likely to give us any of their ideas in exchange. All I will say is that untiring vigilance and mind-searching must be devoted to the subject, because the enemy is crafty and cunning and full of novel treacheries and stratagems. The House may be assured that the utmost ingenuity is being displayed and imagination is being evoked from large numbers of competent officers, well trained in tactics and thoroughly up to date, to measure and counterwork novel possibilities. Untiring vigilance and untiring searching of the mind is being, and must be, devoted to the subject, because, remember, the enemy is crafty and there is no dirty trick he will not do.

Some people will ask why, then, was it that the British Navy was not able to prevent the movement of a large army from Germany into Norway across the Skaggerak? But the conditions in the Channel and in the North Sea are in no way like those which prevail in the Skaggerak. In the Skaggerak, because of the distance, we could give no air support to our surface ships, and consequently, lying as we did close to the enemy's main air power, we were compelled to use only our submarines. We could not enforce the decisive blockade or interruption which is possible from surface vessels. Our submarines took a heavy toll but could not, by themselves, prevent the invasion of Norway. In the Channel and in the North Sea, on the other hand, our superior naval surface forces, aided by our submarines, will operate with close and effective air assistance.

This brings me, naturally, to the great question of invasion from the air, and of the impending struggle between the British and German Air Forces. It seems quite clear that no invasion on a scale beyond the capacity of our land forces to crush speedily is likely to take place from the air until our Air Force has been definitely overpowered. In the meantime, there may be raids by parachute troops and attempted descents of airborne soldiers. We should be able to give those gentry a warm reception, both in the air and on the ground, if they reach it in any condition to continue the dispute. But the great question is: Can we break Hitler's air weapon? Now, of course, it is a very great pity that we have not got an Air Force at least equal to that of the most powerful enemy within striking distance of these shores. But we have a very powerful Air Force which has proved itself far superior in quality, both in men and in many types of machine, to what we have met so far in the numerous and fierce air battles which have been fought with the Germans. In France, where we were at a considerable disadvantage and lost many machines on the ground when they were standing round the aerodromes, we were accustomed to inflict in the air losses of as much as two to two-and-a-half to one. In the fighting over Dunkirk, which was a sort of no-man's land, we undoubtedly beat the German Air Force, and gained the mastery of the local air, inflicting here a loss of three or four to one day after day. Anyone who looks at the photographs which were published a week or so ago of the re-embarkation, showing the masses of troops assembled on the beach and forming an ideal target for hours at a time, must realize that this re-embarkation would not have been possible unless the enemy had resigned all hope of recovering air superiority at that time and at that place.

In the defence of this island the advantages to the defenders will be much greater than they were in the fighting around Dunkirk. We hope to improve on the rate of three or four to one which was realized at Dunkirk; and in addition all our injured machines and their crews which get down safe—and, surprisingly, a very great many injured machines and men do get down safely in modern air fighting—all of these will fall, in an attack upon these islands, on friendly soil and live to fight another day; whereas all the injured enemy machines and their complements will be total losses as far as the war is concerned.

During the great battle in France, we gave very powerful and continuous aid to the French Army, both by fighters and bombers; but in spite of every kind of pressure we never would allow the entire metropolitan fighter strength of the Air Force to be consumed. This decision was painful, but it was also right, because the fortunes of the battle in France could not have been decisively affected even if we had thrown in our entire fighter force. That battle was lost by the unfortunate strategical opening, by the extraordinary and unforeseen power of the armoured columns and by the great preponderance of the German Army in numbers. Our fighter Air Force might easily have been exhausted as a mere accident in that great struggle, and then we should have found ourselves at the present time in a very serious plight. But as it is, I am happy to inform the House that our fighter strength is stronger at the present time relatively to the Germans, who have suffered terrible losses, than it has ever been; and consequently we believe ourselves possessed of the capacity to continue the war in the air under better conditions than we have ever experienced before. I look forward confidently to the exploits of our fighter pilots—these splendid men, this brilliant youth—who will have the glory of saving their native land, their island home, and all they love, from the most deadly of all attacks.

There remains, of course, the danger of bombing attacks, which will certainly be made very soon upon us by the bomber forces of the enemy. It is true that the German bomber force is superior in numbers to ours; but we have a very large bomber force also, which we shall use to strike at military targets in Germany without intermission. I do not at all underrate the severity of the ordeal which lies before us; but I believe our countrymen will show themselves capable of standing up to it, like the brave men of Barcelona, and will be able to stand up to it, and carry on in spite of it, at least as well as any other people in the world. Much will depend upon this; every man and every woman will have the chance to show the finest qualities of their race, and render the highest service to their cause. For all of us, at this time, whatever our sphere, our station, our occupation or our duties, it will be a help to remember the famous lines:

He nothing common did or mean, upon that memorable scene. I have thought it right upon this occasion to give the House and the country some indication of the solid, practical grounds upon which we base our inflexible resolve to continue the war. There are a good many people who say, 'Never mind. Win or lose, sink or swim, better die than submit to tyranny—and such a tyranny.' And I do not dissociate myself from them. But I can assure them that our professional advisers of the three Services unitedly advise that we should carry on the war, and that there are good and reasonable hopes of final victory. We have fully informed and consulted all the self-governing Dominions, these great communities far beyond the oceans who have been built up on our laws and on our civilization, and who are absolutely free to choose their course, but are absolutely devoted to the ancient Motherland, and who feel themselves inspired by the same emotions which lead me to stake out all upon duty and honour. We have fully consulted them, and I have received from their Prime Ministers, Mr Mackenzie King of Canada, Mr Menzies of Australia, Mr Fraser of New Zealand, and General Smuts of South Africa—that wonderful man, with his immense profound mind, and his eye watching from a distance the whole panorama of European affairs—I have received from all these eminent men, who all have Governments behind them elected on wide franchises, who are all there because they represent the will of their people, messages couched in the most moving terms in which they endorse our decision to fight on, and declare themselves ready to share our fortunes and to persevere to the end. That is what we are going to do.

We may now ask ourselves: In what way has our position worsened since the beginning of the war? It has worsened by the fact that the Germans have conquered a large part of the coastline of Western Europe, and many small countries have been overrun by them. This aggravates the possibilities of air attack and adds to our naval preoccupations. It in no way diminishes, but on the contrary definitely increases, the power of our long-distance blockade. Similarly, the entrance of Italy into the war increases the power of our long-distance blockade. We have stopped the worst leak by that. We do not know whether military resistance will come to an end in France or not, but should it do so, then of course, the Germans will be able to concentrate their forces, both military and industrial, upon us. But for the reasons I have given to the House these will not be found so easy to apply. If invasion has become more imminent, as no doubt it has, we, being relieved from the task of maintaining a large army in France, have far larger and more efficient forces to meet it.

If Hitler can bring under his despotic control the industries of the countries he has conquered, this will add greatly to his already vast armament output. On the other hand, this will not happen immediately, and we are now assured of immense, continuous and increasing support in supplies and munitions of all kinds from the United States; and especially of airplanes and pilots from the Dominions and across the oceans, coming from regions which are beyond the reach of enemy bombers.

I do not see how any of these factors can operate to our detriment on balance before the winter comes; and the winter will impose a strain upon the Nazi regime, with almost all Europe writhing and starving under its cruel heel, which, for all their ruthlessness, will run them very hard. We must not forget that from the moment when we declared war on the 3 September it was always possible for Germany to turn all her air force upon this country, together with any other devices of invasion she might conceive, and that France could have done little or nothing to prevent her doing so. We have, therefore, lived under this danger, in principle and in a slightly modified form, during all these months. In the meanwhile, however, we have enormously improved our methods of defence, and we have learned, what we had no right to assume at the beginning, namely, that the individual aircraft and the individual British pilot have a sure and definite superiority. Therefore, in casting up this dread balance sheet and contemplating our dangers with a disillusioned eye, I see great reason for intense vigilance and exertion but none whatever for panic or despair.

During the first four years of the last war the Allies experienced nothing but disaster and disappointment. That was our constant fear: one blow after another, terrible losses, frightful dangers. Everything miscarried. And yet at the end of those four years the morale of the Allies was higher than that of the Germans, who had moved from one aggressive triumph to another, and who stood everywhere triumphant invaders of the lands into which they had broken. During that war we repeatedly asked ourselves the question: How are we going to win? And no one was able ever to answer it with much precision, until at the end, quite suddenly, quite unexpectedly, our terrible foe collapsed before us, and we were so glutted with victory that in our folly we threw it away.

We do not yet know what will happen in France or whether the French resistance will be prolonged, both in France and in the French Empire overseas. The French Government will be throwing away great opportunities and casting adrift their future if they do not continue the war in accordance with their Treaty obligations, from which we have not felt able to release them. The House will have read the historic declaration in which, at the desire of many Frenchmen—and of our own hearts—we have proclaimed our willingness at the darkest hour in French history to conclude a union of common citizenship in this struggle. However matters may go in France or with the French Government, or other French Governments, we in this island and in the British Empire will never lose our sense of comradeship with the French people. If we are now called upon to endure what they have been suffering, we shall emulate their courage, and if final victory rewards our toils they shall share the gains, aye, and freedom shall be restored to all. We abate nothing of our just demands; not one jot or title do we recede. Czechs, Poles, Norwegians, Dutch, Belgians have joined their causes to our own. All these shall be restored.

What General Weygand called the Battle of France is over. I expect that the Battle of Britain is about to begin. Upon this battle depends the survival of Christian civilization. Upon it depends our own British life, and the long continuity of our institutions and our Empire. The whole fury and might of the enemy must very soon be turned on us. Hitler knows that he will have to break us in this island or lose the war. If we can stand up to him, all Europe may be free and the life of the world may move forward into broad, sunlit uplands. But if we fail, then the whole world, including the United States, including all that we have known and cared for, will sink into the abyss of a new Dark Age made more sinister, and perhaps more protracted, by the lights of perverted science. Let us therefore brace ourselves to our duties and so bear ourselves that, if the British Empire and its Commonwealth last for a thousand years, men will still say, 'This was their finest hour.'

Heinrich Himmler, "Speech to SS Officers"

Heinrich Himmler (1900-1945) headed the SS, or the Schutzstaffel (protection echelon), the elite militia of the Nazi party. The group had its origins in the 1920s when they first served as Hitler's bodyguards. With the growth and expansion of the party, the SS evolved into a policing force of more than 50,000 men. The SS routinely used intimidation tactics and coercion to eliminate political opposition, even perceived threats from within the Nazi party itself. In the 1930s the SS, under Hitler's express orders, executed Ernst Roehm (18871934) a high level political official along with many other officers, in a purge designed to ensure Hitler's control over the party. This address made by Himmler to the SS comes in 1943 during World War II after the tide had turned against the Germans, when their troops were not faring well, particularly on the Russian front. By 1943, the Holocaust was also well underway, with Nazi troops and the SS overseeing the mass killings of European Jews and other "non-

Aryan" groups held in war camps. In the following document, Himmler lays out the role of the SS and the code of behavior expected of them.

Source: Heinrich Himmler,"Speech to SS Officers, 1943" in A Holocaust Reader, ed. Lucy Dawidowicz (New York: Berman House, 1976), 130-135; reprinted in *Reading the Global Past: Selected Historical Documents*, eds. Russell J. Barber, Cheryl A. Riggs, vol. 2 (Boston: Bedford Books, 1998), 145-147.

FOCUS QUESTIONS:

1. How did Himmler define "Germans" and "Germany" in this speech? What groups did he deem to be "foreigners," and how did he characterize these groups?
2. What ideas and beliefs informed Himmler's views? How did the war, and the course of the war by 1943, possibly affect his views?
3 .For Himmler, what was the role of the SS in the war, in the Nazi party, and in the German nation?

... In 1941 the Führer attacked Russia. That was, as we probably can assert now, shortly—perhaps three to six months— before Stalin was winding up for his great push into Central and Western Europe. I can sketch this first year in a very few lines. The attack cut through. The Russian army was herded together in great pockets, ground down, captured. At that time we did not value this human mass the way we value it today, as raw material, as labor. In the long run, viewed in terms of generations, it is no loss, but today, because of the loss of manpower, it is regrettable that the prisoners died by the tens and hundreds of thousands of exhaustion, of hunger....

GOOD NATURE IN THE WRONG PLACE

It is a basic mistake for us to infuse our inoffensive soul and feeling, our good nature, our idealism, into alien peoples. This has been true since the time of Herder, who must have written Stimmen der Völker in a boozy hour,[1] and who thereby brought such immeasurable sorrow and misery on us later generations. This has been true since the case of the Czechs and Slovenes, to whom, after all, we gave their sense of nationality. They themselves were not capable of achieving it; we invented it for them.

One basic principle must be absolute for the SS man: we must be honest, decent, loyal, and comradely to members of our own blood and to nobody else.

1 Johann Gottfried von Herder (1744-1803), German philospher and poet, has been called the father of German nationalism. As a champion of the idea of nationalism, he published an anthology of folk songs of various peoples called Stimmen der Völker (Voices of the Peoples).

What happens to the Russians, what happens to the Czechs, is a matter of total indifference to me. What there is among the nations is the way of good blood of our kind, we will take for ourselves—if necessary, by kidnapping their children and raising them among us. Whether the other nations live in prosperity or croak from hunger interests me only insofar as we need them as slaves for our culture; otherwise, it does not interest me. Whether 10,000 Russian females drop from exhaustion while building an anti-tank ditch interests me only insofar as the anti-tank ditch gets finished for Germany's sake. We shall never be brutal and heartless where it is not necessary—obviously not. We Germans, the only people in the world who have a decent attitude toward animals, will also take a decent attitude toward these human animals. But it is a crime against our own blood to worry about them and to give them ideals that will make it still harder for our sons and grandsons to cope with them. If someone were to come to me and say, "I cannot build the anti-tank ditch with women or children; it is inhuman, they will die in the process," then I would have to say, "You are a murderer of your own blood, for if the anti-tank ditch is not built, German soldiers will die, and they are sons of German mothers. They are our own blood." This is what I want to instill into the SS and what I believe I have instilled into them as one of the most sacred laws of the future: Our concern, our duty is to our people and our blood; it is for them that we have to provide and to plan, to work and to fight, and for nothing else. Toward anything else we can be indifferent. I wish the SS to take this attitude in confronting the problem of all alien, non-Germanic peoples, especially the Russians. All else is just soap bubbles, is a fraud against our own nation and an obstacle to the earlier winning of the war....

FOREIGNERS IN THE REICH

We must also realize that we have between six and seven million foreigners in Germany, perhaps even eight million by now. We have prisoners in Germany. They are none of them dangerous so long as we hit them hard at the smallest trifle. Shooting ten Poles today is a mere nothing when compared with the fact that we might later have to shoot tens of thousands in their place, and that the shooting of these tens of thousands would also cost German blood. Every little fire will immediately be stamped out and quenched and extinguished; others— as with a real conflagration—a political and psychological fire may break out among the people.

THE COMMUNISTS IN THE REICH

I do not believe the Communists could risk any action, for their leading elements, like most criminals, are in our concentration camps. Here something needs saying: After the war it will be possible to see what a blessing it was for Germany that, regardless of all humanitarian sentimentality, we imprisoned this whole criminal substratum of the German people in the concentration camps;

and for this I claim the credit. If these people were going about free, we would be having a harder time of it. For then the subhumans would have their NCO's and commanding officers, they would have their workers' and soldiers' councils. As it is, they are locked up, and are making shells or projectile cases or other important things, and are very useful members of human society....

THE EVACUATION OF THE JEWS

I also want to make reference before you here, in complete frankness, to a really grave matter. Among ourselves, this once, it shall be uttered quite frankly; but in public we will never speak of it. Just as we did not hesitate on June 30, 1934, to do our duty as ordered, to stand up against the wall comrades who had transgressed, and shoot them,[2] so we have never talked about this and never will. It was the tact which I am glad to say is a matter of course to us that made us never discuss it among ourselves, never talk about it. Each of us shuddered, and yet each one knew that he would do it again if it were ordered and if it were necessary.

I am referring to the evacuation of the Jews, the annihilation of the Jewish people. This is one of those things that are easily said. "The Jewish people is going to be annihilated," says every party member. "Sure, it's in our program, elimination of the Jews, annihilation—we'll take care of it." And then they all come trudging, 80 million worthy Germans, and each one has his own decent Jew. Sure, the others are swine, but this one is an A1 Jew. Of all those who talk this way, not one has seen it happen, not one has been through it. Most of you must know what it means to see a hundred corpses lie side by side, or five hundred, or a thousand. To have stuck this out and—excepting cases of human weakness—to have kept our integrity, that is what has made us hard. In our history, this is an unwritten and never-to-be-written page of glory, for we know how difficult we would have made it for ourselves if today—amid the bombing raids, the hardships and the deprivations of war—we still had the Jews in every city as secret saboteurs, agitators, and demagogues. If the Jews were still ensconced in the body of the German nation, we probably would have reached the 1916-17 stage by now.[3]

The wealth they had we have taken from them. I have issued a strict order, Carried out by SS-Obergruppenführer Pohl, that this wealth in its entirety is to be turned over to the Reich as a matter of course. We have taken none of it for ourselves. Individuals who transgress will be punished in accordance with an order I issued at the beginning, threatening that whoever takes so much as a mark of it for himself is a dead man. A number of SS men—not very many—have

2 A reference to the purge of the SA [Sturmabteilung, "storm troopers," the Nazi Party militia] and the murder of its top leaders by SS officers and men.

3 The reference is to the time when the tide of World War I began to turn against Germany. German nationalists and rightists then attributed Germany's losses and ultimate defeat to the Dolchstoss, the "stab in the back" by the Jews.

transgressed, and they will die, without mercy. We had the moral right, we had the duty toward our people, to kill this people which wanted to kill us. But we do not have the right to enrich ourselves with so much as a fur, a watch, a mark, or a cigarette or anything else. Having exterminated a germ, we do not want, in the end, to be infected by the germ, and die of it. I will not stand by and let even a small rotten spot develop or take hold. Wherever it may form, we together will cauterize it. All in all, however, we can say that we have carried out this heaviest of our tasks in a spirit of love for our people. And our inward being, our soul, or character has not suffered injury from it.

Franklin D. Roosevelt, "Call for Sacrifice"

With the Japanese surprise attack on Pearl Harbor in December of 1941, the US entered World War II fighting on the side of the British and Allies, which after Hitler's invasion of Russia in June of 1941 also included the USSR. In the wake of the Pearl Harbor attack, Hitler honored an earlier treaty he had made with the Japanese emperor, and came to the defense of Japan making it a member of the Axis powers. The entry of the US and Japan created another theater of war, one in the Pacific, in addition to the European front which by 1942 extended into the Mediterranean, North Africa and the Middle East. In this 1942 speech, entitled "Call for Sacrifice," President Roosevelt asked all Americans to contribute to the war. Roosevelt made this appeal during one of his regular informal speeches, which he called "fireside chats," that were broadcast to a wide American radio listening audience.

Source: Russell D. Buhite and David W. Levy, eds., *FDR's Firesides Chats* (Norman: University of Oklahoma Press. 1992), 219-229.

Focus Questions:

1. What "sacrifices" did Roosevelt request from Americans and from what segments of the public?
2. What did he see as the greatest threats to the war effort and the Allies' success? How did Roosevelt present these threats?
3. What does this tell us about the nature of warfare in World War II and its affect on civilian populations, even in the US which was far removed from the theaters of war?

My Fellow Americans, it is nearly five months since we were attacked at Pearl Harbor. For the two years prior to that attack this country had been gearing itself up to a high level of production of munitions. And yet our war efforts had done little to dislocate the normal lives of most of us.

Since then we have dispatched strong forces of our Army and Navy, several hundred thousands of them, to bases and battlefronts thousands of miles from home. We have stepped up our war production on a scale that is testing our industrial power, our engineering genius, and our economic structure to the utmost. We have had no illusions about the fact that this is a tough job—and a long one.

American warships are now in combat in the North and South Atlantic, in the Arctic, in the Mediterranean, in the Indian Ocean, and in the North and South Pacific. American troops have taken stations in South America, Greenland, Iceland, the British Isles, the Near East, the Middle East and the Far East, the continent of Australia, and many islands of the Pacific. American war planes, manned by Americans, are flying in actual combat over all the continents and all the oceans.

On the European front the most important development of the past year has been without question the crushing counteroffensive on the part of the great armies of Russia against the powerful German army. These Russian forces have destroyed and are destroying more armed power of our enemies—troops, planes, tanks, and guns— than all the other United Nations put together.

In the Mediterranean area, matters remain on the surface much as they were. But the situation there is receiving very careful attention. Recently, we've received news of a change in government in what we used to know as the Republic of France—a name dear to the hearts of all lovers of liberty, a name and an institution which we hope will soon be restored to full dignity.

Throughout the Nazi occupation of France, we have hoped for the maintenance of a French government which would strive to regain independence, to reestablish the principles of "Liberty, Equality, and Fraternity," and to restore the historic culture of France. Our policy has been consistent from the very beginning. However, we are now greatly concerned lest those who have recently come to power may seek to force the brave French people into submission to Nazi despotism.

The United Nations will take measures, if necessary, to prevent the use of French territory in any part of the world for military purposes by the Axis powers. The good people of France will readily understand that such action is essential for the United Nations to prevent assistance to the armies or navies or air forces of Germany or Italy or Japan. The overwhelming majority of the French people understand that the fight of the United Nations is fundamentally their fight, that our victory means the restoration of a free and independent France—and the saving of France from the slavery which would be imposed upon her by her external enemies and by her internal traitors.

We know how the French people really feel. We know that a deep-seated determination to obstruct every step in the Axis plan extends from occupied France through Vichy France all the way to the people of their colonies in every ocean and on every continent.

Our planes are helping in the defense of French colonies today, and soon American Flying Fortresses will be fighting for the liberation of the darkened continent of Europe itself.

In all the occupied countries there are men and women, and even little children, who have never stopped fighting, never stopped resisting, never stopped proving to the Nazis that their so-called new order will never be enforced upon free peoples.

In the German and Italian peoples themselves there's a growing conviction that the cause of Nazism and Fascism is hopeless—that their political and military leaders have led them along the bitter road which leads not to world conquest but to final defeat. They cannot fail to contrast the present frantic speeches of these leaders with their arrogant boastings of a year ago, and two years ago.

And on the other side of the world, in the Far East, we have passed through a phase of serious losses.

We have inevitably lost control of a large portion of the Philippine Islands. But this whole nation pays tribute to the Filipino and American officers and men who held out so long on Bataan Peninsula, to those grim and gallant fighters who still hold Corregidor, where the flag flies, and to the forces that are still striking effectively at the enemy on Mindanao and other islands.

The Malayan Peninsula and Singapore are in the hands of the enemy; the Netherlands East Indies are almost entirely occupied, though resistance there continues. Many other islands are in the possession of the Japanese. But there is good reason to believe that their southward advance has been checked. Australia, New Zealand, and much other territory will be bases for offensive action—and we are determined that the territory that has been lost will be regained.

The Japanese are pressing their northward advance against Burma with considerable power, driving toward India and China. They have been opposed with great bravery by small British and Chinese forces aided by American fliers.

The news in Burma tonight is not good. The Japanese may cut the Burma Road;[1] but I want to say to the gallant people of China that no matter what advances the Japanese may make, ways will be found to deliver airplanes and munitions of war to the armies of Generalissimo Chiang Kai-shek.[2]

1 The Burma Road ran seven hundred miles from a Burmese railhead, through very difficult mountain terrain, and into China's Yunnan province. It was a main supply route to the beleaguered Chinese, especially after the Japanese closed China's east-coast ports.

2 Chiang Kai-shek (1887–1975) was the leader of the Chinese Nationalists, opposed both to the Japanese invaders and to the native Chinese Communists. During World War II his prestige was at its height as he and his wife were befriended by President Roosevelt, despite accusations in some quarters of incompetence and corruption.

We remember that the Chinese people were the first to stand up and fight against the aggressors in this war; and in the future a still unconquerable China will play its proper role in maintaining peace and prosperity, not only in eastern Asia but in the whole world.

For every advance that the Japanese have made since they started their frenzied career of conquest, they have had to pay a very heavy toll in warships, in transports, in planes, and in men. They are feeling the effects of those losses.

It is even reported from Japan that somebody has dropped bombs on Tokyo, and on other principal centers of Japanese war industries.

If this be true, it is the first time in history that Japan has suffered such indignities.[3]

Although the treacherous attack on Pearl Harbor was the immediate cause of our entry into the war, that event found the American people spiritually prepared for war on a worldwide scale. We went into this war fighting. We know what we are fighting for. We realize that the war has become what Hitler originally proclaimed it to be—a total war.

Not all of us can have the privilege of fighting our enemies in distant parts of the world.

Not all of us can have the privilege of working in a munitions factory or a shipyard, or on the farms or in oil fields or mines, producing the weapons or the raw materials that are needed by our armed forces.

But there is one front and one battle where everyone in the United States—every man, woman, and child—is in action, and will be privileged to remain in action throughout this war. That front is right here at home, in our daily lives, in our daily tasks. Here at home everyone will have the privilege of making whatever self-denial is necessary, not only to supply our fighting men, but to keep the economic structure of our country fortified and secure during the war and after the war.

This will require, of course, the abandonment not only of luxuries but of many other creature comforts.

Every loyal American is aware of his individual responsibility. Whenever I hear anyone saying, "The American people are complacent—they need to be aroused," I feel like asking him to come to Washington to read the mail that floods into the White House and into all departments of this government. The one question that recurs through all these thousands of letters and messages is, "What more can I do to help my country in winning this war?"

3 This passage, delivered by Roosevelt with sly sarcasm in his voice, was a vague reference to the bombing raid by Army airmen under the command of Colonel James Doolittle only ten days before this speech. Sixteen B-25 bombers, taking off from the carrier Hornet, carried out attacks on Tokyo and other Japanese cities. Damage in Japan was negligible.

To build the factories, to buy the materials, to pay the labor, to provide the transportation, to equip and feed and house the soldiers and sailors and marines, and to do all the thousands of things necessary in a war—all cost a lot of money, more money than has ever been spent by any nation at anytime in the long history of the world.

We are now spending, solely for war purposes, the sum of about $100 million every day in the week. But, before this year is over, that almost unbelievable rate of expenditure will be doubled.

All of this money has to be spent—and spent quickly—if we are to produce within the time now available the enormous quantities of weapons of war which we need. But the spending of these tremendous sums presents grave danger of disaster to our national economy.

When your government continues to spend these unprecedented sums for munitions month by month and year by year, that money goes into the pocketbooks and bank accounts of the people of the United States. At the same time raw materials and many manufactured goods are necessarily taken away from civilian use; and machinery and factories are being converted to war production.

You do not have to be a professor of mathematics or economics to see that if people with plenty of cash start bidding against each other for scarce goods, the price of those goods goes up.

Yesterday I submitted to the Congress of the United States a seven-point program, a program of general principles which taken together could be called the national economic policy for attaining the great objective of keeping the cost of living down.

I repeat them now to you in substance:

First, we must, through heavier taxes, keep personal and corporate profits at a low reasonable rate.

Second, we must fix ceilings on prices and rents.

Third, we must stabilize wages.

Fourth, we must stabilize farm prices.

Fifth, we must put more billions into war bonds.

Sixth, we must ration all essential commodities which are scarce.

And seventh, we must discourage installment buying, and encourage paying off debts and mortgages.

I do not think it is necessary to repeat what I said yesterday to the Congress in discussing these general principles.

The important thing to remember is that each one of these points is dependent on the others if the whole program is to work.

Some people are already taking the position that every one of the seven points is correct except the one point which steps on their own individual toes. A few seem very willing to approve self-denial—on the part of their neighbors. The only effective course of action is a simultaneous attack on all of the factors which increase the cost of living, in one comprehensive, all-embracing program covering prices and profits and wages and taxes and debts.

The blunt fact is that every single person in the United States is going to be affected by this program. Some of you will be affected more directly by one or two of these restrictive measures, but all of you will be affected indirectly by all of them.

Are you a businessman, or do you own stock in a business corporation? Well, your profits are going to be cut down to a reasonably low level by taxation. Your income will be subject to higher taxes. Indeed in these days, when every available dollar should go to the war effort, I do not think that any American citizen should have a net income in excess of $25,000 per year after payment of taxes.

Are you a retailer or a wholesaler or a manufacturer or a farmer or a landlord? Ceilings are being placed on the prices at which you can sell your goods or rent your property.

Do you work for wages? You will have to forgo higher wages for your particular job for the duration of the war.

All of us are used to spending money for things that we want, things, however, which are not absolutely essential. We will all have to forgo that kind of spending. Because we must put every dime and every dollar we can possibly spare out of our earnings into war bonds and stamps. Because the demands of the war effort require the rationing of goods of which there is not enough to go around. Because the stopping of purchases of nonessentials will release thousands of workers who are needed in the war effort.

As I told the Congress yesterday, "sacrifice" is not exactly the proper word with which to describe this program of self-denial. When, at the end of this great struggle, we shall have saved our free way of life, we shall have made no "sacrifice."

The price for civilization must be paid in hard work and sorrow and blood. The price is not too high. If you doubt it, ask those millions who live today under the tyranny of Hitlerism.

Ask the workers of France and Norway and the Netherlands, whipped to labor by the lash, whether the stabilization of wages is too great a "sacrifice."

Ask the farmers of Poland and Denmark and Czechoslovakia and France, looted of their livestock, starving while their own crops are stolen from their land, ask them whether parity prices are too great a "sacrifice."

Ask the businessmen of Europe, whose enterprises have been stolen from their owners, whether the limitation of profits and personal incomes is too great a "sacrifice."

Ask the women and children whom Hitler is starving whether the rationing of tires and gasoline and sugar is too great a "sacrifice."

We do not have to ask them. They have already given us their agonized answers.

This great war effort must be carried through to its victorious conclusion by the indomitable will and determination of the people as one great whole.

It must not be impeded by the faint of heart.

It must not be impeded by those who put their own selfish interests above the interests of the nation.

It must not be impeded by those who pervert honest criticism into falsification of fact.

It must not be impeded by self-styled experts either in economics or military problems who know neither true figures nor geography itself.

It must not be impeded by a few bogus patriots who use the sacred freedom of the press to echo the sentiments of the propagandists in Tokyo and Berlin.

And, above all, it shall not be imperiled by the handful of noisy traitors—betrayers of America, betrayers of Christianity itself—would-be dictators who in their hearts and souls have yielded to Hitierism and would have this republic do likewise.

I shall use all of the executive power that I have to carry out the policy laid down. If it becomes necessary to ask for any additional legislation in order to attain our objective of preventing a spiral in the cost of living, I shall do so.

I know the American farmer, the American workman, and the American businessman. I know that they will gladly embrace this economy and equality of sacrifice—satisfied that it is necessary for the most vital and compelling motive in all their lives—winning through to victory.

Never in the memory of man has there been a war in which the courage, the endurance, and the loyalty of civilians played so vital a part.

Many thousands of civilians all over the world have been and are being killed or maimed by enemy action. Indeed, it is the fortitude of the common people of Britain under fire which enabled that island to stand and prevented Hitler from winning the war in 1940. The ruins of London and Coventry and other cities are today the proudest monuments to British heroism.

Our own American civilian population is now relatively safe from such disasters. And, to an ever increasing extent, our soldiers, sailors, and marines are fighting with great bravery and great skills on far distant fronts to make sure that we shall remain safe.

I should like to tell you one or two stories about the men we have in our armed forces:

There is, for example, Dr. Corydon M. Wassell. He was a missionary, well known for his good works in China. He is a simple, modest, retiring man, nearly sixty years old, but he entered the service of his country and was commissioned a lieutenant commander in the navy.

Dr. Wassell was assigned to duty in Java caring for wounded officers and men of the cruisers Houstonand Marbleheadwhich had been in heavy action in the Java seas.

When the Japanese advanced across the island, it was decided to evacuate as many as possible of the wounded to Australia. But about twelve of the men were so badly wounded that they couldn't be moved. Dr. Wassell remained with them, knowing that he would be captured by the enemy. But he decided to make a last desperate attempt to get the men out of Java. He asked each of them if he wished to take the chance, and every one agreed.

He first had to get the twelve men to the seacoast—fifty miles away. To do this, he had to improvise stretchers for the hazardous journey. The men were suffering severely, but Dr. Wassell kept them alive by his skill, inspired them by his own courage.

And as the official report said, Dr. Wassell was "almost like a Christ-like shepherd devoted to his flock."

On the seacoast, he embarked the men on a little Dutch ship. They were bombed, they were machine-gunned by waves of Japanese planes. Dr. Wassell took virtual command of the ship, and by great skill avoided destruction, hiding in little bays and little inlets.

A few days later, Dr. Wassell and his small flock of wounded men reached Australia safely.

And today Dr. Wassell wears the Navy Cross.

Another story concerns a ship, a ship rather than an individual man. You may remember the tragic sinking of the submarine, the United States Ship Squalus, off the New England coast in the summer of 1939. Some of the crew were lost, but others were saved by the speed and the efficiency of the surface rescue crews.

The Squalusitself was tediously raised from the bottom of the sea.

She was repaired, put back into commission, and eventually she sailed again under a new name, the United States Ship Sailfish. Today, she is a potent and effective unit of our submarine fleet in the Southwest Pacific.

The Sailfishhas covered many thousands of miles in operations in those far waters.

She has sunk a Japanese destroyer.

She has torpedoed a Japanese cruiser.

She has made torpedo hits—two of them—on a Japanese aircraft carrier.

Three of the enlisted men of our Navy who went down with the Squalusin 1939 and were rescued are today serving on the same ship, the United States Ship Sailfish, in this war. It seems to me that it is heartening to know that the Squalus, once given up as lost, rose from the depths to fight for our country in time of peril.

One more story that I heard only this morning.

This is a story of one of our Army Flying Fortresses operating in the western Pacific. The pilot of this plane is a modest young man, proud of his crew for one of the toughest fights a bomber has yet experienced.

The bomber departed from its base, as part of a flight of five bombers, to attack Japanese transports that were landing troops against us in the Philippines. When they had gone about halfway to their destination, one of the motors of this bomber went out of commission. The young pilot lost contact with the other bombers. The crew, however, got the motor working, got it going again and the plane proceeded on its mission alone.

By the time it arrived at its target the other four Flying Fortresses had already passed over, had dropped their bombs, and had stirred up the hornets' nest of Japanese "Zero" planes. Eighteen of these Zero fighters attacked our one Flying Fortress. Despite this mass attack, our plane proceeded on its mission, and dropped all of its bombs on six Japanese transports which were lined up along the docks.

As it turned back on its homeward journey a running fight between the bomber and the eighteen Japanese pursuit planes continued for seventy-five miles. Four pursuit planes of the Japs attacked simultaneously at each side. Four were shot down with the side guns. During this fight, the bomber's radio operator was killed, the engineer's right hand was shot off, and one gunner was crippled, leaving only one man available to operate both side guns. Although wounded in one hand, this gunner alternately manned both side guns, bringing down three more Japanese Zero planes. While this was going on, one engine on the American bomber was shot out, one gas tank was hit, the radio was shot off, and the oxygen system was entirely destroyed. Out of eleven control cables all but four were shot away. The rear landing wheel was blown off entirely, and the two front wheels were both shot flat.

The fight continued until the remaining Japanese pursuit ships exhausted their ammunition and turned back. With two engines gone and the plane practically out of control, the American bomber returned to its base after dark and made an emergency landing. The mission had been accomplished.

The name of that pilot is Captain Hewitt T. Wheless, of the United States Army. He comes from a place called Menard, Texas—with a population of 2,375. He has been awarded the Distinguished Service Cross. And I hope that he is listening.

These stories I have told you are not exceptional. They are typical examples of individual heroism and skill.

As we here at home contemplate our own duties, our own responsibilities, let us think and think hard of the example which is being set for us by our fighting men.

Our soldiers and sailors are members of well-disciplined units. But they're still and forever individuals—free individuals. They are farmers and workers, businessmen, professional men, artists, clerks. They are the United States of America.

That is why they fight.

We too are the United States of America. That is why we must work and sacrifice. It is for them. It is for us. It is for victory.

Franklin D. Roosevelt and Winston Churchill, "The Atlantic Charter"

President Franklin D. Roosevelt's concern over the war in Europe sharply increased in 1940 with the collapse of France and the potential expansion of Hitler's empire to the New World if Britain fell. In September, Roosevelt tried to strengthen Britain's ability to resist by exchanging American destroyers for the right to lease naval and air bases in British Commonwealth territories. The following spring, although the United States was technically neutral, Roosevelt urged the passage of the Lend-Lease Act to provide war materials to those nations fighting the Axis powers. While taking these important steps on the road to war, President Roosevelt outlined his objectives and the national interest in his 1941 State of the Union Address, which became known as his "Four Freedoms" speech.

Later that summer, Roosevelt and Churchill met for a shipboard conference off Argentia, Newfoundland, and forged a closer alignment with their joint statement of war aims known as the Atlantic Charter.

Source: U.S. Department of State, *Peace and War: United States Foreign Policy, 1931–1941*, Publication 1983 (Washington, DC: Government Printing Office, 1943), pp. 718–19.

Focus Questions:

1. Why would the influential Japanese newspaper Asahi regard the Atlantic Charter, particularly its fourth article, as a de facto declaration of war by the United States and Great Britain?
2 .Would Woodrow Wilson approve of this charter? Why? Why not?

Joint declaration of the President of the United States of America and the Prime Minister, Mr. Churchill, representing His Majesty's Government in the United Kingdom, being met together, deem it right to make known certain common principles in the national policies of their respective countries on which they base their hopes for a better future for the world.

First, their countries seek no aggrandizement, territorial or other;

Second, they desire to see no territorial changes that do not accord with the freely expressed wishes of the peoples concerned;

Third, they respect the right of all peoples to choose the form of government under which they will live; and they wish to see sovereign rights and self-government restored to those who have been forcibly deprived of them;

Fourth, they will endeavor, with due respect for their existing obligations, to further the enjoyment by all states, great or small, victor or vanquished, of access, on equal terms, to the trade and to the raw materials of the world which are needed for their economic prosperity;

Fifth, they desire to bring about the fullest collaboration between all nations in the economic field with the object of securing, for all, improved labor standards, economic advancement, and social security;

Sixth, after the final destruction of the Nazi tyranny, they hope to see established a peace which will afford to all nations the means of dwelling in safety within their own boundaries, and which will afford assurance that all the men in all the lands may live out their lives in freedom from fear and want;

Seventh, such a peace should enable all men to traverse the high seas and oceans without hindrance;

Eighth, they believe that all the nations of the world, for realistic as well as spiritual reasons, must come to the abandonment of the use of force. Since no future peace can be maintained if land, sea, or air armaments continue to be employed by nations which threaten, or may threaten, aggression outside of their frontiers, they believe, pending the establishment of a wider and permanent system of general security, that the disarmament of such nations is essential. They will likewise aid and encourage all other practicable measures which will lighten for peace-loving peoples the crushing burden of armaments.

Franklin D. Roosevelt

Winston S. Churchill

American Investigators, from *The Effects of Atomic Bombs on Hiroshima and Nagasaki*

Although heavy fighting had been waged on the mainland of Asia since the Japanese invasion of Manchuria in 1931, the beginning of the Second World War is usually dated from September 1, 1939, when Nazi Germany launched its surprise attack on Poland. Unlike the First World War, in which hostilities were generally confined to relatively small areas of Europe, the Second World War was virtually global in extent. Land, sea, and aerial combat spread throughout most of Europe, large areas of Asia and Africa, along the coastlines of both North and South America, and on innumerable islands scattered across the Pacific Ocean. The United States entered the war following the Japanese surprise attack on the Pacific Fleet at Pearl Harbor, Hawaii, on December 7, 1941. The war finally came to an end, first with the German collapse in May 1945, and then the Japanese surrender three months later, following the American atomic bomb attacks on Hiroshima and Nagasaki. One of the unanswerable questions of history is that of how long the war would have continued and how many lives would have been lost had the United States not dropped the two atomic bombs.

The bomb had been developed over several years by American scientists and engineers working in great secrecy under the code name "Manhattan Project." It had been tested only once—in the desert of New Mexico—before being released over Hiroshima. The decision to drop the bomb in Japan, probably the most awesome decision ever to face a human being, was made by President Harry S. Truman.

It is difficult to describe in words the effects of the atomic explosions over the two Japanese cities. Nevertheless, the following selection, although written largely in factual, unemotional terms, succeeds in capturing something of the essence not only of the material destruction wreaked but also of the human suffering, both physical and psychological, of the victims of the attacks. It is taken from a report prepared shortly after the war by a team of American investigators who visited both cities, examined the effects of the bombing, and questioned many survivors of the attacks.

Source: *The Effects of Atomic Bombs on Hiroshima and Nagasaki* (Washington, D.C.: U.S. Government Printing Office, 1946).

Focus Questions:

1. What is the purpose of this report?
2. What unexpected effects of the bombings did the investigators find?

I. INTRODUCTION

The available facts about the power of the atomic bomb as a military weapon lie in the story of what it did at Hiroshima and Nagasaki. Many of these facts have been published, in official and unofficial form, but mingled with distortions or errors. The United States Strategic Bombing Survey, therefore, in partial fulfillment of the mission for which it was established, has put together in these pages a fairly full account of just what the atomic bombs did at Hiroshima and Nagasaki. Together with an explanation of how the bomb achieved these effects, this report states the extent and nature of the damage, the casualties, and the political repercussions from the two attacks. The basis is the observation, measurement, and analysis of the Survey's investigators. The conjecture that is necessary for understanding of the complex phenomena and for applying the findings to the problems of defense of the United States is clearly labelled.

When the atomic bombs fell, the United States Strategic Bombing Survey was completing a study of the effects of strategic bombing on Germany's ability and will to resist. A similar study of the effects of strategic bombing on Japan was being planned. The news of the dropping of the atomic bomb gave a new urgency to this project, for a study of the air war against Japan clearly involved new weapons and new possibilities of concentration of attack that might qualify or even change the conclusions and recommendations of the Survey as to the effectiveness of air power. The directors of the Survey, therefore, decided to examine exhaustively the effects of the atomic bombs, in order that the full impact on Japan and the implications of their results could be

confidently analyzed. Teams of experts were selected to study the scenes of the bombings from the special points of emphasis of physical damage, civilian defense, morale, casualties, community life, utilities and transportation, various industries, and the general economic and political repercussions. In all, more than 110 men—engineers, architects, fire experts, economists, doctors, photographers, draftsmen—participated in the field study at each city, over a period of 10 weeks from October to December, 1945. Their detailed studies are now being published.

* * *

II. THE EFFECTS OF THE ATOMIC BOMBINGS

A. The Attacks and Damage

1. The attacks.

A single atomic bomb, the first weapon of its type ever used against a target, exploded over the city of Hiroshima at 0815 on the morning of 6 August 1945. Most of the industrial workers had already reported to work, but many workers were enroute and nearly all the school children and some industrial employees were at work in the open on the program of building removal to provide fire-breaks and disperse valuables to the country. The attack came 45 minutes after the "all clear" had been sounded from a previous alert. Because of the lack of warning and the populace's indifference to small groups of planes, the explosion came as an almost complete surprise, and the people had not taken shelter. Many were caught in the open, and most of the rest in flimsily constructed homes or commercial establishments.

The bomb exploded slightly northwest of the center of the city. Because of this accuracy and the flat terrain and circular shape of the city, Hiroshima was uniformly and extensively devastated. Practically the entire densely or moderately built-up portion of the city was leveled by blast and swept by fire. A "firestorm," a phenomenon which has occurred infrequently in other conflagrations, developed in Hiroshima: fires springing up almost simultaneously over the wide flat area around the center of the city drew in air from all directions. The inrush of air easily overcame the natural ground wind, which had a velocity of only about 5 miles per hour. The "firewind" attained a maximum velocity of 30 to 40 miles per hour 2 to 3 hours after the explosion. The "fire-wind" and the symmetry of the built-up center of the city gave a roughly circular shape to the 4.4 square miles which were almost completely burned out. The surprise, the collapse of many buildings, and the conflagration contributed to an unprecedented casualty rate. Seventy to eighty thousand people were killed, or missing and presumed dead, and an equal number were injured.

At Nagasaki, 3 days later, the city was scarcely more prepared, though vague references to the Hiroshima disaster had appeared in the newspaper of 8 August. From the Nagasaki Prefectural Report on the bombing, something of the shock of the explosion can be inferred:

The day was clear with not very much wind—an ordinary midsummer's day. The strain of continuous air attack on the city's population and the severity of the summer had vitiated enthusiastic air raid precautions. Previously, a general alert had been sounded at 0748, with a raid alert at 0750; this was canceled at 0830, and the alertness of the people was dissipated by a great feeling of relief.

The city remained on the warning alert, but when two B-29s were again sighted coming in the raid signal was not given immediately; the bomb was dropped at 1102 and the raid signal was given a few minutes later, at 1109. Thus only about 400 people were in the city's tunnel shelters, which were adequate for about 30 percent of the population.

When the atomic bomb exploded, an intense flash was observed first, as though a large amount of magnesium had been ignited, and the scene grew hazy with white smoke. At the same time at the center of the explosion, and a short while later in other areas, a tremendous roaring sound was heard and a crushing blast wave and intense heat were felt. The people of Nagasaki, even those who lived on the outer edge of the blast, all felt as though they had sustained a direct hit, and the whole city suffered damage such as would have resulted from direct hits everywhere by ordinary bombs.

The zero area, where the damage was most severe, was almost completely wiped out and for a short while after the explosion no reports came out of that area. People who were in comparatively damaged areas reported their condition under the impression that they had received a direct hit. If such a great amount of damage could be wreaked by a near miss, then the power of the atomic bomb is unbelievably great.

In Nagasaki, no fire-storm arose, and the uneven terrain of the city confined the maximum intensity of damage to the valley over which the bomb exploded. The area of nearly complete devastation was thus much smaller; only about 1.8 square miles. Casualties were lower also; between 35,000 and 40,000 were killed, and about the same number injured. People in the tunnel shelters escaped injury, unless exposed in the entrance shaft.

* * *

Hiroshima before the war was the seventh largest city in Japan, with a population of over 340,000, and was the principal administrative and commercial center of the southwestern part of the country. As the headquarters of the Second Army and of the Chugoku Regional Army, it was one of the most important military command stations in Japan, the site of one of the largest military supply depots, and the foremost military shipping point for both troops and supplies. Its shipping activities had virtually ceased by the time of the attack, however, because of sinkings and the mining of the Inland Sea. It had been relatively unimportant industrially before the war, ranking only twelfth, but during the war new plants were built that increased its significance. These factories were not concentrated, but spread over the outskirts of the city; this location, we shall see, accounts for the slight industrial damage.

The impact of the atomic bomb shattered the normal fabric of community life and disrupted the organizations for handling the disaster. In the 30 percent of the population killed and the additional 30 per-cent seriously injured were included corresponding proportions of the civic authorities and rescue groups. A mass flight from the city took place, as persons sought safety from the conflagration and a place for shelter and food. Within 24 hours, however, people were streaming back by the thousands in search of relatives and friends and to determine the extent of their property loss. Road blocks had to be set up along all routes leading into the city, to keep curious and unauthorized people out. The bulk of the dehoused population found refuge in the surrounding countryside; within the city the food supply was short and shelter virtually nonexistent.

On 7 August, the commander of the Second Army assumed general command of the counter-measures, and all military units and facilities in the area were mobilized for relief purposes. Army buildings on the periphery of the city provided shelter and emergency hospital space, and dispersed Army supplies supplemented the slight amounts of food and clothing that had escaped destruction. The need far exceeded what could be made available. Surviving civilians assisted; although casualties in both groups had been heavy, 190 policemen and over 2,000 members of the Civilian Defense Corps reported for duty on 7 August.

The status of medical facilities and personnel dramatically illustrates the difficulties facing authorities. Of more than 200 doctors in Hiroshima before the attack, over 90 percent were casualties and only about 30 physicians were able to perform their normal duties a month after the raid. Out of 1,780 nurses, 1,654 were killed or injured. Though some stocks of supplies had been dispersed, many were destroyed. Only three out of 45 civilian hospitals could be used, and two large Army hospitals were rendered unusable. Those within 3,000 feet of ground zero were totally destroyed, and the mortality rate of the occupants was practically 100 percent. Two large hospitals of reinforced concrete construction were located 4,900 feet from ground zero. The basic structures remained erect but there was such severe interior damage that neither was able to resume operation as a hospital for some time and the casualty rate was approximately 90 percent, due primarily to falling plaster, flying glass, and fire. Hospitals and clinics beyond 7,000 feet, though often remaining standing, were badly damaged and contained many casualties from flying glass or other missiles.

With such elimination of facilities and personnel, the lack of care and rescue activities at the time of the disaster is understandable; still, the eyewitness account of Father Siemes8 shows how this lack of first-aid contributed to the seriousness of casualties. At the improvised first-aid stations, he reports:

...Iodine is applied to the wounds but they are left uncleansed. Neither ointment nor other therapeutic agents are available. Those that have been brought in are laid on the floor and no one can give them any further care. What could one do when all means are lacking? Among the passersby, there are many who are uninjured. In a purposeless, insensate manner, distraught by the magnitude of the disaster, most of them rush by and none conceives the thought of organizing help on his own initiative. They are concerned only with the welfare of their own families—in the official aid stations and hospitals, a good third or half of those that had been brought in died. They lay about there almost without care, and a very high percentage succumbed. Everything was lacking, doctors, assistants, dressings, drugs, etc...

Effective medical help had to be sent in from the outside, and arrived only after a considerable delay.

Fire-fighting and rescue units were equally stripped of men and equipment. Father Siemes reports that 30 hours elapsed before any organized rescue parties were observed. In Hiroshima, only 16 pieces of fire-fighting equipment were available for fighting the conflagration, three of them borrowed. However, it is unlikely that any public fire department in the world, even without damage to equipment or casualties to personnel, could have prevented development of a conflagration in Hiroshima, or combatted it with success at more than a few locations along its perimeter. The total fire damage would not have been much different.

When the atomic bomb fell, Nagasaki was comparatively intact. Because the most intense destruction was confined to the Urukami Valley, the impact of the bomb on the city as a whole was less shattering than at Hiroshima. In addition, no fire-storm occurred; indeed, a shift in wind direction helped control the fires. Medical personnel and facilities were hard-hit, however. Over 80 percent of the city's hospital beds and the Medical College were located within 3,000 feet of the center of the explosion, and were completely gutted by fire; buildings of wooden construction were destroyed by fire and blast. The mortality rate in this group of buildings was between 75 and 80 percent. Exact casualty figures for medical personnel are unknown, but the city seems to have fared better than Hiroshima: 120 doctors were at work on 1 November, about one-half of the pre-raid roster. Casualties were undoubtedly high: 600 out of 850 medical students at the Nagasaki Medical College were killed and most of the others injured; and of the 20 faculty members, 12 were killed and 4 others injured.

The city's repair facilities were completely disorganized by the atomic bomb, so that with the single exception of shutting off water to the affected areas no repairs were made to roads, bridges, water mains, or transportation installations by city forces. The prefecture took full responsibility for such restoration as was accomplished, delegating to the scattered city help the task of assisting in relief of victims. There were only 3 survivors of 115 employees of the street car company, and as late as the middle of November 1945 no cars were running. A week after the explosion, the water works officials made an effort to supply water to persons attempting to live in the bombed-out areas, but the leakage was so great that the effort was abandoned. It fell to the prefecture, therefore, to institute recovery measures even in those streets normally the responsibility of the city. Of the entire public works construction group covering the Nagasaki city area, only three members appeared for work and a week was required to locate and notify other survivors. On the morning of 10 August, police rescue units and workers from the Kawaminami shipbuilding works began the imperative task of clearing the Omura-Nagasaki pike, which was impassable for 8,000 feet. A path 6-1/2 feet wide was cleared despite the intense heat from smouldering fires, and by 15 August had been widened to permit two-way traffic. No trucks, only rakes and shovels, were available for clearing the streets, which were filled with tile, bricks, stone, corrugated iron, machinery, plaster, and stucco. Street areas affected by blast and not by fire were littered with wood. Throughout the devastated area, all wounded had to be carried by stretcher, since no motor vehicles were able to proceed through the cluttered streets for several days. The plan for debris removal required clearance of a few streets leading to the main highway; but there were frequent delays caused by the heat of smouldering fires and by calls for relief work. The debris was simply raked and shoveled off the streets. By 20 August the job was considered complete. The streets were not materially damaged by the bomb nor were the surface or the abutments of the concrete bridges, but many of the wooden bridges were totally or partially destroyed by fire.

Under the circumstances—fire, flight of entire families, destruction of official records, mass cremation— identification of dead and the accurate count of casualties was impossible. As at Hiroshima, the season of the year made rapid disposal of bodies imperative, and mass cremation and mass burial were resorted to in the days immediately after the attack. Despite the absence of sanitary measures, no epidemics broke out here. The dysentery rate rose from 25 per 100,000 to 125 per 100,000. A census taken on 1 November 1945 found a population of 142,700 in the city.

At Nagasaki, the scale of destruction was greater than at Hiroshima, though the actual area destroyed was smaller because of the terrain and the point of fall of the bomb. The Nagasaki Prefectural Report described vividly the impress of the bomb on the city and its inhabitants:

Within a radius of 1 kilometer from ground zero, men and animals died almost instantaneously from the tremendous blast pressure and heat; houses and other structures were smashed, crushed and scattered; and fires broke out. The strong complex steel members of the structures of the Mitsubishi Steel Works were bent and twisted like jelly and the roofs of the reinforced concrete National Schools were crumpled and collapsed, indicating a force beyond imagination.

Trees of all sizes lost their branches or were uprooted or broken off at the trunk.

Outside a radius of 1 kilometer and within a radius of 2 kilometers from ground zero, some men and animals died instantly from the great blast and heat, but the great majority were seriously or superficially injured. Houses and other structures were completely destroyed while fires broke out everywhere. Trees were uprooted and withered by the heat.

Outside a radius of 2 kilometers and within a radius of 4 kilometers from ground zero, men and animals suffered various degrees of injury from window glass and other fragments scattered about by the blast and many were burned by the intense heat. Dwelling and other structures were half damaged by blast.

Outside a radius of 4 kilometers and within a radius of 8 kilometers from ground zero, living creatures were injured by materials blown about by the blast; the majority were only superficially wounded. Houses were half or only partially damaged.

While the conflagration with its uniformly burnt-out area caught the attention at Hiroshima, the blast effects, with their resemblance to the aftermath of a hurricane, were most striking at Nagasaki. Concrete buildings had their sides facing the blast stove in like boxes. Long lines of steel-framed factory sheds, over a mile from ground zero, leaned their skeletons away from the explosion. Blast resistant objects such as telephone poles leaned away from the center of the explosion; on the surrounding hills trees were blown down within considerable areas. Although there was no general conflagration, fires contributed to the total damage in nearly all concrete structures. Evidence of primary fire is more frequent than at Hiroshima.

* * *

B. General Effects

1. Casualties.

The most striking result of the atomic bombs was the great number of casualties. The exact number of dead and injured will never be known because of the confusion after the explosions. Persons unaccounted for might have been burned beyond recognition in the falling buildings, disposed of in one of the mass cremations of the first week of recovery, or driven out of the city to die or recover without any record remaining. No sure count of even the pre-raid population existed. Because of the decline in activity in the two port cities, the constant threat of incendiary raids, and the formal evacuation programs of the Government, an unknown number of the inhabitants had either drifted away from the cities or been removed according to plan. In this uncertain situation, estimates of casualties have generally ranged between 100,000 and 180,000 for Hiroshima, and between 50,000 and 100,000 for Nagasaki. The Survey believes the dead at Hiroshima to have been between 70,000 and 80,000 with an equal number injured; at Nagasaki over 35,000 dead and somewhat more than that injured seems the most plausible estimate.

Most of the immediate casualties did not differ from those caused by incendiary or high-explosive raids. The outstanding difference was the presence of radiation effects, which became unmistakable about a week after the bombing. At the time of impact, however, the causes of death and injury were flash burns, secondary effects of blast and falling debris, and burns from blazing buildings. No records are available that give the relative importance of the various types of injury, especially for those who died immediately after the explosion. Indeed, many of these people undoubtedly died several times over, theoretically, since each was subjected to several injuries, any one of which would have been fatal.

Radiation disease. The radiation effects upon survivors resulted from the gamma rays liberated by the fission process rather than from induced radio-activity or the lingering radio-activity of deposits of primary fission products. Both at Nagasaki and at Hiroshima, pockets of radioactivity have been detected where fission products were directly deposited, but the degree of activity in these areas was insufficient to produce casualties. Similarly, induced radio-activity from the interaction of neutrons with matter caused no authenticated fatalities. But the effects of gamma rays—here used in a general sense to include all penetrating high-frequency radiations and neutrons that caused injury—are well established, even though the Allies had no observers in the affected areas for several weeks after the explosions.

Our understanding of radiation casualties is not complete. In part the deficiency is in our basic knowledge of how radiation effects animal tissue.

According to the Japanese, those individuals very near the center of the explosion but not affected by flash burns or secondary injuries became ill within 2 or 3 days. Bloody diarrhea followed, and the victims expired, some within 2 to 3 days after the onset and the majority within a week. Autopsies showed remarkable changes in the blood picture—almost complete absence of white blood cells, and deterioration of bone marrow. Mucous membranes of the throat, lungs, stomach, and the intestines showed acute inflammation.

The majority of the radiation cases, who were at greater distances, did not show severe symptoms until 1 to 4 weeks after the explosion, though many felt weak and listless on the following day. After a day or two of mild nausea and vomiting, the appetite improved and the person felt quite well until symptoms reappeared at a later date. In the opinion of some Japanese physicians, those who rested or subjected themselves to less physical exertion showed a longer delay before the onset of subsequent symptoms. The first signs of recurrence were loss of appetite, lassitude, and general discomfort. Inflammation of the gums, mouth, and pharynx appeared next. Within 12 to 48 hours, fever became evident. In many instances it reached only 100° Fahrenheit and remained for only a few days. In other cases, the temperature went as high as 104° or 106° Fahrenheit. The degree of fever apparently had a direct relation to the degree of exposure to radiation. Once developed, the fever was usually well sustained, and in those cases terminating fatally it continued high until the end. If the fever subsided, the patient usually showed a rapid disappearance of other symptoms and soon regained his feeling of good health. The other symptoms commonly seen were shortage of white corpuscles, loss of hair, inflammation and gangrene of the gums, inflammation of the mouth and pharynx, ulceration of the lower gastro-intestinal tract, small livid spots (petechiae) resulting from escape of blood into the tissues of the skin or mucous membrane, and larger hemorrhages of gums, nose and skin.

Loss of hair usually began about 2 weeks after the bomb explosion, though in a few instances it is reported to have begun as early a 4 to 5 days afterward. The areas were involved in the following order of frequency with variations depending on the degree of exposure: scalp, armpits, beard, pubic region, and eyebrows. Complete baldness was rare. Microscopic study of the body areas involved has shown atrophy of the hair follicles. In those patients who survived after 2 months, however, the hair has commenced to re-grow. An interesting but unconfirmed report has it that loss of the hair was less marked in persons with grey hair than in those with dark hair…

The effects of the bomb on pregnant women are marked, however. Of women in various stages of pregnancy who were within 3,000 feet of ground zero, all known cases have had miscarriages. Even up to 6,500 feet they have had miscarriages or premature infants who died shortly after birth. In the group between 6,500 and 10,000 feet, about one-third have given birth to apparently normal children. Two months after the explosion, the city's total incidence of miscarriages, abortions, and premature births was 27 percent as compared with a normal rate of 6 percent. Since other factors than radiation contributed to this increased rate, a period of years will be required to learn the ultimate effects of mass radiation upon reproduction.

Treatment of victims by the Japanese was limited by the lack of medical supplies and facilities. Their therapy consisted of small amounts of vitamins, liver extract, and an occasional blood transfusion. Allied doctors used penicillin and plasma with beneficial effects. Liver extract seemed to benefit the few patients on whom it was used: It was given in small frequent doses when available. A large percentage of the cases died of secondary disease, such as septic bronchopneumonia or tuberculosis, as a result of lowered resistance. Deaths from radiation began about a week after exposure and reached a peak in 3 to 4 weeks. They had practically ceased to occur after 7 to 8 weeks.

Unfortunately, no exact definition of the killing power of radiation can yet be given, nor a satisfactory account of the sort and thickness of concrete or earth that will shield people. From the definitive report of the Joint Commission will come more nearly accurate statements on these matters. In the meanwhile the awesome lethal effects of the atomic bomb and the insidious additional peril of the gamma rays speak for themselves.

* * *

2. MORALE.

As might be expected, the primary reaction to the bomb was fear—uncontrolled terror, strengthened by the sheer horror of the destruction and suffering witnessed and experienced by the survivors. Between one-half and two-thirds of those interviewed in the Hiroshima and Nagasaki areas confessed having such reactions, not just for the moment but for some time. As two survivors put it:

Whenever a plane was seen after that, people would rush into their shelters; they went in and out so much that they did not have time to eat. They were so nervous they could not work.

After the atomic bomb fell, I just couldn't stay home. I would cook, but while cooking I would always be watching out and worrying whether an atomic bomb would fall near me.

The behavior of the living immediately after the bombings, as described earlier, clearly shows the state of shock that hindered rescue efforts. A Nagasaki survivor illustrates succinctly the mood of survivors: All I saw was the flash and I felt my body get warm and then I saw everything flying around. My grandmother was hit on the head by a flying piece of roof and she was bleeding…I became hysterical seeing my grandmother bleeding and we just ran around without knowing what to do.

I was working at the office. I was talking to a friend at the window. I saw the whole city in a red flame, then I ducked. The pieces of the glass hit my back and face. My dress was torn off by the glass. Then I got up and ran to the mountain where the good shelter was.

The two typical impulses were these: Aimless, even hysterical activity or flight from the city to shelter and food.

The Charter of the United Nations, 1945

As the Second World War was drawing to a close, representatives of most of the nations of the world came together in San Francisco in April of 1945 and drafted the Charter of the United Nations. It was organized with a Security Council including the United States, Great Britain, France, the Soviet Union and China, each of which have veto power over any proposed action. Whether its authority and its ability to maintain peace and security in the future will prove effective remains to be seen.

Source: The Charter of the United Nations, drafted in San Francisco, 1945.

Focus Questions:

1. What are the requirements for joining the United Nations?
2. What is the purpose of the United Nations?
3. What is the function of the General Assembly? The Security Council?

We the Peoples of the United Nations Determined

to save succeeding generations from the scourge of war, which twice in our lifetime has brought untold sorrow to mankind, and

to reaffirm faith in fundamental human rights, in the dignity and worth of the human person, in the equal rights of men and women and of nations large and small, and

to establish conditions under which justice and respect for the obligations arising from treaties and other sources of international law can be maintained, and

to promote social progress and better standards of life in larger freedom,

And for These Ends

to practice tolerance and live together in peace with one another as good neighbours, and

to unite our strength to maintain international peace and security, and

to ensure by the acceptance of principles and the institution of methods, that armed force shall not be used, save in the common interest, and

to employ international machinery for the promotion of the economic and social advancement of all peoples,

Have Resolved to Combine Our Efforts to Accomplish These Aims

Accordingly, our respective Governments, through representatives assembled in the city of San Francisco, who have exhibited their full powers found to be in good and due form, have agreed to the present Charter of the United Nations and do hereby establish an international organization to be known as the United Nations.

CHAPTER I
Purposes and Principles

Article 1. The Purposes of the United Nations are:

1 To maintain international peace and security, and to that end: to take effective collective measures for the prevention and removal of threats to the peace, and for the suppression of acts of aggression or other breaches of the peace, and to bring about by peaceful means, and in conformity with the principles of justice and international law, adjustment or settlement of international disputes or situations which might lead to a breach of the peace;

2 To develop friendly relations among nations based on respect for the principle of equal rights and self-determination of peoples, and to take other appropriate measures to strengthen universal peace;

3 To achieve international cooperation in solving international problems of an economic, social, cultural or humanitarian character, and in promoting and encouraging respect for human rights and for fundamental freedoms for all without distinction as to race, sex, language, or religion; and

4 To be a centre for harmonizing the actions of nations in the attainment of these common ends.

Article 2.

The Organization and its Members, in pursuit of the Purposes stated in Article 1, shall act in accordance with the following Principles.

1 The Organization is based on the principle of the sovereign equality of all its Members.

2 All Members, in order to ensure to all of them the rights and benefits resulting from membership, shall fulfill in good faith the obligations assumed by them in accordance with the present Charter.

3 All Members shall settle their international disputes by peaceful means in such a manner that international peace and security, and justice, are not endangered.

4 All Members shall refrain in their international relations from the threat or use of force against the territorial integrity or political independence of any state, or in any other manner inconsistent with the Purposes of the United Nations.

5 All Members shall give the United Nations every assistance in any action it

takes in accordance with the present Charter, and shall refrain from giving assistance to any state against which the United Nations is taking preventive or enforcement action.

6 The Organization shall ensure that states which are not Members of the United Nations act in accordance with these Principles so far as may be necessary for the maintenance of international peace and security.

7 Nothing contained in the present Charter shall authorize the United Nations to intervene in matters which are essentially within the domestic jurisdiction of any state or shall require the Members to submit such matters to settlement under the present Charter; but this principle shall not prejudice the application of enforcement measures under Chapter VII.

CHAPTER II
Membership

Article 3.

The original Members of the United Nations shall be the states which, having participated in the United Nations Conference on International Organization at San Francisco, or having previously signed the Declaration by United Nations of 1 January 1942, sign the present Charter and ratify it in accordance with Article 110.

Article 4.

1 Membership to the United Nations is open to all other peace-loving states which accept the obligations contained in the present Charter and, in the judgment of the Organization, are able and willing to carry out these obligations.

2 The admission of any such state to membership in the United Nations will be effected by a decision of the General Assembly upon the recommendation of the Security Council.

Article 5.

A member of the United Nations against which preventive or enforcement action has been taken by the Security Council may be suspended from the exercise of the rights and privileges of membership by the General Assembly upon the recommendation of the Security Council. The exercise of these rights and privileges may be restored by the Security Council.

Article 6.

A member of the United Nations which has persistently violated the Principles contained in the present Charter may be expelled from the Organization by the General Assembly upon the recommendation of the Security Council.

CHAPTER III
Organs

Article 7.

1 There are established as the principal organs of the United Nations: a General Assembly, a Security Council, an Economic and Social Council, a Trusteeship Council, an International Court of Justice, and a Secretariat. 2 Such subsidiary organs as may be found necessary may be established in accordance with the present Charter.

Article 8. The United Nations shall place no restrictions on the eligibility of men and women to participate in any capacity and under conditions of equality in its principal and subsidiary organs.

CHAPTER IV
The General Assembly
Composition

Article 9.

1 The General Assembly shall consist of all the members of the United Nations. 2 Each Member shall have not more than five representatives in the General Assembly.

Functions and Powers

Article 10.

The General Assembly may discuss any questions or any matters within the scope of the pres-ent Charter or relating to the powers and functions of any organs provided for in the present Charter, and except as provided in Article 12, may make recommendations to the Members of the United Nations or to the Security Council or to both on any such questions or matters.

Article 11.

1 The General Assembly may consider the general principles of cooperation in the maintenance of international peace and security, including the principles governing disarmament and the regulation of armaments, and may make recommendations with regard to such principles to the Members or to the Security Council or to both.

2 The General Assembly may discuss any questions relating to the maintenance of international peace and security brought before it by any Member of the United Nations, or by the Security Council, or by a state which is not a Member of the United Nations in accordance with Article 35, paragraph 2, and, except as provided in Article 12, may make recommendations with

regard to any such question to the state or states concerned or to the Security Council or to both. Any such question on which action is necessary shall be referred to the Security Council by the General Assembly either before or after discussion.

3 The General Assembly may call the attention of the Security Council to situations which are likely to endanger international peace and security.

4 The powers of the General Assembly set forth in this Article shall not limit the general scope of Article 10.

Article 12.

1 While the Security Council is exercising in respect of any dispute or situation the functions assigned to it in the present Charter, the General Assembly shall not make any recommendation with regard to that dispute or situation unless the Security Council so requests.

2 The Secretary-General, with the Security Council, shall notify the General Assembly at each session of any matters relative to the maintenance of international peace and security which are being dealt with by the Security Council and shall similarly notify the General Assembly or the Members of the United Nations if the General Assembly is not in session, immediately the Security Council ceases to deal with such matters.

Article 13.

1. The General Assembly shall initiate studies and make recommendations for the purpose of:

    a. promoting international cooperation in the political field and encouraging the progressive developments of international law and its codification;

    b. promoting international cooperation in the economic, social, cultural, educational, and health fields, and assisting in the realization of human rights and fundamental freedoms for all without distinction as to race, sex, language, or religion.

2. The further responsibilities, functions and powers of the General Assembly with respect to matters mentioned in paragraph lb above are set forth in Chapters IX and X.

Article 14.

Subject to the provisions of Article 12, the General Assembly may recommend measures for the peaceful adjustment of any situation, regardless of origin, which it deems likely to impair the general welfare or friendly relations among nations, including situations resulting from a violation of the provisions of the present Charter setting forth the Purposes and Principles of the United Nations.

Article 15.

1 The General Assembly shall receive and consider annual and special reports from the Security Council; these reports shall include an account of the measures that the Security Council has decided upon or taken to maintain international peace and security.

2 The General Assembly shall receive and consider reports from the other organs of the United Nations.

Article 16.

The General Assembly shall perform such functions with respect to the international trustee-ship system as are assigned to it under Chapters XII and XIII, including the approval of the trusteeship agreements for areas not designed as strategic.

Article 17.

1 The General Assembly shall consider and approve the budget of the Organization.

2 The expenses of the Organization shall be borne by the Members as apportioned by the General Assembly.

3 The General Assembly shall consider and approve any financial and budgetary arrangements with specialized agencies referred to in Article 57 and shall examine the administrative budgets of such specialized agencies with a view to making recommendations to the agencies concerned.

Voting

Article 18.

1. Each member of the General Assembly shall have one vote.

1 Decisions of the General Assembly on important questions shall be made by a two-thirds majority of the members present and voting. These questions shall include: recommendations with respect to the maintenance of international peace and security, the election of the nonpermanent members of the Security Council, the election of the members of the Economic and Social Council, the election of members of the Trusteeship Council in accordance with paragraph 1c of Article 86, the admission of new members to the United Nations, the suspension of the rights and privileges of membership, the expulsion of Members, questions relating to the operation of the trusteeship system, and budgetary questions.

2 Decisions on other questions including the determination of additional categories of questions to be decided by a two-thirds majority, shall be made by a majority of the members present and voting.

Article 19.

A member of the United Nations which is in arrears in the payment of its financial contributions to the Organization shall have no vote in the General Assembly if the amount of its arrears equals or exceeds the amount of the contributions due from it for the preceding two full years. The General Assembly may, nevertheless, permit such a Member to vote if it is satisfied that the failure to pay is due to conditions beyond the control of the Member.

Procedure

Article 20.

The General Assembly shall meet in regular annual sessions and in such special sessions as occasion may require. Special sessions shall be convoked by the Secretary-General at the request of the Security Council or of a majority of the Members of the United Nations.

Article 21.

The General Assembly shall adopt its own rules of procedure. It shall elect its President for each session.

Article 22.

The General Assembly may establish such subsidiary organs as it deems necessary for the performance of its functions.

CHAPTER V
The Security Council Composition

Article 23.

1 The Security Council shall consist of fifteen members of the United Nations. The Republic of China, France, the Union of Soviet Socialist Republics, the United Kingdom of Great Britain and Northern Ireland, and the United States of America shall be permanent members of the Security Council. The General Assembly shall elect ten other Members of the United Nations to be nonpermanent members of the Security Council, due regard being specially paid, in the first instance to the contribution of Members of the United Nations to the maintenance of international peace and security and to the other purposes of the Organization, and also to equitable geographical distribution.

2 The nonpermanent members of the Security Council shall be elected for a term of two years. In the first election of the nonpermanent members after the increase of the membership of the Security Council from eleven to fifteen, two of the four additional members shall be chosen for a term of one year. A

retiring member shall not be eligible for immediate re-election.

3 Each member of the Security Council shall have one representative.

Functions and Powers

Article 24.

1 In order to ensure prompt and effective action by the United Nations, its Members confer on the Security Council primary responsibility for the maintenance of international peace and security, and agree that in carrying out its duties under this responsibility the Security Council acts on their behalf.

2 In discharging these duties the Security Council shall act in accordance with the Purposes and Principles of the United Nations. The specific powers granted to the Security Council for the discharge of these duties are laid down in Chapters VI, VII, VIII, and XII.

3 The Security Council shall submit annual and, when necessary, special reports to the General Assembly for its consideration.

Article 25.

The Members of the United Nations agree to accept and carry out the decisions of the Security Council in accordance with the present Charter.

Article 26.

In order to promote the establishment and maintenance of international peace and security with the least diversion for armaments of the world's human economic resources, the Security Council shall be responsible for formulating, with the assistance of the Military Staff Committee referred to in Article 47, plans to be submitted to the Members of the United Nations for the establishment of a system for the regulation of armaments.

Voting

Article 27.

1 Each member of the Security Council shall have one vote.

2 Decisions of the Security Council on procedural matters shall be made by an affirmative vote of nine members.

3 Decisions of the Security Council on all other matters shall be made by an affirmative vote of nine members including the concurring votes of the permanent members; provided that, in decisions under Chapter VI, and under paragraph 3 of Article 52, a party to a dispute shall abstain from voting.

Procedure

Article 28.

1 The Security Council shall be so organized as to be able to function continuously. Each member of the Security Council shall for this purpose be represented at all times at the seat of the Organization.

2 The Security Council shall hold periodic meetings at which each of its members may, if it so desires, be represented by a member of the government or by some other specially designated representative.

3 The Security Council may hold meetings at such places other than the seat of the Organization as in its judgment will best facilitate its work.

Article 29.

The Security Council may establish such subsidiary organs as it deems necessary for the performance of its functions.

Article 30.

The Security Council shall adopt its own rules of procedure, including the method of selecting its President.

Article 31.

Any Member of the United Nations which is not a member of the Security Council may participate, without vote, in the discussion of any question brought before the Security Council whenever the latter considers that the interests of that Member are specially affected.

Article 32.

Any Member of the United Nations which is not a member of the Security Council or any state which is not a Member of the United Nations, if it is a party to a dispute under consideration by the Security Council, shall be invited to participate, without vote, in the discussion relating to the dispute. The Security Council shall lay down such conditions as it deems just for the participation of such a state which is not a Member of the United Nations.

CHAPTER VI
Pacific Settlement of Disputes

Article 33.

1 The parties to any dispute, the continuance of which is likely to endanger the maintenance of international peace and security, shall, first of all, seek a solution by negotiation, enquiry, mediation, conciliation, arbitration, judicial settlement, resort to regional agencies or arrangements, or other peaceful means of their own choice.

2 The Security Council shall, when it deems necessary, call upon the parties to settle their dispute by such means.

Article 34.

The Security Council may investigate any dispute, or any situation which might lead to inter-national friction or give rise to a dispute, in order to determine whether the continuance of the dispute or situation is likely to endanger the maintenance of international peace and security.

Article 35.

1 Any Member of the United Nations may bring any dispute, or any situation of the nature referred to in Article 34, to the attention of the Security Council or of the General Assembly.

2 A state which is not a Member of the United Nations may bring to the attention of the Security Council or of the General Assembly any dispute to which it is a party if it accepts in advance, for the purposes of the dispute, the obligations of pacific settlement provided in the present Charter.

3 The proceedings of the General Assembly in respect of matters brought to its attention under this Article will be subject to the provisions of Articles 11 and 12.

Article 36.

1 The Security Council may, at any stage of a dispute of the nature referred to in Article 33 or of a situation of like nature, recommend appropriate procedures or methods of adjustment.

2 The Security Council should take into consideration any procedures for the settlement of the dispute which have already been adopted by the parties.

3 In making recommendations under this Article the Security Council should also take into consideration that legal disputes should as a general rule be referred by the parties to the International Court of Justice in accordance with the provisions of the Statute of the Court.

Article 37.

1 Should the parties to a dispute of the nature referred to in Article 33 fail to settle it by the means indicated in that Article, they shall refer it to the Security Council.

2 If the Security Council deems that the continuance of the dispute is in fact likely to endanger the maintenance of international peace and security, it shall decide whether to take action under Article 36 or to recommend such terms of settlement as it may consider appropriate.

Article 38.

Without prejudice to the provisions of Article 33 to 37, the Security Council may, if all the parties to any dispute so request, make recommendations to the parties with a view to a pacific settlement of the dispute.

CHAPTER VII
Action with Respect to Threats to the Peace, Breaches of the Peace, and Acts of Aggression

Article 39.

The Security Council shall determine the existence of any threat to the peace, breach of the peace, or act of aggression and shall make recommendations, or decide what measures shall be taken in accordance with Articles 41 and 42, to maintain or restore international peace and security.

Article 40.

In order to prevent an aggravation of the situation, the Security Council may, before making the recommendations or deciding upon the measures provided for in Article 39, call upon the parties concerned to comply with such provisional measures as it deems necessary or desirable. Such provisional measures shall be without prejudice to the rights, claims, or position of the parties concerned. The Security Council shall duly take account of failure to comply with such provisional measures.

Article 41.

The Security Council may decide what measures not involving the use of armed forces are to be employed to give effect to its decisions, and it may call upon the Members of the United Nations to apply such measures. These may include complete or partial interruption of economic relations and of rail, sea, air, postal, telegraphic, radio, and other means of communication, and the severance of diplomatic relations.

Article 42.

Should the Security Council consider that measures provided for in Article 41 would be inadequate or have proved to be inadequate, it may take such action by air, sea, or land forces as may be necessary to maintain or restore international peace and security. Such action may include demonstrations, blockade, and other operations by air, sea, or land forces of Members of the United Nations.

Article 43.

1 All Members of the United Nations, in order to contribute to the maintenance of international peace and security, undertake to make available to the

Security Council, on its call and in accordance with a special agreement or agreements, armed forces, assistance, and facilities, including rights of passage, necessary for the purpose of maintaining international peace and security.

2 Such agreement or agreements shall govern the numbers and types of forces, the degree of readiness and general location, and the nature of the facilities and assistance to be provided.

3 The agreement or agreements shall be negotiated as soon as possible on the initiative of the Security Council. They shall be concluded between the Security Council and Members or between the Security Council and groups of Members and shall be subject to ratification by the signatory states in accordance with their respective constitutional processes.

Article 44.

When the Security Council has decided to use force it shall, before calling upon a Member not represented on it to provide armed forces in fulfillment of the obligations assumed under Article 43, invite that Member, if the Member so desires, to participate in the decisions of the Security Council concerning the employment of contingents of that Member's armed forces.

Article 45.

In order to enable the United Nations to take urgent military measures, Members shall hold immediately available national air-force contingents for combined international enforcement action. The strength and degree of readiness of these contingents and plans for their combined action shall be deter-mined, within the limits laid down in the special agreement or agreements referred to in Article 43, by the Security Council with the assistance of the Military Staff Committee.

Article 46.

Plans for the application of armed force shall be made by the Security Council with the assistance of the Military Staff Committee.

Article 47.

1 There shall be established a Military Staff Committee to advise and assist the Security Council on all questions relating to the Security Council's military requirements for the maintenance of international peace and security, the employment and command of forces placed at its disposal, the regulation of armaments, and possible disarmament.

2 The Military Staff Committee shall consist of the Chiefs of Staff, of the permanent members of the Security Council or their representatives. Any Member of the United Nations not permanently represented on the Committee shall

be invited by the Committee to be associated with it when the efficient discharge of the Committee's responsibilities requires the participation of that Member in its work.

3 The Military Staff Committee shall be responsible under the Security Council for the strategic direction of any armed forces placed at the disposal of the Security Council. Questions relating to the command of such forces shall be worked out subsequently.

4 The Military Staff Committee, with the authorization of the Security Council and after consultation with appropriate regional agencies, may establish regional subcommittees.

Article 48.

1 The action required to carry out the decisions of the Security Council for the maintenance of international peace and security shall be taken by all the Members of the United Nations or by some of them, as the Security Council may determine.

2 Such decisions shall be carried out by the Members of the United Nations directly and through their action in the appropriate international agencies of which they are members.

Article 49.

The Members of the United Nations shall join in affording mutual assistance in carrying out the measures decided upon by the Security Council.

Article 50.

If preventive or enforcement measures against any state are taken by the Security Council, any other state, whether a Member of the United Nations or not, which finds itself confronted with special economic problems arising from the carrying out of those measures shall have the right to consult the Security Council with regard to a solution of those problems.

Article 51.

Nothing in the present Charter shall impair the inherent right of individual or collective self-defence if an armed attack occurs against a Member of the United Nations until the Security Council has taken measures necessary to maintain international peace and security. Measures taken by Members in the exercise of this right of self-defence shall be immediately reported to the Security Council and shall not in any way affect the authority and responsibility of the Security Council under the present Charter to take at any time such action as it deems necessary in order to maintain or restore international peace and security.

CHAPTER 27

The Cold War

Winston Churchill, from "The Iron Curtain Speech"

The term "Cold War" describes the era of uneasy relations between the Western Allies and the Soviet Union after World War II. Each was competing for influence in Europe through propaganda and troop placement. In the first excerpt, the Soviet leader Joseph Stalin offered a glimpse of the ideological combat that was to be waged in the future. A month later, Winston Churchill, who had largely directed the British war effort, warned the West of the deceptive Soviet Union in his famous "Iron Curtain" speech.

Source: "An Iron Curtain Has Descended Across the Continent," from Congressional Record, 79th Congress, 2nd session, pp. A1145–A1147.

Focus Questions:

1. What policy was Churchill advocating in his "Iron Curtain" speech?
2. Was he pessimistic or optimistic about the possibility of war?

I now come to the…danger which threatens the cottage home and ordinary people, namely tyranny. We cannot be blind to the fact that the liberties enjoyed by individual citizens throughout the United States and British Empire are not valid in a considerable number of countries, some of which are very powerful. In these states control is forced upon the common people by various kinds of all-embracing police governments, to a degree which is overwhelming and contrary to every principle of democracy. The power of the state is exercised without restraint, either by dictators or by compact oligarchies operating through a privileged party and a political police. It is not our duty at this time, when difficulties are so numerous, to interfere forcibly in the internal affairs of countries whom we have not conquered in war, but we must never cease to proclaim in fearless tones the great principles of freedom and the rights of man, which are the joint inheritance of the English-speaking world and which, through Magna Carta, the Bill of Rights, the habeas corpus, trial by jury, and the English common law find their famous expression in the Declaration of Independence…

A shadow has fallen upon the scenes so lately lighted by the Allied victory. Nobody knows what Soviet Russia and its Communist international organization intends to do in the immediate future, or what are the limits, if any, to their expansive and proselytizing tendencies…From Stettin in the Baltic to Trieste in the Adriatic, an iron curtain has descended across the continent. Behind that line lie all the capitals of the ancient states of central and eastern Europe. Warsaw, Berlin, Prague, Vienna, Budapest, Belgrade, Bucharest, and Sofia, all these famous cities and the populations around them lie in the Soviet sphere and all are subject, in one form or another, not only to Soviet influence but to a very high and increasing measure of control from Moscow. Athens alone, with its immortal glories, is free to decide its future at an election under British, American, and French observation. In a great number of countries, far from the Russian frontiers and throughout the world, Communist fifth columns are established and work in complete unity and absolute obedience to the directions they receive from the Communist center. Except in the British Commonwealth, and in the United States, where communism is in its infancy, the Communist parties and fifth columns constitute a growing challenge and peril to Christian civilization. These are somber facts for anyone to have to recite on the morrow of a victory gained by so much splendid comradeship in arms and in the cause of freedom and democracy, and we should be most unwise not to face them squarely while time remains…

On the other hand, I repulse the idea that, a new war is inevitable, still more that it is imminent. It is because I am so sure that our fortunes are in our own hands and that we hold the power to save the future, that I feel the duty to speak out now that I have occasion to do so. I do not believe that Soviet Russia desires war. What they desire is the fruits of war and the indefinite expansion of their power and doctrines. But what we have to consider here today while time remains, is the permanent prevention of war and the establishment of conditions of freedom and democracy as rapidly as possible in all countries.

Our difficulties and dangers will not be removed by closing our eyes to them; they will not be removed by mere waiting to see what happens; nor will they be relieved by a policy of appeasement. What is needed is a settlement, and the longer this is delayed, the more difficult it will be and the greater our dangers will become. From what I have seen of our Russian friends and allies during the war, I am convinced that there is nothing they admire so much as strength, and there is nothing for which they have less respect than for military weakness. For that reason the old doctrine of a balance of power is unsound. We cannot afford, if we can help it, to work on narrow margins, offering temptations to a trial of strength. If the western democracies stand together in strict adherence to the principles of the United Nations Charter, their influence for furthering these principles will be immense and no one is likely to molest them. If, however, they become divided or falter in their duty, and if these all-important years are allowed to slip away, then indeed catastrophe may overwhelm us all.

George C. Marshall, The Marshall Plan, 1947

In the first months of 1946, President Truman received urgent requests from the Greek government for economic assistance, which, it was hoped, would put an end to the chaos and strife hindering its recovery from the war. Hoping to forestall Communist dissidents who were threatening the stability of the government, Truman appealed to Congress to appropriate such financial assistance. He also asked for military as well as economic aid to Turkey. The controversial Truman Doctrine, as it came to be called, committed the United States to an active policy of promoting ideological divisions between it and the Soviet Union and further escalated Cold War tensions. The Marshall Plan of 1947, which advocated the rebuilding of West Germany after the war, is an example of this policy of Soviet containment.

Source: "The Marshall Plan" in *Department of State Bulletin* (June 15, 1947), pp. 1159–1160.

Focus Questions:

1. How does this plan fit into the context of "containment"?
2. The plan states "our policy is not directed against any country or doctrine, but against hunger, poverty, desperation, and chaos." Was this true? Why was it necessary to articulate a disclaimer? What relation do hunger, poverty, desperation, and chaos have to political instability or political agendas?

The truth of the matter is that Europe's requirements for the next three or four years of foreign food and other essential products—principally from America—are so much greater than her present ability to pay that she must have substantial additional help or face economic, social, and political deterioration of a very grave character.

The remedy lies in breaking the vicious circle and restoring the confidence of the European people in the economic future of their own countries and of Europe as a whole. The manufacturer and the farmer throughout wide areas must be able and willing to exchange their products for currencies the continuing value of which is not open to question.

Aside from the demoralizing effect on the world at large and the possibilities of disturbances arising as a result of the desperation of the people concerned, the consequences to the economy of the United States should be apparent to all. It is logical that the United States should do whatever it is able to do to assist in the return of normal economic health in the world, without which there can be no political stability and no assured peace. Our policy is directed not against any country or doctrine but against hunger, poverty, desperation, and chaos. Its purpose should be the revival of a working economy in the world so as to permit the emergence of political and social conditions in which free institutions can exist. Such assistance, I am convinced, must not be on a piecemeal basis as various crises develop. Any assistance that this Government may render in the future should provide a cure rather than a mere palliative. Any government that is willing to assist in the task of recovery will find full cooperation, I am sure, on the part of the United States Government. Any government which maneuvers to block the recovery of other countries cannot expect help from us. Furthermore, governments, political parties, or groups which seek to perpetuate human misery in order to profit therefrom politically or otherwise will encounter the opposition of the United States.

It is already evident that, before the United States Government can proceed much further in its efforts to alleviate the situation and help start the European world on its way to recovery, there must be some agreement among the countries of Europe as to the requirements of the situation and the part those countries themselves will take in order to give proper effect to whatever action might be undertaken by this Government. It would be neither fitting nor efficacious for this Government to undertake to draw up unilaterally a program designed to place Europe on its feet economically. This is the business of the Europeans. The initiative, I think, must come from Europe. The role of this country should consist of friendly aid in the drafting of a European program and of later support of such a program so far as it may be practical for us to do so. The program should be a joint one, agreed to by a number, if not all, European nations.

An essential part of any successful action on the part of the United States is an understanding on the part of the people of America of the character of the problem and the remedies to be applied. Political passion and prejudice should have no part. With foresight, and a willingness on the part of our people to face up to the vast responsibility which history has clearly placed upon our country, the difficulties I have outlined can and will be overcome.

Harry S Truman, The Truman Doctrine, 1947

In the first months of 1946, President Truman received urgent requests from the Greek government for economic assistance, which, it was hoped, would put an end to the chaos and strife hindering its recovery from the war. Hoping to forestall Communist dissidents who were threatening the stability of the government, Truman appealed to Congress to appropriate such financial assistance. He also asked for military as well as economic aid to Turkey. The controversial Truman Doctrine, as it came to be called, committed the United States to an active policy of promoting ideological divisions between it and the Soviet Union and further escalated Cold War tensions. The Marshall Plan of 1947, which advocated the rebuilding of West Germany after the war, is an example of this policy of Soviet containment.

Source: Harry S. Truman,"The Truman Doctrine,"in *Public Papers of the President*, 1947 (Washington, DC: Government Printing Office, 1963), pp. 177–180.

Focus Questions:

1. What prompted Truman to choose this course of action?
2. How much of the philosophy of the Truman Doctrine was vested in America's need to help free peoples and how much was vested in issues considered vital to national interests?

To ensure the peaceful development of nations, free from coercion, the United States has taken a leading part in establishing the United Nations. The United Nations is designed to make possible lasting freedom and independence for all its members. We shall not realize our objectives, however, unless we are willing to help free peoples to maintain their free institutions and their national integrity against aggressive movements that seek to impose upon them totalitarian regimes. This is no more than a frank recognition that totalitarian regimes imposed upon free peoples, by direct or indirect aggression, undermine the foundations of international peace and hence the security of the United States.

The peoples of a number of countries of the world have recently had totalitarian regimes forced upon them against their will. The Government of the United States has made frequent protests against coercion and intimidation, in violation of the Yalta agreement, in Poland, Rumania, and Bulgaria. I must also state that in a number of other countries there have been similar developments.

At the present moment in world history nearly every nation must choose between alternative ways of life. The choice is too often not a free one.

One way of life is based upon the will of the majority, and is distinguished by free institutions, representative government, free elections, guarantees of individual liberty, freedom of speech and religion, and freedom from political oppression.

The second way of life is based upon the will of a minority forcibly imposed upon the majority. It relies upon terror and oppression, a controlled press and radio, fixed elections, and the suppression of personal freedoms.

I believe that it must be the policy of the United States to support free peoples who are resisting attempted subjugation by armed minorities or by outside pressures. I believe that we must assist free peoples to work out their own destinies in their own way. I believe that our help should be primarily through economic and financial aid which is essential to economic stability and orderly political processes.

The world is not static, and the status quo is not sacred. But we cannot allow changes in the status quo in violation of the Charter of United Nations by such methods as coercion, or by such subterfuges as political infiltration. In helping free and independent nations to maintain their freedom, the United States will be giving effect to the principles of the Charter of the United Nations…

The seeds of totalitarian regimes are nurtured by misery and want. They spread and grow in the evil soil of poverty and strife. They reach their full growth when the hope of a people for a better life has died. We must keep that hope alive. The free peoples of the world look to us for support in maintaining their freedoms.

If we falter in our leadership, we may endanger the peace of the world—and we shall surely endanger the welfare of this Nation. Great responsibilities have been placed upon us by the swift movement of events. I am confident that the Congress will face these responsibilities squarely.

Robert Schuman, "The Schuman Declaration"

Robert Schuman (1886-1963) was a French statesman who was born and raised in Luxembourg and attended several leading universities in Germany. He first became active in French politics after World War I, and then went on to become increasingly prominent in the aftermath of the Second World War, assuming several cabinet-level positions, including that of Prime Minister in 1947-48. As French Foreign Minister in 1950, Schuman gave the following speech proposing the unification of the coal and steel producing capacities of France and West Germany as a step toward greater cooperation among European countries. Schuman's declaration directly inspired the 1951 creation of the European Coal and Steel Community (ECSC), which became a central predecessor to the European Union.

Source: http://europa.eu/abc/symbols/9-may/decl_en.htm

Focus Questions:

1. Why is the relationship between France and Germany so important, according to Schuman?
2. What reasons does Schuman give for focusing on coal and steel production as a vehicle for forging closer relations between France and Germany?
3. How were collective decisions regarding coal and steel production to be made?

Declaration of 9 May 1950

This is the full text of the proposal, which was presented by the French foreign minister Robert Schuman and which led to the creation of what is now the European Union.

World peace cannot be safeguarded without the making of creative efforts proportionate to the dangers which threaten it.

The contribution which an organized and living Europe can bring to civilization is indispensable to the maintenance of peaceful relations. In taking upon herself for more than 20 years the role of champion of a united Europe, France has always had as her essential aim the service of peace. A united Europe was not achieved and we had war.

Europe will not be made all at once, or according to a single plan. It will be built through concrete achievements which first create a de facto solidarity. The coming together of the nations of Europe requires the elimination of the age-old opposition of France and Germany. Any action taken must in the first place concern these two countries.

With this aim in view, the French Government proposes that action be taken immediately on one limited but decisive point.

It proposes that Franco-German production of coal and steel as a whole be placed under a common High Authority, within the framework of an organization open to the participation of the other countries of Europe. The pooling of coal and steel production should immediately provide for the setting up of common foundations for economic development as a first step in the federation of Europe, and will change the destinies of those regions which have long been devoted to the manufacture of munitions of war, of which they have been the most constant victims.

The solidarity in production thus established will make it plain that any war between France and Germany becomes not merely unthinkable, but materially impossible. The setting up of this powerful productive unit, open to all countries willing to take part and bound ultimately to provide all the member countries with the basic elements of industrial production on the same terms, will lay a true foundation for their economic unification.

This production will be offered to the world as a whole without distinction or exception, with the aim of contributing to raising living standards and to promoting peaceful achievements. [...]

In this way, there will be realized simply and speedily that fusion of interest which is indispensable to the establishment of a common economic system; it may be the leaven from which may grow a wider and deeper community between countries long opposed to one another by sanguinary divisions.

By pooling basic production and by instituting a new High Authority, whose decisions will bind France, Germany and other member countries, this proposal will lead to the realization of the first concrete foundation of a European federation indispensable to the preservation of peace.

To promote the realization of the objectives defined, the French Government is ready to open negotiations on the following bases.

The task with which this common High Authority will be charged will be that of securing in the shortest possible time the modernization of production and the improvement of its quality; the supply of coal and steel on identical terms to the French and German markets, as well as to the markets of other member countries; the development in common of exports to other countries; the equalization and improvement of the living conditions of workers in these industries.

To achieve these objectives, starting from the very different conditions in which the production of member countries is at present situated, it is proposed that certain transitional measures should be instituted, such as the application of a production and investment plan, the establishment of compensating machinery for equating prices, and the creation of a restructuring fund to facilitate the rationalization of production. The movement of coal and steel between member countries will immediately be freed from all customs duty, and will not be affected by differential transport rates. Conditions will gradually be created which will spontaneously provide for the more rational distribution of production at the highest level of productivity.

In contrast to international cartels, which tend to impose restrictive practices on distribution and the exploitation of national markets, and to maintain high profits, the organization will ensure the fusion of markets and the expansion of production.

The essential principles and undertakings defined above will be the subject of a treaty signed between the States and submitted for the ratification of their parliaments. The negotiations required to settle details of applications will be undertaken with the help of an arbitrator appointed by common agreement. He will be entrusted with the task of seeing that the agreements reached conform with the principles laid down, and, in the event of a deadlock, he will decide what solution is to be adopted.

The common High Authority entrusted with the management of the scheme will be composed of independent persons appointed by the governments, giving equal representation. A chairman will be chosen by common agreement between the governments. The Authority's decisions will be enforceable in France, Germany and other member countries. Appropriate measures will be provided for means of appeal against the decisions of the Authority.

A representative of the United Nations will be accredited to the Authority, and will be instructed to make a public report to the United Nations twice yearly, giving an account of the working of the new organization, particularly as concerns the safeguarding of its objectives.

The institution of the High Authority will in no way prejudge the methods of ownership of enterprises. In the exercise of its functions, the common High Authority will take into account the powers conferred upon the International Ruhr Authority and the obligations of all kinds imposed upon Germany, so long as these remain in force.

Mikhail Gorbachev, Speech to the 27th Congress of the Communist Party of the Soviet Union

Between 1985 and its collapse in late 1991, the Soviet Union was led by Mikhail Gorbachev (b. 1931), Time Magazine's "Man of the Year" in 1988. Gorbachev began his political career in the 1950s and worked his way up the ranks of the internal hierarchy of the Communist Party, emerging by the early 1980s as one of the more dynamic political figures in the Soviet Union. He succeeded Konstantin Chernenko (1911-1985) as Soviet Premier in March 1985, and proceeded to launch a series of major reforms designed to reinvigorate the Soviet economy. These reforms, most notably associated with the terms *Glasnost* ("openness") and *Perestroika* ("restructuring"), set in motion a series of events that ultimately contributed to the collapse of the Soviet system in the early 1990s, an outcome Gorbachev did not initially envision. In the following speech, given before the 27th Congress of the Communist Party in early 1986, Gorbachev provides an early glimpse into some of the major reform impulses that were to become increasingly visible over the next few years.

Source: Mikhail S. Gorbachev, *Political Report of the CPSU Central Committee to the 27th Congress of the Communist Party of the Soviet Union* (Moscow: Novosti Press Agency Publishing House, 1986), 125-30.

Focus Questions:

1. How does Gorbachev attempt maintain a connection between the current need for drastic reform and the older trajectory of the Communist Party's history?
2. What sorts of changes does Gorbachev have in mind when speaking of a policy of "socio-economic acceleration"?
3. What goals does Gorbachev express regarding relations with the United States?

Dear Comrades, The 27th Congress is about to close. It is up to history to give an objective evaluation of its importance. But already today we can say: the Congress has been held in an atmosphere of Party fidelity to principle, in a spirit of unity, exactingness, and Bolshevik truth; it has frankly pointed out shortcomings and deficiencies, and made a profound analysis of the internal and external conditions in which our society develops. It has set a lofty moral and spiritual tone for the Party's activity and for the life of the entire country.

Coming to this rostrum, delegates put all questions frankly, and did not mince words in showing what is impeding our common cause, what is holding us back. Not a few critical statements were made about the work of all links of the Party, of government and economic organisations, both at the centre and locally. In fact, not a single sphere of our life has escaped critical analysis. All this, comrades, is in the spirit of the Party's finest traditions, in the Bolshevik spirit.

More than sixty years ago, when summing up the discussion on the Political Report of the RCP(B) Central Committee to the 11th Party Congress, Lenin expressed a thought that is of fundamental importance. He said: "All the revolutionary parties that have perished so far, perished because they became conceited, because they failed to see the source of their strength and were afraid to discuss their weaknesses. We, however, shall not perish, because we are not afraid to discuss our weaknesses and will learn to overcome them."

It is in this way, in Lenin's way, that we have acted here at our Congress. And that is the way we shall continue to act!

The Congress has answered the vital questions that life itself has put before the Party, before society, and has equipped every Communist, every Soviet citizen, with a clear understanding of the coming tasks. It has shown that we were right when we advanced the concept of socio-economic acceleration at the April 1985 Plenary Meeting. The idea of acceleration imbued all our pre-Congress activity. It was at the centre of attention at the Congress. It was embodied in the

Political Report of the Central Committee, the new edition of the Party Programme, and the amendments to the Party Rules, as well as in the Guidelines for the Economic and Social

Development of the USSR for the 12th Five-Year Plan Period and for the Period Ending in the Year 2000. These documents were wholeheartedly endorsed and approved by the delegates to the Congress.

The adopted and approved general line of the Party's domestic and foreign policy – that of the country's accelerated socio-economic development, and of consolidating world peace – is the main political achievement of the 27th CPSU Congress. From now on it will be the law of life for the Party, for its every organisation, and a guide to action for Communists, for all working people.

We are aware of the great responsibility to history that the CPSU is assuming, of the huge load it has taken on by adopting the strategy of acceleration. But we are convinced of the vital necessity of this strategy. We are confident that this strategy is a realistic one. Relying on the inexhaustible potentials and advantages of socialism, on the vigorous creative activity of the people, we shall be able to carry out all the projected objectives.

To secure the country's accelerated socio-economic development means to provide new powerful stimuli to the growth of the productive forces and to scientific and technological progress through the improvement of socialism's economic system, and to set in motion the tremendous untapped potentials of our national economy.

To secure acceleration means conducting an active and purposeful social policy by closely linking the improvement of the working people's well-being with the efficiency of labour, and by combining all-round concern for people with the consistent implementation of the principles of social justice.

To secure acceleration means to provide scope for the initiative and activity of every working person, every work collective, by deepening democracy, by steadily developing the people's socialist self-government, and by ensuring more openness in the life of the Party and society.

To secure acceleration means to bring ideological and organisational work closer to the people and direct it towards the elimination of difficulties and the practical solution of our tasks by associating this work more closely with the actual problems of life, by getting rid of hollow verbiage and didacticism, and by increasing people's responsibility for their job.

Comrades, we can and must accomplish all this!

The CPSU is entering the post-Congress period better organised, more cohesive, more efficient, with a well-considered long-term policy. It is determined to act with purpose, aware of all the complexity, the great scope and novelty of the tasks it faces, undaunted by difficulties and obstacles.

It is up to us to reach every Soviet citizen and bring home the essence and spirit of the Congress decisions. Not only must we explain the basic concepts of the Congress; we must also organise in practice all work in line with present-day demands.

Very many interesting proposals were made and many profound thoughts expressed at our Congress and in the pre-Congress period. They must be carefully examined, and everything valuable and useful should be put into effect.

The most important thing now is to convert the energy of our plans into the energy of concrete action. This idea was very well expressed by a delegate to our Congress, Vasily Gorin, chairman of a Belgorod collective farm.

"All over our country," he said, "in every work collective, a difficult but, we are sure, irreversible process of renovation and reconstruction is now under way. It passes through the hearts and minds of Soviet people and calls for complete dedication on the part of each and everyone. Above all in their work."

Yes, comrades, acceleration and radical changes in all spheres of our life are not just a slogan but a course that the Party will follow firmly and undeviatingly.

Many delegates noted that departmentalism, localism, paper work, and other bureaucratic practices are a big obstacle to what is new and progressive. I wish to assure you, comrades, that the Central Committee will resolutely eliminate all the obstacles standing in the way of accelerating socio-economic progress, strengthen discipline and order, and create the organisational, moral and material prerequisites for the maximum development of creative activity, bold search, and socialist enterprise. I am confident that this will meet with broad and active support on the part of the entire Party and of all working people.

The Party committees, from top to bottom, are the organisers of the work of implementing the instructions of the Congress. What we now need are a concrete, businesslike and consistent style of work, unity of words and deeds, use of the most effective ways and means, a thorough consideration of people's opinions, and efficient coordination of the actions of all social forces.

Sluggishness, formalism, indifference, the habit of letting good ideas get bogged down in empty and endless round-about discussions and attempts to "adjust to readjustment" must be completely overcome.

One of the main conclusions of the Congress is that all Party committees should act as genuine bodies of political leadership. In the final analysis, the success of all our efforts to implement the general line of the 27th Party Congress will be determined by the conscious participation of the broadest masses of the people in building communism. Everything depends on us, comrades! The time has come for vigorous and united actions. The Party calls on every Communist, every Soviet citizen, to join actively in the large-scale work of putting our plans into practice, of perfecting Soviet society, of renovating our socialist home.

Comrades, the congress has strongly reaffirmed that socialism and peace, and peace and constructive endeavour, are indivisible. Socialism would fail to carry out its historic mission if it did not lead the struggle to deliver mankind from the burden of military threats and violence. The main goal of Soviet policy is security and a just peace for all nations. We regard the struggle against war and military preparations, against the propagation of hatred and violence as an inseparable part of the democratisation of all international relations, of the genuine normalisation of the political climate in the world.

In one respect the nuclear danger has put all states on an equal footing: in a big war nobody will be able to stand aside or to profit from the misfortunes of others. Equal security is the imperative of the times. Ensuring this security is becoming increasingly a political issue, one that can be resolved only by political means. It is high time to replace weapons by a more stable foundation for the relations among states. We see no alternative to this, nor are we trying to find one.

Unfortunately, however, in the international community there are still some who lay claims to a special security, one that is suited only to themselves. This is illustrated by the thinking in Washington. Calls for strength are still in fashion there, and strength continues to be regarded as the most convincing argument in world politics. It looks as though some people are simply afraid of the possibility that has appeared for a serious and long-term thaw in Soviet-American relations and in international relations as a whole.

This is not the first time we have come up against this kind of situation. Now, too, the militaristic, aggressive forces would of course prefer to preserve and perpetuate the confrontation. But what should we do, comrades?

Slam the door? It is possible that this is just what we are being pushed into doing. But we very clearly realise our responsibility for the destinies of our country and for the destinies of the world. We do not intend, therefore, to play into the hands of those who would like to force mankind to get used to the nuclear threat and to the arms race.

Soviet foreign policy is oriented towards a search for mutual understanding, towards dialogue, and the establishment of peaceful coexistence as the universal norm in relations among states. We have both a clear idea of how to achieve this and a concrete programme for maintaining and consolidating peace.

The Soviet Union is acting and will continue to act in the world arena in an open and responsible way, energetically and in good faith. We intend to work persistently and constructively to eliminate nuclear weapons, radically to limit the arms race, and to build reliable international security that is equal for all countries. A mandate to preserve peace and to curb the arms race resounded forcefully in speeches by delegates to our Congress. The Party will unswervingly carry out this mandate.

We call on the leaders of countries that have a different social system to take a responsible approach to the key issue of world politics today: the issue of war and peace.

The leadership of the CPSU and the Soviet state will do its utmost to secure for our people the opportunity to work under the conditions of freedom and a lasting peace. As reaffirmed by the Congress, our Party and the Soviet Union have many allies, supporters and partners abroad in the struggle for peace, freedom, and the progress of mankind.

We are sincerely happy to see here the leaders of the socialist countries. Allow me, on behalf of the Congress, wholeheartedly to thank the Communist Parties and peoples of these countries for their solidarity with the CPSU and the Soviet Union!

For a number of the fraternal parties in socialist countries this is also a congress year. The problems and tasks that the very course of history has set before the ruling Communist Parties are similar in many respects. And by responding to them, each party contributes to the treasure-chest of world socialism's combined experience. We wish you every success, dear friends!

The CPSU is grateful for the warm greetings addressed to it by the representatives of communist, revolutionary-democratic, socialist and social-democratic parties, of democratic, liberation, and anti-war forces and movements. We highly appreciate their understanding and support of the idea advanced by the Congress of establishing a comprehensive system of international security and the plan for eliminating nuclear arms before the end of this century. The CPSU is convinced that they are consonant with the true interests of all nations, all countries and all humanity.

Comrades, our Congress has shown that at the present stage, which is a turning point in our country's social development, the Leninist Party is equal to its historic tasks. On behalf of the delegates representing our entire Party I should like to say from this rostrum that we Communists set great store by the confidence placed in us by the workers, the farmers, the intelligentsia, by all Soviet people. We put above all else the interests of the people, of our Motherland, of socialism and peace. We will spare neither effort nor energy to translate into life the decisions of the 27th Congress of the Communist Party of the Soviet Union.

Nikita S. Krushchev, "Address to the Party Twentieth Congress"

In 1953, Nikita S. Khrushchev (1894-1971) took over as first party secretary of the Communist Party in the Soviet Union following the death of Joseph Stalin (1879-1953). By 1956, Khrushchev was the recognized leader of the USSR. At the Twentieth Party Congress in 1956, he delivered a speech to the party leaders, denouncing the brutal excesses of Stalin's regime and paving the way for a break them. Khrushchev's criticisms of Stalin shocked some of the party elite, but did result in a "thaw" for some the domestic policies of the Stalin era, including the liquidation of forced labor camps and reforms for the collectivized farming system. Under Khrushchev's direction, the Soviet Union also began a process of pardoning and "rehabilitating" those whom Stalin had exiled or imprisoned as political dissidents. While Khrushchev's speech initially was a secret speech meant only to spur discussion among the \Communist Party elite, it was leaked and published abroad. Khrushchev's "de-Stalinization" policies had a great impact within the Soviet Union, but also led some mistakenly to expect a "thaw" in Soviet international policies as well.

Source: *Congressional Record,* 84th Congress, 2nd Session, 1956, vol. CII, 9389-9403.

Focus Questions:

1. What criticisms did Khrushchev make regarding Stalin and his policies?
2. What steps did he propose to end the "cult of the individual" in the USSR?
3. What impact would this policy change have for domestic policies within the Soviet Union? For relations with Eastern bloc countries, and in the Cold War?

When we analyze the practice of Stalin in regard to the direction of the party and of the country, when we pause to consider everything which Stalin perpetrated, we must be convinced that Lenin's fears were justified. The negative characteristics of Stalin, which, in Lenin's time, were only incipient, transformed themselves during the last years into a grave abuse of power by Stalin, which caused untold harm to our party.

We have to consider seriously and analyze correctly this matter in order that we may preclude any possibility of a repetition in any form whatever of what took place during the life of Stalin, who absolutely did not tolerate collegiality in leadership and in work, and who practiced brutal violence, not only toward everything which opposed him, but also toward that which seemed to his capricious and despotic character, contrary to his concepts.

Stalin acted not through persuasion, explanation, and patient cooperation with people, but by imposing his concepts and demanding absolute submission to his opinion. Whoever opposed this concept or tried to prove his viewpoint, and the correctness of his position— was doomed to removal from the leading collective and to subsequent moral and physical annihilation. This was especially true during the period following the 17th party congress, when many prominent party leaders and rank-and-file party workers, honest and dedicated to the cause of communism, fell victim to Stalin's despotism....

Lenin's traits—patient work with people; stubborn and painstaking education of them; the ability to induce people to follow him without using compulsion, but rather through the ideological influence on them of the whole collective—were entirely foreign to

Stalin. He (Stalin) discarded the Leninist method of convincing and educating; he abandoned the method of ideological struggle for that of administrative violence, mass repressions, and terror. He acted on an increasingly larger scale and more stubbornly through punitive organs, at the same time often violating all existing norms of morality and of Soviet laws.... During Lenin's life party congresses were convened regularly; always when a radical turn in the development of the party and the country took place Lenin considered it absolutely necessary that the party discuss at length all the basic matters pertaining to internal and foreign policy and to questions bearing on the development of party and government.. . .

Were our party's holy Leninist principles observed after the death of Vladimir Ilyich?

Whereas during the first few years after Lenin's death party congresses and central committee plenums took place more or less regularly; later, when Stalin began increasingly to abuse his power, these principles were brutally violated. This was especially evident during the last 15 years of his life. Was it a normal situation when 13 years elapsed between the 18th and 19th party congresses, years during which our party and our country had experienced so many important events? These events demanded categorically that the party should have passed resolutions pertaining to the country's defense during the patriotic war and to peacetime construction after the war. Even after the end of the war a congress was not convened for over 7 years.

Central committee plenums were hardly ever called. It should be sufficient to mention that during all the years of the patriotic war not a single central committee plenum took place.... In practice Stalin ignored the norms of party life and trampled on the Leninist principle of collective party leadership....

Facts prove that many abuses were made on Stalin's orders without reckoning with any norms of party and Soviet legality. Stalin was a very distrustful man.... He could look at a man and say: "Why are your eyes so shifty today," or "Why are you turning so much today and avoiding to look me directly in the eyes?" The sickly suspicion created in him a general distrust even toward eminent party workers whom he had known for years. Everywhere and in everything he saw enemies, "two-facers" and spies.

Possessing unlimited power he indulged in great willfulness and choked a person morally and physically. A situation was created where one could not express one's own will....

The willfulness of Stalin showed itself not only in decisions concerning the internal life of the country but also in the international relations of the Soviet Union.

The July plenum of the Central Committee studied in detail the reasons for the development of conflict with Yugoslavia. It was a shameful role which Stalin played here. The "Yugoslav affair" contained no problems which could not have been solved through party discussions among comrades. There was no significant basis for the development of this affair"; it was completely possible to have prevented the rupture of relations with that country. This does not mean, however, that the Yugoslav leaders did not make mistakes or did not have shortcomings. But these mistakes and shortcomings were magnified in a monstrous manner by Stalin, which resulted in a break of relations with a friendly country.

I recall the first days when the conflict between the Soviet Union and Yugoslavia began artificially to be blown up. Once, when I came from Kiev to Moscow, I was invited to visit Stalin who, pointing to the copy of a letter lately sent to Tito, asked me, "Have you read this?"

Not waiting for my reply he answered, "I will shake my little finger and there will be no more Tito. He will fall."

We have dearly paid for this "shaking of the little finger." This statement reflected Stalin's mania for greatness, but he acted just that way: "I shall shake my little finger and there will be no Kossior"; "I will shake my little finger once more and Postyshev and Chubar will be no more"; "I will shake my little finger again and Voznesensky, Kuznetsov and many others will disappear."

But this did not happen to Tito. No matter how much or how little Stalin shook, not only his little finger but everything else that he could shake, Tito did not fall. Why? The reason was that, in this case of disagreement with the Yugoslav comrades, Tito had behind him a state and a people who had gone through a severe school of fighting for liberty and independence, a people which gave support to its leaders.

You see to what Stalin's mania for greatness led. He had completely lost consciousness of reality; he demonstrated his suspicion and haughtiness not only in relation to individuals in the U.S.S.R., but in relation to whole parties and nations.

We have carefully examined the case of Yugoslavia and have found a proper solution which is approved by the peoples of the Soviet Union and of Yugoslavia as well as by the working masses of all the people's democracies and by all progressive humanity. The liquidation of the abnormal relationship with Yugoslavia was done in the interest of the whole camp of socialism, in the interest of strengthening peace in the whole world....

If we are to consider this matter as Marxists and as Leninists, then we have to state unequivocably that the leadership practice which came into being during the last years of Stalin's life became a serious obstacle in the path of Soviet social development.

Stalin often failed for months to take up some unusually important problems concerning the life of the party and of the state whose solution could not be postponed. During Stalin's leadership our peaceful relations with other nations were often threatened, because one-man decisions could cause and often did cause great complications.

In the last years, when we managed to free ourselves of the harmful practice of the cult of the individual and took several proper steps in the sphere of internal and external policies, everyone saw how activity grew before their very eyes, how the creative activity of the broad working masses developed, how favorably all this acted upon the development of economy and of culture. [Applause.] Some comrades may ask us: Where were the members of the Political Bureau of the Central Committee? Why did they not assert themselves against the cult of the individual in time? And why is this being done only now?

First of all we have to consider the fact that the members of the Political Bureau viewed these matters in a different way at different times. Initially, many of them backed Stalin actively because Stalin was one of the strongest Marxists and his logic, his strength, and his will greatly influenced the cadres and party work....

Later, however, abusing his power more and more, [Stalin] began to fight eminent party and government leaders and to use terroristic methods against honest Soviet people....

It is clear that such conditions put every member of the Political Bureau in a very difficult situation. And when we also consider the fact that in the last years the Central Committee plenary sessions were not convened, and that the sessions of the Political Bureau occurred only occasionally, from time to time, then we will understand how difficult it was for any member of the Political Bureau to take a stand against one or another unjust or improper procedure, against serious errors and shortcomings in the practices of leadership.. . .

Comrades, we must abolish the cult of the individual decisively, once and for all; we must draw the proper conclusions concerning both ideological-theoretical and practical work.

It is necessary for this purpose: First, in a Bolshevik manner to condemn and to eradicate the cult of the individual as alien to Marxism-Leninism and not consonant with the principles of party leadership and the norms of party life, and to fight inexorably all attempts at bringing back this practice....

Secondly, to continue systematically and consistently the work done by the party's central committee during the last years, a work characterized by minute observation in all party organizations, from the bottom to the top, of the Leninist principles of party leadership, characterized, above all, by the main principle of collective leadership, characterized by the observation of the norms of party life described in the statutes of our party, and, finally, characterized by the wide practice of criticism and self-criticism.

Thirdly, to restore completely the Leninist principles of Soviet Socialist democracy, expressed in the constitution of the Soviet Union, to fight willfulness of individuals abusing their power. The evil caused by acts violating revolutionary Socialist legality which have accumulated during a long time as a result of the negative influence of the cult of the individual has to be completely corrected....

We are absolutely certain that our party, armed with the historical resolutions of the 20th Congress, will lead the Soviet people along the Leninist path to new successes, to new victories. [Tumultuous, prolonged applause.] Long live the victorious banner of our party—Leninism. [Tumultuous, prolonged applause ending in ovation. All rise.]

Joseph Stalin, Excerpts from the "Soviet Victory" Speech, 1946

The term "Cold War" describes the era of uneasy relations between the Western Allies and the Soviet Union after World War II. Each was competing for influence in Europe through propaganda and troop placement. In the first excerpt, the Soviet leader Joseph Stalin offered a glimpse of the ideological combat that was to be waged in the future. A month later, Winston Churchill, who had largely directed the British war effort, warned the West of the deceptive Soviet Union in his famous "Iron Curtain" speech.

Source: "The Soviet Victory," from Embassy of the U.S.S.R., speech delivered by J.V. Stalin at a Meeting of Voters of the Stalin Electoral Area of Moscow (Washington, DC: Government Printing Office, 1946).

Focus Question:

1. What did Stalin mean in his speech of February 1946 by the phrase "Soviet victory"?

PART 26
The Cold War

It would be wrong to believe that the Second World War broke out accidentally or as a result of the mistakes of some or other statesmen, though mistakes certainly were made. In reality, the war broke out as an inevitable result of the development of world economic and political forces on the basis of modern monopoly capitalism.

Marxists have stated more than once that the capitalist system of world economy conceals in itself the elements of general crisis and military clashes, that in view of this in our time the development of world capitalism takes place not as a smooth and even advance but through crises and war catastrophes.

The reason is that the unevenness of the development of capitalist countries usually results, as time passes, in an abrupt disruption of the equilibrium within the world system of capitalism, and that a group of capitalist countries which believes itself to be less supplied with raw materials and markets usually attempts to alter the situation and redivide the "spheres of influence" in its own favour by means of armed force…

This results in the splitting of the capitalist world into two hostile camps and in war between them. Perhaps the catastrophes of war could be avoided if there existed the possibility of re-distributing periodically raw materials and markets among the countries in accordance with their economic weight—by means of adopting coordinated and peaceful decisions. This, however, cannot be accomplished under present capitalist conditions of the development of world economy…

As to our country, for her the war was the severest and hardest of all the wars our Motherland has ever experienced in her history. But the war was not only a curse. It was at the same time a great school in which all the forces of the people were tried and tested. The war laid bare all the facts and events in the rear and at the front, it mercilessly tore off all the veils and covers which had concealed the true faces of States, governments, and parties, and placed them on the stage without masks, without embellishments, with all their shortcomings and virtues.

And so, what are the results of the war?…

Our victory means, in the first place, that our Soviet social system has won, that the Soviet social system successfully withstood the trial in the flames of war and proved its perfect viability. It is well known that the foreign press more than once asserted that the Soviet social system is a "risky experiment" doomed to failure, that the Soviet system is a "house of cards," without any roots in life, imposed upon the people by the organs of the "Cheka" [secret police], that a slight push from outside would be enough to blow this "house of cards" to smithereens.

Now we can say that the war swept away all these assertions of the foreign press as groundless. The war has shown that the Soviet social system is a truly popular system, which has grown from the people and enjoys its powerful support, that the Soviet social system is a perfectly viable and stable form of organisation of society.

More than that, the point is now not whether the Soviet social system is viable or not, since after the objective lessons of the war no single skeptic now ventures to come out with doubts concerning the viability of the Soviet social system. The point now is that the Soviet social system has proved more viable and stable than a non-Soviet social system, that the Soviet social system is a better form of organisation of society than any non-Soviet social system.

John F. Kennedy, Address Before the General Assembly of the United Nations, 1961

Kennedy, John Fitzgerald (1917–1963 CE) was the 35th President of the United States. Born in Massachusetts to a prominent family, Kennedy graduated from Harvard University in 1940. He was severely injured in Pacific naval combat during World War II. Kennedy held a seat in the U.S. House of Representatives, followed by election to the U.S. Senate in 1953. In 1960, he became the youngest person to be elected President of the United States. He created the U.S. Peace Corps to support developing countries, challenged Soviet advances in East Germany and Cuba, spurred American exploration of outer space, and sought to halt the Cold War nuclear arms race. Kennedy was assassinated on November 22, 1963.

Source: Address Before the General Assembly of the United Nations (Sections I–VI), by President John F. Kennedy, 1961.

Focus Question:

1. According to President Kennedy, what kind of responsibilities has the "age of mass extermination" placed on individual countries and the United Nations Organization?
2. What solutions does Kennedy propose to reduce the threat of nuclear weapons?

ADDRESS BEFORE THE GENERAL ASSEMBLY OF THE UNITED NATIONS

President John F. Kennedy

New York City

September 25, 1961

Mr. President, honored delegates, ladies and gentlemen:

We meet in an hour of grief and challenge. Dag Hammarskjold is dead. But the United Nations lives. His tragedy is deep in our hearts, but the task for which he died is at the top of our agenda. A noble servant of peace is gone. But the quest for peace lies before us.

The problem is not the death of one man—the problem is the life of this organization. It will either grow to meet the challenges of our age, or it will be gone with the wind, without influence, without force, without respect. Were we to let it die, to enfeeble its vigor, to cripple its powers, we would condemn our future.

For in the development of this organization rests the only true alternative to war—and war appeals no longer as a rational alternative. Unconditional war can no longer lead to unconditional victory. It can no longer serve to settle disputes. It can no longer concern the great powers alone. For a nuclear disaster, spread by wind and water and fear, could well engulf the great and the small, the rich and the poor, the committed and the uncommitted alike. *Mankind must put an end to war—or war will put an end to mankind.*

So let us here resolve that Dag Hammarskjold did not live, or die, in vain. Let us call a truce to terror. Let us invoke the blessings of peace. And as we build an international capacity to keep peace, let us join in dismantling the national capacity to wage war.

II

This will require new strength and new roles for the United Nations. For disarmament without checks is but a shadow—and a community without law is but a shell. Already the United Nations has become both the measure and the vehicle of man's most generous impulses. Already it has provided—in the Middle East, in Asia, in Africa this year in the Congo—a means of holding man's violence within bounds.

But the great question which confronted this body in 1945 is still before us: whether man's cherished hopes for progress and peace are to be destroyed by terror and disruption, whether the "foul winds of war" can be tamed in time to free the cooling winds of reason, and whether the pledges of our Charter are to be fulfilled or defied—pledges to secure peace, progress, human rights and world law.

In this Hall, there are not three forces, but two. One is composed of those who are trying to build the kind of world described in Articles I and II of the Charter. The other, seeking a far different world, would undermine this organization in the process.

Today, of all days our dedication to the Charter must be maintained. It must be strengthened first of all by the selection of an outstanding civil servant to carry forward the responsibilities of the Secretary General—a man endowed with both the wisdom and the power to make meaningful the moral force of the world community. The late Secretary General nurtured and sharpened the United Nations' obligation to act. But he did not invent it. It was there in the Charter. It is still there in the Charter.

However difficult it may be to fill Mr. Hammarskjold's place, it can better be filled by one man rather than three. Even the three horses of the Troika did not have three drivers, all going in different directions. They had only one—and so must the United Nations executive. To install a triumvirate, or any panel, or any rotating authority, in the United Nations administrative offices would replace order with anarchy, action with paralysis, confidence with confusion.

The Secretary General, in a very real sense, is the servant of the General Assembly. Diminish his authority and you diminish the authority of the only body where all nations, regardless of power, are equal and sovereign. Until all the powerful are just, the weak will be secure only in the strength of this Assembly.

Effective and independent executive action is not the same question as balanced representation. In view of the enormous change in membership in this body since its founding, the American delegation will join in any effort for the prompt review and revision of the composition of United Nations bodies.

But to give this organization three drivers—to permit each great power to decide its own case, would entrench the Cold War in the headquarters of peace. Whatever advantages such a plan may hold out to my own country, as one of the great powers, we reject it. For we far prefer world law, in the age of self-determination, to world war, in the age of mass extermination.

III

Today, every inhabitant of this planet must contemplate the day when this planet may no longer be habitable. Every man, woman and child lives under a nuclear sword of Damocles, hanging by the slenderest of threads, capable of being cut at any moment by accident or miscalculation or by madness. The weapons of war must be abolished before they abolish us.

Men no longer debate whether armaments are a symptom or a cause of tension. The mere existence of modern weapons—ten million times more powerful than any that the world has ever seen, and only minutes away from any target on earth—is a source of horror, and discord and distrust. Men no longer maintain that disarmament must await the settlement of all disputes—for disarmament must be a part of any permanent settlement. And

men may no longer pretend that the quest for disarmament is a sign of weakness—for in a spiraling arms race, a nation's security may well be shrinking even as its arms increase.

For fifteen years this organization has sought the reduction and destruction of arms. Now that goal is no longer a dream—it is a practical matter of life or death. The risks inherent in disarmament pale in comparison to the risks inherent in an unlimited arms race.

It is in this spirit that the recent Belgrade Conference—recognizing that this is no longer a Soviet problem or an American problem, but a human problem—endorsed a program of "general, complete and strictly an internationally controlled disarmament." It is in this same spirit that we in the United States have labored this year, with a new urgency, and with a new, now statutory agency fully endorsed by the Congress, to find an approach to disarmament which would be so far-reaching, yet realistic, so mutually balanced and beneficial, that it could be accepted by every nation. And it is in this spirit that we have presented with the agreement of the Soviet Union—under the label both nations now accept of "general and complete disarmament"—a new statement of newly-agreed principles for negotiation.

But we are well aware that all issues of principle are not settled, and that principles alone are not enough. It is therefore our intention to challenge the Soviet Union, not to an arms race, but to a peace race—to advance together step by step, stage by stage, until general and complete disarmament has been achieved. We invite them now to go beyond agreement in principle to reach agreement on actual plans.

The program to be presented to this assembly—for general and complete disarmament under effective international control—moves to bridge the gap between those who insist on a gradual approach and those who talk only of the final and total achievement. It would create machinery to keep the peace as it destroys the machinery of war. It would proceed through balanced and safeguarded stages designed to give no state a military advantage over another. It would place the final responsibility for verification and control where it belongs, not with the big powers alone, not with one's adversary or one's self, but in an international organization within the framework of the United Nations. It would assure that indispensable condition of disarmament—true inspection—and apply it in stages proportionate to the stage of disarmament. It would cover delivery systems as well as weapons. It would ultimately halt their production as well as their testing, their transfer as well as their possession. It would achieve under the eyes of an international disarmament organization, a steady reduction in force, both nuclear and conventional, until it has abolished all armies and all weapons except those needed for internal order and a new United Nations Peace Force. And it starts that process now, today, even as the talks begin.

In short, general and complete disarmament must no longer be a slogan, used to resist the first steps. It is no longer to be a goal without means of achieving it, without means of verifying its progress, without means of keeping the peace. It is now a realistic plan, and a test—a test of those only willing to talk and a test of those willing to act.

Such a plan would not bring a world free from conflict and greed—but it would bring a world free from the terrors of mass destruction. It would not usher in the era of the super state—but it would usher in an era in which no state could annihilate or be annihilated by another.

In 1945, this Nation proposed the Baruch Plan to internationalize the atom before other nations even possessed the bomb or demilitarized their troops. We proposed with our allies the Disarmament plan of 1951 while still at war in Korea. And we make our proposals today, while building up our defenses over Berlin, not because we are inconsistent or insincere or intimidated, but because we know the rights of free men will prevail—because while we are compelled against our will to rearm, we look confidently beyond Berlin to the kind of disarmed world we all prefer.

I therefore propose on the basis of this Plan, that disarmament negotiations resume promptly, and continue without interruption until an entire program for general and complete disarmament has not only been agreed but has actually been achieved.

The logical place to begin is a treaty assuring the end of nuclear tests of all kinds, in every environment, under workable controls. The United States and the United Kingdom have proposed such a treaty that is both reasonable, effective and ready for signature. We are still prepared to sign that treaty today.

We also proposed a mutual ban on atmospheric testing, without inspection or controls, in order to save the human race from the poison of radioactive fallout. We regret that the offer has not been accepted.

For 15 years we have sought to make the atom an instrument of peaceful growth rather than of war. But for 15 years our concessions have been matched by obstruction, our patience by intransigence. And the pleas of mankind for peace have met with disregard.

Finally, as the explosions of others beclouded the skies, my country was left with no alternative but to act in the interests of its own and the free world's security. We cannot endanger that security by refraining from testing while others improve their arsenals. Nor can we endanger it by another long, uninspected ban on testing. For three years we accepted those risks in our open society while seeking agreement on inspection. But this year, while we were negotiating in good faith in Geneva, others were secretly preparing new experiments in destruction.

Our tests are not polluting the atmosphere. Our deterrent weapons are guarded against accidental explosion or use. Our doctors and scientists stand ready to help any nation measure and meet the hazards to health which inevitably result from the tests in the atmosphere.

But to halt the spread of these terrible weapons, to halt the contamination of the air, to halt the spiralling nuclear arms race, we remain ready to seek new avenues of agreement, our new Disarmament Program thus includes the following proposals:

—First, signing the test-ban treaty by all nations. This can be done now. Test ban negotiations need not and should not await general disarmament.

—Second, stopping the production of fissionable materials for use in weapons, and preventing their transfer to any nation now lacking in nuclear weapons.

—Third, prohibiting the transfer of control over nuclear weapons to states that do not own them.

—Fourth, keeping nuclear weapons from seeding new battlegrounds in outer space.

—Fifth, gradually destroying existing nuclear weapons and converting their materials to peaceful uses; and

—Finally, halting the unlimited testing and production of strategic nuclear delivery vehicles, and gradually destroying them as well.

V

To destroy arms, however, is not enough. We must create even as we destroy—creating worldwide law and law enforcement as we outlaw worldwide war and weapons. In the world we seek, the United Nations Emergency Forces which have been hastily assembled, uncertainly supplied, and inadequately financed, will never be enough.

Therefore, the United States recommends that all member nations earmark special peace-keeping units in their armed forces—to be on call of the United

Nations, to be specially trained and quickly available, and with advanced provision for financial and logistic support.

In addition, the American delegation will suggest a series of steps to improve the United Nations' machinery for the peaceful settlement of disputes—for on-the-spot fact-finding, mediation and adjudication—for extending the rule of international law. For peace is not solely a matter of military or technical problems— it is primarily a problem of politics and people. And unless man can match his strides in weaponry and technology with equal strides in social and political development, our great strength, like that of the dinosaur, will become incapable of proper control—and like the dinosaur vanish from the earth.

VI

As we extend the rule of law on earth, so must we also extend it to man's new domain—outer space.

All of us salute the brave cosmonauts of the Soviet Union. The new horizons of outer space must not be driven by the old bitter concepts of imperialism and sovereign claims. The cold reaches of the universe must not become the new arena of an even colder war.

To this end, we shall urge proposals extending the United Nations Charter to the limits of man's exploration of the universe, reserving outer space for peaceful use, prohibiting weapons of mass destruction in space or on celestial bodies, and opening the mysteries and benefits of space to every nation. We shall propose further cooperative efforts between all nations in weather prediction and eventually in weather control. We shall propose, finally, a global system of communications satellites linking the whole world in telegraph and telephone and radio and television. The day need not be far away when such a system will televise the proceedings of this body to every corner of the world for the benefit of peace…

CHAPTER 28

Identity and Power in a Decolonizing World

The United Nations, "Universal Declaration of Human Rights," 1948

One of the early acts of the United Nations was to proclaim a *Universal Declaration of Human Rights.* Work on the document began soon after the international organization was established and continued for approximately three years before the *Declaration* was formally promulgated by the General Assembly in December, 1948. In the Assembly ballot forty-eight member states voted approval of the *Declaration* and eight abstained. There were no negative votes.

The sessions of the drafting committees, which all together held hundreds of meetings to prepare the document, were far from harmonious. The topic of human rights is one not just of fundamental concern but also one about which different nations of the world held (and still hold) quite divergent opinions. The aim throughout the drafting sessions was to formulate a document that, although it would not satisfy the wishes of every nation entirely, would still embrace enough of these to meet with general acceptance. That it was almost completely successful in doing so is revealed by the final vote. As the president of the General Assembly pointed out at the time: "It was the first occasion on which the organized community of nations had made a declaration of human rights and fundamental freedoms."

The *Declaration* is a compilation of political, social, and cultural ideals to which all nations can aspire. It should be clear from a close reading of its text that no country in the world today fully realizes these ideals and, indeed, that many fall far short of doing so. Yet, although the Articles of the Declaration are not legally binding on its signatories, it has, as many delegates to the United Nations emphasized at the time, a moral force that can lead the nations of the world away from oppression toward more humane and liberal forms of society.

Source: U.N."Universal Declaration of Human Rights", 1948.

FOCUS QUESTIONS:

1. What rights are considered universal in the Declaration?
2. Do you think all of the rights enumerated in the Declaration should be included? Do you think they left any important rights out?

UNIVERSAL DECLARATION OF HUMAN RIGHTS PREAMBLE

Whereas recognition of the inherent dignity and of the equal and inalienable rights of all members of the human family is the foundation of freedom, justice and peace in the world,

Whereas disregard and contempt for human rights have resulted in barbarous acts which have outraged the conscience of mankind, and the advent of a world in which human beings shall enjoy freedom of speech and belief and freedom from fear and want has been proclaimed as the highest aspiration of the common people,

Whereas it is essential, if man is not to be compelled to have recourse, as a last resort, to rebellion against tyranny and oppression, that human rights should be protected by the rule of law,

Whereas it is essential to promote the development of friendly relations between nations,

Whereas the peoples of the United Nations have in the Charter reaffirmed their faith in fundamental human rights, in the dignity and worth of the human person and in the equal rights of men and women and have determined to promote social progress and better standards of life in larger freedom,

Whereas Member States have pledged themselves to achieve, in cooperation with the United Nations, the promotion of universal respect for and observance of human rights and fundamental freedoms,

Whereas a common understanding of these rights and freedoms is of the greatest importance for the full realization of this pledge,

Now, therefore, The General Assembly

Proclaims this Universal Declaration of Human Rights as a common standard of achievement for all peoples and all nations, to the end that every individual and every organ of society, keeping this Declaration constantly in mind, shall strive by teaching and education to promote respect for these rights and freedoms and by progressive measures, national and international, to secure their universal and effective recognition and observance, both among the peoples of Member States themselves and among the peoples of territories under their jurisdiction.

ARTICLE 1

All human beings are born free and equal in dignity and rights. They are endowed with reason and conscience and should act towards one another in a spirit of brotherhood.

ARTICLE 2

Everyone is entitled to all the rights and freedoms set forth in this Declaration, without distinction of any kind, such as race, colour, sex, language, religion, political or other opinion, national or social ori-gin, property, birth, or other status.

Furthermore, no distinction shall be made on the basis of the political, jurisdictional or international status of the country or territory to which a person belongs, whether it be independent, trust, non-self-governing, or under any other limitation of sovereignty.

ARTICLE 3

Everyone has the right to life, liberty, and the security of person.

ARTICLE 4

No one shall be held in slavery or servitude; slavery and the slave trade shall be prohibited in all their forms.

ARTICLE 5

No one shall be subjected to torture or to cruel, inhuman, or degrading treatment or punishment.

ARTICLE 6

Everyone has the right to recognition everywhere as a person before the law.

ARTICLE 7

All are equal before the law and are entitled without any discrimination to equal protection of the law. All are entitled to equal protection against any discrimination in violation of this Declaration and against any incitement to such discrimination.

ARTICLE 8

Everyone has the right to an effective remedy by the competent national tribunals for acts violating the fundamental rights granted him by the constitution or by law.

ARTICLE 9

No one shall be subjected to arbitrary arrest, detention, or exile.

ARTICLE 10

Everyone is entitled in full equality to a fair, and public hearing by an independent and impartial tribunal, in the determination of his rights and obligations and of any criminal charge against him.

ARTICLE 11

1. Everyone charged with a penal offence has the right to be presumed innocent until proved guilty according to law in a public trial at which he has had all the guarantees necessary for his defence.
2. No one shall be held guilty of any penal offence on account of any act or omission which did not constitute a penal offence, under national or international law, at the time when it was committed. Nor shall a heavier penalty be imposed than the one that was applicable at the time the penal offence was committed.

ARTICLE 12

No one shall be subjected to arbitrary interference with his privacy, family, home, or correspondence, nor to attacks upon his honour and reputation. Everyone has the right to the protection of the law against such interference or attacks.

ARTICLE 13

1. Everyone has the right to freedom of movement and residence within the borders of each State.
2. Everyone has the right to leave any country, including his own, and to return to his country.

ARTICLE 14

1. Everyone has the right to seek and to enjoy in other countries asylum from persecution.
2. This right may not be invoked in the case of prosecutions genuinely arising from non-political crimes or from acts contrary to the purposes and principles of the United Nations.

ARTICLE 15

1. Everyone has the right to a nationality.

2. No one shall be arbitrarily deprived of his nationality nor denied the right to change his nationality.

ARTICLE 16

1. Men and women of full age, without any limitation due to race, nationality, or religion, have the right to marry and to found a family. They are entitled to equal rights as to marriage, during marriage, and at its dissolution.
2. Marriage shall be entered into only with the free and full consent of the intending spouses.
3. The family is the natural and fundamental group unit of society and is entitled to protection by society and the State.

ARTICLE 17

1. Everyone has the right to own property alone as well as in association with others.
2. No one shall be arbitrarily deprived of his property.

ARTICLE 18

Everyone has the right to freedom of thought, conscience and religion; this right includes freedom to change his religion or belief, and freedom, either alone or in community with others and in public or private, to manifest his religion or belief in teaching, practice, worship, and observance.

ARTICLE 19

Everyone has the right to freedom of opinion and expression; this right includes freedom to hold opinions without interference and to seek, receive and impart information and ideas through any media and regardless of frontiers.

ARTICLE 20

1. Everyone has the right to freedom of peaceful assembly and association.
2. No one may be compelled to belong to an association.

ARTICLE 21

1. Everyone has the right to take part in the government of his country, directly or through freely chosen representatives.
2. Everyone has the right of equal access to public service in his country.
3. The will of the people shall be the basis of the authority of government; this will shall be expressed in periodic and genuine elections which shall be by

universal and equal suffrage and shall be held by secret vote or by equivalent free voting procedures.

ARTICLE 22

Everyone, as a member of society, has the right to social security and is entitled to realization, through national effort and international co-operation and in accordance with the organization and resources of each. State, of the economic, social and cultural rights indispensable for his dignity and the free development of his personality.

ARTICLE 23

1. Everyone has the right to work, to free choice of employment, to just and favourable conditions of work and to protection against unemployment.
2. Everyone, without any discrimination, has the right to equal pay for equal work.
3. Everyone who works has the right to just and favourable remuneration ensuring for himself and his family an existence worthy of human dignity, and supplemented, if necessary, by other means of social protection.

The United Nations, "Declaration on the Granting of Independence to Colonial Countries and Peoples"

This document comprises one of the central landmarks in the history of decolonization. Known officially as United Nations Resolution 1514, it was formulated in December 1960 and made specific reference to earlier United Nations declarations, such as the UN Charter of 1945 and the Universal Declaration of Human Rights of 1948. Although no UN member states voted against Resolution 1514 in 1960, several major powers – including Britain, France, and the United States – abstained. A UN special committee was formed in 1962 to oversee the application and implementation of the ideals contained in Resolution 1514.

Source: www.unhchr.ch/html/menu3/b/c_coloni.htm

Focus Questions:

1. What similarities and differences exist between this declaration and earlier UN declarations, such as the UN Charter and the Universal Declaration of Human Rights?
2. How is the legacy of colonialism characterized here?

3. After discussing the "passionate yearning for freedom in all dependent peoples," the declaration goes on to state that "the process of liberation is irresistible and irreversible." To what extent do you believe these statements apply to the world of the early 21st century?

Declaration on the Granting of Independence to Colonial Countries and Peoples Adopted by General Assembly resolution 1514 (XV) of 14 December 1960

The General Assembly,

Mindful of the determination proclaimed by the peoples of the world in the Charter of the United Nations to reaffirm faith in fundamental human rights, in the dignity and worth of the human person, in the equal rights of men and women and of nations large and small and to promote social progress and better standards of life in larger freedom,

Conscious of the need for the creation of conditions of stability and well-being and peaceful and friendly relations based on respect for the principles of equal rights and self-determination of all peoples, and of universal respect for, and observance of, human rights and fundamental freedoms for all without distinction as to race, sex, language of religion,

Recognizing the passionate yearning for freedom in all dependent peoples and the decisive role of such peoples in the attainment of their independence,

Aware of the increasing conflicts resulting from the denial of or impediments in the way of the freedom of such peoples, which constitute a serious threat to world peace,

Considering the important role of the United Nations in assisting the movement for independence in Trust and Non-Self-Governing Territories,

Recognizing that the peoples of the world ardently desire the end of colonialism in all its manifestations,

Convinced that the continued existence of colonialism prevents the development of international economic cooperation, impedes the social, cultural and economic development of dependent peoples and militates against the United Nations ideal of universal peace,

Affirming that peoples may, for their own ends, freely dispose of their natural wealth and resources without prejudice to any obligations arising out of international economic co-operation, based upon the principle of mutual benefit, and international law,

Believing that the process of liberation is irresistible and irreversible and that, in order to avoid serious crises, an end must be put to colonialism and all practices of segregation and discrimination associated therewith,

Welcoming the emergence in recent years of a large number of dependent territories into freedom and independence, and recognizing the increasingly powerful trends towards freedom in such territories which have not yet attained independence,

Convinced that all peoples have an inalienable right to complete freedom, the exercise of their sovereignty and the integrity of their national territory,

Solemnly proclaims the necessity of bringing to a speedy and unconditional end colonialism in all its forms and manifestations;

And to this end Declares that:

1. The subjection of peoples to alien subjugation, domination and exploitation constitutes a denial of fundamental human rights, is contrary to the Charter of the United Nations and is an impediment to the promotion of world peace and co-operation.

2. All peoples have the right to self-determination; by virtue of that right they freely determine their political status and freely pursue their economic, social and cultural development.

3. Inadequacy of political, economic, social or educational preparedness should never serve as a pretext for delaying independence.

4. All armed action or repressive measures of all kinds directed against dependent peoples shall cease in order to enable them to exercise peacefully and freely their right to complete independence, and the integrity of their national territory shall be respected.

5. Immediate steps shall be taken, in Trust and Non-Self-Governing Territories or all other territories which have not yet attained independence, to transfer all powers to the peoples of those territories, without any conditions or reservations, in accordance with their freely expressed will and desire, without any distinction as to race, creed or colour, in order to enable them to enjoy complete independence and freedom.

6. Any attempt aimed at the partial or total disruption of the national unity and the territorial integrity of a country is incompatible with the purposes and principles of the Charter of the United Nations.

7. All States shall observe faithfully and strictly the provisions of the Charter of the United Nations, the Universal Declaration of Human Rights and the present Declaration on the basis of equality, non-interference in the internal affairs of all States, and respect for the sovereign rights of all peoples and their territorial integrity.

Jomo Kenyatta, *from Facing Mt. Kenya: The Tribal Life of the Gokuyu,* 1938

Born in 1893, Kenyatta early campaigned for land rights for his Kikuyu tribe in Kenya. He spent sixteen years in England, studying at the University of London and linking with other African leaders. In 1946 he and Kwame Nkrumah, later the first leader of independent Ghana, formed the Pan-African Federation. Kenyatta returned to Kenya in 1946 and was jailed for a role in a violent uprising against white settlers. Released in 1961, he negotiated independence arrangements with the British while also reconciling two main tribal factions in Kenya. Kenyatta stands as one of the earliest and most revered African nationalist leaders.

Source: Jomo Kenyatta, *Facing Mt. Kenya: The Tribal Life of the Gikuyu* (London: Sedser and Warburg, 1938), pp. 47–52.

Focus Questions:

1. Why has Kenyatta made his argument mostly in the form of a parable? What does this imply about his intended audience(s)? What moral are these audiences supposed to draw?
2. What does Kenyatta think valuable about European culture? What parts are not valuable? How does he illustrate these in the parable?
3. How is the document an illustration of Kenyatta himself as a product of both African and European culture?

And the Europeans, having their feet firm on the soil, began to claim the absolute right to rule the country and to have the ownership of the lands under the title of "Crown Lands," where the Gikuyu, who are the original owners, now live as "tenants at will of the Crown." The Gikuyu lost most of their lands through their magnanimity, for the Gikuyu country was never wholly conquered by force of arms, but the people were put under the ruthless domination of European imperialism through the insidious trickery of hypocritical treaties.

The relation between the Gikuyu and the Europeans can well be illustrated by a Gikuyu story which says: That once upon a time an elephant made a friendship with a man. One day a heavy thunderstorm broke out, the elephant went to his friend, who had a little hut at the edge of the forest, and said to him: "My dear good man, will you please let me put my trunk inside your hut to keep it out of this torrential rain?" The man, seeing what situation his friend was in, replied: "My dear good elephant, my hut is very small, but there is room for your trunk and myself. Please put your trunk in gently." The elephant thanked his friend, saying: "You have done me a good deed and one day I shall return your kindness." But what followed? As soon as the elephant put his trunk inside the hut, slowly he pushed his head inside, and finally flung the man out in the rain, and then lay down comfortably inside his friend's hut, saying: "My dear good friend, your skin is harder than mine, and as there is not enough room for both of us, you can afford to remain in the rain while I am protecting my delicate skin from the hailstorm."

The man, seeing what his friend had done to him, started to grumble, the animals in the nearby forest heard the noise and came to see what was the matter. All stood around listening to the heated argument between the man and his friend the elephant. In this turmoil the lion came along roaring, and said in a loud voice: "Don't you all know that I am the King of the Jungle! How dare anyone disturb the peace of my kingdom?" On hearing this the elephant, who was one of the high ministers in the jungle kingdom, replied in a soothing voice, and said: "My Lord, there is no disturbance of the peace in your kingdom. I have only been having a little discussion with my friend here as to the possession of this little hut which your lordship sees me occupying." The lion, who wanted to have "peace and tranquillity" in his kingdom, replied in a noble voice, saying: "I command my ministers to appoint a Commission of Enquiry to go thoroughly into this matter and report accordingly." He then turned to the man and said: "You have done well by establishing friendship with my people, especially with the elephant who is one of my honourable ministers of state. Do not grumble any more, your hut is not lost to you. Wait until the sitting of my Imperial Commission, and there you will be given plenty of opportunity to state your case. I am sure that you will be pleased with the findings of the Commission." The man was very pleased by these sweet words from the King of the Jungle, and innocently waited for his opportunity, in the belief, that naturally, the hut would be returned to him.

The elephant, obeying the command of his master, got busy with other ministers to appoint the Commission of Enquiry. The following elders of the jungle were appointed to sit in the Commission: (1) Mr. Rhinoceros; (2) Mr. Buffalo; (3) Mr. Alligator; (4) The Rt. Hon. Mr. Fox to act as chairman; and (5) Mr. Leopard to act as Secretary to the Commission. On seeing the personnel, the man protested and asked if it was not necessary to include in this Commission a member from his side. But he was told that it was impossible, since no one from his side was well enough educated to understand the intricacy of jungle law. Further, that there was nothing to fear, for the members of the Commission were all men of repute for their impartiality in justice, and as they were gentlemen chosen by God to look after the interests of races less adequately endowed with teeth and claws, he might rest assured that they would investigate the matter with the greatest care and report impartially.

The Commission sat to take the evidence. The Rt. Hon. Mr. Elephant was first called. He came along with a superior air, brushing his tusks with a sapling which Mrs. Elephant had provided, and in an authoritative voice said: "Gentlemen of the Jungle, there is no need for me to waste your valuable time in relating a story which I am sure you all know. I have always regarded it as my duty to protect the interests of my friends, and this appears to have caused the misunderstanding between myself and my friend here. He invited me to save his hut from being blown away by a hurricane. As the hurricane had gained access owing to the unoccupied space in the hut, I considered it necessary, in my friend's own interests, to turn the undeveloped space to a more economic use by sitting in it myself; a duty which any of you would undoubtedly have performed with equal readiness in similar circumstances."

After hearing the Rt. Hon. Mr. Elephant's conclusive evidence, the Commission called Mr. Hyena and other elders of the jungle, who all supported what Mr. Elephant had said. They then called the man, who began to give his own account of the dispute. But the Commission cut him short, saying: "My good man, please confine yourself to relevant issues. We have already heard the circumstances from various unbiased sources; all we wish you to tell us is whether the undeveloped space in your hut was occupied by anyone else before Mr. Elephant assumed his position?" The man began to say: "No, but—" But at this point the Commission declared that they had heard sufficient evidence from both sides and retired to consider their decision. After enjoying a delicious meal at the expense of the Rt. Hon. Mr. Elephant, they reached their verdict, called the man, and declared as follows: "In our opinion this dispute has arisen through a regrettable misunderstanding due to the backwardness of your ideas. We consider that Mr. Elephant has fulfilled his sacred duty of protecting your interests. As it is clearly for your good that the space should be put to its most economic use, and as you yourself have not yet reached the stage of expansion which would enable you to fill it, we consider it necessary to arrange a compromise to suit both parties. Mr. Elephant shall continue his occupation of your hut, but we give you permission to look for a site where you can build another hut more suited to your needs, and we will see that you are well protected."

The man, having no alternative, and fearing that his refusal might expose him to the teeth and claws of members of the Commission, did as they suggested. But no sooner had he built another hut than Mr. Rhinoceros charged in with his horn lowered and ordered the man to quit. A Royal Commission was again appointed to look into the matter, and the same finding was given. This procedure was repeated until Mr. Buffalo, Mr. Leopard, Mr. Hyena and the rest were all accommodated with new huts. Then the man decided that he must adopt an effective method of protection, since Commissions of Enquiry did nor seem to be of any use to him. He sat down and said: "Ng'enda thi mieagaga motegi," which literally means "there is nothing that treads on the earth that cannot be trapped," or in other words, you can fool people for a time, but not for ever.

Early one morning, when the huts already occupied by the jungle lords were all beginning to decay and fall to pieces, he went out and built a bigger and better hut a little distance away. No sooner had Mr. Rhinoceros seen it than he came rushing in, only to find that Mr. Elephant was already inside, sound asleep. Mr. Leopard next came in at the window, Mr. Lion, Mr. Fox, and Mr. Buffalo entered the doors, while Mr. Hyena howled for a place in the shade and Mr. Alligator basked on the roof. Presently they all began disputing about their rights of penetration, and from disputing they came to fighting, and while they were all embroiled together the man set the hut on fire and burnt it to the ground, jungle lords and all. Then he went home, saying: "Peace is costly, but it's worth the expense," and lived happily ever after...

There certainly are some progressive ideas among the Europeans. They include the ideas of material prosperity, of medicine, and hygiene, and literacy which enables people to take part in world culture. But so far the Europeans who visit Africa have not been conspicuously zealous in imparting these parts of their inheritance to the Africans, and seem to think that the only way to do it is by police discipline and armed force. They speak as if it was somehow beneficial to an African to work for them instead of for himself, and to make sure that he will receive this benefit they do their best to take away his land and leave him with no alternative. Along with his land they rob him of his government, condemn his religious idea, and ignore his fundamental conceptions of justice and morals, all in the name of civilisation and progress.

If Africans were left in peace on their own lands, Europeans would have to offer them the benefits of white civilisation in real earnest before they could obtain the African labour which they want so much. They would have to offer the African a way of life which was really superior to the one his fathers lived before him, and a share in the prosperity given them by their command of science. They would have to let the African choose what parts of European culture could be beneficially transplanted, and how they could be adapted. He would probably not choose the gas bomb or the armed police force, but he might ask for some other things of which he does not get so much today. As it is, by driving him off his ancestral lands, the Europeans have robbed him of the material foundations of his culture, and reduced him to a state of serfdom incompatible with human happiness. The African is conditioned, by the cultural and social institutions of centuries, to a freedom of which Europe has little conception, and it is not in his nature to accept serfdom for ever. He realises that he must fight unceasingly for his own complete emancipation, for without this he is doomed to remain the prey of rival imperialisms, which in every successive year will drive their fangs more deeply into his vitality and strength.

Gamal Abdel Nasser, Speech on the Suez Canal

Beginning in the 1880s Egypt fell increasingly under the control of the British, who were intent on maintaining access to Asian markets through the Suez Canal, a key commercial artery which opened in 1869 and ran through Egyptian territory and linked the Mediterranean with the Red Sea. Although Egypt was officially granted independence in 1922, British dominance of Egyptian political and economic life continued through less official channels, until a revolution in 1952 deposed Egypt's King Farouk I (1920-1965), who was largely seen as a British puppet. A central figure in the revolution was Gamal Abdel Nasser (1918-1970), an army officer who became president of the newly-founded Republic of Egypt in 1954. In July 1956, following a successful British campaign to stop the United States from loaning Egypt money to build the Aswan High Dam, Nasser made the controversial move to nationalize the Suez Canal, with the goal of keeping the income generated by the canal in Egypt. The British responded harshly, insisting that a British-led international consortium would be better suited to adminster the canal than the Egyptians, whose scientific and technical capabilities were questioned. In response, Nasser gave the following speech on September 15, 1956. Following a short-lived and ultimately unsuccessful attempt by Britain, France, and Israel to occupy the canal zone later in the Fall of 1956, Nasser emerged from the "Suez Crisis" with increased prestige as perhaps the most influential spokesman for Arab and Middle Eastern interests in a decolonizing world.

Source: U.S. Department of State, *The Suez Canal Problem, 26 July – 22 September 1956,* Publication No. 6392 (Washington D.C.: Government Printing Office, 1956), 345-51.

Focus Questions:

1. How does Nasser justify the nationalization of the Suez Canal?
2. How does Nasser describe the motives of the imperial powers? Are those motives primarily economic, or is a broader agenda being pursued by the "imperialists"?
3. What measures is Nasser prepared to use to ensure Egyptian sovereignty?

Speech by President Nasser of the United Arab Republic, September 15, 1956

In these decisive days in the history of mankind, these days in which truth struggles to have itself recognized in international chaos where powers of evil domination and imperialism have prevailed, Egypt stands firmly to preserve her sovereignty. Your country stands solidly and staunchly to preserve her dignity against imperialistic schemes of a number of nations who have uncovered their desires for domination and supremacy. In these days and in such circumstances Egypt has resolved to show the world that when small nations decide to preserve their sovereignty, they will do that all right and that when these small nations are fully determined to defend their rights and maintain their dignity, they will undoubtedly succeed in achieving their ends. . . .

I am speaking in the name of every Egyptian Arab and in the name of all free countries and of all those who believe in liberty and are ready to defend it. I am speaking in the name of principles proclaimed by these countries in the Atlantic Charter. But they are now violating these principles and it has become our lot to shoulder the responsibility of reaffirming and establishing them anew. . . .

We have tried by all possible means to cooperate with those countries which claim to assist smaller nations and which promised to collaborate with us but they demanded their fees in advance. This we refused so they started to fight with us. They said they will pay toward building the High Dam and then they withdrew their offer and cast doubts on the Egyptian economy. Are we to declaim [disclaim?] our sovereign right? Egypt insists her sovereignty must remain intact and refuses to give up any part of that sovereignty for the sake of money.

Egypt nationalized the Egyptian Suez Canal company. When Egypt granted the concession to de Lesseps it was stated in the concession between the Egyptian Government and the Egyptian company that the company of the Suez Canal is an Egyptian company subject to Egyptian authority. Egypt nationalized this Egyptian company and declared freedom of navigation will be preserved.

But the imperialists became angry. Britain and France said Egypt grabbed the Suez Canal as if it were part of France or Britain. The British Foreign Secretary forgot that only two years ago he signed an agreement stating the Suez Canal is an integral part of Egypt. Egypt declared she was ready to negotiate. But as soon as negotiations began threats and intimidations started. . . .

Eden stated in the House of Commons there shall be no discrimination between states using the canal. We on our part reaffirm that and declare there is no discrimination between canal users. He also said Egypt shall not be allowed to succeed because that would spell success for Arab nationalism and would be against their policy, which aims at the protection of Israel.

Today they are speaking of a new association whose main objective would be to rob Egypt of the canal and deprive her of rightful canal dues. Suggestions made by Eden in the House of Commons which have been backed by France and the United States are a clear violation of the 1888 convention, since it is impossible to have two bodies organizing navigation in the canal. . . .

By stating that by succeeding, Abdel Nasser would weaken Britain's stand against Arab nationalism, Eden is in fact admitting his real objective is not Abdel Nasser as such but rather to defeat Arab nationalism and crush its cause. Eden speaks and finds his own answer. A month ago he let out the cry that be was after Abdel Nasser. Today the Egyptian people are fully conscious of their sovereign rights and Arab nationalism is fully awakened to its new destiny....

Those who attack Egypt will never leave Egypt alive. We shall fight a regular war, a total war, a guerrilla war. Those who attack Egypt will soon realize they brought disaster upon themselves. He who attacks Egypt attacks tile whole Arab world. They say in their papers the whole thing will be over in forty-eight hours. They do not know how strong we really are.

We believe in international law. But we will never submit. We shall show the world bow a small country can stand in the face of great powers threatening with armed might. Egypt might be a small power but she is great inasmuch as she has faith in her power and convictions. I feel quite certain every Egyptian shares the same convictions as I do and believes in everything I am stressing now.

We shall defend our freedom and independence to the last drop of our blood. This is the stanch feeling of every Egyptian. The whole Arab nation will stand by us in our common fight against aggression and domination. Free peoples, too, people who are really free will stand by us and support us against the forces of tyranny.

CHAPTER 29

Freedom, Conflict, and New Directions

Treaty on European Union

Following the 1951 formation of the European Coal and Steel Community (ECSC), which had built upon the ideals of the Schuman Declaration and included six founding member states, Western Europe continued over the ensuing decades to progress toward greater economic and political integration, eventually forming what became known as the European Community (EC). In late 1991, representatives from each of the EC member states, which numbered twelve at the time, met in the city of Maastricht in the Netherlands to formulate the following treaty, which was finally completed and signed in February 1992. The treaty laid the groundwork for monetary union through a common currency (the "Euro") and established the European Union, which went on to expand by 2007 to include 27 countries in both eastern and western Europe.

Source: http://europa.eu.int/en/record/mt/top.html, excerpts from Titles I, V, and VI.

Focus Questions:

1. The nineteenth-century French writer Victor Hugo had dreamed of a "United States of Europe" that would parallel, and in many ways serve as a European counterpart to, the United States of America. To what extent does this treaty create a United States of Europe?
2. In addition to a common currency, what types of common foreign and security policies are to be pursued by the European Union?
3. What powers are to be given up by the individual member states?

TITLE I COMMON PROVISIONS
ARTICLE A

By this Treaty, the High Contracting Parties establish among themselves a European Union, hereinafter called "the Union". This Treaty marks a new stage in the process of creating an ever closer union among the peoples of Europe, in which decisions are taken as closely as possible to the citizen. The Union shall be founded on the European Communities, supplemented by the policies and forms of cooperation established by this Treaty. Its task shall be to organize, in a manner demonstrating consistency and solidarity, relations between the Member States and between their peoples.

ARTICLE B

The Union shall set itself the following objectives:

to promote economic and social progress which is balanced and sustainable, in particular through the creation of an area without internal frontiers, through the strengthening of economic and social cohesion and through the establishment of economic and monetary union, ultimately including a single currency in accordance with the provisions of this Treaty; to assert its identity on the international scene, in particular through the implementation of a common foreign and security policy including the eventual framing of a common defence policy, which might in time lead to a common defence; to strengthen the protection of the rights and interests of the nationals of its Member States through the introduction of a citizenship of the Union; to develop close cooperation on justice and home affairs; to maintain in full the "acquis communautaire" and build on it with a view to considering, through the procedure referred to in Article N(2), to what extent the policies and forms of cooperation introduced by this Treaty may need to be revised with the aim of ensuring the effectiveness of the mechanisms and the institutions of the Community.

The objectives of the Union shall be achieved as provided in this Treaty and in accordance with the condition and the timetable set out therein while respecting the principle of subsidiarity as defined in Article 3b of the Treaty establishing the European Community.

ARTICLE C

The Union shall be served by a single institutional framework which shall ensure the consistency and the continuity of the activities carried out in order to attain its objectives while respecting and building upon the "acquis communautaire". The Union shall in particular ensure the consistency of its external activities as a whole in the context of its external relations, security, economic and development policies. The Council and the Commission shall be responsible for ensuring such consistency. They shall ensure the implementation of these policies, each in accordance with its respective powers.

ARTICLE D

The European Council shall provide the Union with the necessary impetus for its development and shall define the general political guidelines thereof. The European Council shall bring together the Heads of State or of Government of the Member States and the President of the Commission. They shall be assisted by the Ministers for Foreign Affairs of the Member States and by a Member of the Commission. The European Council shall meet at least twice a year, under the chairmanship of the Head of State or of Government of the Member State which holds the Presidency of the Council.The European Council shall submit to the European Parliament a report after each of its meetings and a yearly written report on the progress achieved by the Union.

ARTICLE E

The European Parliament, the Council, the Commission and the Court of Justice shall exercise their powers under the conditions and for the purposes provided for, on the one hand, by the provisions of the Treaties establishing the European Communities and of the subsequent Treaties and Acts modifying and supplementing them and, on the other hand, by the other provisions of this Treaty.

ARTICLE F

1. The Union shall respect the national identities of its Member States, whose systems of government are founded on the principles of democracy.
2. The Union shall respect fundamental rights, as guaranteed by the European Convention for the Protection of Human Rights and Fundamental Freedoms signed in Rome on 4 November 1950 and as they result from the constitutional traditions common to the Member States, as general principles of Community law.
3. The Union shall provide itself with the means necessary to attain its objectives and carry through its policies.

TITLE V

PROVISIONS ON A COMMON FOREIGN AND SECURITY POLICY

ARTICLE J

A common foreign and security policy is hereby established which shall be governed by the following provisions.

ARTICLE J.1

The union and its Member States shall define and implement a common foreign and security policy, governed by the provisions of the Title and covering all areas of foreign and security policy. The objectives of the common foreign and security policy shall be: to safeguard the common values, fundamental interests and independence of the Union; to strengthen the security of the Union and its Member States in all ways; to preserve peace and strengthen international security, in accordance with the principles of the United Nations Charter as well as the principles of the Helsinki Final Act and the objectives of the Paris Charter; to promote international cooperation; to develop and consolidate democracy and the rule of law, and respect for human rights and fundamental freedoms. The Union shall pursue these objectives; by establishing systematic cooperation between Member States in the conduct of policy, in accordance with Article J.2; by gradually implementing, in accordance with Article J.3, joint action in the areas in which the Member States have important interests in common.

The Member States shall support the Union's external and security policy actively and unreservedly in a spirit of loyalty and mutual solidarity. They shall refrain from any action which is contrary to the interests of the Union or likely to impair its effectiveness as a cohesive force in international relations. The Council shall ensure that these principles are complied with.

ARTICLE J.2

Member States shall inform and consult one another within the Council on any matter of foreign and security policy of general interest in order to ensure that their combined influence is exerted as effectively as possible by means of concerted and convergent action. Whenever it deems it necessary, the Council shall define a common position. Member States shall ensure that their national policies conform on the common positions. Member States shall coordinate their action in international organizations and at international conferences. They shall uphold the common positions in such fora. In international organizations and at international conferences where not all the Member States participate, those which do take part shall uphold the common positions.

ARTICLE J.3

The procedure for adopting joint action in matters covered by foreign and security policy shall be the following:

The Council shall decide, on the basis of general guidelines from the European Council, that a matter should be the subject of joint action. Whenever the Council decides on the principle of joint action, it shall lay down the specific scope, the Union's general and specific objectives in carrying out such action, if necessary its duration, and the means, procedures and conditions for its implementation.

The Council shall, when adopting the joint action and at any stage during its development, define those matters on which decisions are to be taken by a qualified majority.

Where the Council is required to act by a qualified majority pursuant to the preceding subparagraph, the votes of its members shall be weighted in accordance with Article 148(2) of the Treaty establishing the European Community, and for their adoption, acts of the Council shall require at least fifty-four votes in favour, cast by at least eight members.

If there is a change in circumstances having a substantial effect on a question subject to joint action, the Council shall review the principles and objectives of that action and take the necessary decisions. As long as the Council has not acted, the joint action shall stand.

Joint actions shall commit the Member States in the positions they adopt and in the conduct of their activity. Whenever there is any plan to adopt a national position or take national action pursuant to a joint action, information shall be provided in time to allow, if necessary, for prior consultations within the Council. The obligation to provide prior information shall not apply to measures which are merely a national transposition of Council decisions.

In cases of imperative need arising from changes in the situation and failing a Council decision, Member States may take the necessary measures as a of urgency having regard to the general objectives of the joint action. The Member State concerned shall inform the Council immediately of any such measures.

Should there be any major difficulties in implementing a joint action, a Member State shall refer them to the Council which shall discuss them and seek appropriate solutions. Such solu-tions shall not run counter to the objectives of the joint action or impair its effectiveness.

ARTICLE J.4

The common foreign and security policy shall include all questions related to the security of the Union, including the eventual framing of a common defence policy, which might in time lead to a common defence.

The union requests the Western European Union (WEU), which is an integral part of the development of the Union, to elaborate and implement decisions and actions of the Union which have defence implications. The Council shall, in agreement with the institutions of the WEU, adopt the necessary practical arrangements. Issues having defence implications dealt with under this Article shall not be subject to the procedures set out in Article J.3. The policy of the

Union in accordance with this Article shall not prejudice the specific character of the security and defence policy of certain Member States and shall respect the obligations of certain Member States under the North Atlantic Treaty and be compatible with the common security and defence policy established within that framework.

The provisions of this Article shall not prevent the development of closer cooperation between two or more Member States on a bilateral level, in the framework of the WEU and the Atlantic Alliance, provided such cooperation does not run counter to or impede that provided for in this Title. With a view to furthering the objective of this Treaty, and having in view the date of 1998 in the context of Article XII of the Brussels Treaty, the provisions of this Article may be revised as provided for in Article N(2) on the basis of a report to be presented in 1996 by the Council to the European Council, which shall include an evaluation of the progress made and the experience gained until then.

ARTICLE J.5

The Presidency shall represent the Union in matters coming within the common foreign and security policy. The Presidency shall be responsible for the implementation of common measures; in that capacity it shall in principle express the position of the Union in international organizations and international conferences. In the tasks referred to in paragraphs 1 and 2, the presidency shall be assisted if needs be by the previous and next Member States to hold the Presidency. The Commission shall be fully associated in these tasks. Without prejudice to Article J.2(3) and Article J.3(4), Member States represented in international organizations or international conferences where not all the Member States participate shall keep the latter informed of any matter of common interest. Member States which are also members of the United Nations Security Council will concert and keep the other Member States fully informed. Member States which are permanent members of the Security Council will, in the execution of their functions, ensure the defence of the positions and the interests of the union, without prejudice to their responsibilities under the provisions of the United Nations Charter.

ARTICLE J.6

The diplomatic and consular missions of the Member States and the Commission Delegations in third countries and international conferences, and their representations to international organizations, shall cooperate in ensuring that the common positions and common measures adopted by the Council are complied with and implemented. They shall step up cooperation by exchanging information, carrying out joint assessments and contributing to the implementation of the provisions referred to in Article 8c of the Treaty establishing the European Community.

ARTICLE J.7

The Presidency shall consult the European Parliament on the main aspects and the basic choices of the common foreign and security policy and shall ensure that the views of the European Parliament are duly taken into consideration. The European Parliament shall be kept regularly informed by the Presidency and the Commission of the development of the Union's foreign and security policy. The European Parliament may ask questions of the Councils or make recommendations to it. It shall hold an annual debate on progress in implementing the common foreign and security policy.

ARTICLE J.8

The European Council shall define the principles of and general guidelines for the common foreign and security policy. The Council shall take the decisions necessary for defining and implementing the common foreign and security policy on the basis of the general guidelines adopted by the European Council. It shall ensure the unity, consistency and effectiveness of action by the Union. The Council shall act unanimously, except for procedural questions and in the case referred to in Article J.3(2).

Any Member State or the Commission may refer to the Council any question relating to the common foreign policy and may submit proposals to the Council. In cases requiring a rapid decision, the Presidency, of its own motion, or at the request of the Commission or a Member State, shall convene an extraordinary Council meeting within forty-eight hours or, in an emergency, within a shorter period. Without prejudice to Article 151 of the Treaty establishing the European Community, a Political Committee consisting of Political Directors shall monitor the international situation in the areas covered by common foreign and security policy and contribute to the definition of policies by delivering opinions to the Council at the request of the Council or on its own initiative. It shall also monitor the implementation of agreed policies, without prejudice to the responsibility of the Presidency and the Commission.

ARTICLE J.9

The Commission shall be fully associated with the work carried out in the common foreign and security policy field.

ARTICLE J.10

On the occasion of any review of the security provisions under Article J.4, the Conference which is convened to that effect shall also examine whether any other amendments need to be made to provisions relating to the common foreign and security policy.

ARTICLE J.11

The provisions referred to in Articles 137, 138, 139 to 142, 146, 147, 150 to 153, 157 to 163 and 217 of the Treaty establishing the European Community shall apply to the provisions relating to the areas referred to in this Title. Administrative expenditure which the provisions relating to the areas referred to in this Title entail for the institutions shall be charged to the budget of the European Communities. The Council may also: either decide unanimously that operational expenditure to which the implementation of those provisions gives rise is to be charged to the budget of the European Communities; in that event, the budgetary procedure laid down in the Treaty establishing the European Community shall be applicable; or determine that such expenditure shall be charged to the Member States, where appropriate in accordance with a scale to be decided.

TITLE VI

PROVISIONS ON COOPERATION IN THE FIELDS OF JUSTICE AND HOME AFFAIRS

ARTICLE K

Cooperation in the fields of justice and home affairs shall be governed by the following provisions.

ARTICLE K.1

For the purposes of achieving the objectives of the Union, in particular the free movement of persons, and without prejudice to the powers of the European Community, Member States shall regard the following areas as matters of common interest: asylum policy; rules governing the crossing by persons of the external borders of the Member States and the exercise of controls thereon; immigration policy and policy regarding nationals of third countries; (a) conditions of entry and movement by nationals of third countries on the territory of Member States; (b) conditions of residence by nationals of third countries on the territory of Member States, including family reunion and access to employment; (c) combatting unauthorized immigration, residence and work by nationals of third countries on the territory of Member States; combating drug addiction in so far as this is not covered by 7 to 9; combating fraud on an international scale in so far as this is not covered by 7 to 9; judicial cooperation in civil matters; judicial cooperation in criminal matters; customs cooperation; police cooperation for the purposes of preventing and combating terrorism, unlawful drug trafficking and other serious forms of international crime, including if necessary certain aspects of customs cooperation, in connection with the organization of a Union-wide system for exchanging information within a European Police Office (Europol).

ARTICLE K.2

The matters referred to in Article K.1 shall be dealt with in compliance with the European Convention for the Protection of Human Rights and Fundamental Freedoms of 4 November 1950 and the Convention relating to the Status of Refugees of 28 July 1951 and having regard to the protection afforded by Member States to persons persecuted on political grounds. This Title shall not affect the exercise of the responsibilities incumbent upon Member States with regard to the maintenance of law and order and the safeguarding of internal security.

ARTICLE K.3

In the areas referred to in Article K.1, Member States shall inform and consult one another within the Council with a view to coordinating their action. To that end, they shall establish collaboration between the relevant departments of their administrations.

The Council may: on the initiative of any Member State of the Commission, in the areas referred to in Article K.1(1) to (6);on the initiative of any Member State, in the areas referred to Article K1(7) to (9): (a) adopt joint positions and promote, using the appropriate form and procedures, any cooperation contributing to the pursuit of the objectives of the Union; (b) adopt joint action in so far as the objectives of the Union can be attained better by joint action than by the Member States acting individually on account of the scale or effects of the action envisaged; it may decide that measures implementing joint action are to be adopted by a qualified majority; (c) without prejudice to Article 220 of the Treaty establishing the European Community, draw up conventions which it shall recommend to the Member States for adoption in accordance with their respective constitutional requirements. Unless otherwise provided by such conventions, measures implementing them shall be adopted within the Council by a majority of two-thirds of the High Contracting Parties. Such conventions may stipulate that the Court of Justice shall have jurisdiction to interpret their provisions and to rule on any disputes regarding their application, in accordance with such arrangements as they may lay down.

ARTICLE K.4

A Coordinating Committee shall be set up consisting of senior officials. In additions to its coordinating role, it shall be the task of the Committee to; give opinions for the attention of the Council, either at the Councils request or on its own initiative. Contribute, without prejudice to Article 151 of the Treaty establishing the European Community, to the preparation of the Council's discussions in the areas referred to in Article K.1 and, in accordance with the conditions laid down in Article 100d of the Treaty establishing the European Community, in the areas referred to in Article 100c of that Treaty.

The Commission shall be fully associated with the work in the areas referred to in this Title. The Council shall act unanimously, except on matters of procedure and in cases where Article K.3 expressly provides for other voting rules. Where the Council is required to act by a qualified majority, the votes of its members shall be weighted as laid down in Article 148(2) of the Treaty establishing the European Community, and for their adoption, acts of the Council shall require at least fifty-four votes in favour, cast by at least eight members.

ARTICLE K.5

Within international organizations and at international conferences in which they take part, Member States shall defend the common positions adopted under the provisions of this Title.

ARTICLE K.6

The Presidency and the Commission shall regularly inform the European Parliament of discussions in the areas covered by this Title. The Presidency shall consult the European Parliament on the principal aspects of activities in the areas referred to in this Title and shall ensure that the views of the European Parliament are duly taken into consideration. The European Parliament may ask questions of the Council or make recommendations to it. Each year, it shall hold a debate on the progress made in implementation of the areas referred to in this Title.

ARTICLE K.

7 The provisions of this Title shall not prevent the establishment or development of closer cooperation between two or more Member States in so far as such cooperation does not conflict with, or impede, that provided for in this Title.

ARTICLE K.8

The provisions referred to in Article 137,138,139 top 142, 146, 147, 150 to 153, 157 to 163 and 217 of the Treaty establishing the European Community shall apply to the provisions relating to the areas referred to in this Title.

Administrative expenditure which the provisions relating to the areas referred to in this Title entail for the institutions shall be charged to the budget of European Communities. The Council may also: either decide unanimously that operational expenditure to which the implementation of those provisions gives rise is to be charged to the budget of the European Communities; in that event, the budgetary procedure laid down in the treaty establishing the European Community shall be applicable; or determine that such expenditure shall be charged to the Member States, where appropriate in accordance with a scale to be decided.

ARTICLE K.9

The Council, acting unanimously on the initiative of the Commission or a Member State, may decide to apply Article 100c of the Treaty establishing the European Community to action in areas referred to in Article K.1(1) to (6), at the same time determine the relevant voting conditions relating to it. It shall recommend the Member States to adopt that decision in accordance with their respective constitutional requirements.

George W. Bush, Addresses

Basking in the faint glow of Cold War victory and somewhat adrift in foreign affairs during the 1990s, the United States, its image as a bastion of security and freedom now tarnished, had entered a new era. No longer the invulnerable "superpower," the United States once again was given purpose and direction—an evil to confront. The war against terrorism provided a new forum for the confirmation of its values as a nation and for its leadership in the Western world, as these excerpts from President Bush's speeches following the disaster indicate.

Source: "We Wage a War to Save Civilization Itself," speeches delivered to the people of the United States and to the General Assembly of the United Nations on September 11, November 8 and 10, 2001. Contained in *Vital Speeches of the Day,* October 1, 2001, p. 738 and December 1, 2001, pp. 98–99, 103–104.

Focus Questions:

1. In his speech of September 11, Bush states that the U.S. was attacked "because we're the brightest beacon for freedom and opportunity in the world." Do you agree with this assessment? Why or why not?
2. Can you think of any instances in history where terrorism worked to achieve a political goal?

ADDRESS DELIVERED TO THE NATION (September 11, 2001)

Today, our fellow citizens, our way of life, our very freedom came under attack in a series of deliberate and deadly terrorist acts. The victims were in airplanes, or in their offices; secretaries, businessmen and women, military and federal workers; moms and dads, friends and neighbors. Thousands of lives were suddenly ended by evil, despicable acts of terror. The pictures of airplanes flying into buildings, fires burning, huge structures collapsing, have filled us with disbelief, terrible sadness and a quiet, unyielding anger. These acts of mass murder were intended to frighten our nation into chaos and retreat, but they have failed; our country is strong. A great people has been moved to defend a great nation. Terrorist attacks can shake the foundations of our biggest buildings, but they cannot touch the foundation of America. These acts shattered steel, but they cannot dent the steel of American resolve. American was targeted for attack because we're the brightest beacon for freedom and opportunity in the world. And no one will keep that light from shining…

ADDRESS TO THE NATION (NOVEMBER 8, 2001)

We are a different country than we were on September the 10th—sadder and less innocent; stronger and more united; and in the face of ongoing threats, determined and courageous. Our nation faces a threat to our freedoms, and the stakes could not be higher. We are the target of enemies who boast they want to kill—kill all Americans, kill all Jews, and kill all Christians. We've seen that type of hate before—and the only possible response is to confront it, and to defeat it.

This new enemy seeks to destroy our freedom and impose its views. We value life; the terrorists ruthlessly destroy it. We value education; the terrorists do not believe women should be educated or should have health care, or should leave their homes. We value the right to speak our minds; for the terrorists, free expression can be grounds for execution. We respect people of all faiths and welcome the free practice of religion; our enemy wants to dictate how to think and how to worship even to their fellow Muslims.

The enemy tries to hide behind a peaceful faith. But those who celebrate the murder of innocent men, women, and children have no religion, have no conscience, and have no mercy. We wage war to save civilization, itself. We did not seek it, but we must fight it—and we will prevail.

This is a different war from any our nation has ever faced, a war on many fronts, against terrorists who operate in more than 60 different countries. And this is a war that must be fought not only overseas, but also here at home…

ADDRESS TO THE UNITED NATIONS GENERAL ASSEMBLY (NOVEMBER 10, 2001)

We're asking for a comprehensive commitment to this fight. We must unite in opposing all terrorists, not just some of them. In this world there are good causes and bad causes, and we may disagree on where the line is drawn. Yet, there is no such thing as good terrorist. No national aspiration, no remembered wrong can ever justify the deliberate murder of the innocent. Any government that rejects this principle, trying to pick and choose its terrorist friends, will know the consequences.

We must speak the truth about terror. Let us never tolerate outrageous conspiracy theories concerning the attacks of September the 11th; malicious lies that attempt to shift the blame away from the terrorists, themselves, away from the guilty. To inflame ethnic hatred is to advance the cause of terror. The war against terror must not serve as an excuse to persecute ethnic and religious minorities in any country. Innocent people must be allowed to live their own lives, by their own customs, under their own religion. And every nation must have avenues for the peaceful expression of opinion and dissent. When these avenues are closed, the temptation to speak through violence grows…

As I've told the American people, freedom and fear are at war. We face enemies that hate not our policies, but our existence; the tolerance of openness and creative culture that defines us. But the outcome of this conflict is certain: There is a current in history and it runs toward freedom. Our enemies resent it and dismiss it, but the dreams of mankind are defined by liberty—the natural right to create and build and worship and live in dignity. When men and women are released from oppression and isolation, they find fulfillment and hope, and they leave poverty by the millions. These aspirations are lifting up the peoples of Europe, Asia, Africa, and the Americas, and they can lift up all of the Islamic world. We stand for the permanent hopes of humanity, and those hopes will not be denied. We're confident, too, that history has an author who fills time and eternity with His purpose. We know that evil is real, but good will prevail against it. This is the teaching of many faiths, and in that assurance we gain strength for a long journey…

We did not ask for this mission, yet there is honor in history's call. We have a chance to write the story of our times, a story of courage defeating cruelty and light overcoming darkness. This calling is worthy of any life, and worthy of every nation. So let us go forward, confident, determined, and unafraid.

A Constitution for Europe

Representatives of the member states of the European Union met in 2004 to formulate a Constitution. The treaty establishing the constitution was signed in Rome by all the member state representatives in October 2004, but before the constitution could officially come into force it had to be ratified via referenda in each of the individual member states. Following negative votes in France (in May 2005) and the Netherlands (in June 2005), the constitutional process stalled, despite the fact that many of the EU member states voted in favor of the constitution. Some opponents of the constitution argue that it forces individual member states to give up too much sovereignty to a new European "super-state," while others oppose such aspects as the lack of specific reference to Europe's Christian heritage. While its future is currently uncertain, the European Constitution represents an important development in the attempt to forge greater unity among the states of Europe.

Source: http://europa.eu/constitution/en/lstoc1_en/htm

Focus Questions:

1. How is the nature of Europe's cultural and religious heritage portrayed?
2. What balance is struck between the sovereignty of the inidividual member states and then broader collectivity? Can you envision any problems with the principle of "unity in diversity?"
3. Do you find anything interesting or noteworthy about the nature of the signatories to the Constitution?

PREAMBLE

HIS MAJESTY THE KING OF THE BELGIANS, THE PRESIDENT OF THE CZECH REPUBLIC, HER MAJESTY THE QUEEN OF DENMARK, THE PRESIDENT OF THE FEDERAL REPUBLIC OF GERMANY, THE PRESIDENT OF THE REPUBLIC OF ESTONIA, THE PRESIDENT OF THE HELLENIC REPUBLIC, HIS MAJESTY THE KING OF SPAIN, THE PRESIDENT OF THE FRENCH REPUBLIC, THE PRESIDENT OF IRELAND, THE PRESIDENT OF THE ITALIAN REPUBLIC, THE PRESIDENT OF THE REPUBLIC OF CYPRUS, THE PRESIDENT OF THE REPUBLIC OF LATVIA, THE PRESIDENT OF THE REPUBLIC OF LITHUANIA, HIS ROYAL HIGHNESS THE GRAND DUKE OF LUXEMBOURG, THE PRESIDENT OF THE REPUBLIC OF HUNGARY, THE PRESIDENT OF MALTA, HER MAJESTY THE QUEEN OF THE NETHERLANDS, THE FEDERAL PRESIDENT OF THE REPUBLIC OF AUSTRIA, THE PRESIDENT OF THE REPUBLIC OF POLAND, THE PRESIDENT OF THE PORTUGUESE REPUBLIC, THE PRESIDENT OF THE REPUBLIC OF SLOVENIA, THE PRESIDENT OF THE SLOVAK REPUBLIC, THE PRESIDENT OF THE REPUBLIC OF FINLAND, THE GOVERNMENT OF THE KINGDOM OF SWEDEN, HER MAJESTY THE QUEEN OF THE UNITED KINGDOM OF GREAT BRITAIN AND NORTHERN IRELAND,

DRAWING INSPIRATION from the cultural, religious and humanist inheritance of Europe, from which have developed the universal values of the inviolable and inalienable rights of the human person, freedom, democracy, equality and the rule of law,

BELIEVING that Europe, reunited after bitter experiences, intends to continue along the path of civilisation, progress and prosperity, for the good of all its inhabitants, including the weakest and most deprived; that it wishes to remain a continent open to culture, learning and social progress; and that it wishes to deepen the democratic and transparent nature of its public life, and to strive for peace, justice and solidarity throughout the world,

CONVINCED that, while remaining proud of their own national identities and history, the peoples of Europe are determined to transcend their former divisions and, united ever more closely, to forge a common destiny,

CONVINCED that, thus 'United in diversity', Europe offers them the best chance of pursuing, with due regard for the rights of each individual and in awareness of their responsibilities towards future generations and the Earth, the great venture which makes of it a special area of human hope,

DETERMINED to continue the work accomplished within the framework of the Treaties establishing the European Communities and the Treaty on European Union, by ensuring the continuity of the Community acquis, GRATEFUL to the members of the European Convention for having prepared the draft of this Constitution on behalf of the citizens and States of Europe,

HIS MAJESTY THE KING OF THE BELGIANS,
Guy VERHOFSTADT
Prime Minister

Karel DE GUCHT
Minister for Foreign Affairs

THE PRESIDENT OF THE CZECH REPUBLIC,
Stanislav GROSS
Prime Minister

Cyril SVOBODA
Minister for Foreign Affairs

HER MAJESTY THE QUEEN OF DENMARK,
Anders Fogh RASMUSSEN
Prime Minister

Per Stig MØLLER
Minister for Foreign Affairs
THE PRESIDENT OF THE FEDERAL REPUBLIC OF GERMANY,
Gerhard SCHRÖDER Federal Chancellor
Joseph FISCHER
Federal Minister for Foreign Affairs and Deputy Federal Chancellor

THE PRESIDENT OF THE REPUBLIC OF ESTONIA,
Juhan PARTS
Prime Minister
Kristiina OJULAND
Minister for Foreign Affairs

THE PRESIDENT OF THE HELLENIC REPUBLIC,
Kostas KARAMANLIS
Prime Minister

Petros G. MOLYVIATIS
Minister of Foreign Affairs

HIS MAJESTY THE KING OF SPAIN,
JosŽ Luis RODRÊGUEZ ZAPATERO
President of the Government
Miguel Angel MORATINOS CUYAUBÉ
Minister for External Affairs and Cooperation

THE PRESIDENT OF THE FRENCH REPUBLIC,
Jacques CHIRAC
President
Jean-Pierre RAFFARIN Prime Minister
Michel BARNIER
Minister for Foreign Affairs
Bertie AHERN Taoiseach

Dermot AHERN
Minister for Foreign Affairs

THE PRESIDENT OF THE ITALIAN REPUBLIC,
Silvio BERLUSCONI
Prime Minister
Franco FRATTINI
Minister for Foreign Affairs

THE PRESIDENT OF THE REPUBLIC OF CYPRUS,
Tassos PAPADOPOULOS
President

George IACOVOU
Minister for Foreign Affairs

THE PRESIDENT OF THE REPUBLIC OF LATVIA,
Vaira VĪĶE FREIBERGA
President

Indulis EMSIS
Prime Minister
Artis PABRIKS Minister for Foreign Affairs
THE PRESIDENT OF THE REPUBLIC OF LITHUANIA,

Valdas ADAMKUS President
Algirdas Mykolas BRAZAUSKAS
Prime Minister

Antanas VALIONIS
Minister of Foreign Affairs

HIS ROYAL HIGHNESS THE GRAND DUKE OF LUXEMBOURG,
Jean-Claude JUNCKER
Prime Minister, Ministre d'Etat
Jean ASSELBORN
Deputy Prime Minister, Minister for Foreign Affairs and Immigration

THE PRESIDENT OF THE REPUBLIC OF HUNGARY,
Ferenc GYURCSÁNY
Prime Minister

László KOVÁCS
Minister for Foreign Affairs

THE PRESIDENT OF MALTA,
The Hon Lawrence GONZI
Prime Minister

The Hon Michael FRENDO
Minister for Foreign Affairs

Dr. J. P. BALKENENDE
Prime Minister
Dr. B. R. BOT
Minister for Foreign Affairs

THE FEDERAL PRESIDENT OF THE REPUBLIC OF AUSTRIA,
Dr. Wolfgang SCHÜSSEL
Federal Chancellor

Dr. Ursula PLASSNIK
Federal Minister for Foreign Affairs

THE PRESIDENT OF THE REPUBLIC OF POLAND,
Marek BELKA
Prime Minister

Włodzimierz CIMOSZEWICZ
Minister for Foreign Affairs

THE PRESIDENT OF THE PORTUGUESE REPUBLIC,
Pedro Miguel DE SANTANA LOPES
Prime Minister
Ant—nio Victor MARTINS MONTEIRO
Minister for Foreign Affairs and the Portuguese Communities

THE PRESIDENT OF THE REPUBLIC OF SLOVENIA,
Anton ROP
President of the Government
Ivo VAJGL
Minister for Foreign Affairs

THE PRESIDENT OF THE SLOVAK REPUBLIC,
Mikuláš DZURINDA
Prime Minister

Eduard KUKAN
Minister for Foreign Affairs

THE PRESIDENT OF THE REPUBLIC OF FINLAND,
Matti VANHANEN
Prime Minister

Erkki TUOMIOJA
Minister for Foreign Affairs

THE GOVERNMENT OF THE KINGDOM OF SWEDEN,
Göran PERSSON
Prime Minister
Laila FREIVALDS
Minister for Foreign Affairs
The Rt. Hon Tony BLAIR
Prime Minister

The Rt. Hon Jack STRAW
Secretary of State for Foreign and Commonwealth Affairs

WHO, having exchanged their full powers, found in good and due form, have agreed as follows: